SQL Server 2005 T-SQL Recipes

A Problem-Solution Approach

Joseph Sack

Apress®

SQL Server 2005 T-SQL Recipes: A Problem-Solution Approach

Copyright © 2006 by Joseph Sack

ISBN-13 (pbk): 978-1-59059-570-1
ISBN-10 (pbk): 1-59059-570-X

Printed and bound in the United States of America 9 8 7 6 5 4 3 2

Lead Editor: Tony Davis
Technical Reviewer: Evan Terry
Editorial Board: Steve Anglin, Dan Appleman, Ewan Buckingham, Gary Cornell, Tony Davis, Jason Gilmore, Jonathan Hassell, Chris Mills, Dominic Shakeshaft, Jim Sumser
Project Manager: Beth Christmas
Copy Edit Manager: Nicole LeClerc
Copy Editor: Julie M. Smith
Assistant Production Director: Kari Brooks-Copony
Production Editor: Katie Stence
Compositor and Artist: Kinetic Publishing Services, LLC
Proofreader: Patrick Vincent
Indexer: Brenda Miller
Cover Designer: Kurt Krames
Manufacturing Director: Tom Debolski

Distributed to the book trade worldwide by Springer-Verlag New York, Inc., 233 Spring Street, 6th Floor, New York, NY 10013. Phone 1-800-SPRINGER, fax 201-348-4505, e-mail orders-ny@springer-sbm.com, or visit http://www.springeronline.com.

For information on translations, please contact Apress directly at 2560 Ninth Street, Suite 219, Berkeley, CA 94710. Phone 510-549-5930, fax 510-549-5939, e-mail info@apress.com, or visit http://www.apress.com.

The source code for this book is available to readers at http://www.apress.com in the Source Code section. You will need to answer questions pertaining to this book in order to successfully download the code.

Contents at a Glance

Contents

About the Author

JOSEPH SACK is an independent consultant based in Minneapolis, Minnesota. Since 1997, he has been developing and supporting SQL Server environments for clients in the financial services, multimedia distribution, IT consulting, manufacturing, and real estate industries. Joseph received his bachelor's degree in psychology from the University of Minnesota. He is the author of *SQL Server 2000 Fast Answers for DBAs and Developers* and is a Microsoft Certified Database Administrator (MCDBA). For questions or consulting needs, he can be reached at joe.sack@gmail.com.

About the Technical Reviewer

EVAN TERRY has been in the IT industry for over 15 years, serving the government and the private sector as a Programmer/Analyst, Systems Engineer, Custom Software Consultant, Senior Developer, Data Analyst, and Data Architect. He firmly believes that in order to succeed at developing complex systems, the IT professional must truly understand the business processes we support. Evan also tries to bridge the gap between the technical and the non-technical by understanding the perspectives of both and by helping the two groups communicate effectively. Evan is also the co-author of Apress' *Beginning Relational Data Modeling*.

Acknowledgments

This book is dedicated to David Hatch. His continuing help, encouragement, advice, and support made it all possible.

Thank you to Tony Davis for his ability to see the big picture, for providing insight and clarity, and for helping me formulate a meaningful narrative. Tony gave me the straight truth, and as a result, pushed me to do my very best.

Thank you to Evan Terry, who took an amazing amount of care in making sure that not only the technical side of the book was reviewed, but made sure to look at the content as a whole. Evan has a gift for clarity and for asking the right questions. It was a comfort knowing that I had both Tony and Evan watching over my shoulder.

Also, thank you to Beth Christmas for her wonderful attitude, her talent for keeping things rolling, and her rapid responses to my burning questions. Beth cared just as much as I did about keeping this book on schedule, and I'm very grateful for that.

Thank you to the very talented Julie Smith, who helped me find the right words, stay consistent, and make the narrative flow. Like Evan, Julie also went above and beyond her role by evaluating the text at multiple levels.

Thank you also to Katie Stence, Kari Brooks, and the rest of the Apress team—some of whom I didn't get to meet, but whose contributions I'm thankful to have received. It is nice to know I had so many people watching out for me.

Lastly, thank you to Gary Cornell, who purchased the rights to my last book, made good on the previous publisher's commitments, and continues to show integrity and support for my future projects. If all publishing companies were run by people like Gary, there would be a lot more happy technical authors out there!

Introduction

When it comes to performing your daily SQL Server tasks, technical documentation tends to tell you *more* than you need to know.

Let's say that you're in a hurry, and you want to add a unique constraint to a table before someone inserts a duplicate value into it. Where do you look?

One obvious choice is SQL Server Books Online. With its massive amounts of useful information, you know that the answer has to be there somewhere. Unfortunately, finding this information may involve several click-throughs and red herrings. Once you *do* arrive at the correct page, the information you need may be integrated into a larger syntax block, with unrelated functionality or examples.

SQL Server 2005 T-SQL Recipes was written in order to address the need for fast information retrieval and use. Topics are presented in a task-based format. Each topic (recipe) provides the necessary background to get you started, presents one or more examples, and then concisely explains how it all works.

Whether you need to brush up on a topic you haven't used for a while, or whether you're new to Transact-SQL, you can easily pick and choose the areas you need to work on. This book covers the basics and beyond, demonstrating the more complex techniques and functionality offered in SQL Server 2005's flavor of Transact-SQL.

Want to learn more about what's new in SQL Server 2005? This book will also demonstrate the new Transact-SQL features and functionality introduced in SQL Server 2005, allowing you to quickly test out features with a minimal amount of fuss.

Written to be index-friendly, the book does not need to be read front to back in order for readers to benefit from it. Whether you are a novice, part-time, or seasoned SQL Server professional, *SQL Server 2005 T-SQL Recipes* will provide you with the fast facts needed to help you get the job done.

CHAPTER 1

■■■

SELECT

In this chapter, I include recipes for returning data from a SQL Server database using the SELECT statement. At the beginning of each chapter you'll notice that most of the basic concepts are covered first. This is for those of you who are new to the SQL Server 2005 Transact-SQL query language. In addition to the basics, I'll also provide recipes that can be used in your day-to-day development and administration. These recipes will also help you learn about the new functionality introduced in SQL Server 2005. A majority of the examples in this book use the AdventureWorks database, which is an optional install with SQL Server 2005.

Tip The AdventureWorks database is a sample database provided with SQL Server 2005. It's similar to the Northwind and Pubs databases found in previous versions of SQL Server. For instructions on installing this database, see SQL Server 2005 Books Online's topic, "Running Setup to Install AdventureWorks Sample Databases and Samples."

You can read the recipes in this book in almost any order. You can skip to the topics that interest you, or read it through sequentially. If you see something that is useful to you, perhaps a code chunk or example that you can modify for your own purposes or integrate into a stored procedure or function, then this book has been successful.

The Basic SELECT Statement

The SELECT command is the cornerstone of the Transact-SQL language, allowing you to retrieve data from a SQL Server database (and more specifically from database objects within a SQL Server database). Although the full syntax of the SELECT statement is enormous, the basic syntax can be presented in a more boiled down form:

```
SELECT select_list
FROM table_list
```

The select_list argument shown in the previous code listing is the list of columns that you wish to return in the results of the query. The table_list arguments are the actual tables and or views that the data will be retrieved from.

The next few recipes will demonstrate how to use a basic SELECT statement.

Selecting Specific Columns for Every Row

This example demonstrates a very simple SELECT query against the AdventureWorks database, whereby four columns are returned, along with several rows. Explicit column naming is used in the query:

```
USE AdventureWorks
GO

SELECT   ContactID,
      Title,
      FirstName,
      LastName
FROM   Person.Contact
```

The query returns the following abridged results:

ContactID	Title	FirstName	LastName
1	Mr.	Gustavo	Achong
2	Ms.	Catherine	Abel
3	Ms.	Kim	Abercrombie
4	Sr.	Humberto	Acevedo
5	Sra.	Pilar	Ackerman
...			

```
(19972 row(s) affected)
```

How It Works

The first line of code sets the context database context of the query. Your initial database context, when you first login to SQL Server Management Studio (SSMS), is defined by your login's default database. USE followed by the database name changes your connection context:

```
USE AdventureWorks
GO
```

The SELECT query was used next. The next five lines of code define which four columns to display in the query results:

```
SELECT   ContactID,
      Title,
      FirstName,
      LastName
```

The next line of code is the FROM clause:

```
FROM   Person.Contact
```

The FROM clause is used to specify the data source, which in this example is a table. Notice the two-part name of Person.Contact. The first part (the part before the period) is the *schema* and the second part (after the period) is the actual table name. In SQL Server 2000, the first part of the two part name was called the *object owner*. Now, with SQL Server 2005, users are separated from direct ownership of database objects. Instead of owning the object directly, a *schema* contains the object, and that schema is then *owned* by a user. In SQL Server 2000, if an object was owned by Jane, and Jane left the company, you would not be able to drop her login until you reassigned all of the objects that Jane owned to another user. Now with users owning a schema instead, and the schema containing the object, you can change the owner of the schema and drop Jane's login without having to modify object ownership.

Selecting Every Column for Every Row

If you wish to show *all* columns from the data sources in the FROM clause, you can use the following query:

```
USE AdventureWorks
GO

SELECT    *
FROM    Person.Contact
```

The abridged column and row output is shown here:

ContactID	NameStyle	Title	FirstName	MiddleName	LastName
1	0	Mr.	Gustavo	NULL	Achong
2	0	Ms.	Catherine	R.	Abel
3	0	Ms.	Kim	NULL	Abercrombie
...					

How It Works

The asterisk symbol (*) returns all columns for every row of the table or view you are querying. All other details are as explained in the previous recipe.

Please remember that, as good practice, it is better to explicitly reference the columns you want to retrieve instead of using SELECT *. If you write an application that uses SELECT *, your application may expect the same columns (in the same order) from the query. If later on you add a new column to the underlying table or view, or if you reorder the table columns, you could break the calling application, because the new column in your result-set is unexpected. Using SELECT * can also negatively impact performance, as you may be returning more data than you need over the network, increasing the result set size and data retrieval operations on the SQL Server instance.

Selective Querying Using a Basic WHERE Clause

In a SELECT query, the WHERE clause is used to restrict rows returned in the query result set. The simplified syntax for including the WHERE clause is as follows:

```
SELECT select_list
FROM table_list
[WHERE search_conditions]
```

The WHERE clause uses search conditions which determine the rows returned by the query. Search conditions use predicates, which are expressions that evaluate to TRUE, FALSE, or UNKNOWN. UNKNOWN values can make their appearance when NULL data is used in the search conditions. A NULL value doesn't mean that the value is blank or zero—only that the value is unknown.

The next few recipes will demonstrate how to use the WHERE clause to specify which rows are and aren't returned in the result set.

Using the WHERE Clause to Specify Rows Returned in the Result Set

This basic example demonstrates how to select which rows are returned in the query results:

```
SELECT    Title,
    FirstName,
    LastName
FROM    Person.Contact
WHERE Title = 'Ms.'
```

This example returns the following (abridged) results:

```
Title     FirstName                                         LastName
--------  ------------------------------------------------  ---------------------
Ms.       Catherine                                         Abel
Ms.       Kim                                               Abercrombie
Ms.       Frances                                           Adams
Ms.       Margaret                                          Smith
...

(415 row(s) affected)
```

How It Works

In this example, you can see that only rows where the person's title was equal to "Ms." were returned. This search condition was defined in the WHERE clause of the query:

```
WHERE Title = 'Ms.'
```

Only one search condition was used in this case; however, an almost unlimited number of search conditions can be used in a single query, as you'll see in the next recipe.

Combining Search Conditions

This recipe will demonstrate connecting multiple search conditions by utilizing the AND, OR, and NOT logical operators. The AND logical operator joins two or more search conditions and returns the row or rows only when each of the search conditions is true. The OR logical operator joins two or more search conditions and returns the row or rows in the result set when any of the conditions are true.

In this first example, two search conditions are used in the WHERE clause, separated by the AND operator. The AND means that for a given row, both search conditions must be true for that row to be returned in the result set:

```
SELECT   Title,
         FirstName,
         LastName
FROM   Person.Contact
WHERE Title = 'Ms.' AND
      LastName = 'Antrim'
```

This returns the following results:

```
Title     FirstName                                         LastName
--------  ------------------------------------------------  ---------------------
Ms.       Ramona                                            Antrim

(1 row(s) affected)
```

In this second example, an OR operator is used for the two search conditions instead of an AND, meaning that if *either* search condition evaluates to TRUE for a row, that row will be returned:

```
SELECT   Title,
         FirstName,
         LastName
FROM   Person.Contact
WHERE Title = 'Ms.' OR
      LastName = 'Antrim'
```

This returns the following (abridged) results:

Title	FirstName	LastName
Ms.	Ramona	Antrim
Ms.	Frances	Adams
Ms.	Margaret	Smith
Ms.	Carla	Adams
Ms.	Kim	Akers

...

(415 row(s) affected)

How It Works

In the first example, two search conditions were joined using the AND operator:

```
WHERE Title = 'Ms.' AND
      LastName = 'Antrim'
```

As you add search conditions to your query, you join them by the logical operators AND and OR. For example, if both the Title equals Ms. *and* the LastName equals Antrim, that row or rows will be returned. The AND operator dictates that *both* joined search conditions must be true in order for the row to be returned.

The OR operator, on the other hand, returns rows if *either* search condition is TRUE, as the third example demonstrated:

```
WHERE Title = 'Ms.' OR
      LastName = 'Antrim'
```

So instead of a single row as the previous query returned, rows with a Title of Ms. or a LastName of Antrim were returned.

Negating a Search Condition

The NOT logical operator, unlike AND and OR, isn't used to combine search conditions, but instead is used to negate the expression that follows it.

This next example demonstrates using the NOT operator for reversing the result of the following search condition and qualifying the Title to be equal to 'Ms.' (reversing it to anything *but* 'Ms.'):

```
SELECT   Title,
         FirstName,
         LastName
FROM   Person.Contact
WHERE NOT Title = 'Ms.'
```

This returns the following (abridged) results:

Title	FirstName	LastName
Mr.	Gustavo	Achong
Sr.	Humberto	Acevedo
Sra.	Pilar	Ackerman

...

(594 row(s) affected)

How It Works

This example demonstrated the NOT operator:

```
WHERE NOT Title = 'Ms.'
```

NOT specifies the reverse of a search condition, in this case specifying that only rows that *don't* have the Title = 'Ms.' be returned.

Keeping Your WHERE Clause Unambiguous

You can use multiple operators (AND, OR, NOT) in a single WHERE clause, but it is important to keep your intentions clear by properly embedding your ANDs and ORs in parentheses. The AND operator limits the result set, and the OR operator expands the conditions for which rows will be returned. When multiple operators are used in the same WHERE clause, operator precedence is used to determine how the search conditions are evaluated. For example, the NOT operator takes precedence (is evaluated first) before AND. The AND operator takes precedence over the OR operator. Using both AND and OR operators in the same WHERE clause without using parentheses can return unexpected results.

For example, the following query may return unintended results:

```
SELECT   Title,
    FirstName,
    LastName
FROM   Person.Contact
WHERE   Title = 'Ms.' AND
    FirstName = 'Catherine' OR
    LastName = 'Adams'
```

This returns the following (abridged) results:

Title	FirstName	LastName
Ms.	Catherine	Abel
Ms.	Frances	Adams
Ms.	Carla	Adams
Mr.	Jay	Adams
...		

Was the author of this query's intention to return results for all rows with a Title of Ms., and of those rows, only include those with a FirstName of Catherine or a LastName of Adams? Or did the author wish to search for all people named Ms. with a FirstName of Catherine, *as well as* anyone with a LastName of Adams?

A query that uses both AND and OR should use parentheses to clarify exactly what rows should be returned. For example, this next query returns anyone with a Title of Ms. *and* a FirstName equal to Catherine. It also returns anyone else with a LastName of Adams—regardless of Title and FirstName:

```
SELECT   ContactID,
     Title,
     FirstName,
     MiddleName,
     LastName
FROM   Person.Contact
WHERE   (Title = 'Ms.' AND
     FirstName = 'Catherine') OR
     LastName = 'Adams'
```

How It Works

Use parentheses to clarify multiple operator WHERE clauses. Parentheses assist in clarifying a query as they help SQL Server identify the order that expressions should be evaluated. Search conditions enclosed in parentheses are evaluated in an inner to outer order, so in the example from this recipe, the following search conditions were evaluated first:

```
(Title = 'Ms.' AND
FirstName = 'Catherine')
```

before evaluating the outside OR search expression:

```
LastName = 'Adams'
```

Using Operators and Expressions

So far this chapter has used the = (equals) operator to designate what the value of a column in the result set should be. The = comparison operator tests the equality of two expressions. An *expression* is a combination of values, identifiers, and operators evaluated by SQL Server in order to return a result (for example, return TRUE or FALSE or UNKNOWN).

Table 1-1 lists some of the operators you can use in a search condition.

Table 1-1. *Operators*

Operator	Description
!=	Tests two expressions not being equal to each other.
!>	Tests that the left condition is not greater than the expression to the right.
!<	Tests that the right condition is not greater than the expression to the right.
<	Tests the left condition as less than the right condition.
<=	Tests the left condition as less than or equal to the right condition.
<>	Tests two expressions not being equal to each other.
=	Tests equality between two expressions.
>	Tests the left condition being greater than the expression to the right.
>=	Tests the left condition being greater than or equal to the expression to the right.
ALL	When used with a comparison operator and subquery, if all retrieved values satisfy the search condition, the rows will be retrieved.
ANY	When used with a comparison operator and subquery, if any retrieved values satisfy the search condition, the rows will be retrieved.
BETWEEN	Designates an inclusive range of values. Used with the AND clause between the beginning and ending values.
CONTAINS	Does a fuzzy search for words and phrases.
ESCAPE	Takes the character used prior to a wildcard character to designate that the literal value of the wildcard character should be searched, rather than use the character as a wildcard.
EXISTS	When used with a subquery, EXISTS tests for the existence of rows in the subquery.
FREETEXT	Searches character-based data for words using meaning, rather than literal values.
IN	Provides an inclusive list of values for the search condition.
IS NOT NULL	Evaluates if the value is NOT null.
IS NULL	Evaluates whether the value is null.

(Continued)

Table 1-1. *(Continued)*

Operator	Description
LIKE	Tests character string for pattern matching.
NOT BETWEEN	Specifies a range of values NOT to include. Used with the AND clause between the beginning and ending values.
NOT IN	Provides a list of values for which NOT to return rows for.
NOT LIKE	Tests character string, excluding those with pattern matches.
SOME	When used with a comparison operator and subquery, if any retrieved values satisfy the search condition, the rows will be retrieved.

As you can see from Table 1-1, SQL Server 2005 includes several operators which can be used within query expressions. Specifically, in the context of a WHERE clause, operators can be used to compare two expressions, and also check whether a condition is TRUE, FALSE, or UNKNOWN. The next few recipes will demonstrate how the different operators are used within search expressions.

Using BETWEEN for Date Range Searches

This example demonstrates the BETWEEN operator, used to designate sales orders that occurred between the dates 7/28/2002 and 7/29/2002:

```
SELECT   SalesOrderID,
      ShipDate
FROM Sales.SalesOrderHeader
WHERE ShipDate BETWEEN '7/28/2002' AND '7/29/2002'
```

The query returns the following (abridged) results:

```
SalesOrderID ShipDate
------------ -----------------------
46845        2002-07-28 00:00:00.000
46846        2002-07-28 00:00:00.000
46847        2002-07-28 00:00:00.000
more rows
46858        2002-07-29 00:00:00.000
46860        2002-07-29 00:00:00.000
46861        2002-07-29 00:00:00.000

(17 row(s) affected)
```

How It Works

The exercise demonstrated the BETWEEN operator, which tested whether or not a column's ShipDate value fell between two dates:

```
WHERE ShipDate BETWEEN '7/28/2002' AND '7/29/2002'
```

Using Comparisons

This next example demonstrates the < Less Than operator which is used in this query to only show products with a standard cost below $110.00:

```
SELECT   ProductID,
   Name,
```

```
      StandardCost
FROM    Production.Product
WHERE     StandardCost < 110.0000
```

This query returns the following (abridged) results:

ProductID	Name	StandardCost
1	Adjustable Race	0.00
2	Bearing Ball	0.00
3	BB Ball Bearing	0.00
4	Headset Ball Bearings	0.00
more rows		
952	Chain	8.9866
994	LL Bottom Bracket	23.9716
995	ML Bottom Bracket	44.9506
996	HL Bottom Bracket	53.9416
more rows		
(317 row(s) affected)		

How It Works

This example demonstrated the < Less Than operator, returning all rows with a StandardCost less than 110.0000:

```
WHERE     StandardCost < 110.0000
```

Checking for NULL Values

This next query tests for the NULL value of a specific column. A NULL value does *not* mean that the value is blank or zero—only that the value is *unknown*. This query returns any rows where the value of the product's weight is unknown:

```
SELECT    ProductID,
    Name,
    Weight
FROM    Production.Product
WHERE    Weight IS NULL
```

This query returns the following (abridged) results:

ProductID	Name	Weight
1	Adjustable Race	NULL
2	Bearing Ball	NULL
3	BB Ball Bearing	NULL
4	Headset Ball Bearings	NULL
more rows		
(299 row(s) affected)		

How It Works

This example demonstrated the IS NULL operator, returning any rows where the Weight value was unknown (not available):

```
WHERE    Weight IS NULL
```

Returning Rows Based on a List of Values

In this example, the IN operator validates the equality of the Color column to a list of expressions:

```
SELECT   ProductID,
       Name,
       Color
FROM Production.Product
WHERE Color IN ('Silver', 'Black', 'Red')
```

This returns the following (abridged) results:

```
ProductID   Name                                              Color
----------- ------------------------------------------------- -----
317         LL Crankarm                                       Black
318         ML Crankarm                                       Black
319         HL Crankarm                                       Black
more results
988         Mountain-500 Silver, 52                           Silver
790         Road-250 Red, 48                                  Red
```

How It Works

This example demonstrated the IN operator, returning all products that had a Silver, Black, or Red color:

```
WHERE Color IN ('Silver', 'Black', 'Red')
```

Using Wildcards with LIKE

Wildcards are used in search expressions to find pattern matches within strings. In SQL Server 2005, you have the following wildcard options described in Table 1-2.

Table 1-2. *Wildcards*

Wildcard	Usage
%	Represents a string of zero or more characters.
_	Represents a single character.
[]	Specifies a single character, from a selected range or list.
[^]	Specifies a single character not within the specified range.

This example demonstrates using the LIKE operation with the % wildcard, searching for any product with a name starting with the letter B:

```
SELECT   ProductID,
     Name
FROM   Production.Product
WHERE Name LIKE 'B%'
```

This returns the following results:

```
ProductID    Name
-----------  -------------------------------------------------
3            BB Ball Bearing
2            Bearing Ball
877          Bike Wash - Dissolver
316          Blade
(4 row(s) affected)
```

What if you want to search for the literal value of the % percentage sign or an _ underscore in your character column? For this, you can use the ESCAPE operator.

This next query searches for any product name with a literal _ underscore value in it. The ESCAPE operator allows you to search for the wildcard symbol as an actual character:

```
SELECT ProductID,
     Name
FROM Production.Product
WHERE Name LIKE '%/_%' ESCAPE '/'
```

How It Works

Wildcards allow you to search for patterns in character-based columns. In the example from this recipe, the % percentage sign was used to represent a string of zero or more characters:

```
WHERE Name LIKE 'B%'
```

If searching for a literal value that would otherwise be interpreted by SQL Server as a wildcard, you can use the ESCAPE keyword. The example from this recipe searched for a literal underscore in the Name column:

```
WHERE Name LIKE '%/_%' ESCAPE '/'
```

A backslash embedded in single quotes was put after the ESCAPE command. This designates the backslash symbol as the escape character. If an escape character precedes the underscore within a search condition, it is treated as a literal value instead of a wildcard.

Ordering Results

The ORDER BY clause orders the results of a query based on designated columns or expressions. The basic syntax for ORDER BY is as follows:

```
SELECT select_list
[INTO new_table_name]
FROM table_list
[WHERE search_conditions]
[GROUP BY group_by_list]
[HAVING search_conditions]
[ORDER BY order_list [ASC | DESC] ]
```

ORDER BY must appear after the required FROM clause, as well as the optional WHERE, GROUP BY, and HAVING clauses.

Using the ORDER BY Clause

This example demonstrates ordering the query results by columns `ProductID` and `EndDate`:

```
SELECT    p.Name,
      h.EndDate,
      h.ListPrice
FROM    Production.Product p
INNER JOIN Production.ProductListPriceHistory h ON
   p.ProductID = h.ProductID
ORDER BY p.Name, h.EndDate
```

This query returns:

Name	EndDate	ListPrice
All-Purpose Bike Stand	NULL	159.00
AWC Logo Cap	NULL	8.99
AWC Logo Cap	2002-06-30 00:00:00.000	8.6442
AWC Logo Cap	2003-06-30 00:00:00.000	8.6442
more rows		
Women's Tights, L	2003-06-30 00:00:00.000	74.99
Women's Tights, M	2003-06-30 00:00:00.000	74.99
Women's Tights, S	2003-06-30 00:00:00.000	74.99

(395 row(s) affected)

The default sorting order of `ORDER BY` is ascending order, which can be explicitly designated as `ASC` too. In this next example, `DESC` is used to return the results in reverse (descending) order:

```
SELECT    p.Name,
      h.EndDate,
      h.ListPrice
FROM    Production.Product p
INNER JOIN Production.ProductListPriceHistory h ON
   p.ProductID = h.ProductID
ORDER BY p.Name DESC, h.EndDate DESC
```

This returns the following abridged results:

Name	EndDate	ListPrice
Women's Tights, S	2003-06-30 00:00:00.000	74.99
Women's Tights, M	2003-06-30 00:00:00.000	74.99
Women's Tights, L	2003-06-30 00:00:00.000	74.99
...		
AWC Logo Cap	2002-06-30 00:00:00.000	8.6442
AWC Logo Cap	NULL	8.99
All-Purpose Bike Stand	NULL	159.00

(395 row(s) affected)

This third example demonstrates ordering results based on a column that is not used in the `SELECT` clause:

```
SELECT    p.Name
FROM    Production.Product p
ORDER BY p.Color
```

This returns the following abridged results:

```
name
Guide Pulley
LL Grip Tape
ML Grip Tape
HL Grip Tape
Thin-Jam Hex Nut 9
...
```

How It Works

Although queries sometimes appear to return data properly without an ORDER BY clause, the natural ordering of results is determined by the physical key column order in the clustered index (see Chapter 5 for more information on clustered indexes). If the row order of your result sets is critical, you should never depend on the implicit physical order.

In the first example, the Production.Product and Production.ProductListPriceHistory tables were queried to view the history of product prices over time.

Note The full details of INNER JOIN are provided later in the chapter.

The following line of code sorted the results first alphabetically by product name, and then by the end date:

```
ORDER BY p.Name, h.EndDate
```

You can designate one or more columns in your ORDER BY clause, so long as the columns do not exceed 8,060 bytes in total.

The second example demonstrated returning results in descending order (ascending is the default order). The DESC keyword was referenced behind each column that required the descending sort:

```
ORDER BY p.Name DESC, h.EndDate DESC
```

The third example demonstrated ordering the results by a column that was not used in the SELECT statement:

```
ORDER BY p.Color
```

One caveat when ordering by unselected columns is that ORDER BY items must appear in the select list if SELECT DISTINCT is specified.

Using the TOP Keyword with Ordered Results

The TOP keyword allows you to return the first n number of rows from a query based on the number of rows or percentage of rows that you define. The first rows returned are also impacted by how your query is ordered.

Note SQL Server 2005 also provides new ranking functions which can be used to rank each row within the partition of a result set. For a review of ranking functions, see Chapter 8.

In this example, the top ten rows are retrieved from the Purchasing.Vendor table for those rows with the highest value in the CreditRating column:

```
SELECT TOP 10 v.Name,
    v.CreditRating
FROM Purchasing.Vendor v
ORDER BY v.CreditRating DESC, v.Name
```

This returns:

Name	CreditRating
Merit Bikes	5
Victory Bikes	5
Proseware, Inc.	4
Recreation Place	4
Consumer Cycles	3
Continental Pro Cycles	3
Federal Sport	3
Inner City Bikes	3
Northern Bike Travel	3
Trey Research	3

```
(10 row(s) affected)
```

The next example demonstrates limiting the *percentage* of rows returned in a query using a local variable (using local variables in TOP is a new feature in SQL Server 2005):

```
DECLARE @Percentage float

SET @Percentage = 1

SELECT TOP (@Percentage) PERCENT
        Name
FROM Production.Product
ORDER BY Name
```

This returns the top 1 percent of rows from the Production.Product table, ordered by product name:

Name
Adjustable Race
All-Purpose Bike Stand
AWC Logo Cap
BB Ball Bearing
Bearing Ball
Bike Wash - Dissolver

```
(6 row(s) affected)
```

How It Works

In previous versions of SQL Server, developers used SET ROWCOUNT to limit how many rows the query would return or impact. In SQL Server 2005, you should use the TOP keyword instead of SET ROWCOUNT, as the TOP will usually perform faster. Also, *not* having the ability to use local variables in the TOP clause was a major reason why people still used SET ROWCOUNT over TOP in previous versions of SQL Server. With these functionality barriers removed, there is no reason not to start using TOP.

▉Tip The TOP keyword can also now be used with INSERT, UPDATE, and DELETE statements—something that will not be supported with SET ROWCOUNT future versions of SQL Server. For more information about TOP used in conjunction with data modifications, see Chapter 2.

The key to the first example was the TOP keyword, followed by the number of rows to be returned:

```
SELECT TOP 10 v.Name
```

Also important was the ORDER BY clause, which ordered the results prior to the TOP *n* rows being returned:

```
ORDER BY v.CreditRating DESC, v.Name
```

The second example demonstrated how to use the new local variable assignment functionality with TOP PERCENT:

```
DECLARE @Percentage float

SET @Percentage = 1

SELECT TOP (@Percentage) PERCENT
```

The new local variable functionality allows you to create scripts, functions, or procedures that can determine the number of rows returned by a query based on the value set by the caller, instead of having to hardcode a set TOP number or percentage of rows.

Grouping Data

The GROUP BY clause is used in a SELECT query to determine the groups that rows should be put in. The simplified syntax is as follows:

```
SELECT select_list
FROM table_list
[WHERE search_conditions]
[GROUP BY group_by_list]
```

GROUP BY follows the optional WHERE clause, and is most often used when aggregate functions are referenced in the SELECT statement (aggregate functions are reviewed in more detail in Chapter 8).

Using the GROUP BY Clause

This example uses the GROUP BY clause to summarize total amount due by order date from the Sales.SalesOrderHeader table:

```
SELECT   OrderDate,
   SUM(TotalDue) TotalDueByOrderDate
FROM   Sales.SalesOrderHeader
WHERE OrderDate BETWEEN '7/1/2001' AND '7/31/2001'
GROUP BY OrderDate
```

This returns the following (abridged) results:

```
OrderDate                TotalDueByOrderDate
-----------------------  --------------------
2001-07-01 00:00:00.000  665262.9599
2001-07-02 00:00:00.000  15394.3298
2001-07-03 00:00:00.000  16588.4572
2001-07-04 00:00:00.000  7907.9768
2001-07-05 00:00:00.000  16588.4572
...
2001-07-27 00:00:00.000  30985.659
2001-07-28 00:00:00.000  21862.8284
2001-07-29 00:00:00.000  19545.3176
2001-07-30 00:00:00.000  15914.584
2001-07-31 00:00:00.000  16588.4572

(31 row(s) affected)
```

How It Works

In this recipe's example, the GROUP BY clause was used in a SELECT query to determine the groups that rows should be put in.

Stepping through the first line of the query, the SELECT clause designated that the OrderDate should be returned, as well as the SUM total of values in the TotalDue column. SUM is an aggregate function. An aggregate function performs a calculation against a set of values (in this case TotalDue), returning a single value (the total of TotalDue by OrderDate):

```
SELECT   OrderDate,
    SUM(TotalDue) TotalDueByOrderDate
```

Notice that a *column alias* for the SUM(TotalDue) aggregation was used. A column alias returns a name for a calculated, aggregated, or regular column. This is another method of sending information to the calling application—allowing you to change the underlying source column without the application being aware. Aside from application situations, providing a separate interface from the table structures can also be useful to other referencing database objects (such as views, functions, and stored procedures, which are demonstrated in future chapters).

In the next part of the query, the Sales.SalesOrderHeader table was referenced in the FROM clause:

```
FROM   Sales.SalesOrderHeader
```

Next, the OrderDate was qualified to return rows for the month of July, and the year 2001:

```
WHERE OrderDate BETWEEN '7/1/2001' AND '7/31/2001'
```

The result set was grouped by OrderDate:

```
GROUP BY OrderDate
```

Note that grouping can occur against one or more columns.

Had the GROUP BY clause been left out of the query, using an aggregate function in the SELECT clause would have raised the following error:

```
Msg 8120, Level 16, State 1, Line 1
Column 'Sales.SalesOrderHeader.OrderDate' is invalid in the select list because
it is not contained in either an aggregate function or the GROUP BY clause.
```

This error is raised because any column that is *not* used in an aggregate function in the SELECT list must be listed in the GROUP BY clause.

Using GROUP BY ALL

By adding the ALL keyword after GROUP BY, all row values are used in the grouping, even if they were not qualified to appear via the WHERE clause.

This example executes the same query as the previous recipe's example, except it includes the ALL clause:

```
SELECT   OrderDate,
    SUM(TotalDue) TotalDueByOrderDate
FROM    Sales.SalesOrderHeader
WHERE OrderDate BETWEEN '7/1/2001' AND '7/31/2001'
GROUP BY ALL OrderDate
```

This returns the following (abridged) results:

```
OrderDate                TotalDueByOrderDate
----------------------   ---------------------
2001-07-22 00:00:00.000  42256.626
2004-06-15 00:00:00.000  NULL
2002-01-07 00:00:00.000  NULL
more rows
2002-11-14 00:00:00.000  NULL
2002-08-12 00:00:00.000  NULL
Warning: Null value is eliminated by an aggregate or other SET operation.

(1124 row(s) affected)
```

How It Works

In the results returned by the GROUP BY ALL example, notice that TotalDueByOrderDate was NULL for those order dates not included in the WHERE clause. This does not mean they have zero rows, but instead, that data is not *displayed* for them.

This query also returned a warning along with the results:

```
Warning: Null value is eliminated by an aggregate or other SET operation.
```

This means the SUM aggregate encountered NULL values and didn't include them in the total. For the SUM aggregate function, this was okay, however NULL values in other aggregate functions can cause undesired results. For example, the AVG function ignores NULL values but the COUNT function does not. If your query uses both these functions, you may think that the NULL value included in COUNT helps make up the AVG results—which it doesn't.

Selectively Querying Grouped Data Using HAVING

The HAVING clause of the SELECT statement allows you to specify a search condition on a query using GROUP BY and/or an aggregated value. The syntax is as follows:

```
SELECT select_list
[ INTO new_table_name ]
FROM table_list
[ WHERE search_conditions ]
[ GROUP BY group_by_list ]
[ HAVING search_conditions ]
```

The HAVING clause is used after the GROUP BY clause. The WHERE clause, in contrast, is used to qualify the rows that are returned *before* the data is aggregated or grouped. HAVING qualifies the aggregated data *after* the data has been grouped or aggregated.

This example queries two tables, Production.ScrapReason and Production.WorkOrder. The Production.ScrapReason is a lookup table that contains manufacturing failure reasons, while the Production.WorkOrder table contains the manufacturing work orders that control which products are manufactured in the quantity and time period, in order to meet inventory and sales needs.

This example reports to management which "failure reasons" have occurred fifty or more times:

```
SELECT  s.Name,
    COUNT(w.WorkOrderID) Cnt
FROM Production.ScrapReason s
INNER JOIN Production.WorkOrder w ON
    s.ScrapReasonID = w.ScrapReasonID
GROUP BY s.Name
HAVING COUNT(*)>50
```

This query returns:

Name	Cnt
Gouge in metal	54
Stress test failed	52
Thermoform temperature too low	63
Trim length too long	52
Wheel misaligned	51

(5 row(s) affected)

How It Works

In this recipe, the SELECT clause requested a count of WorkOrderIDs by failure name:

```
SELECT  s.Name,
    COUNT(w.WorkOrderID)
```

Two tables were joined by the ScrapReasonID column:

```
FROM Production.ScrapReason s
INNER JOIN Production.WorkOrder w ON
    s.ScrapReasonID = w.ScrapReasonID
```

Since an aggregate function was used in the SELECT clause, the non-aggregated columns must appear in the GROUP BY Clause:

```
GROUP BY s.Name
```

Lastly, using the HAVING query determines that, *of the selected and grouped data*, only those rows in the result set with a count of fifty or higher will be returned:

```
HAVING COUNT(*)>50
```

SELECT Clause Techniques

The SELECT clause is primarily used to define which columns are returned in the result set, but its functionality isn't limited to just that. This next set of queries will detail a number of SELECT clause techniques, including:

- Using the DISTINCT keyword to remove duplicate values

- Renaming columns using column aliases

- Concatenating string values into a single column

- Creating a SELECT statement that itself creates an executable Transact-SQL script

- Creating a comma-delimited array list of values

Using DISTINCT to Remove Duplicate Values

The default behavior of a SELECT statement is to use the ALL keyword (although because it is the default, you'll rarely see this being used in a query), meaning that duplicate rows will be retrieved and displayed if they exist. Using the DISTINCT keyword instead of ALL allows you to only return unique rows in your results.

This example shows you how to use the DISTINCT keyword to remove duplicate values from a set of selected columns, so that only unique rows appear:

```
SELECT   DISTINCT HireDate
FROM   HumanResources.Employee
```

The results show all unique hire dates from the HumanResources.Employee table:

```
HireDate
-----------------------
1996-07-31 00:00:00.000
1997-02-26 00:00:00.000
1997-12-12 00:00:00.000
1998-01-05 00:00:00.000
more rows
2002-11-01 00:00:00.000
2003-04-15 00:00:00.000
2003-07-01 00:00:00.000

(164 row(s) affected)
```

How It Works

Use the DISTINCT keyword to return distinct values in the result set. In this recipe, DISTINCT was used to return unique HireDate column values. Be sure to only use DISTINCT when actually needed or necessary, as it can slow the query down on larger result sets.

Using DISTINCT in Aggregate Functions

You can also use DISTINCT for a column that is used within an aggregate function (aggregate functions are reviewed in more detail in Chapter 8). You may wish to do this in order to perform aggregations on only the unique values of a column.

For example, if you wanted to calculate the average product list price, you could use the following query:

```
SELECT   AVG(ListPrice)
FROM Production.Product
```

This returns:

```
--------------------
438.6662

(1 row(s) affected)
```

But the previous query calculated the average list price across *all* products. What if some product types are more numerous than others? What if you are only interested in the average price of *unique* price points?

In this case you would write the query as:

```
SELECT   AVG(DISTINCT ListPrice)
FROM Production.Product
```

This returns the unique set of price points first, *and then* averages them:

```
--------------------
437.4042

(1 row(s) affected)
```

How It Works

DISTINCT can be used to return unique rows from a result set, as well as force unique column values within an aggregate function. In this example, the DISTINCT keyword was put within the parentheses of the aggregate function.

Using Column Aliases

For column computations or aggregate functions, you can use a column alias to explicitly name the columns of your query output. You can also use column aliases to rename columns that already *have* a name, which helps obscure the underlying column from the calling application (allowing you to swap out underlying columns without changing the derived column name). You can designate a column alias by using the AS keyword, or by simply following the column or expression with the column alias name.

This example demonstrates producing column aliases using two different techniques:

```
SELECT   Color AS 'Grouped Color',
         AVG(DISTINCT ListPrice) AS 'Average Distinct List Price',
         AVG(ListPrice) 'Average List Price'
FROM Production.Product
GROUP BY Color
```

This returns the following abridged results:

Grouped Color	Average Distinct List Price	Average List Price
Silver	726.2907	850.3053
Grey	125.00	125.00
...		
Silver/Black	61.19	64.0185

```
(10 row(s) affected)
```

How It Works

This example shows three examples of using column aliasing. The first example demonstrated how to rename an *existing* column using the AS clause. The AS clause is used to change a column name in the results, or add a name to a derived (calculated or aggregated) column:

```
SELECT Color AS 'Grouped Color',
```

The second example demonstrated how to add a column name to an aggregate function:

```
AVG(DISTINCT ListPrice) AS 'Average Distinct List Price',
```

The third example demonstrated how to add a column alias without using the AS keyword (it can simply be omitted):

```
AVG(ListPrice) 'Average List Price'
```

Using SELECT to Create a Script

As a DBA or developer, you sometimes need a Transact-SQL script to run against several objects within a database or against several databases across a SQL Server instance. Or perhaps you have a very large table with several columns, which you need to validate in search conditions, but you don't want to have to hand type each column.

This next recipe offers a time-saving technique, using SELECT to write out Transact-SQL for you. You can adapt this recipe to all sorts of purposes.

In this example, assume that you wish to check for rows in a table where all values are NULL. There are many columns in the table, and you want to avoid hand-coding them. Instead, you can create a script to do the work for you:

```
SELECT column_name + ' IS NULL AND '
FROM INFORMATION_SCHEMA.columns
WHERE table_name = 'Employee'
ORDER BY ORDINAL_POSITION
```

This returns code that you can integrate into a WHERE clause (after you remove the trailing AND at the last WHERE condition):

```
------------------------------
EmployeeID IS NULL AND
NationalIDNumber IS NULL AND
ContactID IS NULL AND
LoginID IS NULL AND
ManagerID IS NULL AND
Title IS NULL AND
BirthDate IS NULL AND
MaritalStatus IS NULL AND
Gender IS NULL AND
HireDate IS NULL AND
SalariedFlag IS NULL AND
VacationHours IS NULL AND
SickLeaveHours IS NULL AND
CurrentFlag IS NULL AND
rowguid IS NULL AND
ModifiedDate IS NULL AND

(16 row(s) affected)
```

How It Works

The example used string concatenation and the `INFORMATION_SCHEMA.columns` system view to generate a list of columns from the `Employee` table. For each column, `IS NULL AND` was concatenated to its name. The results can then be copied to the `WHERE` clause of a query, allowing you to query for rows where each column has a `NULL` value.

This general technique of concatenating SQL commands to various system data columns can be used in numerous ways, including for creating scripts against tables or other database objects. Do be careful when scripting an action against multiple objects or databases—make sure that the change is what you intended, and that you are fully aware of the script's outcome.

Performing String Concatenation

String concatenation is performed by using the + operator to join two expressions, as this example demonstrates:

```
SELECT    'The ' +
          p.name +
          ' is only ' +
          CONVERT(varchar(25),p.ListPrice) +
          '!'
FROM    Production.Product p
WHERE    p.ListPrice between 100 AND 120
ORDER BY p.ListPrice
```

This returns:

```
--------------------------------------------------------------------------------
The ML Bottom Bracket is only 101.24!
The ML Headset is only 102.29!
The Rear Brakes is only 106.50!
The Front Brakes is only 106.50!
The LL Road Rear Wheel is only 112.57!
The Hitch Rack - 4-Bike is only 120.00!

(6 row(s) affected)
```

How It Works

When used with character data types, the + operator is used to concatenate expressions together. In this example, literal values were concatenated to columns from the `Production.Product` table. Each row formed a sentence celebrating the low price of each row's product.

String concatenation is often used when generating end-user reports (such as displaying the First and Last Name in a single column), or when you need to combine multiple data columns into a single column (as you'll see in the next recipe).

Creating a Comma Delimited List Using SELECT

This next recipe demonstrates how to create a comma delimited list using a `SELECT` query. You can use this recipe in several ways. For example, you could integrate it into a user-defined function that returns a comma delimited list of the regions that a salesperson sells to into a single column (see Chapter 11).

This example demonstrates returning one-to-many table data into a single presentable string:

```
DECLARE @Shifts varchar(20)
SET @Shifts = ''

SELECT   @Shifts = @Shifts + s.Name + ','
FROM   HumanResources.Shift s
ORDER BY s.EndTime

SELECT @Shifts
```

This query returns:

```
--------------------
Night,Day,Evening,

(1 row(s) affected)
```

How It Works

In the first part of this script, a local variable was created to hold a comma delimited list:

```
DECLARE @Shifts varchar(20)
```

After a variable is declared, but before it is set, it is given a NULL value. Because we cannot concatenate NULL values with strings, the variable should be set to an initial blank value instead, as was done in the recipe:

```
SET @Shifts = ''
```

In the query itself, a list of shifts are gathered from the HumanResources.Shift table, ordered by EndTime. At the core of this example, you see that the local variable is assigned to the value of itself concatenated to the shift name, and then concatenated to a comma. The query loops through each value ordered by EndTime, appending each one to the local variable:

```
SELECT   @Shifts = @Shifts + s.Name + ','
FROM   HumanResources.Shift s
ORDER BY s.EndTime
```

SELECT is used to display the final contents of the local variable:

```
SELECT @Shifts
```

Using the INTO Clause

The INTO clause of the SELECT statement allows you to create a new table based on the columns and rows of the query results. Ideally you should be creating your tables using the CREATE TABLE command: however using INTO provides a quick-and-dirty method of creating a new table without having to explicitly define the column names and data types.

The INTO clause allows you to create a table in a SELECT statement based on the columns and rows the query returns. The syntax for INTO is as follows:

```
SELECT select_list
[INTO new_table_name]
FROM table_list
```

The INTO clause comes after the SELECT clause but before the FROM clause, as the next recipe will demonstrate.

In this first example, a new table is created based on the results of a query:

```
SELECT    CustomerID,
    Name,
    SalesPersonID,
    Demographics
INTO    Store_Archive
FROM    Sales.Store
```

The query returns the number of rows inserted into the new Store_Archive table, but does not return query results:

```
(701 row(s) affected)
```

In the second example, a table is created without inserting rows into it:

```
SELECT    CustomerID,
        Name,
        SalesPersonID,
        Demographics
INTO    Store_Archive
FROM    Sales.Store
WHERE    1=0
```

This returns the number of rows inserted into your new Store_Archive table (which in this case is zero):

```
(0 row(s) affected)
```

How It Works

This recipe's example looked like a regular SELECT query, only between the SELECT and FROM clauses the following instructions were inserted:

```
INTO    Store_Archive
```

The INTO clause is followed by the new table name (which must not already exist). This can be a permanent, temporary, or global temporary table (See Chapter 4 for more information). The columns you select determine the structure of the table.

This is a great technique for quickly "copying" the base table structure and data of an existing table. Using INTO, you are not required to pre-define the new table's structure explicitly (for example, you do not need to issue a CREATE TABLE statement).

■Caution Although the structure of the selected columns is reproduced, the constraints, indexes, and other separate objects dependent on the source table are *not* copied.

In the second example, a new table was created without also populating it with rows. This was achieved by using a WHERE clause condition that always evaluates to FALSE:

```
WHERE    1=0
```

Since the number 1 will never equal the number 0, no rows will evaluate to TRUE, and therefore no rows will be inserted into the new table. However, the new table is created anyway.

SubQueries

A subquery is a SELECT query that is nested within another SELECT, INSERT, UPDATE, or DELETE statement. A subquery can also be nested inside another subquery. Subqueries can often be re-written into regular JOINs, however sometimes an existence subquery (demonstrated in this recipe) can perform better than equivalent non-subquery methods.

A *correlated* subquery is a subquery whose results depend on the values of the outer query.

Using Subqueries to Check for the Existence of Matches

This first example demonstrates checking for the existence of matching rows within a correlated subquery:

```
SELECT DISTINCT s.PurchaseOrderNumber
FROM Sales.SalesOrderHeader s
WHERE EXISTS (   SELECT SalesOrderID
         FROM Sales.SalesOrderDetail
         WHERE UnitPrice BETWEEN 1000 AND 2000 AND
              SalesOrderID = s.SalesOrderID)
```

This returns the following abridged results:

```
PurchaseOrderNumber
-------------------------
PO8410140860
PO12325137381
PO1160166903
PO1073122178
...
PO15486173227
PO14268145224

(1989 row(s) affected)
```

This second example demonstrates a regular non-correlated subquery:

```
SELECT   SalesPersonID,
     SalesQuota CurrentSalesQuota
FROM     Sales.SalesPerson
WHERE    SalesQuota IN
           (SELECT MAX(SalesQuota)
            FROM Sales.SalesPerson)
```

This returns the three salespeople who had the maximum sales quota of 300,000:

```
SalesPersonID CurrentSalesQuota
------------- --------------------
275           300000.00
279           300000.00
287           300000.00
Warning: Null value is eliminated by an aggregate or other SET operation.

(3 row(s) affected)
```

How It Works

The critical piece of the first example was the subquery in the WHERE clause, which checked for the existence of SalesOrderIDs that had products with a UnitPrice between 1000 and 2000. A JOIN was used in the WHERE clause of the subquery, between the outer query and the inner query, by stating SalesOrderID = s.SalesOrderID. The subquery used the SalesOrderID from each returned row in the outer query.

In the second example, there is no WHERE clause in the subquery used to join to the outer table. It is not a correlated subquery. Instead, a value is retrieved from the query to evaluate against in the IN operator of the WHERE clause.

Querying from More Than One Data Source

The previous recipes retrieved data from a single table. Most normalized databases have more than one table in them, so more often than not you'll need to retrieve data from multiple tables using a single query. The JOIN keyword allows you to combine data from multiple tables and/or views into a single result set. It joins a column or columns from one table to another table, evaluating whether there is a match.

With the JOIN keyword, you join two tables based on a join condition. Most often you'll see a join condition testing the equality of one column in one table compared to another column in the second table (joined columns do not need to have the same name, only compatible data types).

■**Tip** As a query performance best practice, try to avoid having to convert data types of the columns in your join clause (using CONVERT or CAST, for example). Opt instead for modifying the underlying schema to match data types (or convert the data beforehand in a separate table, temp table, table variable, or Common Table Expression (CTE)).

SQL Server 2005 join types fall into three categories: *inner*, *outer*, and *cross*. Inner joins use the INNER JOIN keywords. INNER JOIN operates by matching common values between two tables. Only table rows satisfying the join conditions are used to construct the result set. INNER JOINs are the default JOIN type, so if you wish, you can use just the JOIN keyword in your INNER JOIN operations.

Outer joins have three different join types: LEFT OUTER, RIGHT OUTER, and FULL OUTER joins. LEFT OUTER and RIGHT OUTER JOINs, like INNER JOINs, return rows that match the conditions of the join condition. *Unlike* INNER JOINs, LEFT OUTER JOINs return unmatched rows from the first table of the join pair, and RIGHT OUTER JOINs return unmatched rows from the second table of the join pair. The FULL OUTER JOIN clause returns unmatched rows on both the left *and* right tables.

A lesser used join type is CROSS JOIN. A CROSS JOIN returns a Cartesian product when a WHERE clause isn't used. A *Cartesian product* produces a result set based on every possible combination of rows from the left table, multiplied against the rows in the right table. For example, if the Stores table has 7 rows, and the Sales table has 22 rows, you would receive 154 rows (or 7 times 22) in the query results (each possible combination of row displayed).

The next few recipes will demonstrate the different join types.

Using INNER Joins

This inner join joins three tables in order to return discount information on a specific product:

```
SELECT   p.Name,
         s.DiscountPct
FROM Sales.SpecialOffer s
INNER JOIN Sales.SpecialOfferProduct o ON
```

```
    s.SpecialOfferID = o.SpecialOfferID
INNER JOIN Production.Product p ON
    o.ProductID = p.ProductID
WHERE p.Name = 'All-Purpose Bike Stand'
```

The results of this query:

Name	DiscountPct
All-Purpose Bike Stand	0.00

(1 row(s) affected)

How It Works

A join starts after the first table in the FROM clause. In this example, three tables were joined together: Sales.SpecialOffer, Sales.SpecialOfferProduct, and Production.Product.

Sales.SpecialOffer, the first table referenced in the FROM clause, contains a lookup of sales discounts:

```
FROM Sales.SpecialOffer s
```

Notice the letter "s" which trails the table name. This is a table alias. Once you begin using more than one table in a query, it is important to understand the data source of the individual columns. If the same column names exist in two different tables, you could get an error from the SQL compiler asking you to clarify which column you really wanted to return.

As a best practice, it is a good idea to use aliases whenever column names are specified in a query. For each of the referenced tables, a character was used to symbolize the table name—saving you the trouble of spelling it out each time. This query used a single character as a table alias, but you can use any valid identifier. A *table alias*, aside from allowing you to shorten or clarify the original table name, allows you to swap out the base table name if you ever have to replace it with a different table or view, or if you need to self-join the tables. Table aliases are optional, but recommended when your query has more than one table. A table alias follows the table name in the statement FROM clause.

But back to the example... The INNER JOIN keywords followed the first table reference, then the table being joined to it, followed by its alias:

```
INNER JOIN Sales.SpecialOfferProduct o
```

After that, the ON keyword prefaces the column joins:

```
ON
```

This particular INNER JOIN is based on the equality of two columns—one from the first table and another from the second:

```
s.SpecialOfferID = o.SpecialOfferID
```

Next, the Production.Product table is INNER JOIN'd too:

```
INNER JOIN Production.Product p ON
    o.ProductID = p.ProductID
```

Lastly, a WHERE clause is used to filter rows returned:

```
WHERE Name = 'All-Purpose Bike Stand'
```

Using OUTER Joins

This recipe compares the results of an INNER JOIN versus a LEFT OUTER JOIN. This first query displays the tax rates states and provinces using the Person.StateProvince table and the Sales.SalesTaxRate table. The following query uses an INNER JOIN:

```
SELECT   s.CountryRegionCode,
         s.StateProvinceCode,
         t.TaxType,
         t.TaxRate
FROM Person.StateProvince s
INNER JOIN Sales.SalesTaxRate t ON
    s.StateProvinceID = t.StateProvinceID
```

This returns the following (abridged) results:

CountryRegionCode	StateProvinceCode	TaxType	TaxRate
CA	AB	1	14.00
CA	ON	1	14.25
CA	QC	1	14.25
CA	AB	2	7.00
more rows			

But with the INNER JOIN, you are only seeing those records from Person.StateProvince that *have* rows in the Sales.SalesTaxRate table. In order to see *all* rows from Person.StateProvince, whether or not they have associated tax rates, LEFT OUTER JOIN is used:

```
SELECT   s.CountryRegionCode,
         s.StateProvinceCode,
         t.TaxType,
         t.TaxRate
FROM Person.StateProvince s
LEFT OUTER JOIN Sales.SalesTaxRate t ON
    s.StateProvinceID = t.StateProvinceID
```

This returns the following (abridged) results:

CountryRegionCode	StateProvinceCode	TaxType	TaxRate
CA	AB	1	14.00
CA	AB	2	7.00
US	AK	NULL	NULL
US	AL	NULL	NULL
more rows			

How It Works

This recipe's example demonstrated an INNER JOIN query versus a LEFT OUTER JOIN query. The LEFT OUTER JOIN query returned unmatched rows from the first table of the join pair. Notice how this query returned NULL values for those rows from Person.StateProvince that didn't have associated rows in the Sales.SalesTaxRate table.

Using CROSS Joins

In this example, the `Person.StateProvince` and `Sales.SalesTaxRate` tables are CROSS JOIN'd:

```
SELECT   s.CountryRegionCode,
         s.StateProvinceCode,
         t.TaxType,
         t.TaxRate
FROM Person.StateProvince s
CROSS JOIN Sales.SalesTaxRate t
```

This returns the following (abridged) results:

CountryRegionCode	StateProvinceCode	TaxType	TaxRate
FR	01	1	14.00
FR	01	1	14.25
FR	01	1	14.25
...			
CA	YT	3	19.60
CA	YT	3	17.50

```
(5249 row(s) affected)
```

How It Works

A CROSS JOIN without a WHERE clause returns a Cartesian product. The results of this CROSS JOIN show StateProvince and SalesTaxRate information that doesn't logically go together. Since the Person. StateProvince table had 181 rows, and the Sales.SalesTaxRate had 29 rows, the query returned 5249 rows.

Performing Self-Joins

Sometimes you may need to treat the same table as two separate tables. This may be because the table contains nested hierarchies of data (for example, employees reporting to managers in the Employees table), or perhaps you wish to reference the same table based on different time periods (compare sales records from the year 1999 versus the year 2005). You can achieve this joining of a table with itself through the use of table aliases.

In this example, a self-join is demonstrated by joining the Employee table's ManagerID with the Employee table's EmployeeID:

```
SELECT   e.EmployeeID,
         e.Title,
         m.Title AS ManagerTitle
FROM   HumanResources.Employee e
LEFT OUTER JOIN HumanResources.Employee m ON
         e.ManagerID = m.EmployeeID
```

This returns the following (abridged) results:

EmployeeID	Title	ManagerTitle
1	Production Technician - WC60	Production Supervisor - WC60
2	Marketing Assistant	Marketing Manager
3	Engineering Manager	Vice President of Engineering
4	Senior Tool Designer	Engineering Manager
more rows		
288	Pacific Sales Manager	Vice President of Sales
289	Sales Representative	European Sales Manager
290	Sales Representative	Pacific Sales Manager

(290 row(s) affected)

How It Works

This example queried the HumanResources.Employee table, returning the EmployeeID of the employee, the employee's title, and the title of his or her manager. The HumanResource.Employee table has a recursive foreign key column called ManagerID, which points to the manager's EmployeeID , and which is the key to another row in the same table. Managers and employees have their data stored in the same table.

Almost all employees have a manager in this table, so using a recursive query, you can establish a nested hierarchy of employees and their managers. There is only one employee that does not have a manager, and that's the Chief Executive Officer.

In the example, the EmployeeID and Title were both taken from the first table aliased with an e. The third column was the title of the Manager, and that table was aliased with an m:

```
SELECT   e.EmployeeID,
       e.Title,
       m.Title AS ManagerTitle
```

The two tables (really the same table, but represented twice using aliases) were joined by EmployeeID to ManagerID using a LEFT OUTER JOIN, so that the Chief Executive Officer would be returned too:

```
FROM   HumanResources.Employee e
LEFT OUTER JOIN HumanResources.Employee m ON
       e.ManagerID = m.EmployeeID
```

Although the same table was referenced twice in the FROM clause, by using a table alias, SQL Server treats them as separate tables.

■Tip New to SQL Server 2005, Comment Table Expressions (CTEs) are also reviewed in this chapter, and provide a more sophisticated method of handling recursive queries.

Using Derived Tables

Derived tables are SELECT statements that act as tables in the FROM clause. Derived tables can sometimes provide better performance than using temporary tables (see Chapter 4 for more on temporary tables).

This example demonstrates how to use a derived table in the FROM clause of a SELECT statement:

```
SELECT DISTINCT s.PurchaseOrderNumber
FROM Sales.SalesOrderHeader s
INNER JOIN (SELECT SalesOrderID
        FROM Sales.SalesOrderDetail
        WHERE UnitPrice BETWEEN 1000 AND 2000) d ON
    s.SalesOrderID = d.SalesOrderID
```

This returns the following abridged results:

```
PurchaseOrderNumber
------------------------
PO8410140860
PO12325137381
PO1160166903
PO1073122178
...
PO15486173227
PO14268145224

(1989 row(s) affected)
```

How It Works

This example's query searches for the `PurchaseOrderNumber` from the `Sales.SalesOrderHeader` table for any order containing products with a `UnitPrice` between 1000 and 2000.

The query joins a table to a derived table using `INNER JOIN`. The derived table query is encapsulated in parentheses, and followed by a table alias. The derived table is a separate query in itself, and doesn't require the use of a temporary table to store the results. Thus, queries that use derived tables can sometimes perform significantly better than temporary tables, as you eliminate the steps needed for SQL Server to create and allocate the temporary table prior to use.

Combining Result Sets with UNION

The `UNION` operator is used to append the results of two or more `SELECT` statements into a single result set. Each `SELECT` statement being merged must have the same number of columns, with the same or compatible data types in the same order, as this example demonstrates:

```
SELECT    SalesPersonID, GETDATE() QuotaDate, SalesQuota
FROM      Sales.SalesPerson
WHERE     SalesQuota > 0
UNION
SELECT    SalesPersonID, QuotaDate, SalesQuota
FROM      Sales.SalesPersonQuotaHistory
WHERE     SalesQuota > 0
ORDER BY  SalesPersonID DESC, QuotaDate DESC
```

This returns the following (abridged) results:

```
SalesPersonID QuotaDate                SalesQuota
------------- ----------------------- ---------------------
290             2005-02-27 10:10:12.587 250000.00
290             2004-04-01 00:00:00.000 421000.00
290             2004-01-01 00:00:00.000 399000.00
289             2004-01-01 00:00:00.000 366000.00
289             2003-10-01 00:00:00.000 566000.00
...
268             2002-01-01 00:00:00.000 91000.00
268             2001-10-01 00:00:00.000 7000.00
268             2001-07-01 00:00:00.000 28000.00

(177 row(s) affected)
```

How It Works

This query appended two result sets into a single result set. The first result set returned the SalesPersonID, the current date function (see Chapter 8 for more information on this) and the SalesQuota. Since GETDATE() is a function, it doesn't naturally return a column name—so a QuotaDate column alias was used in its place:

```
SELECT    SalesPersonID, GETDATE() QuotaDate, SalesQuota
FROM      Sales.SalesPerson
```

The WHERE clause filtered data for those salespeople with a SalesQuota greater than zero:

```
WHERE     SalesQuota > 0
```

The next part of the query was the UNION operator, which appended the *distinct* results with the second query:

```
UNION
```

The second query pulled data from the Sales.SalesPersonQuotaHistory, which keeps history for a salesperson's sales quota as it changes through time:

```
SELECT    SalesPersonID, QuotaDate, SalesQuota
FROM      Sales.SalesPersonQuotaHistory
WHERE     SalesQuota > 0
```

The ORDER BY clause sorted the result set by SalesPersonID and QuotaDate, both in descending order. The ORDER BY clause, when needed, must appear at the bottom of the query and cannot appear after queries prior to the final UNION'd query. The ORDER BY clause should also only refer to column names from the *first* result set:

```
ORDER BY SalesPersonID DESC, QuotaDate DESC
```

Looking at the results again, for a single salesperson, you can see that the current QuotaDate of '2005-02-27' is sorted at the top. This was the date retrieved by the GETDATE() function. The other rows for SalesPersonID 290 are from the Sales.SalesPersonQuotaHistory table:

SalesPersonID	QuotaDate	SalesQuota
290	2005-02-27 10:10:12.587	250000.00
290	2004-04-01 00:00:00.000	421000.00
290	2004-01-01 00:00:00.000	399000.00
290	2003-10-01 00:00:00.000	389000.00

Keep in mind that the default behavior of the UNION operator is to remove *all duplicate rows*, and display column names based on the first result set. For large result sets, this can be a very costly operation, so if you don't need to de-duplicate the data, or if the data is naturally distinct, you can add the ALL keyword to the UNION:

```
UNION ALL
```

With the ALL clause added, duplicate rows are NOT removed.

Using APPLY to Invoke a Table-Valued Function for Each Row

New to SQL Server 2005, APPLY is used to invoke a table-valued function for each row of an outer query. A table-valued function returns a result set based on one or more parameters. Using APPLY, the input of these parameters are the columns of the left referencing table. This is useful if the left table contains columns and rows that must be evaluated by the table-valued function.

CROSS APPLY works like an INNER JOIN in that unmatched rows between the left table and the table-valued function don't appear in the result set. OUTER APPLY is like an OUTER JOIN, in that non-matched rows are still returned in the result set with NULL values in the function results.

The next two recipes will demonstrate both CROSS and OUTER APPLY.

■**Note** This next example covers both the FROM and JOIN examples, and user-defined table-valued functions functionality. Table-valued functions are reviewed in more detail in Chapter 11.

Using CROSS APPLY

In this example, a table-valued function is created that returns work order routing information based on the WorkOrderID passed to it:

```
CREATE FUNCTION dbo.fn_WorkOrderRouting
  (@WorkOrderID int) RETURNS TABLE
AS
RETURN
  SELECT WorkOrderID,
         ProductID,
         OperationSequence,
         LocationID
   FROM Production.WorkOrderRouting
   WHERE WorkOrderID = @WorkOrderID
GO
```

Next, the WorkOrderID is passed from the Production.WorkOrder table to the new function:

```
SELECT   w.WorkOrderID,
         w.OrderQty,
         r.ProductID,
         r.OperationSequence
FROM Production.WorkOrder w
  CROSS APPLY dbo.fn_WorkOrderRouting
  (w.WorkOrderID) AS r
ORDER BY   w.WorkOrderID,
         w.OrderQty,
         r.ProductID
```

This returns the following (abridged) results:

WorkOrderID	OrderQty	ProductID	OperationSequence
13	4	747	1
13	4	747	2
13	4	747	3
13	4	747	4
13	4	747	6
13	4	747	7
14	2	748	1
14	2	748	2
...			
72585	6	802	1
72585	6	802	6
72586	1	803	1
72586	1	803	6
72587	19	804	1
72587	19	804	6

How It Works

The first part of this example was the creation of a table-valued function. The function accepts a single parameter, @WorkOrderID, and when executed, returns the WorkOrderID, ProductID, OperationSequence, and LocationID from the Production.WorkOrderRouting table for the specified WorkOrderID.

The next query in the example returned the WorkOrderID and OrderQty from the Production.WorkOrder table. In addition to this, two columns from the table-valued function were selected:

```
SELECT    w.WorkOrderID,
        w.OrderQty,
        r.ProductID,
        r.OperationSequence
```

The heart of this example comes next. Notice that in the FROM clause, the Production.WorkOrder table is joined to the new table-valued function using CROSS APPLY, only unlike a JOIN clause, there isn't an ON followed by join conditions. Instead, in the parentheses after the function name, the w.WorkOrderID is passed to the table-valued function from the left Production.WorkOrder table:

```
FROM Production.WorkOrder w
  CROSS APPLY dbo.fn_WorkOrderRouting
  (w.WorkOrderID) AS r
```

The function was aliased like a regular table, with the letter "r."

Lastly, the results were sorted:

```
ORDER BY    w.WorkOrderID,
        w.OrderQty,
        r.ProductID
```

In the results for WorkOrderID 13, each associated WorkOrderRouting row was returned next to the calling tables WorkOrderID and OrderQty:

WorkOrderID	OrderQty	ProductID	OperationSequence
13	4	747	1
13	4	747	2
13	4	747	3
13	4	747	4
13	4	747	6
13	4	747	7

Each row of the WorkOrder table was duplicated for each row returned from fn_WorkOrderRouting—all were based on the WorkOrderID.

Using OUTER APPLY

In order to demonstrate OUTER APPLY, a new row is inserted into Production.WorkOrder:

```
INSERT INTO [AdventureWorks].[Production].[WorkOrder]
          ([ProductID]
          ,[OrderQty]
          ,[ScrappedQty]
          ,[StartDate]
          ,[EndDate]
          ,[DueDate]
          ,[ScrapReasonID]
          ,[ModifiedDate])
     VALUES
          (1,
          1,
          1,
          GETDATE(),
          GETDATE(),
          GETDATE(),
          1,
          GETDATE())
```

Because this is a new row, and because Production.WorkOrder has an IDENTITY column for the WorkOrderID, the new row will have the maximum WorkOrderID in the table. Also, this new row will *not* have an associated value in the Production.WorkOrderRouting table, because it was just added.

Next, a CROSS APPLY query is executed, this time qualifying it to only return data for the newly inserted row:

```
SELECT   w.WorkOrderID,
      w.OrderQty,
      r.ProductID,
      r.OperationSequence
FROM Production.WorkOrder AS w
  CROSS APPLY dbo.fn_WorkOrderRouting
  (w.WorkOrderID) AS r
WHERE w.WorkOrderID IN
      (SELECT MAX(WorkOrderID)
       FROM Production.WorkOrder)
```

This returns nothing, because the left table's new row is unmatched:

```
WorkOrderID OrderQty    ProductID   OperationSequence
----------- ----------- ----------- ------------------

(0 row(s) affected)
```

Now an OUTER APPLY is tried instead, which then returns the row from WorkOrder in spite of there being no associated value in the table-valued function:

```
SELECT    w.WorkOrderID,
      w.OrderQty,
      r.ProductID,
      r.OperationSequence
FROM Production.WorkOrder AS w
  OUTER APPLY dbo.fn_WorkOrderRouting
  (w.WorkOrderID) AS r
WHERE w.WorkOrderID IN
      (SELECT MAX(WorkOrderID)
       FROM Production.WorkOrder)
```

This returns:

```
WorkOrderID OrderQty    ProductID   OperationSequence
----------- ----------- ----------- ------------------
72592       1           NULL        NULL

(1 row(s) affected)
```

How It Works

SQL Sever 2005 has increased the expressiveness of the Transact-SQL language with CROSS and OUTER APPLY, providing a new method for applying lookups against columns, using a table-valued function.

CROSS APPLY was demonstrated against a row without a match in the table-valued function results. Since CROSS APPLY works like an INNER JOIN, no rows were returned. In the second query of this example, OUTER APPLY was used instead, this time returning unmatched NULL rows from the table-valued function, similar to an OUTER JOIN.

Data Source Advanced Techniques

This next set of recipes shows you a few advanced techniques for sampling, manipulating, and comparing data sources (a data source being any valid data source reference in a FROM clause), including:

- Returning a sampling of rows using TABLESAMPLE

- Using PIVOT to convert values into columns, and using an aggregation to group the data by the new columns

- Using UNPIVOT to normalize repeating column groups

- Using INTERSECT and EXCEPT operands to return distinct rows that only exist in either the left query (using EXCEPT), or only distinct rows that exist in both the left and right queries (using INTERSECT)

These recipes all happen to be new features introduced in SQL Server 2005.

Using the TABLESAMPLE to Return Random Rows

Introduced in SQL Server 2005, TABLESAMPLE allows you to extract a sampling of rows from a table in the FROM clause. This sampling can be based on a percentage of number of rows. You can use TABLESAMPLE when only a sampling of rows is necessary for the application instead of a full result set.

This example demonstrates a query that returns a percentage of random rows from a specific data source using TABLESAMPLE:

```
SELECT FirstName,LastName
FROM Person.Contact TABLESAMPLE SYSTEM (1 PERCENT)
```

This returns the following (abridged) results:

```
FirstName                                    LastName
----------------------------------------     ---------------------------------
Pat                                          Coleman
Takiko                                       Collins
John                                         Colon
Scott                                        Colvin
more rows
Gerald                                       Lopez
Sydney                                       Johnson
Gerald                                       Martinez

(216 row(s) affected)
```

Executing it again returns a new set of (abridged) results:

```
FirstName                                    LastName
----------------------------------------     ---------------------------------
Reinout                                      Hillmann
Mike                                         Hines
Matthew                                      Hink
Nancy                                        Hirota
more rows
Jason                                        Ross
Jake                                         Zhang
Jason                                        Coleman

(291 row(s) affected)
```

How It Works

TABLESAMPLE works by extracting a sample of rows from the query result set. In this example, 1 percent of rows were sampled from the Person.Contact table. However don't let the "percent" fool you. That percentage is the percentage of the table's data pages. Once the sample pages are selected, all rows for the selected pages are returned. Since the fill-state of pages can vary, the number of rows returned will also vary—you'll notice that the first time the query is executed in this example there were 216 rows, and the second time there were 291 rows.

If you designate the number of rows, this is actually converted by SQL Server into a percentage, and then the same method used by SQL Server to identify the percentage of data pages is used.

Using PIVOT to Convert Single Column Values into Multiple Columns and Aggregate Data

Introduced in SQL Server 2005, the new PIVOT operator allows you to create cross-tab queries that convert values into columns, using an aggregation to group the data by the new columns.

PIVOT uses the following syntax:

```
FROM  table_source
PIVOT    ( aggregate_function ( value_column )
     FOR pivot_column
     IN ( <column_list>)
   ) table_alias
```

The arguments of PIVOT are described in the Table 1-3.

Table 1-3. *PIVOT arguments*

Argument	Description
table_source	The table where the data will be pivoted.
aggregate_function	
(value_column)	The aggregate function that will be used against the specified column.
pivot_column	The column that will be used to create the column headers.
column_list	The values to pivot from the pivot column.
table_alias	The table alias of the pivoted result set.

This next example shows you how to PIVOT and aggregate data similar to Microsoft Excel functionality—such as shifting values in a single column into multiple columns, with aggregated data shown in the results.

The first part of the example displays the data pre-pivoted. The query results show employee shifts, as well as the departments that they are in:

```
SELECT    s.Name ShiftName,
     h.EmployeeID,
     d.Name DepartmentName
FROM   HumanResources.EmployeeDepartmentHistory h
INNER JOIN HumanResources.Department d ON
     h.DepartmentID = d.DepartmentID
INNER JOIN HumanResources.Shift s ON
     h.ShiftID = s.ShiftID
WHERE    EndDate IS NULL AND
     d.Name IN ('Production', 'Engineering', 'Marketing')
ORDER BY ShiftName
```

Notice that the varying departments are all listed in a single column:

ShiftName	EmployeeID	DepartmentName
Day	3	Engineering
Day	9	Engineering
Day	11	Engineering
Day	12	Engineering
Day	267	Engineering
Day	270	Engineering
...		
Night	234	Production
Night	245	Production
Night	262	Production
Night	252	Production

(194 row(s) affected)

The next query moves the department values into columns, along with a count of employees by shift:

```
SELECT   ShiftName,
      Production,
      Engineering,
      Marketing
FROM
(SELECT   s.Name ShiftName,
      h.EmployeeID,
      d.Name DepartmentName
FROM   HumanResources.EmployeeDepartmentHistory h
INNER JOIN HumanResources.Department d ON
      h.DepartmentID = d.DepartmentID
INNER JOIN HumanResources.Shift s ON
      h.ShiftID = s.ShiftID
WHERE   EndDate IS NULL AND
      d.Name IN ('Production', 'Engineering', 'Marketing')) AS a
PIVOT
(
COUNT(EmployeeID)
FOR DepartmentName IN ([Production], [Engineering], [Marketing]))
AS b
ORDER BY ShiftName
```

This returns:

ShiftName	Production	Engineering	Marketing
Day	79	6	9
Evening	54	0	0
Night	46	0	0

(3 row(s) affected)

How It Works

The result of the PIVOT query returned employee counts by shift and department. The query began by naming the fields to return:

```
SELECT   ShiftName,
      Production,
      Engineering,
      Marketing
```

Notice that these fields were actually the converted rows, but turned into column names.

The FROM clause referenced the subquery (the query used at the beginning of this example. The subquery was aliased with an arbitrary name of "a":

```
FROM
(SELECT   s.Name ShiftName,
      h.EmployeeID,
      d.Name DepartmentName
FROM   HumanResources.EmployeeDepartmentHistory h
INNER JOIN HumanResources.Department d ON
      h.DepartmentID = d.DepartmentID
INNER JOIN HumanResources.Shift s ON
      h.ShiftID = s.ShiftID
WHERE    EndDate IS NULL AND
      d.Name IN ('Production', 'Engineering', 'Marketing')) AS a
```

Inside the parentheses, the query designated which columns would be aggregated (and how). In this case, the number of employees would be counted:

```
PIVOT
(COUNT(EmployeeID)
```

After the aggregation section, the FOR statement determined which row values would be converted into columns. Unlike regular IN clauses, single quotes aren't used around each string character, instead using square brackets. DepartmentName was the data column where values are converted into pivoted columns:

```
FOR DepartmentName IN ([Production], [Engineering], [Marketing]))
```

■**Note** The list of column names cannot already exist in the query results being pivoted.

Lastly, a closed parenthesis closed off the PIVOT operation. The PIVOT operation was then aliased like a table with an arbitrary name (in this case "b"):

```
AS b
```

The results were then ordered by ShiftName:

```
ORDER BY ShiftName
```

The results took the three columns fixed in the FOR part of the PIVOT operation and aggregated counts of employees by ShiftName.

Normalizing Data with UNPIVOT

The UNPIVOT command does *almost* the opposite of PIVOT by changing columns into rows. It also uses the same syntax as PIVOT, only UNPIVOT is designated instead.

This example demonstrates how UNPIVOT can be used to remove column-repeating groups often seen in denormalized tables. For the first part of this example, a denormalized table is created with repeating, incrementing phone number columns:

```
CREATE TABLE dbo.Contact
   (EmployeeID int NOT NULL,
    PhoneNumber1 bigint,
    PhoneNumber2 bigint,
    PhoneNumber3 bigint)
GO

INSERT dbo.Contact
(EmployeeID, PhoneNumber1, PhoneNumber2, PhoneNumber3)
VALUES(   1, 2718353881, 3385531980, 5324571342)

INSERT dbo.Contact
(EmployeeID, PhoneNumber1, PhoneNumber2, PhoneNumber3)
VALUES(   2, 6007163571, 6875099415, 7756620787)

INSERT dbo.Contact
(EmployeeID, PhoneNumber1, PhoneNumber2, PhoneNumber3)
VALUES(   3, 9439250939, NULL, NULL)
```

Now using UNPIVOT, the repeating phone numbers are converted into a more normalized form (re-using a single PhoneValue field instead of repeating the phone column multiple times):

```
SELECT   EmployeeID,
      PhoneType,
      PhoneValue
FROM
(SELECT   EmployeeID, PhoneNumber1, PhoneNumber2, PhoneNumber3
FROM dbo.Contact) c
UNPIVOT
   (PhoneValue FOR PhoneType IN ([PhoneNumber1], [PhoneNumber2], [PhoneNumber3])
) AS p
```

This returns:

EmployeeID	PhoneType	PhoneValue
1	PhoneNumber1	2718353881
1	PhoneNumber2	3385531980
1	PhoneNumber3	5324571342
2	PhoneNumber1	6007163571
2	PhoneNumber2	6875099415
2	PhoneNumber3	7756620787
3	PhoneNumber1	9439250939

(7 row(s) affected)

How It Works

This UNPIVOT example began by selecting three columns. The EmployeeID came from the subquery. The other two columns, PhoneType and PhoneValue—were defined later on in the UNPIVOT statement:

```
SELECT   EmployeeID,
      PhoneType,
      PhoneValue
```

Next, the FROM clause referenced a subquery. The subquery selected all four columns from the contact table. The table was aliased with the letter "c" (table alias naming was arbitrary however):

```
FROM
(SELECT    EmployeeID, PhoneNumber1, PhoneNumber2, PhoneNumber3
FROM dbo.Contact) c
```

A new column called PhoneValue (referenced in the SELECT) holds the individual phone numbers across the three denormalized phone columns:

```
UNPIVOT
(PhoneValue FOR PhoneType IN ([PhoneNumber1], [PhoneNumber2], [PhoneNumber3])
```

FOR references the name of the pivot column, PhoneType, which holds the column names of the denormalized table. The IN clause following PhoneType lists the columns from the original table to be narrowed into a single column.

Lastly, a closing parenthesis is used, then alias it with an arbitrary name, in this case "p":

```
) AS p
```

This query returned the phone data merged into two columns, one to describe the phone type, and another to hold the actual phone numbers. Also notice that there are seven rows, instead of nine. This is because for EmployeeID "3", only non-NULL values were returned. UNPIVOT does not process NULL values from the pivoted result set.

Returning Distinct or Matching Rows Using EXCEPT and INTERSECT

Introduced in SQL Server 2005, the INTERSECT and EXCEPT operands allow you to return distinct rows that only exist in either the left query (using EXCEPT), or only distinct rows that exist in both the left and right queries (using INTERSECT).

INTERSECT and EXCEPT are useful in dataset comparison scenarios; for example, if you need to compare rows between test and production tables, you can use EXCEPT to easily identify and populate rows that existed in one table and not the other. These operands are also useful for data recovery, because you could restore a database from a period prior to a data loss, compare data with the current production table, and then recover the deleted rows accordingly.

For this example, demonstration tables are created which are partially populated from the Production.Product table:

```
-- First two new tables based on ProductionProduct will be
-- created, in order to demonstrate EXCEPT and INTERSECT.
-- See Chapter 8 for more on ROW_NUMBER

-- Create TableA
SELECT    prod.ProductID,
       prod.Name
INTO dbo.TableA
FROM
(SELECT ProductID,
      Name,
       ROW_NUMBER() OVER (ORDER BY ProductID) RowNum
FROM Production.Product) prod
WHERE RowNum BETWEEN 1 and 20

-- Create TableB
SELECT    prod.ProductID,
       prod.Name
INTO dbo.TableB
```

```
FROM
(SELECT ProductID,
      Name,
      ROW_NUMBER() OVER (ORDER BY ProductID) RowNum
FROM Production.Product) prod
WHERE RowNum BETWEEN 10 and 29
```

This returns:

```
(20 row(s) affected)

(20 row(s) affected)
```

Now the EXCEPT operator will be used to determine which rows exist *only* in the left table of the query, TableA, and not in TableB:

```
SELECT    ProductID,
      Name
FROM    TableA
EXCEPT
SELECT    ProductID,
      Name
FROM    TableB
```

This returns:

```
ProductID   Name
----------- ---------------------------------------------------
1           Adjustable Race
2           Bearing Ball
3           BB Ball Bearing
4           Headset Ball Bearings
316         Blade
317         LL Crankarm
318         ML Crankarm
319         HL Crankarm
320         Chainring Bolts

(9 row(s) affected)
```

To show distinct values from *both* result sets that match, use the INTERSECT operator:

```
SELECT    ProductID,
      Name
FROM    TableA
INTERSECT
SELECT    ProductID,
      Name
FROM    TableB
```

This returns:

```
ProductID    Name
-----------  ------------------------------------------------
321          Chainring Nut
322          Chainring
323          Crown Race
324          Chain Stays
325          Decal 1
326          Decal 2
327          Down Tube
328          Mountain End Caps
329          Road End Caps
330          Touring End Caps
331          Fork End

(11 row(s) affected)
```

How It Works

The example started off by creating two tables (using INTO) that contain overlapping sets of rows. The first table, TableA, contained the first twenty rows (ordered by ProductID) from the Production. Product table. The second table, TableB, also received another twenty rows, half of which overlapped with TableA's rows.

To determine which rows exist *only* in TableA, the EXCEPT operand was placed after the FROM clause of the first query and before the second query:

```
SELECT    ProductID,
       Name
FROM    TableA
EXCEPT
SELECT    ProductID,
       Name
FROM    TableB
```

In order for EXCEPT to be used, both queries must have the same number of columns. Those columns also need to have compatible data types (it's not necessary that the column names from each query match). The power of EXCEPT is that *all* columns are evaluated to determine if there is a match, which is much more efficient than using INNER JOIN (which would require explicitly joining the tables on each column in both data sources).

The results of the EXCEPT query show the first nine rows from TableA that were not also populated into TableB.

In the second example, INTERSECT was used to shows rows that *overlap* between the two tables. Like EXCEPT, INTERSECT is placed between the two queries:

```
SELECT    ProductID,
       Name
FROM    TableA
INTERSECT
SELECT    ProductID,
       Name
FROM    TableB
```

The query returned the eleven rows that overlapped between both tables. The same rules about compatible data types and number of columns apply to INTERSECT as for EXCEPT.

Summarizing Data

In these next three recipes, I will demonstrate summarizing data within the result set using the following operators:

- Use WITH CUBE to add summarizing total values to a result-set based on columns in the GROUP BY clause.

- Use WITH ROLLUP with GROUP BY to add hierarchical data summaries based on the ordering of columns in the GROUP BY clause.

I also demonstrate the GROUPING function. GROUPING is used to determine which of these summarized total value rows are based on the summarized or original data set data.

Summarizing Data with WITH CUBE

WITH CUBE adds rows to your result-set, summarizing total values based on the columns in the GROUP BY clause.

This example demonstrates a query that returns the total quantity of a product, grouped by the shelf the product is kept on:

```
SELECT   i.Shelf,
      SUM(i.Quantity) Total
FROM   Production.ProductInventory i
GROUP BY i.Shelf
WITH CUBE
```

This returns the following (abridged) results:

Shelf	Total
A	26833
B	12672
C	19868
D	17353
E	31979
F	21249
G	40195
H	20055
more rows	
W	2908
Y	437
NULL	335974

How It Works

Because the query in this example groups by Shelf, a total will be displayed, displaying the total for all shelves in the final row. With WITH CUBE added after the GROUP BY clause, an extra row with a NULL Shelf value is added at the end of the results, along with the SUM total of all quantities in the Total column.

If you added additional columns to the query, included in the GROUP BY clause, WITH CUBE would attempt to aggregate values for each grouping combination. WITH CUBE is often used for reporting purposes, providing an easy method of reporting totals by grouped column.

■**Note** In SQL Server 2000, you may have used COMPUTE BY to also provide similar aggregations for your query. Microsoft has deprecated this functionality for SQL Server 2005 backward compatibility. Unlike WITH CUBE, COMPUTE BY created an entirely new summarized result set after the original query results which were often difficult for calling applications to consume.

Using GROUPING with WITH CUBE

In the previous example, WITH CUBE was used to aggregate values for each grouping combination. Extra NULL values were included in the result set for those rows that contained the WITH CUBE aggregate totals.

What if one of the values in the SHELF column was actually NULL? In order to distinguish between a NULL that comes from the source data versus a NULL generated by a WITH CUBE aggregation, you can use the GROUPING function. This function returns a "0" value when the data is derived from the data, and a "1" when generated by a WITH CUBE.

This example modifies the previous recipe's example to include GROUPING:

```
SELECT   i.Shelf,
    GROUPING(i.Shelf) Source,
    SUM(i.Quantity) Total
FROM   Production.ProductInventory i
GROUP BY i.Shelf
WITH CUBE
```

This returns the following (abridged) results:

Shelf	Source	Total
A	0	26833
B	0	12672
Y	0	437
NULL	1	335974

How It Works

In this recipe, GROUPING was used to discern a natural NULL versus a NULL generated by the WITH CUBE function. You can also use the GROUPING function with the ROLLUP function, which is reviewed next.

Summarizing Data with WITH ROLLUP

WITH ROLLUP is used in conjunction with GROUP BY to add hierarchical data summaries based on the ordering of columns in the GROUP BY clause.

This example retrieves the shelf, product name, and total quantity of the product:

```
SELECT   i.Shelf,
       p.Name,
       SUM(i.Quantity) Total
FROM   Production.ProductInventory i
INNER JOIN Production.Product p ON
    i.ProductID = p.ProductID
GROUP BY i.Shelf, p.Name
WITH ROLLUP
```

This returns the following (abridged) results:

```
Shelf      Name                                           Total
---------- ---------------------------------------------- -----------
A          Adjustable Race                                761
A          BB Ball Bearing                                909
A          Bearing Ball                                   791
...
A          NULL                                           26833
...
W          Rear Derailleur Cage                           121
W          Reflector                                       121
W          Touring Pedal                                  388
W          NULL                                           2908
Y          HL Spindle/Axle                                228
Y          LL Spindle/Axle                                209
Y          NULL                                           437
NULL       NULL                                           335974
```

How It Works

The order you place the columns in the GROUP BY impacts how WITH ROLLUP aggregates the data. The WITH ROLLUP in this query aggregated total quantity for each change in Shelf. Notice the row with Shelf "A" and the NULL name; this holds the total quantity for Shelf A. Also notice that the final row was the grand total of all product quantities.

Hints

SQL Server's query optimization process is responsible for producing a query execution plan when a SELECT query is executed. The goal of the query optimizer is to generate an efficient (but not always the best) query execution plan. Under rare circumstances SQL Server may choose an inefficient plan over a more efficient one. If this happens you would be advised to investigate the query execution plan, table statistics, and other factors that are explored in more detail in Chapter 28.

After researching the query performance, you may decide to override the decision making process of the SQL Server query optimizer by using *hints*. The next three recipes will demonstrate three types of hints: *query*, *table*, and *join*.

Using Join Hints

A join "hint" is a misnomer in this case, as a join hint will *force* the query optimizer to join the tables in the way you command. Join hints force the internal JOIN operation used to join two tables in a query. Available join hints are described in Table 1-4.

Table 1-4. *Join Hints*

Hint Name	Description
LOOP	LOOP joins operate best when one table is small and the other is large, with indexes on the joined columns.
HASH	HASH joins are optimal for large unsorted tables.
MERGE	MERGE joins are optimal for medium or large tables that are sorted on the joined column.
REMOTE	REMOTE forces the join operation to occur at the site of the table referenced on the right (the second table referenced in a JOIN clause). For performance benefits, the left table should be the local table, and should have fewer rows than the remote right table.

Before showing how the join hint works, the example starts off with the original, non-hinted query:

```
-- (More on SHOWPLAN_TEXT in Chapter 28)
SET SHOWPLAN_TEXT ON
GO

SELECT    p.Name,
        r.ReviewerName,
        r.Rating
FROM    Production.Product p
INNER JOIN Production.ProductReview r ON
    r.ProductID = p.ProductID
GO

SET SHOWPLAN_TEXT OFF
GO
```

This returns the following abridged results (SHOWPLAN_TEXT returns information about how the query *may be* processed, but it doesn't actually execute the query):

StmtText

```
  |--Nested Loops(Inner Join, OUTER REFERENCES:([r].[ProductID]))
       |--Clustered Index
Scan(OBJECT:([AdventureWorks].[Production].[ProductReview].[PK_ProductReview_
ProductReviewID] AS [r]))
       |--Clustered Index
Seek(OBJECT:([AdventureWorks].[Production].[Product].[PK_Product_ProductID]
AS [p]), SEEK:([p].[ProductID]=[AdventureWorks].[Production].[ProductReview].
[ProductID] as [r].[ProductID]) ORDERED FORWARD)
```

The next example submits the same query, only this time using a join hint:

```
SET SHOWPLAN_TEXT ON
GO

SELECT    p.Name,
        r.ReviewerName,
        r.Rating
FROM    Production.Product p
INNER HASH JOIN Production.ProductReview r ON
    r.ProductID = p.ProductID
GO

SET SHOWPLAN_TEXT OFF
GO
```

This returns the following abridged results:

StmtText

```
|--Hash Match(Inner Join, HASH:([p].[ProductID])=([r].[ProductID]))
       |--Index Scan(OBJECT:([AdventureWorks].[Production].[Product].
[AK_Product_Name] AS [p]))
       |--Clustered Index Scan(OBJECT:([AdventureWorks].[Production].
[ProductReview].
[PK_ProductReview_ProductReviewID] AS [r]))
```

How It Works

In the first, non-hinted query, SET SHOWPLAN_TEXT was used to view how the query may be executed by SQL Server.

■**Caution** You should almost always let SQL Server do the decision-making for the join type. Even if your hint works for the short term, there is no guarantee that in the future there may be more efficient query plans that could be used, but won't be, because you have overridden the optimizer with the specified hint. Also, the validity of or effectiveness of a hint may change when new service packs or editions of SQL Server are released.

The StmtText section, shown next, tells us how the query will be executed. For this example, the most important information was in the first line of the results, telling us that a Nested Loop would be used to join the two tables:

```
|--Nested Loops(Inner Join, OUTER REFERENCES:([r].[ProductID]))
```

In the second query, a hint was added to force the nested loop join to perform a hash join operation instead. To do this, HASH was added between the INNER and JOIN keywords:

```
INNER HASH JOIN Production.ProductReview r ON
   r.ProductID = p.ProductID
```

Now in the second SHOWPLAN_TEXT results, the query execution now uses a hash join to join the two tables:

```
|--Hash Match(Inner Join, HASH:([p].[ProductID])=([r].[ProductID]))
```

Using Query Hints

Some query hints, like the join hints discussed in the previous recipe, are instructions sent with the query to override SQL Server's query optimizer decision-making. Using query hints may provide a short term result that satisfies your current situation, but may not always be the most efficient result over time. Nonetheless, there are times when you may decide to use them, if only to further understand the choices that the query optimizer automatically makes.

Query hints can be used in SELECT, INSERT, UPDATE, and DELETE statements, described in Table 1-5.

Table 1-5. *Query Hints*

Hint Name	Description
{HASH | ORDER} GROUP	When used in conjunction with the GROUP BY clause, specifies whether hashing or ordering is used for GROUP BY and COMPUTE aggregations.
{CONCAT | HASH | MERGE} UNION	Designates the strategy used to join all result sets for UNION operations.
{LOOP | MERGE | HASH} JOIN	Forces *all* join operations to perform the loop, merge, or hash join in the entire query.
FAST integer	Speeds up the retrieval of rows for the top *integer* value designated.
FORCE ORDER	When designated, table joins are performed in the order in which the tables appear.

(Continued)

Table 1-5. *(Continued)*

Hint Name	Description
MAXDOP number_of_processors	This option overrides the "max degree of parallelism" server configuration option for the query. See Chapter 21 for more information on this server option.
OPTIMIZE FOR (@variable_name = literal_constant) [,...n]	The OPTIMIZE FOR option directs SQL Server to use a particular variable value or values for a variable when the query is compiled and optimized . You could, for example, plug in a literal constant that returns the best performance across the range of expected parameters.
ROBUST PLAN	Creates a query plan with the assumption that the row size of a table will be at maximum width.
MAXDOP integer	This determines the max degree of parallelism for your query (overriding the server level setting).
KEEP PLAN	The recompile threshold for the query is "relaxed" when this hint is used.
KEEPFIXED PLAN	When this hint is used, the query optimizer is forced NOT to recompile due to statistics or indexed column changes. Only schema changes or sp_recompile will cause the query plan to be recompiled.
EXPAND VIEWS	This hint keeps the query optimizer from using indexed views when the base table is referenced.
MAXRECURSION number	Designates the maximum number of recursions (1 to 32757) allowed for the query. If 0 is chosen, no limit is applied. The default recursion limit is 100. This option is used in conjunction with Common Table Expressions (CTE).
USE PLAN 'xml_plan'	USE PLAN directs SQL SERVER to use a potentially better performing query plan (provided in the xml_plan literal value) that you know can cause the query to perform better. See Chapter 28 for more detail.
PARAMETERIZATION { SIMPLE | FORCED }	This hint relates to the new PARAMETERIZATION database setting which controls whether or not all queries are parameterized (literal values contained in a query get substituted with parameters in the cached query plan). When PARAMETERIZATION SIMPLE is chosen, SQL Server decides which queries are parameterized or not. When PARAMETERIZATION FORCED is used, all queries in the database will be parameterized. For more information on this database setting, see Chapter 28.
RECOMPILE	This forces SQL Server 2005 to throw out the query execution plan after it is executed, meaning that the next time the query executes, it will be forced to recompile a new query plan. Although usually SQL Server re-uses effective query plans—sometimes a less efficient query plan is re-used. Recompiling forces SQL Server to come up with a fresh plan (but with the overhead of a recompile).

This example uses a new SQL Server 2005 RECOMPILE query hint to recompile the query, forcing SQL Server to discard the plan generated for the query after it executes. With the RECOMPILE query hint, a new plan will be generated the next time the same or similar query is executed. You may decide you wish to do this for volatile query plans, where differing search condition values for the same plan cause extreme fluctuations in the number of rows returned. In that scenario, using a compiled query plan may hurt, not help the query performance. The benefit of a cached and reusable query execution plan may occasionally be outweighed by a fresh, recompiled plan.

■Note SQL Server 2005 has introduced statement-level stored procedure recompilation. Now instead of an entire stored procedure recompiling when indexes are added or data is changed to the referenced tables, only individual statements within the procedure impacted by the change are recompiled. See Chapter 10 for more information.

Typically, you will want to use this RECOMPILE query hint within a stored procedure—so that you can control which statements automatically recompile—instead of having to recompile the entire stored procedure. Now for the example:

```
SELECT   SalesOrderID,
   ProductID,
   UnitPrice,
   OrderQty
FROM Sales.SalesOrderDetail
WHERE CarrierTrackingNumber = '5CE9-4D75-8F'
ORDER BY   SalesOrderID,
         ProductID
OPTION (RECOMPILE)
```

This returns:

```
SalesOrderID ProductID   UnitPrice              OrderQty
------------ -----------  --------------------  --------
47964        760          469.794               1
47964        789          1466.01               1
47964        819          149.031               4
47964        843          15.00                 1
47964        844          11.994                6

(5 row(s) affected)
```

How It Works

This query demonstrated using a query hint, which was referenced in the OPTION clause at the end of the query:

```
OPTION (RECOMPILE)
```

SQL Server 2005 should be relied upon most of the time to make the correct decisions when processing a query; however query hints provide you with more control for those exceptions when you need to override SQL Server's choices.

Using Table Hints

Table hints, like query hints, can be used to override SELECT, INSERT, UPDATE, and DELETE default processing behavior. You can use multiple table hints for one query, separated by commas, so long as they do not belong to the same category grouping. Be sure to test the performance of your queries with and without the query hints (see Chapter 28 for more details on examining query performance).

Table 1-6 lists available table hints. Some hints cannot be used together, so they have been grouped in the table accordingly. You can't, for example, use both NOLOCK and HOLDLOCK for the same query:

Table 1-6. *Table Hints*

Hint Name	Description
FASTFIRSTROW	This hint optimizes the query to pull the first row of the result set very quickly. Whether or not this hint will work depends on the size of your table, indexing used, and the type of data you are returning. Test your results with and without the hint, to be sure that the hint is necessary. Use this hint in order to begin returning results to the client faster – not to improve the speed of the entire result set.
INDEX (index_val [,... n])	Overrides SQL Server's index choice and forces a specific index for the table to be used.
NOEXPAND	When an indexed view is referenced, the query optimizer will treat the view like a table with a clustered index.
HOLDLOCK. SERIALIZABLE. REPEATABLEREAD. READCOMMITTED. READCOMMITTEDLOCK. READUNCOMMITTED. NOLOCK	Selecting one of these hints determines the isolation level for the table. For example, designating NOLOCK means that the operation (SELECT for example) will place no locking on the table.
ROWLOCK. PAGLOCK. TABLOCK. TABLOCKX. NOLOCK	Designates the granularity of locking for the table, for example, selecting ROWLOCK to force only row locks for a query.
READPAST	Skips locked rows, and does not read them.
UPDLOCK	The hint will force update locks instead of shared locks to be generated (not compatible with NOLOCK or XLOCK).
XLOCK	This hint forces exclusive locks on the resources being referenced (not compatible with NOLOCK or UPDLOCK).
KEEPIDENTITY	This option applies to the OPENROWSET function's new SQL Server 2005 BULK insert functionality (see Chapter 27) and impacts how rows are inserted into a table with an IDENTITY column. If you use this hint, SQL Server will use the identity values from the data file, instead of generating its own. For more on the IDENTITY column, see Chapter 4, "Tables."
KEEPDEFAULTS	Like KEEPIDENTITY, this table hint applies to the OPENROWSET function. Using this hint specifies that columns not included in the bulk-load operation will be assigned to the column default. For more on default columns, see Chapter 4.
IGNORE_CONSTRAINTS	Another OPENROWSET hint, IGNORE_CONSTRAINTS directs SQL Server to ignore CHECK constraints when importing data. See Chapter 4 for more on CHECK constraints.
IGNORE_TRIGGERS	This query hint directs INSERT triggers *not* to fire when importing using the new SQL Server 2005 BULK option of OPENROWSET.

This example returns the `DocumentID` and `Title` from the `Production.Document` table where the `Status` column is equal to "1." It uses the `NOLOCK` table hint, which means the query will not place shared locks on the `Production.Document` table (for a review of locking, see Chapter 3):

```
SELECT DocumentID,
     Title
FROM Production.Document
WITH (NOLOCK)
WHERE Status = 1
```

How It Works

The crux of this example is the `WITH` keyword, which uses the `NOLOCK` table hint in parentheses:

```
WITH (NOLOCK)
```

`NOLOCK` causes the query not to place shared locks on the impacted rows/data pages—allowing you to read without being blocked or blocking others (although you are now subject to "dirty reads").

Common Table Expressions

A Common Table Expression (CTE) is similar to a view or derived query, allowing you to create a temporary query that can be referenced within the scope of a `SELECT`, `INSERT`, `UPDATE`, or `DELETE` query. Unlike a derived query, you don't need to copy the query definition multiple times each time it is used. You can also use local variables within a CTE definition—something you can't do in a view definition.

The basic syntax for a CTE is as follows:

```
WITH expression_name [ ( column_name [ ,...n ] ) ]
AS ( CTE_query_definition )
```

The arguments of a CTE are described in the Table 1-7.

Table 1-7. *CTE Arguments*

Argument	Description
expression_name	The name of the common table expression.
column_name [,...n]	The unique column names of the expression.
CTE_query_definition	The SELECT query that defines the common table expression.

A *non-recursive* CTE is one that is used within a query without referencing itself. It serves as a temporary result set for the query. A *recursive* CTE is defined similarly to a non-recursive CTE, only a recursive CTE returns hierarchical self-relating data. Using a CTE to represent recursive data can minimize the amount of code needed compared to other methods.

The next two recipes will demonstrate both non-recursive and recursive CTEs.

Using a Non-Recursive Common Table Expression (CTE)

This example of a common table expression demonstrates returning vendors in the `Purchasing.Vendor` table—returning the first five and last five results ordered by name:

```
WITH VendorSearch (RowNumber, VendorName, AccountNumber)
AS
(
```

```
SELECT ROW_NUMBER() OVER (ORDER BY Name) RowNum,
       Name,
       AccountNumber
FROM Purchasing.Vendor
)

SELECT    RowNumber,
       VendorName,
       AccountNumber
FROM VendorSearch
WHERE RowNumber BETWEEN 1 AND 5
UNION
SELECT    RowNumber,
       VendorName,
       AccountNumber
FROM VendorSearch
WHERE RowNumber BETWEEN 100 AND 104
```

This returns:

RowNumber	VendorName	AccountNumber
1	A. Datum Corporation	ADATUM0001
2	Advanced Bicycles	ADVANCED0001
3	Allenson Cycles	ALLENSON0001
4	American Bicycles and Wheels	AMERICAN0001
5	American Bikes	AMERICAN0002
100	Vista Road Bikes	VISTARO0001
101	West Junction Cycles	WESTJUN0001
102	WestAmerica Bicycle Co.	WESTAMER0001
103	Wide World Importers	WIDEWOR0001
104	Wood Fitness	WOODFIT0001

(10 row(s) affected)

The previous example used UNION, however non-recursive CTEs can be used like any other SELECT query too:

```
WITH VendorSearch (VendorID, VendorName)
AS
(
SELECT VendorID,
       Name
FROM Purchasing.Vendor
)

SELECT    v.VendorID,
       v.VendorName,
       p.ProductID,
       p.StandardPrice
FROM VendorSearch v
INNER JOIN Purchasing.ProductVendor p ON
   v.VendorID = p.VendorID
ORDER BY v.VendorName
```

This returns the following (abridged) results:

VendorID	VendorName	ProductID	StandardPrice
32	Advanced Bicycles	359	45.41
32	Advanced Bicycles	360	43.41
32	Advanced Bicycles	361	47.48
...			
91	WestAmerica Bicycle Co.	363	41.26
28	Wide World Importers	402	45.21
57	Wood Fitness	2	39.92

(406 row(s) affected)

How It Works

In this example, WITH defined the CTE name and the columns it returned. This was a non-recursive CTE because CTE data wasn't being joined to itself. The CTE in this example was only using a query that UNION'd two data sets:

```
WITH VendorSearch (RowNumber, VendorName, AccountNumber)
```

The column names defined in the CTE can match the actual names of the query within—or you can create your own alias names. For example in this example, the Purchasing.Vendor column Name has been referenced as VendorName in the CTE.

Next in the recipe, AS marked the beginning of the CTE query definition:

```
AS
(
```

Inside the parentheses, the query used a new SQL Server 2005 function that returned the sequential row number of the result set—ordered by the vendor name (see Chapter 8 for a review of ROW_NUMBER):

```
SELECT ROW_NUMBER() OVER (ORDER BY Name) RowNum,
    Name,
    AccountNumber
FROM Purchasing.Vendor)
```

The Vendor Name and AccountNumber from the Purchasing.Vendor table were also returned. The CTE definition finished after marking the closing parentheses.

Following the CTE definition was the query that used the CTE. Keep in mind that a SELECT, INSERT, UPDATE, or DELETE statement that references some or all the CTE columns *must* follow the definition of the CTE:

```
SELECT   RowNumber,
    VendorName,
    AccountNumber
FROM VendorSearch
WHERE RowNumber BETWEEN 1 AND 5
```

The SELECT column names were used from the new VendorSearch CTE. In the WHERE clause, the first query returns rows 1 through 5. Next the UNION operator was used prior to the second query:

```
UNION
```

This second query displayed the last five rows in addition to the first five rows. The VendorSearch CTE was referenced twice—but the full query definition only had to be defined a single time (unlike derived queries)—thus reducing code.

In the second example of the recipe, a simple CTE was defined without using any functions, just VendorID and VendorName from the Purchasing.Vendor table:

```
WITH VendorSearch (VendorID, VendorName)
AS
(
SELECT VendorID,
       Name
FROM Purchasing.Vendor)
```

In the query following this CTE definition, the CTE "VendorSearch" was joined just like a regular table (only without specifying the owning schema):

```
SELECT   v.VendorID,
         v.VendorName,
         p.ProductID,
         p.StandardPrice
FROM VendorSearch v
INNER JOIN Purchasing.ProductVendor p ON
   v.VendorID = p.VendorID
ORDER BY v.VendorName
```

One gotcha that you should be aware of—if the CTE is part of a batch of statements, the statement before its definition must be followed by a *semicolon*.

■**Note** With SQL Server 2005, you can use a semicolon as a SQL Server statement terminator. Doing so isn't mandatory, but is ANSI compliant, and you'll see it being used in some of the documentation coming from Microsoft.

Using a Recursive Common Table Expression (CTE)

In this example, the new Company table will define the companies in a hypothetical giant mega conglomerate. Each company has a CompanyID and an optional ParentCompanyID. The example will demonstrate how to display the company hierarchy in the results using a recursive CTE. First, the table is created:

```
CREATE TABLE dbo.Company
    (CompanyID int NOT NULL PRIMARY KEY,
     ParentCompanyID int NULL,
     CompanyName varchar(25) NOT NULL)
```

Next, rows are inserted into the new table:

```
INSERT dbo.Company (CompanyID, ParentCompanyID, CompanyName)
VALUES (1, NULL, 'Mega-Corp')
INSERT dbo.Company (CompanyID, ParentCompanyID, CompanyName)
VALUES (2, 1, 'Mediamus-Corp')
INSERT dbo.Company (CompanyID, ParentCompanyID, CompanyName)
VALUES (3, 1, 'KindaBigus-Corp')
INSERT dbo.Company (CompanyID, ParentCompanyID, CompanyName)
VALUES (4, 3, 'GettinSmaller-Corp')
INSERT dbo.Company (CompanyID, ParentCompanyID, CompanyName)
VALUES (5, 4, 'Smallest-Corp')
INSERT dbo.Company (CompanyID, ParentCompanyID, CompanyName)
VALUES (6, 5, 'Puny-Corp')
INSERT dbo.Company (CompanyID, ParentCompanyID, CompanyName)
VALUES (7, 5, 'Small2-Corp')
```

Now the actual example:

```
WITH CompanyTree(ParentCompanyID, CompanyID, CompanyName, CompanyLevel)
AS
(
    SELECT    ParentCompanyID,
        CompanyID,
        CompanyName,
        0 AS CompanyLevel
    FROM dbo.Company
    WHERE ParentCompanyID IS NULL
    UNION ALL
    SELECT    c.ParentCompanyID,
        c.CompanyID,
        c.CompanyName,
        p.CompanyLevel + 1
    FROM dbo.Company c
        INNER JOIN CompanyTree p
        ON c.ParentCompanyID = p.CompanyID
)
SELECT ParentCompanyID, CompanyID, CompanyName, CompanyLevel
FROM CompanyTree
```

This returns:

```
ParentCompanyID CompanyID  CompanyName              CompanyLevel
--------------- ---------- ------------------------ ------------
NULL            1          Mega-Corp                0
1               2          Mediamus-Corp            1
1               3          KindaBigus-Corp          1
3               4          GettinSmaller-Corp       2
4               5          Smallest-Corp            3
5               7          Small2-Corp              4
5               6          Puny-Corp                4

(7 row(s) affected)
```

How It Works

In this example, the CTE name and columns are defined first:

```
WITH CompanyTree(ParentCompanyID, CompanyID, CompanyName, CompanyLevel)
```

The CTE query definition began with AS and an open parenthesis:

```
AS
(
```

The SELECT clause began with the "anchor" SELECT statement. When using recursive CTEs, "anchor" refers to the fact that it defines the base of the recursion—in this case the top level of the corporate hierarchy (the parentless "Mega-Corp"). This SELECT also includes a CompanyLevel column alias, preceded with the number zero. This column will be used in the recursion to display how many levels deep a particular company is in the company hierarchy:

```
SELECT ParentCompanyID,
    CompanyID,
    CompanyName,
    0 AS CompanyLevel
FROM dbo.Company
WHERE ParentCompanyID IS NULL
```

Next was the UNION ALL, to join the second, recursive query to the anchor member (UNION ALL, and not just UNION, is required for the last anchor member and the first recursive member in a recursive CTE):

```
UNION ALL
```

After that was the recursive query. Like the anchor, the SELECT clause references the ParentCompanyID, CompanyID, and CompanyName from the dbo.Company table. Unlike the anchor, the CTE column references p.CompanyLevel (from the anchor query), adding + 1 to its total at each level of the hierarchy:

```
SELECT    c.ParentCompanyID,
    c.CompanyID,
    c.CompanyName,
    p.CompanyLevel + 1
```

The dbo.Company table was joined to the CompanyTree CTE, joining the CTE's recursive query's ParentCompanyID to the CTE's CompanyID:

```
FROM dbo.Company c
    INNER JOIN CompanyTree p
    ON c.ParentCompanyID = p.CompanyID
)
```

After the closing of the CTE's definition, the query selected from the CTE based on the columns defined in the CTE definition.

```
SELECT ParentCompanyID, CompanyID, CompanyName, CompanyLevel
FROM CompanyTree
```

In the results, for each level in the company hierarchy, the CTE increased the CompanyLevel column.

With this useful new feature come some cautions, however. If you create your recursive CTE incorrectly, you could cause an infinite loop. While testing, and to avoid infinite loops, use the MAXRECURSION hint mentioned earlier in the chapter.

For example, you can stop the previous example from going further than 2 levels by adding the OPTION clause with MAXRECURSION at the end of the query:

```
WITH CompanyTree(ParentCompanyID, CompanyID, CompanyName, CompanyLevel) AS
(
    SELECT ParentCompanyID, CompanyID, CompanyName, 0 AS CompanyLevel
    FROM dbo.Company
    WHERE ParentCompanyID IS NULL
    UNION ALL
    SELECT c.ParentCompanyID, c.CompanyID, c.CompanyName, p.CompanyLevel + 1
    FROM dbo.Company c
        INNER JOIN CompanyTree p
        ON c.ParentCompanyID = p.CompanyID
)
SELECT ParentCompanyID, CompanyID, CompanyName, CompanyLevel
FROM CompanyTree
OPTION (MAXRECURSION 2)
```

This returns:

```
ParentCompanyID CompanyID   CompanyName                CompanyLevel
--------------- ----------- -------------------------- ------------
NULL            1           Mega-Corp                  0
1               2           Mediamus-Corp              1
1               3           KindaBigus-Corp            1
3               4           GettinSmaller-Corp         2
Msg 530, Level 16, State 1, Line 1
Statement terminated. Maximum recursion 2 has been exhausted
before statement completion
```

As a best practice, set the MAXRECURSION based on your understanding of the data. If you know that the hiearchy cannot go more than 10 levels deep, for example, then set MAXRECURSION to that value.

CHAPTER 2

■ ■ ■

INSERT, UPDATE, DELETE

In this chapter, I review how to modify data using the Transact-SQL INSERT, UPDATE, and DELETE commands. I'll review the basics of each command and cover specific techniques such as inserting data from a stored procedure, and importing an image file into a table using the new OPENROWSET BULK functionality (added to OPENROWSET in SQL Server 2005.) The new SQL Server 2005 features I cover in this chapter include:

- The new OUTPUT clause, which allows you to capture inserted and deleted rows from a data modification into a table for reporting.

- The TOP clause, which in previous versions of SQL Server was only useable within a SELECT statement. Now it can be used in conjunction with data modification commands.

- Easier data modification methods for large object data type data (SQL Server 2005 introduces new, large object data types intended to replace the deprecated text, ntext, and image data types).

Before going into the new features, however, I'll start the chapter off by reviewing basic INSERT concepts.

INSERT

The simplified syntax for the INSERT command is as follows:

```
INSERT
   [ INTO]
   table_or_view_name
   [ ( column_list ) ]
   VALUES ({DEFAULT | NULL | expression } [ ,...n ])
```

The arguments of this command are described in Table 2-1:

Table 2-1. *INSERT Command Arguments*

Argument	Description
table_or_view_name	The name of the table or updateable view that you are inserting a row into.
column_list	The explicit comma-separated list of columns on the insert table which will be populated with values.
(DEFAULT | NULL | expression } [,...n])	The comma-separated list of values to be inserted as a row into the table. Each value can be an expression, NULL value, or DEFAULT value (if a default was defined for the column). Defaults are described later in the chapter.

Inserting a Row into a Table

In this recipe, I demonstrate the use of INSERT to add new rows into a table (as specified by table_name), specifying a column_list of columns into which the data should be inserted, and a corresponding comma-separated list of values to be inserted, [,....n], in the VALUES clause. Specifically, a single row is inserted into the AdventureWorks Production.Location table:

```
INSERT Production.Location
(Name, CostRate, Availability)
VALUES ('Wheel Storage', 11.25, 80.00)
```

This returns:

```
(1 row(s) affected)
```

This next query then searches for any row with the name "Wheel Storage":

```
SELECT  Name,
    CostRate,
    Availability
FROM Production.Location
WHERE Name = 'Wheel Storage'
```

This returns:

```
Name                                             CostRate       Availability
------------------------------------------------ -------------- ------------
Wheel Storage                                    11.25                 80.00

(1 row(s) affected)
```

How It Works

In this recipe, a new row was inserted into the Production.Location table.

The query began with the INSERT command and the name of the table that will receive the inserted data (the INTO keyword is optional):

```
INSERT Production.Location
```

The next line of code explicitly lists the columns of the destination table that we wish to insert the data into:

```
(Name, CostRate, Availability)
```

A comma must separate each column. Columns don't need to be listed in the same order as they appear in the base table—as long as the order in which you specify the values in the VALUES clause exactly matches the order of the column list. Column lists are not necessary if your INSERT statement provides all values in the same internal physical order as they appear in the table. However, using column lists should be required for your production code, particularly if the base schema undergoes periodic changes. This is because explicitly listing columns allows you to add new columns to the base table without changing the referencing code (assuming the new column has a default value).

The next line of code is the VALUES clause, and a comma-separated list of values (expressions) to insert:

```
VALUES ('Wheel Storage', 11.25, 80.00)
```

As I've noted previously, the values in this list must be provided in the same order as the listed columns, or, if no columns are listed, the same order of the columns in the table.

Inserting a Row Using Default Values

In this recipe, I'll show you how to load a row into a table such that it takes a default value for a certain column (or columns), using the DEFAULT keyword. In the previous recipe, the Production.Location table had a row inserted into it. The Production.Location table has two other columns which were not explicitly referenced in the INSERT statement. If you look at the column definition of Table 2-2, you'll see that there is also a LocationID and a ModifiedDate column that were not included in the previous example's INSERT:

■**Note** See Chapter 4 for more information on the CREATE TABLE command, IDENTITY columns, and DEFAULT values.

Table 2-2. *Production.Location Table Definition*

Column Name	Data Type	Nullability	Default Value	Identity Column?
LocationID	smallint	NOT NULL		Yes
Name	dbo.Name (user-defined data type)	NOT NULL		No
CostRate	smallmoney	NOT NULL	0.00	No
Availability	decimal(8,2)	NOT NULL	0.00	No
ModifiedDate	datetime	NOT NULL	GETDATE() (function to return the current date and time)	No

The ModifiedDate column has a default value which populates the current date and time for new rows if the column value wasn't explicitly inserted. The INSERT could have been written to update this column too. For example:

```
INSERT Production.Location
(Name, CostRate, Availability, ModifiedDate)
VALUES ('Wheel Storage 2', 11.25, 80.00, '1/1/2005')
```

When a column has a default value specified in a table, you can use the DEFAULT keyword in the VALUES clause, in order to explicitly trigger the default value.

For example:

```
INSERT Production.Location
(Name, CostRate, Availability, ModifiedDate)
VALUES ('Wheel Storage 3', 11.25, 80.00, DEFAULT)
```

If each column in the table uses defaults for all columns, you can trigger an insert that inserts a row using only the defaults by using DEFAULT VALUES option. For example:

```
INSERT dbo.ExampleTable
DEFAULT VALUES
```

How It Works

The DEFAULT keyword allows you to explicitly set a column's default value in an INSERT statement. The DEFAULT VALUES keywords can be used in your INSERT statement to explicitly set all the column's default values (assuming the table is defined with a default on each column).

The LocationID column from the Production.Location table, however, is an IDENTITY column (not a defaulted column). An IDENTITY property on a column causes the value in that column to automatically populate with an incrementing numeric value. Because LocationID is an IDENTITY column, an INSERT statement cannot explicitly add its value (unlike with a default). You can, however, explicitly insert values into an IDENTITY column, but only after performing the steps detailed in the next recipe.

Explicitly Inserting a Value into an IDENTITY Column

In this recipe, I'll demonstrate how to explicitly insert values into an IDENTITY property column. A column using an IDENTITY property automatically increments, based on a numeric seed value and incrementing value for every row inserted into the table. IDENTITY columns are often used as surrogate keys (a surrogate key is a unique, primary key generated by the database that holds no business-level significance other then to ensure uniqueness within the table).

In data load or recovery scenarios, you may find that you need to manually insert explicit values into an IDENTITY column. For example, if a row with the key value of "4" was deleted accidentally, and you need to manually reconstruct that row preserving the original value of "4" with the old business information, you'll need to be able to explicitly insert this value into the table.

To explicitly insert a numeric value into a column using an IDENTITY property, you must use the SET IDENITTY_INSERT command. The syntax is as follows:

```
SET IDENTITY_INSERT [ database_name . [ schema_name ] . ] table { ON | OFF }
```

The arguments of this command are described in Table 2-3:

Table 2-3. *SET IDENTITY_INSERT Command*

Argument	Description
[database_name . [schema_name] .] table	The optional database name, optional schema name, and required table name for which explicit values will be allowed to be inserted into an IDENTITY property column.
ON	OFF	When set ON, explicit value inserts are allowed. When OFF, explicit value inserts are *not* allowed.

In this recipe, I'll demonstrate how to explicitly insert the value of an IDENTITY column into a table. The following query first demonstrates what happens if you try to do an explicit insert into an identity column without first using IDENTITY_INSERT:

```
INSERT HumanResources.Department
(DepartmentID,  Name,  GroupName)
VALUES (17,  'Database Services',  'Information Technology')
```

This returns an error, keeping you from inserting an explicit value for the identity column:

```
Msg 544, Level 16, State 1, Line 2
Cannot insert explicit value for identity column in table 'Department' when
IDENTITY_INSERT is set to OFF.
```

Using SET IDENTITY_INSERT removes this barrier, as this next example demonstrates:

```
SET IDENTITY_INSERT HumanResources.Department ON

INSERT HumanResources.Department
(DepartmentID,  Name,  GroupName)
VALUES (17,  'Database Services',  'Information Technology')

SET IDENTITY_INSERT HumanResources.Department OFF
```

How It Works

In the recipe, this property was set ON prior to the insert:

```
SET IDENTITY_INSERT HumanResources.Department ON
```

The INSERT was then performed, using a value of "17." When inserting into an identity column, you must also explicitly list the column names after the INSERT table_name clause:

```
INSERT HumanResources.D epartment
(DepartmentID,  Name,  GroupName)
VALUES (17,  'Database Services',  'Information Technology')
```

IDENTITY_INSERT should be set OFF once you are finished explicitly inserting values:

```
SET IDENTITY_INSERT HumanResources.Department OFF
```

You should set this OFF once you are finished, as only one table in the session (your database connection session) can have IDENTITY_INSERT ON at the same time (assuming that you wish to insert explicit values for multiple tables). Closing your session will remove the ON property.

Inserting a Row into a Table with a Uniqueidentifier Column

In this recipe, I'll show you how to insert data into a table that uses a uniqueidentifier column.

A uniqueidentifier data type stores a 16-byte globally unique identifier (GUID) that is often used to ensure uniqueness across tables within the same or a different database. GUIDs offer an alternative to integer value keys, although their width compared to integer values can sometimes result in slower query performance for bigger tables.

To generate this value for a new INSERT, the NEWID system function is used.

NEWID generates a unique uniqueidentifier data type value, as this recipe demonstrates:

```
INSERT Purchasing.ShipMethod
(Name,  ShipBase,  ShipRate,  rowguid)
VALUES('MIDDLETON CARGO TS1',  8.99,  1.22,  NEWID())

SELECT rowguid,  name
FROM Purchasing.ShipMethod
WHERE Name = 'MIDDLETON CARGO TS1'
```

This returns:

```
(1 row(s) affected)
rowguid                              name
-----------------------------------  ------------------------------------------------
174BE850-FDEA-4E64-8D17-C019521C6C07 MIDDLETON CARGO TS1

(1 row(s) affected)
```

How It Works

The rowguid column in the Purchasing.ShipMethod table is a uniqueidentifier data type column. Here is an excerpt from the table definition:

```
rowguid uniqueidentifier ROWGUIDCOL  NOT NULL DEFAULT (newid()),
```

To generate a new, unique uniqueidentifier data type value for this inserted row, the NEWID() function is used in the VALUES clause:

```
VALUES('MIDDLETON CARGO TS1', 8.9 9,  1.2 2,  NEWID())
```

Selecting the new row that was just created, the rowguid was given a uniqueidentifier value of 174BE850-FDEA-4E64-8D17-C019521C6C07 (although when you test it yourself, you'll get a different value because NEWID creates a new value each time it is executed).

Inserting Rows Using an INSERT...SELECT Statement

The previous recipes showed you how to insert a single row of data. In this recipe, I'll show you how to insert multiple rows into a table using INSERT..SELECT. The syntax for performing an INSERT..SELECT operation is as follows:

```
INSERT
    [ INTO]
    table_or_view_name
    [ ( column_list ) ]
    SELECT column_list FROM data_source
```

The syntax for using INSERT...SELECT is almost identical to inserting a single row, only instead of using the VALUES clause, you designate a SELECT query that will populate the columns and rows into the table or updateable view. The SELECT query can be based on one or more data sources, so long as the column list conforms to the expected data types of the destination table.

For the purposes of this example, a new table will be created for storing the rows. The example populates values from the HumanResources.Shift table into the new dbo.Shift_Archive table:

```
CREATE TABLE [dbo]. [Shift_Archive](
  [ShiftID] [tinyint] NOT NULL,
  [Name] [dbo]. [Name] NOT NULL,
  [StartTime] [datetime] NOT NULL,
  [EndTime] [datetime] NOT NULL,
  [ModifiedDate] [datetime] NOT NULL DEFAULT (getdate()),
 CONSTRAINT [PK_Shift_ShiftID] PRIMARY KEY CLUSTERED
([ShiftID] ASC)
)
GO
```

Next, an INSERT..SELECT is performed:

```
INSERT Shift_Archive
(ShiftID, Name, StartTime, EndTime, ModifiedDate)
SELECT ShiftID, Name, StartTime, EndTime, ModifiedDate
FROM HumanResources.Shift
ORDER BY ShiftID
```

The results show that three rows were inserted:

```
(3 row(s) affected)
```

Next, a query is executed to confirm the inserted rows in the Shift_Archive table:

```
SELECT ShiftID, Name
FROM Shift_Archive
```

This returns:

```
ShiftID Name
------- ------------------------------------------------
1       Day
2       Evening
3       Night

(3 row(s) affected)
```

How It Works

Using the INSERT...SELECT statement, you can insert multiple rows into a table based on a SELECT query. Just like a regular, single-value INSERTs, you begin by using INSERT table_name and the list of columns to be inserted into the table (in parentheses):

```
INSERT Shift_Archive
(ShiftID, Name, StartTime, EndTime, ModifiedDate)
```

Following this is the query used to populate the table. The SELECT statement must return columns in the same order as the columns appear in the new table. The columns list must also have data type compatibility with the associated INSERT column list:

```
SELECT ShiftID, Name, StartTime, EndTime, ModifiedDate
FROM HumanResources.Shift
ORDER BY ShiftID
```

When the column lists aren't designated, the SELECT statement must provide values for *all* the columns of the table into which the data is being inserted.

Inserting Data from a Stored Procedure Call

In this recipe, I demonstrate how to insert table data by using a stored procedure. A *stored procedure* groups one or more Transact-SQL statements into a logical unit, and stores it as an object in a SQL Server database. Stored procedures allow for more sophisticated result set creation (for example you can use several intermediate result sets built in temporary tables before returning the final result set). Reporting system stored procedures (those that come with SQL Server 2005) that return a result set can also be used for INSERT...EXEC, which is useful if you wish to retain SQL Server information in tables.

This recipe also teaches you how to add rows to a table based on the output of a stored procedure. A stored procedure can only be used in this manner if it returns data via a SELECT command from within the procedure definition—it can't be used if it performs data modifications or database object operations.

■Note For more information on stored procedures, see Chapter 10.

The syntax for inserting data from a stored procedure is as follows:

```
INSERT
   [ INTO]
   table_or_view_name
   [ ( column_list ) ]
   EXEC stored_procedure_name
```

The syntax is almost identical to the previously demonstrated INSERT examples, only this time the data is populated via an executed stored procedure.

In this example, a stored procedure is created that returns rows from the Production. TransactionHistory table, based on the begin and end dates passed to the stored procedure. These results returned by the procedure also only return rows that don't exist in the Production. TransactionHistoryArchive:

```
CREATE PROCEDURE usp_SEL_Production_TransactionHistory
   @ModifiedStartDT datetime,
   @ModifiedEndDT datetime
AS

SELECT TransactionID, ProductID, ReferenceOrderID, ReferenceOrderLineID,
 TransactionDate, TransactionType, Quantity, ActualCost, ModifiedDate
FROM Production.TransactionHistory
WHERE ModifiedDate BETWEEN @ModifiedStartDT AND @ModifiedEndDT AND
    TransactionID NOT IN
      (SELECT TransactionID
         FROM Production.TransactionHistoryArchive)

GO
```

Next, this example tests the stored procedures to pre-check which rows will be inserted:

```
EXEC usp_SEL_Production_TransactionHistory '6/2/04', '6/3/04'
```

This returns 568 rows based on the date range passed to the procedure. In the next example, this stored procedure is used to insert the 568 rows into the Production.TransactionHistoryArchive table:

```
INSERT Production.TransactionHistoryArchive
(TransactionID, ProductID, ReferenceOrderID, ReferenceOrderLineID, TransactionDate,
TransactionType, Quantity, ActualCost, ModifiedDate)
EXEC usp_SEL_Production_TransactionHistory '6/2/04', '6/3/04'
```

How It Works

This example demonstrated using a stored procedure to populate a table using INSERT and EXEC. The INSERT began with the name of the table to be inserted into:

```
INSERT Production.TransactionHistoryArchive
```

Next was the list of columns to be inserted into:

```
(TransactionID, ProductID, ReferenceOrderID, ReferenceOrderLineID,
TransactionDate, TransactionType, Quantity, ActualCost, ModifiedDate)
```

Last was the EXEC statement, which executed the stored procedures. Any parameters the stored procedure expects follow the stored procedure name:

```
EXEC usp_SEL_Production_TransactionHistory '6/2/04', '6/3/04'
```

UPDATE

The following is basic syntax for the UPDATE statement:

```
UPDATE <table_or_view_name>
SET column_name = {expression | DEFAULT | NULL} [ ,...n ]
WHERE <search_condition>
```

The arguments of this command are described in Table 2-4:

Table 2-4. *UPDATE Command Arguments*

Argument	Description
table_or_view_name	The table or updateable view containing data to be updated.
column_name = {expression | DEFAULT | NULL}	The name of the column or columns to be updated. The column can be set to an expression, the DEFAULT value of the column, or a NULL.
search_condition	The search condition that defines *what* rows are modified. If this isn't included, all rows from the table or updateable view will be modified.

Updating a Single Row

In this recipe, I'll demonstrate how to use the UPDATE statement to modify data. With the UPDATE statement, you can apply changes to single or multiple columns, as well as to single or multiple rows. In this example, a single row is updated by designating the SpecialOfferID, which is the primary key of the table (for more on primary keys, see Chapter 4):

```
UPDATE Sales.SpecialOffer
SET DiscountPct = 0.15
WHERE SpecialOfferID = 10
```

Querying that specific row after the update confirms that the value of DiscountPct was indeed modified:

```
SELECT DiscountPct
FROM Sales.SpecialOffer
WHERE SpecialOfferID = 10
```

This returns:

```
DiscountPct
---------------------
0.15
```

How It Works

In this example, the query started off with UPDATE and the table name Sales.SpecialOffer:

```
UPDATE Sales.SpecialOffer
```

Next, SET was used, followed by the column name to be modified, and an equality operator to modify the DiscountPct to a value of 0.15. Relating back to the syntax at the beginning of the recipe, this example is setting the column to an expression value, and not a DEFAULT or NULL value:

```
SET DiscountPct = 0.15
```

Had this been the end of the query, *all* rows in the Sales.SpecialOffer table would have been modified, because the UPDATE clause works at the table level, not the row level. But the intention of this query was to only update the discount percentage for a specific product. The WHERE clause was used in order to achieve this:

```
WHERE SpecialOfferID = 10
```

After executing this query, only one row is modified. Had there been multiple rows that met the search condition in the WHERE clause, those rows would have been modified too.

■Tip Performing a SELECT query with the FROM and WHERE clauses of an UPDATE, prior to the UPDATE, allows you to see what rows you will be updating (an extra validation that you are updating the proper rows).

Updating Rows Based on a FROM and WHERE Clause

In this recipe, I'll show you how to use the UPDATE statement to modify rows based on a FROM clause and associated WHERE clause search conditions. The basic syntax, elaborating from the last example, is:

```
UPDATE <table_or_view_name>
SET column_name = {expression | DEFAULT | NULL}  [ ,...n ]
FROM <table_source>
WHERE <search_condition>
```

The FROM and WHERE clauses are not mandatory, however you will find that they are almost always implemented in order to specify exactly which rows are to be modified, based on joins against one or more tables.

In this example, assume that a specific product, "Full-Finger Gloves, M" from the Production. Product table has a customer purchase limit of two units per customer. For this query's requirement, any shopping cart with a quantity of more than two units for this product should immediately be adjusted back to the required limit:

```
UPDATE Sales.ShoppingCartItem
SET   Quantity =2,
  ModifiedDate = GETDATE()
FROM Sales.ShoppingCartItem c
INNER JOIN Production.Product p ON
  c.ProductID = p.ProductID
WHERE p.Name = 'Full-Finger Gloves,  M ' AND
  c.Quantity > 2
```

How It Works

Stepping through the code, the first line shows the table to be updated:

```
UPDATE Sales.ShoppingCartItem
```

Next, the columns to be updated are designated in the SET clause:

```
SET   Quantity =2,
  ModifiedDate = GETDATE()
```

Now here comes the optional FROM clause where the Sales.ShoppingCartItem and Production.Product tables are joined by ProductID. As you can see, the object being updated can also be referenced in the FROM clause. The reference in the UPDATE and in the FROM are treated as the same table:

```
FROM Sales.ShoppingCartItem c
INNER JOIN Production.Product p ON
  c.ProductID = p.P roductID
```

Using the updated table in the FROM clause allows you to join to other tables. Presumably, those other joined tables will be used to filter the updated rows, or to provide values for the updated rows.

The WHERE clause specifies that only the "Full-Finger Gloves, M" product in the Sales.ShoppingCartItem should be modified, and only if the Quantity is greater than 2 units:

```
WHERE p.Name = 'Full-Finger Gloves,  M ' AND
  c.Quantity > 2
```

Updating Large Value Data Type Columns

In this recipe, I'll show you how to modify large value data type column values. SQL Server 2005 has introduced new large value data types intended to replace the deprecated text, ntext, and image data types in SQL Server 2000. These new data types include:

- varchar(max), which holds non-Unicode variable length data.

- nvarchar(max), which holds Unicode variable length data.

- varbinary(max), which holds variable length binary data.

These data types can store up to $2^{31}-1$ bytes of data (for more information on data types, see Chapter 4).

One of the major drawbacks of the old text and image data types is that they required you to use separate functions such as WRITETEXT and UPDATETEXT in order to manipulate the image/text data. Using the new large value data types, you can now use regular INSERT and UPDATEs instead.

The syntax for inserting a large value data type is no different from a regular insert. For updating large value data types, however, the UPDATE command now includes the .WRITE method:

```
UPDATE <table_or_view_name>
SET column_name = .WRITE ( expression , @Offset , @Length )
FROM <table_source>
WHERE <search_condition>
```

The parameters of the .WRITE method are described in Table 2-5:

Table 2-5. *UPDATE Command With .WRITE Clause*

Argument	Description
expression	The expression defines the chunk of text to be placed in the column.
@Offset	@Offset determines the starting position in the existing data the new text should be placed. If @Offset is NULL, it means the new expression will be appended to the end of the column (also ignoring the second @Length parameter).
@Length	@Length determines the length of the section to overlay.

This example starts off by creating a table called RecipeChapter:

```
CREATE TABLE RecipeChapter
  (ChapterID int NOT NULL,
   Chapter varchar(max)  NOT NULL)
```

Next, a row is inserted into the table. Notice that there is nothing special about the string being inserted into the Chapter varchar(max) column:

```
INSERT RecipeChapter
(ChapterID,  Chapter)
VALUES
(1,  'At the beginning of each chapter you'll notice that basic concepts are covered
first.' )
```

This next example updates the newly inserted row, adding a sentence to the end of the existing sentence:

```
UPDATE RecipeChapter
SET Chapter .WRITE ('  In addition to the basics,  this chapter will also provide recipes
that can be used in your day to day development and administration.' ,  NULL,  NULL)
WHERE ChapterID = 1
```

Next, for that same row, the phrase "day to day" is replaced with the single word "daily":

```
UPDATE RecipeChapter
SET Chapter .WRITE('daily',  178,  10)
WHERE ChapterID = 1
```

Lastly, the results are returned for that row:

```
SELECT Chapter
FROM RecipeChapter
WHERE ChapterID = 1
```

This returns:

```
Chapter
-----------------------------------------------------------------------
At the beginning of each chapter you'll notice that basic concepts are covered
first.  In addition to the basics, this chapter will also provide recipes that can
be used in your daily development and administration.
```

How It Works

The recipe began by creating a table where book chapter descriptions would be held. The Chapter column used a varchar(max) data type:

```
CREATE TABLE RecipeChapter
 (ChapterID int NOT NULL,
  Chapter varchar(max)  NOT NULL)
```

Next, a new row was inserted. Notice that the syntax for inserting a large object data type doesn't differ from inserting data into a regular non-large value data type:

```
 INSERT RecipeChapter
(ChapterID,  Chapter)
VALUES
(1,  'At the beginning of each chapter you'll
notice that basic concepts are covered first.' )
```

Next, an UPDATE was performed against the RecipeChapter table to add a second sentence after the end of the first sentence:

```
UPDATE RecipeChapter
```

The SET command was followed by the name of the column to be updated (Chapter), and the new .WRITE command. The .WRITE command is followed by an open parenthesis, a single quotation, and the sentence to be appended to the end of the column:

```
SET Chapter .WRITE('  In addition to the basics,
this chapter will also provide recipes that can be
used in your day to day development and administration.' ,
NULL,  NULL)
```

The WHERE clause specified that only ChapterID "1" be modified:

```
WHERE ChapterID = 1
```

The next example of .WRITE demonstrated replacing data within the body of the column. In the example, the expression day to day was replaced with daily. The bigint value of @Offset and @Length are measured in bytes for varbinary(max) and varchar(max) data types. For nvarchar(max), these parameters measure the actual number of characters. For the example, the .WRITE had a value for @Offset (178 bytes into the text) and @Length (10 bytes long):

```
UPDATE RecipeChapter
SET Chapter .WRITE('daily',  178,  10)
WHERE ChapterID = 1
```

Inserting or Updating an Image File Using OPENROWSET and BULK

In this recipe, I demonstrate how to insert or update an image file from the file system into a SQL Server table. Adding images to a table in SQL Server 2000 usually required the use of external application tools or scripts. There was no elegant way to insert images using just Transact-SQL. With new functionality added in SQL Server 2005, UPDATE and OPENROWSET can be used together to import an image into a table.

OPENROWSET can be used to import a file into a single row, single column value. The basic syntax for OPENROWSET as it applies to this recipe is as follows:

```
OPENROWSET
( BULK 'data_file' ,
        | SINGLE_BLOB | SINGLE_CLOB | SINGLE_NCLOB )
```

The parameters for this command are described in Table 2-6:

Table 2-6. *The OPENROWSET Command Arguments*

Parameter	Description
data_file	The name and path of the file to read.
SINGLE_BLOB | SINGLE_CLOB | SINGLE_NCLOB	Designate the SINGLE_BLOB object for importing into a varbinary(max) data type, SINGLE_CLOB for ASCII data into a varchar(max) data type, and SINGLE_NCLOB for importing into a nvarchar(max) UNICODE data type.

See Chapter 27 for a detailed review of the syntax of OPENROWSET.

The first part of the recipe creates a new table which will be used to store gif image files:

```
CREATE TABLE StockGifs
  (StockGifID int NOT NULL,
   Gif varbinary(max)  NOT NULL)
```

Next, a row containing the image file will be inserted into the table:

```
INSERT StockGifs
(StockGifID,  Gif)
SELECT  1,
    BulkColumn
FROM OPENROWSET(BULK
'C:\Program Files\Microsoft SQL Server\90\Tools\Binn\VSShell\Common7\
IDE\DataWarehouseDesigner\KPIsBrowserPage\Images\Gauge_Asc0.gif',
SINGLE_BLOB) AS x
```

This next query selects the row from the table:

```
SELECT Gif
FROM StockGifs
WHERE StockGifID = 1
```

The returns:

```
Gif
------------------------------------------------------------------------------------
0x47494638396130001800E6FF00FFFFFFC0C0C0FF0000F7F7F7F70000EFEFEFEF0000E7E7E7DE00E7
D600E7C600E70000DEC600DEBD00DEAD00DE0000D6D6D6D6A5A5D6A500D69C00D69400D68C00D60000CE
CECECEA500CE0000C6C6C6C6B500C68400C67B73C60000BDBDBDBD8400BD5A5ABD0000B5B5B5B
5AD00B50000
```

The last example in this recipe updates an existing gif, changing it to a different gif file:

The second part of the recipe demonstrates how to update an existing gif:

```
UPDATE StockGifs
SET Gif =
(SELECT BulkColumn
FROM OPENROWSET(BULK
'C:\Program Files\Microsoft SQL Server\90\Tools\Binn\VSShell\Common7\IDE\
DataWarehouseDesigner\KPIsBrowserPage\Images\Cylinder2.gif',
SINGLE_BLOB) AS x)
WHERE StockGifID =1
```

How It Works

In this recipe, I've demonstrated using OPENROWSET with the BULK option to insert a row containing a gif image file, and then the way to update it to a different gif file.

First, a table was created to hold the gif files using a varbinary(max) data type:

```
CREATE TABLE StockGifs
  (StockGifID int NOT NULL,
   Gif varbinary(max)  NOT NULL)
```

Next, a new row was inserted using INSERT:

```
INSERT #StockGifs
(StockGifID,  Gif)
```

The INSERT was populated using a SELECT query against the OPENROWSET function to bring in the file data. The BulkColumn referenced in the query represents the varbinary value to be inserted into the varbinary(max) row from the OPENROWSET data source:

```
SELECT  1,
   BulkColumn
```

In the FROM clause, OPENROWSET was called. OPENROWSET allows you to access remote data from a data source:

```
FROM OPENROWSET(BULK 'C:\Program Files\Microsoft SQL
Server\90\Tools\Binn\VSShell\Common7\IDE\
DataWarehouseDesigner\KPIsBrowserPage\Images\Gauge_Asc0.gif',  SINGLE_BLOB) AS x
```

The BULK option was used inside the function, followed by the file name, and the SINGLE_BLOB keyword. The BULK option within OPENROWSET means that data will be read from a file (in this case the gif file specified after BULK). The SINGLE_BLOB switch tells OPENROWSET to return the contents of the data file as a single-row, single-column varbinary(max) rowset.

This recipe also demonstrates an UPDATE of the varbinary(max) column from an external file. The UPDATE designated the StockGifs table, and used SET to update the Gif column:

```
UPDATE StockGifs
SET Gif =
```

The expression to set the new image to Cylinder2.gif from the previous Gauge_Asc0.gif occurs in a subquery. It uses almost the same syntax as the previous INSERT, only this time the only value returned in the SELECT is the BulkColumn column:

```
(SELECT BulkColumn
FROM OPENROWSET(BULK 'C:\Program Files\Microsoft SQL
Server\90\Tools\Binn\VSShell\Common7\IDE\DataWarehouseDesigner\
KPIsBrowserPage\Images\Cylinder2.gif',  SINGLE_BLOB)
AS g)
WHERE StockGifID =1
```

The image file on the machine is then stored in the column value for that row as varbinary data.

DELETE

The simple syntax for DELETE is as follows:

```
DELETE [FROM] table_or_view_name
WHERE search_condition
```

The arguments of this command are described in Table 2-7:

Table 2-7. *The DELETE Command Arguments*

Argument	Description
table_or_view_name	The name of the table or updateable view that you are deleting rows from.
search_condition	The search condition(s) in the WHERE clause defines which rows will be deleted from the table or updateable view.

Deleting Rows

In this recipe, I show you how to use the DELETE statement to remove one or more rows from a table. First, take an example table this is populated with rows:

```
SELECT *
INTO Production.Example_ProductProductPhoto
FROM Production.ProductProductPhoto
```

This returns:

```
(504 row(s) affected)
```

Next, all rows are deleted from the table:

```
DELETE Production.Example_ProductProductPhoto
```

This returns:

```
(504 row(s) affected)
```

This next example demonstrates using DELETE with a WHERE clause. Let's say that the relationship of keys between two tables gets dropped, and the users were able to delete data from the primary key table and not the referencing foreign key tables (see Chapter 4 for a review of primary and foreign keys). In this example search condition, only rows that *do not* exist in the Production.Product table are deleted from the Production.ExampleProductProductPhoto table (which in this example, there are none that do not exist):

```
-- Repopulate the Example_ProductProductPhoto table
INSERT Production.Example_ProductProductPhoto
SELECT *
FROM Production.ProductProductPhoto

DELETE Production.Example_ProductProductPhoto
WHERE ProductID NOT IN
    (SELECT ProductID
     FROM Production.Product)
```

This third example demonstrates the same functionality of the previous example, only the DELETE has been re-written to use a FROM clause, instead of a subquery:

```
DELETE Production.ProductProductPhoto
FROM Production.Example_ProductProductPhoto ppp
LEFT OUTER JOIN Production.Product p ON
  ppp.ProductID = p.ProductID
WHERE p.ProductID IS NULL
```

How It Works

In the first example of the recipe, all rows were deleted from the Example_ProductProductPhoto table:

```
DELETE Production.Example_ProductProductPhoto
```

This is because there was no WHERE clause to specify which rows would be deleted.

In the second example, the WHERE clause was used to specify rows to be deleted based on a subquery lookup to another table:

```
WHERE ProductID NOT IN
    (SELECT ProductID
     FROM Production.Product)
```

The third example used a LEFT OUTER JOIN instead of a subquery, joining the ProductID of the two tables:

```
FROM Production.Example_ProductProductPhoto ppp
LEFT OUTER JOIN Production.Product p ON
  ppp.ProductID = p.ProductID
```

Because the same object that is being deleted from Production.ProductProductPhoto is also the same object in the FROM clause, and since there is only *one* reference to that table in the FROM clause, it is assumed that rows identified in the FROM and WHERE clause will be one and the same—it will associate to the rows deleted from the Production.ProductProductPhoto table.

Because a LEFT OUTER JOIN was used, if any rows did *not* match between the left and right tables, the right table would have NULL values for the unmatched ProductIDs. Thus, to show rows in Production.Example_ProductProductPhoto that don't have a matching ProductID in the Production. Product table, you can qualify the Production.Product as follows:

```
WHERE p.ProductID IS NULL
```

Any rows without a match to the Production.Product table will be deleted from the Production. Example_ProductProductPhoto table.

Truncating a Table

In this recipe, I show you how to delete rows from a table in a minimally logged fashion (hence, much quicker). Generally you should use DELETE for operations that should be fully logged, however for test or throw-away data, this is a fast technique for removing the data. Minimal logging references how much recoverability information is written to the database's transaction log (see Chapter 22). To achieve this, use the TRUNCATE command.

The syntax is as follows:

```
TRUNCATE TABLE table_name
```

This command takes just the table name to truncate. Since it always removes *all* rows from a table, there is no FROM or WHERE clause, as this recipe demonstrates:

```
-- First populating the example
SELECT *
INTO Sales.Example_StoreContact
FROM Sales.StoreContact

-- Next, truncating ALL rows from the example table
TRUNCATE TABLE Sales.Example_StoreContact
```

Next, the table's row count is queried:

```
SELECT COUNT(*)
FROM Sales.Example_StoreContact
```

This returns:

```
-----------
0
```

How It Works

The `TRUNCATE TABLE` statement, like the `DELETE` statement, can delete rows from a table. `TRUNCATE TABLE` deletes rows faster than `DELETE`, because it is minimally logged. Unlike `DELETE` however, the `TRUNCATE TABLE` must be used to remove `ALL` rows in the table (no `WHERE` clause).

Although `TRUNCATE TABLE` is a faster way to delete rows, you can't use it if the table columns are referenced by a foreign key constraint (see Chapter 4 for more information on foreign keys), if the table is published using transactional or merge replication, or if the table participates in an indexed view (see Chapter 7 for more information). Also, if the table has an `IDENTITY` column, keep in mind that the column will be reset to the seed value defined for the column (if no seed was explicitly set, it is set to 1).

The OUTPUT Clause

The syntax for using `OUTPUT` in a data modification operation is as follows:

```
OUTPUT { DELETED | INSERTED | from_table_name } . { * | column_name } [ ,...n ]
    INTO { @table_variable | output_table }
```

The arguments of this command are described in Table 2-8:

Table 2-8. *OUTPUT Clause Arguments*

Argument	Description
DELETED | INSERTED | from_table_name	Like triggers (see Chapter 12), two "virtual" tables exist for the OUTPUT to use - INSERTED and DELETED, which hold the original and modified values for the updated table. The INSERTED and DELETED virtual tables share the same column names of the modified table.
* | column_name	You can select all columns from the updated table using * or one or more specified columns.
@table_variable | output_table	The table variable or regular table that will receive the rows from the OUTPUT operation.

Using the OUTPUT Clause with INSERT, UPDATE, DELETE

In this recipe, I show you how to return information about rows that are impacted by an `INSERT`, `UPDATE`, or `DELETE` operation using the new `OUTPUT` clause introduced in SQL Server 2005. In this first example, an `UPDATE` statement modifies the name of a specific product. `OUTPUT` is then used to return information on the original and updated column names:

```
DECLARE @ProductChanges TABLE
  (DeletedName nvarchar(50),
   InsertedName nvarchar(50))
```

```
UPDATE Production.Product
SET Name = 'HL Spindle/Axle XYZ'
OUTPUT DELETED.Name,
      INSERTED.Name
 INTO @ProductChanges
WHERE ProductID = 524

SELECT DeletedName,
    InsertedName
FROM @ProductChanges
```

This query returns:

DeletedName	InsertedName
HL Spindle/Axle	HL Spindle/Axle XYZ

This next example uses OUTPUT for a DELETE operation. First, an example table to hold the data is created:

```
SELECT *
INTO Sales.Example_SalesTaxRate
FROM Sales.SalesTaxRate
```

Next, this batch creates a table variable to hold the data, deletes rows from the table, and then selects from the table variable to see which rows were deleted:

```
DECLARE @SalesTaxRate TABLE(
   [SalesTaxRateID] [int]  NOT NULL,
   [StateProvinceID] [int]  NOT NULL,
   [TaxType] [tinyint] NOT NULL,
   [TaxRate] [smallmoney] NOT NULL,
   [Name] [dbo]. [Name] NOT NULL,
   [rowguid] [uniqueidentifier]  ,
   [ModifiedDate] [datetime] NOT NULL )

DELETE Sales.Example_SalesTaxRate
OUTPUT DELETED.*
INTO @SalesTaxRate

SELECT  SalesTaxRateID,
    Name
FROM @SalesTaxRate
```

This returns the following abridged results:

SalesTaxRateID	Name
19	California State Sales Tax
5	Canadian GST
1	Canadian GST + Alberta Provincial Tax
12	Canadian GST
...	
29	Germany Output Tax
8	Canadian GST
2	Canadian GST + Ontario Provincial Tax

```
(29 row(s) affected)
```

In the third example, an INSERT is demonstrated with OUTPUT. A new row is inserted into a table and the operation is captured to a table variable table:

```
DECLARE @NewDepartment TABLE
  (DepartmentID smallint NOT NULL,
   Name nvarchar(50)  NOT NULL,
   GroupName nvarchar(50)  NOT NULL,
   ModifiedDate datetime NOT NULL)

INSERT HumanResources.Department
(Name,  GroupName)
OUTPUT INSERTED.*
INTO @NewDepartment
VALUES ('Accounts Receivable',  'Accounting')

SELECT  DepartmentID,
    ModifiedDate
FROM  @NewDepartment
```

This returns:

```
DepartmentID ModifiedDate
------------ ----------------------------
18           2005-03-06 12:46:40.653
```

How It Works

The first example used a temporary table variable to hold the OUTPUT results (See Chapter 4 for more information on temporary table variables):

```
DECLARE @ProductChanges TABLE
  (DeletedName nvarchar(50),
   InsertedName nvarchar(50))
```

Next, the first part of the UPDATE changed the product name to "HL Spindle/Axle XYZ":

```
UPDATE Production.Product
SET Name = 'HL Spindle/Axle XYZ'
```

After the SET clause, but *before* the WHERE clause, the OUTPUT defined which columns to return:

```
OUTPUT DELETED.Name,
    INSERTED.Name
```

Like triggers (covered in Chapter 12), two "virtual" tables exist for the OUTPUT to use—INSERTED and DELETED—both of which hold the original and modified values for the updated table. The INSERTED and DELETED virtual tables share the same column names of the modified table—in this case returning the original name (DELETED.Name), and the new name (INSERTED.Name).

The values of this OUTPUT are placed into the temporary table variable by using INTO, followed by the table name:

```
 INTO @ProductChanges
```

The UPDATE query qualified that only ProductID 524 would be modified to the new name:

```
WHERE ProductID = 524
```

After the update, a query was executed against the @ProductChanges temporary table variable to show the before/after changes:

```
SELECT DeletedName,
  InsertedName
FROM @ProductChanges
```

The DELETE and INSERT examples were variations on the first example, where OUTPUT pushes the deleted rows (for DELETE) or the inserted rows (for INSERT) into a table variable.

Chunking Data Modifications with TOP

I demonstrated using TOP in Chapter 1. In SQL Server 2005, TOP can also be used in DELETE, INSERT, or UPDATE statements. This recipe further demonstrates using TOP to "chunk" data modifications; meaning instead of executing a very large operation, you can break the modification into smaller pieces, potentially increasing performance and improving database concurrency for larger, highly-accessed tables. This technique is often used for large data loads to reporting or data warehouse applications.

Large, single set updates can cause the database transaction log to grow considerably. When processing in chunks, each chunk is committed after completion, allowing SQL Server to potentially reuse that transaction log space. In addition to transaction log space, on a very large data update, if the query must be cancelled, you may have to wait a long time while the transaction rolls back. With smaller chunks, you can continue with your update more quickly. Also, chunking allows more concurrency against the modified table, allowing user queries to jump in, instead of waiting several minutes for a large modification to complete.

Deleting Rows in Chunks

In this recipe, I show you how to modify data in blocks of rows in multiple executions, instead of an entire result set in one large transaction. First, I create an example deletion table for this example:

```
SELECT *
INTO Production.Example_BillOfMaterials
FROM Production.BillOfMaterials
```

Next, all rows will be deleted from the table in 500 row chunks:

```
WHILE (SELECT COUNT(*)FROM Production.Example_BillOfMaterials)>  0
BEGIN

  DELETE TOP(500)
  FROM Production.Example_BillOfMaterials

END
```

This returns:

```
(500 row(s) affected)

(500 row(s) affected)

(500 row(s) affected)

(500 row(s) affected)

(500 row(s) affected)

(179 row(s)  affected)
```

How It Works

In this example, I used a WHILE condition to keep executing the DELETE while the count of rows in the table was greater than zero (see Chapter 9 for more information on WHILE):

```
WHILE (SELECT COUNT(*)FROM Production.Example_BillOfMaterials)> 0
BEGIN
```

Next was the DELETE, followed by the TOP clause, and the row limitation in parentheses:

```
DELETE TOP(500)
FROM Production.BillOfMaterials
```

This recipe didn't use a WHERE clause, so no filtering was applied and *all* rows were deleted from the table—but only in 500 row chunks. Once the WHILE condition no longer evaluated to TRUE, the loop ended. After executing, the row counts affected in each batch were displayed. The first five batches deleted 500 rows, and the last batch deletes the remaining 179 rows.

This "chunking" method can be used with INSERTs and UPDATEs too. For INSERT and UPDATE, the TOP clause follows right after the INSERT and UPDATE keyword, for example:

```
INSERT TOP(100)
...
```

```
UPDATE TOP(25)
...
```

The expanded functionality of TOP adds a new technique for managing large data modifications against a table.

■■■

Transactions, Locking, Blocking, and Deadlocking

In the last two chapters, I covered Data Modification Language, and provided recipes for SELECT, INSERT, UPDATE, and DELETE statements. Before moving on to Data Definition Language (creating/altering/dropping tables, indexes, views, and more), in this chapter I'll review recipes for handling transactions, lock-monitoring, blocking, and deadlocking. I'll demonstrate the new SQL Server 2005 snapshot isolation level, as well as dynamic management views that are used to monitor and troubleshoot blocking and locking.

Transaction Control

Transactions are an integral part of a relational database system and they help define a single unit of work. This unit of work can include one or more Transact-SQL statements, which are either committed or rolled-back as a group. This all-or-none functionality helps prevent partial updates or inconsistent data states. A partial update occurs when one part of an interrelated process is rolled back or cancelled without rolling back or reversing all of the other parts of the interrelated processes.

A transaction is bound by the ACID test. ACID stands for Atomicity, Consistency, Isolation (or Independence), and Durability:

- *Atomicity* means that the transactions are an all-or-nothing entity—carrying out all steps or none at all

- *Consistency* ensures that the data is valid both before and after the transaction. Data integrity must be maintained (foreign key references, for example) and internal data structures need to be in a valid state.

- *Isolation* is a requirement that transactions not be dependent on other transactions that may be taking place concurrently (either at the same time or overlapping). One transaction can't see another transaction's data that is in an intermediate state, but instead sees the data as it was either before the transaction began or after.

- *Durability* means that the transaction's effects are permanent after the transaction has committed, and any changes will survive system failures.

In this chapter, I demonstrate and review the SQL Server 2005 mechanisms and functionality that are used to ensure ACID test compliance, namely locking and transactions.

There are three possible transactions types in SQL Server 2005: autocommit, explicit, or implicit.

Autocommit is the default behavior for SQL Server 2005, where each separate Transact-SQL statement you execute is automatically committed after it is finished. For example, if you have two INSERT statements, with the first one failing and the second one succeeding, the second change is maintained because each INSERT is automatically contained in its own transaction. Although this mode frees the developer from having to worry about explicit transactions, depending on this mode for transactional activity can be a mistake. For example if you have two transactions, one that credits an account, and another that debits it, and the first transaction failed, you'll have a debit without the credit. This may make the bank happy, but not necessarily the customer, who had their account debited! Autocommit is even a bit dangerous for ad hoc administrative changes—for example if you accidentally delete all rows from a table, you don't have the option of rolling back the transaction after you've realized the mistake.

Implicit transactions occur when the SQL Server session is in implicit transaction mode, and when one of the following statements is first executed:

ALTER TABLE	FETCH	REVOKE
CREATE	GRANT	SELECT
DELETE	INSERT	TRUNCATE TABLE
DROP	OPEN	UPDATE

A new transaction is automatically created (opened) once any of the aforementioned statements are executed, and remains open until either a ROLLBACK or COMMIT statement is issued. The initiating command is included in the open transaction. Implicit mode is activated by executing the following command in your query session:

```
SET IMPLICIT_TRANSACTIONS ON
```

To turn this off (back to explicit mode), execute:

```
SET IMPLICIT_TRANSACTIONS OFF
```

Implicit mode can be *very* troublesome in a production environment, as application designers and end-users could forget to commit transactions, leaving them open to block other connections (more on blocking later in the chapter).

Explicit transactions are those that you define yourself. This is by far the recommended mode of operation when performing data modifications for your database application. This is because you explicitly control which modifications belong to a single transaction, as well as the actions that are performed if an error occurs. Modifications which must be grouped together are done using your own instruction.

Explicit transactions use the following Transact-SQL commands and keywords described in Table 3-1:

Table 3-1. *Explicit Transaction Commands*

Command	Description
BEGIN TRANSACTION	Sets the starting point of an explicit transaction.
ROLLBACK TRANSACTION	Restores original data modified by a transaction, and brings data back to the state it was in at the start of the transaction. Resources held by the transaction are freed.
COMMIT TRANSACTION	Ends the transaction if no errors were encountered and makes changes permanent. Resources held by the transaction are freed.
BEGIN DISTRIBUTED TRANSACTION	Allows you to define the beginning of a distributed transaction to be managed by Microsoft Distributed Transaction Coordinator (MS DTC). MS DTC must be running locally and remotely.
SAVE TRANSACTION	SAVE TRANSACTION issues a savepoint within a transaction, which allows one to define a location to which a transaction can return if part of the transaction is cancelled. A transaction must be rolled back or committed immediately after rolling back to a savepoint.
@@TRANCOUNT	Returns the number of active transactions for the connection. BEGIN TRANSACTION increments @@TRANCOUNT by 1, and ROLLBACK TRANSACTION and COMMIT TRANSACTION decrements @@TRANCOUNT by 1. ROLLBACK TRANSACTION to a savepoint has no impact.

Using Explicit Transactions

This recipe's example demonstrates how to use explicit transactions to commit or rollback the data modification depending on the return of an error in a batch of statements:

```
-- Before count
SELECT COUNT(*) BeforeCount FROM HumanResources.Department

-- Variable to hold the latest error integer value
DECLARE @Error int

BEGIN TRANSACTION

INSERT HumanResources.Department
(Name, GroupName)
VALUES ('Accounts Payable', 'Accounting')

SET @Error = @@ERROR
IF (@Error<> 0) GOTO Error_Handler

INSERT HumanResources.Department
(Name, GroupName)
VALUES ('Engineering', 'Research and Development')

SET @Error = @@ERROR
IF (@Error <> 0) GOTO Error_Handler

COMMIT TRAN

Error_Handler:
IF @Error <> 0
```

```
BEGIN
    ROLLBACK TRANSACTION
END

-- After count
SELECT COUNT(*) AfterCount FROM HumanResources.Department
```

This returns:

```
BeforeCount
-----------
18

(1 row(s) affected)


(1 row(s) affected)

Msg 2601, Level 14, State 1, Line 14
Cannot insert duplicate key row in object 'HumanResources.Department'
➥ with unique index 'AK_Department_Name'.
The statement has been terminated.

AfterCount
-----------
18

(1 row(s) affected)
```

How It Works

The first statement in this example validated the count of rows in the HumanResources.Department table, returning 18 rows:

```
-- Before count
SELECT COUNT(*) BeforeCount FROM HumanResources.Department
```

A local variable is created to hold the value of the @@ERROR function (which captures the latest error state of a SQL statement):

```
-- Variable to hold the latest error integer value
DECLARE @Error int
```

Next, an explicit transaction was started:

```
BEGIN TRANSACTION
```

The next statement attempted an INSERT into the HumanResources.Department table. There was a unique key on the department name, but because the department name didn't already exist in the table, the insert succeeded:

```
INSERT HumanResources.Department
(Name, GroupName)
VALUES ('Accounts Payable', 'Accounting')
```

Next was an error handler for the INSERT:

```
SET @Error = @@ERROR
IF (@Error <> 0) GOTO Error_Handler
```

This line of code evaluates the @@ERROR function. The @@ERROR system function returns the last error number value for the last executed statement within the scope of the current connection. The IF statement says that *if* an error occurs, the code should jump to (using GOTO) the Error_Handler section of the code.

Note For a review of GOTO, see Chapter 9. For a review of @@Error, see Chapter 16. Chapter 16 also introduces a new error handling command, TRY...CATCH.

GOTO is a keyword that helps you control the flow of statement execution. The identifier after GOTO, Error_Handler, is a user-defined code section.

Next, another insert is attempted, this time for a department that already exists in the table. Because the table has a unique constraint on the name column, this insert will fail:

```
INSERT HumanResources.Department
(Name, GroupName)
VALUES ('Engineering', 'Research and Development')
```

The failure will cause the @@ERROR following this INSERT to be set to a non-zero value. The IF statement will then evaluate to TRUE, which will invoke the GOTO, thus skipping over the COMMIT TRAN to the Error_Handler section:

```
SET @Error = @@ERROR
IF (@Error <> 0) GOTO Error_Handler

COMMIT TRAN
```

Following the Error_Handler section is a ROLLBACK TRANSACTION:

```
Error_Handler:
IF @Error <> 0
BEGIN
    ROLLBACK TRANSACTION
END
```

Another count is performed after the rollback, and again, there are only 18 rows in the database. This is because both INSERTs were in the same transaction, and one of the INSERTs failed. Since a transaction is all-or-nothing, no rows were inserted:

```
-- After count
SELECT COUNT(*) AfterCount FROM HumanResources.Department
```

Some final thoughts and recommendations regarding how to handle transactions in your Transact-SQL code or through your application:

- Keep transaction time short as possible for the business process at hand. Transactions that remain open can hold locks on resources for an extended period of time, which can block other users from performing work or reading data (see later on in the chapter for a review of locking and blocking).

- Minimize resources locked by the transaction. For example, update only tables that are related to the transaction at hand. If the data modifications are logically dependent on each other, they belong in the same transaction. If not, the unrelated updates belong in their own transaction.

- Add only *relevant* Transact-SQL statements to a transaction. Don't add extra lookups or updates that are not germane to the specific transaction. Executing SELECT statement within a transaction can create locks on the referenced tables, which can in turn block other users/sessions from performing work or reading data.

- Do not open new transactions that require user or external feedback within the transaction. Open transactions can hold locks on resources, and user feedback can take an indefinite amount of time to receive. Instead, gather user feedback *before* issuing an explicit transaction.

Displaying the Oldest Active Transaction with DBCC OPENTRAN

If a transaction remains open in the database, whether intentionally or not, this transaction can block other processes from performing activity against the modified data. Also, backups of the transaction log can only truncate the inactive portion of a transaction log, so open transactions can cause the log to grow (or reach the physical limit) until that transaction is committed or rolled back.

In order to identify the oldest active transactions in a database, you can use the DBCC OPENTRAN command. The syntax is as follows:

```
DBCC OPENTRAN
     [ (    [ 'database_name' | database_id | 0 ] ) ]
     [ WITH TABLERESULTS
     [ , NO_INFOMSGS ]
     ]
```

The arguments of this command are described in Table 3-2:

Table 3-2. *DBCC OPENTRAN Command Arguments*

Argument	Description
'database_name' | database_id | 0	The database name or database id to check for the oldest active transaction. If 0 is designated, the current database is used.
WITH TABLERESULTS	When designated, the results are returned in a tabular format.
NO_INFOMSGS	When included in the command, WITH NO_INFOMSGS suppresses informational messages from the DBCC output.

This example demonstrates using DBCC OPENTRAN to identify the oldest active transaction in the database:

```
BEGIN TRANSACTION

DELETE Production.ProductProductPhoto
WHERE ProductID = 317

DBCC OPENTRAN('AdventureWorks')

ROLLBACK TRAN
```

This returns:

```
(1 row(s) affected)
Transaction information for database 'AdventureWorks'.

Oldest active transaction:
    SPID (server process ID): 52
    UID (user ID) : -1
    Name          : user_transaction
    LSN           : (44:6363:17)
    Start time    : Mar  9 2005  8:46:49:610PM
    SID           : 0x0105000000000005150000005527a777bf094b3850ff83d06eb030000
DBCC execution completed. If DBCC printed error messages, contact your system
administrator.
```

How It Works

The recipe started off by opening up a new transaction, and then deleting a specific row from the Production.ProductProductPhoto table:

```
BEGIN TRANSACTION

DELETE Production.ProductProductPhoto
WHERE ProductID = 317
```

Next, the DBCC OPENTRAN was executed, with the database name in parentheses:

```
DBCC OPENTRAN(AdventureWorks)
```

Last, the transaction containing a DELETE was rolled back:

```
ROLLBACK TRAN
```

These results showed information regarding the oldest active transaction, including the server process id, user id, and start time of the transaction:

```
Oldest active transaction:
    SPID (server process ID): 52
    UID (user ID) : -1
    Name          : user_transaction
    LSN           : (44:6363:17)
    Start time    : Mar  9 2005  8:46:49:610PM
    SID           : 0x0105000000000005150000005527a777bf094b3850ff83d06eb030000
DBCC execution completed. If DBCC printed error messages,
➥ contact your system administrator.
```

The key pieces of information from the results are the SPID (server process id) and Start time.

■**Note** SQL Server 2005 has renamed server process id to *server session id*. Not all references to "server process id" have been purged from command and documentation references yet.

Using these, you can check the Transact-SQL that the process is executing using DBCC INPUTBUFFER (demonstrated later in the chapter), figure out how long the process has been running for, and if necessary, shut down the process. DBCC OPENTRAN is very useful for troubleshooting orphaned connections (connections still open in the database but disconnected from the application or client), and the identification of transactions missing a COMMIT or ROLLBACK.

This command also returns the oldest distributed and undistributed replicated transactions, if any exist within the database. If there are no active transactions, no data will be returned.

Locking

Locking is a normal and necessary part of a relation database system, ensuring the integrity of the data by not allowing concurrent updates to the same data. Locking can also prevent users from reading data while it is being updated. SQL Server 2005 manages locking dynamically; however it is still important to understand how Transact-SQL queries impact locking in SQL Server. Before proceeding to the recipe, I'll describe SQL Server 2005 locking fundamentals briefly.

Locks help prevent concurrency problems from occurring. Concurrency problems (discussed in detail in the next section on Transaction, Locking, and Concurrency) can occur when one user attempts to read data that another is modifying, modify data that another is reading, or modify data that another transaction is trying to modify.

Locks are placed against SQL Server resources. How a resource is locked is called its *lock mode*. Table 3-3 reviews the main lock modes that SQL Server 2005 has at its disposal:

Table 3-3. *SQL Server 2005 Lock Modes*

Name	Description
Shared lock	Shared locks are issued during read, non-modifying queries. They allow data to be read, but not updated by other processes while being held.
Intent lock	Intent locks effectively create a lock queue, designating the order of connections and their associated right to update or read resources. SQL Server uses intent locks to show future intention of acquiring locks on a specific resource.
Update lock	Update locks are acquired prior to modifying the data. When the row is modified, this lock is escalated to an exclusive lock. If not modified, it is downgraded to a shared lock. This lock type prevents deadlocks if two connections hold a Shared (S) lock on a resource, and attempt to convert to an Exclusive (X) lock, but cannot because they are each waiting for the other transaction to release the Shared (S) lock.
Exclusive lock	Issues a lock on the resource that bars any kind of access (reads or writes). Issued during INSERT, UPDATE, or DELETE statements.
Schema modification	Issued when a DDL statement is executed.
Schema stability	Issued when a query is being compiled. Keeps DDL operations from being performed on the table.
Bulk update	This type of lock is issued during a bulk-copy operation. Performance is increased for the bulk copy operation, but table concurrency is reduced.
Key-range	Key-range locks protect a range of rows (based on the index key). For example, protecting rows in an UPDATE statement with a range of dates from '1/1/2005' to '12/31/2005'. Protecting the range of data prevents row inserts into the date range that would be missed by the current data modification.

You can lock all manner of objects in SQL Server, from a single row in a database, to a table, to the database itself. Lockable resources vary in granularity, from small (at the row level) to large (the entire database). Small grain locks allow for greater database concurrency, because users can execute queries against specified unlocked rows. Each lock placed by SQL Server requires memory, however, so thousands of individual row locks can also affect SQL Server performance. Larger grained locks reduce concurrency, but take up fewer resources. Table 3-4 details the resources SQL Server 2005 can apply locks to:

Table 3-4. *SQL Server 2005 Lock Resources*

Resource Name	Description
RID	Row Identifier, designating a single table row.
Key	Index row lock, helping prevent phantom reads. Also called Key-range lock, this lock type uses both a range and a row component. The range represents the range of index keys between two consecutive index keys. The row component represents the lock type on the index entry.
Page	Referring to an 8KB data or index page.
Extent	Allocation unit of eight 8KB data or index pages.
HOPT	A heap (table without a clustered index) or B-tree.
Allocation unit	A set of related pages grouped by data type, for example data rows, index rows, and large object data rows.
Table	Entire table, data, and indexes locked.
Object	A database object (for example a view, stored procedure, function).
File	The database file.
DB	Entire database lock.
Application	An application-specified resource.
Metadata	System metadata.

Not all lock types are compatible with each other. For example, no other locks can be placed on a resource that has already been locked by an Exclusive lock. The other transaction must wait or time out until the exclusive lock is released. A resource locked by an Update lock can only have a Shared lock placed on it by another transaction. A resource locked by a Shared lock can have other Shared or Update locks placed on it.

Locks are allocated and escalated automatically by SQL Server. Escalation means that finer grain locks (row or page locks) are converted into coarse-grain table locks. SQL Server will attempt to initialize escalation when a single Transact-SQL statement has more than 5,000 locks on a single table or index, or if the amount of locks on the SQL Server instance exceeds the available memory threshold. Locks take up system memory, so converting many locks into one larger lock can free up memory resources. The drawback to freeing up the memory resources, however, is reduced concurrency.

Viewing Lock Activity

This recipe shows you how to monitor locking activity in the database using the new SQL Server 2005 `sys.dm_tran_locks` dynamic management view. It uses a table locking hint (for a review of hints, see Chapter 1's "Using Table Hints" section).

▪**Note** The `sys.dm_tran_locks` view is a replacement of the deprecated `sp_lock` system stored procedure used to monitor activity in SQL Server 2000.

In the first part of this recipe, a new query editor window is opened, and the following command is executed:

```
USE AdventureWorks

BEGIN TRAN
SELECT ProductID, DocumentID, ModifiedDate
FROM Production.ProductDocument
WITH (TABLOCKX)
```

In a second query editor window, the following query is executed:

```
SELECT request_session_id sessionid,
       resource_type type,
       resource_database_id dbid,
       OBJECT_NAME(resource_associated_entity_id) objectname,
       request_mode rmode,
       request_status rstatus
FROM sys.dm_tran_locks
```

This returns information about the locking session identifier (server process id spid), the resource being locked, the database, object, resource mode, and lock status:

sessionid	rtype	dbname	objectname	rmode	rstatus
53	DATABASE	AdventureWorks	NULL	S	GRANT
52	DATABASE	AdventureWorks	NULL	S	GRANT
52	OBJECT	AdventureWorks	ProductDocument	X	GRANT

```
(3 row(s) affected)
```

How It Works

The example began by starting a new transaction and executing a query against the `Production.ProductDocument` table using a `TABLOCKX` locking hint (this hint places an exclusive lock on the table). In order to monitor what locks are open for the current SQL Server instance, the `sys.dm_tran_locks` dynamic management view was queried. It returned a list of active locks in the AdventureWorks database. The exclusive lock on the ProductDocument table could be seen in the third row of the results.

Use `sys.dm_tran_locks` to troubleshoot unexpected concurrency issues. For example, a query session may be holding locks longer than desired, or issuing a lock resource granularity or lock mode that you hadn't expected (perhaps a table lock instead of a finer grained row or page lock). Understanding what is happening at the locking level can help you troubleshoot your queries more effectively.

Transaction, Locking, and Concurrency

One of the listed ACID properties was *isolation*. Transaction isolation refers to the extent to which changes made by one transaction can be seen by other transactions occurring in the database (i.e., under conditions of concurrent database access). At the highest possible degree of isolation, each transaction occurs as if it was the only transaction taking place at that time. No changes made by other transactions are visible to it. At the lowest level, anything done in one transaction, whether committed or not, can been seen by another transaction.

The ANSI/ISO SQL standard defines three types of interactions between concurrent transactions. These are:

- **Dirty Reads**. These occur while a transaction is updating a row, and a second transaction reads the row before the first transaction is committed. If the original update rolls back, the data read by the second transaction is not the same, hence a "dirty" read has occurred

- **Nonrepeatable reads**. These occur when a transaction is updating data while a second transaction is reading the same data, both before and after a change. Data retrieved from the first query does not match the second query (this presumes that the second transaction reads the data twice: once before, and once after).

- **Phantom reads**. These occur when a transaction retrieves a set of rows once, another transaction inserts or deletes a row from that same table, and the first transaction re-executes the query again only to find a row that wasn't there before, or see that a row retrieved in the original query is no longer returned in consecutive result sets. The "phantom" is the missing or new row.

- **Lost updates**. This occurs when two transactions update a row's value, and the transaction to last update the row "wins." Thus the first update is lost.

The SQL standard also identifies four isolation levels, *read uncommitted, read committed, repeatable read*, and *serializable*. These levels determine which of these interactions are allowed, as described in Table 3-5 (note that SQL Server 2005 adds additional isolation levels to this standard):

Table 3-5. *SQL Standard Isolation Levels*

Isolation Level	Dirty Read	Non-Repeatable Read	Phantom Read
READ UNCOMMITTED	YES	YES	YES
READ COMMITTED	NO	YES	YES
REPEATABLE READ	NO	NO	YES
SERIALIZABLE	NO	NO	NO

SQL Server uses locking mechanisms to control the competing activity of simultaneous transactions. In order to avoid the concurrency issues such as dirty read, non-repeatable reads, and so on, it implements locking to control access to database resources and to impose a certain level of transaction isolation. Table 3-6 describes the available isolation levels in SQL Server 2005:

Table 3-6. *SQL Server 2005 Isolation Levels*

Isolation level	Description
READ COMMITTED (this is the default behavior of SQL Server)	While READ COMMITTED is set, uncommitted data modifications can't be read. Shared locks are used during a query, and data cannot be modified by other processes while the query is retrieving the data. Data inserts and modifications to the same table are allowed by other transactions, so long as the rows involved are not locked by the first transaction.
READ UNCOMMITTED	This is the least restrictive isolation level, issuing no locks on the data selected by the transaction. This provides the highest concurrency but the lowest amount of data integrity, as the data that you read can be changed while you read it (these reads are known as "dirty reads"), or new data can be added or removed that would change your original query results. This option allows you to read data without blocking others but with the danger of reading data "in flux" that could be modified during the read itself (including reading data changes from a transaction that ends up getting rolled back). For relatively static and unchanging data, this isolation level can potentially improve performance by instructing SQL Server not to issue unnecessary locking on the accessed resources.
REPEATABLE READ	When enabled, dirty and nonrepeatable reads are not allowed. This is achieved by placing Shared locks on all read resources. New rows that may fall into the range of data returned by your query can, however, still be inserted by other transactions.
SERIALIZABLE	When enabled, this is the most restrictive setting. Range locks are placed on the data based on the search criteria used to produce the result set. This ensures that actions such as insertion of new rows, modification of values, or deletion of existing rows that would have been returned within the original query and search criteria are not allowed.
SNAPSHOT	New to SQL Server 2005, this isolation level allows you to read a transactionally consistent version of the data as it existed at the *beginning* of a transaction. Data reads do not block data modifications—however, the SNAPSHOT session will not detect changes being made.

Transactions and locking go hand in hand. Depending on your application design, your transactions can significantly impact database concurrency. Concurrency refers to how many people can query and modify the database and database objects at the same time. For example, the READ UNCOMMITTED isolation level allows the greatest amount of concurrency since it issues no locks—with the drawback that you can encounter a host of data isolation anomalies (dirty reads, for example). The SERIALIZABLE mode, however, offers very little concurrency with other processes when querying a larger range of data.

Using SET TRANSACTION ISOLATION LEVEL

This recipe demonstrates how to use the SET TRANSACTION ISOLATION LEVEL command to set the default transaction locking behavior for Transact-SQL statements used in a connection. You can only have one isolation level set at a time and the isolation level does not change unless explicitly set. SET TRANSACTION ISOLATION LEVEL allows you to change the locking behavior for a specific database connection. The syntax for this command is as follows:

```
SET TRANSACTION ISOLATION LEVEL
    { READ UNCOMMITTED
    | READ COMMITTED
    | REPEATABLE READ
    | SNAPSHOT
    | SERIALIZABLE
    }
```

In this first example, SERIALIZABLE isolation is used to query the contents of a table. In the *first query editor window*, the following code is executed:

```
USE AdventureWorks
GO

SET TRANSACTION ISOLATION LEVEL SERIALIZABLE
GO

BEGIN TRAN

SELECT   AddressTypeID, Name
FROM Person.AddressType
WHERE AddressTypeID BETWEEN 1 AND 6
```

This returns the following results (while still leaving a transaction open for the query session):

```
AddressTypeID Name
------------- --------------------------------------------------
1             Billing
2             Home
3             Main Office
4             Primary
5             Shipping
6             Archive
```

In a *second query editor*, the following query is executed to view the kinds of locks generated by the SERIALIZABLE isolation level:

```
SELECT resource_associated_entity_id, resource_type,
➡ request_mode, request_session_id
FROM sys.dm_tran_locks
```

This shows several key locks being held for request_session_id 52 (which is the other session's id):

resource_associated_entity_id	resource_type	request_mode	request_session_id
0	DATABASE	S	52
0	DATABASE	S	53
72057594043039744	PAGE	IS	52
101575400	OBJECT	IS	52
72057594043039744	KEY	RangeS-S	52
72057594043039744	KEY	RangeS-S	52
72057594043039744	KEY	RangeS-S	52
72057594043039744	KEY	RangeS-S	52
72057594043039744	KEY	RangeS-S	52
72057594043039744	KEY	RangeS-S	52
72057594043039744	KEY	RangeS-S	52

Back in the first query editor window, execute the following code to end the transaction and remove the locks:

```
COMMIT TRAN
```

In contrast, the same query is executed again in the first query editor window, this time using the READ UNCOMMITTED isolation level to read the range of rows:

```
SET TRANSACTION ISOLATION LEVEL READ UNCOMMITTED
GO

BEGIN TRAN

SELECT   AddressTypeID, Name
FROM Person.AddressType
WHERE AddressTypeID BETWEEN 1 AND 6
```

In a second query editor, the following query is executed to view the kinds of locks generated by the READ UNCOMMITTED isolation level:

```
SELECT resource_associated_entity_id, resource_type,
➥ request_mode, request_session_id
FROM sys.dm_tran_locks
```

This returns:

resource_associated_entity_id	resource_type	request_mode	request_session_id
0	DATABASE	S	52
0	DATABASE	S	53

Unlike SERIALIZABLE, the READ UNCOMMITTED isolation level creates no additional locks on the keys of the Person.AddressType table.

Returning back to the first query editor with the READ UNCOMMITTED query, the transaction is ended for cleanup purposes:

```
COMMIT TRAN
```

SQL Server 2005 introduced a new SNAPSHOT isolation level, and it is this level that will be demonstrated here in this example. In the first query editor window, the following code is executed:

```
ALTER DATABASE AdventureWorks
SET ALLOW_SNAPSHOT_ISOLATION ON
GO

USE AdventureWorks
GO

SET TRANSACTION ISOLATION LEVEL SNAPSHOT
GO

BEGIN TRAN

SELECT   CurrencyRateID,
      EndOfDayRate
FROM Sales.CurrencyRate
WHERE CurrencyRateID = 8317
```

This returns:

```
CurrencyRateID EndOfDayRate
-------------- --------------------
8317           0.6862

(1 row(s) affected)
```

In a second query editor, the following query is executed:

```
USE AdventureWorks
GO

UPDATE Sales.CurrencyRate
SET EndOfDayRate = 1.00
WHERE CurrencyRateID = 8317
```

Now back to the first query editor, the following query is re-executed:

```
SELECT   CurrencyRateID,
    EndOfDayRate
FROM Sales.CurrencyRate
WHERE CurrencyRateID = 8317
```

This returns:

```
CurrencyRateID EndOfDayRate
-------------- --------------------
8317           0.6862

(1 row(s) affected)
```

The same results are returned as before, even though the row was updated by the second query editor query. The SELECT was not blocked from reading the row, nor was the UPDATE blocked from making the modification.

How It Works

In this recipe, I demonstrated how to change the locking isolation level of a query session by using the SET TRANSACTION ISOLATION LEVEL. Executing this command isn't necessary if you wish to use the default SQL Server 2005 isolation level, which is READ COMMITTED. Otherwise, once you set an isolation level, it remains in effect for the connection until explicitly changed again.

The first example in the recipe demonstrated using the SERIALIZABLE isolation level:

```
SET TRANSACTION ISOLATION LEVEL SERIALIZABLE
GO
```

An explicit transaction was then started and a query was executed against the Person.AddressType table for all rows that fell between a specific range of AddressTypeID values:

```
BEGIN TRAN

SELECT   AddressTypeID, Name
FROM Person.AddressType
WHERE AddressTypeID BETWEEN 1 AND 6
```

In a separate connection, a query was then executed against the sys.dm_tran_locks dynamic management view, which returned information about active locks being held for the SQL Server instance. In this case, we saw a number of key range locks, which served the purpose of prohibiting other connections from inserting, updating, or deleting data that would cause different results in the query's search condition (WHERE AddressTypeID BETWEEN 1 AND 6).

In the second example, the isolation level was set to READ UNCOMMITTED:

```
SET TRANSACTION ISOLATION LEVEL READ UNCOMMITTED
GO
```

Querying sys.dm_tran_locks again, we saw that this time no row, key, or page locks were held at all on the table, allowing the potential for other transactions to modify the queried rows while the original transaction remained open. With this isolation level, the query performs "dirty reads," meaning that the query could read data with in-progress modifications, whether or not the actual modification is committed or rolled back later on.

In the third example from the recipe, the database setting ALLOW_SNAPSHOT_ISOLATION was enabled for the database (see Chapter 22, "Creating and Configuring Databases" for more information on ALTER DATABASE):

```
ALTER DATABASE AdventureWorks
SET ALLOW_SNAPSHOT_ISOLATION ON
GO
```

This option had to be ON in order to start a snapshot transaction. In the next line of code, the database context was changed and SET TRANSACTION ISOLATION LEVEL was set to SNAPSHOT:

```
USE AdventureWorks
GO
SET TRANSACTION ISOLATION LEVEL SNAPSHOT
GO
```

A transaction was then opened and a query against Sales.CurrencyRate was performed:

```
BEGIN TRAN

SELECT   CurrencyRateID,
      EndOfDayRate
FROM Sales.CurrencyRate
WHERE CurrencyRateID = 8317
```

In the second query editor session, the same Sales.CurrencyRate row being selected in the first session query was modified:

```
USE AdventureWorks
GO

UPDATE Sales.CurrencyRate
SET EndOfDayRate = 1.00
WHERE CurrencyRateID = 8317
```

Back at the first query editor session, although the EndOfDayRate was changed to 1.0 in the second session, executing the query again in the SNAPSHOT isolation shows that the value of that column was still 0.6862. This new isolation level provided a consistent view of the data as of the beginning of the transaction.

What if you decide to UPDATE a row in the snapshot session that was updated in a separate session? Had the snapshot session attempted an UPDATE against CurrencyRateID 8317 instead of a SELECT, an error would have been raised warning you that an update was made against the original row while in snapshot isolation mode:

```
Msg 3960, Level 16, State 1, Line 2
Cannot use snapshot isolation to access table 'Sales.CurrencyRate'
directly or indirectly in database 'AdventureWorks'.
Snapshot transaction aborted due to update conflict.
Retry transaction.
```

Blocking

Blocking occurs when one transaction in a database session is locking resources that one or more other session transactions wants to read or modify. Short term blocking is usually OK, depending on your application requirements. However, poorly designed applications can cause long term blocking, unnecessarily keeping locks on resources and blocking other sessions from reading or updating them.

In SQL Server 2005, a blocked process remains blocked indefinitely or until it times-out (based on SET LOCK_TIMEOUT), the server goes down, the process is killed, the connection finishes its updates, or something happens to the original transaction to cause it to release its locks on the resource.

Some reasons why long term blocking can happen:

- Without proper indexing, blocking issues can grow. Excessive row locks on a table without an index can cause SQL Server to acquire a table lock, blocking out other transactions.

- Applications that open a transaction then request user feedback or interaction while the transaction stays open. This is usually when an end user is allowed to enter data in a GUI while a transaction remains open. While open, any resources referenced by the transaction may be held with locks.

- Transactions that BEGIN and then look up data that could have been referenced prior to the transaction starting.

- Queries that use locking hints inappropriately, for example if the application uses only a few rows, but uses a table lock hint instead (for a review of locking hints, see Chapter 1, "SELECT," in the recipe "Use Table Hints," which include a list of the available locking hints).

- The application uses long-running transactions that update many rows or many tables within one transaction (chunking large updates into smaller update transactions can help improve concurrency).

Identifying and Resolving Blocking Processes

In this recipe, I'll demonstrate how to identify a blocking process, view the Transact-SQL being executed by the process, and then forcefully shut down the active sessions connection (thus rolling back any open work not yet committed by the blocking session). First, however, let's go to a quick background on the commands used in this example...

This recipe demonstrates how to identify blocking processes with the new SQL Server 2005 dynamic management view, sys.dm_os_waiting_tasks. This view is intended to be used instead of the sp_who system stored procedure, which was used in previous versions of SQL Server.

After identifying the blocking process, this recipe will then use DBCC INPUTBUFFER to view the query that is being executed—and then as a last resort, forcefully end the process. The syntax for DBCC INPUTBUFFER is as follows:

```
DBCC INPUTBUFFER ( session_id [ , request_id ] )
[WITH NO_INFOMSGS ]
```

The arguments for this command are described in Table 3-7:

Table 3-7. *DBCC INPUTBUFFER Command Arguments*

Argument	Description
session_id	The session id associated with the active database connection.
request_id	The batch to identify within the session.
WITH NO_INFOMSGS	When included in the command, WITH NO_INFOMSGS suppresses informational messages from the DBCC output.

To forcefully shut down a wayward active query session, the KILL command is used. KILL should only be used if other methods can't be, including waiting for the process to stop on its own or shutting down or canceling the operation via the calling application. The syntax for KILL is as follows:

```
KILL {spid | UOW} [WITH STATUSONLY]
```

The arguments for this command are described in Table 3-8:

Table 3-8. *KILL Command arguments*

Argument	Description
spid	The session id associated with the active database connection to be shut down.
UOW	The unit-of-work identifier for a distributed transaction. This is the unique identifier of a specific distributed transaction process.
WITH STATUSONLY	Some KILL statements take longer to roll back a transaction than others (depending on the scope of updates being performed by the session). In order to check the status of a rollback, you can use WITH STATUSONLY to get an estimate of rollback time.

Beginning the example, the following query is executed in the first query editor session in order to set up a blocking process:

```
BEGIN TRAN

UPDATE Production.ProductInventory
SET Quantity = 400
WHERE ProductID = 1 AND
LocationID = 1
```

Next, in a second Query Editor window, the following query is executed:

```
BEGIN TRAN

UPDATE Production.ProductInventory
SET Quantity = 406
WHERE ProductID = 1 AND
LocationID = 1
```

Now in a third query editor window, the following query is executed:

```
SELECT blocking_session_id, wait_duration_ms, session_id
FROM  sys.dm_os_waiting_tasks
WHERE blocking_session_id IS NOT NULL
```

This returns:

blocking_session_id	wait_duration_ms	session_id
52	158568	53

(1 row(s) affected)

This query identified that session id "52" is blocking session "53." To see what session id 52 is doing, execute the following query in the same window as the previous query:

```
DBCC INPUTBUFFER(52)
```

This returns:

EventType	Parameters	EventInfo
Language Event	0	BEGIN TRAN

```
UPDATE Production.ProductInventory
SET Quantity = 400
WHERE ProductID = 1 AND
   LocationID = 1
```

(1 row(s) affected)

```
DBCC execution completed. If DBCC printed error messages,
contact your system administrator.
```

Next, to forcibly shut down the session, execute this query:

```
KILL 52
```

This returns:

```
Command(s) completed successfully.
```

The second session's UPDATE is then allowed to proceed once the other session's connection is removed.

How It Works

The recipe demonstrated blocking by executing an UPDATE against the Production.ProductInventory table with a transaction that was opened but *not* committed. In a different session, a similar query was executed against the same table and the same row. Because the other connection's transaction never committed, the second connection must wait in line indefinitely before it has a chance to update the record.

In a third Query Editor connection, the sys.dm_os_waiting_tasks dynamic management view was queried, returning information on the session being blocked by another session:

blocking_session_id	wait_duration_ms	session_id
52	158568	53

(1 row(s) affected)

This query identified that session id 52 was blocking session 53.

When troubleshooting blocks, you'll want to see exactly what the blocking spid is doing. To view this, the recipe used the DBCC INPUTBUFFER function, putting the blocking spid in parentheses. The DBCC INPUTBUFFER command was used to view the last statement sent by the client connection to SQL Server.

■**Note** Sometimes blocks "pile up," and you must work your way through each blocked process up to the original blocking process using the blocking_session_id and session_id columns.

KILL was then used to forcibly end the blocking process, but in a production scenario, you'll want to see if the process is valid, and if so, whether it should be allowed to complete, or if it can be shut down using the application (by the application end-user, for example). Prior to stopping the process, be sure that you are not stopping a long-running transaction that is critical to the business, like a payroll update, for example. If there is no way to stop the transaction (for example, the application that spawned it cannot commit the transaction), you can use the KILL command (followed by the spid to terminate).

Using SET LOCK TIMEOUT

When a transaction or statement is being "blocked," this means it is waiting for a lock on a resource to be released. This recipe demonstrates the SET LOCK_TIMEOUT option, which specifies how long the blocked statement should wait for a lock to be released before returning an error.

The syntax is as follows:

```
SET LOCK_TIMEOUT timeout_period
```

The timeout period is the number of milliseconds before a locking error will be returned. This example demonstrates setting up a lock timeout period of one second (1000 milliseconds):

```
SET LOCK_TIMEOUT 1000

UPDATE Production.ProductInventory
SET Quantity = 406
WHERE ProductID = 1 AND
LocationID = 1
```

How It Works

In this recipe, the lock timeout is set to 1000 milliseconds (1 second). This setting doesn't impact how long a resource can be *held* by a process, only how long it has to wait for another process to release access to the resource.

If the lock timeout threshold is exceeded, you'll get the following error:

```
Msg 1222, Level 16, State 51, Line 3
Lock request time out period exceeded.
The statement has been terminated.
```

Deadlocking

Deadlocking occurs when one user session (let's call it Session 1) has locks on a resource that another user session (let's call it Session 2) wants to modify, and Session 2 has locks on resources that Session 1 needs to modify. Neither Session 1 nor Session 2 can continue until the other releases the locks, so SQL Server chooses one of the sessions in the deadlock as the "deadlock victim":

■**Note** A deadlock victim has its session killed and transactions rolled back.

Some reasons why deadlocks can happen:

- The application accesses tables in different orders. For example, Session 1 updates Customers and then Orders, whereas Session 2 updates Orders and then Customers. This increases the chance of two processes deadlocking, rather than them accessing and updating a table in a serialized (in order) fashion.

- The application uses long-running transactions, updating many rows or many tables within one transaction. This increases the surface area of rows that can cause deadlock conflicts.

- In some situations, SQL Server issues several row locks, which it later decides must be escalated to a table lock. If these rows exist on the same data pages, and two sessions are both trying to escalate the lock granularity on the same page, a deadlock can occur.

Identifying Deadlocks with a Trace Flag

If you are having deadlock trouble in your SQL Server instance, this recipe demonstrates how to make sure deadlocks are logged to the SQL Server Management Studio SQL log appropriately using the DBCC TRACEON, DBCC TRACEOFF, and DBCC TRACESTATUS commands. These functions enable, disable, and check the status of trace flags.

■**Tip** There are other methods in SQL Server 2005 for troubleshooting deadlocks, such as SQL Profiler, but since this book is Transact-SQL focused, they are out of scope.

Trace flags are used within SQL server to enable or disable specific behaviors for the SQL Server instance. By default, SQL Server doesn't return significant logging when a deadlock event occurs. Using trace flag 1222, information about locked resources and types participating in a deadlock are returned in an XML format, helping you troubleshoot the event.

The DBCC TRACEON command enables trace flags. The syntax is as follows:

```
DBCC TRACEON ( trace# [ ,...n ][ ,-1 ] ) [ WITH NO_INFOMSGS ]
```

The arguments for this command are described in Table 3-9:

Table 3-9. *DBCC TRACEON Command Arguments*

Argument	Description
trace#	One or more trace flag numbers to enable.
-1	When -1 is designated, the specified trace flags are enabled globally.
WITH NO_INFOMSGS	When included in the command, WITH NO_INFOMSGS suppresses informational messages from the DBCC output.

The DBCC TRACESTATUS command is used to check on the status (enabled or disabled) for a specific flag or flags. The syntax is as follows:

```
DBCC TRACESTATUS ( [ [ trace# [ ,...n ] ] [ , ] [ -1 ] ] ) [ WITH NO_INFOMSGS ]
```

The arguments for this command are described in Table 3-10:

Table 3-10. *DBCC TRACESTATUS Command Arguments*

Argument	Description
trace#	One or more trace flag numbers to check the status of.
-1	Shows globally enabled flags.
WITH NO_INFOMSGS	When included in the command, WITH NO_INFOMSGS suppresses informational messages from the DBCC output.

The DBCC TRACEOFF command disables trace flags. The syntax is as follows:

```
DBCC TRACEOFF ( trace# [ ,...n ] [ , -1 ] ) [ WITH NO_INFOMSGS ]
```

The arguments for this command are described in Table 3-11:

Table 3-11. *DBCC TRACEOFF Command Arguments*

Argument	Description
trace#	One or more trace flag numbers to disable.
-1	Disables the globally set flags.
WITH NO_INFOMSGS	When included in the command, WITH NO_INFOMSGS suppresses informational messages from the DBCC output.

In order to demonstrate this recipe, a deadlock will be simulated. In a **new query editor** window, the following query is executed:

```
SET NOCOUNT ON
SET TRANSACTION ISOLATION LEVEL SERIALIZABLE

WHILE 1=1
BEGIN
BEGIN TRAN

    UPDATE Purchasing.Vendor
    SET CreditRating = 1
    WHERE VendorID = 2

    UPDATE Purchasing.Vendor
    SET CreditRating = 2
    WHERE VendorID = 1

COMMIT TRAN
END
```

In a second query editor window, the following query is executed:

```
SET NOCOUNT ON
SET TRANSACTION ISOLATION LEVEL SERIALIZABLE
```

```
WHILE 1=1
BEGIN
BEGIN TRAN

    UPDATE Purchasing.Vendor
    SET CreditRating = 2
    WHERE VendorID = 1

    UPDATE Purchasing.Vendor
    SET CreditRating = 1
    WHERE VendorID = 2

COMMIT TRAN
END
```

After a few seconds, check each query editor window until the following error message appears on one of the query editors:

```
Msg 1205, Level 13, State 51, Line 9
Transaction (Process ID 53) was deadlocked on lock
resources with another process and has been chosen
as the deadlock victim. Rerun the transaction.
```

Looking at the SQL Log in SQL Server Management Studio, the deadlock event was not logged. A third query editor window is opened and the following command is executed:

```
DBCC TRACEON (1222, -1)
GO
DBCC TRACESTATUS
```

DBCC TRACESTATUS shows the active traces running for both the local session and globally:

```
DBCC execution completed. If DBCC printed error messages, contact your system
administrator.
TraceFlag Global Session
--------- ------ -------
1222      1      0

(1 row(s) affected)

DBCC execution completed. If DBCC printed error messages, contact your system
administrator.
```

To simulate another deadlock, the "winning" connection query (the one that wasn't killed in the deadlock) is restarted, and then the deadlock losing session is restarted, causing another deadlock after a few seconds.

After the deadlock has occurred, stop the other executing query. Now the SQL log in SQL Server Management Studio contains a detailed error message from the deadlock event, including the database and object involved, the lock mode, and the Transact-SQL statements involved in the deadlock.

For example, when deadlocks occur, you'll want to make sure to find out the queries that are involved in the deadlock, so you can troubleshoot them accordingly. The following excerpt from the log shows a deadlocked query:

```
07/28/2005 20:20:00,spid20s,Unknown,
UPDATE [Purchasing].[Vendor] set [CreditRating] = @1
WHERE [VendorID]=@2
```

From this we can tell which query was involved in the deadlocking, which is often enough to get started with a solution. Other important information you can retrieve by using trace 1222 includes the login name of the deadlocked process, the client application used to submit the query, and the isolation level used for its connection (letting you know if that connection is using an isolation level that doesn't allow for much concurrency):

```
... clientapp=Microsoft SQL Server Management Studio -
Query hostname=JOEPROD hostpid=3884
loginname=JOEPROD\Owner isolationlevel=serializable
(4) xactid=223338311933 currentdb=5 lockTimeout=4294967295
clientoption1=673187936 clientoption2=390200
```

After examining the SQL Log, disable the trace flag in the query editor:

```
DBCC TRACEOFF (1222, -1)
GO
DBCC TRACESTATUS
```

How It Works

In this recipe, I simulated a deadlock using two separate queries that updated the same rows repeatedly: updating two rows in the opposite order. When a deadlock occurred, the error message was logged to the query editor window, but nothing was written to the SQL Log.

To enable deadlock logging to the SQL log, the recipe enabled the trace flag 1222. Trace 1222 was introduced in SQL Server 2005 and returns detailed deadlock information to the SQL log. The -1 flag indicated that trace flag 1222 should be enabled globally for all SQL Server connections. To turn on a trace flag, DBCC TRACEON was used, with the 1222 flag in parentheses:

```
DBCC TRACEON (1222, -1)
```

To verify that the flag was enabled, DBCC TRACESTATUS was executed:

```
DBCC TRACESTATUS
```

After encountering another deadlock, the deadlock information was logged in the SQL log. The flag was then disabled using DBCC TRACEOFF:

```
DBCC TRACEOFF (1222, -1)
```

Setting Deadlock Priority

You can increase a query session's chance of being chosen as a deadlock victim by using the SET DEADLOCK_PRIORITY command. The syntax for this command is as follows:

```
SET DEADLOCK_PRIORITY { LOW | NORMAL | HIGH | <numeric-priority> }
```

The arguments for this command are described in Table 3-12:

Table 3-12. *SET DEADLOCK_PRIORITY Command Arguments*

Argument	Description
LOW |	LOW | makes the current connection the likely deadlock victim.
NORMAL |	NORMAL | lets SQL Server decide based on which connection seems least expensive to roll back.
HIGH |	HIGH | lessens the chances of the connection being chosen as the victim, unless the other connection is also HIGH or has a numeric priority greater than 5.
<numeric-priority>	The numeric priority allows you to use a range of values from -10 to 10, where -10 is the most likely deadlock victim, up to 10 being the least likely to be chosen as a victim. The higher number between two participants in a deadlock wins.

For example, had the first query from the previous recipe used the following deadlock priority command, it would almost certainly have been chosen as the victim (normally, the default deadlock victim is the connection SQL Server deems least expensive to cancel and roll back):

```
SET NOCOUNT ON
SET TRANSACTION ISOLATION LEVEL SERIALIZABLE
SET DEADLOCK_PRIORITY LOW

WHILE 1=1
BEGIN
BEGIN TRAN

    UPDATE Purchasing.Vendor
    SET CreditRating = 1
    WHERE VendorID = 2

    UPDATE Purchasing.Vendor
    SET CreditRating = 2
    WHERE VendorID = 1

COMMIT TRAN
END
```

How It Works

You can also set the deadlock priority to HIGH and NORMAL. HIGH means that unless the other session is of the same priority, it will not be chosen as the victim. NORMAL is the default behavior, and will be chosen if the other session is HIGH, but not chosen if the other session is LOW. If both sessions have the same priority, the least expensive transaction to roll back will be chosen.

■ ■ ■

Tables

In this chapter, I'll present recipes that demonstrate table creation and manipulation. Tables are used to store data in the database and make up the central unit upon which most SQL Server database objects depend. Tables are uniquely named within a database and schema, and contain one or more columns. Each column has an associated data type that defines the kind of data that can be stored within it.

As I've done in the previous chapters, I'll provide basic table recipes throughout, and break them up by more complex functionality as well as new SQL Server 2005 features.

■Caution If you decide to follow along with some of these exercises, consider backing up the AdventureWorks database beforehand, so that you can restore it back to a clean version once you are finished.

Table Basics

You can create a table using the CREATE TABLE command. The full syntax is quite large, so this chapter will build upon the different areas of the command as the chapter progresses. The simplified syntax is as follows:

```
CREATE TABLE
    [ database_name . [ schema_name ] . | schema_name . ] table_name
        ( column_name <data_type> [ NULL | NOT NULL ] [ ,...n ]  )
```

The arguments of this command are described in Table 4-1.

Table 4-1. *CREATE TABLE Arguments*

Argument	Description
database_name . [schema_name] . | schema_name .] table_name	This argument indicates that you can qualify the new table name using the database, schema, and table name or just the schema and table name.
column_name	The name of the column.
data_type	The column's data type (data types are described next).
NULL | NOT NULL	The NULL | NOT NULL option refers to the column nullability. Nullability defines whether a column can contain a NULL value. A NULL value means that the value is unknown. It does not mean that the column is zero, blank, or empty.

Each column requires a defined data type. The data type defines and restricts the type of data the column can hold. Table 4-2 details the system data types available in SQL Server 2005:

Table 4-2. *SQL Server 2005 Data Types*

Data Type	Value Range
bigint	Whole number from –2^63 (-9,223,372,036,854,775,808) through 2^63-1 (9,223,372,036,854,775,807).
binary	Fixed-length binary data with a maximum of 8000 bytes.
bit	Whole number either 0 or 1.
char	Fixed-length character data with maximum length of 8000 characters.
datetime	Date and time from January 1, 1753, through December 31, 9999. (1753 was the year following the adoption of the Gregorian calendar, which produced a difference in days to the previous calendar of 12 days. Beginning with the year 1753 sidesteps all sorts of calculation problems.) Decimal or numeric (no difference between the two) range from –10^38 +1 through 10^38-1. Decimal uses precision and scale. Precision determines maximum total number of decimal digits both left and right of the decimal point. Scale determines maximum decimal digits to the right of the decimal point.
float	Floating precision number from - 1.79E + 38 to -2.23E - 38, 0 and 2.23E -38 to 1.79E + 38.
image	Variable-length binary data from 0 through 2^31 –1. This data type will be removed in a future version of SQL Server. Instead of using this data type, use varbinary(max) instead.
int	Whole number from –2^31 (-2,147,483,648) through 2^31-1 (2,147,483,647).
money	Monetary value between –2^63 (-922,377,203,685,477.5808) through 2^63-1 (+922,337,203,685,477.5807).
nchar	Fixed-length Unicode character data with a maximum length of 4000 characters.
ntext	Variable-length Unicode character data with a maximum length of 1,073,741,823 characters. This data type will be removed in a future version of SQL Server. Instead of using this data type, use nvarchar(max) instead.
nvarchar	Variable-length Unicode character data with maximum length of 4000 characters. SQL Server 2005 has also added a "max" option which allows you to store up to 2^31-1bytes. This new option allows you to use the regular data types instead of SQL Server 2000's text, ntext, and image.
real	Floating precision number from -1.18E - 38, 0 and 1.18E - 38 to 3.40E + 38.
smalldatetime	Date and time from January 1, 1900, through June 6, 2079.
smallint	Whole number from –32,768 through 32,767.
smallmoney	Monetary value between –214,748.3648 through +214,748.3647.
sql_variant	A data type which can store all data types except text, ntext, timestamp, varchar(max), nvarchar(max), varbinary(max), xml, image, user-defined types, and another sql_variant.
table	The table data type can't be used in CREATE TABLE as a column type. Instead it is used for table variables or for storage of rows for a table-valued function.
text	Variable-length data with maximum length of 2,147,483,647 characters. This data type will be removed in a future version of SQL Server. Instead of using this data type, use varchar(max) instead.
timestamp	Database-wide unique number that is updated when a row is modified.

Data Type	Value Range
`tinyint`	Whole number from 0 through 255.
`uniqueidentifier`	Stores a 16-byte GUID (globally-unique identifier).
`varbinary`	Variable-length data with a maximum of 8000 bytes. SQL Server 2005 has also added a max value, which allows you to store up to 2^31-1bytes. This new option allows you to use the regular data types instead of SQL Server 2000's `text`, `ntext`, and `image`.
`varchar`	Variable-length character data with a maximum length of 8,000 characters. SQL Server 2005 has also added a max value, which allows you to store up to 2^31-1bytes. This new option allows you to use the regular data types instead of SQL Server 2000's `text`, `ntext`, and `image`.
`xml`	New to SQL Server 2005, this data type stores native xml data.

Some basic guidelines when selecting data types for your columns:

- Store character data types in character type columns (`char`, `nchar`, `varchar`, `nvarcht`), numeric data in numeric type columns (`int`, `bigint`, `tinyint`, `smallmoney`, `money`, `decimal\numeric`, `float`), and date and/or time data in `smalldate` or `datetime` data types. For example, although you *can* store numeric and datetime information in character-based fields, doing so may slow down your performance when attempting to utilize the column values within mathematical or other Transact-SQL functions.

- If your character data type columns use the same or a similar number of characters consistently, use fixed length data types (`char`, `nchar`). Fixed length columns consume the same amount of storage for each row, whether or not they are fully utilized. If, however, you expect that your character columns length will vary significantly from row to row, use variable length data types (`varchar`, `nvarchar`). Variable length columns have some storage overhead tacked on, however, they will only consume storage for characters used. Only use `char` or `nchar` if you are sure that you will have consistent lengths in your strings, and that most of your string values will be present.

- Choose the smallest numeric or character data type required to store the data. You may be tempted to select data types for columns that use more storage than is necessary, resulting in wasted storage. Conserving column space, particularly for very large tables, can increase the number of rows that can fit on an 8KB data page, reduce total storage needed in the database, and potentially improve index performance (smaller index keys).

A table can have up to 1024 columns, but can't exceed a total of 8060 actual used bytes per row. A data page size is 8KB, with a 96-byte header that stores information about the page. This byte limit is not applied to the large object data types `varchar(max)`, `nvarchar(max)`, `varbinary(max)`, `text`, `image`, or `xml`.

Another exception to the 8060-byte limit rule is that SQL Server 2005 introduces "over-flow" functionality for regular `varchar`, `nvarchar`, `varbinary`, and `sql_variant` data types. If the lengths of these individual data types do not exceed 8000 bytes, but the combined width of more than one of these columns together in a table exceeds the 8060 byte row limit, the largest width column will be dynamically moved to another 8KB page and replaced in the original table with a 24-byte pointer. Row "overflow" provides extra flexibility for managing large row sizes, but you should still limit your potential maximum variable data type length in your table definition when possible, as reliance on page overflow may decrease query performance as more data pages need to be retrieved by a single query.

Creating a Table

In this recipe, I create a simple table called EducationType owned by the Person schema:

```
CREATE TABLE Person.EducationType
    (EducationTypeID int NOT NULL,
    EducationTypeNM varchar(40) NOT NULL)
GO
```

How It Works

In this example, a very simple, two-column table was created within the AdventureWorks database using the Person schema. The first line of code shows the schema and table name:

```
CREATE TABLE Person.EducationType
```

The column definition follows on the second line of code within the parentheses:

```
(EducationTypeID int NOT NULL,
    EducationTypeNM varchar(40) NOT NULL)
```

The first column name, EducationTypeID, was defined with an integer data type and NOT NULL specified (meaning that NULL values are not allowed for this column). The second column was the EducationTypeNM column name with a data type of varchar(40) and the NOT NULL option.

In the next recipe, you'll learn how to add additional columns to an existing table.

Adding a Column to an Existing Table

After a table is created, you can modify it using the ALTER TABLE command. Like CREATE TABLE, this chapter will demonstrate the ALTER TABLE and CREATE TABLE functionality in task-based parts. In this recipe, I demonstrate how to add a column to an existing table.

The specific syntax for adding a column is as follows:

```
ALTER TABLE table_name
ADD { column_name data_type } NULL
```

Table 4-3 details the arguments of this command.

Table 4-3. *ALTER TABLE ADD Column Arguments*

Argument	Description
table_name	The table name you are adding the column to.
column_name	The name of the column.
data_type	The column's data type.

This example demonstrates adding a column to an existing table (not that using this method adds the column to last column position in the table definition):

```
ALTER TABLE HumanResources.Employee
ADD Latest_EducationTypeID int NULL
```

How It Works

ALTER TABLE was used to make modifications to an existing table. The first line of code designated the table to have the column added to:

```
ALTER TABLE HumanResources.Employee
```

The second line of code defined the new column and data type:

```
ADD Latest_EducationTypeID int NULL
```

When adding columns to a table that already has data in it, you will be required to add the column with NULL values allowed. You can't specify that the column be NOT NULL, because you must first add the column to the table before you can put a value in that column for existing rows.

Changing a Column Definition

In addition to adding new columns to a table, you can also use ALTER TABLE to modify an existing column's definition.

The syntax for doing this is as follows:

```
ALTER TABLE table_name
ALTER COLUMN column_name
[type_name] [NULL | NOT NULL] [COLLATE collation_name]
```

Table 4-4 details the arguments of this command.

Table 4-4. *ALTER TABLE...ALTER COLUMN Arguments*

Argument	Description
table_name	The table name containing the column to be modified.
column_name	The name of the column to modify.
type_name	The column's data type to modify.
NULL | NOT NULL	The nullability option to modify.
COLLATE collation_name	The column collation (for character-based data types) to modify. Collations define three settings: a code page used to store non-Unicode character data types, the sort order for non-Unicode character data types, and the sort order for Unicode data types. Collations are reviewed later on in the chapter.

This example demonstrates how to change an existing table column's nullability and data type. The Gender column in the HumanResources.Employee table is originally NOT NULL and the original data type of the LoginID column is nvarchar(256):

```
-- Make it Nullable
ALTER TABLE HumanResources.Employee
ALTER COLUMN Gender nchar(1) NULL

-- Expanded nvarchar(256) to nvarchar(300)
ALTER TABLE HumanResources.Employee
ALTER COLUMN LoginID nvarchar(300) NOT NULL
```

How It Works

In this recipe, two columns were modified in the HumanResources.Employee table. The ALTER COLUMN modified the Gender column to allow NULL values, although the data type remained the same:

```
ALTER COLUMN Gender nchar(1) NULL
```

In the second ALTER TABLE, the LoginID column's data type of nvarchar(256) was expanded to nvarchar(300):

```
ALTER COLUMN LoginID nvarchar(300) NOT NULL
```

There are limitations to the kind of column changes that can be made. For example, you can't alter a column that is used in an index unless the column data type is varchar, nvarchar, or varbinary—and even then, the new size of that data type must be *larger* than the original size. You also can't use ALTER COLUMN on columns referenced in a primary key or foreign key constraint. The full list of other column modification limitations (and there are quite a few) are documented in SQL Server 2005 Books Online.

Creating a Computed Column

A column defined within a CREATE TABLE or ALTER TABLE statement can be derived from a freestanding or column-based calculation. Computed columns are sometimes useful when a calculation must be recomputed on the same data repeatedly in referencing queries. A computed column is based on an expression defined when you create or alter the table, and is not physically stored in the table unless you use the SQL Server 2005 PERSISTED keyword.

In this recipe, I'll give a demonstration of creating a computed column, as well as presenting ways to take advantage of SQL Server 2005's new PERSISTED option.

The syntax for adding a computed column either by CREATE or ALTER TABLE is as follows:

```
column_name AS computed_column_expression
[ PERSISTED ]
```

The column_name is the name of the new column. The computed_column_expression is the calculation you wish to be performed in order to derive the column's value. Adding the PERSISTED keyword actually causes the results of the calculation to be physically stored.

In this example, a new, calculated column is added to an existing table:

```
ALTER TABLE Production.TransactionHistory
ADD CostPerUnit AS (ActualCost/Quantity)
```

The previous example created a calculated column called CostPerUnit. This next query takes advantage of it, returning the highest CostPerUnit for quantities over 10:

```
SELECT TOP 1 CostPerUnit, Quantity, ActualCost
FROM Production.TransactionHistory
WHERE Quantity > 10
ORDER BY ActualCost DESC
```

This returns:

CostPerUnit	Quantity	ActualCost
132.0408	13	1716.5304

(1 row(s) affected)

The next example creates a PERSISTED calculated column, which means the calculated data will actually be physically stored in the database (but still automatically calculated by SQL Server):

```
CREATE TABLE HumanResources.CompanyStatistic
(CompanyID int NOT NULL,
 StockTicker char(4) NOT NULL,
 SharesOutstanding int NOT NULL,
 Shareholders int NOT NULL,
 AvgSharesPerShareholder AS (SharesOutStanding/Shareholders) PERSISTED)
```

How It Works

The first example added a new, non-persisted column called CostPerUnit to the Production.TransactionHistory table, allowing it to be referenced in SELECT queries like a regular table column:

```
ADD CostPerUnit AS (ActualCost/Quantity)
```

Computed columns can't be used within a DEFAULT or FOREIGN KEY constraint. A calculated column can't be explicitly updated or inserted into (since its value is always derived).

Computed columns can be used within indexes, but must meet certain requirements, such as being deterministic (always returning the same result for a given set of inputs) and precise (not containing float values).

The second example demonstrated using a computed column in a CREATE TABLE command:

```
AvgSharesPerShareholder AS (SharesOutStanding/Shareholders) PERSISTED
```

Unlike the first example, adding the PERSISTED keyword means that the data is actually physically stored in the database. Any changes made to columns that are used in the computation will cause the stored value to be updated again. The stored data still can't be modified directly—the data is still computed. Storing the data does mean, however, that the column can be used to partition a table (see later in the chapter for more on partitioning), or can be used in an index with an imprecise (float-based) value—unlike its non-persisted version.

Dropping a Table Column

You can use ALTER TABLE to drop a column from an existing table.

The syntax for doing so is as follows:

```
ALTER TABLE table_name
DROP COLUMN column_name
```

Table 4-5 details the arguments of this command.

Table 4-5. *ALTER TABLE...DROP COLUMN Arguments*

Argument	Description
table_name	The table name containing the column to be dropped.
column_name	The name of the column to drop from the table.

This recipe demonstrates how to drop a column from an existing table:

```
ALTER TABLE HumanResources.Employee
DROP COLUMN Latest_EducationTypeID
```

How It Works

The first line of code designated the table for which the column would be dropped:

```
ALTER TABLE HumanResources.Employee
```

The second line designates the column to be dropped from the table (along with any data stored in it):

```
DROP COLUMN Latest_EducationTypeID
```

You can drop a column only if it isn't being used in a PRIMARY KEY, FOREIGN KEY, UNIQUE, or CHECK CONSTRAINT (these constraint types are all covered in this chapter). You also can't drop a column being used in an index or that has a DEFAULT value bound to it.

Reporting Table Information

The system stored procedure sp_help returns information about the specified table, including the column definitions, IDENTITY column, ROWGUIDCOL, filegroup location, indexes (and keys), CHECK, DEFAULT, and FOREIGN KEY constraints, and referencing views.

The syntax for this system stored procedure is as follows:

```
sp_help [ [ @objname = ] ' name ' ]
```

This example demonstrates how to report detailed information about the object or table (the results aren't shown here as they include several columns and multiple result sets):

```
EXEC sp_help 'HumanResources.Employee'
```

How It Works

The sp_help system stored procedure returns several different result sets with useful information regarding the specific object (in this example, it returns data about the table HumanResources.Employee. This system stored procedure can be used to gather information regarding other database object types as well.

Dropping a Table

In this recipe, I'll demonstrate how to drop a table. The DROP command uses the following syntax:

```
DROP TABLE schema.tablename
```

The DROP TABLE takes a single argument, the name of the table. In this example, the HumanResources.EWCompany table is dropped:

```
DROP TABLE HumanResources.EWCompany
```

How It Works

The DROP command removes the table definition and its data permanently from the database. In this example, the DROP command would have failed had another table been referencing the table's primary key in a foreign key constraint. If there are foreign key references, you must drop them first before dropping the primary key table.

Collation Basics

If your database requires international or multilingual data storage, your default SQL Server instance settings may not be sufficient for the task. This recipe describes how to view and manipulate code pages and sort order settings using collations. SQL Server collations determine how data is sorted, compared, presented, and stored.

SQL Server 2005 allows two types of collations: Windows or SQL. Windows collations are the preferred selection for SQL Server 2005, as they offer more options and match the same support provided with Microsoft Windows locales. SQL collations are used in earlier versions of SQL Server and are maintained for backward compatibility.

In addition to SQL Server and database level collation settings, you can also configure individual columns with their own collation settings. If you need to store character data in a column that uses a different default collation than your database or server-level collation, you use the COLLATE command within the column definition.

The Windows or SQL collation can be explicitly defined during a CREATE TABLE or ALTER TABLE operation for columns that use the varchar, char, nchar, and nvarchar data types.

Collations define three settings:

- A code page used to store non-Unicode character data types

- The sort order for non-Unicode character data types

- The sort order for Unicode data types

Your SQL Server instance's default collation was determined during the install, where you either used the default-selected collation, or explicitly changed it. The next two recipes will demonstrate how to view information about the collations on your SQL Server instance, as well as define an explicit collation for a table column.

Viewing Collation Metadata

You can determine your SQL Server instance's default collation by using the SERVERPROPERTY function and the Collation option. For example:

```
SELECT SERVERPROPERTY('Collation')
```

This returns (for this example's SQL Server instance):

```
SQL_Latin1_General_CP1_CI_AS

(1 row(s) affected)
```

In addition to the SQL Server instance's default collation settings, your database can also have a default collation defined for it. You can use the DATABASEPROPERTYEX system function to determine a database's default collation. For example, this next query determines the default database collation for the AdventureWorks database (first parameter is database name, second is the Collation option to be viewed):

```
SELECT DATABASEPROPERTYEX ( 'AdventureWorks' , 'Collation' )
```

This returns the following collation information for the database (which in this example is going to be the same as the SQL Server instance default until explicitly changed):

```
SQL_Latin1_General_CP1_CI_AS

(1 row(s) affected)
```

■**Note** See Chapter 8 for more information on the SERVERPROPERTY and DATABASEPROPERTYEX functions.

But what do the results of these collation functions mean? To determine the actual settings that a collation applies to the SQL Server instance or database, you can query the table function fn_helpcollations for a more user-friendly description. In this example, the collation description is returned from the SQL_Latin1_General_CP1_CI_AS collation:

```
SELECT description
FROM fn_helpcollations()
WHERE name = 'SQL_Latin1_General_CP1_CI_AS'
```

This returns the collation description:

```
description
--------------------------------------------------------------------------------
Latin1-General, case-insensitive, accent-sensitive, kanatype-insensitive, width-
insensitive for Unicode Data, SQL Server Sort Order 52 on Code Page 1252 for non-Unicode
Data
```

The results show a more descriptive break-down of the collation's code page, case sensitivity, sorting, and Unicode options.

How It Works

This recipe demonstrated how to view the default collation for a SQL Server instance and for specific databases. We also reviewed how to list the collation's code page, case sensitivity, sorting, and Unicode options using fn_helpcollations. Once you know what settings your current database environment is using, you may decide to apply different collations to table columns when internationalization is required. This is demonstrated in the next recipe.

Designating a Column's Collation

In this recipe, I'll demonstrate how to designate the collation of a table column using the ALTER TABLE command:

```
ALTER TABLE Production.Product
ADD IcelandicProductName nvarchar(50) COLLATE Icelandic_CI_AI,
UkrainianProductName nvarchar(50) COLLATE Ukrainian_CI_AS
```

How It Works

In this recipe, two new columns were added to the Production.Product table. The query began by using ALTER TABLE and the table name:

```
ALTER TABLE Production.Product
```

After that, ADD was used, followed by the new column name, data type, COLLATE keyword and collation name (for a list of collation names, use the fn_helpcollations function described earlier):

```
ADD IcelandicProductName nvarchar(50) COLLATE Icelandic_CI_AI,
UkrainianProductName nvarchar(50) COLLATE Ukrainian_CI_AS
```

Be aware that when you define different collations within the same database or across databases in the same SQL Server instance, you can sometimes encounter compatibility issues. Cross-collation joins don't always work, and data transfers can result in lost or misinterpreted data.

Keys

A *primary key* is a special type of constraint, which identifies a single column or set of columns, which in turn uniquely identifies all rows in the table.

Constraints place limitations on the data that can be entered into a column or columns. A primary key enforces *entity integrity*, meaning that rows are guaranteed to be unambiguous and unique. Best practices for database normalization dictate that every table should have a primary key. A primary key provides a way to access the record, and ensures that the key is unique. A primary key column can't contain NULL values.

Only one primary key is allowed for a table and when a primary key is designated, an underlying table *index* is automatically created, defaulting to a clustered index (index types are reviewed in Chapter 5). You can also explicitly designate a nonclustered index be created when the primary key is created instead, if you have a better use for the single clustered index allowed for a table. An index created on primary key counts against the total indexes allowed for a table, the limit being one clustered index and up to 249 nonclustered indexes.

To designate a primary key on a single column, use the following syntax in the column definition:

```
( column_name <data_type> [ NULL | NOT NULL ] PRIMARY KEY  )
```

The token PRIMARY KEY is included at the end of the column definition.

A *composite primary key* is the unique combination of *more* than one column in the table. In order to define a composite primary key, you must use a *table constraint* instead of a *column constraint*. Setting a single column as the primary key within the column definition is called a column constraint. Defining the primary key (single or composite) outside of the column definition is referred to as a table constraint.

The syntax for a table constraint for a primary key is as follows:

```
 CONSTRAINT constraint_name  PRIMARY KEY
(column [ ASC | DESC ] [ ,...n ] )
```

Table 4-6 details the arguments of this command.

Table 4-6. *Table Constraint,Primary Key Arguments*

Argument	Description
constraint_name	The unique name of the constraint to be added.
column [ASC	DESC] [,...n]	The column or columns that make up the primary key must uniquely identify a single row in the table (no two rows can have the same values for all the specified columns). The ASC (ascending) and DESC (descending) options define the sorting order of the columns within the clustered or nonclustered index.

Foreign key constraints establish and enforce relationships between tables and help maintain referential integrity, which means that every value in the foreign key column must exist in the corresponding column for the referenced table.

Foreign key constraints also help define domain integrity, in that they define the range of potential and allowed values for a specific column or columns. Domain integrity defines the validity of values in a column.

The basic syntax for a foreign key constraint is:

```
CONSTRAINT constraint_name
FOREIGN KEY (column_name)
REFERENCES [ schema_name.] referenced_table_name [ ( ref_column ) ]
```

Table 4-7 details the arguments of this command.

Table 4-7. *Foreign Key Constraint Arguments*

Argument	Description
constraint_name	The name of the foreign key constraint.
column_name	The column in the current table referencing the primary key column of the primary key table.
[schema_name.] referenced_table_name	The table name containing the primary key being referenced by the current table.
ref_column	The primary key column being referenced.

The next few recipes will demonstrate primary and foreign key usage in action.

Creating a Table with a Primary Key

In this recipe, I'll create a table with a single column primary key:

```
CREATE TABLE Person.CreditRating(
   CreditRatingID int NOT NULL PRIMARY KEY,
   CreditRatingNM varchar(40) NOT NULL)
GO
```

In the previous example, a primary key was defined on a single column. You can, however, create a composite primary key.

In this example, a new table is created with a PRIMARY KEY table constraint formed from two columns:

```
CREATE TABLE Person.EmployeeEducationType (
   EmployeeID int NOT NULL,
   EducationTypeID int NOT NULL,
   CONSTRAINT PK_EmployeeEducationType
   PRIMARY KEY (EmployeeID, EducationTypeID))
```

How It Works

In the first example of the recipe, I created the Person.CreditRating table with a single column primary key. The column definition had the PRIMARY KEY keywords following the column definition:

```
CreditRatingID int NOT NULL PRIMARY KEY,
```

The primary key column was defined at the column level, whereas the second example defines the primary key at the table level:

```
CONSTRAINT PK_EmployeeEducationType
   PRIMARY KEY (EmployeeID, EducationTypeID))
```

The constraint definition followed the column definitions. The constraint was named, and then followed by the constraint type (PRIMARY KEY), and the columns forming the primary key in parentheses.

Adding a Primary Key Constraint to an Existing Table

In this recipe, I'll demonstrate how to add a primary key to an existing table using `ALTER TABLE` and `ADD CONSTRAINT`:

```
ALTER TABLE Person.EducationType
ADD CONSTRAINT PK_EducationType
PRIMARY KEY (EducationTypeID)
```

How It Works

In this recipe, `ALTER TABLE` was used to add a new primary key to an existing table that doesn't already have one defined. The first line of code defined the table to add the primary key to:

```
ALTER TABLE Person.EducationType
```

The second line of code defined the constraint name:

```
ADD CONSTRAINT PK_EducationType
```

On the last line of code in the previous example, the constraint type `PRIMARY KEY` was declared, followed by the column defining the key column in parentheses:

```
PRIMARY KEY (EducationTypeID)
```

Creating a Table with a Foreign Key Reference

In this recipe, I'll demonstrate how to create a table with a foreign key. In this example, a foreign key reference is included in a `CREATE TABLE` statement:

```
CREATE TABLE Person.EmployeeCreditRating(
    EmployeeCreditRating int NOT NULL PRIMARY KEY,
    EmployeeID int NOT NULL,
    CreditRatingID int NOT NULL,
    CONSTRAINT FK_EmployeeCreditRating_Employee
    FOREIGN KEY(EmployeeID)
    REFERENCES HumanResources.Employee(EmployeeID),
    CONSTRAINT FK_EmployeeCreditRating_CreditRating
    FOREIGN KEY(CreditRatingID)
    REFERENCES Person.CreditRating(CreditRatingID)
)
```

How It Works

In this example, a table was created with two foreign key references. The first four lines of code defined the table name and its three columns:

```
CREATE TABLE Person.EmployeeCreditRating(
    EmployeeCreditRating int NOT NULL PRIMARY KEY,
    EmployeeID int NOT NULL,
    CreditRatingID int NOT NULL,
```

On the next line, the name of the first foreign key constraint is defined (must be a unique name in the current database):

```
CONSTRAINT FK_EmployeeCreditRating_Employee
```

The constraint type is defined, followed by the table's column (which will be referencing an outside primary key table):

```
    FOREIGN KEY(EmployeeID)
```

The referenced table is defined, with that table's primary key column defined in parentheses:

```
REFERENCES HumanResources.Employee(EmployeeID),
```

A second foreign key is then created for the CreditRatingID column, which references the primary key of the Person.CreditRating table:

```
CONSTRAINT FK_EmployeeCreditRating_CreditRating
FOREIGN KEY(CreditRatingID)
REFERENCES Person.CreditRating(CreditRatingID)
)
```

As I demonstrated in this example, a table can have multiple foreign keys—and each foreign key can be based on a single or multiple (composite) key that references more then one column (referencing composite primary keys or unique indexes). Also, although the column names needn't be the same between a foreign key reference and a primary key, the primary key/unique columns must have the same data type. Also, you can't define foreign key constraints that reference tables across databases or servers.

Adding a Foreign Key to an Existing Table

Using ALTER TABLE and ADD CONSTRAINT, you can add a foreign key to an existing table. The syntax for doing so is as follows:

```
ALTER TABLE table_name
ADD CONSTRAINT  constraint_name
FOREIGN KEY (column_name)
REFERENCES [ schema_name.] referenced_table_name [ ( ref_column ) ]
```

Table 4-8 details the arguments of this command.

Table 4-8. *ALTER TABLE...ADD CONSTRAINT Arguments*

Argument	Description
table_name	The name of the table receiving the new foreign key constraint.
constraint_name	The name of the foreign key constraint.
column_name	The column in the current table referencing the primary key column of the primary key table.
[schema_name.] referenced_table_name	The table name containing the primary key being referenced by the current table.
ref_column	The primary key column being referenced.

This example adds a foreign key constraint to an existing table:

```
ALTER TABLE Person.EmergencyContact
ADD CONSTRAINT FK_EmergencyContact_Employee
FOREIGN KEY (EmployeeID)
REFERENCES HumanResources.Employee (EmployeeID)
```

How It Works

This example demonstrated adding a foreign key constraint to an existing table. The first line of code defined the table where the foreign key would be added:

```
ALTER TABLE Person.EmergencyContact
```

The second line defines the constraint name:

```
ADD CONSTRAINT FK_EmergencyContact_Employee
```

The third line defines the column from the table that will reference the primary key of the primary key table:

```
FOREIGN KEY (EmployeeID)
```

The last line of code defines the primary key table, and primary key column name:

```
REFERENCES HumanResources.Employee (EmployeeID)
```

Creating Recursive Foreign Key References

A foreign key column in a table can be defined to reference its own primary/unique key. This technique is often used to represent recursive relationships, as I'll demonstrate in this next example.

In this example, a table is created with a foreign key reference to its own primary key:

```
CREATE TABLE HumanResources.Company
   (CompanyID int NOT NULL PRIMARY KEY,
    ParentCompanyID int NULL,
    CompanyName varchar(25) NOT NULL,
    CONSTRAINT FK_Company_Company
    FOREIGN KEY (ParentCompanyID)
    REFERENCES HumanResources.Company(CompanyID))
GO
```

A row specifying CompanyID and CompanyName is added to the table:

```
INSERT HumanResources.Company
(CompanyID, CompanyName)
VALUES(1, 'MegaCorp')
```

A second row is added, this time referencing the ParentCompanyID, which is equal to the previously inserted row:

```
INSERT HumanResources.Company
(CompanyID, ParentCompanyID, CompanyName)
VALUES(2, 1, 'Medi-Corp')
```

A third row insert is attempted, this time specifying a ParentCompanyID for a CompanyID that does *not* exist in the table:

```
INSERT HumanResources.Company
(CompanyID, ParentCompanyID, CompanyName)
VALUES(3, 8, 'Tiny-Corp')
```

The following error message is returned:

```
Msg 547, Level 16, State 0, Line 1
The INSERT statement conflicted with the FOREIGN KEY SAME TABLE constraint
 "FK_Company_Company". The conflict occurred in database "AdventureWorks", table
"Company", column 'CompanyID'.
The statement has been terminated.
```

How It Works

In this example, the HumanResources.Company table was created with the CompanyID column defined as the primary key, and with a foreign key column defined on ParentCompanyID that references CompanyID:

```
CONSTRAINT FK_Company_Company
    FOREIGN KEY (ParentCompanyID)
    REFERENCES HumanResources.Company(CompanyID)
```

The foreign key column `ParentCompanyID` must be nullable in order to handle a parent-child hierarchy. A company with a `NULL` parent is at the top of the company hierarchy (which means it doesn't have a parent company). After the table was created, three new rows were inserted.

The first row inserted a company without designating the `ParentCompanyID` (which means the value for the `ParentCompanyID` column for this company is `NULL`):

```
INSERT HumanResources.Company
(CompanyID, CompanyName)
VALUES(1, 'MegaCorp')
```

The second insert created a company that references the first MegaCorp Company defined in the previous `INSERT` statement. The value of "1" was valid in the `ParentCompanyID` column, as it refers to the previously inserted row:

```
INSERT HumanResources.Company
(CompanyID, ParentCompanyID, CompanyName)
VALUES(2, 1, 'Medi-Corp')
```

The third insert tries to create a new company with a `ParentCompanyID` of 8, which does not exist in the table:

```
INSERT HumanResources.Company
(CompanyID, ParentCompanyID, CompanyName)
VALUES(3, 8, 'Tiny-Corp')
```

Because there is no company with a `CompanyID` of 8 in the table, the foreign key constraint prevents the row from being inserted and reports an error. The row is not inserted.

Allowing Cascading Changes in Foreign Keys

Foreign keys restrict the values that can be placed within the foreign key column or columns. If the associated primary key or unique value does not exist in the reference table, the `INSERT` or `UPDATE` to the table row fails. This restriction is bi-directional in that if an attempt is made to delete a primary key, but a row referencing that specific key exists in the foreign key table, an error will be returned. All referencing foreign key rows must be deleted prior to deleting the primary key or unique value in question, otherwise an error will be raised.

SQL Server 2005 provides an automatic mechanism for handling changes in the primary key/unique key column, called *cascading changes*.

In previous recipes, cascading options weren't used. You can allow cascading changes for deletions or updates using `ON DELETE` and `ON UPDATE`. The basic syntax for cascading options are as follows:

```
[ ON DELETE { NO ACTION | CASCADE | SET NULL | SET DEFAULT } ]
[ ON UPDATE { NO ACTION | CASCADE | SET NULL | SET DEFAULT } ]
[ NOT FOR REPLICATION ]
```

Table 4-9 details the arguments of this command.

Table 4-9. *Cascading Change Arguments*

Argument	Description
NO ACTION	The default setting for a new foreign key is NO ACTION, meaning if an attempt to delete a row on the primary key/unique column occurs when there is a referencing value in a foreign key table, the attempt will raise an error and prevent the statement from executing.
CASCADE	For ON DELETE, if CASCADE is chosen, foreign key rows referencing the deleted primary key are also deleted. For ON UPDATE, foreign key rows referencing the updated primary key are also updated.
SET NULL	New in SQL Server 2005, if the primary key row is deleted, the foreign key referencing row(s) can also be set to NULL (assuming NULL values are allowed for that foreign key column).
SET DEFAULT	New in SQL Server 2005, if the primary key row is deleted, the foreign key referencing row(s) can also be set to a DEFAULT value. The new cascade SET DEFAULT option assumes the column has a default value set for a column. If not, and the column is nullable, a NULL value is set.
NOT FOR REPLICATION	The NOT FOR REPLICATION option is used to prevent foreign key constraints from being enforced by SQL Server Replication Agent processes (allowing data to arrive via replication potentially out-of-order from the primary key data).

In this example, a table is created using cascading options:

```
CREATE TABLE Person.EmployeeEducationType(
   EmployeeEducationTypeID int NOT NULL PRIMARY KEY,
   EmployeeID int NOT NULL,
   EducationTypeID int NULL,
   CONSTRAINT FK_EmployeeEducationType_Employee
   FOREIGN KEY(EmployeeID)
   REFERENCES HumanResources.Employee(EmployeeID)
   ON DELETE CASCADE,
   CONSTRAINT FK_EmployeeEducationType_EducationType
   FOREIGN KEY(EducationTypeID)
   REFERENCES Person.EducationType(EducationTypeID)
   ON UPDATE SET NULL)
```

How It Works

In this recipe, one of the foreign key constraints uses ON DELETE CASCADE in a CREATE TABLE definition:

```
CONSTRAINT FK_EmployeeEducationType_Employee
   FOREIGN KEY(EmployeeID)
   REFERENCES HumanResources.Employee(EmployeeID)
   ON DELETE CASCADE
```

Using this cascade option, if a row is deleted on the HumanResources.Employee table, any referencing EmployeeID in the Person.EmployeeEducationType table will also be deleted.

A second foreign key constraint was also defined in the CREATE TABLE using ON UPDATE:

```
CONSTRAINT FK_EmployeeEducationType_EducationType
   FOREIGN KEY(EducationTypeID)
   REFERENCES Person.EducationType(EducationTypeID)
   ON UPDATE SET NULL
```

If an update is made to the primary key of the `Person.EducationType` table, the `EducationTypeID` column in the referencing `Person.EmployeeEducationType` table will be set to `NULL`.

Surrogate Keys

Surrogate keys, also called artificial keys, can be used in place of primary keys and have no inherent business/data meaning. Surrogate keys are independent of the data itself and are used to provide a single unique record locator in the table. A big advantage to surrogate primary keys is that they don't need to change. If you use business data to define your key (natural key), such as first name and last name, these values can change over time and change arbitrarily. Surrogate keys don't have to change, as their only meaning is within the context of the table itself.

The next few recipes will demonstrate methods for generating and managing surrogate keys using `IDENTITY` property columns and `uniqueidentifier` data type columns.

The `IDENTITY` column property, allows you to define an automatically incrementing numeric value for a single column in a table. An `IDENTITY` column is most often used for surrogate primary key columns, as they are more compact than non-numeric data type natural keys. When a new row is inserted into a table with an `IDENTITY` column property, the column is inserted with a unique incremented value. The data type for an `IDENTITY` column can be `int`, `tinyint`, `smallint`, `bigint`, `decimal`, or `numeric` data type. Tables may only have one identity column defined and the defined `IDENTITY` column can't have a `DEFAULT` or rule settings associated with it.

The basic syntax for an `IDENTITY` property column is as follows:

```
[ IDENTITY [ ( seed ,increment ) ] [NOT FOR REPLICATION] ]
```

The `IDENTITY` property takes two values: seed and increment. *Seed* defines the starting number for the `IDENTITY` column, and *increment* defines the value added to the previous `IDENTITY` column value to get the value for the next row added to the table. The default for both seed and increment is 1.The `NOT FOR REPLICATION` option preserves the original values of the Publisher `IDENTITY` column data when replicated to the Subscriber, retaining any values referenced by foreign key constraints (preventing the break of relationships between tables that may use the `IDENTITY` column as a primary key and foreign key reference).

Unlike the `IDENTITY` column, which guarantees uniqueness within the defined table, the `ROWGUIDCOL` property ensures a very high level of uniqueness (Microsoft claims that it can be unique for every database networked in the world). This is important for those applications which merge data from multiple sources, where the unique values cannot be duplicated across tables. This unique ID is stored in a `uniqueidentifier` data type and is generated by the `NEWID` system function.

The `ROWGUIDCOL` is a marker designated in a column definition, allowing you to query a table not only by the column's name, but by the `ROWGUIDCOL` designator, as this recipe demonstrates.

Which surrogate key data type is preferred? Although using a `uniqueidentifier` data type with a `NEWID` value for a primary key may be more unique, it takes up more space than an integer based `IDENTITY` column. If you only care about unique values within the table, you may be better off using an integer surrogate key, particularly for very large tables. However if uniqueness is an absolute requirement, with the expectation that you may be merging data sources in the future, `uniqueidentifier` with `NEWID` may be your best choice.

The next set of recipes will demonstrate `IDENTITY` and `ROWGUIDCOL` properties in action.

Using the IDENTITY Property During Table Creation

In this example, I'll demonstrate how to create a new table with a primary key `IDENTITY` column. The `IDENTITY` keyword is placed after the nullability option but before the `PRIMARY KEY` keywords:

```
CREATE TABLE HumanResources.CompanyAuditHistory
   (CompanyAuditHistory int NOT NULL IDENTITY(1,1) PRIMARY KEY,
    CompanyID int NOT NULL ,
    AuditReasonDESC varchar(50) NOT NULL,
    AuditDT datetime NOT NULL DEFAULT GETDATE())
```

Two rows are inserted into the new table:

```
INSERT HumanResources.CompanyAuditHistory
(CompanyID, AuditReasonDESC, AuditDT)
VALUES
(1, 'Bad 1099 numbers.', '6/1/2005')

INSERT HumanResources.CompanyAuditHistory
(CompanyID, AuditReasonDESC, AuditDT)
VALUES
(1, 'Missing financial statement.', '7/1/2005')
```

Even though the CompanyAuditHistory column wasn't explicitly populated with the two inserts, querying the table shows that the IDENTITY property on the column caused the values to be populated:

```
SELECT CompanyAuditHistory, AuditReasonDESC
FROM HumanResources.CompanyAuditHistory
```

This returns:

```
CompanyAuditHistory AuditReasonDESC
------------------- --------------------------------------------------
1                   Bad 1099 numbers.
2                   Missing financial statement.

(2 row(s) affected)
```

How It Works

In this example, an IDENTITY column was defined for a new table. The IDENTITY property was designated after the column definition, but before the PRIMARY KEY definition:

```
CompanyAuditHistory int NOT NULL IDENTITY(1,1) PRIMARY KEY
```

After creating the table, two rows were inserted without explicitly inserting the CompanyAuditHistory column value. After selecting from the table, these two rows were automatically assigned values based on the IDENTITY property, beginning with a seed value of 1, and incrementing by 1 for each new row.

Using DBCC CHECKIDENT to View and Correct IDENTITY Seed Values

In this recipe, I'll show you how to check the current IDENTITY value of a column for a table by using the DBCC CHECKIDENT command. DBCC CHECKIDENT checks the current maximum value for the specified table. The syntax for this command is as follows:

```
DBCC CHECKIDENT
(
'table_name'
    [ , {
    NORESEED | { RESEED [ , new_reseed_value ] }
        }
```

```
        ]
)
[ WITH NO_INFOMSGS ]
```

Table 4-10 details the arguments of this command.

Table 4-10. *CHECKIDENT Arguments*

Argument	Description
table_name	The name of the table to check IDENTITY values for.
NORESEED | RESEED	NORESEED means that no action is taken other then to report the maximum identity value. RESEED specifies what the current IDENTITY value should be.
new_reseed_value	The new current IDENTITY value.
WITH NO_INFOMSGS	When included in the command, WITH NO_INFOMSGS suppresses informational messages from the DBCC output.

In this example, the current table IDENTITY value is checked:

```
DBCC CHECKIDENT('HumanResources.CompanyAuditHistory', NORESEED)
```

This returns:

```
Checking identity information: current identity value '2', current column value '2'.
DBCC execution completed. If DBCC printed error messages, contact your system
administrator.
```

This second example resets the seed value to a higher number:

```
DBCC CHECKIDENT ('HumanResources.CompanyAuditHistory', RESEED, 50)
```

This returns:

```
Checking identity information: current identity value '2',
 current column value '50'.
DBCC execution completed. If DBCC printed error messages,
contact your system administrator.
```

How It Works

The first example demonstrated checking the current IDENTITY value using the DBCC CHECKIDENT and the NORESEED option. The second example demonstrated actually resetting the IDENTITY value to a higher value. Any future inserts will begin from that value.

Why make such a change? DBCC CHECKIDENT with RESEED is often used to fill primary key gaps. If you deleted rows from the table that had the highest value for the IDENTITY column, the used identity values will not be reused the next time records are inserted into the table. For example if the last row inserted had a value of "22," and you deleted that row, the next inserted row would be "23." Just because the value is deleted doesn't mean the SQL Server will backfill the gap. If you need to re-use key values (which is generally OK to do in the test-phase of your database—as in production you really shouldn't reuse primary key values), you can use DBCC CHECKIDENT to re-use numbers after a large row deletion.

Using the ROWGUIDCOL Property

First, a table is created using ROWGUIDCOL identified after the column data type definition, but before the default definition (populated via the NEWID system function):

```
CREATE TABLE HumanResources.BuildingAccess
(   BuildingEntryExitID uniqueidentifier ROWGUIDCOL DEFAULT NEWID(),
    EmployeeID int NOT NULL,
    AccessTime datetime NOT NULL,
    DoorID int NOT NULL)
```

Next, a row is inserted into the table:

```
INSERT HumanResources.BuildingAccess
(EmployeeID, AccessTime, DoorID)
VALUES (32, GETDATE(), 2)
```

The table is then queried, using the ROWGUIDCOL designator instead of the original BuildingEntryExitID column name (although the original name can be used too—ROWGUIDCOL just offers a more generic means of pulling out the identifier in a query):

```
SELECT   ROWGUIDCOL,
         EmployeeID,
         AccessTime,
         DoorID
FROM     HumanResources.BuildingAccess
```

This returns:

BuildingEntryExitID	EmployeeID	AccessTime	DoorID
4E7B0E4B-BE1C-44B6-80E0-E852B775940C	32	2005-07-04 15:29:39.930	2

(1 row(s) affected)

How It Works

The recipe started by creating a new table with a uniqueidentifier data type column:

```
BuildingEntryExitID uniqueidentifier ROWGUIDCOL DEFAULT NEWID(),
```

The column was bound to a default of the function NEWID—which returns a unique, uniqueidentifier data type value. In addition to this, the ROWGUIDCOL property was assigned. Only one ROWGUIDCOL column can be defined for a table. You can still, however, have multiple uniqueidentifier columns in the table.

A SELECT query then used ROWGUIDCOL to return the uniqueidentifier column, although the column name could have been used instead.

Constraints

Constraints are used by SQL Server to enforce column data integrity. Both primary and foreign keys are forms of constraints. Other forms of constraints used for a column include:

- UNIQUE constraints, which enforce uniqueness within a table on non-primary key columns.
- DEFAULT constraints, which can be used when you don't know the value of a column in a row when it is first inserted into a table, but still wish to populate that column with an anticipated value.
- CHECK constraints, which are used to define the data format and values allowed for a column.

The next few recipes will discuss how to create and manage these constraint types.

Creating a Unique Constraint

You can only have a single primary key defined on a table. If you wish to enforce uniqueness on other non-primary key columns, you can use a UNIQUE constraint. A unique constraint, by definition, creates an alternate key.

Unlike a PRIMARY KEY constraint, you can create multiple UNIQUE constraints for a single table and are also allowed to designate a UNIQUE constraint for columns that allow NULL values (although only one NULL value is allowed for a single column key, per table). Like primary keys, UNIQUE constraints enforce entity integrity by ensuring that rows can be uniquely identified.

The UNIQUE constraint creates an underlying table index when it is created. This index can be CLUSTERED or NONCLUSTERED, although you can't create the index as CLUSTERED if a clustered index already exists for the table.

As with PRIMARY KEY constraints, you can define a UNIQUE constraint when a table is created either on the column definition, or at the table constraint level.

The syntax for defining a UNIQUE constraint during a table's creation is as follows:

```
( column_name <data_type> [ NULL | NOT NULL ] UNIQUE   )
```

This example demonstrates creating a table with both a PRIMARY KEY and UNIQUE key defined:

```
CREATE TABLE HumanResources.EmployeeAnnualReview(
    EmployeeAnnualReviewID int NOT NULL PRIMARY KEY,
    EmployeeID int NOT NULL,
    AnnualReviewSummaryDESC varchar(900) NOT NULL UNIQUE)
```

You can apply a unique constraint across multiple columns by creating a table constraint:

```
 CONSTRAINT constraint_name  UNIQUE
(column [ ASC | DESC ] [ ,...n ] )
```

Table 4-11 details the arguments of this command.

Table 4-11. *UNIQUE Constraint Arguments*

Argument	Description
constraint_name	The unique name of the constraint to be added.
column [ASC	DESC] [,...n]	The values stored in the column(s) must uniquely identify a single row in the table (i.e. no two rows can have the same values for all the specified columns). The ASC (ascending) and DESC (descending) options define the sorting order of the columns within the clustered or nonclustered index.

In this example, a new table is created with a UNIQUE constraint based on three table columns:

```
CREATE TABLE Person.EmergencyContact (
    EmergencyContactID int NOT NULL PRIMARY KEY,
    EmployeeID int NOT NULL,
    ContactFirstNM varchar(50) NOT NULL,
    ContactLastNM varchar(50) NOT NULL,
    ContactPhoneNBR varchar(25) NOT NULL,
    CONSTRAINT UNQ_EmergencyContact_FirstNM_LastNM_PhoneNBR
    UNIQUE (ContactFirstNM, ContactLastNM, ContactPhoneNBR))
```

How It Works

In the first example, a UNIQUE constraint was defined in the CREATE TABLE for a specific column:

```
AnnualReviewSummaryDESC varchar(900) NOT NULL UNIQUE
```

The UNIQUE keyword follows the column definition and indicates that a UNIQUE constraint is to be created on the column AnnualReviewSummaryDESC.

In the second example, a UNIQUE constraint is created based on three table columns defined in CREATE TABLE. The constraint is defined after the column definitions. The first line of code defines the constraint name:

```
CONSTRAINT UNQ_EmergencyContact_FirstNM_LastNM_PhoneNBR
```

The second line of code defines the constraint type (UNIQUE) and a list of columns that make up the constraint in parentheses:

```
UNIQUE (ContactFirstNM, ContactLastNM, ContactPhoneNBR)
```

Adding a UNIQUE Constraint to an Existing Table

Using ALTER TABLE, you can add a UNIQUE constraint to an existing table. The syntax is as follows:

```
ALTER TABLE table_name
ADD CONSTRAINT  constraint_name
UNIQUE  (column [ ASC | DESC ] [ ,...n ] )
```

Table 4-12 details the arguments of this command.

Table 4-12. *ALTER TABLE...ADD CONSTRAINT (Unique) Arguments*

Argument	Description
table_name	The name of the table receiving the new unique key index.
constraint_name	The unique name of the constraint to be added.
column [ASC | DESC] [,...n]	The values stored in the column(s) must uniquely identify a single row in the table (i.e. no two rows can have the same values for all the specified columns). The ASC (ascending) and DESC (descending) options define the sorting order of the columns within the clustered or nonclustered index.

This example demonstrates adding a UNIQUE key to the Production.Culture table:

```
ALTER TABLE Production.Culture
ADD CONSTRAINT UNQ_Culture_Name
UNIQUE (Name)
```

How It Works

In this example, the first line of code defined the table to be modified:

```
ALTER TABLE Production.Culture
```

The second line of code defined the name of the constraint:

```
ADD CONSTRAINT UNQ_Culture_Name
```

The third line of code defined the constraint type, followed by the column name it will apply to:

```
UNIQUE (Name)
```

The columns specified in the UNIQUE constraint definition can't have duplicate values occurring in the table, otherwise the operation will fail with an error that a duplicate key value was found.

Using CHECK Constraints

CHECK constraint is used to define what format and values are allowed for a column. The syntax of the CHECK constraint is as follows:

```
CHECK ( logical_expression )
```

If the logical expression of CHECK evaluates to TRUE, the row will be inserted. If the CHECK constraint expression evaluates to FALSE, the row insert will fail.

This example demonstrates adding a CHECK constraint to a CREATE TABLE definition. The GPA column's values will be restricted to a specific numeric range:

```
CREATE TABLE Person.EmployeeEducationType(
    EmployeeEducationTypeID int NOT NULL PRIMARY KEY,
    EmployeeID int NOT NULL,
    EducationTypeID int NULL,
    GPA numeric(4,3) NOT NULL CHECK (GPA > 2.5 AND GPA <=4.0))
```

In the previous example, the CHECK constraint expression was defined at the column constraint level. A CHECK constraint can also be defined at the table constraint level—where you are allowed to reference multiple columns in the expression, as this next example demonstrates:

```
CREATE TABLE Person.EmployeeEducationType(
    EmployeeEducationTypeID int NOT NULL PRIMARY KEY,
    EmployeeID int NOT NULL,
    EducationTypeID int NULL,
    GPA numeric(4,3) NOT NULL,
    CONSTRAINT CK_EmployeeEducationType
    CHECK (EducationTypeID > 1 AND GPA > 2.5 AND GPA <=4.0))
```

How It Works

In the first example, a CHECK column constraint was placed against the GPA column in the Person.EmployeeEducationType table:

```
GPA numeric(4,3) NOT NULL CHECK (GPA > 2.5 AND GPA <=4.0)
```

Only a GPA column value greater than 2.5 or less than/equal to 4.0 is allowed in the table—anything else out of that range will cause any INSERT or UPDATE to fail.

In the second example, the CHECK table constraint evaluates two table columns:

```
CHECK (EducationTypeID > 1 AND GPA > 2.5 AND GPA <=4.0)
```

This CHECK constraint requires that the EducationTypeID value must be greater than 1, in addition to the GPA requirements.

Adding a CHECK Constraint to an Existing Table

Like other constraint types, you can add a CHECK constraint to an existing table using ALTER TABLE and ADD CONSTRAINT. The syntax is as follows:

```
ALTER TABLE table_name
WITH CHECK | WITH NOCHECK
ADD CONSTRAINT  constraint_name
CHECK ( logical_expression )
```

Table 4-13 details the arguments of this command.

Table 4-13. *ALTER TABLE...ADD CONSTRAINT (Check) Arguments*

Argument	Description
table_name	The name of the table receiving the new CHECK constraint.
CHECK | WITH NOCHECK	With the CHECK option (the default), existing data is validated against the new CHECK constraint. NOCHECK skips validation of new data, limiting the constraint to validation of new values (inserted or updated).
constraint_name	The name of the CHECK constraint.
logical_expression	The logical expression used to restrict values that are allowed in the column.

In this example, a new CHECK request is added to the Person.ContactType table:

```
ALTER TABLE Person.ContactType WITH NOCHECK
ADD CONSTRAINT  CK_ContactType
CHECK (Name NOT LIKE '%assistant%')
```

How It Works

A new constraint was added to the Person.ContactType table to not allow any name like "assistant." The first part of the ALTER TABLE statement included WITH NOCHECK:

```
ALTER TABLE Person.ContactType WITH NOCHECK
```

Had this statement been executed without WITH NOCHECK, it would have failed because there are already rows in the table with "assistant" in the name. Adding WITH NOCHECK means that existing values are ignored going forward, and only new values are validated against the CHECK constraint.

■**Caution** Using WITH NOCHECK may cause problems later on, as you cannot depend on the data in the table conforming to the constraint.

The next part of the statement defined the new constraint name:

```
ADD CONSTRAINT  CK_ContactType
```

The constraint type CHECK was used followed by the logical expression to limit the Name column's contents:

```
CHECK (Name NOT LIKE '%assistant%')
```

Disabling and Enabling a Constraint

The previous exercise demonstrated using NOCHECK to ignore existing values that disobey the new constraints rule when adding a new constraint to the table. Constraints are used to maintain data integrity, although sometimes you may need to relax the rules while performing a one-off data import or non-standard business operation.

NOCHECK can also be used to disable a CHECK or FOREIGN KEY constraint, allowing you to insert rows that disobey the constraints rules.

In the setup of this example, an insert is attempted to the Purchasing.VendorContact table:

```
INSERT Purchasing.VendorContact
(VendorID, ContactID, ContactTypeID)
VALUES (93, 643, 888)
```

The insert fails, returning the following error message:

```
Msg 547, Level 16, State 0, Line 1
The INSERT statement conflicted with the FOREIGN KEY constraint
"FK_VendorContact_ContactType_ContactTypeID". The conflict occurred in database
"AdventureWorks", table "ContactType", column 'ContactTypeID'.
The statement has been terminated.
```

Next, the foreign key constraint that caused the previous error message will be disabled using NOCHECK:

```
ALTER TABLE Purchasing.VendorContact
NOCHECK CONSTRAINT FK_VendorContact_ContactType_ContactTypeID
```

The insert is then attempted again:

```
INSERT Purchasing.VendorContact
(VendorID, ContactID, ContactTypeID)
VALUES (93, 643, 888)
```

This time it succeeds:

```
(1 row(s) affected)
```

We can then DELETE the newly inserted row, so as not to leave data integrity issues once the constraint is re-enabled:

```
DELETE Purchasing.VendorContact
WHERE VendorID = 93 AND
ContactID = 643 AND
ContactTypeID = 888
```

To re-enable checking of the foreign key constraint, CHECK is used in an ALTER TABLE statement:

```
ALTER TABLE Purchasing.VendorContact
CHECK CONSTRAINT FK_VendorContact_ContactType_ContactTypeID
```

To disable or enable all CHECK and FOREIGN KEY constraints for the table, you should use the ALL keyword, as this example demonstrates:

```
-- disable checking on all constraints
ALTER TABLE Purchasing.VendorContact
NOCHECK CONSTRAINT ALL
```

```
-- enable checking on all constraints
ALTER TABLE Purchasing.VendorContact
CHECK CONSTRAINT ALL
```

■**Caution** Disabling all CHECK and FOREIGN KEY constraints for a table should only be performed when absolutely necessary. Re-enable all constraints when you are finished.

How It Works

In this recipe, an insert was attempted against Purchasing.VendorContact with a ContactTypeID that didn't exist in the primary key table. The insert causes a conflict with the FK_VendorContact_ContactType_ContactTypeID foreign key constraint.

To disable the constraint from validating new values, ALTER TABLE and NOCHECK CONSTRAINT were used:

```
ALTER TABLE Purchasing.VendorContact
NOCHECK CONSTRAINT FK_VendorContact_ContactType_ContactTypeID
```

After disabling the constraint with NOCHECK, the ContactTypeID value was then allowed to be inserted, even though it doesn't exist in the primary key table.

The recipe finished by re-enabling the constraint again, and deleting the value just inserted (using CHECK instead of NOCHECK):

```
ALTER TABLE Purchasing.VendorContact
CHECK CONSTRAINT FK_VendorContact_ContactType_ContactTypeID
```

The next example demonstrated disabling all foreign key and check constraints on a table using the ALL keyword:

```
NOCHECK CONSTRAINT ALL
```

All constraints for the table were then re-enabled using the following code:

```
CHECK CONSTRAINT ALL.
```

Using a DEFAULT Constraint During Table Creation

If you don't know the value of a column in a row when it is first inserted into a table, you can use a DEFAULT constraint to populate that column with an anticipated or non-NULL value. The syntax for designating the default value in the column definition of a CREATE TABLE is as follows:

```
DEFAULT constant_expression
```

The constant_expression is the default value you wish to populate into the column when the column's value isn't explicitly specified in an INSERT.

This example demonstrates setting the default value of the EducationTypeID column to "1":

```
CREATE TABLE Person.EmployeeEducationType(
   EmployeeEducationTypeID int NOT NULL PRIMARY KEY,
   EmployeeID int NOT NULL,
   EducationTypeID int NOT NULL DEFAULT 1,
   GPA numeric(4,3) NOT NULL )
```

How It Works

In this example, the default value of EducationTypeID was set to a default of "1." The keyword DEFAULT was placed after the column definition and followed by the default value (which must match the data type of the column):

```
EducationTypeID int NOT NULL DEFAULT 1
```

Since this column has a DEFAULT value, if the value isn't explicitly inserted with an INSERT statement, the value "1" will be inserted instead of a NULL value.

Adding a DEFAULT Constraint to an Existing Table

Like other constraint types, you can add a default constraint to an existing table column using ALTER TABLE and ADD CONSTRAINT. The syntax for doing this is as follows:

```
ALTER TABLE table_name
ADD CONSTRAINT  constraint_name
DEFAULT default_value
FOR column_name
```

Table 4-14 details the arguments of this command.

Table 4-14. *ALTER TABLE...ADD CONSTRAINT (Default) Arguments*

Argument	Description
table_name	The name of the table receiving the new DEFAULT constraint.
constraint_name	The name of the DEFAULT constraint.
default_value	The default value to be used for the column.
column_name	The name of the column the default is being applied to.

This example demonstrates adding a default to an existing table column:

```
ALTER TABLE HumanResources.Company
ADD CONSTRAINT DF_Company_ParentCompanyID
DEFAULT 1
FOR ParentCompanyID
```

How It Works

In this example, a new default was applied to an existing table column. The first line of ALTER TABLE defines the impacted table:

```
ALTER TABLE HumanResources.Company
```

The second line of the statement adds a constraint and defines the constraint name:

```
ADD CONSTRAINT DF_Company_ParentCompanyID
```

The third line of code defines the constraint type, DEFAULT, followed by the value to use for the default:

```
DEFAULT 1
```

Lastly, the column that the default is applied to is used in the FOR clause:

```
FOR ParentCompanyID
```

Dropping a Constraint from a Table

Now that I've reviewed several constraints that can be added to a table, in this recipe I'll demonstrate how to now *drop* a constraint using ALTER TABLE and DROP CONSTRAINT. The basic syntax for dropping a constraint is as follows:

```
ALTER TABLE table_name
DROP CONSTRAINT constraint_name
```

The table_name designates the table you are dropping the constraint from, and the constraint_name designates the name of the constraint to be dropped.

In this example, a default constraint is dropped from the HumanResources.Company table:

```
ALTER TABLE HumanResources.Company
DROP CONSTRAINT DF_Company_ParentCompanyID
```

How It Works

In the first line of code in this example, the table to drop the constraint from is designated:

```
ALTER TABLE HumanResources.Company
```

In the second line of code, the name of the constraint to drop is designated:

```
DROP CONSTRAINT DF_Company_ParentCompanyID
```

Notice that the constraint type wasn't needed, and that only the constraint name was used. To find out the constraint name, use the system stored procedure sp_help.

Temporary Tables and Table Variables

Temporary tables are defined just like regular tables, only they are automatically stored in the tempdb database (no matter which database context you create them in). Temporary tables are often used in the following scenarios:

- As a replacement to cursors. For example, instead of using a Transact-SQL cursor to loop through a result set, performing tasks based on each row, you can populate a temporary table instead. Using a WHILE loop, you can loop through each row in the table, perform the action for the specified row, and then delete the row from the temp table.

- As an incremental storage of result sets. For example, let's say you have a single SELECT query that performs a join against ten tables. Sometimes queries with several joins can perform badly. One technique to try is to break down the large query into smaller, incremental queries. Using temporary tables, you can create intermediate result sets based on smaller queries, instead of trying to execute a single, very large and multi-joined query.

- As a temporary, low-overhead lookup table. For example, imagine that you are using a query that takes several seconds to execute, but only returns a small result set. You wish to use the small result set in several areas of your stored procedure, but each time you reference it, you incur the query execution time overhead. To resolve this, you can execute the query just once within the procedure, populating the temporary table. Then you can reference the temporary table in multiple places in your code, without incurring the extra overhead.

There are two different temporary table types: *global* and *local*. Local temporary tables are prefixed with a single # sign, and global temporary tables with a double ## sign.

Local temporary tables are available for use by the current user connection that created them. Multiple connections can create the same-named temporary table for local temporary tables without encountering conflicts. The internal representation of the local table is given a unique name, so as not to conflict with other temporary tables with the same name created by other connections in the tempdb database. Local temporary tables are dropped by using the DROP statement or are automatically removed from memory when the user connection is closed.

Global temporary tables have a different scope from local temporary tables. Once a connection creates a global temporary table, any user with proper permissions access to the current database they are in can access the table. Unlike local temporary tables, you can't create simultaneous versions of a global temporary table, as this will generate a naming conflict. Global temporary tables are removed from SQL Server if explicitly dropped by DROP TABLE. They are also automatically removed after the connection that created it exits and the global temporary table is no longer referenced by other connections. As an aside, I rarely see global temporary tables used in the field. When a table must be shared across connections, a real table is created, instead of a global temporary table. Nonetheless, Microsoft offers this as a choice anyway.

Temporary tables are much maligned by the DBA community due to performance issues—some of these complaints are valid, and some aren't. It is true that temporary tables may cause unwanted disk overhead in tempdb, locking of tempdb during their creation, as well as cause stored procedure recompilations, when included within a stored procedure's definition (a recompilation is when an execution plan of the stored procedure is recreated instead of being reused).

Microsoft recommends table variables as a replacement of temporary tables when the data set is not very large (which is a vague instruction—in the end it is up to you to test which table types work best in your environment). A *table variable* is a data type that can be used within a Transact-SQL batch, stored procedure, or function—and is created and defined similarly to a table, only with a strictly defined lifetime scope.

Unlike regular tables or temporary tables, table variables can't have indexes or FOREIGN KEY constraints added to them. Table variables do allow some constraints to be used in the table definition (PRIMARY KEY, UNIQUE, CHECK).

Reasons to use table variables include:

- Well scoped. The lifetime of the table variable only lasts for the duration of the batch, function, or stored procedure.

- Shorter locking periods (because of the tighter scope).

- Less recompilation when used in stored procedures.

There are drawbacks to using table variables though. Table variable performance suffers when the result set becomes too large (defined by your hardware, database design, and query). When encountering performance issues, be sure to test all alternative solutions and don't necessarily assume that one option (temporary tables) is less desirable than others (table variables).

Using a Temporary Table for Multiple Lookups Within a Batch

In this example, I'll demonstrate creating a local temporary table that is then referenced multiple times in a batch of queries. This technique can be helpful if the query used to generate the lookup values takes several seconds to execute. Rather then execute the SELECT query multiple times, we can query the pre-aggregated temp table instead:

```
CREATE TABLE #ProductCostStatistics
( ProductID int NOT NULL PRIMARY KEY,
  AvgStandardCost money NOT NULL,
  ProductCount int NOT NULL)
GO
```

```
INSERT #ProductCostStatistics
(ProductID, AvgStandardCost, ProductCount)
SELECT ProductID,
       AVG(StandardCost) AvgStandardCost,
       COUNT(ProductID) Rowcnt
FROM Production.ProductCostHistory
GROUP BY ProductID
GO

SELECT TOP 3 *
FROM #ProductCostStatistics
ORDER BY AvgStandardCost ASC

SELECT TOP 3 *
FROM #ProductCostStatistics
ORDER BY AvgStandardCost DESC

SELECT AVG(AvgStandardCost) Average_of_AvgStandardCost
FROM #ProductCostStatistics

DROP TABLE #ProductCostStatistics
```

This returns three result sets from the temporary table:

ProductID	AvgStandardCost	ProductCount
873	0.8565	1
922	1.4923	1
870	1.8663	1

ProductID	AvgStandardCost	ProductCount
749	2171.2942	1
750	2171.2942	1
751	2171.2942	1

Average_of_AvgStandardCost
423.0001

How It Works

In this recipe, a temporary table called #ProductCostStatistics was created. The table had rows inserted into it like a regular table, and then the temporary table was queried three times (again, just like a regular table), and then dropped. The table was created and queried with the same syntax as a regular table, only the temporary table name was prefixed with a # sign. In situations where the initial population query execution time takes too long to execute, this is one technique to consider.

Creating a Table Variable to Hold a Temporary Result Set

Table variables were first demonstrated in Chapter 2, in the "Using the OUTPUT clause with INSERT, UPDATE, DELETE" recipe. There you learned to use them to hold the results of the OUTPUT command

The syntax to creating a table variable is similar to creating a table, only the DECLARE keyword is used and the table name is prefixed with an @ symbol:

```
DECLARE @TableName TABLE
   (column_name <data_type> [ NULL | NOT NULL ] [ ,...n ]  )
```

In this example, a table variable is used in a similar fashion to the temporary table of the previous recipe. This example demonstrates how the implementation differs (including how you don't explicitly DROP the table):

```
DECLARE @ProductCostStatistics TABLE
( ProductID int NOT NULL PRIMARY KEY,
  AvgStandardCost money NOT NULL,
  ProductCount int NOT NULL)

INSERT @ProductCostStatistics
(ProductID, AvgStandardCost, ProductCount)
SELECT ProductID,
     AVG(StandardCost) AvgStandardCost,
     COUNT(ProductID) Rowcnt
FROM Production.ProductCostHistory
GROUP BY ProductID

SELECT TOP 3 *
FROM @ProductCostStatistics
ORDER BY ProductCount
```

This returns:

ProductID	AvgStandardCost	ProductCount
710	3.3963	1
709	3.3963	1
731	352.1394	1

How It Works

This recipe used a table variable in much the same way as the previous recipe did with temporary tables. There are important distinctions between the two recipes however.

First, this time a table variable was defined using DECLARE @Tablename TABLE instead of CREATE TABLE. Secondly, unlike the temporary table recipe, there isn't a GO after each statement, as temporary tables can only be scoped within the batch, procedure, or function.

In the next part of the recipe, you'll use inserts and selects from the table variable as you would a regular table, only this time using the @tablename format:

```
INSERT @ProductCostStatistics
...

SELECT TOP 3 *
FROM @ProductCostStatistics
...
```

No DROP TABLE was necessary at the end of the example, as the table variable is eliminated from memory after the end of the batch/procedure/function execution.

Manageability for Very Large Tables

These next few recipes will demonstrate methods for managing very large tables (with millions of rows, for example). Specifically, we'll discuss SQL Server 2005's table-partitioning functionality, and then file group placement.

New to SQL Server 2005, table partitioning provides you with a built-in method of horizontally partitioning data within a table and/or index while still maintaining a single logical object. Horizontal partitioning involves keeping the same number of columns in each partition, but reducing the number of rows. Partitioning can ease management of very large tables and/or indexes, decrease load time, improve query time, and allow smaller maintenance windows. These next few recipes in this section will demonstrate how to use new SQL Server 2005 Transact-SQL commands to create, modify, and manage partitions and partition database objects.

■**Note** SQL Server 2005 partitioning is only available in the Enterprise and Developer edition.

We'll also cover *filegroup* placement. Database data files belong to filegroups. Every database has a primary filegroup and you can add additional filegroups as needed. Adding new filegroups to a database is often used for *very large databases (VLDB)* as they can ease backup administration and potentially improve performance by distributing data over multiple arrays. I'll demonstrate placing a table on a specific filegroup in the last recipe of this chapter.

Before diving in to the partitioning-related recipes, I'll discuss the two new commands CREATE PARTITION FUNCTION and CREATE PARTITION SCHEME.

The CREATE PARTITION FUNCTION maps columns to partitions based on the value of a specified column. For example, if you are evaluating a column with a datetime data type, you can partition data to separate filegroups based on the year or month.

The basic syntax for CREATE PARTITION FUNCTION is:

```
CREATE PARTITION FUNCTION partition_function_name(input_parameter_type)
AS RANGE [ LEFT | RIGHT ]
FOR VALUES ( [ boundary_value [ ,...n ] ] )
```

Table 4-15 details the arguments of this command.

Table 4-15. *CREATE PARTITION FUNCTION Arguments*

Argument	Description
partition_function_name	The partition function name.
input_parameter_type	The data type of the partitioning column. You cannot use large value data types (text, ntext, image, xml, timestamp, varchar(max), varbinary(max), nvarchar(max)), CLR user-defined data types, or aliased data types. If you wished to partition table data by a datetime column, you would designate datetime for the input_parameter_type.
LEFT | RIGHT	You also have a choice of LEFT or RIGHT, which defines which boundary the defined values in the boundary_value argument belong to (see the upcoming How It Works section for a review of LEFT versus RIGHT).
[boundary_value [,...n]]	This argument defines the range of values in each partition. You can defined up to 999 partitions (however that many isn't recommended due to potential performance concerns). The number of values you choose in this argument amounts to a total of n + 1 partitions (again, see the How It Works section for a more in depth explanation).

Once a partition function is created, it can be used with one or more partition schemes. A partition scheme maps partitions defined in a partition function to actual filegroups.

The basic syntax for CREATE PARTITION SCHEME is as follows:

```
CREATE PARTITION SCHEME partition_scheme_name
AS PARTITION partition_function_name
[ ALL ] TO ( { file_group_name | [PRIMARY] } [ ,...n] )
```

Table 4-16 details the arguments of this command.

Table 4-16. *CREATE PARTITION SCHEME Arguments*

Argument	Description
partition_scheme_name	The name of the partition scheme.
partition_function_name	The name of the partition function that the scheme will bind to.
ALL	If ALL is designated, all partitions will map to the filegroup designated in the file_group_name argument.
{ file_group_name	[PRIMARY] } [,...n]	The filegroup or filegroups assigned to each partition. When PRIMARY is designated, the partition will be stored on the primary filegroup.

Implementing Table Partitioning

In this recipe, I'll show you how to:

- Create a filegroup or filegroups to hold the partitions.
- Add files to each filegroup used in the partitioning.
- Use the CREATE PARTITION FUNCTION command to determine how the table's data will be partitioned.
- Use the CREATE PARTITION SCHEME command to bind the PARTITION FUNCTION to the specified filegroups.
- Create the table, binding a specific partitioning column to a PARTITION SCHEME.

The recipe creates a table called Sales.WebSiteHits, which is used to track each hit to a hypothetical website. In this scenario, the table is expected to become very large, very fast. Because of the potential size, queries may not perform as well as they could, and backup operations against the entire database take longer than the current maintenance window allows.

The data from this table will be partitioned horizontally, which means that groups of rows based on a selected column (in this case HitDate) will be mapped into separate underlying physical files on the disk. The first part of this example demonstrates adding the new filegroups to the AdventureWorks database:

```
ALTER DATABASE AdventureWorks
ADD FILEGROUP hitfg1

ALTER DATABASE AdventureWorks
ADD FILEGROUP hitfg2

ALTER DATABASE AdventureWorks
ADD FILEGROUP hitfg3
```

```
ALTER DATABASE AdventureWorks
ADD FILEGROUP hitfg4
```

Next, for each new filegroup created, a new database file is added to it:

```
ALTER DATABASE AdventureWorks
ADD FILE
(   NAME = awhitfg1,
    FILENAME = 'c:\Program Files\Microsoft SQL
Server\MSSQL.1\MSSQL\Data\aw_hitfg1.ndf',
    SIZE = 1MB
)
TO FILEGROUP hitfg1
GO

ALTER DATABASE AdventureWorks
ADD FILE
(   NAME = awhitfg2,
    FILENAME = 'c:\Program Files\Microsoft SQL
Server\MSSQL.1\MSSQL\Data\aw_hitfg2.ndf',
    SIZE = 1MB
)
TO FILEGROUP hitfg2
GO

ALTER DATABASE AdventureWorks
ADD FILE
(   NAME = awhitfg3,
    FILENAME = 'c:\Program Files\Microsoft SQL
Server\MSSQL.1\MSSQL\Data\aw_hitfg3.ndf',
    SIZE = 1MB
)
TO FILEGROUP hitfg3
GO

ALTER DATABASE AdventureWorks
ADD FILE
(   NAME = awhitfg4,
    FILENAME = 'c:\Program Files\Microsoft SQL
Server\MSSQL.1\MSSQL\Data\aw_hitfg4.ndf',
    SIZE = 1MB
)
TO FILEGROUP hitfg4
GO
```

Now that the filegroups are ready for their partitioned data, the partition function will be created which determines how the table will have its data horizontally partitioned (in this case, by date range):

```
CREATE PARTITION FUNCTION HitDateRange (datetime)
AS RANGE LEFT FOR VALUES ('1/1/2003', '1/1/2004', '1/1/2005')
GO
```

After creating the partition function, the partition scheme is created in order to bind the partition function to the new filegroups:

```
CREATE PARTITION SCHEME HitDateRangeScheme
AS PARTITION HitDateRange
TO ( hitfg1, hitfg2, hitfg3, hitfg4 )
```

Lastly, a table is created that uses the partition scheme on the HitDate column in the ON clause of the CREATE TABLE statement:

```
CREATE TABLE Sales.WebSiteHits
(WebSiteHitID bigint NOT NULL IDENTITY(1,1),
 WebSitePage varchar(255) NOT NULL,
 HitDate datetime NOT NULL,
 CONSTRAINT PK_WebSiteHits
 PRIMARY KEY (WebSiteHitID, HitDate))
ON [HitDateRangeScheme] (HitDate)
```

How It Works

In the first part of the recipe, four new filegroups were added to the AdventureWorks database. After that, a database file was added to each filegroup.

Next, a partition function was created which defined the partition boundaries for the partition function and the expected partition column data type. On the first line of the CREATE PARTITION FUNCTION command, the datetime data type was selected:

```
CREATE PARTITION FUNCTION HitDateRange (datetime)
```

The next line defined the ranges for values for the partition function, creating partitions by year:

```
AS RANGE LEFT FOR VALUES ('1/1/2003', '1/1/2004', '1/1/2005')
```

You can define up to 999 partitions (however, that many isn't recommended due to potential performance concerns). The number of values you choose amounts to a total of n + 1 partitions. You also have a choice of LEFT or RIGHT, which defines the boundary that the defined values belong to. In this recipe, LEFT was chosen. Table 4-17 shows the partition boundaries (or partitions where rows will be placed) in this case.

Table 4-17. *LEFT Boundaries*

Partition #	Lower bound datetime	Upper bound datetime
1	Lowest allowed datetime	1/1/2003 00:00:00
2	1/1/2003 00:00:01	1/1/2004 00:00:00
3	1/1/2004 00:00:01	1/1/2005 00:00:00
4	1/1/2005 00:00:01	Highest allowed datetime

Had RIGHT been chosen instead, the partition boundaries would have been as shown in Table 4-18.

Table 4-18. *RIGHT Boundaries*

Partition #	Lower bound date	Upper bound date
1	Lowest allowed datetime	12/31/2002 12:59:59
2	1/1/2003 00:00:00	12/31/2003 12:59:59
3	1/1/2004 00:00:00	12/31/2004 12:59:59
4	1/1/2005 00:00:00	Highest allowed datetime

Once a partition function is created, it can be used with one or more partition schemes. A partition scheme maps the partitions defined in a partition function to actual filegroups. The first line of the new partition scheme defined the partition scheme name:

```
CREATE PARTITION SCHEME HitDateRangeScheme
```

The second line of code defined the partition function of the partition scheme it is bound to (the function created in the previous step):

```
AS PARTITION HitDateRange
```

The TO clause defines which filegroups map to the four partitions defined in the partition function, in order of partition sequence:

```
TO ( hitfg1, hitfg2, hitfg3, hitfg4 )
```

After a partition scheme is created, it can then be bound to a table. In the CREATE TABLE statement's ON clause (last row of the table definition), the partition scheme is designated with the column to partition in parentheses:

```
CREATE TABLE Sales.WebSiteHits
(WebSiteHitID bigint NOT NULL IDENTITY(1,1),
 WebSitePage varchar(255) NOT NULL,
 HitDate datetime NOT NULL,
 CONSTRAINT PK_WebSiteHits
 PRIMARY KEY (WebSiteHitID, HitDate))
ON [HitDateRangeScheme] (HitDate)
```

Notice that the primary key is made up of both the WebSiteHitID and HitDate. The partitioned key column (HitDate) must be part of the primary key.

The Sales.WebSiteHits table is now partitioned—and can be worked with just like a single regular table. You needn't do anything special to your SELECT, INSERT, UPDATE, or DELETE statements. In the background, as data is added, rows are inserted into the appropriate filegroups based on the partition function and scheme.

Determining the Location of Data in a Partition

Because partitioning happens in the background, you don't actually query the individual partitions directly. In order to determine which partition the data belongs to, you can use the $PARTITION function.

The syntax for $PARTITION is as follows:

```
$PARTITION.partition_function_name(expression)
```

Table 4-19 details the arguments of this command.

Table 4-19. *$PARTITION Function Arguments*

Argument	Description
partition_function_name	The name of the partition function used to partition the table.
expression	The column used as the partitioning key.

This example demonstrates how to use this function. To begin with, four rows are inserted into the Sales.WebSiteHits partitioned table:

```
INSERT Sales.WebSiteHits
(WebSitePage, HitDate)
VALUES ('Home Page', '10/22/2004')
```

```
INSERT Sales.WebSiteHits
(WebSitePage, HitDate)
VALUES ('Home Page', '10/2/2001')

INSERT Sales.WebSiteHits
(WebSitePage, HitDate)
VALUES ('Sales Page', '5/9/2005')

INSERT Sales.WebSiteHits
(WebSitePage, HitDate)
VALUES ('Sales Page', '3/4/2003')
```

The table is then queried using SELECT and the $PARTITION function:

```
SELECT  HitDate,
    $PARTITION.HitDateRange (HitDate) Partition
FROM  Sales.WebSiteHits
```

This returns:

HitDate	Partition
2001-10-02 00:00:00.000	1
2003-03-04 00:00:00.000	2
2004-10-22 00:00:00.000	3
2005-05-09 00:00:00.000	4

How It Works

The recipe starts out by inserting four rows into the partitioned Sales.WebSiteHits table. Each insert is for a row with a different HitDate year (in order to demonstrate the function).

Next, a query is executed against the table using the $PARTITION function:

```
SELECT  HitDate,
    $PARTITION.HitDateRange (HitDate) Partition
FROM  Sales.WebSiteHits
```

The partition_function_name is the name of the function created in the last recipe. The expression in parentheses is the HitDate, which is the column used to partition the data.
The $PARTITION function evaluates each HitDate and determines what partition it is stored in based on the partition function. This allows you to see how data is distributed across the different partitions. If one partition is uneven with the rest, you can explore creating or removing existing partitions—both functions of which are demonstrated next.

Adding a New Partition

Over time you may decide that your partitioned table needs additional partitions (for example, you can create a new partition for each new year). To add a new partition, the ALTER PARTITION SCHEME and ALTER PARTITION FUNCTION commands are used.

Before a new partition can be created on an existing partition function, you must first prepare a filegroup for use in holding the new partition data (a new or already used filegroup can be used). The first step is designating the next partition filegroup to use with ALTER PARTITION SCHEME.

The syntax for ALTER PARTITION SCHEME is as follows:

```
ALTER PARTITION SCHEME partition_scheme_name
NEXT USED [ filegroup_name ]
```

Table 4-20 details the arguments of this command.

Table 4-20. *ALTER PARTITION SCHEME Arguments*

Argument	Description
partition_scheme_name	The name of the partition scheme to modify.
NEXT USED [filegroup_name]	The NEXT USED keywords queues the next filegroup to be used by any new partition.

After adding a reference to the next filegroup, ALTER PARTITION FUNCTION is used to create (split) the new partition (and also remove/merge a partition). The syntax for ALTER PARTITION FUNCTION is as follows:

```
ALTER PARTITION FUNCTION partition_function_name()
{
    SPLIT RANGE ( boundary_value )
  | MERGE RANGE ( boundary_value )
}
```

Table 4-21 details the arguments of this command.

Table 4-21. *ALTER PARTITION FUNCTION Arguments*

Argument	Description
partition_function_name	The name of the partition function to add or remove a partition from.
SPLIT RANGE (boundary_value) | MERGE RANGE (boundary_value)	SPLIT RANGE is used to create a new partition by defining a new boundary value. MERGE RANGE is used to remove an existing partition.

This example demonstrates how to create (split) a new partition. The first step is creating a new filegroup to be used by the new partition. In this example, the PRIMARY filegroup is used:

```
ALTER PARTITION SCHEME HitDateRangeScheme
NEXT USED [PRIMARY]
```

Next, the partition function is modified to create a new partition, defining a boundary of January 1, 2006:

```
ALTER PARTITION FUNCTION HitDateRange ()
SPLIT RANGE ('1/1/2006')
```

After the new partition is created, a new row is inserted to test the new partition:

```
INSERT Sales.WebSiteHits
(WebSitePage, HitDate)
VALUES ('Sales Page', '3/4/2006')
```

The table is queried using $PARTITION:

```
SELECT  HitDate,
$PARTITION.HitDateRange (HitDate) Partition
FROM  Sales.WebSiteHits
```

This shows the newly inserted row has been stored in the new partition (partition number 5):

```
HitDate                 Partition
----------------------- -----------
2001-10-02 00:00:00.000 1
2003-03-04 00:00:00.000 2
2004-10-22 00:00:00.000 3
2005-05-09 00:00:00.000 4
2006-03-04 00:00:00.000 5

(5 row(s) affected)
```

How It Works

In this recipe's example, the HitDateRangeScheme was altered using ALTER PARTITION SCHEME and the NEXT USED keywords. The NEXT USED keywords queue the next filegroup to be used by any new partition. The default PRIMARY filegroup was selected as the destination for the new partition:

```
ALTER PARTITION SCHEME HitDateRangeScheme
NEXT USED [PRIMARY]
```

ALTER PARTITION FUNCTION was then used with SPLIT RANGE in order to add a new partition boundary:

```
ALTER PARTITION FUNCTION HitDateRange ()
SPLIT RANGE ('1/1/2006')
```

Only one value was used to add the new partition, which essentially splits an existing partition range into two, using the original boundary type (LEFT or RIGHT). You can only use SPLIT RANGE for a single split at a time—and you can't add multiple partitions in a statement.

This example's split added a new partition, partition #5, as shown in Table 4-22.

Table 4-22. *New Partition Layout*

Partition #	Lower bound datetime	Upper bound datetime
1	Lowest allowed datetime	1/1/2003 00:00:00
2	1/1/2003 00:00:01	1/1/2004 00:00:00
3	1/1/2004 00:00:01	1/1/2005 00:00:00
4	1/1/2005 00:00:01	1/1/2006 00:00:00
5	1/1/2006 00:00:01	Highest allowed datetime

A new row was inserted into the Sales.WebSiteHits table, which used the partition function. A query was executed to view the partitions that each row belongs in, and it is confirmed that the new row was inserted into the fifth partition.

Removing a Partition

The previous recipe showed the syntax for ALTER PARTITION FUNCTION, including a description of the MERGE RANGE functionality which is used to remove an existing partition. Removing a partition essentially merges two partitions into one, with rows relocating to the resulting merged partition.

This example demonstrates removing the '1/1/2004' partition from the HitDateRange partition function:

```
ALTER PARTITION FUNCTION HitDateRange ()
MERGE RANGE ('1/1/2004')
```

Next, the partitioned table is queried using the $PARTITION function:

```
SELECT   HitDate,
    $PARTITION.HitDateRange (HitDate) Partition
FROM  Sales.WebSiteHits
```

This returns the following results:

```
HitDate                 Partition
----------------------- -----------
2001-10-02 00:00:00.000 1
2004-10-22 00:00:00.000 2
2003-03-04 00:00:00.000 2
2005-05-09 00:00:00.000 3
2006-03-04 00:00:00.000 4

(5 row(s) affected)
```

How It Works

ALTER PARTITION FUNCTION is used for both splitting and merging partitions. In this case, the MERGE RANGE keywords were used to eliminate the '1/1/2004' partition boundary:

```
ALTER PARTITION FUNCTION HitDateRange ()
MERGE RANGE ('1/1/2004')
```

A query was executed to view which rows belong to which partitions. After the MERGE, the boundaries became the following as shown in Table 4-23.

Table 4-23. *New Partition Layout*

Partition #	Lower bound datetime	Upper bound datetime
1	Lowest allowed datetime	1/1/2003 00:00:00
2	1/1/2003 00:00:01	1/1/2005 00:00:00
3	1/1/2005 00:00:01	1/1/2006 00:00:00
4	1/1/2006 00:00:01	Highest allowed datetime

Partition #2 now encompasses the data for two years instead of one.

You can only merge one partition per ALTER PARTITION FUNCTION execution, and you can't convert a partitioned table into a non-partitioned table using ALTER PARTITION FUNCTION—you can only reduce the number of partitions down to a single partition.

Moving a Partition to a Different Table

With SQL Server 2005's new partitioning functionality, you can now transfer partitions between different tables with a minimum of effort or overhead. You can transfer partitions between tables using ALTER TABLE... SWITCH. Transfers can take place in three different ways: switching a partition from a partitioned table to another partitioned table (both needing to be partitioned on the same column), transferring an entire table from a non-partitioned table to a partitioned table, or moving a partition from a partitioned table to a non-partitioned table.

The basic syntax for switching partitions between tables is as follows:

```
ALTER TABLE tablename
SWITCH [ PARTITION source_partition_number_expression ]
TO [ schema_name. ] target_table
[ PARTITION target_partition_number_expression ]
```

Table 4-24 details the arguments of this command.

Table 4-24. *ALTER TABLE...SWITCH Arguments*

Argument	Description
tablename	The source table to move the partition from.
source_partition_number_expression	The partition number being relocated.
[schema_name.] target_table	The target table to receive the partition.
partition.target_partition_number_expression	The destination partition number.

This example demonstrates moving a partition between Sales.WebSiteHits and a new table called Sales.WebSiteHitsHistory. In the first step, a new table is created to hold historical website hit information:

```
CREATE TABLE Sales.WebSiteHitsHistory
(WebSiteHitID bigint NOT NULL IDENTITY(1,1),
 WebSitePage varchar(255) NOT NULL,
 HitDate datetime NOT NULL,
 CONSTRAINT PK_WebSiteHitsHistory
 PRIMARY KEY (WebSiteHitID, HitDate))
ON [HitDateRangeScheme] (HitDate)
```

Next, ALTER TABLE is used to move partition 3 from Sales.WebSiteHits to partition 3 of the new Sales.WebSiteHitsHistory table:

```
ALTER TABLE Sales.WebSiteHits SWITCH PARTITION 3
TO Sales.WebSiteHitsHistory PARTITION 3
```

Next, a query is executed using $PARTITION to view the transferred data in the new table:

```
SELECT   HitDate,
$PARTITION.HitDateRange (HitDate) Partition
FROM   Sales.WebSiteHitsHistory
```

This returns:

```
HitDate                 Partition
----------------------- -----------
2005-05-09 00:00:00.000 3
```

How It Works

The first part of the recipe created a new table called Sales.WebSiteHitsHistory and used the same partition scheme as the Sales.WebSiteHits table.

The source table and partition number to transfer was referenced in the first line of the ALTER TABLE command:

```
ALTER TABLE Sales.WebSiteHits SWITCH PARTITION 3
```

The TO keyword designated the destination table and partition to move the data to:

```
TO Sales.WebSiteHitsHistory PARTITION 3
```

Moving partitions between tables is much faster then performing a manual row operation (INSERT..SELECT, for example) because you aren't actually moving physical data. Instead you are only changing the metadata regarding where the partition is currently stored.

Also, keep in mind that the target partition of any existing table needs to be empty for the destination partition. If it is a non-partitioned table, it must also be empty.

Removing Partition Functions and Schemes

If you try to drop a partition function or scheme while it is still bound to an existing table or index, you'll get an error message. You also can't directly remove a partition scheme or function while it is bound to a table (unless you drop the entire table as will be done in this recipe). If you had originally created the table as a heap (a table without a clustered index), and then created a clustered index bound to a partition scheme, you can use the CREATE INDEX DROP_EXISTING option (see Chapter 5) to rebuild the index without the partition scheme reference.

Dropping a partition scheme uses the following syntax:

```
DROP PARTITION SCHEME partition_scheme_name
```

This command takes the name of the partition scheme to drop.

Dropping a partition function uses the following syntax:

```
DROP PARTITION FUNCTION partition_function_name
```

Again, this command only takes the partition function name that should be dropped.

This example demonstrates how to drop a partition function and scheme, assuming that it is okay in this scenario to drop the source tables (which often times in a production scenario will *not* be acceptable!):

```
DROP TABLE Sales.WebSiteHitsHistory
DROP TABLE Sales.WebSiteHits

-- Dropping the partition scheme and function
DROP PARTITION SCHEME HitDateRangeScheme
DROP PARTITION FUNCTION HitDateRange
```

How It Works

This example demonstrated dropping a partition scheme and function, which required for this example that the source tables be dropped beforehand.

One alternative solution was to copy out the results to an external table, drop the tables, drop the partition scheme and partition function, and then rename the tables that you copied the data to. If your goal is just to get the table down to a single partition, you can merge all partitions, while still keeping the partition scheme and function. A single partitioned table is functionally equivalent to a regular, non-partitioned table.

Placing a Table on a Filegroup

Filegroups are often used for very large databases (VLDB),because they can ease backup administration and potentially improve performance by distributing data over multiple arrays. When creating a table, you can specify that it be created on a specific filegroup. For example if you have a table that you know will become very large, you can designate that it be created on a specific filegroup.

■Note This recipe includes some filegroup techniques and concepts covered in more detail in Chapter 22.

The basic syntax for designating a table's filegroup is as follows:

```
CREATE TABLE ...
    [ ON filegroup
        | " DEFAULT " } ]
    [ { TEXTIMAGE_ON { filegroup | " DEFAULT " } ]
```

Table 4-25 details the arguments of this command.

Table 4-25. *Arguments for Creating a Table on a Filegroup*

Argument	Description
filegroup	The name of the filegroup on which the table will be created.
"DEFAULT"	This sets the table to be created on the default filegroup defined for the database.
TEXTIMAGE_ON { filegroup | "DEFAULT" }	This option stores in a separate filegroup the data from text, ntext, image, xml, varchar(max), nvarchar(max), varbinary(max) data types.

This example demonstrates how to place a table on a non-default, user created filegroup. The first step involves creating a new filegroup in the AdventureWorks database (see Chapter 22 for more information on this):

```
ALTER DATABASE AdventureWorks
ADD FILEGROUP AW_FG2
GO
```

Next, a new file is added to the filegroup:

```
ALTER DATABASE AdventureWorks
ADD FILE
(    NAME = AW_F2,
     FILENAME = 'c:\Program Files\Microsoft SQL Server\MSSQL.1\MSSQL\Data\aw_f2.ndf',
     SIZE = 1MB
)
TO FILEGROUP AW_FG2
GO
```

A table is then created on the new filegroup (and hence its data will be stored in the new file, contained within the filegroup):

```
CREATE TABLE HumanResources.AWCompany(
    AWCompanyID int IDENTITY(1,1) NOT NULL PRIMARY KEY,
    ParentAWCompanyID int NULL,
    AWCompanyNM varchar(25) NOT NULL,
    CreateDT datetime NOT NULL DEFAULT (getdate())
) ON AW_FG2
```

In the second example, a table is created by specifying that large object data columns be stored on a separate filegroup (AW_FG2) from the regular data (on the PRIMARY filegroup):

```
CREATE TABLE HumanResources.EWCompany(
    EWCompanyID int IDENTITY(1,1) NOT NULL PRIMARY KEY,
    ParentEWCompanyID int NULL,
    EWCompanyName varchar(25) NOT NULL,
    HeadQuartersImage varbinary(max) NULL,
    CreateDT datetime NOT NULL DEFAULT (getdate())
) ON [PRIMARY]
TEXTIMAGE_ON AW_FG2
```

How It Works

The recipe starts by creating a new filegroup called AW_FG2. This is done using the ALTER DATABASE command. After that, a new database file was added to the AdventureWorks database, which was placed into the new filegroup.

CREATE TABLE was then executed normally, only in the last part of the table definition, ON AW_FG2 is used in order to place it into the AW_FG2 filegroup:

```
ON AW_FG2
```

If an ON filegroup clause isn't used in a CREATE TABLE, it's assumed that the table will be placed on the default filegroup (which if you haven't changed it, is called PRIMARY).

If this table becomes very large, and you've placed it on its own filegroup, a filegroup backup can be used to specifically back up the table and any other tables or indexes that are placed in it (see Chapter 5 for more on placing an index into a filegroup and Chapter 29 for a review of filegroup backups).

For the second example, a table was created with filegroup options placing regular data on the PRIMARY filegroup, and text/image data on the AW_FG2 filegroup (doing so requires that your table actually *have* a large value data type):

```
ON [PRIMARY]
TEXTIMAGE_ON AW_FG2
```

Separating out large object data may ease database maintenance and improve performance depending on your database design and physical hardware, the types of queries accessing it, and the location of the file(s) in the filegroup.

Indexes

Indexes assist with query processing by speeding up access to the data stored in tables and views. Indexes allow for ordered access to data based on an ordering of data rows. These rows are ordered based upon the values stored in certain columns. These columns comprise the "index key columns" and their values (for any given row) are a row's "index key."

This chapter contains recipes for creating, altering, and dropping different types of indexes. SQL Server 2005 has introduced several new changes to how indexes can be created, including a new syntax for index options, support for partition schemes, the INCLUDE command, page and row lock disabling, index disabling, and the ability to perform online operations. For exercises performed in this chapter, you may wish to back up the AdventureWorks database beforehand, so that you can restore it to its original state after going through the recipes.

■Note For coverage of index maintenance, re-indexing, and rebuilding (ALTER INDEX), see Chapter 23. Indexed views are covered in Chapter 7. For coverage of index performance troubleshooting and fragmentation, see Chapter 31.

Indexes Overview

An index is a database object that, when created on a table, can provide faster access paths to data and can facilitate faster query execution. Indexes are used to provide SQL Server with a more efficient method of accessing the data. Instead of always searching every data page in a table, an index facilitates retrieving specific rows without having to read a table's entire content.

By default, rows in a regular un-indexed table aren't stored in any particular order. A table in an order-less state is called a *heap*. In order to retrieve rows from a heap based on a matching set of search conditions, SQL Server would have to read through all the rows in the table. Even if only one row matched the search criteria and that row just happened to be the first row the SQL Server database engine read, SQL Server would still need to evaluate every single table row, since there is no other way for it to know if other matching rows exist. Such a scan for information is known as a *full* table scan. For a large table, that might mean reading hundreds or thousands or millions and billions of rows just to retrieve a single row.

However, if SQL Server knows that there is an index on a column (or columns) of a table, then it may be able to use that index to search for matching records more efficiently.

In SQL Server 2005, a table is contained in one or more *partitions*. A partition is a user-defined unit of organization which allows you to horizontally partition data within a table and/or index, while still maintaining a single logical object. When a table is created, by default, all of its data is contained within a single partition. A partition contains heaps, or, when indexes are created, *B-tree structures*.

When an index is created, its index key data is stored in a B-tree structure. A B-tree structure starts with a root node which is the beginning of the index. This *root node* has index data which contains a range of index key values that point to the next level of index nodes, called the *intermediate leaf level*.

The bottom level of the node is called the *leaf level*. The leaf level differs based on whether the actual index type is *clustered* or *nonclustered*. If it is a clustered index, the leaf level is the actual data pages itself. If a nonclustered index, the leaf level contains pointers to the heap or clustered index data pages.

A clustered index determines how the actual table data is physically stored. You can only designate *one* clustered index. This index type stores the data according to the designated index key column or columns. Figure 5-1 demonstrates the B-tree structure of the clustered index. Notice that the leaf level is the actual data pages itself.

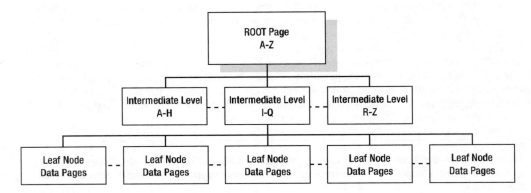

Figure 5-1. *B-tree structure of a clustered index*

Clustered index selection is a critical choice, as you can only have one clustered index for a single table. In general, good candidates for clustered indexes include columns that are queried often in range queries because the data is then physically organized in a particular order. Range queries use the BETWEEN keyword and the greater than > and less than < operators. Other columns to consider are those used to order large result sets, those used in aggregate functions, and those that contain entirely unique values. Frequently updated columns and non-unique columns are usually *not* a good choice for a clustered index key, because the clustered index key is contained in the leaf level of all dependent nonclustered indexes, causing excessive reordering and modifications. For this same reason you should also avoid creating a clustered index with too many or very wide (many bytes) index keys.

Nonclustered indexes store index pages separately from the physical data, with pointers to the physical data located in the index pages and nodes. Nonclustered index columns are stored in the order of the index key column values. You can have up to 249 nonclustered indexes on a table or indexed view. For nonclustered indexes, the leaf node level is the index key coupled to a row locater which points to either the row of a heap or the clustered index row key, as shown in Figure 5-2:

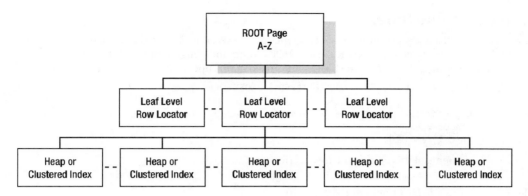

Figure 5-2. *B-tree structure of a nonclustered index*

When selecting columns to be used for nonclustered indexes, look for those columns that are frequently referenced in WHERE, JOIN, and ORDER BY clauses. Search for highly selective columns that would return smaller result sets (less than 20 percent of all rows in a table). Selectivity refers to how many rows exist for each unique index key value. If a column has poor selectivity, for example only containing zeros or ones, it is unlikely that SQL Server will take advantage of that query when creating the query execution plan, because of its poor selectivity.

An index, either clustered or nonclustered, is based on one or more key values. The index key refers to columns used to define the index itself. SQL Server 2005 also has a new feature which allows the addition of non-key columns to the leaf level of the index by using the new INCLUDE clause demonstrated later on in the chapter. This new feature allows more of your query's selected columns to be returned or "covered" by a single nonclustered index, thus reducing total I/O, as SQL Server doesn't have to access the clustered leaf level data pages at all.

You can use up to 16 key columns in a single index, so long as you don't exceed 900 bytes of all index key columns combined. You also can't use large object data types within the index key, including varchar(max), nvarchar(max), varbinary(max), xml, ntext, text, and the image data types.

A clustered or nonclustered index can either be specified as unique or non-unique. Choosing a unique index makes sure that the data values inserted into the key column or columns are unique. For unique indexes using multiple keys (called a **composite** index), the combination of the key values have to be unique for every row in the table.

As noted earlier, indexes can be massively beneficial in terms of your query performance, but there are costs associated with them. You should only add indexes based on expected query activity, and you must continually monitor whether or not indexes are still being used. If not, they should be removed. Too many indexes on a table can cause performance overhead whenever data modifications are performed to the table, as SQL Server must maintain the index changes alongside the data changes.

These next few recipes will demonstrate how to create, modify, disable, view, and drop indexes.

■**Note** See Chapter 28 to learn how to view which indexes are being used for a query. This chapter also covers how to view index fragmentation and identify whether or not an index is being used over time. To learn how to rebuild or reorganize indexes, see Chapter 23.

Create a Table Index

In this recipe, I'll show you how to create two types of indexes, one clustered and the other nonclustered. An index is created by using the CREATE INDEX command. This chapter will review the many facets of this command, however the basic syntax used in this upcoming example is as follows:

```
CREATE [ UNIQUE ] [ CLUSTERED | NONCLUSTERED ] INDEX index_name
    ON {
    [ database_name. [ schema_name ] . | schema_name. ]
        table_or_view_name}
( column [ ASC | DESC ] [ ,...n ] )
```

The arguments of this command are described in Table 5-1:

Table 5-1. *CREATE INDEX Command Arguments*

Argument	Description
[UNIQUE]	You can only have one primary key on each table. However, if you wish to enforce uniqueness in other non-key columns, you can designate that the index be created with the UNIQUE constraint. You can create multiple UNIQUE indexes for a single table and can include columns that contain NULL values (although only one NULL value is allowed per column combo).
[CLUSTERED	NONCLUSTERED]	Specifies the index type, either CLUSTERED or NONCLUSTERED. You can only have one CLUSTERED index, but up to 249 NONCLUSTERED indexes.
index_name	The name of the new index.
[database_name. [schema_name] .	schema_name.] table_or_view_name}	The table or view to be indexed.
column	The column or columns to be used as part of the index key.
[ASC	DESC]	The specific column order of indexing, either ASC for ascending order or DESC for descending order.

I'll also show you a few examples of modifying an existing index using the ALTER INDEX command. This command includes many of the same options of CREATE INDEX, only you cannot use it to change which columns are used and their ordering. This command is also used to rebuild or reorganize an index (which is covered in Chapter 23):

```
ALTER INDEX index_name
ON object_name
...
```

Starting off this example, a new table is created in the AdventureWorks database:

```
CREATE TABLE HumanResources.TerminationReason(
    TerminationReasonID smallint IDENTITY(1,1) NOT NULL,
    TerminationReason varchar(50) NOT NULL,
    DepartmentID smallint NOT NULL,
 CONSTRAINT FK_TerminationReason_DepartmentID
    FOREIGN KEY (DepartmentID) REFERENCES
    HumanResources.Department(DepartmentID)
)
GO
```

Before I demonstrate how to use `CREATE INDEX`, it is important to remember that when a primary key is created on a column using `CREATE TABLE` or `ALTER TABLE`, that primary key also creates an index. In this example, a `CLUSTERED` index is created on the `TerminationReasonID` using `ALTER TABLE`:

```
ALTER TABLE HumanResources.TerminationReason
ADD CONSTRAINT PK_TerminationReason PRIMARY KEY CLUSTERED (TerminationReasonID)
```

Next, a nonclustered index is created on the `DepartmentID` column:

```
CREATE NONCLUSTERED INDEX NCI_TerminationReason_DepartmentID ON
HumanResources.TerminationReason (DepartmentID)
```

How It Works

In this exercise, the `TerminationReason` table was created without a primary key defined, meaning that initially, the table was a "heap."

The primary key was then added afterwards using `ALTER TABLE`. The word `CLUSTERED` follows the `PRIMARY KEY` statement, thus also creating a clustered index with the new constraint:

```
ALTER TABLE HumanResources.TerminationReason
ADD CONSTRAINT PK_TerminationReason PRIMARY KEY CLUSTERED (TerminationReasonID)
```

Had the `TerminationReasonID` column not been chosen as the primary key, you could have still defined a clustered index on it by using `CREATE INDEX`:

```
CREATE CLUSTERED INDEX CI_TerminationReason_TerminationReasonID ON
HumanResources.TerminationReason (TerminationReasonID)
```

Had a nonclustered index already existed for the table, the creation of the new clustered index would have caused the nonclustered index to be rebuilt, in order to swap the nonclustered leaf level row identifier with the clustered key.

The nonclustered index in the example was created as follows:

```
CREATE NONCLUSTERED INDEX NCI_TerminationReason_DepartmentID ON
HumanResources.TerminationReason (DepartmentID)
```

The only difference in syntax between the two index types was that the word `NONCLUSTERED` is designated between `CREATE` and `INDEX`.

Enforce Uniqueness on Non-Key Columns

In this recipe, I'll show you how to enforce uniqueness for non-key table columns. The syntax for `CREATE INDEX` in the previous recipe showed the `UNIQUE` keyword. This example shows you how to create a unique index on the `HumanResources.TerminationReason` table `TerminationReason` column:

```
CREATE UNIQUE NONCLUSTERED INDEX UNI_TerminationReason ON
HumanResources.TerminationReason (TerminationReason)
```

Now, two new rows are inserted into the table with success:

```
INSERT HumanResources.TerminationReason
(DepartmentID, TerminationReason)
VALUES (1, 'Bad Engineering Skills')

INSERT HumanResources.TerminationReason
(DepartmentID, TerminationReason)
VALUES (2, 'Breaks Expensive Tools')
```

Attempting to insert a row with a duplicate, already existing `TerminationReason` value, raises an error:

```
INSERT HumanResources.TerminationReason
(DepartmentID, TerminationReason)
VALUES (2, 'Bad Engineering Skills')
```

This returns:

```
Msg 2601, Level 14, State 1, Line 9
Cannot insert duplicate key row in object 'HumanResources.TerminationReason'
with unique index 'UNI_TerminationReason'.
The statement has been terminated.
```

Selecting the current rows from the table shows that only the first two rows were inserted:

```
SELECT TerminationReasonID, TerminationReason, DepartmentID
FROM HumanResources.TerminationReason
```

This returns:

```
TerminationReasonID TerminationReason                                   DepartmentID
------------------- --------------------------------------------------- ------------
1                   Bad Engineering Skills                              1
2                   Breaks Expensive Tools                              2
```

How It Works

A unique index was created on the TerminationReason column, which means that each row must have a unique value. You can choose multiple unique constraints for a single table. NULL values are permitted in a unique index; however, they must only occur once. Like a primary key, unique indexes enforce entity integrity by ensuring that rows can be uniquely identified.

Create a Composite Index

In this recipe, I'll show you how to create a multiple-column index. In previous recipes, I've shown you how to create an index on a single column, however many times you will want more than one column to be used in a single index. Use composite indexes when two or more columns are often searched within the same query, or are often used in conjunction with one another.

In this example, we're assuming that TerminationReason and the DepartmentID will often be used in the same WHERE clause of a SELECT query. With that in mind, the following NONCLUSTERED INDEX is created:

```
CREATE NONCLUSTERED INDEX NI_TerminationReason_TerminationReason_DepartmentID
ON HumanResources.TerminationReason(TerminationReason, DepartmentID)
```

How It Works

Choosing which columns to index is a bit of an art. You'll want to add indexes to columns that you'll know will be commonly queried, however you must always keep a column's selectivity in mind. *Selectivity* refers to how many rows exist for each unique index key value. If a column has poor selectivity, for example only containing zeros or ones, it is unlikely that SQL Server will take advantage of that query when creating the query execution plan.

One general rule of thumb when creating a composite index is to put the most selective columns at the beginning, followed by the other less selective columns. In this recipe's example, the TerminationReason was chosen as the first column, followed by the DepartmentID. Both are guaranteed to be totally unique in the table, and therefore are equally selective.

■**Tip** If you're new to SQL Server or need assistance in a poorly performing query, use Database Tuning Advisor to help make index suggestions for you. Also, see Chapter 28 for more information on index usage and performance.

You can use up to 16 columns in a single index, so long as you don't exceed 900 bytes of all index key columns combined. You also can't use large object data types within the index key, including varchar(max), nvarchar(max), varbinary(max), xml, ntext, text, and the image data types.

The index key refers to columns used to define the index itself. SQL Server 2005 *does* however, allow the addition of non-key columns to the leaf level of the index by using the new INCLUDE clause demonstrated later on in the chapter.

Define Index Column Sort Direction

In this recipe, I'll show you how to set the sort direction of an index column. The default sort for an indexed column is ascending order. You can explicitly set the ordering using ASC or DESC in the column definition of CREATE INDEX:

```
( column [ ASC | DESC ] [ ,...n ] )
```

In this example, a new column is added to a table and then indexed in descending order:

```
ALTER TABLE HumanResources.TerminationReason
ADD ViolationSeverityLevel smallint
GO

CREATE NONCLUSTERED INDEX NI_TerminationReason_ViolationSeverityLevel
ON HumanResources.TerminationReason (ViolationSeverityLevel DESC)
```

How It Works

In this recipe's example, a new column ViolationSeverityLevel was added to the TerminationReason table:

```
ALTER TABLE HumanResources.TerminationReason
ADD ViolationSeverityLevel smallint
GO
```

Query authors may want to most commonly sort on this value, showing ViolationSeverityLevel from highest to lowest. Matching index order to how you think users will use ORDER BY in the query can improve query performance, as SQL Server isn't then required to re-sort the data when the query is processed.

The index is created with the DESC instruction after the column name:

```
(ViolationSeverityLevel DESC)
```

If you have multiple key columns in your index, each can have its own separate sort order.

View Index Meta Data

In this recipe, I'll show you how to view helpful information about indexes. Once you've created indexes on your tables, you'll need some mechanism for tracking where they are, what their names are, types, and the columns that define them. For this, use the sp_helpindex system stored procedure to view the index names, descriptions, and keys for indexes on a specific table. This system stored procedure only takes a single argument, the name of the table to view indexes on.

This example demonstrates viewing all indexes on the Employee table:

```
EXEC sp_helpindex 'HumanResources.Employee'
```

This returns the following abridged results:

index_name	index_description	index_keys
AK_Employee_LoginID	nonclustered, unique located on PRIMARY	LoginID
...		
AK_Employee_rowguid	nonclustered, unique located on PRIMARY	rowguid
IX_Employee_ManagerID	nonclustered located on PRIMARY	ManagerID
PK_Employee_EmployeeID	clustered, unique, primary key located on PRIMARY	EmployeeID

For more in-depth index analysis of indexes, you can use the sys.indexes system catalog view. For example the following query shows index options (which will be discussed later in the chapter) for the HumanResources.Employee table:

```
SELECT SUBSTRING(name, 1,30) index_name,
       allow_row_locks,
       allow_page_locks,
       is_disabled,
       fill_factor
FROM sys.indexes
WHERE object_id = OBJECT_ID('HumanResources.Employee')
```

This returns:

index_name	allow_row_locks	allow_page_locks	is_disabled	fill_factor
PK_Employee_EmployeeID	1	1	0	0
AK_Employee_LoginID	1	1	0	0
AK_Employee_NationalIDNumber	1	1	0	0
AK_Employee_rowguid	1	1	0	0
IX_Employee_ManagerID	1	1	0	0

How It Works

You can use the system stored procedure sp_helpindex call to list the indexes on a specific table. The output also returns a description of the indexes, including the type and filegroup location. The key columns defined for the index are also listed.

The sys.indexes system catalog view can also be used to find out more about the configured settings of a specific index. Several of the options shown in this system catalog view haven't been covered yet, but some of them that I've discussed are described in Table 5-2:

Table 5-2. *A Sub-Set of the sys.indexes System Catalog Columns*

Column	Description
object_id	The object identifier of the table or view for which the index belongs. You can use the OBJECT_NAME function to show the table or view name, or OBJECT_ID to convert a table or view name into its database object identifier.
name	The index name.
index_id	When index_id = 0, the index is a heap. When index_id = 1, the index is a clustered index. When index_id > 1, it is a nonclustered index.

Column	Description
type	The index type, which can be 0 for heap, 1 for clustered index, 2 for nonclustered, and 3 for an XML index (see Chapter 14).
type_desc	The index type description.
is_unique	When is_unique = 1, the index is a unique index.
is_primary_key	When is_primary_key = 1, the index is the result of a primary key constraint.
is_unique_constraint	When is_unique_constraint = 1, the index is the result of a unique constraint.

Disable an Index

In this recipe, I'll show you how to disable an index from being used in SQL Server queries. Disabling an index retains the metadata definition data in SQL Server but makes the index unavailable for use. Consider disabling an index as an index troubleshooting technique or if a disk error has occurred and you would like to defer the index's re-creation. If you disable a clustered index, keep in mind that the table index data will no longer be accessible. This is because the leaf level of a clustered index is the actual table data itself.

An index is disabled by using the ALTER INDEX command. The syntax is as follows:

```
ALTER INDEX index_name ON
table_or_view_name DISABLE
```

The command takes two arguments, the name of the index, and the name of the table or view that the index is created on.

In this example, the UNI_TerminationReason index is disabled on the TerminationReason table:

```
ALTER INDEX UNI_TerminationReason ON
HumanResources.TerminationReason DISABLE
```

How It Works

This recipe demonstrated how to disable an index. If an index is disabled, the index definition remains in the system tables, although the user can no longer use the index. For nonclustered indexes on a table, the index data is actually removed from the database. For a clustered index on a table, the data remains on disk, but because the index is disabled, you can't query it. For a clustered or nonclustered index on the view, the index data is removed from the database.

To re-enable the index, you can use either the CREATE INDEX with DROP_EXISTING command (see later in this chapter) or ALTER INDEX REBUILD (described in Chapter 23). Rebuilding a disabled nonclustered index reuses the existing space used by the original index.

Dropping Indexes

In this recipe, I'll show you how to drop an index from a table or view. When you drop an index, it is physically removed from the database. If this is a clustered index, the table's data remains in an unordered (heap) form. You can remove an index entirely from a database by using the DROP INDEX command. The basic syntax is as follows:

```
DROP INDEX <table_or_view_name>.<index_name> [ ,...n ]
```

This example demonstrates dropping a single index from a table:

```
DROP INDEX HumanResources.TerminationReason.UNI_TerminationReason
GO
```

How It Works

You can drop one or more indexes for a table using the DROP INDEX command. Dropping an index frees up the space taken up by the index and removes the index definition from the database. You can't use DROP INDEX to remove indexes that result from the creation of a PRIMARY KEY or UNIQUE CONSTRAINT. If you drop a clustered index that has nonclustered indexes on it, those nonclustered indexes will also be rebuilt in order to swap the clustered index key for a row identifier of the heap.

Change an Existing Index with DROP_EXISTING

In this recipe, I'll show you how to drop and recreate an index within a single execution, as well as change the key column definition of an existing index. The ALTER INDEX can be used to change index options, rebuild and reorganize indexes (reviewed in Chapter 23), and disable an index, but it is not used to actually add, delete, or rearrange columns in the index.

You can, however, change the column definition of an existing index by using CREATE INDEX...DROP_EXISTING. This option also has the advantage of dropping and recreating an index within a single command (instead of using both DROP INDEX and CREATE INDEX). Also, using DROP_EXISTING on a clustered index will not cause existing nonclustered indexes to be automatically rebuilt, unless the index column definition has changed.

This first example demonstrates just rebuilding an existing nonclustered index (no change in the column definition):

```
CREATE NONCLUSTERED INDEX NCI_TerminationReason_DepartmentID ON
HumanResources.TerminationReason
(DepartmentID ASC)
WITH (DROP_EXISTING = ON)
GO
```

Next, a new column is added to the existing nonclustered index:

```
CREATE NONCLUSTERED INDEX NCI_TerminationReason_DepartmentID ON
HumanResources.TerminationReason
(ViolationSeverityLevel, DepartmentID DESC)
WITH (DROP_EXISTING = ON)
GO
```

How It Works

In the first example, the CREATE INDEX didn't change anything about the existing index definition, but instead just rebuilds it by using the DROP_EXISTING clause. Rebuilding an index can help defragment the data, something which is discussed in more detail in Chapter 23.

In the second statement, a new column was added to the existing index, and placed right before the DepartmentID. The index was recreated with the new index key column, making it a composite index.

You can't use DROP_EXISTING to change the name of the index, however. For that, use DROP INDEX and CREATE INDEX with the new index name.

Controlling Index Build Performance and Concurrency

So far in this chapter I've reviewed how an index is defined, but note that you can also determine under what circumstances an index is built. For example, when creating an index in SQL Server 2005, in order to improve the performance, you can designate that a parallel plan of execution is used, instantiating multiple processors to help complete a time-consuming build. In addition to this, you could also direct SQL Server to create the index in tempdb, instead of causing file growth operations in the index's home database.

If you are using SQL Server 2005 Enterprise Edition, you can now also allow concurrent user query access to the underlying table during the index creation by using the new ONLINE option.

The next three recipes will demonstrate methods for improving the performance of the index build, as well as improving user concurrency during the operation.

Intermediate Index Creation in Tempdb

In this recipe, I'll show you how to push index creation processing to the tempdb system database. The tempdb system database is used to manage user connections, temporary tables, temporary stored procedures, or temporary work tables needed to process queries on the SQL Server instance. Depending on the database activity on your SQL Server instance, you can sometimes reap performance benefits by isolating the tempdb database on its own disk array, separate from other databases. If index creation times are taking too long for what you expect, you can try to use the index option SORT_IN_TEMPDB to improve index build performance (for larger tables). This option pushes the intermediate index build results to the tempdb database instead of using the user database where the index is housed.

The syntax for this option, which can be used in both CREATE INDEX and ALTER INDEX, is as follows:

```
WITH (SORT_IN_TEMPDB = { ON | OFF })
```

The default for this option is OFF. In this example, a new nonclustered index is created with this option enabled:

```
CREATE NONCLUSTERED INDEX NI_Address_PostalCode ON
Person.Address (PostalCode)
WITH (SORT_IN_TEMPDB = ON)
```

How It Works

The SORT_IN_TEMPDB option enables the use of tempdb database for intermediate index results. This option may decrease the amount of time it takes to create the index for a large table, but with the trade-off that the tempdb system database will need additional space to participate in this operation.

Controlling Parallel Plan Execution for Index Creation

In this recipe, I'll show you how to control the number of processors used to process a single query. If using SQL Server 2005 Enterprise Edition with a multiprocessor server, you can control/limit the number of processors potentially used in an index creation operation by using the MAXDOP index option. The use of *parallelism*, which is the use of two or more processors to fulfill a single query statement, can potentially improve the performance of the index creation operation.

The syntax for this option, which can be used in both CREATE INDEX and ALTER INDEX, is as follows:

```
MAXDOP = max_degree_of_parallelism
```

The default value for this option is 0, which means that SQL Server can choose any or all of the available processors for the operation. A MAXDOP value of 1 disables parallelism on the index creation.

This example demonstrates how to control the number of processors used in parallel plan execution (parallelism) during an index creation:

```
CREATE NONCLUSTERED INDEX NI_Contact_Phone ON
Person.Contact(Phone)
WITH (MAXDOP = 4)
```

How It Works

In this recipe, the index creation was limited to 4 processors:

```
WITH (MAXDOP = 4)
```

This option overrides the "max degree of parallelism" option discussed in Chapter 21. Just because you set MAXDOP, doesn't make any guarantee that SQL Server will actually *use* the number of processors that you designate. It only ensures that SQL Server will not exceed the MAXDOP threshold.

Allowing User Table Access During Index Creation

In this recipe, I'll show you how to allow query activity to continue to access the index even while an index creation process is executing. If you are using SQL Server 2005 Enterprise Edition, you can allow concurrent user query access to the underlying table during the index creation by using the new ONLINE option, which is demonstrated in this next recipe:

```
CREATE NONCLUSTERED INDEX NCI_ProductVendor_MinOrderQty ON
Purchasing.ProductVendor(MinOrderQty)
WITH (ONLINE = ON)
```

How It Works

With the new ONLINE option in the WITH clause of the index creation, long-term table locks are not held during the index creation. This can provide better concurrency on larger indexes that contain frequently accessed data. When the ONLINE option is set ON, only Intent Share locks are held on the source table for the duration of the index creation, instead of the default behavior of a longer term table lock held for the duration of the index creation.

Index Options

The next three recipes cover options which impact performance, although each in their own different ways.

For example the new INCLUDE keyword allows you to add non-key columns to a nonclustered index. This allows you to create a covering index which can be used to return data to the user without having to access the clustered index data.

The PAD_INDEX and FILLFACTOR options determine how to set the initial percentage of rows to fill the index leaf level pages and intermediate levels of an index. The recipe will discuss how the fill factor impacts not only the performance of queries, but also of insert, update, and delete operations.

The third recipe will cover how to disable certain locking types for a specific index. As will be discussed in the recipe, using these options allows you to control both concurrency and resource usage when queries access the index.

Using an Index INCLUDE

In this recipe, I'll show you how to include non-key columns within a nonclustered index. A *covering query* is a query whose referenced columns are found entirely within a nonclustered index. Often this scenario results in superior query performance, as SQL Server need not retrieve the actual data from the clustered index or heap—it only needs to read the data stored in the non-clustered index. The drawback, however, is that you can only include up to 16 columns or up to 900 bytes for an index key.

One solution to this problem is the newly introduced INCLUDE keyword, which allows you to add up to 1023 *non-key* columns to the nonclustered index, helping you improve query performance by creating a covered index. These non-key columns are not stored at each level of the index, but instead are only found in the leaf level of the nonclustered index.

The syntax for using INCLUDE with CREATE NONCLUSTERED INDEX is as follows:

```
CREATE NONCLUSTERED INDEX index_name
    ON table_or_view_name ( column [ ASC | DESC ] [ ,...n ] )
INCLUDE ( column [ ,... n ] )
```

Whereas the first column list is for key index columns, the column list after INCLUDE is for non-key columns.

In this example, a new large object data type column is added to the TerminationReason table. An existing index on DepartmentID is dropped and recreated, this time adding the new non-key value to the index:

```
ALTER TABLE HumanResources.TerminationReason
ADD LegalDescription varchar(max)

DROP INDEX HumanResources.TerminationReason.NI_TerminationReason_
➥ TerminationReason_DepartmentID

GO

CREATE NONCLUSTERED INDEX NI_TerminationReason_TerminationReason_DepartmentID
ON HumanResources.TerminationReason (TerminationReason, DepartmentID)
INCLUDE (LegalDescription)
```

How It Works

This recipe demonstrated a new SQL Server 2005 technique for enhancing a nonclustered index's usefulness. The example started off by creating a new varchar(max) data type column. Because of its data type, it cannot be used as a key value in the index, however using it within the INCLUDE keyword will allow you to reference the new large object data types. The existing index on the TerminationReason table was then dropped and recreated using INCLUDE with the new non-key column.

You can only use INCLUDE with a nonclustered index (where a covered query comes in handy) and you still can't include the image, ntext, and text data types. Also, if the index size increases too significantly because of the additional non-key values, you may lose some of the query benefits that a covering query can give you, so be sure to test comparative before/after performance.

Using PAD_INDEX and FILLFACTOR

In this recipe, I'll show you how to set the initial percentage of rows to fill the index leaf level pages and intermediate levels of an index. The fill factor percentage of an index refers to how full the leaf level of the index pages should be when the index is first created. The default fill factor, if not explicitly set, is 0, which equates to filling the pages as full as possible (SQL Server does leave *some* space available—enough for a single index row). Leaving some space available, however, allows new rows to be inserted without resorting to page splits. A page split occurs when a new row is added to a full index page. In order to make room, half the rows are moved from the existing full page to a new page. Numerous page splits can slow down INSERT operations. On the other hand, however, fully packed data pages allow for faster read activity, as the database engine can retrieve more rows from less data pages.

The PAD_INDEX option, used only in conjunction with FILLFACTOR, specifies that the specified percentage of free space be left open on the intermediate level pages of an index.

These options are set in the WITH clause of the CREATE INDEX and ALTER INDEX commands. The syntax is as follows:

```
WITH (PAD_INDEX  = { ON | OFF }
  | FILLFACTOR = fillfactor)
```

In this example, an index is dropped and recreated with a 50% fill factor and PAD_INDEX enabled:

```
DROP INDEX
HumanResources.TerminationReason.NI_TerminationReason_TerminationReason_DepartmentID
GO

CREATE NONCLUSTERED INDEX NI_TerminationReason_TerminationReason_DepartmentID
ON HumanResources.TerminationReason
(TerminationReason ASC, DepartmentID ASC)
WITH (FILLFACTOR=50, PAD_INDEX=ON)
```

How It Works

In this recipe, the fill factor was configured to 50%, leaving 50% of the index pages free for new rows. PAD_INDEX was also enabled, so the intermediate index pages will also be left half free. Both options are used in the WITH clause of the CREATE INDEX syntax:

```
WITH (FILLFACTOR=50, PAD_INDEX=ON)
```

Using FILLFACTOR can be a balancing act between reads and writes. For example, a 100% fill factor can improve reads, but slow down write-activity, causing frequent page splitting as the database engine must continually shift row locations in order to make space in the data pages. Having too *low* of a fill factor can benefit row inserts, but it can also slow down read operations, as more data pages must be accessed in order to retrieve all required rows. If you're looking for a general rule of thumb, use a 100% fill factor for tables with almost no data modification activity, 90% for low activity, 70% for medium activity, and 50% or lower for high activity.

Disabling Page and/or Row Index Locking

In this recipe, I'll show you how to change the lock resource types that can be locked for a specific index. In Chapter 3, I discussed various lock types and resources within SQL Server. Specifically, various resources can be locked by SQL Server from small (row and key locks) to medium (page locks, extents) to large (table, database). Multiple, smaller-grained locks help with query concurrency, assuming there are a significant number of queries simultaneously requesting data from the same table and associated indexes. Numerous locks take up memory, however, and can lower performance for the SQL Server instance as a whole. The trade-off is larger-grained locks which increase memory resource availability but also reduce query concurrency.

Now in SQL Server 2005, you can create an index that restricts certain locking types when it is queried. Specifically, you can designate whether page or row locks are allowed.

In general you should allow SQL Server to automatically decide which locking type is best; however, there may be situations where you wish to temporarily restrict certain resource locking types, for troubleshooting, or a severe performance issue.

The syntax for configuring these options for both CREATE INDEX and ALTER INDEX is as follows:

```
WITH ( ALLOW_ROW_LOCKS = { ON | OFF }
  | ALLOW_PAGE_LOCKS = { ON | OFF })
```

This recipe shows you how to disable the database engine's ability to place row or page locks on an index, forcing it to use table locking instead:

```
-- Disable page locks. Table and row locks can still be used.
CREATE INDEX NI_EmployeePayHistory_Rate ON
```

```
HumanResources.EmployeePayHistory (Rate)
WITH (ALLOW_PAGE_LOCKS=OFF)
GO

-- Disable page and row locks. Only table locks can be used.
ALTER INDEX NI_EmployeePayHistory_Rate ON
HumanResources.EmployeePayHistory
SET (ALLOW_PAGE_LOCKS=OFF,ALLOW_ROW_LOCKS=OFF )
GO

-- Allow page and row locks.
ALTER INDEX NI_EmployeePayHistory_Rate ON
HumanResources.EmployeePayHistory
SET (ALLOW_PAGE_LOCKS=ON,ALLOW_ROW_LOCKS=ON )
GO
```

How It Works

This recipe demonstrated three variations. The first query created a new index on the table, configured so that the database engine couldn't issue page locks against the index:

```
WITH (ALLOW_PAGE_LOCKS=OFF)
```

In the next statement, both page and row locks were turned OFF (the default for an index is for both to be set to ON):

```
ALTER INDEX NI_EmployeePayHistory_Rate ON
HumanResources.EmployeePayHistory
SET (ALLOW_PAGE_LOCKS=OFF,ALLOW_ROW_LOCKS=OFF )
```

In the last statement, page and row locking is re-enabled:

```
SET (ALLOW_PAGE_LOCKS=ON,ALLOW_ROW_LOCKS=ON )
```

Removing locking options should only be done if you have a good reason to do so—for example you may have activity that causes too many row locks, which can eat up memory resources. Instead of row locks, you may wish to have SQL Server use larger grained page or table locks instead.

Managing Very Large Indexes

The last two recipes for this chapter cover methods for managing very large indexes. For example, you can designate that an index is created on a separate filegroup. Doing so can provide benefits from both the manageability and performance sides, as you can then perform separate backups by filegroup, as well as improving I/O performance of a query if the filegroup has files that exist on a separate array.

As was initially reviewed in Chapter 4, you can also implement index partitioning. Partitioning allows you to break down the index data set into smaller subsets of data. As will be discussed in the recipe, if large indexes are separated onto separate partitions, this can positively impact the performance of a query (particularly for very large indexes).

Creating an Index on a Filegroup

In this recipe, I'll show you how to create an index on a specific filegroup. If not explicitly designated, an index is created on the same filegroup as the underlying table. This is accomplished using the ON clause of the CREATE INDEX command:

```
ON  filegroup_name    | default
```

This option can take an explicit filegroup name, or the database default filegroup (for more information on filegroups, see Chapter 22).

This example demonstrates how to explicitly define which filegroup an index is stored on. First, a new filegroup is added to the database:

```
ALTER DATABASE AdventureWorks
ADD FILEGROUP FG2
GO
```

Next, a new file is added to the database and the newly created filegroup:

```
ALTER DATABASE AdventureWorks
ADD FILE
(   NAME = AW2,
    FILENAME = 'c:\Program Files\Microsoft SQL Server\MSSQL.1\MSSQL\Data\aw2.ndf',
    SIZE = 1MB
)
TO FILEGROUP FG2
GO
```

A new index is then created, designating that it be stored on the newly created filegroup:

```
CREATE INDEX NI_ProductPhoto_ThumnailPhotoFileName ON
Production.ProductPhoto (ThumbnailPhotoFileName)
ON [FG2]
```

How It Works

The first part of the recipe creates a new filegroup in the AdventureWorks database called FG2 using the ALTER DATABASE command. After that a new database data file is created on the new filegroup. Lastly, a new index is created on the FG2 filegroup. The ON clause designated the filegroup name for the index in square brackets:

```
ON [FG2]
```

Filegroups can be used to help manage very large databases, both by allowing separate backups by filegroup, as well as improving I/O performance if the filegroup has files that exist on a separate array.

Implementing Index Partitioning

In this recipe, I'll show you how to apply partitioning to a nonclustered index. In Chapter 4, I demonstrated table partitioning. Partitioning can provide manageability, scalability, and performance benefits for large tables. This is because partitioning allows you to break down the data set into smaller subsets of data. Depending on the index key(s), an index on a table can also be quite large. Applying the partitioning concept to indexes, if large indexes are separated onto separate partitions, this can positively impact the performance of a query. Queries that target data from just one partition will benefit because SQL Server will target just the selected partition, instead of accessing all partitions for the index.

This recipe will now demonstrate index partitioning using the HitDateRangeScheme partition scheme that was created in Chapter 4 on the Sales.WebSiteHits table:

```
CREATE NONCLUSTERED INDEX NI_WebSiteHits_WebSitePage ON
Sales.WebSiteHits (WebSitePage)
ON [HitDateRangeScheme] (HitDate)
```

How It Works

The partition scheme is applied using the ON clause.

```
ON [HitDateRangeScheme] (HitDate)
```

Notice that although the HitDate column wasn't a nonclustered index key, it was included in the partition scheme, matching that of the table. When the index and table use the same partition scheme, they are said to be "aligned."

You can choose to use a different partitioning scheme for the index than the table; however that scheme must use the same data type argument, number of partitions, and boundary values. Unaligned indexes can be used to take advantage of collocated joins—meaning if you have two columns from two tables that are frequently joined that also use the same partition function, same data type, number of partitions and boundaries, you can potentially improve query join performance. However, the common approach will most probably be to use aligned partition schemes between the index and table, for administration and performance reasons.

■ ■ ■

Full-Text Search

Full-text search functionality allows you to issue intelligent word—and phrase—searches against character and binary data, using full-text enabled operators, which can perform significantly better than a regular LIKE operator search. In this chapter, I'll present recipes that teach you how to enable full-text search capabilities in your database using Transact-SQL.

■Note In SQL Server 2005, Microsoft deprecated several of the full-text system stored procedures in favor of more consistent Transact-SQL CREATE/ALTER/DROP commands. Deprecated procedures include: sp_fulltext_catalog, sp_fulltext_column, sp_fulltext_database, sp_fulltext_table, sp_help_fulltext_catalogs, sp_help_fulltext_catalogs_cursor, sp_help_fulltext_columns, sp_help_fulltext_tables, and sp_help_fulltext_table_cursor.

Full-Text Indexes and Catalogs

Full-text indexes allow you to search against unstructured textual data using more sophisticated functions and a higher level of performance than using just the LIKE operator. Unlike regular B-tree clustered or nonclustered indexes, full-text indexes are compressed index structures that are comprised of *tokens* from the indexed textual data. Tokens are words or character strings that SQL Server has identified in the indexing process. Using special full-text functions, you can extend word or phrase searches beyond the character pattern, and search based on inflection, synonyms, wildcards, and proximity to other words.

Full-text catalogs are used to contain zero or more full-text indexes, and are stored on the local hard drive of the SQL Server instance server. A full-text catalog can contain full-text indexes that index one or more tables in a single database.

SQL Server 2005 has two internal components that are used to generate and process the full-text functionality. The Microsoft Full-Text Engine for SQL Server (MSFTESQL) is used to populate the full-text indexes and catalogs and facilitate full-text searches against the database tables. The Microsoft Full-Text Engine Filter Daemon (MSFTEFD) is used to extract textual information from the document, removing non-textual data and retaining meaningful words and phrases.

SQL Server 2005 introduces a number of new Transact-SQL commands used to create, modify, and remove full-text catalog and full-text index objects. System-stored procedures used in previous versions of SQL Server have been deprecated in place of these new commands. Also new in SQL Server 2005, full-text catalogs are now backed up along with regular database backups, and thus can be restored with a database RESTORE command as well.

Creating a Full-Text Catalog

In its simplest form, you can create a new catalog just by defining its name. There are other options however, and the extended syntax for CREATE FULLTEXT CATALOG is as follows:

```
CREATE FULLTEXT CATALOG catalog_name
     [ON FILEGROUP 'filegroup']
     [IN PATH 'rootpath']
     [WITH ACCENT_SENSITIVITY = {ON|OFF}]
     [AS DEFAULT]
     [AUTHORIZATION owner_name ]
```

The arguments of this command are described in Table 6-1.

Table 6-1. *CREATE FULLTEXT CATALOG Arguments*

Argument	Description
catalog_name	The name of the new full-text catalog.
filegroup	Designates that the catalog will be placed on a specific filegroup. If this isn't designated, the default filegroup for the database is used.
rootpath	Allows you to specify a non-default root directory for the catalog. For example in this recipe, the new catalog will be created by default on the local C:\Program Files\Microsoft SQL Server\MSSQL.1\MSSQL\FTData\cat_Production_Document directory.
ACCENT_SENSITIVITY = {ON|OFF}	This option allows you to choose whether the indexes will be created within the catalog as accent sensitive or accent insensitive. Accent sensitivity defines whether or not SQL Server will distinguish between accented and unaccented characters.
AS DEFAULT	This option sets the catalog as the default catalog for all full-text indexes which are created in the database without explicitly defining an owning full-text catalog.
owner_name	The AUTHORIZATION option determines the owner of the new full-text catalog, allowing you to choose either a database user or a role.

In this first example, a new full-text catalog is created in the AdventureWorks database (note that a full-text catalog only belongs to a *single* database):

```
USE AdventureWorks
GO
CREATE FULLTEXT CATALOG cat_Production_Document
```

In the second example, a new full-text catalog is created designating a non-default file path, and with accent sensitivity enabled:

```
USE AdventureWorks
GO
CREATE FULLTEXT CATALOG cat_Production_Document_EX2
IN PATH 'C:\Apress\Recipes\FTC'
WITH ACCENT_SENSITIVITY = ON
```

How It Works

In this recipe, I demonstrated how to create a new full-text catalog using the CREATE FULLTEXT CATALOG command. This command creates related files on the local server of the SQL Server instance. Once it's created, you'll see a new folder created with the name of the new full-text catalog. This folder will contain a subfolder and system files, none of which should be opened or modified outside of SQL Server.

Once a full-text catalog is created, you can then proceed with full-text indexes, which are reviewed in the next recipe.

Creating a Full-Text Index

In this recipe, I'll demonstrate how to create a full-text index on columns in a table, so that you can then take advantage of the more sophisticated search capabilities shown later on in the chapter.

The command for creating a full-text index is CREATE FULLTEXT INDEX. The syntax is as follows:

```
CREATE FULLTEXT INDEX ON table_name
[(column_name [TYPE COLUMN type_column_name]
[LANGUAGE language_term] [,...n])]
KEY INDEX index_name
[ON fulltext_catalog_name]
[WITH
{CHANGE_TRACKING {MANUAL | AUTO | OFF [, NO POPULATION]}}
]
```

The arguments of this command are described in Table 6-2.

Table 6-2. *CREATE FULLTEXT INDEX Arguments*

Argument	Description
table_name	The name of the table that you are creating the full-text index on. There can only be one full-text index on a single table.
column_name	The listed column or columns to be indexed, which can be of the data types varchar, nvarchar, char, nchar, xml, varbinary, text, ntext, and image.
type_column_name	The TYPE COLUMN keyword token is used to designate a column in the table that tells the full-text index what type of data is held in the varbinary(max) or image data type column. SQL Server can interpret different file types, but must know exactly how to do so. In this case, the FileExtension table has ".doc" in it for each row. This tells SQL Server that the data held in Document will be of a Word Document format.
language_term	The optional LANGUAGE keyword can also be used within the column list to indicate the language of the data stored in the column. Specifying the language will help SQL Server determine how the data is parsed in the full-text indexing process and how it will be linguistically interpreted. For a list of available languages, query the sys.fulltext_languages table.
index_name	In order for the full-text index to be created on a table, that table must have a single-key, unique, non-nullable column. This can be, for example, a single column primary key, or a column defined with a UNIQUE constraint that is also non-nullable. The KEY INDEX clause in the CREATE FULLTEXT INDEX command identifies the required unique key column on the specified table.

(Continued)

Table 6-2. (*Continued*)

Argument	Description
fulltext_catalog_name	The ON clause designates the catalog where the full-text index will be stored. If a default catalog was identified before creation of the index, and this option isn't used, the index will be stored on the default catalog. However if no default was defined, the index creation will fail.
CHANGE_TRACKING {MANUAL | AUTO | OFF [, NO POPULATION]}	This argument determines how user data changes will be detected by the full-text service. Based on this configuration, indexes can be automatically updated as data is changed in the table. You also have the option of only manually repopulating the indexes at a time or on a schedule of your choosing. The AUTO option is designated to automatically update the full-text index as table data is modified. The MANUAL option means that changes will either be propagated manually by the user or initiated via a SQL Server Agent schedule. The OFF option means that SQL Server will not keep a list of user changes. Using OFF with NO POPULATION means that SQL Server will not populate the index after it is created. Under this option, full-text index population will only occur after someone executes ALTER FULLTEXT INDEX, which is reviewed in the next recipe.

In this recipe's example, a new full-text index is created on the AdventureWorks database's Production.Document table (we'll demonstrate how to query the index in future recipes). DocumentSummary is the column to be indexed, and FileExtension is the column that contains a pointer to the column's document type:

```
CREATE FULLTEXT INDEX ON Production.Document
(DocumentSummary, Document TYPE COLUMN FileExtension)
KEY INDEX PK_Document_DocumentID
ON cat_Production_Document
WITH CHANGE_TRACKING AUTO
```

How It Works

In this recipe, a new full-text index was created for the Production.Document table, on the DocumentSummary column (which has a varchar(max) data type). Note that more than one column can be designated for one full-text index. Stepping through the code, the first line designated the table the full-text index would be based on:

```
CREATE FULLTEXT INDEX ON Production.Document
```

The second line of code designated the column to be indexed, and then a pointer to the column that tells SQL Server what document type is stored in the DocumentSummary column:

```
(DocumentSummary, Document TYPE COLUMN FileExtension)
```

Keep in mind that the TYPE COLUMN clause is only necessary if you are indexing a varchar(max) or image type column, as you'll be assisting SQL Server with interpreting the stored data. Regular text data types such as char, varchar, nchar, nvarchar, text, ntext and xml don't require the TYPE COLUMN clause.

Next, the name of the key, non-null, unique column for the table is identified:

```
KEY INDEX PK_Document_DocumentID
```

The ON clause designates which full-text catalog the full-text index will be stored in:

```
ON cat_Production_Document
```

Lastly, the method of ongoing index population is designated for the index:

```
WITH CHANGE_TRACKING AUTO
```

Once the full-text index is created, you can begin querying it. Before we get to this however, there are other commands used for modifying or removing indexes and catalogs you should be aware of.

Modifying a Full-Text Catalog

In this recipe, I'll demonstrate ALTER FULLTEXT CATALOG, which you can use to:

- Change accent sensitive settings. Accent sensitivity defines whether or not SQL Server will distinguish between accented and unaccented characters, or treat them as equivalent characters in the search.

- Set the catalog as the default database catalog.

- REBUILD the entire catalog with all indexes in it.

- REORGANIZE the catalog, which optimizes internal index and catalog full-text structures. Microsoft calls this process a "master merge," which means that smaller indexes are physically processed (not logically, however) into one large index in order to improve performance.

The syntax for ALTER FULLTEXT CATALOG is as follows:

```
ALTER FULLTEXT CATALOG catalog_name
{ REBUILD [WITH ACCENT_SENSITIVITY = {ON|OFF} ]
    | REORGANIZE
    | AS DEFAULT
}
```

The arguments for this command are described in Table 6-3.

Table 6-3. *ALTER FULLTEXT CATALOG Arguments*

Argument	Description
REBUILD	The REBUILD option deletes the existing full-text file system files and replaces it with a new catalog (with the indexes still intact).
[WITH ACCENT_SENSITIVITY = {ON|OFF}]	The ACCENT_SENSITIVITY option can only be configured when used in conjunction with a REBUILD.
REORGANIZE	This causes SQL Server to optimize catalog structures and internal indexes, freeing up disk and memory resources for those full-text indexes based on frequently updated columns.
AS DEFAULT	Sets the catalog as the default database catalog.

In this first example in the recipe, a full-text catalog is optimized using the REORGANIZE keyword:

```
ALTER FULLTEXT CATALOG cat_Production_Document
REORGANIZE
```

In this second example, a full-text catalog is set to be the default full-text catalog for the database:

```
ALTER FULLTEXT CATALOG cat_Production_Document
AS DEFAULT
```

In this example, a full-text catalog (and all indexes within), is rebuilt along with disabling accent sensitivity:

```
ALTER FULLTEXT CATALOG cat_Production_Document
REBUILD WITH ACCENT_SENSITIVITY = OFF
```

How It Works

In this recipe, `ALTER FULLTEXT CATALOG` was used to optimize the indexes and internal data structures, set the catalog to the default database, and rebuild the catalog and indexes within. This command is used to maintain existing catalogs, and keep them performing at their best as data modifications are made to the underlying indexed tables.

Modifying a Full-Text Index

The `ALTER FULLTEXT INDEX` command can be used both to change the properties of an index and also control/initiate index population. The syntax is as follows:

```
ALTER FULLTEXT INDEX ON table_name
{    ENABLE
    | DISABLE
    | SET CHANGE_TRACKING {MANUAL|AUTO|OFF}
    | ADD (column_name
    [TYPE COLUMN type_column_name ]
    [LANGUAGE language_term] [,...n] )
    [WITH NO POPULATION]
    | DROP (column_name [,...n] )
    [WITH NO POPULATION]
    | START {FULL|INCREMENTAL|UPDATE} POPULATION
    | STOP POPULATION
}
```

The arguments of this command are described in Table 6-4.

Table 6-4. *ALTER FULLTEXT INDEX Arguments*

Argument	Description
table_name	The name of the table of the index to be modified.
ENABLE | DISABLE	The ENABLE option activates the full-text index. DISABLE deactivates a full-text index. Deactivating a full-text index means that changes to the table columns are no longer tracked and moved to the full-text index (however full-text search conditions are still allowed against the index).
SET CHANGE TRACKING {MANUAL|AUTO|OFF}	MANUAL specifies that change tracking on the source indexed data will be enabled on a schedule or manually executed basis. AUTO specifies that the full-text index is modified automatically when the indexed column(s) values are modified. OFF disabled change tracking from occurring on the full-text index.

Argument	Description
`ADD (column_name [,...n] )`	The name of the column or columns to add to the existing full-text index.
`type_column_name`	The column used to designate the full-text index file type of the data stored in the varbinary(max) or image data type column.
`language_term`	The optional LANGUAGE keyword used within the column list to indicate the language of the data stored in the column.
`WITH NO POPULATION`	When designated, the full-text index isn't populated after the addition or removal of a table column.
`DROP (column_name [,...n] )`	The name of the column or columns to remove from the existing full-text index.
`START {FULL|INCREMENTAL|UPDATE} POPULATION`	This option initiates the population of the full-text index based on the option of FULL, INCREMENTAL, and UPDATE. FULL refreshes every row from the table into the index. INCREMENTAL only refreshes the index for those rows that were modified since the last population and in order for INCREMENTAL to be used, the indexed table requires a column with a timestamp data type. The UPDATE token refreshes the index for any rows that were inserted, updated, or deleted since the last index update.
`STOP POPULATION`	For very large tables, full-text index population can consume significant system resources. Because of this, you may need to stop a population process while it is in progress. For indexes created with the MANUAL or OFF change tracking setting, you can use the STOP POPULATION option.

In this first example, a new column is added to the existing full-text index on the Production.Document table:

```
ALTER FULLTEXT INDEX ON Production.Document
ADD (Title)
```

Next, a full-text index population is initiated:

```
ALTER FULLTEXT INDEX ON Production.Document
START FULL POPULATION
```

This returns a warning because the full-text index population was already underway for the table (we didn't designate the WITH NO POPULATION option when adding the new column to the full-text index):

```
Warning: Request to start a full-text index population on table or indexed view
'Production.Document' is ignored because a population is currently active for this
table or indexed view.
```

This next example demonstrates disabling change tracking for the table's full-text index:

```
ALTER FULLTEXT INDEX ON Production.Document
SET CHANGE_TRACKING OFF
```

This returns the following warning:

```
Warning: Request to stop change tracking has deleted all changes tracked on table or
indexed view 'Production'.
```

In this last example for the recipe, the Title column is dropped from the full-text index:

```
ALTER FULLTEXT INDEX ON Production.Document
DROP (Title)
```

How It Works

In this recipe, `ALTER FULLTEXT INDEX` was used to perform the following actions:

- Add a new column to an existing full-text index. This is useful if you wish to add additional columns to the full-text index which would benefit from more advanced searching functionality.

- Start a full-text index population (which works if the population isn't already set to automatically update). For very large tables, you may wish to manually control when the full-text index is populated, instead of allowing SQL Server to manually populate the index over time.

- Disable change tracking. This removes a log of any changes that have occurred to the indexed data.

- Drop a column from a full-text index. For example, if you have a column which isn't benefiting from the full-text index functionality, it is best to remove it in order to conserve space (from the stored indexing results) and resources (from the effort it takes SQL Server to update the data).

Other actions `ALTER FULLTEXT INDEX` can perform include disabling an enabled index using the `DISABLE` option, thus making it unavailable for us (but keeping the meta data in the system tables). You can then enable a disabled index using the `ENABLE` keyword.

Dropping a Full-Text Catalog

In this recipe, I demonstrate how to remove a full-text catalog from the database using the `DROP FULLTEXT CATALOG` command. The syntax is as follows:

```
DROP FULLTEXT CATALOG catalog_name
```

This command takes a single argument, the name of the catalog to drop. For example:

```
DROP FULLTEXT CATALOG cat_Production_Document
```

How It Works

The `DROP FULLTEXT CATALOG` references the catalog name, and doesn't require any further information to remove it from the database. If the full-text catalog was set as the `DEFAULT` catalog, you'll see the following warning:

```
Warning: The fulltext catalog 'cat_Production_Document'
is being dropped and is currently set as default.
```

Dropping a Full-Text Index

In this recipe, I'll demonstrate how to remove a full-text index from the full-text catalog using the DROP FULLTEXT INDEX command. The syntax is as follows:

```
DROP FULLTEXT INDEX ON table_name
```

This command only takes a single argument, the name of the table on which the full-text index should be dropped. For example:

```
DROP FULLTEXT INDEX ON Production.Document
```

How It Works

The DROP FULLTEXT INDEX ON command references the full-text indexed table. Since only one index is allowed on a single table, no other information is required to drop the full-text index.

Retrieving Full-Text Catalog and Index Metadata

This recipe shows you how to retrieve useful information regarding the full-text catalogs and indexes in your database by using system catalog views.

The sys.fulltext_catalogs system catalog view returns information on all full-text catalogs in the current database. For example,

```
SELECT name, path, is_default, is_accent_sensitivity_on
FROM sys.fulltext_catalogs
```

returns this:

name	path	is_default	is_accent_sensitivity_on
cat_Production_Document_EX2	C:\Apress\Recipes\FTC\ cat_Production_Document_EX2	0	1
cat_Production_Document	C:\Program Files\ Microsoft SQL Server\MSSQL.4\ MSSQL\FTData\ cat_Production_Document	0	1

The sys.fulltext_indexes system catalog view lists all full-text indexes in the database. For example,

```
SELECT object_name(object_id) table_name, is_active, change_tracking_state_desc
FROM sys.fulltext_indexes
```

returns this:

table_name	is_active	change_tracking_state_desc
Document	1	AUTO

The sys.fulltext_index_columns system catalog view lists all full-text indexed columns in the database. For example,

```
SELECT object_name(object_id) tblname, column_id
FROM sys.fulltext_index_columns
```

returns the table name, and the indexed columns (using the ordinal position of the column in the table):

tblname	column_id
Document	2
Document	8
Document	9

Also, the FULLTEXTCATALOGPROPERTY system function can be used to return information about a specific catalog. The syntax is as follows:

```
FULLTEXTCATALOGPROPERTY ('catalog_name' ,'property')
```

The function takes two arguments, the name of the catalog, and the name of the property to evaluate. Some of the more useful options for the property option are described in Table 6-5.

Table 6-5. *FULLTEXTCATALOGPROPERTY Property Options*

Property	Description
AccentSensitivity	Returns 1 for accent sensitive, 0 for insensitive.
IndexSize	Returns the size of the full-text catalog in megabytes.
MergeStatus	Returns 1 when a reorganization is in process, and 0 when it is not.
PopulateStatus	Returns a numeric value representing the current population status of a catalog. For example, 0 for idle, 1 for an in progress population, 2 for paused, 7 for building an index, and 8 for a full disk.

In this example, the full-text catalog population status is returned:

```
SELECT FULLTEXTCATALOGPROPERTY ('cat_Production_Document','PopulateStatus')
PopulationStatus
```

This returns "0" for idle:

```
PopulationStatus
0
```

How It Works

This recipe used three different catalog views and a system function to return information about full-text catalogs and indexes in the current database. You'll need this information in order to keep track of their existence, as well as track the current state of activity and settings.

Basic Searching

Once you've created the full-text catalog and full-text indexes, you can get down to the business of querying the data with more sophisticated Transact-SQL predicates. Predicates are used in expressions in the WHERE or HAVING clauses, or join conditions of the FROM clause. Predicates return a TRUE, FALSE, or UNKNOWN response.

Beginning with the more simple commands, the FREETEXT command is used to search unstructured text data based on inflectional, literal, or synonymous matches. It is more intelligent than using LIKE because the text data is searched by meaning and not necessarily the exact wording.

The CONTAINS predicate is used to search unstructured textual data for precise or less precise word and phrase matches. This command can also take into consideration the proximity of words to one another, allowing for weighted results.

These next two recipes will demonstrate basic searches using the FREETEXT and CONTAINS predicates.

Using FREETEXT to Search Full-Text Indexed Columns

The FREETEXT predicate is used to search full-text columns based on inflectional, literal, or synonymous matches. The syntax is as follows:

```
FREETEXT ( { column_name | (column_list) | * }
        , 'freetext_string' [ , LANGUAGE language_term ] )
```

The arguments for this predicate are described in Table 6-6.

Table 6-6. *FREETEXT Arguments*

Argument	Description
column_name | column_list | *	The name of the column or columns that are full-text indexed and that you wish to be searched. Designating * designates that all searchable columns are used.
freetext_string	The text to search for.
language_term	Directs SQL Server to use a specific language for performing the search, accessing thesaurus information, and removing noise words. Noise words are words that, depending on the language, cause unnecessary index bloat and do not assist with the search: for example "a" and "the."

In this example, FREETEXT is used to search data based on the *meaning* of the search term. SQL Server looks at the individual words and searches for exact matches, inflectional forms, or extensions/replacements based on the specific language's thesaurus:

```
SELECT DocumentID, DocumentSummary
FROM Production.Document
WHERE FREETEXT (DocumentSummary, 'change pedal' )
```

This returns:

DocumentID	DocumentSummary
4	Detailed instructions for replacing pedals with Adventure Works Cycles replacement pedals. Instructions are applicable to all Adventure Works Cycles bicycle models and replacement pedals. Use only Adventure Works Cycles parts when replacing worn or broken components.

How It Works

In this recipe, FREETEXT was used to search the DocumentSummary column for the phrase "change pedal." Though neither the exact word "change" nor "pedal" exists in the data, a row was returned because of a match on the plural form of pedal ("pedals").

FREETEXT is, however, a less precise way of searching full-text indexes compared to CONTAINS, which is demonstrated in the next few recipes.

Using CONTAINS for Word Searching

In this recipe, I demonstrate using the CONTAINS command to perform word searches. The CONTAINS allows for more sophisticated full-text term searches than the FREETEXT predicate. The basic syntax is as follows:

```
CONTAINS
  ( { column_name | (column_list) | * } ,
'< contains_search_condition >'    [ , LANGUAGE language_term ] )
```

The arguments are identical to FREETEXT, only CONTAINS allows for a variety of search conditions (some demonstrated later on in the "Advanced Searching" section of this chapter.

This example demonstrates a simple search of rows with a DocumentSummary searching for the words "replacing" or "pedals":

```
SELECT DocumentID, DocumentSummary
FROM Production.Document
WHERE CONTAINS (DocumentSummary, '"replacing" OR "pedals"' )
```

This returns:

DocumentID	DocumentSummary
4	Detailed instructions for replacing pedals with Adventure Works Cycles replacement pedals. Instructions are applicable to all Adventure Works Cycles bicycle models and replacement pedals. Use only Adventure Works Cycles parts when replacing worn or broken components.
8	Worn or damaged seats can be easily replaced following these simple instructions. Instructions are applicable to these Adventure Works Cycles models: Mountain 100 through Mountain 500. Use only Adventure Works Cycles parts when replacing worn or broken components.

How It Works

In this recipe, I performed a search against the DocumentSummary finding any summary that contained either the words "replacing" OR "pedals ." Unlike FREETEXT, the literal words are searched, and not the synonyms or inflectional form. Any noise words like "a" or "the" are ignored, as well as punctuation. Noise words are defined by the specified language. You can find noise word files under the SQL Server instance directory $SQL_Server_Install_Path\Microsoft SQL Server\MSSQL.1\MSSQL\FTDATA\, for filenames prefixed by "noise." For example the "noiseFRA.txt" contains French noise words.

OR was used to search for rows with either of the words, but AND could also have been used to return rows only if both words existed for the DocumentSummary value.

For a single term word, double quotes are not necessary, just the outer single quotes, for example:

```
SELECT DocumentID, DocumentSummary
FROM Production.Document
WHERE CONTAINS (DocumentSummary, 'pedals' )
```

Advanced Searching

So far this chapter has demonstrated examples of fairly straightforward word searches. However, using CONTAINS you can perform more advanced searches against words or phrases. Some examples of this include:

- Using a wildcard search to match words or phrases that match a specific text prefix.
- Search for words or phrases based on inflections of a specific word.
- Search for words or phrases based on the proximity of words near to one another.

These next three recipes will demonstrate these more advanced searches using the CONTAINS predicate.

Using CONTAINS to Search with Wildcards

In this recipe, I demonstrate how to use wildcards within a CONTAINS search. A prefix term is designated, followed by the asterisk symbol:

```
SELECT DocumentID, DocumentSummary
FROM Production.Document
WHERE CONTAINS (DocumentSummary, '"import*"' )
```

This returns:

DocumentID	DocumentSummary
7	It is important that you maintain your bicycle and keep it in good repair. Detailed repair and service guidelines are provided along with instructions for adjusting the tightness of the suspension fork.

How It Works

This recipe uses the asterisk symbol to represent a wildcard of one or more characters. This is similar to using LIKE, only you can benefit from the inherent performance of full-text indexing. Any match on a word that starts with "import" will be returned. In this case, one row that matches on the word "important" was returned.

When using a wildcard, the term must be embedded in double quotes; otherwise SQL Server interprets the asterisk as a literal value to be searched for. For example searching for 'import*' without the embedded quotes looks for the literal asterisk value as part of the search term.

Using CONTAINS to Search for Inflectional Matches

In this recipe, I'll demonstrate how to search for rows that match a search term based on inflectional variations. The syntax for searching for inflectional variations is as follows:

```
FORMSOF ( { INFLECTIONAL | THESAURUS } , < simple_term > [ ,...n ] )
```

In this example, the inflectional variation of "replace" is searched:

```
SELECT DocumentID, DocumentSummary
FROM Production.Document
WHERE CONTAINS(DocumentSummary, ' FORMSOF  (INFLECTIONAL, replace) ')
```

This returns:

DocumentID	DocumentSummary
3	Reflectors are vital safety components of your bicycle. Always ensure your front and back reflectors are clean and in good repair. Detailed instructions and illustrations are included should you need to replace the front reflector or front reflector bracket of your Adventure Works Cycles bicycle.
4	Detailed instructions for replacing pedals with Adventure Works Cycles replacement pedals. Instructions are applicable to all Adventure Works Cycles bicycle models and replacement pedals. Use only Adventure Works Cycles parts when replacing worn or broken components.
8	Worn or damaged seats can be easily replaced following these simple instructions. Instructions are applicable to these Adventure Works Cycles models: Mountain 100 through Mountain 500. Use only Adventure Works Cycles parts when replacing worn or broken components.

How It Works

This recipe searches for any rows with the inflectional version of "replace." Although the literal value is not always found in that column, a row will also be returned that contains "replaced" or "replacing."

THESAURUS is the other option for the FORMSOF clause, allowing you to search based on synonymous terms (which are maintained in XML files in the $SQL_Server_Install_Path\Microsoft SQL Server\MSSQL.1\MSSQL\FTDATA\ directory). For example, the French thesaurus XML file is called tsFRA.xml. These XML files are updateable, so you can customize them according to your own application requirements.

Using CONTAINS for Searching Results by Term Proximity

This recipe demonstrates how CONTAINS is used to find rows with specified words that are near one another. The syntax is as follows:

```
{ < simple_term > | < prefix_term > }
{ { NEAR | ~ }
{ < simple_term > | < prefix_term > }
```

In this example, rows are returned where the word "oil" is near to "grease":

```
SELECT DocumentSummary
FROM Production.Document
WHERE CONTAINS(DocumentSummary, 'oil NEAR grease')
```

This returns:

DocumentSummary
Guidelines and recommendations for lubricating the required components of your Adventure Works Cycles bicycle. Component lubrication is vital to ensuring a smooth and safe ride and should be part of your standard maintenance routine. Details instructions are provided for each bicycle component requiring regular lubrication including the frequency at which oil or grease should be applied.

How It Works

This recipe looked for any text that had the word grease near the word oil.

This example searched for proximity between two words, although you can also test for proximity between multiple words, for example:

```
SELECT DocumentSummary
FROM Production.Document
WHERE CONTAINS(DocumentSummary, 'oil NEAR grease AND frequency')
```

Ranked Searching

The previous examples demonstrated full-text index searches conducted in the WHERE clause of a SELECT query. SQL Server 2005 also has ranking functions available which are referenced in the FROM clause of a query instead. Instead of just returning those rows that meet the search condition, the ranking functions CONTAINSTABLE and FREETEXTTABLE are used to return designated rows by relevance. The closer the match, the higher the system generated rank, as these next two recipes will demonstrate.

Returning Ranked Search Results by Meaning

In this recipe, I demonstrate FREETEXTTABLE, which can be used to return search results ordered by rank, based on a search string.

The syntax and functionality between FREETEXT and FREETEXTTABLE is still very similar:

```
FREETEXTTABLE (table , { column_name | (column_list) | * }
            , 'freetext_string'
        [, LANGUAGE language_term ]
        [ ,top_n_by_rank ] )
```

The two additional arguments that differentiate FREETEXTTABLE from FREETEXT are the table and top_n_by_rank arguments. The table argument is the name of the table containing the full-text indexed column or columns. The top_n_by_rank argument, when designated, takes an integer value which represents the top matches in order of rank.

In this example, rows are returned from Production.Document in order of closest rank to the search term "bicycle seat":

```
SELECT    f.RANK, DocumentID, DocumentSummary
FROM Production.Document d
INNER JOIN FREETEXTTABLE(Production.Document, DocumentSummary, 'bicycle seat') f
    ON d.DocumentID = f.[KEY]
ORDER BY RANK DESC
```

This returns:

RANK	DocumentID	DocumentSummary
135	8	Worn or damaged seats can be easily replaced following these simple instructions. Instructions are applicable to these Adventure Works Cycles models: Mountain 100 through Mountain 500. Use only Adventure Works Cycles parts when replacing worn or broken components.
24	3	Reflectors are vital safety components of your bicycle. Always ensure your front and back reflectors are clean and in good repair. Detailed instructions and illustrations are included should you need to replace the front reflector or front reflector bracket of your Adventure Works Cycles bicycle.

(Continued)

RANK	DocumentID	DocumentSummary
24	6	Guidelines and recommendations for lubricating the required components of your Adventure Works Cycles bicycle. Component lubrication is vital to ensuring a smooth and safe ride and should be part of your standard maintenance routine. Details instructions are provided for each bicycle component requiring regular lubrication including the frequency at which oil or grease should be applied.
15	7	It is important that you maintain your bicycle and keep it in good repair. Detailed repair and service guidelines are provided along with instructions for adjusting the tightness of the suspension fork.
15	4	Detailed instructions for replacing pedals with Adventure Works Cycles replacement pedals. Instructions are applicable to all Adventure Works Cycles bicycle models and replacement pedals. Use only Adventure Works Cycles parts when replacing worn or broken components.

How It Works

The FREETEXTTABLE is similar to FREETEXT in that it searches full-text indexed columns by meaning, and not literal value. FREETEXTTABLE is different from FREETEXT however, in that it is referenced like a table in the FROM clause, allowing you to join data by its KEY. KEY and RANK are two columns that the FREETEXTTABLE returns in the result set. KEY is the unique/primary key defined for the full index and RANK is the measure (0 through 1000) of how good a search result the row is estimated to be.

In this recipe, the FREETEXTTABLE result set searched the DocumentSummary column for "bicycle seat," and joined by its KEY value to the Production.Document table's DocumentID column:

```
INNER JOIN FREETEXTTABLE(Production.Document,
DocumentSummary,
'bicycle seat') f
   ON d.DocumentID = f.[KEY]
```

RANK was returned sorted by descending order, based on the strength of the match:

```
ORDER BY RANK DESC
```

Returning Ranked Search Results by Weighted Value

In this recipe, I demonstrate returning search results based on a weighted pattern match value using the CONTAINSTABLE command. CONTAINSTABLE is equivalent to FREETEXTTABLE in that it acts as a table and can be referenced in the FROM clause. CONTAINSTABLE also has the same search capabilities and variations as CONTAINS.

Both CONTAINS and CONTAINSTABLE can be used to designate a row match's "weight," giving one term more importance than another, thus impacting result rank. This is achieved by using ISABOUT in the command, which assigns a weighted value to the search term.

The basic syntax for this is as follows:

```
ISABOUT { <search term> }   [ WEIGHT ( weight_value ) ]
```

This example demonstrates querying Production.Document by rank, giving the term "bicycle" a higher weighting than the term "seat":

```
SELECT f.RANK, d.DocumentID, d.DocumentSummary
FROM Production.Document d
INNER JOIN CONTAINSTABLE(Production.Document, DocumentSummary,
```

```
'ISABOUT ( bicycle weight (.9), seat weight (.1))') f
   ON d.DocumentID = f.[KEY]
ORDER BY RANK DESC
```

This returns:

RANK	DocumentID	DocumentSummary
23	3	Reflectors are vital safety components of your bicycle. Always ensure your front and back reflectors are clean and in good repair. Detailed instructions and illustrations are included should you need to replace the front reflector or front reflector bracket of your Adventure Works Cycles bicycle.
23	6	Guidelines and recommendations for lubricating the required components of your Adventure Works Cycles bicycle. Component lubrication is vital to ensuring a smooth and safe ride and should be part of your standard maintenance routine. Details instructions are provided for each bicycle component requiring regular lubrication including the frequency at which oil or grease should be applied.
11	7	It is important that you maintain your bicycle and keep it in good repair. Detailed repair and service guidelines are provided along with instructions for adjusting the tightness of the suspension fork.
11	4	Detailed instructions for replacing pedals with Adventure Works Cycles replacement pedals. Instructions are applicable to all Adventure Works Cycles bicycle models and replacement pedals. Use only Adventure Works Cycles parts when replacing worn or broken components.

How It Works

The CONTAINSTABLE is a result set, joining to Production.Document by KEY and DocumentID. RANK was returned in the SELECT clause, and sorted in the ORDER BY clause. CONTAINSTABLE can perform the same kinds of searches as CONTAINS, including wildcard, proximity, inflectional, and thesaurus searches.

In this example, a weighted term search was performed, meaning that words are assigned values that impact their weight within the result ranking.

In this recipe, two words were searched, "bicycle" and "seat," with "bicycle" getting a higher rank than "weight":

```
'ISABOUT ( bicycle weight (.9), seat weight (.1))'
```

The weight value can be a number from 0.0 through 1.0 and impacts how each row's matching will be ranked within CONTAINSTABLE. ISABOUT is put within the single quotes and the column definition is within parentheses. Each term was followed by the word "weight" and the value 0.0 to 1.0 value in parentheses.

CHAPTER 7

■ ■ ■

Views

Views allow you to create a virtual representation of table data using a SELECT statement as its definition. The defining SELECT statement can join one or more tables and can include one or more columns. Once created, a view can be referenced in the FROM clause of a query.

Views can be used to simplify data access for query writers, obscuring the underlying complexity of the SELECT statement. Views are also useful for managing security and protecting sensitive data. If you wish to restrict direct table access by the end user, you can grant permissions exclusively to views, rather than to the underlying tables. You can also use views to expose only those columns that you wish the end user to see, including just the necessary columns in the view definition. Views can even allow direct data updates, under specific circumstances that I'll describe later in the chapter. Views also provide a standard interface to the back-end data, which shouldn't need to change unless there are significant changes to the underlying table structures.

In addition to regular views, you can also create indexed views, which are views that actually have index (both clustered and nonclustered) data persisted within the database (regular views do not actually store physical data). Also available are distributed-partitioned views, which allow you to represent one logical table made up of horizontally-partitioned tables, each located across separate SQL Server instances. Table 7-1 shows the three types of views used in SQL Server 2005 (not including the deprecated local-partitioned view).

Table 7-1. *SQL Server 2005 View Types*

View Type	Description
Regular View	Defined by a Transact-SQL query. No data is actually stored in the database, only the view definition.
Indexed View	First defined by a Transact-SQL query, and then, after certain requirements are met, a clustered index is created on it in order to materialize the index data similar to table data. Once a clustered index is created, multiple nonclustered indexes can be created on the indexed view as needed.
Distributed Partitioned View	This is a view that uses UNION ALL to combine multiple, smaller tables separated across two or more SQL Server instances into a single, virtual table for performance purposes and scalability (expansion of table size on each SQL Server instance, for example).

In this chapter, I'll present recipes that create each of these types of views, and I'll also provide methods for reporting view metadata.

Regular Views

Views are a great way to pre-assemble data before presenting it to end-users. Views can be used to obscure numerous table joins and column selections. Views can also be used to implement security by only allowing users authorization access to the view, and not to the actual underlying tables. For all the usefulness of views, there are still some performance shortcomings to watch out for. When considering views for your database, consider the following "best practices":

- Performance-tune your views as you would performance-tune a SELECT query, because a regular view is essentially just a "stored" query. Poorly performing views can have a huge impact on server performance.

- Don't nest your views more than one level deep. Specifically, do not define a view that calls another view, and so on. This can lead to confusion when you attempt to tune inefficient queries, not to mention a performance overhead for each nested level.

- Use stored procedures instead of views, if possible. Stored procedures can offer a performance boost, as the execution plan can reuse them. (In contrast, every time a view is accessed, its execution plan is recompiled.) Stored procedures can also reduce network traffic, provide business logic, and have fewer restrictions than a view (see Chapter 10 for more information).

When a view is created, its definition is stored in the database, but the actual data that the view returns is not stored separately from the underlying tables. The next few recipes will demonstrate how to create and manage views.

Creating a Basic View

A view is created using the CREATE VIEW command. The syntax is as follows:

```
CREATE VIEW [ schema_name . ] view_name [ (column [ ,...n ] ) ]
[ WITH [ ENCRYPTION ] [ SCHEMABINDING ] [ VIEW_METADATA ] [ ,...n ] ]
AS select_statement
[ WITH CHECK OPTION ]
```

The arguments of this command are described in Table 7-2. Some of these arguments will also be reviewed in more detail later on in the chapter.

Table 7-2. *CREATE VIEW Arguments*

Argument	Description
[schema_name .] view_name	The schema and name of the new view.
(column [,...n])	This is the optional list of column names to be used for the view. If not designated, the names used in the SELECT query will be used instead.
ENCRYPTION	Encrypts the Transact-SQL definition in the system tables so that it cannot be viewed without a saved copy of the original CREATE VIEW command.
SCHEMABINDING	SCHEMABINDING binds the view to the schema of the underlying tables, restricting any changes in the base table that would impact the view definition.
VIEW_METADATA	When designated, APIs accessing information about the view will see view information instead of metadata from the underlying table or tables.
select_statement	The SELECT query used to return the rows and columns of the view.

The SELECT statement allows up to 1024 defined columns. You cannot, however, use certain elements in a view definition, including INTO, OPTION, COMPUTE, COMPUTE BY, or references to table variables or temporary tables. You also cannot use ORDER BY, unless used in conjunction with the TOP keyword.

This example demonstrates how to create a view that accesses data from both the Production.TransactionHistory and the Production.Product tables:

```
CREATE VIEW dbo.v_Product_TransactionHistory
AS

SELECT   p.Name ProductName,
         p.ProductNumber,
         c.Name ProductCategory,
         s.Name ProductSubCategory,
         m.Name ProductModel,
         t.TransactionID,
         t.ReferenceOrderID,
         t.ReferenceOrderLineID,
         t.TransactionDate,
         t.TransactionType,
         t.Quantity,
         t.ActualCost
FROM Production.TransactionHistory t
INNER JOIN Production.Product p ON
   t.ProductID = p.ProductID
INNER JOIN Production.ProductModel m ON
   m.ProductModelID = p.ProductModelID
INNER JOIN Production.ProductSubcategory s ON
   s.ProductSubcategoryID = p.ProductSubcategoryID
INNER JOIN Production.ProductCategory c ON
   c.ProductCategoryID = s.ProductCategoryID
WHERE c.Name = 'Bikes'
GO
```

Next, the new view is queried to show transaction history for products by product name and model:

```
SELECT ProductName, ProductModel, ReferenceOrderID, TransactionDate, ActualCost
FROM v_Product_TransactionHistory
ORDER BY ProductName
```

This returns the following abridged results:

ProductName	ProductModel	ReferenceOrderID	TransactionDate	ActualCost
Mountain-200 Black, 38	Mountain-200	53457	2003-09-01 00:00:00.000	1652.3928
Mountain-200 Black, 38	Mountain-200	53463	2003-09-01 00:00:00.000	1652.3928
Mountain-200 Black, 38	Mountain-200	53465	2003-09-01 00:00:00.000	1652.3928
...				
Touring-3000 Yellow, 62	Touring-3000	69467	2004-05-01 00:00:00.000	534.492
Touring-3000 Yellow, 62	Touring-3000	69482	2004-05-01 00:00:00.000	534.492
Touring-3000 Yellow, 62	Touring-3000	66006	2004-05-04 00:00:00.000	0.00

How It Works

In this recipe, I define a view by using a SELECT query that referenced multiple tables in the FROM clause and qualified a specific product category of "Bikes." In this case, the view benefits the query writer, as she or he doesn't need to specify the many table joins each time they write the query.

The view definition also used column aliases, using ProductName instead of just Name—making the column name unambiguous and reducing the possible confusion with other columns called Name. Qualifying what data is returned from the view in the WHERE clause also allows you to restrict the data that the query writer can see—in this case only letting the query writer reference products of a specific product category.

Querying the View Definition

You can view the Transact-SQL definition of a view by querying the sys.sql_modules system catalog view.

This example shows you how to query a view's SQL definition:

```
SELECT definition  FROM   sys.sql_modules
WHERE object_id = OBJECT_ID('v_Product_TransactionHistory')
```

This returns:

```
definition
CREATE VIEW dbo.v_Product_TransactionHistory AS    SELECT   p.Name ProductName,
p.ProductNumber,      c.Name ProductCategory,    s.Name ProductSubCategory,     m.Name
ProductModel,        t.TransactionID,          t.ReferenceOrderID,
t.ReferenceOrderLineID,
t.TransactionDate,          t.TransactionType,          t.Quantity,          t.ActualCost
FROM
Production.TransactionHistory t  INNER JOIN Production.Product p ON      t.ProductID =
p.ProductID  INNER JOIN Production.ProductModel m ON      m.ProductModelID =
p.ProductModelID  INNER JOIN Production.ProductSubcategory s ON
s.ProductSubcategoryID = p.ProductSubcategoryID  INNER JOIN Production.ProductCategory
c ON     c.ProductCategoryID = s.ProductCategoryID  WHERE c.Name = 'Bikes'
```

How It Works

As you just saw, the sys.sql_modules system catalog view allows you to view the SQL text of a view. If the view has been encrypted (see later in the chapter for a review of encryption), the definition column will return a NULL value. This system catalog view can also be used to view other procedural code object types described in later chapters, such as triggers, functions, and stored procedures.

Reporting on Database Views

In this recipe, I use three different queries to return information about views in the current database.

The first query shows all views in the current database:

```
SELECT   s.name SchemaName,
         v.name ViewName
FROM sys.views v
INNER JOIN sys.schemas s ON
   v.schema_id = s.schema_id
ORDER BY s.name,
         v.name
```

This returns the following (abridged) results:

SchemaName	ViewName
HumanResources	vEmployee
HumanResources	vEmployeeDepartment
HumanResources	vEmployeeDepartmentHistory
HumanResources	vJobCandidate
HumanResources	vJobCandidateEducation
HumanResources	vJobCandidateEmployment
...	

This second query displays the columns exposed by each view in the current database:

```
SELECT  v.name ViewName,
        c.name ColumnName
FROM sys.columns c
INNER JOIN sys.views v ON
  c.object_id = v.object_id
ORDER BY v.name,
        c.name
```

This returns the following (abridged) results:

ViewName	ColumnName
vEmployee	AdditionalContactInfo
vEmployee	AddressLine1
vEmployee	AddressLine2
vEmployee	City
vEmployee	CountryRegionName
vEmployee	EmailAddress
vEmployee	EmailPromotion
...	

This next query shows the objects each view is dependent on:

```
SELECT  DISTINCT
        s.name SchemaName,
        v.name ViewName,
        OBJECT_NAME(referenced_major_id) ReferencedObject
FROM sys.sql_dependencies d
INNER JOIN sys.views v ON
  d.object_id = v.object_id
INNER JOIN sys.schemas s ON
  v.schema_id = s.schema_id
ORDER BY s.name, v.name
```

This returns the following (abridged) results:

SchemaName	ViewName	ReferencedObject
HumanResources	vEmployeeDepartmentHistory	Employee
HumanResources	vEmployeeDepartmentHistory	EmployeeDepartmentHistory
HumanResources	vEmployeeDepartmentHistory	Shift
HumanResources	vJobCandidate	JobCandidate
HumanResources	vJobCandidateEducation	JobCandidate
HumanResources	vJobCandidateEmployment	JobCandidate

How It Works

The first query in the recipe references the object catalog views sys.views and sys.schemas to return all views in the database:

```
FROM sys.views v
INNER JOIN sys.schemas s ON
   v.schema_id = s.schema_id
```

The second query reports on all columns returned by each view by querying the object catalog views sys.columns and sys.views:

```
FROM sys.columns c
INNER JOIN sys.views v ON
   c.object_id = v.object_id
```

The last query in the recipe reports on all object dependencies within the view. If a view, for example, selects from two different tables, both base tables are considered view dependencies. The sys.sql_dependencies view tracks dependencies that existed when the view was created:

```
FROM sys.sql_dependencies d
INNER JOIN sys.views v ON
   d.object_id = v.object_id
INNER JOIN sys.schemas s ON
   v.schema_id = s.schema_id
```

Refreshing a View's Definition

When table objects referenced by the view are changed, the view's metadata can become outdated. In this recipe, I'll show you how to refresh a view's metadata if the dependent objects referenced in the view definition have changed:

```
EXEC sp_refreshview 'dbo.v_Product_TransactionHistory'
```

How It Works

If the underlying object references for the view's SELECT query definition changes, you can use the sp_refreshview stored procedure to refresh the view's metadata. The system stored procedure takes only one parameter, the view schema and name.

Modifying a View

The ALTER VIEW command is used to modify the definition of an existing view. The syntax is as follows:

```
ALTER VIEW [ schema_name . ] view_name [ ( column [ ,...n ] ) ]
[ WITH [ ENCRYPTION ] [ SCHEMABINDING ] [ VIEW_METADATA ] [ ,...n ] ]
AS select_statement
[ WITH CHECK OPTION ]
```

ALTER VIEW uses the same arguments as CREATE VIEW. This example demonstrates modifying an existing view:

```
-- Add a WHERE clause and remove
-- the ReferenceOrderID and ReferenceOrderLineID columns

ALTER VIEW dbo.v_Product_TransactionHistory
AS
```

```
SELECT    p.Name,
      p.ProductNumber,
      t.TransactionID,
      t.TransactionDate,
      t.TransactionType,
      t.Quantity,
      t.ActualCost
FROM Production.TransactionHistory t
INNER JOIN Production.Product p ON
   t.ProductID = p.ProductID
WHERE Quantity > 10

GO
```

How It Works

This recipe was used to remove two columns from the original view and add a WHERE clause—both by just redefining the SELECT statement after the AS keyword in the ALTER VIEW command. Note that if you alter an *indexed view* (reviewed later in the chapter), all indexes will be dropped and will need to be manually recreated.

Dropping a View

You can drop a view by using the DROP VIEW command. The syntax is as follows:

```
DROP VIEW [ schema_name . ] view_name [ ...,n ]
```

The command just takes one argument, containing the name or names of the views to drop from the database.

This example demonstrates dropping a view:

```
DROP VIEW dbo.v_Product_Inventory_Location
```

How It Works

Dropping a view will remove its definition from the system catalogs, as well as remove any indexes created for it if it was an *indexed* view.

Modifying Data Through a View

As I mentioned at the beginning of the chapter, you can perform inserts, updates, and deletes against a view, just like you would a regular table. In order to do this, any INSERT/UPDATE/DELETE operations can *only* reference columns from a single table. Also, the columns being referenced in the INSERT/UPDATE/DELETE cannot be derived—for example they can't be calculated, based on an aggregate function, or be affected by a GROUP BY, DISTINCT, or HAVING clause.

As a real world best practice, view updates may be appropriate for situations where the underlying data tables must be obscured from the query writer. For example, if you are building a shrink-wrapped software application that allows users to directly update the data, providing views will allow you to filter the underlying columns that are viewed, or provide more user-friendly column names than what you find used in the base tables.

In this example, a view is created that selects from the Production.Location table. A calculated column is also used in the query definition:

```
CREATE VIEW Production.vw_Location
AS
```

```
SELECT LocationID,
    Name LocationName,
    CostRate,
    Availability,
   CostRate/Availability CostToAvailabilityRatio
FROM Production.Location
GO
```

The following insert is attempted:

```
INSERT Production.vw_Location
(LocationName, CostRate, Availability, CostToAvailabilityRatio)
VALUES ('Finishing Cabinet', 1.22, 75.00, 0.01626 )
```

This returns the following error:

```
Msg 4406, Level 16, State 1, Line 1
Update or insert of view or function 'Production.vw_Location' failed because it contains
a
derived or constant field.
```

This next insert is attempted, this time only referencing the columns that exist in the base table:

```
INSERT Production.vw_Location
(LocationName, CostRate, Availability)
VALUES ('Finishing Cabinet', 1.22, 75.00)
```

The results show that the insert succeeded:

```
(1 row(s) affected)
```

How It Works

In this recipe I demonstrated performing an insert operation against a view. You can perform data modifications against views as long as your data modification and view meet the requirements. If your view can't meet these requirements, you can use an INSTEAD OF trigger to perform updates instead (an example of creating a view on a trigger is demonstrated in Chapter 12).

View Encryption

The ENCRYPTION OPTION in the CREATE VIEW and ALTER VIEW commands allows you to encrypt the Transact-SQL of a view. Once encrypted, you can no longer view the definition in the sys.sql_modules system catalog view. Software producers who use SQL Server in the back-end often encrypt their views or stored procedures in order to prevent tampering or reverse-engineering from clients or competitors. If you use encryption, be sure to save the original, unencrypted definition.

Encrypting a View

This example demonstrates encrypting the view Transact-SQL definition of a new view:

```
CREATE VIEW dbo.v_Product_TopTenListPrice
WITH ENCRYPTION
AS
```

```
SELECT   TOP 10
     p.Name,
     p.ProductNumber,
     p.ListPrice
FROM Production.Product p
ORDER BY p.ListPrice DESC
GO
```

Next, the sys.sql_modules system catalog view is queried for the new view's Transact-SQL definition:

```
SELECT definition
FROM   sys.sql_modules
WHERE object_id = OBJECT_ID('v_Product_TopTenListPrice')
```

This returns:

```
definition
-----------------------------------------------------------------------------------
NULL
```

How It Works

In this recipe, a new view was created using the WITH ENCRYPTION option. If you're using this option, be sure to retain your source code in a safe location, or use a version control program such as Visual Source Safe. In general, if you must encrypt the view, it should be performed just prior to deployment.

Indexed Views

A view is no more efficient than the underlying SELECT query that you use to define it. However, one way you can improve the performance of a frequently accessed view is to add an index to it. To do so, you must first create a unique, clustered index on the view. Once this index on the view has been built, the data used to materialize the view is stored in much the same way as a table's clustered index. After creating the unique clustered index on the view, you can also create additional nonclustered indexes. The underlying (base) tables are not impacted physically by the creation of these view indexes, as they are separate underlying objects.

Indexed views can be created in any edition of SQL Server 2005, although they require SQL Server Enterprise Edition in order for the query optimizer to automatically consider using an indexed view in a query execution plan. In SQL Server 2005 Enterprise Edition, an indexed view can automatically be used by the query optimizer when it deems it useful, even if it is the underlying table or tables referenced in a SELECT query instead of the actual view itself. In editions other than Enterprise Edition, you can manually force an indexed view to be used by the query optimizer by using the NOEXPAND table hint (reviewed later in the chapter).

Indexed views are particularly ideal for SELECT queries view definitions that aggregate data across many rows, as the aggregated values remain updated and materialized, ready to be queried without continuous recalculation. Indexed views are ideal for queries referencing infrequently updated base tables, but creating them on highly volatile tables may result in performance issues related to keeping the indexes updated. Base tables with frequent updates will trigger frequent index updates against the view, meaning that update speed will suffer at the expense of query performance.

Creating an Indexed View

In this recipe, I'll demonstrate how to create an indexed view. First we will create a new view, and then create indexes (clustered and nonclustered) on it. In order to create an indexed view, you are required to use the new WITH SCHEMABINDING option, which binds the view to the schema of the underlying tables. This prevents any changes in the base table that would impact the view definition. The WITH SCHEMABINDING option also adds additional requirements to the view's select definition. Object references in a schema-bound view must include the two-part schema.object naming convention, and all referenced objects have to be located in the same database.

■**Note** Keep in mind that there are also several other requirements which can determine whether or not an index can be created on top of a view. The exhaustive list won't be rehashed in this chapter, so be sure to check out the complete requirements in SQL Server 2005 Books Online.

The recipe begins by creating a new view with the SCHEMABINDING option:

```
CREATE VIEW dbo.v_Product_Sales_By_LineTotal
WITH SCHEMABINDING
AS

SELECT p.ProductID, p.Name ProductName, SUM(LineTotal) LineTotalByProduct, COUNT_BIG(*)
LineItems
FROM Sales.SalesOrderDetail s
INNER JOIN Production.Product p ON
   s.ProductID = p.ProductID
GROUP BY p.ProductID, p.Name

GO
```

Before creating an index, we'll demonstrate querying the regular view, returning the query I/O cost statistics using the SET STATISTICS IO command (see Chapter 28 for more info on this command):

```
SET STATISTICS IO ON
GO

SELECT TOP 5 ProductName, LineTotalByProduct
FROM v_Product_Sales_By_LineTotal
ORDER BY LineTotalByProduct DESC
```

This returns the following results:

```
ProductName                LineTotalByProduct
Mountain-200 Black, 38     4400592.800400
Mountain-200 Black, 42     4009494.761841
Mountain-200 Silver, 38    3693678.025272
Mountain-200 Silver, 42    3438478.860423
Mountain-200 Silver, 46    3434256.941928
```

This also returns I/O information reporting the various scanning activites against the underlying base tables used in the view:

Table 'Product'. Scan count 0, logical reads 10, physical reads 0, read-ahead reads 0, lob
logical reads 0, lob physical reads 0, lob read-ahead reads 0.
Table 'Worktable'. Scan count 0, logical reads 0, physical reads 0, read-ahead reads 0, lob
logical reads 0, lob physical reads 0, lob read-ahead reads 0.
Table 'SalesOrderDetail'. Scan count 1, logical reads 1241, physical reads 0, read-ahead reads
0, lob logical reads 0, lob physical reads 0, lob read-ahead reads 0.

Next, a clustered index will be created on the regular view, based on the unique value of the
ProductID view column:

```
CREATE UNIQUE CLUSTERED INDEX UCI_v_Product_Sales_By_LineTotal
  ON dbo.v_Product_Sales_By_LineTotal (ProductID)
GO
```

Once the clustered index is created, you can then start creating nonclustered indexes as needed:

```
CREATE NONCLUSTERED INDEX NI_v_Product_Sales_By_LineTotal
  ON dbo.v_Product_Sales_By_LineTotal (ProductName)
GO
```

Next, the query executed earlier against the regular view is now executed against the indexed view:

```
SELECT TOP 5 ProductName, LineTotalByProduct
FROM v_Product_Sales_By_LineTotal
ORDER BY LineTotalByProduct DESC
```

This returns the same results as before, but this time the I/O activity is different. Instead of two
base tables being accessed, along with a worktable (tempdb used temporarily to process results),
only a single object is accessed to retrieve results:

Table 'v_Product_Sales_By_LineTotal'. Scan count 1, logical reads 5, physical reads 0,
read-ahead reads 0, lob logical reads 0, lob physical reads 0, lob read-ahead reads 0.

Had this query accessed much larger tables (much larger than our example), the reduction in
I/O would have produced a positive effect on the query's performance.

How It Works

Indexed views allow you to materialize the results of the view as a physical object, similar to a regular
table and associated indexes. This allows the SQL Server query optimizer to retrieve results from
a single physical area instead of having to process the view definition query each time it is called.

In this example, a view was created using the SCHEMABINDING option:

```
CREATE VIEW dbo.v_Product_Sales_By_LineTotal
WITH SCHEMABINDING
AS
```

The remainder of the view was a regular SELECT query which aggregated the sum total of sales
by product:

```
SELECT p.ProductID, p.Name ProductName, SUM(LineTotal) LineTotalByProduct, COUNT_BIG(*)
LineItems
FROM Sales.SalesOrderDetail s
INNER JOIN Production.Product p ON
```

```
    s.ProductID = p.ProductID
GROUP BY p.ProductID, p.Name

GO
```

Notice that the query referenced the COUNT_BIG aggregate function. COUNT_BIG is required in order for SQL Server to maintain the number of rows in each group within the indexed view.

Once the view was successfully created with SCHEMABINDING , a unique clustered index was then created on it:

```
CREATE UNIQUE CLUSTERED INDEX UCI_v_Product_Sales_By_LineTotal
  ON dbo.v_Product_Sales_By_LineTotal (ProductID)
GO
```

In order to index a view, you must first create a unique clustered index on it. Once this index has been built, the view data is stored in much the same way as a clustered index for a table is stored.

After a clustered index is created, you can also create additional nonclustered indexes, as you would for a regular table. In the example, a nonclustered index was created on the ProductName column of the indexed view:

```
CREATE NONCLUSTERED INDEX NI_v_Product_Sales_By_LineTotal
  ON dbo.v_Product_Sales_By_LineTotal (ProductName)
GO
```

Once a view is indexed, view indexes can then be used by SQL Server Enterprise Edition whenever the view or underlying tables are referenced in a query. The SET STATISTICS IO command was used to demonstrate how SQL Server performs the data page retrieval both before and after the view was indexed.

Indexed views can provide performance benefits for relatively static data. Frequently updated base tables, on the other hand, are not an ideal choice for being referenced in an indexed view as the updates will also cause frequent updates to the view's indexes, potentially reducing the benefit of any query performance gained. This is a trade-off between data modification speed and query speed.

Although indexed views can be created using any edition of SQL Server 2005, they will be automatically considered during queries if you are using Enterprise Edition. To make sure SQL Server uses it in other editions, you need to use the view hint NOEXPAND, which is reviewed in the next recipe.

Forcing the Optimizer to Use an Index for an Indexed View

Once you've created an indexed view, if you're running on SQL Server 2005 Enterprise Edition, the query optimizer will automatically decide whether or not to use the indexed view in a query. For other editions however, in order to make SQL Server use a specific indexed view you must use the NOEXPAND keyword.

By adding the WITH (NOEXPAND) view hint after the FROM clause, SQL Server is directed *not* to look for any indexes other then the indexes available for the view.

The view hint syntax is as follows:

```
{ NOEXPAND [ , INDEX ( index_val [ ,...n ] ) ] }
```

This recipe demonstrates how to force an indexed view's index to be used for a query:

```
SELECT ProductID, LocationID, ProductName, LocationName, Shelf
FROM dbo.v_Product_Inventory_Location
WITH (NOEXPAND)
WHERE ProductName = 'Blade'
```

Notice in the syntax that NOEXPAND also allows you to specify one or more indexes to be used for the query, using the INDEX option. For example:

```
SELECT ProductID, LocationID, ProductName, LocationName, Shelf
FROM dbo.v_Product_Inventory_Location
WITH (NOEXPAND, INDEX(NI_v_Product_Inventory_Location_Names))
WHERE ProductName = 'Blade'
```

How It Works

For those using non-Enterprise Edition versions of SQL Server 2005, you can still take advantage of indexed views through the use of the NOEXPAND keyword. The drawback is that you must explicitly use hints whenever the indexed view must be utilized. Another drawback is that your hint usage could nullify a better SQL Server query optimizer choice that would have been made had the hint *not* been used.

Partitioned Views

In SQL Server 2000, you had two options for horizontally partitioning views: local partitioned views and distributed partitioned views. With the introduction of horizontal partitioning functionality in SQL Server 2005 (see Chapter 4), Microsoft no longer recommends that SQL Server 2000 local partitioned views be used.

Distributed partitioned views, however, are alive and well in SQL Server 2005 and allow you to create a single logical representation (view) of two or more horizontally partitioned tables that are located across separate SQL Server instances.

In order to set up a distributed partitioned view, a large table is split into smaller tables based on a range of values defined in a CHECK constraint. This CHECK constraint ensures that each smaller table holds unique data that cannot be stored in the other tables. The distributed partitioned view is then created using a UNION ALL to join each smaller table into a single result set.

The performance benefit is realized when a query is executed against the distributed partitioned view. If the view is partitioned by a date range, for example, and a query is used to return rows that are only stored in a single table of the partition, SQL Server is smart enough to only search that one partition instead of all tables in the distributed-partitioned view.

Creating a Distributed-Partitioned View

In this recipe, I'll demonstrate how to create a distributed-partitioned view that spans two SQL Server instances. It's based on the following business scenario. There are two sibling corporations—MegaCorp and MiniCorp. Each has their own SQL Server instance to house website data, and each wants a table to track website hits. The numbers of hits are voluminous—and would require more storage than a single SQL Server instance could handle. The requirement is to create a unified view that references both tables in a single view. The business wants to be able to query either server, and either return the same data or data just for its own company.

Since more than one SQL Server instance will be accessed in a distributed-partitioned view recipe, linked servers are added to both participating SQL Server instances (see Chapter 27 for a review).

The recipe begins by creating a linked server on the *first SQL Server* instance:

```
USE master
GO
EXEC sp_addlinkedserver
    'JOEPROD',
    N'SQL Server'
GO
```

```
-- skip schema checking of remote tables
EXEC sp_serveroption 'JOEPROD', 'lazy schema validation', 'true'
GO
```

On the second SQL Server instance, a linked server is created to the first SQL Server instance:

```
USE master
GO
EXEC sp_addlinkedserver
    'JOEPROD\SQL2005',
    N'SQL Server'
GO

-- skip schema checking of remote tables
EXEC sp_serveroption 'JOEPROD\SQL2005', 'lazy schema validation', 'true'
GO
```

Back on the first SQL Server instance, the following table is created to hold rows for MegaCorp website hits:

```
Use AdventureWorks
GO

CREATE TABLE dbo.WebHits_MegaCorp
    (WebHitID uniqueidentifier NOT NULL,
     WebSite varchar(20) NOT NULL ,
     HitDT datetime NOT NULL,
     CHECK (WebSite = 'MegaCorp'),
     CONSTRAINT PK_WebHits PRIMARY KEY (WebHitID, WebSite))
```

On the second SQL Server instance, the following table is created to hold rows for MiniCorp website hits:

```
Use AdventureWorks
GO
CREATE TABLE dbo.WebHits_MiniCorp
   (WebHitID uniqueidentifier NOT NULL ,
    WebSite varchar(20) NOT NULL ,
    HitDT datetime NOT NULL,
    CHECK (WebSite = 'MiniCorp') ,
    CONSTRAINT PK_WebHits PRIMARY KEY (WebHitID, WebSite))
```

Back on the first SQL Server instance, the following distributed partitioned view that references the local WebHits_MegaCorp table and the remote WebHits.MiniCorp table is created:

```
CREATE VIEW dbo.v_WebHits AS
   SELECT WebHitID,
          WebSite,
          HitDT
   FROM AdventureWorks.dbo.WebHits_MegaCorp
UNION ALL
   SELECT WebHitID,
          WebSite,
          HitDT
   FROM JOEPROD.AdventureWorks.dbo.WebHits_MiniCorp
GO
```

On the second SQL Server instance, the following distributed partitioned view is created—this time referencing the local WebHits_MiniCorp table and the remote WebHits_MegaCorp table:

```
CREATE VIEW dbo.v_WebHits AS
  SELECT WebHitID,
       WebSite,
       HitDT
  FROM AdventureWorks.dbo.WebHits_MiniCorp
UNION ALL
  SELECT WebHitID,
       WebSite,
       HitDT
  FROM [JOEPROD\SQL2005].AdventureWorks.dbo.WebHits_MegaCorp
GO
```

On the second SQL Server instance, the following batch of queries is executed to insert new rows:

```
-- For these inserts to work the setting XACT_ABORT must be ON and
-- the Distributed Transaction Coordinator service must be running

SET XACT_ABORT ON

INSERT dbo.v_WebHits
(WebHitID, WebSite, HitDT)
VALUES(NEWID(), 'MegaCorp', GETDATE())

INSERT dbo.v_WebHits
(WebHitID, WebSite, HitDT)
VALUES(NEWID(), 'MiniCorp', GETDATE())
```

This returns:

```
(1 row(s) affected)

(1 row(s) affected)
```

Querying from the distributed-partitioned view returns the two newly inserted rows (from both underlying tables):

```
SET XACT_ABORT ON

SELECT WebHitID, WebSite, HitDT
FROM dbo.v_WebHits
```

This returns:

WebHitID	WebSite	HitDT
E5994678-6066-45F4-8AE4-9F10CE412D1A	MegaCorp	2005-08-06 16:56:29.253
E1444A3F-7A2E-4A54-A156-C04FE742B453	MiniCorp	2005-08-06 16:56:29.353

Querying the MiniCorp table directly returns just the one MiniCorp row, as expected:

```
SELECT WebHitID, WebSite, HitDT
FROM JOEPROD.AdventureWorks.dbo.WebHits_MiniCorp
```

This returns:

WebHitID	WebSite	HitDT
E1444A3F-7A2E-4A54-A156-C04FE742B453	MiniCorp	2005-08-06 16:56:29.353

Querying the MegaCorp table also returns the expected, single row:

```
SELECT WebHitID, WebSite, HitDT
FROM [JOEPROD\SQL2005].AdventureWorks.dbo.WebHits_MegaCorp
```

This returns:

WebHitID	WebSite	HitDT
E5994678-6066-45F4-8AE4-9F10CE412D1A	MegaCorp	2005-08-06 16:56:29.253

How It Works

Distributed-partitioned views allow you to partition data across more than one SQL Server instance. This design option can be beneficial for very large databases and SQL Server instances with high volumes of transactions and read activity.

There's a lot going on in this recipe, so I'll walk through each step of the process.

First, linked server references were created on each SQL Server instance so that both instances could use distributed queries to communicate with one another (again, see Chapter 30). Also, the linked server option lazy schema validation was enabled for performance reasons. This setting ensures that schema lookups are skipped prior to query execution.

Next the table dbo.WebHits_MegaCorp was created on SQL Server Instance 1 (JOEPROD\SQL2005) and dbo.WebHits_MiniCorp on SQL Server Instance 2 (JOEPROD). Each was created with a CHECK constraint that restricted what values could be added to it. So that distributed-partitioned view updates are allowed, the CHECK constraints must be defined on the same column and cannot allow overlapping values in the member tables. In addition to this, only the operators <,>, =, >=, <=, AND, OR, and BETWEEN can be used in the CHECK constraint.

Other requirements you'll need to remember in order to allow view updates: the partitioning column, in this case WebSite, cannot allow null values; be a computed column; or be an identity, default, or timestamp column. The partition key, WebSite, also needed to be part of the primary key. Since WebSite wasn't unique by itself, it was added as a composite key with the uniqueidentifier data type WebHitID. Both partitioned tables were required to have primary keys on an identical number of columns:

```
CONSTRAINT PK_WebHits PRIMARY KEY (WebHitID, WebSite))
```

In the next step, the distributed partitioned views were created on each of the SQL Server instances. On the instance with the dbo.WebHits_MegaCorp table, the view referenced that table using the three-part database.schema.viewname format (because the table is local):

```
SELECT WebHitID,
       WebSite,
       HitDT
 FROM AdventureWorks.dbo.WebHits_MegaCorp
```

The table was then joined with UNION ALL (another requirement if you wish to perform data modifications against the distributed partitioned view):

```
UNION ALL
```

The columns defined in the SELECT list can't be referenced more than once in a single list, and should be in the same ordinal position for each SELECT that is UNIONed. Columns across each SELECT should also have the same data types and collations, as this recipe did.

In the FROM clause for the remote dbo.WebHits_MiniCorp table, the four-part name linkedservername.database.schema.viewname was used (since it is a remote table):

```
SELECT WebHitID,
       WebSite,
       HitDT
FROM JOEPROD.AdventureWorks.dbo.WebHits_MiniCorp
GO
```

In the last batches in the recipe, SET XACT_ABORT was set ON in order to allow for the insert of rows into the distributed partitioned view. This option terminates and rolls back a transaction if a runtime error is encountered:

```
SET XACT_ABORT ON
```

As noted in the script comments, the Distributed Transaction Coordinator also needs to be running in order to invoke the distributed transaction of inserting a row across SQL Server instances.

Two inserts were performed against the new distributed partitioned view; the first for a hit to MegaCorp, and the second for MiniCorp:

```
INSERT dbo.v_WebHits
(WebHitID, WebSite, HitDT)
VALUES(NEWID(), 'MegaCorp', GETDATE())

INSERT dbo.v_WebHits
(WebHitID, WebSite, HitDT)
VALUES(NEWID(), 'MiniCorp', GETDATE())
```

Querying the new distributed partitioned views, two rows are returned:

```
SELECT WebHitID, WebSite, HitDT
FROM dbo.v_WebHits
```

Querying the underlying horizontally partitioned tables, one row was automatically routed to the dbo.WebHits_MegaCorp table, and the other to the dbo.WebHits_MiniCorp table.

Based on which view is queried (for example Instance 1 or Instance 2), SQL Server can determine if a particular query request can be fulfilled from just querying the local partitioned table, or whether the remote table need also be queried. The end result is that SQL Server minimizes the amount of data needing to be transferred between the SQL Server instances.

CHAPTER 8

■■■

SQL Server Functions

In this chapter, I'll demonstrate how to use SQL Server 2005 built-in functions in your Transact-SQL code. SQL Server 2005 built-in functions, not to be confused with the user-defined functions covered in Chapter 11, allow you to perform aggregations, mathematical operations, string manipulation, row ranking, and much more.

Aggregate Functions

Aggregate functions are used to perform a calculation on one or more values, resulting in a single value. An example of a commonly used aggregate function is SUM, which is used to return the total value of a set of numeric values. Table 8-1 lists some of the more commonly used aggregate functions available in SQL Server 2005.

Table 8-1. *Aggregate Functions*

Function Name	Description
AVG	The AVG aggregate function calculates the average of non-NULL values in a group.
COUNT	The COUNT aggregate function returns an integer data type showing the count of rows in a group.
COUNT_BIG	Works the same as COUNT, only COUNT_BIG returns a bigint data type value.
MAX	The MAX aggregate function returns the highest value in a set of non-NULL values.
MIN	The MIN aggregate function returns the lowest value in a group of non-NULL values.
SUM	The SUM aggregate function returns the total of all non-NULL values in an expression.
STDEV	The STDEV function returns the standard deviation of all values provided in the expression based on a sample of the data population.
STDEVP	The STDEVP function also returns the standard deviation for all values in the provided expression, only it evaluates the entire data population.
VAR	The VAR function returns the statistical variance of values in an expression based on a sample of the provided population.
VARP	The VARP function also returns the variance of the provided values for the entire data population of the expression.

The next few recipes will demonstrate these aggregate functions.

Returning the Average of Values

The AVG aggregate function calculates the average of non-NULL values in a group.

This first example demonstrates how to use the AVG aggregate function to return the average of non-NULL values in a group:

```
-- Average Product Review by Product
SELECT ProductID,
       AVG(Rating) AvgRating
FROM Production.ProductReview
GROUP BY ProductID
```

This returns:

ProductID	AvgRating
709	5
798	5
937	3

This second example demonstrates averaging the DISTINCT value of the StandardCost column—meaning that only unique StandardCost values are averaged:

```
-- Average DISTINCT Standard Cost
SELECT AVG(DISTINCT StandardCost) AvgDistinctStandardCost
FROM Production.ProductCostHistory
```

This returns:

AvgDistinctStandardCost
287.7111

How It Works

In this recipe, the first example returned the average product rating grouped by ProductID.

The second example took an average of the DISTINCT StandardCost—meaning that only unique StandardCost values were averaged. Without the DISTINCT keyword, the default behavior of the AVG aggregate function is to average all values, duplicate values included.

Returning Row Counts

The COUNT aggregate function returns an integer data type showing the count of the rows in a group.

This example demonstrates using the COUNT aggregate function to return row counts by a group:

```
SELECT  Shelf,
        COUNT(ProductID) ProductCount
FROM  Production.ProductInventory
GROUP BY Shelf
ORDER BY Shelf
```

This returns the following (abridged) results:

Shelf	ProductCount
A	81
B	36
C	55
D	50
E	85
F	59
G	96
...	

If you include the DISTINCT keyword within the COUNT function parentheses, you'll get the count of distinct values for that column. For example:

```
SELECT  COUNT(DISTINCT Shelf) ShelfCount
FROM  Production.ProductInventory
```

This returns:

ShelfCount
21

How It Works

In the first example of this recipe, the number of products per shelf was counted. COUNT is the only aggregate function that does not ignore NULL values, so had ProductID been NULL, it would have still been included in the count. The second example demonstrated counting the number of DISTINCT Shelf values from the Production.ProductInventory table.

If you need to count a value larger than the integer data type can hold, use the COUNT_BIG aggregate function, which returns a bigint data type value.

Finding the Lowest and Highest Values from an Expression

The MAX aggregate function returns the highest value and the MIN aggregate function returns the lowest value in a group of non-NULL values. MIN and MAX can be used with numeric, character, and datetime columns. The minimum and maximum values for character data types are determined by using an ASCII alphabetical sort. MIN and MAX for datetime values are based on the earliest date to the most recent date.

In this example, I'll demonstrate how to use the MIN and MAX functions to find the lowest and highest value in the Rating numeric column from the Production.ProductReview table:

```
SELECT  MIN(Rating) MinRating,
     MAX(Rating) MaxRating
FROM  Production.ProductReview
```

This returns:

MinRating	MaxRating
2	5

How It Works

This recipe demonstrated retrieving the minimum and maximum Rating values from the Product.ProductReview table. As with other aggregate functions, had there also been non-aggregated column references in the SELECT clause, they would have been included in a GROUP BY clause.

Returning the Sum of Values

The SUM aggregate function returns the total of all non-NULL values in an expression.

This example demonstrates how to use the SUM aggregate function to total the value of the TotalDue column for each AccountNumber:

```
SELECT  AccountNumber,
     SUM(TotalDue) TotalDueBySalesOrderID
FROM Sales.SalesOrderHeader
GROUP BY AccountNumber
ORDER BY AccountNumber
```

This returns the following abridged results:

AccountNumber	TotalDueBySalesOrderID
10-4020-000001	113098.7351
10-4020-000002	32733.9695
10-4020-000003	479506.3256
10-4020-000004	780035.2121
10-4020-000005	114218.8006

How It Works

In this recipe, the TotalDue column was totaled by AccountNumber. Since AccountNumber wasn't aggregated itself, it was included in the GROUP BY clause. It was also included in the ORDER BY clause, in order to order the grouped results.

Using Statistical Aggregate Functions

In this recipe, I'll demonstrate using the statistical functions VAR, VARP, STDEV, and STDEVP.

The VAR function returns the statistical variance of values in an expression based on a sample of the provided population (the VARP function also returns the variance of the provided values for the entire data population of the expression).

This first example returns the statistical variance of the TaxAmt value for all rows in the Sales.SalesOrderHeader table:

```
SELECT  VAR(TaxAmt) Variance_Sample,
     VARP(TaxAmt) Variance_EntirePopulation
FROM Sales.SalesOrderHeader
```

This returns:

Variance_Sample	Variance_EntirePopulation
1177342.57277401	1177305.15524429

The STDEV function returns the standard deviation of all the values provided in the expression, based on a sample of the data population. The STDEVP function also returns the standard deviation for all values in the provided expression, only it evaluates the entire data population instead.

This example returns the statistical standard deviation of the UnitPrice value for all rows in the Sales.SalesOrderDetail table:

```
SELECT  STDEV(UnitPrice) StandDevUnitPrice,
     STDEVP(UnitPrice)StandDevPopUnitPrice
FROM  Sales.SalesOrderDetail
```

This returns:

```
StandDevUnitPrice    StandDevPopUnitPrice
751.885080772954     751.881981921885
```

How It Works

Although the use of each statistical function varies, the implementation is similar. Specifically, in this example, each function takes a value expression, using a column name from the table. The function then acts on the set of data (zero or more rows) using the column specified in the SELECT clause, returning a single value.

Mathematical Functions

SQL Server 2005 offers several mathematical functions that can be used in your Transact-SQL code, as described in Table 8-2.

Table 8-2. *Mathematical Functions*

Function	Description
ABS	Calculates the absolute value.
ACOS	Calculates the angle, the cosine of which is the specified argument, in radians.
ASIN	Calculates the angle, the sine of which is the specified argument, in radians.
ATAN	Calculates the angle, the tangent of which is the specified argument, in radians.
ATN2	Calculates the angle, the tangent of which is between two float expressions, in radians.
CEILING	Calculates the smallest integer greater than or equal to the provided argument.
COS	Calculates the cosine.
COT	Calculates the cotangent.
DEGREES	Converts radians to degrees.
EXP	Calculates the exponential value of a provided argument.
FLOOR	Calculates the largest integer less than or equal to the provided argument.
LOG	Calculates the natural logarithm.
LOG10	Calculates the Base-10 logarithm.
PI	Returns the Pi constant.
POWER	Returns the value of the first argument to the power of the second argument.
RADIANS	Converts degrees to radians.
RAND	Produces a random float type value ranging from 0 to 1.
ROUND	Rounds a provided argument's value to a specified precision.
SIGN	Returns –1 for negative values, 0 for zero values, and 1 if the provided argument is positive.
SIN	Calculates the sine for a given angle in radians.
SQUARE	Calculates the square of a provided expression.
SQRT	Calculates the square root.
TAN	Calculates the tangent.

This next recipe will demonstrate mathematical functions in action.

Using Mathematical Functions

This recipe will demonstrate four different mathematical functions, including POWER, SQRT, ROUND, and RAND.

This first example calculates 10 to the 2nd power:

```
SELECT POWER(10,2) Result
```

This returns:

Result
100

This next example calculates the square root of 100:

```
SELECT SQRT(100) Result
```

This returns:

Result
10

This example rounds a number to the third digit right of the decimal place:

```
SELECT ROUND(3.22245, 3) RoundedNumber
```

This returns:

RoundedNumber
3.22200

This example returns a random, float, data-type value between 0 and 1:

```
SELECT RAND() RandomNumber
```

This returns:

RandomNumber
0.497749897248417

This last example in the recipe returns a fixed, float, data-type value based on the provided integer value:

```
SELECT RAND(22) Result
```

This returns:

Result
0.713983285609346

How It Works

In this recipe, I demonstrated four different mathematical functions, including POWER, SQRT, ROUND, and RAND. Each function takes different parameters based on the operation it performs. For some mathematical functions, such as RAND, an input value is optional.

String Functions

This next set of recipes demonstrates SQL Server 2005's string functions. String functions provide a multitude of uses for your Transact-SQL programming, allowing for string cleanup, conversion between ASCII and regular characters, pattern searches, removing trailing blanks, and much more.

Table 8-3 lists the different string functions available in SQL Server 2005.

Table 8-3. *String Functions*

Function Name(s)	Description
ASCII and CHAR	The ASCII function takes the leftmost character of a character expression and returns the ASCII code. The CHAR function converts an integer value for an ASCII code to a character value instead.
CHARINDEX and PATINDEX	The CHARINDEX function is used to return the starting position of a string within another string. The PATINDEX function is similar to CHARINDEX, except that PATINDEX allows the use of wildcards when specifying the string for which to search.
DIFFERENCE and SOUNDEX	The two functions DIFFERENCE and SOUNDEX both work with character strings to evaluate those that sound similar. SOUNDEX assigns a string a four-digit code, and DIFFERENCE evaluates the level of similarity between the SOUNDEX outputs for two separate strings.
LEFT and RIGHT	The LEFT function returns a part of a character string, beginning at the specified number of characters from the left. The RIGHT function is like the LEFT function, only it returns a part of a character string beginning at the specified number of characters from the right.
LEN and DATALENGTH	The LEN function returns the number of characters in a string expression, excluding any blanks after the last character (trailing blanks). DATALENGTH, on the other hand, returns the number of bytes used for an expression.
LOWER and UPPER	The LOWER function returns a character expression in lowercase and the UPPER function returns a character expression in uppercase.
LTRIM and RTRIM	The LTRIM function removes leading blanks and the RTRIM function removes trailing blanks.
NCHAR and UNICODE	The UNICODE function returns the Unicode integer value for the first character of the character or input expression. The NCHAR function takes an integer value designating a Unicode character and converts it to its character equivalent.
QUOTENAME	The QUOTENAME function adds delimiters to a Unicode input string in order to make it a valid delimited identifier.
REPLACE	The REPLACE function replaces all instances of a provided string within a specified string, and replaces it with a new string.
REPLICATE	The REPLICATE function repeats a given character expression a designated number of times.
REVERSE	The REVERSE function takes a character expression and outputs the expression with each character position displayed in reverse order.
SPACE	The SPACE function returns a string of repeated blank spaces, based on the integer you designate for the input parameter.
STR	The STR function converts numeric data into character data.
STUFF	The STUFF function deletes a specified length of characters and inserts a designated string at the specified starting point.
SUBSTRING	The SUBSTRING function returns a defined chunk of a specified expression.

The next few recipes will demonstrate examples of how string functions are used.

Converting a Character Value to ASCII and Back to Character

The ASCII function takes the leftmost character of a character expression and returns the ASCII code, while the CHAR function converts an integer value for an ASCII code to a character value instead. Again, it should be stressed that ASCII only uses the first character of the string. If the string is empty or NULL, ASCII will return a NULL value (although a blank value returns 32).

This first example demonstrates how to convert characters into the integer ASCII value:

```
SELECT ASCII('H'), ASCII('e'), ASCII('l'), ASCII('l'), ASCII('o')
```

This returns:

72	101	108	108	111

Next, the CHAR function is used to convert the integer values back into characters again:

```
SELECT CHAR(72), CHAR(101), CHAR(108), CHAR(108), CHAR(111)
```

This returns:

H	e	l	l	o

How It Works

In this recipe, the word "Hello" was deconstructed one character at a time and then converted into the numeric ASCII value, using the ASCII function. In the second T-SQL statement, the ASCII value was reversed back into character form using the CHAR function.

Returning Integer and Character Unicode Values

The UNICODE function returns the Unicode integer value for the first character of the character or input expression. The NCHAR function takes an integer value designating a Unicode character and converts it to its character equivalent. These functions are useful if you need to exchange data with external processes using the Unicode standard.

This first example converts single characters into an integer value representing the Unicode standard character code:

```
SELECT UNICODE('G'), UNICODE('o'), UNICODE('o'), UNICODE('d'), UNICODE('!')
```

This returns:

71	111	111	100	33

Next, the Unicode integer values are converted back into characters:

```
SELECT NCHAR(71), NCHAR(111), NCHAR(111), NCHAR(100), NCHAR(33)
```

This returns:

G	o	o	d	!

How It Works

In this recipe, the word "Good!" was deconstructed one character at a time and then converted into an integer value using the UNICODE function. In the second T-SQL statement, the integer value was reversed back into character form using the NCHAR function.

Finding the Start Position of a String Within Another String

The CHARINDEX function is used to return the starting position of a string within another string. The syntax is as follows:

```
CHARINDEX ( expression1 ,expression2 [ , start_location ] )
```

The expression1 argument is the string to be searched for. The expresssion2 argument is the string in which you are searching. The optional start_location value indicates the character position where you wish to begin looking.

This example demonstrates how to find the starting position of a string within another string:

```
SELECT CHARINDEX('String to Find', 'This is the bigger string to find something in.')
```

This returns:

```
20
```

How It Works

This function returned the starting character position, in this case the 20th character, where the first argument expression was found in the second expression. You can't use wildcards with this function. Also, note that search matches are based on the rules of your SQL Server instance's collation.

Finding the Start Position of a String Within Another String Using Wildcards

The PATINDEX function is similar to CHARINDEX, except that PATINDEX allows the use of wildcards in the string you are searching for. The syntax for PATINDEX is:

```
PATINDEX ( '%pattern%' ,expression )
```

PATINDEX returns the start position of the first occurrence of the search pattern, but unlike CHARINDEX, it doesn't have a starting position option.

In this example, rows are returned from Person.Address where AddressLine1 contains the word fragment "olive":

```
SELECT  AddressID,
        AddressLine1
FROM  Person.Address
WHERE PATINDEX('%olive%', AddressLine1) > 0
```

This returns the following abridged results:

```
AddressID   AddressLine1
29048       1201 Olive Hill
11768       1201 Olive Hill
15417       1206 Olive St
24480       1480 Oliveria Road
...
```

How It Works

This example returned any row where the AddressLine1 column contained the word "Olive." With the wild card % on both the left and right of the word (without spaces between), the word "Olive" could also have been embedded within another word. The pattern can use different wildcard characters too. For a full review of wildcards, see Chapter 1 and the recipe "Using Wildcards with LIKE."

Determining the Similarity of Strings

The two functions, DIFFERENCE and SOUNDEX, both work with character strings in order to evaluate those that sound similar, based on English phonetic rules. SOUNDEX assigns a string a four-digit code, and then DIFFERENCE evaluates the level of similarity between the SOUNDEX outputs for two separate strings.

DIFFERENCE returns a value of zero to four, with four indicating the closest match in similarity.

This example demonstrates how to identify strings that sound similar—first by evaluating strings individually, and then comparing them in pairs:

```
SELECT  SOUNDEX('Fleas'),
        SOUNDEX('Fleece'),
        SOUNDEX('Peace'),
        SOUNDEX('Peas')
```

This returns:

F420	F420	P200	P200

Next, string pairs are compared using DIFFERENCE:

```
SELECT  DIFFERENCE ( 'Fleas', 'Fleece')
```

This returns:

4

Next, another string pair is compared:

```
SELECT  DIFFERENCE ( 'Fleece', 'Peace')
```

This returns:

2

How It Works

In the first example, SOUNDEX was used to evaluate four similar sounding words. The query results showed four codes, with "Fleas" and "Fleece" equal to F420, and "Peace" and "Peas" equal to P200.

In the second example, DIFFERENCE was used to evaluate "Fleas" and "Fleece" and "Fleece" and "Peace." "Fleas" and "Fleece" were shown to be *more* similar with a value of 4 than "Fleece" and "Peace" which had a comparison value of 2.

Taking the Leftmost or Rightmost Part of a String

The LEFT function returns a part of a character string, beginning at the specified number of characters from the left. The RIGHT function is like the LEFT function, only it returns a part of a character string beginning at the specified number of characters from the right.

This recipe demonstrates how to return a subset of the leftmost and rightmost parts of a string. Also, a common string padding trick is demonstrated using these functions.

In the first example, the leftmost 10 characters are taken from a string:

```
SELECT LEFT('I only want the leftmost 10 characters.', 10)
```

This returns:

```
I only wan
```

Next, the rightmost characters of a string:

```
SELECT RIGHT('I only want the rightmost 10 characters.', 10)
```

This returns:

```
haracters.
```

This next example demonstrates zero-padding the ListPrice column's value:

```
-- Padding a number for business purposes
SELECT  TOP 3
    ProductID, RIGHT('0000000000' + CONVERT(varchar(10), ListPrice),10)
FROM  Production.Product
WHERE ListPrice > 0
```

This returns:

```
ProductID   (No column name)
514         0000133.34
515         0000147.14
516         0000196.92
```

How It Works

This recipe demonstrated three examples of using LEFT and RIGHT. The first two examples demonstrated returning the leftmost or the rightmost characters of a string value.

The third example demonstrated the padding of a string in order to conform to some expected business format. When presenting data to end-users or exporting data to external systems, you may sometimes need to preserve or add leading values, such as leading zeros to fixed length numbers. ListPrice was zero-padded by first concatenating ten zeros in a string to the converted varchar(10) value of the ListPrice. Then, outside of this concatenation, RIGHT was used to grab the last 10 characters of the concatenated string (thus taking leading zeros from the left side with it, when the ListPrice fell short of ten digits):

```
RIGHT('0000000000' + CONVERT(varchar(10), ListPrice),10)
```

Determining the Number of Characters or Bytes in a String

The LEN function returns the number of characters in a string expression, excluding any blanks after the last character (trailing blanks). DATALENGTH, on the other hand, returns the number of bytes used for an expression. In this recipe, I'll demonstrate how to measure the number of characters and bytes in a string.

This first example returns the number of characters in the string:

```
SELECT LEN(N'She sells sea shells by the sea shore.')
```

This returns:

38

This next example returns the number of bytes in the string.

```
SELECT DATALENGTH(N'She sells sea shells by the sea shore.')
```

This returns:

76

How It Works

This recipe used a Unicode string, which is defined by prefixing the string with an N as follows:

```
N'She sells sea shells by the sea shore.'
```

The number of characters for this string is 38 according to LEN, but since it is a Unicode string, DATALENGTH returns 76 bytes. Unicode data takes two bytes for each character, whereas non-Unicode takes only one.

Replacing a Part of a String with Another String

The REPLACE function replaces all instances of a provided string within a specified string, and replaces it with a new string. One real strength of REPLACE is, unlike PATINDEX and CHARINDEX which return a specific location where a pattern is found, REPLACE can find multiple instances of a pattern within a specific character string.

The syntax for REPLACE is:

```
REPLACE ( 'string_expression1' , 'string_expression2' , 'string_expression3' )
```

The first string expression argument is the string that will be modified. The second string expression is the string to be removed from the first string argument. The third string expression is the string to insert into the first argument.

This example demonstrates how to replace all instances of a provided string with a new string:

```
SELECT REPLACE('Zenon is our major profit center. Zenon leads the way.',
          'Zenon',
          'Xerxes')
```

This returns:

```
Xerxes is our major profit center. Xerxes leads the way.
```

How It Works

In this recipe, the first string expression was the string to be searched, "Zenon is our major profit center. Zenon leads the way." The second expression was the expression to replace ("Zenon"), and the third expression was the value to substitute "Zenon" with "Xerxes."

Stuffing a String into a String

The STUFF function deletes a specified length of characters and inserts a designated string at the specified starting point. The syntax is:

```
STUFF ( character_expression, start, length, character_expression )
```

The first argument of this function is the character expression to be modified. The second argument is the starting position of the inserted string. The length is the number of characters to delete within the character expression. The fourth argument is the actual character expression that you want to insert.

This example replaces a part of a string and inserts a new expression into the string body:

```
SELECT STUFF ( 'My cat's name is X. Have you met him?',
        18,
        1,
        'Edgar' )
```

This returns:

```
My cat's name is Edgar. Have you met him?
```

How It Works

The character expression in this recipe was "My cat's name is X'ING Have you met him?". The start value was 18, which means that the replacement will occur at the 18th position within the string (which is X, in this case). The length value was 1, meaning only one character at position 18 would be deleted. The last character expression was Edgar which is the value to stuff into the string.

Changing Character Values to Lower, Upper, and Proper Case

The LOWER function returns a character expression in lowercase and the UPPER function returns a character expression in uppercase. There isn't a built-in proper case function, so a user-defined function will be demonstrated in this recipe instead.

Before showing the different functions in action, the following query I've presented will show the value of DocumentSummary for a specific row in the Production.Document table:

```
SELECT  DocumentSummary
FROM Production.Document
WHERE DocumentID = 4
```

This returns the following sentence case value:

```
Detailed instructions for replacing pedals with Adventure Works Cycles replacement
pedals.  Instructions are applicable to all Adventure Works Cycles bicycle models and
replacement pedals. Use only Adventure Works Cycles parts when replacing worn or broken
components.
```

This first example demonstrates setting values to lowercase:

```
SELECT  LOWER(DocumentSummary)
FROM Production.Document
WHERE DocumentID = 4
```

This returns:

---

detailed instructions for replacing pedals with adventure works cycles replacement pedals. instructions are applicable to all adventure works cycles bicycle models and replacement pedals. use only adventure works cycles parts when replacing worn or broken components.

Now for uppercase:

```
SELECT  UPPER(DocumentSummary)
FROM Production.Document
WHERE DocumentID = 4
```

This returns:

DETAILED INSTRUCTIONS FOR REPLACING PEDALS WITH ADVENTURE WORKS CYCLES REPLACEMENT PEDALS. INSTRUCTIONS ARE APPLICABLE TO ALL ADVENTURE WORKS CYCLES BICYCLE MODELS AND REPLACEMENT PEDALS. USE ONLY ADVENTURE WORKS CYCLES PARTS WHEN REPLACING WORN OR BROKEN COMPONENTS.

In order to set a string to proper case (capitalizing the letter of each word in the string), a user-defined function can be used. The CREATE FUNCTION syntax usage is demonstrated in detail in Chapter 11:

```
CREATE FUNCTION udf_ProperCase(@UnCased varchar(max))
RETURNS varchar(max)
AS
BEGIN

   SET @UnCased = LOWER(@UnCased)

   DECLARE @C int
   SET @C = ASCII('a')

   WHILE @C <= ASCII('z')
   BEGIN

  SET @UnCased = REPLACE( @UnCased, ' ' + CHAR(@C), ' ' +  CHAR(@C-32))
      SET @C = @C + 1
   END

   SET @UnCased = CHAR(ASCII(LEFT(@UnCased, 1))-32) + RIGHT(@UnCased,
LEN(@UnCased)-1)

   RETURN @UnCased
END

GO
```

Once the user-defined function is created, the string to modify to proper case can be used as the function parameter:

```
SELECT  dbo.udf_ProperCase(DocumentSummary)
FROM Production.Document
WHERE DocumentID = 4
```

This returns:

```
Detailed Instructions For Replacing Pedals With Adventure Works Cycles Replacement
Pedals.  Instructions Are Applicable To All Adventure Works Cycles Bicycle Models And
Replacement Pedals. Use Only Adventure Works Cycles Parts When Replacing Worn Or Broken
Components.
```

How It Works

The first example demonstrated the LOWER function, which returned a character expression in lower-case. The second example demonstrated the UPPER function, which returned a character expression in uppercase.

There isn't a built-in proper case function, so a user-defined function was created in this recipe instead.

The first line of the CREATE FUNCTION definition defines the name and parameter expected—in this case a varchar(max) data type parameter:

```
CREATE FUNCTION udf_ProperCase(@UnCased varchar(max))
```

The RETURNS keyword defined what data type would be returned by the function after the logic has been applied:

```
RETURNS varchar(max)
AS
BEGIN
```

Next, the variable passed to the function was first modified to lowercase using the LOWER function:

```
SET @UnCased = LOWER(@UnCased)
```

A new integer local variable @C was set to the ASCII value of the letter 'a':

```
DECLARE @C int
SET @C = ASCII('a')
```

A WHILE loop was initiated to go through every letter in the alphabet, and for each, search for a space preceding that letter, and then replace each occurrence of a letter preceded by a space with the uppercase version of the character:

```
WHILE @C <= ASCII('z')
   BEGIN
   SET @UnCased = REPLACE( @UnCased, ' ' + CHAR(@C), ' ' + CHAR(@C-32))
      SET @C = @C + 1
   END
```

The conversion to uppercase is performed by subtracting 32 from the ASCII integer value of the lowercase character. For example, the ASCII value for a lowercase "a" is 97, while the uppercase A is 65.

```
SET @UnCased = CHAR(ASCII(LEFT(@UnCased, 1))-32) + RIGHT(@UnCased, LEN(@UnCased)-1)
```

The final proper case string value of @UnCased is then returned from the function:

```
   RETURN @UnCased
END
GO
```

Removing Leading and Trailing Blanks

The LTRIM function removes leading blanks and the RTRIM function removes trailing blanks.

This first example demonstrates removing leading blanks from a string:

```
SELECT LTRIM('    String with leading blanks.')
```

This returns:

```
String with leading blanks.
```

This second example demonstrates removing trailing blanks from a string:

```
SELECT RTRIM('"' + 'String with trailing blanks    ') + '"'
```

This returns:

```
"String with trailing blanks"
```

How It Works

Both LTRIM and RTRIM take a single argument—a character expression that trims the leading or trailing blanks. Note that there isn't a TRIM function (as seen in other programming languages) that can be used to remove both leading and trailing characters. To do this, you must use both LTRIM and RTRIM in the same expression.

Repeating an Expression N Number of Times

The REPLICATE function repeats a given character expression a designated number of times.

The syntax is:

```
REPLICATE ( character_expression ,integer_expression )
```

The first argument is the character expression to be repeated. The second argument is the integer value of the number of times the character expression is to be repeated.

This example demonstrates how to use the REPLICATE function to repeat a character expression a set number of times:

```
SELECT REPLICATE ('Z', 30)
```

This returns:

```
ZZZZZZZZZZZZZZZZZZZZZZZZZZZZZZ
```

How It Works

In this recipe's example, the letter Z in the character expression was repeated 30 times. Use REPLICATE to repeat values rather than having to code the characters manually. The maximum return value is 8,000 bytes.

Repeating a Blank Space N Number of Times

The SPACE function returns a string of repeated blank spaces, based on the integer you designate for the input parameter.

This example demonstrates how to repeat a blank space a defined number of times:

```
SELECT  'Give me some' + SPACE(6) + 'space.'
```

This returns:

```
Give me some      space.
```

How It Works

In this recipe, six blank spaces were concatenated in the middle of two strings. The maximum return value is 8,000 bytes.

Outputting an Expression in Reverse Order

The REVERSE function takes a character expression, and outputs the expression with each character position displayed in reverse order.

This example demonstrates how to reverse a string expression:

```
SELECT  TOP 1
    GroupName,
    REVERSE(GroupName) GroupNameReversed
FROM HumanResources.Department
ORDER BY GroupName
```

This returns:

```
GroupName                              GroupNameReversed
Executive General and Administration   noitartsinimdA dna lareneG evitucexE
```

How It Works

This recipe demonstrated using the REVERSE function to output a string's characters in reverse order.

Returning a Chunk of an Expression

The SUBSTRING function returns a defined chunk of a specified expression.

The syntax is as follows:

```
SUBSTRING ( expression, start, length )
```

The first argument of this function is the character expression that you should use to return a defined chunk. The second argument defines the character starting position of the chunk. The third argument is the length of the character chunk that you want to extract.

In this example, assume your application receives a bank account number from a customer. It is your company's policy to only store a masked representation of the bank number, retaining the middle four digits only:

```
DECLARE @BankAccountNumber char(14)
SET @BankAccountNumber = '1424-2342-3536'

SELECT 'XXXX-' + SUBSTRING(@BankAccountNumber, 6,4) + '-XXXX' Masked_BankAccountNumber
```

This returns:

```
Masked_BankAccountNumber
XXXX-2342-XXXX
```

How It Works

In this recipe, the SUBSTRING function was used to get the middle four digits from a longer bank account number. The expression in the SUBSTRING function call was the bank account number, followed by the starting position, and then the number of characters to extract.

Working with NULLs

A NULL value can be tricky to code around because its value is unknown. SQL Server 2005 provides functions used to handle NULLs in your code, as described in Table 8-4.

Table 8-4. *NULL Functions*

Function	Description
ISNULL	ISNULL validates if an expression is NULL, and if so, replaces the NULL value with an alternate value.
COALESCE	The COALESCE function returns the first non-NULL value from a provided list of expressions.
NULLIF	NULLIF returns a NULL value when the two provided expressions have the same value. Otherwise the first expression is returned.

These next few recipes will demonstrate these functions in action.

Replacing a NULL Value with an Alternative Value

ISNULL validates if an expression is NULL, and if so, replaces the NULL value with an alternate value.

In this example, any NULL value will be replaced with a different value:

```
SELECT  LastName,
      ISNULL(Title, 'UNKNOWN') Title
FROM  Person.Contact
WHERE  LastName LIKE 'Sa%'
```

This returns the following (abridged) results:

```
LastName        Title
...
Sam             Mr.
Samant          UNKNOWN
Sandstone       Mr.
```

How It Works

In this example, the LastName column and Samant had a NULL value for the Title column. The ISNULL function replaced that NULL value with the UNKNOWN string expression in the query results.

Performing Flexible Searches Using ISNULL

In this recipe, I'll demonstrate how to perform flexible, dynamic searches in a query when the variables may or may not be populated. This recipe declares three local search variables for ProductID, StartDate, and StandardCost. By using this technique, your query can return results based on all, some, or none of the parameters being used. In this example, only a ProductID is supplied:

```
-- Local variables used for searches
DECLARE @ProductID int
DECLARE @StartDate datetime
DECLARE @StandardCost money

-- Only @ProductID is used
SET @ProductID = 711

SELECT ProductID, StartDate, StandardCost
FROM Production.ProductCostHistory
WHERE ProductID = ISNULL(@ProductID, ProductID) AND
    StartDate = ISNULL(@StartDate, StartDate) AND
    StandardCost = ISNULL(@StandardCost, StandardCost)
```

This returns:

ProductID	StartDate	StandardCost
711	2001-07-01 00:00:00.000	12.0278
711	2002-07-01 00:00:00.000	13.8782
711	2003-07-01 00:00:00.000	13.0863

In this second example, a search is performed by a minimum and maximum StandardCost range:

```
-- Local variables used for searches
DECLARE @ProductID int
DECLARE @MinStandardCost money
DECLARE @MaxStandardCost money

SET @MinStandardCost = 3.3963
SET @MaxStandardCost = 10.0000

SELECT ProductID, StartDate, StandardCost
FROM Production.ProductCostHistory
WHERE ProductID = ISNULL(@ProductID, ProductID) AND
 StandardCost BETWEEN ISNULL(@MinStandardCost, StandardCost) AND
ISNULL(@MaxStandardCost, StandardCost)
ORDER BY StandardCost
```

This returns the following (abridged) results:

ProductID	StartDate	StandardCost
709	2001-07-01 00:00:00.000	3.3963
710	2001-07-01 00:00:00.000	3.3963
712	2001-07-01 00:00:00.000	5.7052
846	2002-07-01 00:00:00.000	5.7709
...		
932	2003-07-01 00:00:00.000	9.3463
860	2002-07-01 00:00:00.000	9.7136
859	2002-07-01 00:00:00.000	9.7136
858	2002-07-01 00:00:00.000	9.7136

How It Works

The benefit of the method demonstrated in this recipe is that your code will be more flexible, allowing for data to be searched in myriad ways, and keeping each search condition optional. The key to this recipe is in the WHERE clause. Each search condition uses ISNULL and the local variable name, followed by the column name itself:

```
WHERE ProductID = ISNULL(@ProductID, ProductID) AND
    StartDate = ISNULL(@StartDate, StartDate) AND
    StandardCost = ISNULL(@StandardCost, StandardCost)
```

If a parameter is not SET, it will remain NULL, and thus the search condition for each column will evaluate the column value against itself—always returning TRUE. Only the parameters that have been specified will be used to filter the results.

Returning the First Non NULL Value in a List of Expressions

The COALESCE function returns the first non-NULL value from a provided list of expressions. The syntax is:

```
COALESCE ( expression [ ,...n ] )
```

This recipe demonstrates how to use COALESCE to return the first occurrence of a non-NULL value:

```
DECLARE @Value1 int
DECLARE @Value2 int
DECLARE @Value3 int

SET @Value2 = 22
SET @Value3 = 955

SELECT COALESCE(@Value1, @Value2, @Value3)
```

This returns:

```
22
```

How It Works

In this recipe, three local variables were created: @Value1, @Value2, and @Value3. Only @Value2 and @Value3 were SET to actual integer values. The variable not SET to a value, @Value2, is NULL. In COALESCE, the three values were checked, from @Value1 to @Value3. Since the @Value2 variable was the first variable with a non-NULL value, "22" was returned.

Returning a NULL Value When Two Expressions Are Equal: Otherwise Return the First Expression

NULLIF returns a NULL value when the two provided expressions have the same value; otherwise the first expression is returned.

This example demonstrates how to use NULLIF to evaluate two expressions. If the two expressions are equal, a NULL value will be returned, otherwise the first evaluated expression is returned:

```
DECLARE @Value1 int
DECLARE @Value2 int

SET @Value1 = 55
SET @Value2 = 955

SELECT NULLIF(@Value1, @Value2)
```

This returns:

```
55
```

The next example tests the values when both are equal:

```
DECLARE @Value1 int
DECLARE @Value2 int

SET @Value1 = 55
SET @Value2 = 55

SELECT NULLIF(@Value1, @Value2)
```

This returns:

```
NULL
```

How It Works

In this recipe, the first batch had two differing values: 55 and 955. Since @Value1 was evaluated first and the values were different, the NULLIF condition is FALSE, and the first evaluated value is returned. In the second batch, both @Value1 and @Value2 were equal, so NULLIF returned a NULL value instead.

Date Functions

As I reviewed earlier in the book, SQL Server 2005 has two different data types used to store date and time data: datetime and smalldatetime. The datetime data type stores dates between January 1st, 1753, through December 31st, 9999, and measures time up to 3.33 milliseconds. The smalldatetime data type stores a smaller range of dates, from January 1st, 1900, through June 6th, 2079, and measures time to the 1 minute granularity. SQL Server 2005 offers several functions used to manipulate and work with these data types, described in Table 8-5.

Table 8-5. *Date Functions*

Function(s)	Description
DATEADD	DATEADD returns a new date that is incremented or decremented based on the interval and number specified.
DATEDIFF	DATEDIFF subtracts the first date from the second date to produce a value in the format of the datepart code specified.
DATENAME	DATENAME returns a string value for the part of a date specified in the datepart code.
DATEPART	This function returns an integer value for the part of a date specified in the datepart code.
DAY, MONTH, and YEAR	DAY returns an integer value for the day, MONTH returns the integer representing the month, and YEAR returns the integer representing the year of the evaluated date.
GETDATE, GETUTCDATE, and CURRENT_TIMESTAMP	GETDATE and CURRENT_TIMESTAMP both return the current date and time. GETUTCDATE returns the Greenwich Mean Time (Universal Time Coordinate).

The next few recipes will demonstrate these date functions.

Returning the Current Date and Time

GETDATE and CURRENT_TIMESTAMP both return the current date and time. GETUTCDATE returns the Greenwich Mean Time   (Universal Time Coordinate).

This example demonstrates how to return the current date and time, as well as the Universal Time Coordinate (Greenwich Mean Time):

```
SELECT  GETDATE(), -- Current Date and Time
    CURRENT_TIMESTAMP, -- Current Date and Time
    GETUTCDATE() -- Universal Time Coordinate or Greenwich Mean Time
```

This returns:

```
2005-08-13 13:15:54.953   2005-08-13 13:15:54.953   2005-08-13 18:15:54.953
```

How It Works

This recipe demonstrated three methods for retrieving the current date and time. All three functions can also be used as a DEFAULT value for date data types within a table column definition.

Incrementing or Decrementing a Date's Value

DATEADD returns a new date, which is the result of having incremented or decremented another date expression. The syntax is:

```
DATEADD (datepart , number, date )
```

The datepart code, used to designate which unit of time the date will be modified by, is described in Table 8-6.

Table 8-6. *Datepart Codes*

Code	Description
yy or yyyy	Year
qq or q	Quarter
mm or m	Month
dy or y	Day of Year
dd or d	Day
wk or ww	Week
dw or w	Weekday
hh	Hour
mi or n	Minute
ss or s	Second
ms	Millisecond

The second argument of the DATEADD function is the numeric value to increment or decrement the date (negative or positive number). The third argument is the date to be modified.

This first example decreases the date by a year:

```
SELECT DATEADD(yy, -1, '4/2/2005')
```

This returns:

```
2004-04-02 00:00:00.000
```

This next example increases the date by a quarter:

```
SELECT DATEADD(q, 1, '4/2/2005')
```

This returns:

```
2005-07-02 00:00:00.000
```

This example decreases a date by six months:

```
SELECT DATEADD(mm, -6, '4/2/2005')
```

This returns:

```
2004-10-02 00:00:00.000
```

This example increases a date by 50 days:

```
SELECT DATEADD(d, 50, '4/2/2005')
```

This returns:

```
2005-05-22 00:00:00.000
```

This example decreases the date and time by 30 minutes:

```
SELECT DATEADD(mi, -30, '2005-09-01 23:30:00.000')
```

This returns:

```
2005-09-01 23:00:00.000
```

How It Works

This recipe demonstrated using the DATEADD function to modify a date based on several granularities. The third argument of DATEADD for each of these examples was a literal date value. However, you can also reference a datetime data type table column or valid date expression.

The first argument, datepart, is also used in different date functions, as you'll see in the next recipe.

Finding the Difference Between Two Dates

DATEDIFF subtracts the first date from the second date, to produce a value in the format of the datepart code specified. The syntax for DATEDIFF is:

```
DATEDIFF ( datepart , startdate , enddate )
```

The first datepart code uses the same datepart codes as DATEADD. The second and third arguments are the date values that are part of the subtraction.

This example demonstrates how to use the DATEDIFF function to find the difference between two dates:

```
-- Find difference in months between now and EndDate
SELECT ProductID,
      EndDate,
      DATEDIFF(m, EndDate, GETDATE()) MonthsFromNow
FROM Production.ProductCostHistory
WHERE EndDate IS NOT NULL
```

This returns the following (abridged) results:

ProductID	EndDate	MonthsFromNow
707	2002-06-30 00:00:00.000	38
707	2003-06-30 00:00:00.000	26
708	2002-06-30 00:00:00.000	38
708	2003-06-30 00:00:00.000	26
...		

How It Works

In this recipe, the difference was calculated between the ProductCostHistory table's EndDate and today's current date, returning the difference by month.

The next recipe demonstrates another function which also uses the datepart argument.

Displaying the String Value for Part of a Date

DATENAME returns a string value for the part of a date specified in the datepart code. The syntax is:

```
DATENAME ( datepart , date )
```

The second parameter designates the date to base the string value on.

In this recipe, I'll demonstrate how to use DATENAME to return the string value for the specified part of a datetime value:

```
-- Show the EndDate's day of the week
SELECT ProductID,
      EndDate,
      DATENAME(dw, EndDate) WeekDay
FROM Production.ProductCostHistory
WHERE EndDate IS NOT NULL
```

This returns the following (abridged) results:

ProductID	EndDate	WeekDay
707	2002-06-30 00:00:00.000	Sunday
707	2003-06-30 00:00:00.000	Monday
708	2002-06-30 00:00:00.000	Sunday
708	2003-06-30 00:00:00.000	Monday
709	2002-06-30 00:00:00.000	Sunday

How It Works

In this recipe, the datepart argument was set to dw (week day), and was based on the EndDate column date, resulting in the day of the week name to be returned.

Displaying the Integer Value for Part of a Date Using DATEPART

This function returns an integer value for the part of a date specified in the date part selection. The syntax for DATEPART is:

```
DATEPART ( datepart , date )
```

The second parameter, date, designates the date for which the integer value is calculated.

This example demonstrates how to return the integer value from a date based on the date part selected. The first example returns the year value:

```
SELECT DATEPART(yy, GETDATE())
```

This returns:

```
2005
```

The next example shows the current month integer value:

```
SELECT DATEPART(m, GETDATE())
```

This returns:

```
8
```

How It Works

In this recipe, the year, month, and day integer values were extracted from the current date and time using the DATEPART function. You can also show these values by using canned functions that don't require the datepart argument, as you'll see in the next recipe.

Displaying the Integer Value for Part of a Date Using YEAR, MONTH, and DAY

There are single parameter functions that you can also use to display the integer values for day, month, and year:

This example returns the current year:

```
SELECT YEAR(GETDATE())
```

This returns:

```
2005
```

This example returns the current month:

```
SELECT MONTH(GETDATE())
```

This returns:

8

This example returns the current day:

```
SELECT DAY(GETDATE())
```

This returns:

13

How It Works

In this recipe, I demonstrated single argument date functions. DAY returns an integer value for the day, MONTH returns the integer representing the month, and YEAR returns the integer representing the year of the evaluated date.

Converting Data Types Using Convert and Cast

The CONVERT and CAST functions are both used to convert multiple data types from one type to another. The syntax for CAST is:

```
CAST ( expression AS data_type [ (length ) ])
```

The first argument is the expression to convert (a table column or literal value, for example). The second argument is the data type to convert the expression to.

The syntax for CONVERT is:

```
CONVERT ( data_type [ ( length ) ] ,expression [ ,style ] )
```

The first argument is the data type that you wish to convert the expression to. The second argument is the expression that you want to be converted. The third argument, style, allows you to configure specific date presentation formats.

Converting Data Types

In this recipe, I'll demonstrate how to convert the data type of an integer to a char(4) data type. In the first example, an integer value is concatenated to a character string:

```
SELECT 2000 + 'Cannot be concatenated'
GO
```

This returns the following error:

```
Msg 245, Level 16, State 1, Line 1
Conversion failed when converting a value of type varchar to type int. Ensure that all
values of the expression being converted can be converted to the target type, or modify
query to avoid this type conversion.
```

In the next example, CONVERT is used to change the integer value into the char data type:

```
SELECT CONVERT(char(4), 2005) + ' Can now be concatenated!'
```

This returns:

```
2005 Can now be concatenated!
```

This example demonstrates performing the same type of conversion, this time using CAST:

```
SELECT EmployeeID, CAST(SickLeaveHours AS char(4)) + ' Sick Leave Hours Left'
FROM HumanResources.Employee
```

This returns the following (abridged) results:

```
EmployeeID     (No column name)
1              30   Sick Leave Hours Left
2              41   Sick Leave Hours Left
3              21   Sick Leave Hours Left
4              80   Sick Leave Hours Left
5              24   Sick Leave Hours Left
```

How It Works

The first query attempts to concatenate an integer and string value together. This results in an error, as the two data types must be compatible or of the same data type. The second attempt used CONVERT to change the data type of the expression to char(4) before concatenating it to the other string. CAST was also used to convert the data type of the smallint column so that it could be concatenated to a string.

Performing Date Conversions

As I mentioned earlier, CONVERT has an optional style parameter which allows you to convert datetime or smalldatetime to specialized character formats. Many people confuse how the date and time is stored with the actual presentation of the date in the query results. When using the style parameter, keep in mind that you are only affecting how the date is presented in its character-based form, and not how it is stored (unless, of course, you choose to store the presented data in a non-datetime data type column).

Some examples of available style formats using the CONVERT function are shown in Table 8-7.

Table 8-7. *CONVERT Style Formats*

Style Code	Format
101	mm/dd/yyyy
102	yy.mm.dd
103	dd/mm/yy
108	hh:mm:ss
110	mm-dd-yy
112	yymmdd

For example:

```
SELECT CONVERT(varchar(20), GETDATE(), 101)
```

returns today's date formatted as:

08/13/2005

When a function like GETDATE() is executed and stored in a datetime column, both the specific date and time data is stored with it. If, however, you only wish to store data at the date level (no specific time), a common trick is to use CONVERT with style to scrub all dates to the 00:00:00.000 time.

The following example converts a datetime value to a character value, and then re-converts it back to the datetime data type:

```
SELECT CONVERT(datetime, CONVERT( varchar(11), '2005-08-13 20:37:22.570', 101))
```

This returns:

2005-08-13 00:00:00.000

How It Works

The 101 value in the style option tells CONVERT to return the date in a mm/dd/yyyy format. Query authors are usually concerned with the style option when presenting data back to the end-user. This presentation is used when a datetime or smalldatetime is converted into a character data type. Keep in mind that if you convert the data type back to datetime and store the reconverted date, you can lose the precision of the original hour, minute, second, etc. depending on the style you chose for the character data!

Evaluating Whether an Expression Is a Date or Is Numeric

When converting data types, it is sometimes useful to figure out what SQL Server thinks an expression's data type is. In this recipe, I'll demonstrate using ISDATE and ISNUMERIC functions to test the data type of an expression:

```
-- Returns 0
SELECT ISDATE('1/1/20000')

-- Returns 1
SELECT ISDATE('1/1/2000')

-- Returns 0
SELECT ISNUMERIC('123ABC')

-- Returns 1
SELECT ISNUMERIC('123')
```

How It Works

ISDATE determines whether an expression is a valid datetime value. ISNUMERIC determines whether or not an expression is a valid numeric data type value. Both ISNUMERIC and ISDATE return a 1 if the expression evaluates to TRUE and 0 if it is FALSE.

Ranking Functions

A very popular feature addition to SQL Server 2005, ranking functions allow you to return values associated to each row in a result set. Table 8-8 describes the four new ranking functions.

Table 8-8. *Ranking Functions*

Function	Description
ROW_NUMBER	Returns an incrementing integer for each row in a set.
RANK	Similar to ROW_NUMBER, RANK increments its value for each row in the set. The key difference is if rows with tied values exist, they will receive the same rank value.
DENSE_RANK	DENSE_RANK is almost identical to RANK, only DENSE_RANK doesn't return gaps in the rank values.
NTILE	NTILE divides the result set into a specified number of groups, based on the ordering and optional partition.

The next four recipes will demonstrate the use of these four ranking functions.

Using an Incrementing Row Number

SQL Server 2005's new ROW_NUMBER function returns an incrementing integer for each row in a set. The syntax for ROW_NUMBER is as follows:

```
ROW_NUMBER ( )    OVER ( [ <partition_by_clause> ] <order_by_clause> )
```

The first optional argument, partition_by_clause, allows you to restart row numbering for each change in the partitioned column. The second argument, order_by_clause, determines the order in which the ROW_NUMBER is applied to the results.

This first example returns the six rows from the middle of the result set, ordered by name:

```
-- Select the rows 255 through 260 in the middle of the result set
SELECT  p.ProductID,
     p.Name,
     p.RowNumber
FROM
   (SELECT     ProductID,
        Name,
        ROW_NUMBER() OVER (ORDER BY Name) RowNumber
   FROM Production.Product) p
WHERE    p.RowNumber BETWEEN 255 AND 260
```

This returns:

ProductID	Name	RowNumber
713	Long-Sleeve Logo Jersey, S	255
716	Long-Sleeve Logo Jersey, XL	256
462	Lower Head Race	257
857	Men's Bib-Shorts, L	258
856	Men's Bib-Shorts, M	259
855	Men's Bib-Shorts, S	260

The optional `partition_by_clause` allows you to restart row numbering for each change in the partitioned column. In this example, the results are partitioned by `Shelf` and ordered by `ProductID`:

```
SELECT  Shelf,
        ProductID,
        ROW_NUMBER() OVER
(PARTITION BY Shelf ORDER BY ProductID) RowNumber
FROM Production.ProductInventory
```

In the returned results, row numbering is incremented by `ProductID`, but with each change in `Shelf`, the row numbering is restarted at 1:

Shelf	ProductID	RowNumber
A	1	1
A	1	2
A	2	3
...		
Shelf	ProductID	RowNumber
B	1	1
B	2	2
B	3	3
...		
Shelf	ProductID	RowNumber
C	317	1
C	318	2
C	319	3
...		

How It Works

In the first example, `ROW_NUMBER` was used to order the results by Product Name and then add an incrementing value for each row. `ROW_NUMBER` was referenced as the third column of the subquery:

```
SELECT     ProductID,
       Name,
       ROW_NUMBER() OVER (ORDER BY Name) RowNumber
   FROM Production.Product
```

The `ORDER BY` clause in parentheses ordered the results by Product Name, which impacted in which order the rows were returned, as well as each row's associated row number. Each row in the record set is given a number, incremented by 1 for each row. Since the query sorts the results by Name, the first product, Adjustable Race will have a row number of "1." This query appeared as a sub query so that the `ROW_NUMBER` column could be referenced in the `WHERE` clause of the outer query, returning rows 255 through 260.

The second example demonstrated using the `partition_by_clause` argument. For each change in `Shelf`, the row numbering was restarted with "1."

With the SQL Server 2005's `ROW_NUMBER` ranking function, you can now page through data (for example, "show me rows 25 through 50") without having to create excessive amounts of code that was necessary in SQL Server 2000.

Returning Rows by Rank

In this recipe, I'll demonstrate SQL Server 2005's new `RANK` function, which is similar to `ROW_NUMBER` in that it increments its value for each row in the set. The syntax for `RANK` is as follows:

```
RANK ( )   OVER ( [ < partition_by_clause > ] < order_by_clause > )
```

The key difference is if rows with tied values exist, they will receive the same rank value, as this example demonstrates:

```
SELECT  SalesPersonID,
      SalesQuota,
RANK() OVER (ORDER BY SalesQuota DESC) as RANK
FROM Sales.SalesPersonQuotaHistory
WHERE SalesQuota BETWEEN 266000.00 AND  319000.00
```

This returns:

SalesPersonID	SalesQuota	RANK
280	319000.00	1
287	304000.00	2
280	301000.00	3
282	288000.00	4
283	284000.00	5
287	281000.00	6
278	280000.00	7
283	280000.00	7
283	267000.00	9
278	266000.00	10

The OVER clause contains an optional partition_by_clause and a required order_by_clause, just like ROW_NUMBER. The order_by_clause determines the order that RANK values are applied to each row and the optional partition_by_clause is used to further divide the ranking groups, as demonstrated in the next example:

```
SELECT  h.SalesPersonID,
    s.TerritoryID,
    h.QuotaDate,
       h.SalesQuota,
RANK() OVER (PARTITION BY  s.TerritoryID ORDER BY h.SalesQuota DESC) as RANK
FROM Sales.SalesPersonQuotaHistory h
INNER JOIN Sales.SalesPerson s ON
    h.SalesPersonID = s.SalesPersonID
WHERE s.TerritoryID IN (5,6,7)
```

This returns ranking of SalesQuota partitioned by the salesperson's TerritoryID:

SalesPersonID	TerritoryID	QuotaDate	SalesQuota	RANK
279	5	2003-07-01 00:00:00.000	950000.00	1
279	5	2001-10-01 00:00:00.000	917000.00	2
...				
282	6	2003-07-01 00:00:00.000	1051000.00	1
282	6	2004-04-01 00:00:00.000	830000.00	2
282	6	2001-10-01 00:00:00.000	767000.00	3
282	6	2003-10-01 00:00:00.000	707000.00	4
282	**6**	**2002-01-01 00:00:00.000**	**583000.00**	**5**
282	**6**	**2002-04-01 00:00:00.000**	**583000.00**	**5**
282	6	2004-01-01 00:00:00.000	569000.00	7
...				

How It Works

RANK increments its values based on the ordered column, only unlike ROWNUMBER which increments on each row, RANK will return the same value for matching ordered values.

For example, in this recipe, the query specified a RANK ordered by SalesQuota with a descending sort. Because two SalesQuota values were equal at 280000.00, they both received a rank of 7:

```
278      280000.00        7
283      280000.00        7
```

Also you should notice that the next SalesQuota value had a rank of 9 (not 8). The RANK function didn't use the 8th position because there were two rows tied for 7th, meaning that the next rank value is 9. If there were three rows tied, the next rank value would be 10, and so on:

```
283      267000.00        9
```

In the second example, RANK was partitioned by TerritoryID, causing the RANK value to restart at "1" for each change in TerritoryID.

Returning Rows by Rank Without Gaps

In this recipe, I'll demonstrate Server 2005's new DENSE_RANK, which is almost identical to RANK, only DENSE_RANK doesn't return gaps in the rank values:

```
SELECT  SalesPersonID,
        SalesQuota,
DENSE_RANK() OVER (ORDER BY SalesQuota DESC) as DENSE_RANK
FROM Sales.SalesPersonQuotaHistory
WHERE SalesQuota BETWEEN 266000.00 AND  319000.00
```

This returns:

```
SalesPersonID    SalesQuota      DENSE_RANK
280              319000.00       1
287              304000.00       2
280              301000.00       3
282              288000.00       4
283              284000.00       5
287              281000.00       6
278              280000.00       7
283              280000.00       7
283              267000.00       8
278              266000.00       9
```

How It Works

The syntax and usage is identical to RANK, only DENSE_RANK doesn't create a gap in the rank value. In this recipe's example, two values were tied with a value of 7 due to the same SalesQuota of 280000.00:

```
278      280000.00        7
283      280000.00        7
283      267000.00        8
```

The next DENSE_RANK value after 7 was 8.

Using NTILE

NTILE divides the result set into a specified number of groups based on the ordering and optional partition. The syntax is very similar to the other ranking functions, only it also includes an integer_expression:

```
NTILE (integer_expression)  OVER ( [ < partition_by_clause > ] < order_by_clause > )
```

The integer_expression is used to determine the number of groups to divide the results into. This example demonstrates the NTILE ranking function against the Sales.SalePersonQuotaHistory table:

```
SELECT  SalesPersonID,
     SalesQuota,
NTILE(4) OVER (ORDER BY SalesQuota DESC) as NTILE
FROM Sales.SalesPersonQuotaHistory
WHERE SalesQuota BETWEEN 266000.00 AND  319000.00
```

This returns:

SalesPersonID	SalesQuota	NTILE
280	319000.00	1
287	304000.00	1
280	301000.00	1
282	288000.00	2
283	284000.00	2
287	281000.00	2
278	280000.00	3
283	280000.00	3
283	267000.00	4
278	266000.00	4

How It Works

In this example, the result set was divided into four percentile groups. The results were ordered by SalesQuota (descending order), and determined the order of NTILE group assignment. Notice that the first two groups, 1, and 2, both had three rows each, whereas groups 3 and 4 had two rows each. If the number of rows isn't divisible by the number of groups, the first few groups will have more rows than the latter groups. Otherwise, if the rows are divisible by the group number, each group will have the same number of rows.

Probing Server, Database, and Connection-Level Settings Using System Functions

SQL Server 2005 includes several system configuration functions that can be used to determine system settings for the SQL Server instance. Some of these functions are prefixed with @@, and were called variables in previous versions of SQL Server. Other system functions don't have the @@ prefix, and accept parameters that help gather information about the SQL Server instance or database.

The next few recipes will demonstrate these system functions in action.

Using SQL Server's First Day of the Week Setting

The @@DATEFIRST function returns the value of the specified first day of the week for the SQL Server Instance. This is important to note because this value defines the calculation for the weekday datepart used in other date functions such as DATEPART and DATEADD. In this example, I'll demonstrate returning the current first day of the week setting for the SQL Server instance:

```
SELECT @@DATEFIRST 'First Day of the Week'
```

This returns:

```
First Day of the Week
7
```

How It Works

The @@DATEFIRST function shows the first day of the week setting. To change the first day value, you can use the SET DATEFIRST command. For example:

```
SET DATEFIRST 7
```

When changing this value, "7" is Sunday and "1" is Monday, and so on. This impacts the returned value for the dw (day of week) code for DATEPART and DATEADD functions.

Viewing the Language Used in the Current Session

The @@LANGID system function returns a smallint data type value representing the local language identifier for the current user session and the @@LANGUAGE system function returns the language name.

This example returns the local language setting currently used in the current query session:

```
SELECT  @@LANGID LanguageID,
        @@LANGUAGE Language
```

This query returns:

```
LanguageID        Language
0                 us_english
```

How It Works

This recipe demonstrated returning the language for the SQL Server instance. This will vary based on the locale and collation used to set up the SQL Server instance.

Viewing and Setting Current Connection Lock Timeout Settings

The SET LOCK_TIMEOUT command configures the number of milliseconds a statement will wait in the current session for locks to be released by other connections. The @@LOCK_TIMEOUT function is used to display the current connection lock timeout setting in milliseconds.

This example demonstrates setting and viewing the current session's lock timeout value:

```
-- 1000 milliseconds, 1 second
SET LOCK_TIMEOUT 1000

SELECT  @@LOCK_TIMEOUT

-- Unlimited
SET LOCK_TIMEOUT -1
```

This returns:

1000

How It Works

The example in this recipe started by setting the lock timeout to 1000 milliseconds. To view the change, @@LOCK_TIMEOUT was used. After that, the lock timeout was changed again to -1, which is an unlimited wait time. A lock timeout value tells us how long a statement will wait on a blocked resource, canceling the statement automatically if the threshold has been exceeded, and then returning an error message.

Displaying the Nesting Level for the Current Stored Procedure Context

@@NESTLEVEL returns the current nesting level for the stored procedure context. A stored procedure nesting level indicates how many times a stored procedure has called another stored procedure. SQL Server 2005 allows stored procedures to make up to a maximum of 32 nested (incomplete) calls.

This recipe demonstrates how to capture the current nesting level for the stored procedure context (see Chapter 10):

```
-- First procedure
CREATE PROCEDURE usp_QuickAndDirty
AS
SELECT @@NESTLEVEL
GO

-- Second procedure
CREATE PROCEDURE usp_Call_QuickAndDirty
AS
SELECT @@NESTLEVEL
EXEC usp_QuickAndDirty
GO
```

After creating the two stored procedures, @@NESTLEVEL function is used prior to calling the usp_Call_QuickAndDirty stored procedure:

```
-- Returns 0 nest level
SELECT @@NESTLEVEL

-- Returns 1 and 2 nest level
EXEC usp_Call_QuickAndDirty
```

This returns three result sets:

0

1

2

How It Works

In this recipe, I created two stored procedures. The first stored procedure, in this case usp_QuickAndDirty, executed @@NESTLEVEL. The second stored procedure also called @@NESTLEVEL, and then executed the first stored procedure. Before calling the procedure, @@NESTLEVEL returned 0. At each execution-nesting, the value of @@NESTLEVEL is incremented.

Returning the Current SQL Server Instance Name and SQL Server Version

@@SERVERNAME displays the local server name and @@VERSION returns the SQL Server instance version, date, and processor information.

This example returns the current SQL Server instance's name and version information:

```
SELECT  @@SERVERNAME ServerName,
    @@VERSION VersionInformation
```

How It Works

In this recipe, I demonstrated returning the current SQL Server instance name and version information. Like the system configuration functions before it, no parameters were required.

Returning the Current Connection's Session ID (SPID)

@@SPID returns the current connection's session ID, which you can use to identify additional information in the sp_who system-stored procedure.

This recipe returns the current SQL connection's server process identifier:

```
SELECT  @@SPID SPID
```

This returns:

```
SPID
52
```

How It Works

In this recipe, I demonstrated returning the SPID of the current connection's query session. Note that in previous versions, SPID was referred to as "server process id," and not "session id."

Returning Number of Open Transactions

The @@TRANCOUNT system function displays active transactions for the current connection. You can use this function to determine the number of open transactions within the current session, and based on that information, either COMMIT or ROLLBACK the transactions accordingly. This recipe demonstrates how to return the number of active transactions in the current connection:

```
BEGIN TRAN t1

SELECT @@TRANCOUNT -- Returns 1

    BEGIN TRAN t2

    SELECT @@TRANCOUNT -- Returns 2
```

```
        BEGIN TRAN t3

        SELECT @@TRANCOUNT -- Returns 3

        COMMIT TRAN

    SELECT @@TRANCOUNT -- Returns 2

    ROLLBACK TRAN

SELECT @@TRANCOUNT -- After ROLLBACK, always Returns 0!
```

This returns:

```
-----------
1

(1 row(s) affected)


-----------
2

(1 row(s) affected)


-----------
3

(1 row(s) affected)


-----------
2

(1 row(s) affected)


-----------
0

(1 row(s) affected)
```

How It Works

In this recipe, each time a BEGIN TRAN was issued, the value of @@TRANCOUNT was incremented. Each time a COMMIT TRAN occurred, @@TRANCOUNT was decremented. When ROLLBACK TRAN was executed, @@ TRANCOUNT was set to 0. ROLLBACK TRAN rolls back all open transactions for the session, no matter how many levels deep the transactions are nested.

Retrieving the Rows Affected by the Previous Statement

@@ROWCOUNT returns the integer value of the number of rows affected by the last Transact-SQL statement in the current scope. @@ROWCOUNT_BIG returns the bigint value.

In this example, I'll demonstrate how to return the rows affected by the previous Transact-SQL statement:

```
SELECT TOP 3 ScrapReasonID
FROM Production.ScrapReason
```

```
SELECT @@ROWCOUNT Int_RowCount, ROWCOUNT_BIG() BigInt_RowCount
```

This returns two result sets:

ScrapReasonID
1
2
4

Int_RowCount	BigInt_RowCount
3	3

How It Works

In this example, the first statement returned three rows from the Production.ScrapReason table—so @@ROWCOUNT returns three rows affected. The ROWCOUNT_BIG function is just like @@ROWCOUNT, only it is capable of returning bigint data type counts, instead of @@ROWCOUNT's integer data type.

@@ROWCOUNT and @@ROWCOUNT_BIG are often used for error handling; for example checking to make sure the desired number of rows were impacted by the previous statement (see Chapter 16).

Using System Statistical Functions

SQL Server 2005 has several built-in system statistical functions, which are described in Table 8-9.

Table 8-9. *System Statistical Functions*

Function	Description
@@CONNECTIONS	Returns the number of connections made to the SQL Server instance since it was last started.
@@CPU_BUSY	Shows the number of busy CPU milliseconds since the SQL Server instance was last started.
@@IDLE	Displays the total idle time of the SQL Server instance in milliseconds, since the instance was last started.
@@IO_BUSY	Displays the number of milliseconds spent performing I/O operations since the SQL Server instance was last started.
@@PACKET_ERRORS	Displays the total network packet errors that have occurred since the SQL Server instance was last started.
@@PACK_RECEIVED	Returns the total input packets read from the network since the SQL Server instance was last started. You can monitor whether the number increments or stays the same, thus surmising if there is a network availability issue.
@@PACK_SENT	Returns the total output packets sent to the network since the SQL Server instance was last started.
@@TIMETICKS	Displays the number of microseconds per tick. A *tick* is a unit of measurement designated by a specified number of milliseconds (31.25 milliseconds for Windows 2000).

Function	Description
@@TOTAL_ERRORS	Displays read/write errors encountered since the SQL Server instance was last started.
@@TOTAL_READ	Displays the number of non-cached disk reads by the SQL Server instance since it was last started.
@@TOTAL_WRITE	Displays the number of disk writes by the SQL Server instance since it was last started.

This example demonstrates using system statistical functions in a query:

```
SELECT  'Connections' FunctionNM, @@CONNECTIONS
UNION
SELECT  'CPUBusy', @@CPU_BUSY
UNION
SELECT  'IDLE', @@IDLE
UNION
SELECT   'IOBusy', @@IO_BUSY
UNION
SELECT   'PacketErrors', @@PACKET_ERRORS
UNION
SELECT   'PackReceived', @@PACK_RECEIVED
UNION
SELECT   'PackSent', @@PACK_SENT
UNION
SELECT   'TimeTicks', @@TIMETICKS
UNION
SELECT   'TotalErrors', @@TOTAL_ERRORS
UNION
SELECT   'TotalRead', @@TOTAL_READ
UNION
SELECT   'TotalWrite', @@TOTAL_WRITE
```

This returns:

```
FunctionNM
------------ -----------
Connections  29374
CPUBusy      3248
IDLE         1135449
IOBusy       901
PacketErrors 0
PackReceived 169
PackSent     574
TimeTicks    31250
TotalErrors  0
TotalRead    1700
TotalWrite   280
```

How It Works

This recipe demonstrated a SELECT query referencing multiple system statistical functions. You can use them to track various statistics in your SQL Server instance.

Displaying Database and SQL Server Settings

The DATABASEPROPERTYEX system function allows you to retrieve information about database options. DATABASEPROPERTYEX uses the following syntax:

```
DATABASEPROPERTYEX ( database , property )
```

The first argument is the database name you want to probe. The second argument is the database property you want to look up.

This example demonstrates how to report the collation, status, and recovery mode for the AdventureWorks database:

```
SELECT  DATABASEPROPERTYEX('AdventureWorks', 'Collation'),
DATABASEPROPERTYEX('AdventureWorks', 'Recovery'),
DATABASEPROPERTYEX('AdventureWorks', 'Status')
```

This returns:

```
SQL_Latin1_General_CP1_CI_AS     SIMPLE   ONLINE
```

The SERVERPROPERTY system function allows you to retrieve information about your SQL Server instance. Its syntax, since not database specific, only requires the property name:

```
SERVERPROPERTY (propertyname )
```

This example demonstrates returning the instance's edition and default collation:

```
SELECT SERVERPROPERTY ('Collation'),
SERVERPROPERTY ('Edition')
```

This returns:

```
SQL_Latin1_General_CP1_CI_AS     Enterprise Edition
```

How It Works

Both DATABASEPROPERTYEX and SERVERPROPERTY can be used to retrieve important system configuration settings. In both examples, the function was referenced in the SELECT clause of a query.

■**Note** I show how these functions are used in this book, but I don't rehash the list of available properties. For a complete list, see SERVERPROPERTY and DATABASEPROPERTYEX topics in SQL Server 2005 Books Online.

Returning the Current Database ID and Name

This DB_ID function returns the database integer ID and DB_NAME returns the database name for the current database (unless there are parameters supplied).

This example demonstrates how to retrieve the current database system ID and name:

```
SELECT  DB_ID() DatabaseID, DB_NAME() DatabaseNM
```

This returns:

```
DatabaseID       DatabaseNM
5                AdventureWorks
```

How It Works

In this example, the internal database ID (assigned by SQL Server when the database was created) is returned along with the database name. The functions will return information based on the current database context.

Both also accept parameters, for example:

```
SELECT  DB_ID('master') DatabaseID, DB_NAME(1) DatabaseNM
```

which you can use to look up explicit database ID or name values without switching the database context to the actual database.

Returning a Database Object Name and ID

OBJECT_ID returns the database object identifier number, as assigned internally within the database. OBJECT_NAME returns the object's name based on its object identifier number.

In this example, I'll demonstrate how to return a database object's name and ID:

```
SELECT OBJECT_ID('Production.Location'), OBJECT_NAME(1253579504)
```

This returns:

1333579789	DF_Illustration_ModifiedDate

How It Works

Both OBJECT_NAME and OBJECT_ID are often used in conjunction with system catalog views or system functions that reference a database object's identifier. The OBJECT_ID function is used to find the internal database identifier of a specific object. Its single argument is the name of the object. OBJECT_NAME is used to return the object name given the object identifier. Note that both functions are database specific—since object ids can be the same for objects across different databases. Object IDs are only unique to the specified database.

Returning the Application and Host for the Current User Session

In this recipe, I'll demonstrate the different functions used to return information about the current connection's context. APP_NAME returns the name of the application for the current SQL Server connection. HOST_ID returns the workstation identification number for the current connection and HOST_NAME returns the workstation name for the current connection.

This example shows how to show the current application and host used to connected to the SQL Server instance:

```
SELECT APP_NAME() as 'Application', HOST_ID() as 'Host ID', HOST_NAME() as 'Host Name'
```

This returns:

Application	Host ID	Host Name
Microsoft SQL Server Management Studio - Query	3388	JOEPROD

How It Works

All three functions used in this example were used without a SELECT clause, and didn't require any arguments. This information is useful for tracking information on a client and application connection, and thus helping you establish identity.

Reporting Current User and Login Context

The SYSTEM_USER function returns the Windows or SQL login name and the USER function returns the current user's database user name.

In this first example, I'll demonstrate how to return the current user and login context:

```
SELECT  SYSTEM_USER, -- Login
    USER -- Database User
```

This returns:

JOEPROD\Owner	dbo

These two functions can also be used as table DEFAULT values, as this next example demonstrates:

```
CREATE TABLE #TempExample
  (ExampleColumn varchar(10) NOT NULL,
   ModifiedByLogin varchar(55) NOT NULL DEFAULT SYSTEM_USER,
   ModifiedByUser varchar(55) NOT NULL DEFAULT USER)
GO

INSERT #TempExample
(ExampleColumn)
VALUES ('Value A')

SELECT ExampleColumn, ModifiedByLogin, ModifiedByUser
FROM #TempExample
```

This returns the following results:

ExampleColumn	ModifiedByLogin	ModifiedByUser
Value A	JOEPROD\Owner	dbo

How It Works

In this recipe, the SYSTEM_USER and USER functions were used within a regular query, and also as the DEFAULT value for a table. These functions are ideal for database change auditing—capturing the current user when a data modification occurs, for example.

Viewing User Connection Options

In this recipe, I'll demonstrate how to view the SET properties for the current user connection using the SESSIONPROPERTY function (for information on SET options see Chapter 22):

```
SELECT  SESSIONPROPERTY ('ANSI_NULLS') ANSI_NULLS,
    SESSIONPROPERTY ('ANSI_PADDING') ANSI_PADDING,
    SESSIONPROPERTY ('ANSI_WARNINGS') ANSI_WARNINGS,
    SESSIONPROPERTY ('ARITHABORT') ARITHABORT,
    SESSIONPROPERTY ('CONCAT_NULL_YIELDS_NULL')  CONCAT_NULL_YIELDS_NULL,
    SESSIONPROPERTY ('NUMERIC_ROUNDABORT') NUMERIC_ROUNDABORT,
    SESSIONPROPERTY ('QUOTED_IDENTIFIER') QUOTED_IDENTIFIER
```

How It Works

SESSIONPROPERTY allows you to see the various database connection settings for the current user. It takes one argument, the name of the property to check. In the example, each available SESSIONPROPERTY option was checked. The function returns a 1 when the option is ON and 0 when it is OFF.

IDENTITY and uniqueidentifier Functions

With the last three recipes of this chapter, I'll review how to work with IDENTITY values for a table and how to generate new uniqueidentifier values.

As you may recall from Chapter 4, the IDENTITY column property is defined on a specific column of a table and allows you to define an automatically incrementing numeric value for a single column in a table.

Unlike the IDENTITY column, which guarantees uniqueness within the defined table, the ROWGUIDCOL property ensures a very high level of uniqueness. This unique ID is stored in a uniqueidentifier data type and is generated by the NEWID system function.

Returning the Last Identity Value

In this recipe, I'll demonstrate three methods for returning last generated identity values. In the first example, the IDENT_CURRENT function is used to return the last generated identity value for a specific table. This command takes a single argument: the name of the table to evaluate:

```
SELECT IDENT_CURRENT('Production.Product') LastIdententityValue
```

This returns:

```
LastIdententityValue
999
```

Next, a new row is inserted into a table that has an IDENTITY column defined within it. Immediately after the INSERT, the last identity value generated is retrieved using the SCOPE_IDENTITY and @@IDENTITY functions (the difference is described after the example):

```
-- Example insert, generates IDENTITY value in the table
INSERT HumanResources.Department
(Name, GroupName)
VALUES ('TestDept', 'TestGroup')

-- Last identity value generated for any table
-- in the current session, for the current scope
SELECT SCOPE_IDENTITY()
```

This returns the last identity value generated from a table INSERT in the current session, for the current scope. Scope means that if this INSERT caused a trigger to fire that inserted another row into a different IDENTITY-based table, we would still only see the last IDENTITY value for the current session (not from the trigger sessions outside our scope):

17

Executing @@IDENTITY generates the last IDENTITY value generated for any table in the current session, but for any scope:

```
-- Last identity value generated for any table
-- in the current session, in any scope
SELECT @@IDENTITY
```

This returns:

17

Although it is the same value for this example query, had a trigger fired off of our INSERT that in turn caused an INSERT into another IDENTITY-based table, we would see the latest identity value for the other table in the trigger's scope.

How It Works

This recipe demonstrated three methods of returning the last identity value generated. The first query used IDENT_CURRENT, which specified the last generated identity value for a specific table.

The next function demonstrated, SCOPE_IDENTITY, is specific to the current user session, and returns the last generated value for the current scope. The current scope, for example, refers to the current batch of SQL statements, current procedure, or current trigger.

In contrast, @@IDENTITY returns the last generated value for any table in the current session, *across any scope*. So if an INSERT in the current scope fires a trigger, which in turn inserts a record into a different table, @@IDENTITY will return the latest value from the inserted row impacted by the trigger, and not the original insert you may have intended to capture.

In short, use IDENT_CURRENT if you care about retrieving the latest IDENTITY value for a specific table, across any session or scope. Use SCOPE_IDENTITY if you wish to retrieve the latest IDENTITY value for any table in the current scope and session. Use @@IDENTITY if you want the last IDENTITY value for any table in the current session, regardless of scope.

Returning an Identity Column's Seed and Incrementing Value

The IDENT_INCR function displays the original increment value for the IDENTITY column of a specific table or referencing view. The IDENT_SEED function displays the originally defined seed value for the IDENTITY column of a specific table or referencing view. These functions are useful to determine at what increment and seed an IDENTITY column's value will progress as rows are inserted.

This example demonstrates returning the identity increment and seed for a specific table:

```
SELECT IDENT_INCR('Production.Product') IdentIncr,
    IDENT_SEED('Production.Product') IdentSeed
```

This returns:

IdentIncr	IdentSeed
1	1

How It Works

In this recipe, the increment and seed for the Production.Product table was returned using IDENT_INCR and IDENT_SEED.

Creating a New uniqueidentifier Value

The NEWID function is used to create a uniqueidentifier data type value. The first example returns a new uniqueidentifier value in a SELECT statement:

```
SELECT NEWID()
```

This returns:

```
D04ED24F-671E-4559-A205-F6864B9C59A7
```

Next, a new temporary table is created that uses the NEWID function as a default:

```
CREATE TABLE #T4
  (MyValue uniqueidentifier NOT NULL DEFAULT NEWID())
```

Next, a new value is inserted into the table:

```
INSERT #T4 DEFAULT VALUES
```

Last, the value is retrieved from the table:

```
SELECT MyValue
FROM #T4
```

This returns:

```
MyValue
2DD54CE0-5D26-42F9-A68D-7392DB89D0EF
```

How It Works

As this recipe shows, NEWID can be used within a SELECT statement or as a DEFAULT column value in a CREATE or ALTER TABLE statement.

CHAPTER 9

■ ■ ■

Conditional Processing, Control-of-Flow, and Cursors

In this chapter, I'll present recipes that demonstrate SQL Server 2005 Transact-SQL for:

- *Conditional processing.* You'll learn how to use the CASE and IF...ELSE statements to evaluate conditions and return values accordingly. I'll review how to use the CASE function to evaluate a single input expression and return a value, and also how to evaluate one or more Boolean expressions. Finally, I'll demonstrate returning a value when the expressions are TRUE.

- *Control-of-flow functionality.* This recipe demonstrates how to control the execution of Transact-SQL statements or batches based on commands such as RETURN, WHILE, WAITFOR, and GOTO. RETURN is used to exit the current Transact-SQL batch immediately, and doesn't allow any code in the batch that executes after it. The WHILE command is used to repeat a specific operation or batch of operations while a condition remains TRUE. The WAITFOR command is used to delay the execution of Transact-SQL code for a specified length of time or until a specific time. GOTO is used to jump to a label in your Transact-SQL batch, passing over the code that follows it.

- *Creating and using cursors.* Here I'll demonstrate Transact-SQL cursors, which allow you to work with one row at a time. Cursors can cause significant performance problems due to memory consumption and code bloat issues if not implemented correctly. However, there still may be rare occasions when the use of a cursor is a better choice than a set-based solution.

An understanding of how and when (and when not) to use these techniques will allow you to create flexible and intelligent Transact-SQL code.

Conditional Processing

Conditional processing allows you to return a value, based on the value of an expression, or group of expressions. The next few recipes will demonstrate SQL Server 2005's conditional processing commands, including CASE and IF...ELSE (note that IF...ELSE also has inherent control-of-flow functionality as well).

The CASE function is used to return a value based on the value of an expression. It is most often used to translate codes into descriptive values or evaluate multiple conditions in order to return a value. (For example, "If the row is from the year 2005 and less than or equal to Current Quarter, return the Total Sales amount.")

The IF...ELSE construct evaluates a Boolean expression, and if TRUE, executes a Transact-SQL statement or batch. The uses for this command are many, allowing you to conditionally return result sets, update data, or execute stored procedures based on one or more search conditions.

The next three recipes will demonstrate conditional processing in action.

Using CASE to Evaluate a Single Input Expression

The CASE function is used to return a value based on the value of an expression. It can also be used to return a value based on the result of one or more Boolean expressions. The syntax for former flavor of CASE is as follows:

```
CASE input_expression
    WHEN when_expression THEN result_expression
    [ ...n ]
    [
    ELSE else_result_expression
    ]
END
```

The arguments of this command are described in Table 9-1.

Table 9-1. *Input Expression CASE Arguments*

Argument	Description
input_expression	The input value to be evaluated in the CASE statement.
when_expression	The expression to compare to the input_expression. For example if the input_expression is the Gender column , then the when_expression could be 'F' or 'M' or NULL. If there is a match between the input_expression and the when_expression, then the result_expression is returned.
result_expression	The value to be returned if the input_expression is equal to the when_expression.

This example demonstrates how to use CASE to evaluate one or more conditions, returning a result based on those conditions that evaluate to TRUE:

```
-- Determine Conference Rooms Based on Department
SELECT DepartmentID,
    Name,
    GroupName,
    CASE GroupName
        WHEN 'Research and Development' THEN 'Room A'
        WHEN 'Sales and Marketing' THEN 'Room B'
        WHEN 'Manufacturing' THEN 'Room C'
        ELSE 'Room D'
    END ConferenceRoom
FROM HumanResources.Department
```

This returns the following (abridged) results:

```
DepartmentID    Name            GroupName                   ConferenceRoom
1               Engineering     Research and Development    Room A
2               Tool Design     Research and Development    Room A
3               Sales           Sales and Marketing         Room B
4               Marketing       Sales and Marketing         Room B
5               Purchasing      Inventory Management        Room D
...
```

How It Works

In this recipe's example, CASE was used to assign a conference room based on the GroupName value. The CASE statement followed the Name column in the SELECT clause:

```
SELECT DepartmentID,
       Name,
       GroupName,
       CASE GroupName
```

The column to evaluate, GroupName, followed the CASE keyword. Next, a set of WHEN expressions was evaluated. Each department was assigned a different room, based on the value of GroupName:

```
       WHEN 'Research and Development' THEN 'Room A'
       WHEN 'Sales and Marketing' THEN 'Room B'
       WHEN 'Manufacturing' THEN 'Room C'
```

The optional ELSE clause is used as a catch-all, assigning a default result expression if none of the WHEN expressions evaluated to TRUE:

```
       ELSE 'Room D'
```

The END keyword is used to mark the end of the CASE statement, and in this recipe, is followed by the aliased column name:

```
       END ConferenceRoom
```

Using CASE to Evaluate Boolean Expressions

CASE offers an alternative syntax which doesn't use an initial input expression. Instead, one or more Boolean expressions is evaluated, returning a result expression when TRUE. The syntax is as follows:

```
CASE
    WHEN Boolean_expression THEN result_expression
    [ ...n ]
    [
    ELSE else_result_expression
    ]
END
```

The additional argument in this syntax, compared to the previous recipe, is the boolean_expression, which is the expression being evaluated. Instead of an input expression, each WHEN evaluates a Boolean expression, and if TRUE, returns a result expression. This flavor of CASE allows for additional expressions above and beyond just evaluating the value of one input expression.

If none of the expressions evaluates to TRUE, the result_expression of the ELSE clause is returned, or a NULL value is returned if no ELSE clause was specified. If a row match is made against more than one Boolean expression, the first Boolean expression to evaluate to TRUE determines the result expression. In this example, the department name is evaluated in addition to other expressions, such as the department identifier and the room name starting with the letter T:

```
SELECT DepartmentID,
       Name,
       CASE
          WHEN Name = 'Research and Development'
              THEN 'Room A'
          WHEN (Name = 'Sales and Marketing' OR
              DepartmentID = 10)
              THEN 'Room B'
          WHEN Name LIKE 'T%'
```

```
            THEN 'Room C'
        ELSE 'Room D'
    END ConferenceRoom
FROM HumanResources.Department
```

This returns the following (abridged) results:

DepartmentID	Name	ConferenceRoom
12	Document Control	Room D
1	Engineering	Room D
16	Executive	Room D
14	Facilities and Maintenance	Room D
10	Finance	Room B
9	Human Resources	Room D
...		
6	Research and Development	Room A
3	Sales	Room D
15	Shipping and Receiving	Room D
17	TestDept	Room C
2	Tool Design	Room C

How It Works

In this example, three Boolean expressions were used. If the department name was Research and Development, Room A would be returned:

```
WHEN Name = 'Research and Development'
        THEN 'Room A'
```

The second Boolean expression stated that if the department name was Sales and Marketing OR the DepartmentID was equal to 10, then Room B would be returned:

```
WHEN (Name = 'Sales and Marketing' OR
        DepartmentID = 10)
        THEN 'Room B'
```

The third Boolean expression looks for any department name that starts with the letter T, causing Room C to be returned if there is a match:

```
WHEN Name LIKE 'T%'
      THEN 'Room C'
```

Using IF...ELSE

IF...ELSE evaluates a Boolean expression, and if TRUE, executes a Transact-SQL statement or batch. The syntax is as follows:

```
IF Boolean_expression
    { sql_statement | statement_block }
[ ELSE
    { sql_statement | statement_block } ]
```

The ELSE clause is invoked if the Boolean expression evaluates to FALSE, executing the Transact-SQL statement or batch that follows the ELSE.

This example demonstrates executing a query conditionally based on the value of a local variable:

```
DECLARE @QuerySelector int
SET @QuerySelector = 3
```

```
IF @QuerySelector = 1
BEGIN
    SELECT TOP 3
        ProductID, Name, Color
    FROM Production.Product
    WHERE Color = 'Silver'
    ORDER BY Name
END
ELSE
BEGIN
    SELECT TOP 3
        ProductID, Name, Color
    FROM Production.Product
    WHERE Color = 'Black'
    ORDER BY Name
END
```

This returns:

ProductID	Name	Color
322	Chainring	Black
863	Full-Finger Gloves, L	Black
862	Full-Finger Gloves, M	Black

How It Works

In this recipe, an integer local variable was created called @QuerySelector, which was set to the value of 3:

```
DECLARE @QuerySelector int
SET @QuerySelector = 3
```

The IF statement began by evaluating if @QuerySelector was equal to 1:

```
IF @QuerySelector = 1
```

If the evaluation determined that @QuerySelector was indeed 1, the next block of code (starting with the BEGIN statement) would be executed:

```
BEGIN
    SELECT TOP 3
        ProductID, Name, Color
    FROM Production.Product
    WHERE Color = 'Silver'
    ORDER BY Name
END
```

BEGIN is optional for single statements following IF, but for multiple statements that must be executed as a group, BEGIN and END must be used. As a best practice, it is easier to use BEGIN...END for single statements too, so that you don't forget to do so if/when the code is changed at a later time.

The optional ELSE clause is used as a catch-all, executing a search on black colored products if the previous IF condition evaluated to FALSE:

```
ELSE
BEGIN
    SELECT TOP 3
        ProductID, Name, Color
    FROM Production.Product
```

```
        WHERE Color = 'Black'
        ORDER BY Name
END
```

Control-of-Flow

In the next few recipes, I'll demonstrate how to use the following SQL Server 2005 control-of-flow functions and commands.

- RETURN. This function is used to unconditionally exit the existing scope and return control to the calling scope. RETURN can also be used to communicate integer values back to the caller. This technique is often used to communicate business logic errors back to the calling procedure, or to confirm that everything in the batch/query/scope executed without error.

- WHILE. You can use this to repeatedly execute the same batch of Transact-SQL code while a Boolean condition evaluates to TRUE. WHILE is often used as an alternative to cursors (also reviewed in this chapter), as you can use it to loop through a result set one row at a time, performing actions for each row until the result set is empty. For example, you could populate a temporary table with a list of the names of indexes that have a fragmentation level greater than 50%. A WHILE statement can be invoked to keep looping for as long as there are rows in this table. For each iteration, you would grab the TOP 1 index row and perform an index rebuild on the first index name grabbed from the table. After that, you could delete that row from the table, and then keep looping through the indexes until the table is empty, ending the WHILE loop.

- GOTO. This function can be used to jump to a label in your Transact-SQL batch. It is often used to jump to a special error handler when an error occurs, or to skip over code if a certain business condition is or isn't met. GOTO has a reputation, which is duly earned, for creating spaghetti code. This is because you have to jump between code blocks in order to fully understand what the batch or procedure is actually doing. Although use of GOTO should be minimal, it is still supported, and thus presented in a recipe here.

- WAITFOR. You can use this function to defer processing of consecutive Transact-SQL commands that follow it—for either a fixed period of time or *until* a specific time. This is useful in situations where activities are synchronous. For example, if your code cannot finish until an external task has completed in a set number of seconds/minutes/hours, or if you cannot perform an action until a specific time (non-business hours, for example).

Using RETURN

RETURN is used to exit the current Transact-SQL batch, query, or stored procedure immediately, and doesn't execute any code in the batch/query/procedure scope that follows after it. RETURN exits only the code executing in the current scope; if you have called stored procedure B from stored procedure A, and stored procedure B issues a RETURN, stored procedure B stops immediately, but stored procedure A continues as though B had completed successfully.

This example demonstrates how to use RETURN to unconditionally stop a query:

```
IF NOT EXISTS
(SELECT ProductID FROM Production.Product WHERE Color = 'Pink')
BEGIN
    RETURN
END

-- Won't execute
SELECT ProductID
```

```
FROM Production.Product
WHERE Color = 'Pink'
```

This returns:

```
Command(s) completed successfully.
```

RETURN also allows for an optional integer expression:

```
RETURN [ integer_expression ]
```

This integer value can be used in a stored procedure to communicate issues to the calling application. For example:

```
-- Create a Stored Procedure that raises an error
CREATE PROCEDURE #usp_TempProc
AS
SELECT 1/0
RETURN @@ERROR
GO
```

Next, the stored procedure is executing, capturing the RETURN code in a local variable:

```
DECLARE @ErrorCode int

EXEC @ErrorCode = #usp_TempProc
PRINT @ErrorCode
```

This returns:

```
Msg 8134, Level 16, State 1, Procedure
#usp_TempProc
                                  00000B72, Line 4
Divide by zero error encountered.
8134
```

How It Works

In this recipe, an IF condition checked for the existence of a pink-colored product:

```
IF NOT EXISTS
(SELECT ProductID FROM Production.Product WHERE Color = 'Pink')
```

If it evaluated to TRUE (no pink products exist), the RETURN statement is executed:

```
BEGIN
    RETURN
END

-- Won't execute
SELECT ProductID
FROM Production.Product
WHERE Color = 'Pink'
```

Since there are no pink products, RETURN is called, and the SELECT query following the IF statement is never executed.

The second example demonstrated creating a temporary stored procedure containing Transact-SQL that creates a divide-by-zero error. RETURN was used to capture the @@ERRORCODE value of 8134, which was passed back to the caller and printed in the @ErrorCode local variable. If an integer value isn't explicitly plugged into the RETURN call, a 0 value is sent by default.

Using WHILE

In this recipe, I demonstrate the WHILE command, which allows you to repeat a specific operation or batch of operations while a condition remains TRUE.

The syntax for WHILE is as follows:

```
WHILE Boolean_expression
    { sql_statement | statement_block }
    [ BREAK ]
    { sql_statement | statement_block }
    [ CONTINUE ]
    { sql_statement | statement_block }
```

WHILE will keep the Transact-SQL statement or batch processing while the Boolean expression remains TRUE. The BREAK keyword allows you to exit from the innermost WHILE loop, and the CONTINUE keyword causes the loop to restart.

In this example, the system stored procedure sp_spaceused is used to return the table space usage for each table in the @AWTables table variable:

```
-- Declare variables
DECLARE @AWTables TABLE (SchemaTable varchar(100))
DECLARE @TableName varchar(100)

-- Insert table names into the table variable
INSERT @AWTables
(SchemaTable)
SELECT TABLE_SCHEMA + '.' + TABLE_NAME
FROM INFORMATION_SCHEMA.tables
WHERE TABLE_TYPE = 'BASE TABLE'
ORDER BY  TABLE_SCHEMA + '.' + TABLE_NAME

-- Report on each table using sp_spaceused
WHILE (SELECT COUNT(*) FROM @AWTables)>0
BEGIN
    SELECT TOP 1 @TableName = SchemaTable
    FROM @AWTables
    ORDER BY SchemaTable

    EXEC sp_spaceused @TableName

    DELETE @AWTables
    WHERE SchemaTable = @TableName

END
```

This returns multiple result sets (one for each table). Three result sets are shown here:

name	rows	reserved	data	index_size	unused
Shift	3	48 KB	8 KB	40 KB	0 KB

name	rows	reserved	data	index_size	unused
Department	20	32 KB	8 KB	24 KB	0 KB

name	rows	reserved	data	index_size	unused
EmployeeAddress	290	48 KB	16 KB	32 KB	0 KB

As you saw in the earlier WHILE syntax, you can also use the keywords BREAK and CONTINUE in your code. BREAK is used to exit the WHILE loop, whereas CONTINUE is used to resume a WHILE loop. For example:

```
WHILE (1=1)
BEGIN
   PRINT 'Endless While, because 1 always equals 1'
   IF 1=1
   BEGIN
      PRINT 'But we didn''t let the endless loop happen'
      BREAK
   END
   ELSE
   BEGIN
      CONTINUE
   END
END
```

This returns:

```
Endless While, because 1 always equals 1
But we didn't let the endless loop happen
```

How It Works

In this recipe, WHILE is used to loop through each table in the AdventureWorks database, reporting information using the sp_spaceused system stored procedure.

This recipe began by declaring two variables:

```
DECLARE @AWTables TABLE (SchemaTable varchar(100))
DECLARE @TableName varchar(100)
```

The table variable @AWTables was used to hold all the table names, and the @TableName variable to hold a single table name's value.

The table variable was populated with all the table names in the AdventureWorks database (populating a schema.table_name value):

```
INSERT @AWTables
(SchemaTable)
SELECT TABLE_SCHEMA + '.' + TABLE_NAME
FROM INFORMATION_SCHEMA.tables
WHERE TABLE_TYPE = 'BASE TABLE'
ORDER BY  TABLE_SCHEMA + '.' + TABLE_NAME
```

The WHILE loop was then started, looping as long as there were rows in the @AWTables table variable:

```
WHILE (SELECT COUNT(*) FROM @AWTables)>0
BEGIN
```

Within the WHILE, the @TableName local variable was populated with the TOP 1 table name from the @AWTables table variable:

```
   SELECT TOP 1 @TableName = SchemaTable
   FROM @AWTables
   ORDER BY SchemaTable
```

Using the @TableName variable, EXEC sp_spaceused was executed:

```
EXEC sp_spaceused @TableName
```

Lastly, the row for the reported table was deleted from the table variable:

```
    DELETE @AWTables
    WHERE SchemaTable = @TableName
END
```

`WHILE` will continue to execute `sp_spaceused` until all rows are deleted from the `@AWTables` table variable.

In the second example of the recipe, `BREAK` was used to exit a loop if a certain condition is met (or threshold tripped). Use `BREAK` as an extra precaution against endless loops.

Using GOTO

This recipe demonstrates `GOTO`, which is used to jump to a label in your Transact-SQL batch, passing over the code that follows it. The syntax is:

```
    GOTO label
label definition: code
```

In this example we check to see if a department name is already in use by an existing department. If so, the `INSERT` is bypassed using `GOTO`. If not, the `INSERT` is performed:

```
DECLARE @Name nvarchar(50)
DECLARE @GroupName nvarchar(50)

SET @Name = 'Engineering'
SET @GroupName = 'Research and Development'

IF EXISTS (SELECT Name
        FROM HumanResources.Department
        WHERE Name = @Name)
BEGIN
   GOTO SkipInsert
END

INSERT HumanResources.Department
(Name, GroupName)
VALUES(@Name , @GroupName)

SkipInsert:
PRINT @Name + ' already exists in HumanResources.Department'
```

This returns:

```
Engineering already exists in HumanResources.Department
```

How It Works

In this recipe's example, two local variables were declared and set to values in preparation for being inserted into the `HumanResources.Department` table:

```
DECLARE @Name nvarchar(50)
DECLARE @GroupName nvarchar(50)

SET @Name = 'Engineering'
SET @GroupName = 'Research and Development'
```

Next, an IF statement was used to check for the existence of any row with the same department name as the local variable. If such a row exists the GOTO command is invoked. GOTO references the label name that you want to skip to, in this case called SkipInsert:

```
IF EXISTS (SELECT Name
        FROM HumanResources.Department
        WHERE Name = @Name)
BEGIN
   GOTO SkipInsert
END
```

An INSERT follows the IF statement, however in our example it is skipped over because the department 'Engineering' does already exist in the HumanResources.Department table:

```
INSERT HumanResources.Department
(Name, GroupName)
VALUES(@Name , @GroupName)
```

The label to be skipped to is then defined, suffixed with a colon. The label defines a printed message to be returned:

```
SkipInsert:
PRINT @Name + ' already exists in HumanResources.Department'
```

As a best practice, when given a choice between using GOTO and other control-of-flow methods, you should choose something other than GOTO. GOTO can cause readability issues and spaghetti code, as you'll have to jump around the batch or stored procedure in order to understand the original intention of the query author.

Using WAITFOR

In this recipe, I demonstrate the WAITFOR command, which delays the execution of Transact-SQL code for a specified length of time.

The syntax for WAITFOR is as follows:

```
WAITFOR
{
    DELAY 'time_to_pass'
  | TIME 'time_to_execute'
  | ( receive_statement ) [ , TIMEOUT timeout ]
}
```

The time_to_pass parameter for WAITFOR DELAY is the number of seconds, minutes, and hours to wait before executing the command. The WAITFOR TIME time_to_execute parameter is used to designate an actual time (hour, minute, second) to execute the batch. The receive_statement and TIMEOUT options are used in conjunction with Service Broker (see Chapter 20).

In this first example, a ten-second delay is created by WAITFOR before a SELECT query is executed:

```
WAITFOR DELAY '00:00:10'
BEGIN
   SELECT TransactionID, Quantity
   FROM Production.TransactionHistory
END
```

In this second example, a query is not executed until a specific time, in this case 7:01PM:

```
WAITFOR TIME '19:01:00'
BEGIN
   SELECT COUNT(*)
   FROM Production.TransactionHistory
END
```

How It Works

In this recipe, two different versions of `WAITFOR` were used to delay processing of a Transact-SQL batch.

The first query waited ten seconds before executing the batch:

```
WAITFOR DELAY '00:00:10'
```

Waiting for a certain amount of time is useful when you know another operation must execute asynchronously while your current batch process must wait. For example if you have kicked off an asynchronous SQL Server Agent job using the `sp_start_job` system stored procedure, control is returned immediately to the batch after the job starts to execute. If you know that the job you just kicked off takes at least five minutes to run, and your consecutive tasks are dependent on the completion of the job, `WAITFOR` can be used to delay processing until the job is complete.

The second query waited until the next instance of the specified time:

```
WAITFOR TIME '19:01:00'
```

`WAITFOR TIME` is useful for when certain operations must occur at specific time periods in the day. For example, say you have a stored procedure which performs data warehouse aggregations from transaction processing tables. The aggregations may take a couple of hours to complete, but you don't want to load the finished data from the staging to the production tables until after business hours. Using `WAITFOR TIME` in the procedure, you can stop the final load of the tables until non-business hours.

Cursors

SQL Server's performance advantage resides in its set-based processing capabilities. Nonetheless, novice query authors with a programming background are often more comfortable using cursors than the set-based alternatives for retrieving or updating rows. Unfortunately, cursors have several strikes against them. Many a time they have been known to eat up a SQL Server instances' memory, lock resources, and create excessive amounts of code. These problems occur when the developer overlooks lower-cost set-based alternatives. Transact-SQL is a set-based language, meaning that it excels at manipulating and retrieving sets of rows, rather than performing single row-by-row processing.

Nevertheless, your application or business requirements may require the single, row-by-row processing that Transact-SQL cursors can provide. In general you should only consider using cursors after exhausting other methods for doing row level processing, such as `WHILE` loops, sub queries, temporary tables, or table variables, to name a few.

The general lifecycle of a Transact-SQL cursor is as follows:

- A cursor is defined via a SQL statement that returns a valid result set.

- The cursor is then populated (opened).

- Once opened, rows can be fetched from the cursor, one at a time or in a block. The rows can also be fetched moving forward or backwards, depending on the original cursor definition.

- Depending on the cursor type, the data can be modified while scrolling through the rows, or read and used with other operations.

- Finally, after the cursor has been used, it should then be explicitly closed and de-allocated from memory.

The `DECLARE CURSOR` command is used to create a cursor, and has many options that impact the flexibility and locking behavior of the cursor. The syntax is as follows:

```
DECLARE cursor_name CURSOR
[ LOCAL | GLOBAL ]
[ FORWARD_ONLY | SCROLL ]
[ STATIC | KEYSET | DYNAMIC | FAST_FORWARD ]
[ READ_ONLY | SCROLL_LOCKS | OPTIMISTIC ]
[ TYPE_WARNING ]
FOR select_statement[ FOR UPDATE [ OF column_name [ ,...n ] ] ]
```

There are several options that can impact whether or not the cursor data can be updated, and whether or not you can move backwards and forwards within the rows populated within the cursor. Table 9-2 briefly describes the available options:

Table 9-2. *Cursor Options*

Option	Description
LOCAL or GLOBAL	If LOCAL is selected, the cursor is only available within the scope of the SQL batch, trigger, or stored procedure. If GLOBAL is selected, the cursor is available to the connection itself (for example, a connection that executes a stored procedure that creates a cursor can use the cursor that was created in the stored procedure execution).
FORWARD_ONLY or SCROLL	The FORWARD_ONLY option only allows you to move forward from the first row of the cursor and onward. SCROLL, on the other hand, allows you to move backwards and forwards through the cursor result set using all fetch options (FIRST, LAST, NEXT, PRIOR, ABSOLUTE, and RELATIVE). If performance is a consideration, stick with FORWARD_ONLY—as this cursor type incurs less overhead than the SCROLL.
STATIC or KEYSET or DYNAMIC or FAST_FORWARD	When STATIC is specified, a snapshot of the cursor data is held in the tempdb database, and any changes made at the original data source aren't reflected in the cursor data. KEYSET allows you to see changes to rows made outside of the cursor, although you can't see inserts that would have met the cursor's SELECT query, or deletes after the cursor has been opened. DYNAMIC allows you to see updates, inserts, and deletes in the underlying data source while the cursor is open. FAST_FORWARD defines two behaviors: settings the cursor to read only and forward only status (this is usually the best performing cursor option, but the least flexible). When faced with a performance decision, and your desired functionality is not complicated, use this option.
READ_ONLY or SCROLL_LOCKS or OPTIMISTIC	The READ_ONLY option means that updates cannot be made through the cursor. If performance and concurrency is a consideration, use this option. SCROLL_LOCKS places locks on rows so that updates or deletes are guaranteed to be made after the cursor is closed. The OPTIMISTIC option places no locks on updated or deleted rows, and will only maintain modifications if an update has not occurred outside of the cursor since the last data read.
TYPE_WARNINGS	When TYPE_WARNINGS is specified, a warning will be sent to the client if the cursor is implicitly converted from one type to a different type.

The select_statement argument is the query used to define the data within the cursor. Avoid using a query that has more columns and rows than will be used, because cursors, while open, are kept in memory. The UPDATE [OF column_name [,...n]] is used to specify those columns that are allowed to be updated by the cursor.

Once a cursor is declared using DECLARE CURSOR, the next step is to open it up and populate it using the OPEN command. The syntax is as follows:

```
OPEN  { [ GLOBAL ] cursor_name }
```

A cursor can be opened locally (the default) or globally. Once opened, you can begin using the FETCH command to navigate through rows in the cursor. The syntax for FETCH NEXT is as follows:

```
FETCH    [ [ NEXT | PRIOR | FIRST | LAST
                   | ABSOLUTE { n | @nvar }
                   | RELATIVE { n | @nvar } ]
           FROM    ]
{ { [ GLOBAL ] cursor_name }
[ INTO @variable_name [ ,...n ] ]
```

FETCH provides several options for navigating through rows in the cursor, by populating the results into local variables for each column in the cursor definition (this is demonstrated in the next recipe).

The @@FETCH_STATUS function is used after a FETCH operation to determine the FETCH status, returning 0 if successful, -1 for unsuccessful, or -2 for missing.

Once you are finished with the opened cursor, execute the CLOSE command to release the result set from memory. The syntax is as follows:

```
CLOSE { [ GLOBAL ] cursor_name }
```

At this point you can still reopen the cursor if you want to. If you are finished however, you should remove internal system references to the cursor by using the DEALLOCATE command. This frees up any resources used by the cursor. For example if scroll locks are held on the cursor referenced in the table, these locks are then released after a DEALLOCATE. The syntax is as follows:

```
DEALLOCATE { [ GLOBAL ] cursor_name }
```

This next recipe will demonstrate each of these commands in action.

Creating and Using Transact-SQL Cursors

Although this book recommends the minimal use of cursors, using cursors for ad hoc, periodic database administration information-gathering, as I demonstrate in this next example, is usually perfectly justified.

This recipe demonstrates a cursor that loops through each session ID (SPID, formerly called "server process ID") currently active on the SQL Server instance, and executes DBCC INPUTBUFFER to see the SQL statements each connection is currently executing (if it is executing anything at that moment):

```
-- Don't show rowcounts in the results
SET NOCOUNT ON

DECLARE @spID smallint

-- Declare the cursor
DECLARE spID_cursor CURSOR
FORWARD_ONLY READ_ONLY
FOR SELECT spID
   FROM sys.sysprocesses
   WHERE status IN ('runnable', 'sleeping')

-- Open the cursor
OPEN spID_cursor

-- Retrieve one row at a time from the cursor
FETCH NEXT
FROM spID_cursor
INTO @spID
```

```
-- Keep retrieving rows while the cursor has them
WHILE @@FETCH_STATUS = 0
BEGIN
-- See what each spID is doing
PRINT 'SpID #: ' + STR(@spID)
EXEC ('DBCC INPUTBUFFER (' + @spID + ')')

-- Grab the next row
FETCH NEXT
FROM spID_cursor
INTO @spID

END

-- Close the cursor
CLOSE spID_cursor

-- Deallocate the cursor
DEALLOCATE spID_cursor
```

This returns the current Transact-SQL activity for each process on the SQL Server instance.

How It Works

The recipe started off by setting SET NOCOUNT ON, which suppresses the SQL Server row count messages in order to provide cleaner output:

```
-- Don't show rowcounts in the results
SET NOCOUNT ON
```

Next, a local variable was defined to hold the individual value of the server process ID to be fetched from the cursor:

```
DECLARE @spID smallint
```

The cursor was then defined using DECLARE CURSOR. The cursor contained the SPID column from the sys.sysprocesses system view:

```
-- Declare the cursor
DECLARE spID_cursor CURSOR
FORWARD_ONLY READ_ONLY
FOR SELECT spID
   FROM sys.sysprocesses
WHERE status IN ('runnable', 'sleeping')
```

After the cursor was defined, it was then opened (populated):

```
OPEN spID_cursor
```

Once opened, the first row value was retrieved into the @SPID local variable using FETCH NEXT:

```
FETCH NEXT
FROM spID_cursor
INTO @spID
```

FETCH NEXT was used to retrieve the first row. After the first fetch, a WHILE condition was defined that told SQL Server to continue the loop of statements until the cursor's fetch status was no longer successful (meaning no more rows could be retrieved).

```
WHILE @@FETCH_STATUS = 0
BEGIN
```

@@FETCH_STATUS was used to return the status of the last cursor FETCH statement last issued against the open cursor, returning 0 if the last FETCH was successful, -1 for unsuccessful, or -2 for missing:

Within the WHILE statement, the @SPID variable is printed, and used with EXEC to create a dynamic query.

```
-- See what each spID is doing
PRINT 'SpID #: ' + STR(@spID)
EXEC ('DBCC INPUTBUFFER (' + @spID + ')')
```

The dynamic query executes DBCC INPUTBUFFER for each individual SPID, returning any SQL Statement that the SPID currently has in the buffer.

After this, another FETCH NEXT was run to populate the next @SPID value:

```
-- Grab the next row
FETCH NEXT
FROM spID_cursor
INTO @spID

END
```

After all SPIDs are retrieved, the WHILE loop exits (because @@FETCH_STATUS will return -1). The cursor was then closed using the CLOSE command:

```
-- Close the cursor
CLOSE spID_cursor
```

At this point, the cursor can still be opened with the OPEN command, however to completely remove the cursor from memory, DEALLOCATE was used:

```
-- Deallocate the cursor
DEALLOCATE spID_cursor
```

Although useful, cursors should be handled with care as they can consume excessive resources, and often don't perform as well as set-based equivalents. Be sure to explore all set-based alternatives before considering cursors in your Transact-SQL development.

■■■

Stored Procedures

A stored procedure groups one or more Transact-SQL statements into a logical unit, stored as an object in a SQL Server database. After the stored procedure is created, its definition is stored in the `sys.sql_module` system catalog view.

Unlike user-defined functions or views, when a stored procedure is executed for the first time (since the SQL Server instance was last started), SQL Server determines the most optimal query access plan and stores it in the plan memory cache. SQL Server can then reuse the plan on subsequent executions of this stored procedure. Plan reuse allows stored procedures to provide fast and reliable performance compared to non-compiled ad hoc query equivalents.

■**Note** In SQL Server 2005, it is also possible to create a stored procedure that utilizes a .NET CLR assembly. This is discussed in Chapter 13. Also, although the creation of extended stored procedures is still supported in SQL Server 2005, it is now deprecated and will be removed from future versions.

This chapter contains recipes for creating and manipulating stored procedures. We'll discuss some of the new features introduced in SQL Server 2005, as well as some best practices.

Stored Procedure Basics

Over the years I have developed a strong bias towards the use of stored procedures whenever possible. There are many good reasons to use stored procedures, and in my experience, very few bad ones. Usually, reasons against using stored procedures come from application developers who are more comfortable using ad hoc SQL within the application tier, and may not be trained in the use of stored procedures. In companies with a separate application and database administration staff, stored procedures also imply a loss of control over the Transact-SQL code from the application developer to the database administration staff. Assuming your database administration team is competent and willing to assist with a move to stored procedures in a timely fashion, the benefits of using them should far outweigh any loss of control.

There are many benefits of using stored procedures:

- Stored procedures help centralize your Transact-SQL code in the data tier. Websites or applications that embed ad hoc SQL are notoriously difficult to modify in a production environment. When ad hoc SQL is embedded in an application, you may spend too much time trying to find and debug the embedded SQL. Once you've found the bug, chances are you'll need to recompile the page or program executable, causing unnecessary application outages or application distribution nightmares. If you centralize your Transact-SQL code in stored procedures, you'll have only one place to look for SQL code or SQL batches. If you document the code properly, you'll also be able to capture the areas that need fixing.

- Stored procedures can help reduce network traffic for larger ad hoc queries. Programming your application call to execute a stored procedure, rather then push across a 500 line SQL call, can have a positive impact on your network and application performance, particularly if the call is repeated thousands of times a minute.

- Stored procedures encourage code reusability. For example, if your web application uses a drop-down menu containing a list of cities, and this drop-down is used in multiple web pages, you can call the stored procedure from each web page rather then embed the same SQL in multiple places.

- Stored procedures allow you to obscure the method of data retrieval. If you change the underlying tables from which the source data is pulled, stored procedures (similar to views) can obscure this change from the application. This allows you to make changes without forcing a code change at the application tier. You can swap in new tables for the old, and so long as the same columns and data types are sent back to the application, the application is none the wiser. Unlike views, stored procedures can take advantage of control-of-flow techniques, temporary tables, table variables, and much more.

- Stored procedures have a stabilizing influence on query response time. If you've worked extensively with ad hoc queries, you may have noticed that sometimes the amount of time it takes to return results from a query can vary wildly. This may be due to external factors, such as concurrent activity against the table (locking) or resource issues (memory, CPU). On the other hand, an ad hoc query may be performing erratically because SQL Server periodically chooses less efficient execution plans. With stored procedures, you gain more reliable query-plan caching, and hence reuse. Notice that I use the word reliable here, rather than quicker or better. Ad hoc queries can sometimes perform better than their stored procedure counterparts, but it all depends on how you have tested, tuned, and then implemented the code within.

If none of these previous reasons convinced you that stored procedures are largely beneficial, let's review the security benefits. Direct table access (or worse, sysadmin access) to the SQL Server instance and its database poses a security risk. Inline ad hoc code is more vulnerable to *SQL injection* attacks. A SQL injection occurs when harmful Transact-SQL is inserted into an existing application's Transact-SQL code prior to being sent to the SQL Server instance. Aside from SQL injection attacks, if someone gets a hold of the inline code, they'll be able to glean information about the underlying schema of your database, and direct their hacking attempts accordingly. Keeping all SQL within stored procedures keeps only the stored procedure reference in the application—instead of each individual column and table name. Another security benefit to stored procedures is that you can grant database users and/or database roles access to them specifically instead of having to grant direct access to tables. The stored procedure can act as a control layer, allowing you to choose which columns and rows can and cannot be modified by the stored procedure (and also by the caller).

Creating a Basic Stored Procedure

Stored procedures can be used for many different activities including simple SELECTs, INSERTs, UPDATEs, DELETEs, and much more. Many of the features or statements reviewed in the chapters of this book can be used within the body of a stored procedure. Transact-SQL activities can be mixed within a single procedure, or you can create stored procedures in a modular fashion, creating multiple stored procedures for each task or set of tasks.

The basic syntax for non-parameterized stored procedures is as follows:

```
CREATE PROCEDURE  [schema_name.] procedure_name
AS { <sql_statement> [ ...n ] }
```

The first arguments of the command are the schema and new procedure name. The sql_statement argument is the Transact-SQL body of your stored procedure. This argument contains one or more tasks that you wish to accomplish.

This example demonstrates how to create a basic stored procedure that queries data from the AdventureWorks database:

```
CREATE PROCEDURE dbo.usp_SEL_ShoppingCartDisplay
AS

SELECT sc.ShoppingCartID,
       sc.ShoppingCartItemID,
       sc.Quantity,
       sc.ProductID,
       p.Name ProductName,
       p.ListPrice
FROM Sales.ShoppingCartItem sc
INNER JOIN Production.Product p ON
       sc.ProductID = p.ProductID

GO
```

Next, the new stored procedure is executed using the EXEC command:

```
EXEC dbo.usp_SEL_ShoppingCartDisplay
```

This returns the following results:

ShoppingCartID	ShoppingCartItemID	Quantity	ProductID	ProductName	ListPrice
14951	2	3	862	Full-Finger Gloves, M	37.99
20621	4	4	881	Short-Sleeve Classic Jersey, S	53.99
20621	5	7	874	Racing Socks, M	8.99

How It Works

In this recipe, I demonstrated creating a stored procedure that queried the contents of two tables, returning a result set. This stored procedure works like a view, only it will now have a cached query plan when executed for the first time, which will also make its runtime consistent in consecutive executions.

The example started off by creating a stored procedure called usp_SEL_ShoppingCartDisplay:

```
CREATE PROCEDURE dbo.usp_SEL_ShoppingCartDisplay
AS
```

The Transact-SQL query definition then followed the AS keyword:

```
SELECT sc.ShoppingCartID,
       sc.ShoppingCartItemID,
       sc.Quantity,
       sc.ProductID,
       p.Name ProductName,
       p.ListPrice
```

```
FROM Sales.ShoppingCartItem sc
INNER JOIN Production.Product p ON
       sc.ProductID = p.ProductID
```

```
GO
```

The GO keyword was used to mark the end of the stored procedure.

After the procedure in this recipe was created, it was then executed using the EXEC command:

```
EXEC dbo.usp_SEL_ShoppingCartDisplay
```

As a side note, during the stored procedure creation process SQL Server checks that the SQL syntax is correct, but it doesn't check for the existence of referenced tables. This means that you can reference a table name incorrectly, and the name will not cause an error until runtime. This is called *deferred name resolution* and it allows you to create or reference the objects in the database that don't exist yet. This also means that you can drop, alter, or modify the objects referenced in the stored procedure without invalidating it.

Creating a Parameterized Stored Procedure

In the previous recipe, I demonstrated a non-parameterized stored procedure, meaning that no external parameters were passed to it. The ability to pass parameters to them is part of why stored procedures are one of the most important database objects in SQL Server. Using parameters, you can pass information into the body of the procedure in order to return customized search information, or use parameters to influence or execute INSERT, UPDATE, or DELETE statements against tables. A procedure can have up to 2100 parameters (although it's unlikely you'll want to use nearly that many).

The syntax for creating a stored procedure is as follows:

```
CREATE PROCEDURE  [schema_name.] procedure_name
    [ { @parameter [ type_schema_name. ] data_type }
      [ = default ] [ [ OUTPUT ]
    ] [ ,...n ]
AS { <sql_statement> [ ...n ] }
```

A parameter is prefixed by the @ sign, followed by the data type and optional default value. Parameters come in two flavors: input and output. Where input parameters are used to pass information into the stored procedure for processing, OUTPUT parameters are used to return information back to the stored procedure caller.

In this example, a new stored procedure is created that can accept three parameters. Based on the values of these parameters, either an existing row in a table will be updated, or a new row will be inserted:

```
CREATE PROCEDURE usp_UPD_ShoppingCartItem
(@ShoppingCartID nvarchar(50),
@Quantity int = 1, -- defaulted to quantity of 1
@ProductID int)
AS
-- If the same ShoppingCartID and ProductID is sent
-- in the parameters, update the new quantity

IF EXISTS(SELECT *
FROM Sales.ShoppingCartItem
WHERE ShoppingCartID = @ShoppingCartID AND
  ProductID = @ProductID )
BEGIN
```

```
        UPDATE Sales.ShoppingCartItem
        SET Quantity = @Quantity
        WHERE ShoppingCartID = @ShoppingCartID AND
           ProductID = @ProductID
END
ELSE
BEGIN
        -- Otherwise insert a new row
        INSERT Sales.ShoppingCartItem
        (ShoppingCartID, ProductID, Quantity)
        VALUES (@ShoppingCartID, @ProductID, @Quantity)
END

GO
```

Next, the new stored procedure is called, passing three values for each expected parameter:

```
EXEC usp_UPD_ShoppingCartItem '1255', 2, 316
```

This returns:

```
(1 row(s) affected)
```

How It Works

This recipe demonstrated the creation of a stored procedure that could accept parameters. In the example, three parameters were defined for the procedure:

```
CREATE PROCEDURE usp_UPD_ShoppingCartItem
(@ShoppingCartID nvarchar(50),
@Quantity int = 1, -- defaulted to quantity of 1
@ProductID int)
AS
```

The first parameter and third parameter are required parameters, as neither designated a default value. The second parameter was optional, however, because it defined a default @Quantity value of 1.

The body of the stored procedure followed the AS keyword, starting with the first block of code, which checks for the existence of rows in an IF statement:

```
IF EXISTS(SELECT *
FROM Sales.ShoppingCartItem
WHERE ShoppingCartID = @ShoppingCartID AND
  ProductID = @ProductID )
BEGIN
```

If the row already existed for that specific ProductID and ShoppingCartID, its quantity would be updated based on the new @Quantity value:

```
        UPDATE Sales.ShoppingCartItem
        SET Quantity = @Quantity
        WHERE ShoppingCartID = @ShoppingCartID AND
           ProductID = @ProductID
END
```

Otherwise, if a row didn't already exist, a new INSERT would be performed:

```
ELSE
BEGIN
        -- Otherwise insert a new row
```

```
    INSERT Sales.ShoppingCartItem
    (ShoppingCartID, ProductID, Quantity)
    VALUES (@ShoppingCartID, @ProductID, @Quantity)
END

GO
```

After the procedure was created, it was then executed along with the required parameter values:

```
EXEC usp_UPD_ShoppingCartItem '1255', 2, 316
```

In this case, since the specific ShoppingCartID and ProductID combination didn't exist in the table yet, a new row was inserted into Sales.ShoppingCartItem.

Using OUTPUT Parameters

In the previous recipe, you saw that there was syntax for including OUTPUT parameters in your stored procedure definition. OUTPUT parameters allow you to pass information back to the caller of the stored procedure, whether it's another stored procedure making the call or an ad hoc call made by an application.

In this example, I create a stored procedure that returns the list of departments for a specific group. In addition to returning the list of departments, an OUTPUT parameter is defined to store the number of departments returned for the specific group:

```
CREATE PROCEDURE dbo.usp_SEL_Department
    @GroupName nvarchar(50),
    @DeptCount int OUTPUT
AS

SELECT Name
FROM HumanResources.Department
WHERE GroupName = @GroupName
ORDER BY Name

SELECT @DeptCount = @@ROWCOUNT

GO
```

Next, the new stored procedure is called. A local variable is defined to hold the OUTPUT parameter value:

```
DECLARE @DeptCount int

EXEC dbo.usp_SEL_Department 'Executive General and Administration',
@DeptCount OUTPUT

PRINT @DeptCount
```

This returns the following result set:

```
Name
Executive
Facilities and Maintenance
Finance
Human Resources
Information Services
```

In addition to the results, the result row count is also returned via the PRINT command:

5

How It Works

In this example, the stored procedure was defined with a parameter called @DeptCount, followed by the data type and OUTPUT keyword:

```
@DeptCount int OUTPUT
```

The parameter was then assigned to the row count value, based on the previous SELECT statement that was executed before it.

```
SELECT @DeptCount = @@ROWCOUNT
```

To use the OUTPUT value in Transact-SQL code, a local variable was declared and used within the EXEC statement:

```
DECLARE @DeptCount int
```

Notice that the OUTPUT keyword followed the second parameter, in order to designate that it was receiving and not sending an actual value:

```
EXEC dbo.usp_SEL_Department 'Executive General and Administration', @DeptCount OUTPUT
```

You can use OUTPUT parameters as an alternative or additional method for returning information back to the caller of the stored procedure. Capturing the OUTPUT results allows you to then pass the variable's value into another stored procedure or process. If you're using OUTPUT just to communicate information back to the calling application, it's usually just as easy to create a second result set containing the information you need. This is because .NET applications, for example, can easily consume the multiple result sets that are returned from a stored procedure. The technique of using OUTPUT parameters versus using an additional result set to return information is really just a matter of preference. However, OUTPUT parameters are limited to returning a specific single value of the specified data type, while using an additional result set will allow you to return multiple rows and columns from the stored procedure.

Modifying a Stored Procedure

The ALTER PROCEDURE command is used to modify the definition of a stored procedure, allowing you to change everything but the original stored procedure name. The syntax is almost identical to CREATE PROCEDURE.

In this recipe, I'll demonstrate modifying the existing stored procedure created in the previous recipe, in order to return the number of departments returned by the query as a separate result set, instead of using an OUTPUT parameter:

```
ALTER PROCEDURE dbo.usp_SEL_Department
   @GroupName nvarchar(50)
AS

SELECT Name
FROM HumanResources.Department
WHERE GroupName = @GroupName
ORDER BY Name

SELECT @@ROWCOUNT DepartmentCount
GO
```

Next, the modified stored procedure is executed:

```
EXEC dbo.usp_SEL_Department 'Research and Development'
```

This returns two result sets:

```
Name
Engineering
Research and Development
Tool Design
```

And:

```
DepartmentCount
3
```

How It Works

In this recipe, ALTER PROCEDURE was used to modify the definition of an existing stored procedure—both removing a parameter and adding a second result set. Using this command, you can change everything but the procedure name itself.

Dropping Stored Procedures

You can drop a stored procedure from the database using the DROP PROCEDURE command.

The syntax for dropping a stored procedure is:

```
DROP PROCEDURE { [ schema_name. ] procedure } [ ,...n ]
```

This command takes one argument; the name of the procedure or procedures to drop. For example:

```
DROP PROCEDURE dbo.usp_SEL_EmployeePayHistory
```

How It Works

Once a stored procedure is dropped, its definition information is removed from the database's system tables. Any cached query execution plans are also removed for that stored procedure. Code references to the stored procedure by other stored procedures or triggers will fail upon execution once the stored procedure has been dropped.

Executing Stored Procedures Automatically at SQL Server Startup

You can designate a stored procedure to be executed whenever the SQL Server service is started. You may wish to do this to perform any cleanup tasks your SQL Server instance requires (for example, documenting when the service started, or clearing out work tables).

This automatic execution of a stored procedure is achieved using the sp_procoption system stored procedure. The command looks like it takes several different options, but in SQL Server 2005, it really only performs a single task, which is setting a stored procedure to execute automatically when the SQL Server service restarts.

In this example, a stored procedure is set to execute automatically whenever SQL Server is started. First, the database context is set to the master database (which is the only place that auto-executable stored procedures can be placed):

```
USE MASTER
GO
```

Next, for the example, a startup logging table is created:

```
CREATE TABLE dbo.SQLStartupLog
(SQLStartupLogID int IDENTITY(1,1) NOT NULL PRIMARY KEY,
 StartupDateTime datetime NOT NULL)
GO
```

Now, a new stored procedure is created to insert a value into the new table (so you can see whenever SQL Server was restarted using the table):

```
CREATE PROCEDURE dbo.usp_INS_TrackSQLStartups
AS

INSERT dbo.SQLStartupLog
(StartupDateTime)
VALUES (GETDATE())

GO
```

Next, the `sp_procoption` stored procedure is used to set this new procedure to execute when the SQL Server service restarts:

```
EXEC sp_procoption @ProcName = 'usp_INS_TrackSQLStartups',
  @OptionName = 'startup',
  @OptionValue = 'true'
```

Once the service restarts, a new row is inserted into the table. To disable the stored procedure again, the following command would need to be executed:

```
EXEC sp_procoption @ProcName = 'usp_INS_TrackSQLStartups',
  @OptionName = 'startup',
     @OptionValue = 'off'
```

How It Works

In this recipe, a new table was created in the master database that tracks SQL Server start-ups. A stored procedure is also created in the master database to insert a row into the table with the current date and time of execution.

■**Caution** I'm not espousing the creation of objects in the system databases. It isn't generally a good idea. Although if you must use auto-execution functionality as discussed in this recipe, you have no choice but to do it (for example, if your IT department requires a log of SQL Server service start times for tracking purposes).

Next, `sp_procoption` was called to set the startup value of the stored procedure:

```
EXEC sp_procoption @ProcName = 'usp_INS_TrackSQLStartups',
  @OptionName = 'startup',
  @OptionValue = 'true'
```

After `sp_procoption` was used, whenever the SQL Server service is restarted, a new row will be inserted into the `dbo.SQLStartupLog` table.

The stored procedure must be created in the master database; otherwise you'll see the following error message when trying to use sp_procoption:

```
Msg 15398, Level 11, State 1, Procedure sp_procoption, Line 73
Only objects in the master database owned by dbo can have the startup setting changed.
```

Reporting Stored Procedure Metadata

You can use the new SQL Server 2005 sys.sql_modules catalog view to explore stored procedure metadata (and other object types as well), as I demonstrate in this example:

```
SELECT definition,
     execute_as_principal_id,
     is_recompiled,
     uses_ansi_nulls,
     uses_quoted_identifier
FROM  sys.sql_modules m
INNER JOIN sys.objects o ON
     m.object_id = o.object_id
WHERE o.type = 'P'
```

How It Works

The sys.sql_modules view is used to view the definition and settings of stored procedures, triggers, views, and other SQL-defined objects. In this recipe, sys.sql_modules is joined to sys.objects so that only sys.objects rows of type P (stored procedures) will be returned.

The query returns the stored procedure definition (if not encrypted), the EXECUTE AS security context ID, whether or not the stored procedure has WITH RECOMPILE set, and a 1 if the ANSI NULL or QUOTED IDENTIFIER options were ON when it was created. Encryption, EXECUTE AS, and WITH RECOMPILE will all be discussed in this chapter.

Documenting Stored Procedures

This next recipe is more of a best practice, rather than a review of a command or function. It is important to comment your stored procedure code well, so that future readers will understand the business rules and intents behind your Transact-SQL code. Although some code may seem "self-evident" at the time of authoring, the original logic may not seem so clear a few months after it was written.

For brevity, the stored procedure examples in this chapter have not included extensive comments or headers. However, in your production database, you should at the very least define headers for each stored procedure created in a production database.

The following is an example of a stored procedure header:

```
CREATE PROCEDURE dbo.usp_IMP_DWP_FactOrder
AS

---------------------------------------------------------
-- Purpose: Populates the data warehouse, Called by Job
--
-- Maintenance Log
--
-- Update By      Update Date     Description
-- -----------    ---------       ----------------------------
-- Joe Sack       8/15/2005       Created
```

```
-- Joe Sack    8/16/2005    A new column was added to
--the base table, so it was added here as well.
... Transact-SQL code here
```

How It Works

This example demonstrated how to include header information within the body of a new stored procedure. It tracks the purpose, the application where it will be called, and a maintenance log.

No doubt you'll see other headers out in the field, with much more information. I'm a firm believer in not demanding more than is realistic though. Too many extraneous fields to update translates into too many fields to maintain. For example, if you include the stored procedure name in the header, in addition to the actual CREATE PROCEDURE, you'll soon start seeing code where the header name doesn't match the stored procedure name. Why not just document the information that isn't already included in the stored procedure definition?

Stored Procedure Security

I mentioned at the beginning of the chapter that stored procedures have inherent security benefits, and I'll go over that again now.

Inline ad hoc code is more susceptible to SQL injection attacks, allowing the hacker to see the embedded SQL calls, and search for words like Social Security Number or Credit Card, for example. Embedding your SQL code in a stored procedure allows you to obscure the schema from any external influences.

Also, using stored procedures instead of direct table access provides greater security for the base tables. You can control how modifications are made, and the data that is retrieved (both at the column and row level). Instead of granting table access, you can grant EXECUTE permissions to the user in order to execute the stored procedure instead. This is also the only call that travels to the database server, so any snooping elements won't see your SELECT statement.

■**Note** For information on how to GRANT permissions, see Chapter 18.

In addition to these inherent benefits (all you have to do is *use* stored procedures in order to benefit from them), there are also a couple of features you should be aware of. The next recipe shows you how to encrypt your stored procedure so that the query definition can't be viewed.

After that recipe, we'll review how to define a custom security context for your stored procedure. In SQL Server 2000, security access always defaulted to the caller of the stored procedure. This was sufficient under certain circumstances, such as when the procedure was performing an INSERT, UPDATE, DELETE, or SELECT operation and if the ownership chain was unbroken (as discussed in the recipe). However, the recipe demonstrates different situations where caller-based security isn't enough and how the new EXECUTE AS can be used to solve any security context issues.

Encrypting a Stored Procedure

Just like a view, stored procedure Transact-SQL definitions can have their contents encrypted in the database, removing the ability to read the procedure's definition. Software producers who use SQL Server in their back-end, often encrypt stored procedures in order to prevent tampering or reverse-engineering from clients or competitors. If you use encryption, be sure to save the original definition, as it can't be decoded later(legally and reliably, anyhow). It should also be encrypted only prior to a push to production.

In order to encrypt the stored procedure, WITH ENCRYPTION is designated after the name of the new stored procedure, as this next example demonstrates:

```
CREATE PROCEDURE usp_SEL_EmployeePayHistory
WITH ENCRYPTION
AS

SELECT EmployeeID, RateChangeDate, Rate, PayFrequency, ModifiedDate
FROM HumanResources.EmployeePayHistory

GO
```

Once you've created WITH ENCRYPTION, you'll be unable to view the procedure's text definition:

```
-- View the procedure's text
EXEC sp_helptext usp_SEL_EmployeePayHistory
```

This returns:

```
The text for object 'usp_SEL_EmployeePayHistory' is encrypted.
```

How It Works

Encryption can be defined using either CREATE PROCEDURE or ALTER PROCEDURE, but be sure to save your source code, as the existing encrypted text cannot be decrypted easily.

Using EXECUTE AS to Specify the Procedure's Security Context

In SQL Server 2005, the WITH EXECUTE AS clause allows you to specify the security context that a stored procedure executes under, overriding the default security of the stored procedure caller. In this case, security context refers to the permissions of the user executing the stored procedure.

■**Note** This recipe discusses several security features and concepts that I also cover in Chapters 17 and 18.

In SQL Server 2000, a stored procedure was *always* executed using the permissions of the caller. In SQL Server 2005, however, you now have the option to execute a stored procedure under the security context of the caller (the 2000 default), the person who authored or last altered the procedure, a specific login (if you have IMPERSONATE permissions for that person's login), or the owner of the stored procedure.

First, let me present you with a quick aside about caller permissions and ownership chaining. An ownership chain occurs when an object, such a stored procedure or view, is created and used to perform an INSERT, UPDATE, DELETE, or SELECT against another database object. If the schema of the stored procedure object is the same as the schema of the object referenced within, SQL Server only checks that the stored procedure caller has EXECUTE permissions to the stored procedure. Again, this ownership chaining only applies to the INSERT, UPDATE, DELETE, or SELECT commands. This is why stored procedures are excellent for securing the database—as you can grant a user access to execute a stored procedure without giving them access to the underlying tables.

An issue arises, however, when you are looking to execute commands that are *not* INSERT, UPDATE, DELETE, or SELECT. In those situations, even if a caller has EXECUTE permissions to a stored procedure that, for example, truncates a table using the TRUNCATE TABLE command, he or she must still have permissions to use the TRUNCATE TABLE command in the first place. For example, the following stored procedure is created, which deletes all data from a table:

```
CREATE PROCEDURE dbo.usp_DEL_ALLEmployeeSalary
AS

-- Deletes all rows prior to the data feed
DELETE dbo.EmployeeSalary

GO
```

Next, EXECUTE permission on this new stored procedure is granted to your employee Boris:

```
GRANT EXEC ON usp_DEL_ALLEmployeeSalary  to Boris
```

Now, if Boris attempts to execute this procedure, ownership chaining has got him covered:

```
EXECUTE  dbo.usp_DEL_ALLEmployeeSalary
```

Boris has no other permissions in the database except to the new stored procedure, but it still works:

```
(25 row(s) affected)
```

But now the procedure is changed to use the TRUNCATE TABLE command instead of DELETE:

```
ALTER PROCEDURE dbo.usp_DEL_ALLEmployeeSalary
AS

-- Deletes all rows prior to the data feed
TRUNCATE TABLE dbo.EmployeeSalary

GO
```

Now, if Boris attempts to execute this procedure again, SQL Server will check Boris's ability to use the TRUNCATE TABLE command, and will return the following error (since he only has permissions to execute the procedure):

```
Msg 1088, Level 16, State 7, Procedure usp_DEL_ALLEmployeeSalary, Line 5
Cannot find the object "EmployeeSalary" because it does not exist or you do not have
permissions.
```

Enter the EXECUTE AS option for stored procedures. Using EXECUTE AS, you can designate that any caller of the stored procedure run under your security context. For example, suppose the previous stored procedure was written as:

```
CREATE PROCEDURE dbo.usp_DEL_ALLEmployeeSalary
WITH EXECUTE AS OWNER
AS

-- Deletes all rows prior to the data feed
TRUNCATE TABLE dbo.EmployeeSalary

GO
```

With the added WITH EXECUTE AS OWNER, Boris only needs EXECUTE permissions on the stored procedure, and can execute the procedure under the stored procedure owner's security context.

The same "gotcha" goes for dynamic SQL (see Chapter 28 for a review of dynamic SQL). SQL Server will ensure that the caller has both EXECUTE *and* the appropriate permissions in order to perform the task the dynamic SQL is attempting to perform, even if that dynamic SQL is performing an INSERT, UPDATE, DELETE, or SELECT.

For example the following procedure contains dynamic SQL, allowing you to select the row count from any table based on the schema and table name designated in the @SchemaAndTable input parameter:

```
CREATE PROCEDURE dbo.usp_SEL_CountRowsFromAnyTable
@SchemaAndTable nvarchar(255)
AS

EXEC ('SELECT COUNT(*) FROM ' + @SchemaAndTable)

GO
```

If you have the permissions to EXECUTE this procedure, and have access to the designated table, SQL Server will allow you to return the row count:

```
EXEC dbo.usp_SEL_CountRowsFromAnyTable 'HumanResources.Department'
```

This returns:

17

However granting the EXECUTE permission isn't enough. Because this is dynamic SQL, if the user doesn't have SELECT permission to the underlying table, SQL Server will check both EXECUTE permissions on the procedure and SELECT permissions on the table. If the user Boris didn't have SELECT permissions, he'd see the following error:

```
Msg 229, Level 14, State 5, Line 1
SELECT permission denied on object 'Department', database 'AdventureWorks', schema
'HumanResources'.
```

Again, this is a situation which can be remedied using EXECUTE AS (if you are comfortable with Boris having these permissions, of course). This time, an explicit user name will be designated as the security context for the procedure:

```
ALTER PROCEDURE dbo.usp_SEL_CountRowsFromAnyTable
    @SchemaAndTable nvarchar(255)
WITH EXECUTE AS 'SteveP'
AS

EXEC ('SELECT COUNT(*) FROM ' + @SchemaAndTable)

GO
```

Assuming SteveP had the proper permissions to any tables passed as dynamic SQL in the procedure, now if Boris executes the procedure, he will see results returned as though Boris were SteveP. SQL Server will not check Boris's permissions, but will use SteveP's security context instead.

How It Works

In this recipe, EXECUTE AS was demonstrated within a stored procedure, allowing you to define the security context under which a stored procedure is executed, regardless of the caller.

The options for EXECUTE AS in a stored procedure are as follows:

```
EXECUTE AS { CALLER | SELF | OWNER | 'user_name' }
```

The default behavior for EXECUTE AS is the CALLER option, which means that the permissions of the executing user are used (and if the user doesn't have proper access, that execution will fail). This was the default behavior of stored procedures in SQL Server 2000 as well. If the SELF option is used, the execution context of the stored procedure will be that of the user that created or last altered the stored procedure. When the OWNER option is designated, the owner of the stored procedure's schema is used. The user_name option is an explicit reference to a database user whose security context the stored procedure will be executed under.

Recompilation and Caching

Stored procedures can provide performance benefits due to the cached query execution plan, allowing SQL Server to reuse an existing plan instead of generating a new one. Stored procedures also have a stabilizing effect on query response time compared to the sometimes varying response times of ad hoc queries.

■**Note** For more information on assessing query performance, see Chapter 28.

With that said, stored procedures are not the magic bullet for query performance. You still need to account for the performance of individual statements within the body of your stored procedure and to make sure that the tables are indexed properly and that the database is designed efficiently. Several of the features discussed in other chapters of this book can be utilized within the body of a stored procedure, but you must use them with the same consideration as you would had they been used outside of a stored procedure.

In the next two recipes, I'll discuss situations where you may *not* want a query execution plan to be cached, the first covering the RECOMPILE option and the second the DBCC FREEPROCCACHE command.

RECOMPILE(ing) a Stored Procedure Each Time It Is Executed

A recompilation occurs when stored procedure's plan is recreated either automatically or explicitly. Recompilations occur automatically during stored procedure execution when underlying table or other object changes occur to objects that are referenced within a stored procedure. They can also occur with changes to indexes used by the plan or after a large number of updates to table keys referenced by the stored procedure. The goal of an automatic recompilation is to make sure SQL Server is tuning towards the current schema and data, and not an older picture of how the data and schema used to be when the plan was last cached.

SQL Server 2005 has added extra efficiency in recompilation by allowing statement level recompiles within the stored procedure, instead of recompiling the entire stored procedure, as was the method in previous versions. Since recompiles cause extra overhead to generate new plans, statement level recompiles help decrease this overhead by only correcting what needs to be corrected.

Although recompilations are costly and should be avoided most of the time, there may sometimes be reasons why you would want to force a recompilation. For example, your procedure may produce wildly different query results based on the application calling it—so much so that the retained execution plan causes performance issues during the majority of procedure calls.

For example, if one parameter value for "City" returns a match of one million rows, while another value for "City" returns a single row, SQL Server may not necessarily cache the correct execution plan. It may end up caching a plan that is optimized for the single row instead of the million rows, causing a long query execution time. If you're looking to use stored procedures for benefits other than caching, you can use the WITH RECOMPILE command.

In this example, I demonstrate how to force a stored procedure to recompile each time it is executed:

```
CREATE PROCEDURE usp_SEL_BackupMBsPerSecond
(@BackupStartDate datetime,
 @BackupFinishDate datetime)
WITH RECOMPILE -- Plan will never be saved
AS

-- Procedure measure db backup throughput
SELECT  (SUM(backup_size)/1024)/1024 as 'MB',
        DATEDIFF ( ss , MIN(backup_start_date),
        MAX(backup_finish_date)) as 'seconds',
        ((SUM(backup_size)/1024)/1024 )/
            DATEDIFF ( ss , MIN(backup_start_date) ,
                MAX(backup_finish_date)) as 'MB per second'
FROM msdb.dbo.backupset
WHERE backup_start_date >= @BackupStartDate AND
backup_finish_date < @BackupFinishDate AND
type = 'd'
GO
```

Now whenever this procedure is called, a new execution plan will be formulated by SQL Server.

How It Works

This procedure used WITH RECOMPILE to ensure that a query plan is not cached for the procedure during creation or execution.

■Note SQL Server 2005 introduces automatic statement-level recompilation within the stored procedure. This means that only the statement within the stored procedure that requires a recompilation (recompilation reason due to several factors) will be recompiled, instead of the entire stored procedure.

You will no doubt only have need to use WITH RECOMPILE under rare circumstances, as generally the cached plan chosen by SQL Server will suffice. Use this option if you still wish to take advantage of a stored procedure's other benefits (such as security and modularization), but don't want SQL Server to store an inefficient plan based on wildly varying result sets.

Flushing the Procedure Cache

In this recipe, I demonstrate how to remove all plans from the procedure cache. This technique is often used in order to test procedure performance in a "cold" cache, reproducing the cache as though SQL Server had just been restarted. This is an option for you on a development SQL Server instance, if you want to make sure existing cached query plans don't have an impact on your stored procedure performance testing. Don't use this command in a production environment, as you could be knocking out several cached query plans that are perfectly fine.

In this example, a count of cached query plans is executed prior to executing DBCC FREEPROCCACHE:

```
SELECT COUNT(*) 'CachedPlansBefore'
FROM sys.dm_exec_cached_plans
```

This returns:

```
CachedPlansBefore
42
```

Next, the procedure cache for the entire SQL Server instance is cleared:

```
DBCC FREEPROCCACHE
```

Next, the first query is executed again to see the number of cached plans:

```
CachedPlansAfter
----------------
0
```

How It Works

DBCC FREEPROCCACHE was used in this recipe to clear out the procedure cache. If you try this yourself, the count of cached plans will vary based on the activity on your SQL Server instance. This includes any background processes or jobs that may be running before or after the clearing of the cache. The dynamic management view sys.dm_exec_cached_plans was used to demonstrate the impact of this DBCC command, showing an original count of 42 plans versus 0 afterwards.

CHAPTER 11

■ ■ ■

User-Defined Functions and Types

In this chapter, I'll present recipes for user-defined functions and types. User-defined *functions* allow you to encapsulate both logic and subroutines into a single function that can then be used within your Transact-SQL queries and programmatic objects. User-defined *types* allow you to create an alias type based on an underlying system data type, enforcing a specific data type, length, and nullability.

■Note This chapter covers how to create both user-defined functions and types using Transact-SQL. However, Chapter 13 briefly discusses how to create these objects using the new Common Language Runtime (CLR) functionality.

UDF Basics

Transact-SQL user-defined functions fall into three categories; *scalar*, *inline table-valued*, and *multi-statement table-valued*.

A scalar user-defined function is used to return a single value based on zero or more parameters. For example, you could create a scalar UDF that accepts a CountryID as a parameter, and returns the CountryNM.

An inline table-valued UDF returns a table data type based on a single SELECT statement that is used to define the returned rows and columns. Unlike a stored procedure, an inline UDF can be referenced in the FROM clause of a query, as well as be joined to other tables. Unlike a view, an inline UDF can accept parameters.

A multi-statement table-valued UDF also returns a result set and is referenced in the FROM clause. Unlike inline table-valued UDFs, they aren't constrained to use a single SELECT statement within the function definition and instead allow multiple Transact-SQL statements in the body of the UDF definition in order to define a single, final result set to be returned.

Like stored procedures, UDFs can perform well because their query execution plans are cached for reuse. UDFs can also be used in places where a stored procedure can't, like in the FROM and SELECT clause of a query. UDFs also encourage code reusability. For example, if you create a scalar UDF that returns the CountryNM based on a CountryID, and the same function is needed across several different stored procedures, rather than repeat the 20 lines of code needed to perform the lookup, you can call the UDF function instead.

In the next few recipes, I'll demonstrate how to create, drop, modify, and view metadata for each of these UDF types.

Creating Scalar User-Defined Functions

A scalar user-defined function accepts zero or more parameters, and returns a single value. Scalar UDFs are often used for converting or translating a current value to a new value, or performing other sophisticated lookups based on specific parameters. Scalar functions can be used within search, column, and join expressions.

The simplified syntax for a scalar UDF is as follows:

```
CREATE FUNCTION [ schema_name. ] function_name
        ( [ { @parameter_name [ AS ]
  [ type_schema_name. ] scalar_parameter_data_type
[ = default ] } [ ,...n ]
      ])
RETURNS scalar_return_data_type
[ AS ]
BEGIN
        function_body
    RETURN scalar_expression
END
```

Note The full syntax for CREATE FUNCTION can be found in SQL Server 2005 Books Online.

Table 11-1 gives a brief description of each argument's intended use.

Table 11-1. *Scalar UDF Arguments*

Argument	Description
[schema_name.] function_name	The optional schema name and required function name of the new scalar UDF.
@parameter_name	This is the name of the parameter to pass to the UDF, and it must be prefixed with an @ sign.
[type_schema_name.] scalar_parameter_data_type	This is the @parameter_name's data type and the optional owning schema (used if you are using a user-defined type as a parameter).
[,...n]	Although not an actual argument, this syntax element indicates that one or more parameters can be defined (up to 1024).
function_body	This function body contains one or more of the Transact-SQL statements that are used to produce and evaluate a scalar value.
scalar_expression	This is the actual value that will be returned by the scalar function (notice that it is defined after the function body).

This example creates a scalar UDF which accepts a varchar(max) data type parameter. It returns a bit value (1 or 0) based on whether the passed parameter contains suspicious values (as defined by the function). So if the input parameter contains a call to a command such as DELETE or SHUTDOWN, the flag is set to 1:

```
-- Create a function to check for any suspicious behaviors
-- from the application
CREATE FUNCTION dbo.udf_CheckForSQLInjection
   (@TSQLString varchar(max))
```

```
RETURNS BIT
AS

BEGIN

DECLARE @IsSuspect bit

-- UDF assumes string will be left padded with a single space
SET @TSQLString = ' ' + @TSQLString

IF    (PATINDEX('% xp_%' , @TSQLString ) <> 0 OR
    PATINDEX('% sp_%' , @TSQLString ) <> 0   OR
    PATINDEX('% DROP %' , @TSQLString ) <> 0 OR
    PATINDEX('% GO %' , @TSQLString ) <> 0 OR
    PATINDEX('% INSERT %' , @TSQLString ) <> 0 OR
    PATINDEX('% UPDATE %' , @TSQLString ) <> 0 OR
    PATINDEX('% DBCC %' , @TSQLString ) <> 0 OR
    PATINDEX('% SHUTDOWN %' , @TSQLString )<> 0 OR
    PATINDEX('% ALTER %' , @TSQLString )<> 0 OR
    PATINDEX('% CREATE %' , @TSQLString ) <> 0OR
    PATINDEX('%;%' , @TSQLString )<> 0 OR
    PATINDEX('% EXECUTE %' , @TSQLString )<> 0 OR
    PATINDEX('% BREAK %' , @TSQLString )<> 0 OR
    PATINDEX('% BEGIN %' , @TSQLString )<> 0 OR
    PATINDEX('% CHECKPOINT %' , @TSQLString )<> 0 OR
    PATINDEX('% BREAK %' , @TSQLString )<> 0 OR
    PATINDEX('% COMMIT %' , @TSQLString )<> 0 OR
    PATINDEX('% TRANSACTION %' , @TSQLString )<> 0 OR
    PATINDEX('% CURSOR %' , @TSQLString )<> 0 OR
    PATINDEX('% GRANT %' , @TSQLString )<> 0 OR
    PATINDEX('% DENY %' , @TSQLString )<> 0 OR
    PATINDEX('% ESCAPE %' , @TSQLString )<> 0 OR
    PATINDEX('% WHILE %' , @TSQLString )<> 0 OR
    PATINDEX('% OPENDATASOURCE %' , @TSQLString )<> 0 OR
    PATINDEX('% OPENQUERY %' , @TSQLString )<> 0 OR
    PATINDEX('% OPENROWSET %' , @TSQLString )<> 0 OR
    PATINDEX('% EXEC %' , @TSQLString )<> 0)

BEGIN
    SELECT @IsSuspect = 1
END
ELSE
BEGIN
    SELECT @IsSuspect = 0
END

    RETURN (@IsSuspect)
END

GO
```

Next, you should test the function by evaluating three different string input values. The first contains a SELECT statement:

```
SELECT dbo.udf_CheckForSQLInjection
('SELECT * FROM HumanResources.Department')
```

This returns:

0

The next string contains the SHUTDOWN command:

```
SELECT dbo.udf_CheckForSQLInjection
(';SHUTDOWN')
```

This returns:

1

The last string tested contains the DROP command:

```
SELECT dbo.udf_CheckForSQLInjection
('DROP HumanResources.Department')
```

This returns:

1

How It Works

This recipe demonstrated a scalar UDF, which accepts zero or more parameters, and returns a single value. Some of the areas where you can use a scalar function in your Transact-SQL code include:

- A column expression in a SELECT or GROUP BY clause
- A search condition for a JOIN in a FROM clause
- A search condition of a WHERE or HAVING clause

The recipe began by defining the UDF name and parameter:

```
CREATE FUNCTION dbo.udf_CheckForSQLInjection
   (@TSQLString varchar(max))
```

The @TSQLString parameter held the varchar(max) string to be evaluated.

In the next line of code, the scalar_return_data_type was defined as bit. This means that the single value returned by the function will be the bit data type:

```
RETURNS BIT
AS
```

The BEGIN marked the start of the function_body, where the logic to return the bit value was formulated:

```
BEGIN
```

A local variable was created to hold the bit value, and was set to a zero default. Ultimately, this is the parameter that will be passed as the function's output:

```
DECLARE @IsSuspect bit
```

Next, the string passed to the UDF has a space concatenated to it:

```
-- UDF assumes string will be left padded with a single space
SET @TSQLString = ' ' + @TSQLString
```

The @TSQLString was padded with an extra space in order to make the search of suspicious words or patterns easier to do. For example, if the suspicious word is at the beginning of the

@TSQLString, and we were searching for the word DROP, you would have to use PATINDEX to search for both '%DROP %' and '% DROP %'. Of course, searching '%DROP %' could give you false positives, such as the word "gumdrop," so you should prevent this confusion by padding the beginning of the string with a space.

In the IF statement, @TSQLString is evaluated using PATINDEX. For each evaluation, if a match is found, the condition will evaluate to TRUE:

```
IF     (PATINDEX('% xp_%' , @TSQLString ) <> 0 OR
    PATINDEX('% sp_%' , @TSQLString ) <> 0  OR
    PATINDEX('% DROP %' , @TSQLString ) <> 0 OR
    PATINDEX('% GO %' , @TSQLString ) <> 0 OR
    PATINDEX('% BREAK %' , @TSQLString )<> 0 OR
...
```

If any of the conditions evaluate to TRUE, the @IsSuspect bit flag will be set to 1:

```
BEGIN
    SELECT @IsSuspect = 1
END
ELSE
BEGIN
    SELECT @IsSuspect = 0
END
```

The RETURN keyword is used to pass the scalar value of the @IsSuspect variable back to the caller:

```
RETURN (@IsSuspect)
```

The END keyword is then used to close the UDF, and GO is used to end the batch:

```
END

GO
```

The new scalar UDF was then used to check three different string values. The first string SELECT * FROM HumanResources.Department comes up clean, but the second strings ; SHUTDOWN and DROP HumanResources.Department both return a bit value of "1" because they match the suspicious word searches in the function's IF clause.

Creating Inline User-Defined Functions

An inline UDF returns a table data type. In the UDF definition, you do not explicitly define the returned table, but use a single SELECT statement for defining the returned rows and columns instead. An inline UDF uses one or more parameters and returns data using a single SELECT statement. Inline UDFs are very similar to views, in that they are referenced in the FROM clause. However unlike views, UDFs can accept parameters that can then be used in the function's SELECT statement.

The basic syntax is as follows:

```
CREATE FUNCTION [ schema_name. ] function_name
        ( [ { @parameter_name [ AS ]
[ type_schema_name. ] scalar_parameter_data_type [ = default ]
        } [ ,...n ]
    ]
    )
RETURNS TABLE
[ AS ]
RETURN [ ( ] select_stmt [ ) ]
```

Note The full syntax for CREATE FUNCTION can be found in SQL Server 2005 Books Online.

Table 11-2 details the arguments of this command.

Table 11-2. *Inline UDF Arguments*

Argument	Description
[schema_name.] function_name	The optional schema name and required function name of the new inline UDF.
@parameter_name	This is the name of the parameter to pass to the UDF. It must be prefixed with an @ sign.
[type_schema_name.] scalar_parameter_data_type	This is the @parameter_name data type and the optional owning schema (used if you are using a user-defined type).
[,...n]	Although not an actual argument, this syntax element indicates that one or more parameters can be defined (up to 1024).
select_stmt	This is the single SELECT statement that will be returned by the inline UDF.

This example demonstrates creating an inline table UDF that accepts an @EmployeeID integer parameter and returns the associated employee addresses:

```
CREATE FUNCTION  dbo.udf_ReturnEmployeeAddress
    ( @EmployeeID int)
RETURNS TABLE
    AS
RETURN (
SELECT AddressLine1, City, StateProvinceID, PostalCode
FROM Person.Address a
INNER JOIN  HumanResources.EmployeeAddress   e ON
    a.AddressID = e.AddressID
WHERE e.EmployeeID = @EmployeeID )

GO
```

Next, the new function is tested in a query, referenced in the FROM clause for the EmployeeID 2:

```
SELECT AddressLine1, City, PostalCode
FROM dbo.udf_ReturnEmployeeAddress(2)
```

This returns:

```
AddressLine1                City     PostalCode
--------------------------- -------- ---------------
7883 Missing Canyon Court   Everett  98201

(1 row(s) affected)
```

How It Works

In this recipe, I created an inline table UDF to retrieve employee address data based on the @EmployeeID value passed. The UDF started off just like a scalar UDF, only the RETURNS command uses a TABLE data type (which is what distinguishes it from a scalar UDF):

```
CREATE FUNCTION  dbo.udf_ReturnEmployeeAddress
   ( @EmployeeID int)
RETURNS TABLE
   AS
```

After the AS keyword, the RETURN statement is issued with a single SELECT statement in parentheses:

```
RETURN (
SELECT AddressLine1, City, StateProvinceID, PostalCode
FROM Person.Address a
INNER JOIN  HumanResources.EmployeeAddress   e ON
   a.AddressID = e.AddressID
WHERE e.EmployeeID = @EmployeeID )

GO
```

After it has been created, the new inline UDF is then used in the FROM clause of a SELECT query. The @EmployeeID value of 2 is passed into the function in parentheses:

```
SELECT AddressLine1, City, PostalCode
FROM dbo.udf_ReturnEmployeeAddress(2)
```

This function then returns a result set, just like when you are querying a view or a table. Also, just like a view or stored procedure, the query you create to define this function must be tuned as you would a regular SELECT statement. Using an inline UDF offers no inherent performance benefits over using a view or stored procedure.

Creating Multi-Statement User-Defined Functions

Multi-statement table UDFs are referenced in the FROM clause just like inline UDFs, but unlike inline UDFs, they are not constrained to use a single SELECT statement within the function definition. Instead, multi-statement UDFs can use multiple Transact-SQL statements in the body of the UDF definition in order to define that a single, final result set be returned.

The basic syntax of a multi-statement table UDF is as follows:

```
CREATE FUNCTION [ schema_name. ] function_name
       ( [ { @parameter_name [ AS ]
                   [ type_schema_name. ] scalar_parameter_data_type [ = default ]
       } [ ,...n ]
    ]
    )
RETURNS @return_variable TABLE < table_type_definition >
[ AS ]
BEGIN
       function_body
    RETURN
END
```

Table 11-3 describes the arguments of this command.

Table 11-3. *Multistatement UDF Arguments*

Argument	Description
[schema_name.] function_name	The optional schema name and required function name of the new inline UDF.
@parameter_name	This is the name of the parameter to pass to the UDF. It must be prefixed with an @ sign.
[type_schema_name.] scalar_parameter_data_type	This is the data type of the @parameter_name and the optional owning schema (used if you are using a user defined type).
[,...n]	Although not an actual argument, this syntax element indicates that one or more parameters can be defined (up to 1024).
@return_variable	This is the user-defined name of the table variable that will hold the results to be returned by the UDF.
< table_type_definition >	This argument contains one or more column definitions for the table variable. Each column definition contains the name and data type, and can optionally define a PRIMARY KEY, UNIQUE, NULL, or CHECK constraint.
function_body	The function body contains one or more Transact-SQL statements that are used to populate and modify the table variable that will be returned by the UDF.

Notice the RETURNS keyword, which defines a *table variable* definition. Also notice the RETURN keyword at the end of the function, which doesn't have any parameter or query after it; as it is assumed that the defined table variable will be returned.

In this example a multi-statement UDF will be created that accepts two parameters: one to hold a string, and the other to define how that string will be delimited. The string is then broken apart into a result set based on the defined delimiter:

```
-- Creates a UDF that returns a string array as a table result set
CREATE FUNCTION dbo.udf_ParseArray
    ( @StringArray varchar(max),
      @Delimiter char(1) )
RETURNS @StringArrayTable  TABLE (Val varchar(50))
AS
BEGIN
    DECLARE @Delimiter_position int

    IF RIGHT(@StringArray,1) != @Delimiter
    SET @StringArray = @StringArray + @Delimiter

    WHILE CHARINDEX(@Delimiter, @StringArray) <> 0
      BEGIN
        SELECT @Delimiter_position =
            CHARINDEX(@Delimiter, @StringArray)

        INSERT @StringArrayTable
        VALUES (left(@StringArray, @Delimiter_position - 1))

        SELECT @StringArray = STUFF(@StringArray, 1,
@Delimiter_position, '')
      END
```

```
RETURN
END

GO
```

Now it will be used to break apart a comma-delimited array of values:

```
SELECT Val
FROM dbo.udf_ParseArray('A,B,C,D,E,F,G', ',')
```

This returns the following results:

```
Val
--------------------------------------------------
A
B
C
D
E
F
G

(7 row(s) affected)
```

How It Works

The multi-statement table UDF in this recipe was created using two parameters, the first to hold a string, and the second to define the character that delimits the string:

```
CREATE FUNCTION dbo.udf_ParseArray
  ( @StringArray varchar(max),
    @Delimiter char(1) )
```

Next, a table variable is defined after the RETURNS token. The @StringArrayTable was used to hold the values of the string array after being shredded into the individual values:

```
RETURNS @StringArrayTable  TABLE (Val varchar(50))
```

The function body started after AS and BEGIN:

```
AS
BEGIN
```

A local variable was created to hold the delimiter position in the string:

```
DECLARE @Delimiter_position int
```

If the last character of the string array wasn't the delimiter value, then the delimiter value was concatenated to the end of the string array:

```
IF RIGHT(@StringArray,1) != @Delimiter
SET @StringArray = @StringArray + @Delimiter
```

A WHILE loop was created, looping until there are no remaining delimiters in the string array:

```
WHILE CHARINDEX(@Delimiter, @StringArray) <> 0
   BEGIN
```

Within the loop, the position of the delimiter was identified using CHARINDEX:

```
SELECT @Delimiter_position =
   CHARINDEX(@Delimiter, @StringArray)
```

The LEFT function was used with the delimiter position to extract the individual-delimited string part into the table variable:

```
INSERT @StringArrayTable
VALUES (left(@StringArray, @Delimiter_position - 1))
```

The inserted chunk was then removed from the string array using the STUFF function:

```
SELECT @StringArray = STUFF(@StringArray, 1, @Delimiter_position, '')
```

STUFF is used to delete a chunk of characters and insert another character string in its place. This first parameter of the STUFF function is the character expression, which in this example is the string array. The second parameter is the starting position of the deleted and inserted text, and in this case we are removing text from the string starting at the first position and stopping at the first delimiter. The third parameter is the length of the characters to be deleted, which for this example is the delimiter-position variable value. The last argument is the string to be inserted, which in this case was a blank string represented by two single quotes. The net effect is that the first comma-separated entry was replaced by an empty string—the same result as if the first entry had been deleted.

This process of inserting values continued until there were no longer delimiters in the string array. After this, the WHILE loop ends and RETURN was called to return the table variable result set.

```
    END
RETURN
END
GO
```

The new UDF was then referenced in the FROM clause. The first parameter of the UDF was a comma-delimited list of letters. The second parameter was the delimiting parameter (a comma):

```
-- Now use it to break apart a comma delimited array
SELECT Val
FROM dbo.udf_ParseArray('A,B,C,D,E,F,G', ',')
```

The list was then broken into a result set, with each individual letter as its own row. As you can see, multi-statement table UDFs allow for much more sophisticated programmability than an inline table value, which can only use a single SELECT statement.

Modifying User-Defined Functions

A function can be modified by using the ALTER FUNCTION command, as I demonstrate in this next recipe:

```
ALTER FUNCTION dbo.udf_ParseArray
   ( @StringArray varchar(max),
 @Delimiter char(1) ,
 @MinRowSelect int,
 @MaxRowSelect int)
RETURNS @StringArrayTable  TABLE (RowNum int IDENTITY(1,1), Val
varchar(50))
AS
BEGIN
   DECLARE @Delimiter_position int

   IF RIGHT(@StringArray,1) != @Delimiter
   SET @StringArray = @StringArray + @Delimiter

   WHILE CHARINDEX(@Delimiter, @StringArray) <> 0
      BEGIN
```

```
        SELECT @Delimiter_position =
            CHARINDEX(@Delimiter, @StringArray)

        INSERT @StringArrayTable
        VALUES (left(@StringArray, @Delimiter_position - 1))

        SELECT @StringArray = stuff(@StringArray, 1,
@Delimiter_position, '')
        END

DELETE @StringArrayTable
WHERE RowNum < @MinRowSelect OR
    RowNum > @MaxRowSelect

RETURN
END

GO

-- Now use it to break apart a comma delimited array
SELECT RowNum, Val
FROM udf_ParseArray('A,B,C,D,E,F,G', ',', 3, 5)
```

This returns:

RowNum	Val
3	C
4	D
5	E

(3 row(s) affected)

How It Works

ALTER FUNCTION allows you to modify an existing UDF by using almost the identical syntax of CREATE FUNCTION (with some limitations, however):

- You can't change the name of the function using ALTER FUNCTION. What you're doing is replacing the code of an *existing* function—therefore the function needs to exist first.

- You can't convert a scalar UDF to a table UDF (either inline or multi-statement), nor can you convert a table UDF to a scalar UDF.

In this recipe, the udf_ParseArray from the previous recipe was modified to add two new parameters, @MinRowSelect and @MaxRowSelect:

```
ALTER FUNCTION dbo.udf_ParseArray
    ( @StringArray varchar(max),
      @Delimiter char(1) ,
      @MinRowSelect int,
      @MaxRowSelect int)
```

The @StringArrayTable table variable also had a new column added to it called RowNum, which was given the IDENTITY property (meaning that it will increment an integer value for each row in the result set):

```
RETURNS @StringArrayTable  TABLE (RowNum int IDENTITY(1,1), Val varchar(50))
```

The other modification came after the WHILE loop was finished. Any RowNum values below the minimum or maximum values were deleted from the @StringArrayTable table array:

```
DELETE @StringArrayTable
WHERE RowNum < @MinRowSelect OR
   RowNum > @MaxRowSelect
```

After altering the function, the function was called using the two new parameters to define the row range to view (in this case rows 3 through 5):

```
SELECT RowNum, Val
FROM udf_ParseArray('A,B,C,D,E,F,G', ',', 3, 5)
```

This returned the third, fourth, and fifth characters from the string array passed to the UDF.

Viewing UDF Metadata

In this recipe, I demonstrate how to view a list of UDFs in the current database:

```
SELECT name, type_desc, definition
FROM sys.sql_modules s
INNER JOIN sys.objects o
   ON s.object_id = o.object_id
WHERE TYPE IN ('IF', -- Inline Table UDF
   'TF', -- Multistatement Table UDF
   'FN') -- Scalar UDF
```

How It Works

The sys.sql_modules and sys.objects system views are used to return the UDF name, type description, and SQL definition in a query result set:

```
FROM sys.sql_modules s
INNER JOIN sys.objects o
   ON s.object_id = o.object_id
```

Because sys.sql_modules contains rows for other object types, sys.objects must also be qualified to only return UDF rows:

```
WHERE TYPE IN ('IF', -- Inline Table UDF
   'TF', -- Multistatement Table UDF
   'FN') -- Scalar UDF
```

Dropping User-Defined Functions

In this recipe, I demonstrate how to drop a user-defined function. The syntax, like other DROP commands, is very straight-forward:

```
DROP FUNCTION { [ schema_name. ] function_name } [ ,...n ]
```

Table 11-4 details the arguments of this command.

Table 11-4. *DROP FUNCTION Arguments*

Argument	Description
[schema_name.] function_name	The optional schema name and required function name of the user-defined function.
[,...n]	Although not an actual argument, this syntax element indicates that one or more user-defined functions can be dropped in a single statement.

This recipe demonstrates how to drop the `dbo.udf_ParseArray` function created in earlier recipes:

```
DROP FUNCTION dbo.udf_ParseArray
```

How It Works

Although there are three different types of user-defined functions (scalar, inline, and multi-statement), you need only drop them using the single `DROP FUNCTION` command.

You can also drop more than one UDF in a single statement, for example:

```
DROP FUNCTION dbo.udf_ParseArray, dbo.udf_ReturnEmployeeAddress,
dbo.udf_CheckForSQLInjection
```

Benefiting From UDFs

User-defined functions are useful for both the performance enhancements they provide because of their cached execution plans and for their ability to encapsulate reusable code. Scalar functions in particular help make code more readable, and allow you to apply look-up rules consistently rather than repeating the same code multiple times throughout different stored procedures or views. Table-valued functions are also useful for allowing you to apply parameters to results, for example, using a parameter to define row-level security for a data set (demonstrated later on).

■**Caution** When designing user-defined functions, consider the multiplier effect. For example, if you create a scalar user-defined function that performs a look-up against a million-row table in order to return a single value, and a single look-up with proper indexing takes 30 seconds, chances are you are going to see a significant performance hit if you use this UDF to return values based on each row of another large table. If scalar user-defined functions reference other tables, make sure that the query you use to access the table information performs well, and doesn't return a result set that is too large.

The next few recipes will demonstrate some of the more common and beneficial ways in which user-defined functions are used in the field.

Using Scalar UDFs to Maintain Reusable Code

Scalar UDFs allow you to reduce code bloat by encapsulating logic within a single function, rather than repeating the logic multiple times wherever it happens to be needed.

For example, the following scalar, user-defined function is used to determine the kind of personal computer that an employee will receive. There are several lines of code that evaluate different parameters, including the title of the employee, who that employee's manager is, and the employee's hire date. Rather then include this logic in multiple areas across your database, you can encapsulate the logic in a single function:

```
CREATE FUNCTION dbo.udf_GET_AssignedEquipment
 (@Title nvarchar(50), @HireDate datetime, @ManagerID int)
RETURNS nvarchar(50)
AS
BEGIN

DECLARE @EquipmentType nvarchar(50)
```

```
IF @Title LIKE 'Chief%' OR
   @Title LIKE 'Vice%' OR
   @Title = 'Database Administrator'
BEGIN
  SET @EquipmentType = 'PC Build A'
END

IF @EquipmentType IS NULL AND @ManagerID IN (3,6,7,12)
BEGIN
  SET @EquipmentType = 'PC Build B'
END

IF @EquipmentType IS NULL AND @HireDate < '1/1/2002'
BEGIN
  SET @EquipmentType = 'PC Build C'
END

IF @EquipmentType IS NULL
BEGIN
  SET @EquipmentType = 'PC Build D'
END

RETURN @EquipmentType
END


GO
```

Once you've created it, you can use this scalar function in many areas of your Transact-SQL code without having to re-code the logic within. For example, the new scalar function is used in the SELECT, GROUP BY, and ORDER BY clauses of a query:

```
SELECT dbo.udf_GET_AssignedEquipment(Title, HireDate,ManagerID)

PC_Build,
    COUNT(*) Employee_Count
FROM HumanResources.Employee
GROUP BY dbo.udf_GET_AssignedEquipment(Title, HireDate,ManagerID)
ORDER BY dbo.udf_GET_AssignedEquipment(Title, HireDate,ManagerID)
```

This returns:

PC_Build	Employee_Count
PC Build A	7
PC Build B	22
PC Build C	254
PC Build D	7

This second query uses the scalar function in both the SELECT and WHERE clause too:

```
SELECT Title,
   EmployeeID,
   dbo.udf_GET_AssignedEquipment(Title, HireDate,ManagerID) PC_Build
FROM HumanResources.Employee
WHERE dbo.udf_GET_AssignedEquipment(Title, HireDate,ManagerID) IN
('PC Build A', 'PC Build B')
```

This returns the following (abridged) results:

Title	EmployeeID	PC_Build
Chief Executive Officer	09	PC Build A
Database Administrator	117	PC Build A
Marketing Specialist	119	PC Build B
Production Technician	WC60122	PC Build B

How It Works

Scalar, user-defined functions can help you encapsulate business logic so that it isn't repeated across your code, providing a centralized location for you to make a single modification to a single function when necessary. This also provides consistency, so that you and other database developers are consistently using and writing the same logic in the same way. One other benefit is code readability, particularly with large queries that perform multiple look-ups or evaluations.

Using Scalar UDFs to Cross Reference Natural Key Values

Recall from Chapter 1 that a *surrogate key* is an artificial primary key, as opposed to a *natural key* which represents a unique descriptor of data (for example, Social Security Number is an example of a natural key, but an IDENTITY property column is a surrogate key). IDENTITY values are often used as surrogate primary keys, but are also referenced as foreign keys.

In my own OLTP and star schema database design, I assign each table a surrogate key by default, unless there is a significant reason not to do so. Doing this helps you abstract your own unique key from any external legacy natural keys. If you are using, for example, an EmployeeNumber that comes from the HR system as your primary key instead, you could run into trouble later on if that HR system decides to change its data type (forcing you to change the primary key, any foreign key references, and composite primary keys). Surrogate keys help protect you from changes like this because they are under your control, and so they make good primary keys. You can keep your natural keys' unique constraints without worrying about external changes impacting your primary or foreign keys.

When importing data from legacy systems into production tables, you'll often still need to reference the natural key in order to determine which rows get inserted, updated, or deleted. This isn't very tricky if you're just dealing with a single column (for example EmployeeID, CreditCardNumber, SSN, UPC). However, if the natural key is made up of multiple columns, the cross-referencing to the production tables may not be quite so easy.

The following demonstrates a scalar, user-defined function that can be used to simplify natural key lookups, by checking for their existence prior to performing an action. To set up the example, I'll execute a few objects and commands will be executed.

First, a new table is created with its own surrogate keys, and the three columns which make up the composite natural key (these three columns form the unique value that we receive from the legacy system):

```
CREATE TABLE dbo.DimProductSalesperson
(DimProductSalespersonID int IDENTITY(1,1) NOT NULL PRIMARY KEY,
 ProductCD char(10) NOT NULL,
 CompanyNBR int NOT NULL,
 SalespersonNBR int NOT NULL
)
```

Next, a staging table is created that holds rows from the external legacy data file. For example this table could be populated from an external text file that is dumped out of the legacy system. This table doesn't have a primary key, as it is just used to hold data prior to being moved to the dbo.DimProductSalesperson table:

```
CREATE TABLE dbo.Staging_PRODSLSP
( ProductCD char(10) NOT NULL,
 CompanyNBR int NOT NULL,
 SalespersonNBR int NOT NULL
)
```

Next, two rows are inserted into this staging table:

```
INSERT dbo.Staging_PRODSLSP
(ProductCD, CompanyNBR, SalespersonNBR)
VALUES ('2391A23904', 1, 24)

INSERT dbo.Staging_PRODSLSP
(ProductCD, CompanyNBR, SalespersonNBR)
VALUES ('X129483203', 1, 34)
```

Now, these two rows can be inserted using the following query that *doesn't* use a scalar UDF:

```
INSERT dbo.DimProductSalesperson
(ProductCD, CompanyNBR, SalespersonNBR)
SELECT s.ProductCD, s.CompanyNBR, s.SalespersonNBR
FROM dbo.Staging_PRODSLSP s
LEFT OUTER JOIN dbo.DimProductSalesperson d ON
    s.ProductCD = d.ProductCD AND
    s.CompanyNBR = d.CompanyNBR AND
    s.SalespersonNBR = d.SalespersonNBR
WHERE d.DimProductSalespersonID IS NULL
```

Because each column forms the natural key, we must LEFT join each column from the inserted table against the staging table, and then check to see if the row does not already exist in the destination table using IS NULL.

An alternative to this, allowing you to reduce the code in each INSERT/UPDATE/DELETE, is to create a scalar UDF like the following:

```
CREATE FUNCTION dbo.udf_GET_Check_NK_DimProductSalesperson
 (@ProductCD char(10),  @CompanyNBR int,  @SalespersonNBR int )
RETURNS bit
AS
BEGIN

DECLARE @Exists bit

IF EXISTS (SELECT DimProductSalespersonID
           FROM dbo.DimProductSalesperson
           WHERE @ProductCD = @ProductCD  AND
                 @CompanyNBR = @CompanyNBR  AND
                 @SalespersonNBR = @SalespersonNBR)
BEGIN
   SET @Exists = 1
END
ELSE
BEGIN
   SET @Exists = 0
END

RETURN @Exists
END

GO
```

The UDF certainly looks like more code up front, but you'll obtain the benefit later during the data import process. For example, now you can rewrite the INSERT operation demonstrated earlier, as follows:

```
INSERT dbo.DimProductSalesperson
(ProductCD, CompanyNBR, SalespersonNBR)
SELECT ProductCD, CompanyNBR, SalespersonNBR
FROM dbo.Staging_PRODSLSP
WHERE dbo.udf_GET_Check_NK_DimProductSalesperson
(ProductCD, CompanyNBR, SalespersonNBR) = 0
```

How It Works

In this recipe, I demonstrated how to create a scalar UDF that returned a bit value based on three parameters. If the three values already existed for a row in the production table, a 1 was returned, otherwise a 0 was returned. Using this function simplifies the INSERT/UPDATE/DELETE code that you must write in situations where a natural key spans multiple columns.

Walking through the UDF code, the first lines define the UDF name and parameters. Each of these parameters is for the composite natural key in the staging and production table:

```
CREATE FUNCTION dbo.udf_GET_Check_NK_DimProductSalesperson
 (@ProductCD char(10),  @CompanyNBR int,  @SalespersonNBR int )
```

Next, a bit data type was defined to be returned by the function:

```
RETURNS bit
AS
BEGIN
```

A local variable is created to hold the bit value:

```
DECLARE @Exists bit
```

An IF is used to check for the existence of a row matching all three parameters for the natural composite key. If there is a match, the local variable is set to 1. If not, it is set to 0:

```
IF EXISTS (SELECT DimProductSalespersonID
           FROM dbo.DimProductSalesperson
           WHERE @ProductCD = @ProductCD   AND
                 @CompanyNBR = @CompanyNBR   AND
                 @SalespersonNBR = @SalespersonNBR)
BEGIN
   SET @Exists = 1
END
ELSE
BEGIN
   SET @Exists = 0
END
```

The local variable is then passed back to the caller:

```
RETURN @Exists
END

GO
```

The function was then used in the WHERE clause, extracting from the staging table those rows that returned a 0 from the scalar UDF, and therefore do not exist in the DimProductSalesperson table:

```
WHERE dbo.udf_GET_Check_NK_DimProductSalesperson
(ProductCD, CompanyNBR, SalespersonNBR) = 0
```

Replacing Views with Multi-Statement UDFs

Multi-statement UDFs allow you to return data in the same way you would from a view, only with the ability to manipulate data like a stored procedure.

In this example, a multi-statement UDF is created to apply row-based security based on the caller of the function. Only rows for the specified salesperson will be returned. In addition to this, the second parameter is a `bit` flag that controls whether rows from the SalesPersonQuotaHistory table will be returned in the results:

```
CREATE FUNCTION dbo.udf_SEL_SalesQuota
   ( @SalesPersonID int,
     @ShowHistory bit )
RETURNS @SalesQuota TABLE
    (SalesPersonID int,
     QuotaDate datetime,
     SalesQuota money)
AS
BEGIN
    INSERT @SalesQuota
    (SalesPersonID, QuotaDate, SalesQuota)
    SELECT SalesPersonID, ModifiedDate, SalesQuota
    FROM Sales.SalesPerson
    WHERE SalespersonID = @SalesPersonID

    IF @ShowHistory = 1
    BEGIN

      INSERT @SalesQuota
      (SalesPersonID, QuotaDate, SalesQuota)
      SELECT SalesPersonID, QuotaDate, SalesQuota
      FROM Sales.SalesPersonQuotaHistory
      WHERE SalespersonID = @SalesPersonID

    END

    RETURN
END

GO
```

After the UDF is created, the following query is executed to show sales quota data for a specific salesperson from the SalesPerson table:

```
SELECT  SalesPersonID, QuotaDate, SalesQuota
FROM dbo.udf_SEL_SalesQuota (275,0)
```

This returns:

SalesPersonID	QuotaDate	SalesQuota
275	2001-06-24 00:00:00.000	300000.00

Next, the second parameter is switched from a 0 to a 1, in order to display additional rows for SalespersonID 275 from the SalesPersonQuotaHistory table:

```
SELECT  SalesPersonID, QuotaDate, SalesQuota
FROM dbo.udf_SEL_SalesQuota (275,1)
```

This returns the following (abridged) results:

SalesPersonID	QuotaDate	SalesQuota
275	2001-06-24 00:00:00.000	300000.00
275	2001-07-01 00:00:00.000	367000.00
275	2001-10-01 00:00:00.000	556000.00
275	2002-01-01 00:00:00.000	502000.00
275	2002-04-01 00:00:00.000	550000.00
...		

How It Works

This recipe demonstrated a multi-statement table-valued UDF to return sales quota data based on the SalespersonID value that was passed. It also included a second bit flag that controlled whether or not history was also returned.

Walking through the function, you'll notice that the first few lines define the input parameters (something that a view doesn't allow):

```
CREATE FUNCTION dbo.udf_SEL_SalesQuota
   ( @SalesPersonID int,
     @ShowHistory bit )
```

After this, the table columns that are to be returned by the function are defined:

```
RETURNS @SalesQuota TABLE
     (SalesPersonID int,
      QuotaDate datetime,
      SalesQuota money)
```

The function body includes two separate batch statements, the first being an INSERT into the table variable of rows for the specific salesperson:

```
AS
BEGIN
     INSERT @SalesQuota
     (SalesPersonID, QuotaDate, SalesQuota)
     SELECT SalesPersonID, ModifiedDate, SalesQuota
     FROM Sales.SalesPerson
     WHERE SalespersonID = @SalesPersonID
```

Next, an IF statement (another construct not allowed in views) evaluates the bit parameter. If equal to 1, quota history will also be inserted into the table variable:

```
IF @ShowHistory = 1
   BEGIN

     INSERT @SalesQuota
     (SalesPersonID, QuotaDate, SalesQuota)
     SELECT SalesPersonID, QuotaDate, SalesQuota
     FROM Sales.SalesPersonQuotaHistory
     WHERE SalespersonID = @SalesPersonID

   END
```

Lastly, the RETURN keyword signals the end of the function (and unlike a scalar function, no local variable is designated after it):

```
   RETURN
END

GO
```

Although the UDF has Transact-SQL not allowed in a view, it is still able to be referenced in the FROM clause:

```
SELECT  SalesPersonID, QuotaDate, SalesQuota
FROM dbo.udf_SEL_SalesQuota (275,0)
```

The results could be returned in a view using a UNION statement, but with that you wouldn't be able to have the control-logic to either show or not show history in a single view.

In this recipe, I demonstrated a method to create your own parameter-based result sets. This can be used to implement row-based security. Row-level security is not built into the SQL Server 2005 security model. You can use functions to return only the rows that are allowed to be viewed by designating input parameters that are used to filter the data.

UDT Basics

User-defined types (UDTs) are useful for defining a consistent data type that is named after a known business attribute, such as "PIN," "PhoneNBR," or "EmailAddress." Once a user-defined type is created in the database, it can be used within columns, parameters, and variable definitions, providing a consistent underlying data type. The next two recipes will show you how to create and drop user-defined types. Note that unlike some other database objects, there isn't a way to modify an existing type using an ALTER command.

Creating and Using User-Defined Types

In previous versions of SQL Server, the system-stored procedure sp_addtype was used to create a user-defined type. This system-stored procedure has been deprecated in SQL Server 2005, and the new CREATE TYPE command should be used instead to create new user-defined types.

This recipe demonstrates how to create a user-defined type (also called an alias data type), which is a data type given a user-specified name, data type, length, and nullability. You can use all base data types except the new xml data type.

The basic syntax for creating a user-defined type is as follows:

```
CREATE TYPE [ schema_name. ] type_name
{
    FROM base_type
  [ (precision [ ,scale ] )  ]
  [ NULL | NOT NULL ] }
```

Table 11-5 details the arguments of these commands.

Table 11-5. *CREATE TYPE Arguments*

Argument	Description
[schema_name.] type_name	The optional schema name and required type name of the new user-defined type.
base_type	The base data type used to define the new user-defined type. You are allowed to use all base system data types except the new xml data type.
(precision [,scale])	If using a numeric base type, precision is the maximum number of digits that can be stored both left and right of the decimal point. Scale is the maximum number of digits to be stored right of the decimal point.
NULL	NOT NULL	Defines whether or not your new user-defined type allows NULL values.

Note This chapter covers how to create user-defined types using Transact-SQL. Chapter 13 briefly discusses how to create these using the new Common Language Runtime (CLR) functionality.

In this example, a new type is created based on a 14 character string:

```
-- In this example, we assume the company's Account number will
-- be used in multiple tables, and that it will always have a fixed
-- 14 character length and will never allow NULL values

CREATE TYPE dbo.AccountNBR
FROM char(14) NOT NULL
GO
```

Next, the new type is used in the column definition of two tables:

```
-- The new data type is now used in two different tables

CREATE TABLE dbo.InventoryAccount
    (InventoryAccountID int NOT NULL,
    InventoryID int NOT NULL,
    InventoryAccountNBR AccountNBR)
GO

CREATE TABLE dbo.CustomerAccount
    (CustomerAccountID int NOT NULL,
    CustomerID int NOT NULL,
    CustomerAccountNBR AccountNBR)
GO
```

This type can also be used in the definition of a local variable or input parameter. For example, the following stored procedure uses the new data type to define the input parameter for a stored procedure:

```
CREATE PROCEDURE dbo.usp_SEL_CustomerAccount
    @CustomerAccountNBR AccountNBR
AS

SELECT CustomerAccountID, CustomerID, CustomerAccountNBR
FROM dbo.CustomerAccount
WHERE CustomerAccountNBR = CustomerAccountNBR
GO
```

Next, a local variable is created using the new data type, and is passed to the stored procedure:

```
DECLARE @CustomerAccountNBR AccountNBR
SET @CustomerAccountNBR = '1294839482'

EXEC dbo.usp_SEL_CustomerAccount @CustomerAccountNBR
```

To view the underlying base type of the user-defined type, you can use the sp_help system stored procedure:

```
EXEC sp_help 'dbo.AccountNBR'
```

This returns (only a few columns are displayed for presentation purposes):

Type_name	Storage_type	Length	Nullable
AccountNbr	char	14	no

How It Works

In this recipe, a new user-defined type called dbo.AccountNBR was created with a char(14) data type and NOT NULL. Once the user-defined type was created, it was than used in the column definition of two different tables:

```
CREATE TABLE dbo.InventoryAccount
   (InventoryAccountID int NOT NULL,
   InventoryID int NOT NULL,
   InventoryAccountNBR AccountNBR)
```

Because NOT NULL was already inherent in the data type, it wasn't necessary to explicitly define it in the column definition.

After creating the tables, a stored procedure was created that used the new data type in the input parameter definition. The procedure was then called using a local variable that also used the new type.

Although Transact-SQL types may be an excellent convenience for some developers, creating your application's data dictionary and abiding by the data types may suit the same purpose. For example if an AccountNBR is always 14 characters, as a DBA/Developer, you can communicate and check to make sure that new objects are using a consistent name and data type. One big "con" for using user-defined data types is their ability to be changed without cascading effects, as you'll see in the last recipe of this chapter.

Identifying Columns and Parameters That Use User-Defined Types

Before showing you how to remove a user-defined data type, you'll need to know how to identify all database objects that depend on that type. As you'll see later on, removing a UDT doesn't automatically cascade changes to the dependent table.

This example shows you how to identify which database objects are using the specified user-defined type. This first query in the recipe displays all columns that use the AccountNBR user-defined type:

```
SELECT OBJECT_NAME(c.object_id) Table_Name, c.name Column_Name
FROM sys.columns c
INNER JOIN sys.types t ON
   c.user_type_id = t.user_type_id
WHERE t.name = 'AccountNBR'
```

This returns:

Table_Name	Column_Name
InventoryAccount	InventoryAccountNBR
CustomerAccount	CustomerAccountNBR

(2 row(s) affected)

This next query shows any procedures or functions that have parameters defined using the AccountNBR user-defined type:

```
-- Now see what parameters reference the AccountNBR data type
SELECT OBJECT_NAME(p.object_id) Table_Name, p.name Parameter_Name
FROM sys.parameters p
INNER JOIN sys.types t ON
   p.user_type_id = t.user_type_id
WHERE t.name = 'AccountNBR'
```

This returns:

Table_Name	Parameter_Name
usp_SEL_CustomerAccount	@CustomerAccountNBR

How It Works

In order to report which table columns use the user-defined type, the system catalog views sys.columns and sys.types are used:

```
FROM sys.columns c
INNER JOIN sys.types t ON
   c.user_type_id = t.user_type_id
```

The sys.columns view contains a row for each column defined for a table-valued function, table, and view in the database. The sys.types view contains a row for each user and system data type.

To identify which function or procedure parameters reference the user-defined type, the system catalog views sys.parameters and sys.types are used:

```
FROM sys.parameters p
INNER JOIN sys.types t ON
   p.user_type_id = t.user_type_id
```

The sys.parameters view contains a row for each database object that can accept a parameter, including stored procedures, for example.

Identifying which objects reference a user-defined type is necessary if you plan on dropping the user-defined type, as the next recipe demonstrates.

Dropping User-Defined Types

In this recipe, I demonstrate how to remove a user-defined type (also called an alias data type) from the database. As with most DROP commands, the syntax for removing a user-defined type is very straightforward:

```
DROP TYPE [ schema_name. ] type_name
```

The DROP TYPE command uses the schema and type name, as this recipe will demonstrate. First however, any references to the user-defined type need to be removed beforehand. In this example, the AccountNBR type is changed to the base equivalent for two tables and a stored procedure:

```
ALTER TABLE dbo.InventoryAccount
ALTER COLUMN InventoryAccountNBR char(14)
GO

ALTER TABLE dbo.CustomerAccount
ALTER COLUMN CustomerAccountNBR char(14)
GO
```

```
ALTER PROCEDURE dbo.usp_SEL_CustomerAccount
   @CustomerAccountNBR char(14)
AS

SELECT CustomerAccountID, CustomerID, CustomerAccountNBR
FROM dbo.CustomerAccount
WHERE CustomerAccountNBR = CustomerAccountNBR
GO
```

With the referencing objects now converted, it is okay to go ahead and drop the type:

```
DROP TYPE dbo.AccountNBR
```

How It Works

In order to remove a type, you must first change or remove any references to the type in a database table. If you are going to change the definition of a UDT, you need to remove *all* references to that UDT everywhere in *all* database objects that use that UDT. That means changing tables, views, stored procedures, etc. first before dropping the type. This can be very cumbersome if your database objects depend very heavily on them. Also, if any schema-bound stored procedures, functions, or triggers use the data type as parameters or variables, these references must be changed/removed. In this recipe, ALTER TABLE... ALTER COLUMN was used to change the data type to the system data type:

```
ALTER TABLE dbo.InventoryAccount
ALTER COLUMN InventoryAccountNBR char(14)
```

A stored procedure parameter was also modified using ALTER PROCEDURE:

```
ALTER PROCEDURE usp_SEL_CustomerAccount
(@CustomerAccountNBR char(14))
...
```

CHAPTER 12

■ ■ ■

Triggers

In this chapter, I'll present recipes for creating and using Data Definition Language (DDL) and Data Manipulation Language (DML) triggers. *DML triggers* contain Transact-SQL code that is used to respond to an INSERT, UPDATE, or DELETE operation against a table or view. *DDL triggers* respond to server or database events instead of data modifications. For example, you can create a DDL trigger that writes to an audit table whenever a database user issues the CREATE TABLE or DROP TABLE command.

Triggers, when used properly, can provide a convenient automatic response to specific actions. They are appropriate for situations where you must create a business-level response to an action. Triggers should not be used in place of constraints (for example primary key or unique constraints) because constraints will perform better and are better-suited to these operations. You should also be cognizant of the Transact-SQL used to define the trigger, being careful to ensure that the code is properly optimized. If a trigger takes several seconds to execute for each UPDATE, overall performance can suffer.

In my experience, triggers always seem to be the forgotten database object when it comes to troubleshooting performance issues. I'll hear complaints about a poorly performing data modification and spend time trying to optimize it, only to find out that it was a poorly tuned trigger that caused the performance issue. It's one of the major reasons that I use DML triggers sparingly—and when I do use them, I take extra care to make sure they are fast and bug-free. Nonetheless, application requirements may dictate that a DML trigger be used. Not to mention that SQL Server 2005 DDL triggers open up a whole new range of functionality not available in previous versions, providing features that can't easily be replaced by other database object types.

In this chapter I'll review the following topics:

- How to create an AFTER DML trigger

- How to create an INSTEAD OF DML trigger

- How to create a DDL trigger

- How to modify or drop an existing trigger

- How to enable or disable triggers

- How to limit trigger nesting, set the firing order, and control recursion

- How to view trigger metadata

First, however, we'll start off with a background discussion of DML triggers.

■**Note** This chapter covers how to create triggers using Transact-SQL. However, Chapter 13 covers how to create triggers using the new Common Language Runtime (CLR) functionality.

DML Triggers

DML Triggers respond to user INSERT, UPDATE, or DELETE operations against a table or a view. When a data modification event occurs, the trigger performs a set of actions defined within the trigger. Similar to stored procedures, triggers are defined in Transact-SQL and allow a full range of activities to be performed.

A DML trigger can be defined specifically as FOR UPDATE, FOR INSERT, FOR DELETE, or any combination of the three. UPDATE triggers respond to modifications against one or more columns within the table, INSERT triggers respond to new data being added to the database, and DELETE triggers respond to data being deleted from the database. There are two types of DML triggers: AFTER and INSTEAD OF.

AFTER triggers are only allowed for tables, and they execute *after* the data modification has been completed against the table. INSTEAD OF triggers execute *instead of* the original data modification and can be created for both tables and views.

DML triggers allow you to perform actions in response to data modifications in a table. For example, you can create a trigger that populates an audit table based on the operation performed, or perhaps use the trigger to decrement the value of a quantity. Although this is a powerful feature, there are a few things to keep in mind before your use of triggers proliferates:

- Triggers can often become a hidden and hence forgotten problem. When troubleshooting performance or logical issues, DBAs can forget that triggers are executing in the background. Make sure that triggers are "visible" in your data documentation.

- If you can ensure that all your data modifications flow through a stored procedure, I would strongly recommend you perform all activities within the stored procedure, rather than use a trigger. For example, if you need to update a quantity in a related table, after inserting a sales record, why not put this logic in the stored procedure instead? The advantages are manageability (one place to look) and supportability (one place to troubleshoot), when the procedure needs modifications or performs unexpected actions.

- Always keep performance in mind, and this means writing triggers that execute quickly. Long-running triggers can significantly slow down data modification operations. Take particular care in putting triggers into databases with frequent data modifications.

- Non-logged updates do not cause a DML trigger to fire (for example WRITETEXT, TRUNCATE TABLE, and bulk insert operations).

- Constraints usually run faster than a DML trigger, so if your business requirements can be fulfilled by a constraint, use constraints instead. AFTER triggers run *after* the data modification has already occurred, so they cannot be used to prevent a constraint violation.

- Don't allow result sets from a SELECT statement to be returned within your trigger. Most applications can't consume these in an elegant fashion, and embedded queries can hurt the trigger's performance.

As long as you keep these general guidelines in mind, and use them properly, triggers are an excellent means of enforcing business rules in your database.

Creating an AFTER DML Trigger

An AFTER DML Trigger executes after an INSERT, UPDATE, and/or DELETE modification has been completed successfully against a table. The specific syntax for an AFTER DML Trigger is as follows:

```
CREATE TRIGGER [ schema_name . ]trigger_name
ON  table
[ WITH <dml_trigger_option> [ ...,n ] ]
```

```
AFTER
{ [ INSERT ] [ , ] [ UPDATE ] [ , ] [ DELETE ] }
[ NOT FOR REPLICATION ]
AS { sql_statement [ ...n ]}
```

Table 12-1 details the arguments of this command.

Table 12-1. *CREATE TRIGGER Arguments*

Argument	Description
[schema_name .]trigger_name	The optional schema owner and required user-defined name of the new trigger.
table	The table name that the trigger applies to.
<dml_trigger_option> [...,n]	Allows you to specify the ENCRYPTION and/or EXECUTE AS clause. ENCRYPTION will encrypt the Transact-SQL definition of the trigger, making it unviewable within the system tables. EXECUTE AS allows you to define the security context that the trigger will be executed under.
[INSERT] [,] [UPDATE] [,] [DELETE]	This defines which DML event or events the trigger will react to, including INSERT, UPDATE, and DELETE. A single trigger can react to one or more of these actions against the table.
NOT FOR REPLICATION	Designates that the trigger should not be executed when a replication modification is performed against the table.
sql_statement [...n]	A trigger allows one or more Transact-SQL statements, which can be used to carry out actions such as performing validations against the DML changes or performing other table DML actions.

Before proceeding to the recipe, it is important to note that SQL Server creates two "virtual" tables that are available specifically for triggers, called the deleted and inserted tables. These two tables capture the before and after pictures of the modified rows. Table 12-2 shows the tables that each DML operation impacts.

Table 12-2. *Inserted and Deleted Virtual Tables*

DML Operation	Inserted Table Holds...	Deleted Table Holds...
INSERT	Inserted rows	
UPDATE	New rows (rows with updates)	Old rows (pre-update)
DELETE		Deleted rows

The inserted and deleted tables can be used within your trigger to access the data both before and after the data modifications that caused the trigger to fire. These tables will store data for both single and multi-row updates. Be sure to program your triggers with both types of updates (single and multi-row) in mind. For example, a DELETE operation can impact either a single row or fifty rows— so make sure that the trigger is programmed to handle this accordingly.

In this recipe, I demonstrate using a trigger to track row inserts or deletes from the Production.ProductInventory table:

```
-- Track all Inserts, Updates, and Deletes
CREATE TABLE Production.ProductInventoryAudit
   (ProductID int NOT NULL  ,
```

```
   LocationID smallint NOT NULL  ,
   Shelf nvarchar(10) NOT NULL  ,
   Bin tinyint NOT NULL  ,
   Quantity smallint NOT NULL  ,
   rowguid uniqueidentifier NOT NULL  ,
   ModifiedDate datetime NOT NULL  ,
   InsOrUPD char(1) NOT NULL  )
GO

-- Create trigger to populate Production.ProductInventoryAudit table
CREATE TRIGGER Production.trg_uid_ProductInventoryAudit
ON  Production.ProductInventory
AFTER  INSERT, DELETE
AS

SET NOCOUNT ON

-- Inserted rows
INSERT Production.ProductInventoryAudit
(ProductID, LocationID, Shelf, Bin, Quantity,
rowguid, ModifiedDate, InsOrUPD)
SELECT DISTINCT i.ProductID, i.LocationID, i.Shelf, i.Bin, i.Quantity,
i.rowguid, GETDATE(),  'I'
FROM inserted i

-- Deleted rows

INSERT Production.ProductInventoryAudit
(ProductID, LocationID, Shelf, Bin, Quantity,
rowguid, ModifiedDate, InsOrUPD)
SELECT d.ProductID, d.LocationID, d.Shelf, d.Bin, d.Quantity,
d.rowguid, GETDATE(), 'D'
FROM deleted d

GO

-- Insert a new row
INSERT Production.ProductInventory
(ProductID, LocationID, Shelf, Bin, Quantity)
VALUES (316, 6, 'A', 4, 22)

-- Delete a row

DELETE Production.ProductInventory
WHERE ProductID = 316 AND
   LocationID = 6

-- Check the audit table
SELECT ProductID, LocationID, InsOrUpd
FROM Production.ProductInventoryAudit
```

This returns:

```
(1 row(s) affected)

(1 row(s) affected)

ProductID   LocationID InsOrUpd
----------- ---------- --------
316         6          I
316         6          D

(2 row(s) affected)
```

How It Works

This recipe started off by having you create a new table for holding inserted or deleted rows from the Production.ProductInventory table. The new table's schema matches the original table, only this time a new column was added called InsOrUPD to indicate whether the row was an INSERT or UPDATE operation:

```
CREATE TABLE Production.ProductInventoryAudit
    (ProductID int NOT NULL   ,
     LocationID smallint NOT NULL   ,
     Shelf nvarchar(10) NOT NULL   ,
     Bin tinyint NOT NULL   ,
     Quantity smallint NOT NULL   ,
     rowguid uniqueidentifier NOT NULL   ,
     ModifiedDate datetime NOT NULL   ,
     InsOrUPD char(1) NOT NULL   )
GO
```

Next, an AFTER DML trigger is created using CREATE TRIGGER. The owning schema and new trigger name is designated in the first line of the statement:

```
CREATE TRIGGER Production.trg_uid_ProductInventoryAudit
```

The table (which when updated will cause the trigger to fire) is designated in the ON clause:

```
ON   Production.ProductInventory
```

Two types of DML activity will be monitored: inserts and deletes:

```
AFTER   INSERT, DELETE
```

The body of the trigger begins after the AS keyword:

```
AS
```

The SET NOCOUNT is set ON in order to suppress the "rows affected" messages from being returned back to the calling application whenever the trigger is fired:

```
SET NOCOUNT ON
```

The first statement inserts a new row into the new audit table for rows that exist in the virtual inserted table:

```
INSERT Production.ProductInventoryAudit
(ProductID, LocationID, Shelf, Bin, Quantity,
rowguid, ModifiedDate, InsOrUPD)
SELECT DISTINCT i.ProductID, i.LocationID, i.Shelf, i.Bin, i.Quantity,
i.rowguid, GETDATE(), 'I'
FROM inserted i
```

The second statement inserts a new row into the new audit table for rows that exist in the virtual deleted table, but not the inserted table:

```
INSERT Production.ProductInventoryAudit
(ProductID, LocationID, Shelf, Bin, Quantity,
rowguid, ModifiedDate, InsOrUPD)
SELECT d.ProductID, d.LocationID, d.Shelf, d.Bin, d.Quantity,
d.rowguid, GETDATE(), 'D'
FROM deleted d

GO
```

After creating the trigger, in order to test it, a new row was inserted into the Production.ProductInventory table and then deleted right afterwards:

```
-- Insert a new row
INSERT Production.ProductInventory
(ProductID, LocationID, Shelf, Bin, Quantity)
VALUES (316, 6, 'A', 4, 22)

-- Delete a row

DELETE Production.ProductInventory
WHERE ProductID = 316 AND
   LocationID = 6
```

As you can see, a query was executed against the audit table, and there were two rows tracking the insert and delete activities against the Production.ProductInventory table:

```
SELECT ProductID, LocationID, InsOrUpd
FROM Production.ProductInventoryAudit
```

Creating an INSTEAD OF DML Trigger

INSTEAD OF DML triggers execute *instead of* the original data modification that fired the trigger and are allowed for both tables and views. INSTEAD OF triggers are often used to handle data modifications to views that do not allow for data modifications (see Chapter 7 for a review of what rules a view must follow in order to be updateable).

DML triggers use the following syntax:

```
CREATE TRIGGER [ schema_name . ]trigger_name
ON { table | view }
[ WITH <dml_trigger_option> [ ...,n ] ]
INSTEAD OF
{ [ INSERT ] [ , ] [ UPDATE ] [ , ] [ DELETE ] }
[ NOT FOR REPLICATION ]
AS { sql_statement [ ...n ] }
```

Table 12-3 details the arguments of this command.

Table 12-3. *INSTEAD OF Trigger Arguments*

Argument	Description
`[ schema_name . ]trigger_name`	The optional schema owner and required user-defined name of the new trigger.
`table | view`	The name of the table or view that the trigger applies to.
`<dml_trigger_option> [ ...,n ]`	Allows you to specify the ENCRYPTION and/or EXECUTE AS clause. ENCRYPTION will encrypt the Transact-SQL definition of the trigger. EXECUTE AS allows you to define the security context under which the trigger will be executed.
`[ INSERT ] [ , ] [ UPDATE ] [ , ] [ DELETE ]`	This defines which DML event or events the trigger will react to, including INSERT, UPDATE, and DELETE. A single trigger can react to one or more of these actions against the table.
`NOT FOR REPLICATION`	Designates that the trigger should not be executed when a replication modification is performed against the table.
`sql_statement [ ...n ]`	A trigger allows one or more Transact-SQL statements which can be used to carry out actions such as performing validations against the DML changes or performing other table DML actions.

In this recipe, you'll create a new table that will hold "pending approval" rows for the `HumanResources.Department` table. These are new departments that require manager approval before being added to the actual table. A view will be created to display all "approved" and "pending approval" departments from the two tables, and an `INSTEAD OF` trigger will be created on the view for inserts, causing inserts to be routed to the new approval table, instead of the actual `HumanResources.Department` table:

```
-- Create Department "Approval" table

CREATE TABLE HumanResources.DepartmentApproval
   (Name nvarchar(50) NOT NULL UNIQUE,
     GroupName nvarchar(50) NOT NULL,
     ModifiedDate datetime NOT NULL DEFAULT GETDATE())
GO
```

```
-- Create view to see both approved and pending approval departments

CREATE VIEW HumanResources.vw_Department
AS

SELECT Name, GroupName, ModifiedDate, 'Approved' Status
FROM HumanResources.Department
UNION
SELECT Name, GroupName, ModifiedDate, 'Pending Approval' Status
FROM HumanResources.DepartmentApproval

GO
```

```
-- Create an INSTEAD OF trigger on the new view

CREATE TRIGGER HumanResources.trg_vw_Department
ON HumanResources.vw_Department
INSTEAD OF
```

```
INSERT
AS

SET NOCOUNT ON
INSERT HumanResources.DepartmentApproval
(Name, GroupName)
SELECT i.Name, i.GroupName
FROM inserted i
WHERE i.Name NOT IN (SELECT Name FROM HumanResources.DepartmentApproval)

GO
```

```
-- Insert into the new view, even though view is a UNION
-- of two different tables

INSERT HumanResources.vw_Department
(Name, GroupName)
VALUES ('Print Production', 'Manufacturing')
```

```
-- Check the view's contents

SELECT Status, Name
FROM   HumanResources.vw_Department
WHERE GroupName = 'Manufacturing'
```

This returns the following result set:

```
Status           Name
---------------- --------------------------------------------------
Approved         Production
Approved         Production Control
Pending Approval Print Production
```

How It Works

The recipe began by creating a separate table to hold "pending approval" department rows:

```
CREATE TABLE HumanResources.DepartmentApproval
   (Name nvarchar(50) NOT NULL UNIQUE,
     GroupName nvarchar(50) NOT NULL,
     ModifiedDate datetime NOT NULL DEFAULT GETDATE())
```

Next, a view was created to display both "approved" and "pending approval" departments:

```
CREATE VIEW HumanResources.vw_Department
AS

SELECT Name, GroupName, ModifiedDate, 'Approved' Status
FROM HumanResources.Department
UNION
SELECT Name, GroupName, ModifiedDate, 'Pending Approval' Status
FROM HumanResources.DepartmentApproval

GO
```

The UNION in the CREATE VIEW prevents this view from being updateable, as any inserts against it will be ambiguous. INSTEAD OF triggers allow you to enable data modifications against non-updateable views.

A trigger was created to react to INSERTs, routing them to the approval table so long as the department name was unique:

```
CREATE TRIGGER HumanResources.trg_vw_Department
ON HumanResources.vw_Department
INSTEAD OF
INSERT
AS

SET NOCOUNT ON
INSERT HumanResources.DepartmentApproval
(Name, GroupName)
SELECT i.Name, i.GroupName
FROM inserted i
WHERE i.Name NOT IN (SELECT Name FROM HumanResources.DepartmentApproval)
```

A new INSERT was tested against the view, to see if it would be inserted in the approval table:

```
INSERT HumanResources.vw_Department
(Name, GroupName)
VALUES ('Print Production', 'Manufacturing')
```

The view was then queried, showing that the row was inserted, and displayed a "pending approval status."

Using DML Triggers and Transactions

In this recipe, I'll demonstrate the use of DML triggers and their interactions with transactions—both within the trigger and within the initiating event that caused the trigger to fire. For these examples, we'll be working with the objects created in the "Creating an AFTER DML Trigger" recipe.

When a trigger is fired, SQL Server always creates a transaction around it, allowing any changes made by the firing trigger, or the caller, to roll back to the previous state. For example, the trg_uid_ProductInventoryAudit trigger has been rewritten to fail if certain Shelf or Quantity values are encountered. If they are, ROLLBACK is used to cancel the trigger and undo any changes:

```
CREATE TRIGGER Production.trg_uid_ProductInventoryAudit
ON  Production.ProductInventory
AFTER  INSERT, DELETE
AS

SET NOCOUNT ON

IF EXISTS
(SELECT Shelf
FROM inserted
WHERE Shelf = 'A')
BEGIN
    PRINT 'Shelf ''A'' is closed for new inventory.'
    ROLLBACK
END

-- Inserted rows
INSERT Production.ProductInventoryAudit
(ProductID, LocationID, Shelf, Bin, Quantity,
```

```
rowguid, ModifiedDate, InsOrUPD)
SELECT DISTINCT i.ProductID, i.LocationID, i.Shelf, i.Bin, i.Quantity,
i.rowguid, GETDATE(), 'I'
FROM inserted i

-- Deleted rows

INSERT Production.ProductInventoryAudit
(ProductID, LocationID, Shelf, Bin, Quantity,
rowguid, ModifiedDate, InsOrUPD)
SELECT d.ProductID, d.LocationID, d.Shelf, d.Bin, d.Quantity,
d.rowguid, GETDATE(), 'D'
FROM deleted d

IF EXISTS
(SELECT Quantity
FROM deleted
WHERE Quantity > 0)
BEGIN
    PRINT 'You cannot remove positive quantity rows!'
    ROLLBACK
END

GO
```

Now an attempt is made to insert a row using Shelf "A":

```
INSERT Production.ProductInventory
(ProductID, LocationID, Shelf, Bin, Quantity)
VALUES (316, 6, 'A', 4, 22)
```

Because this is not allowed based on the trigger logic, the trigger neither inserts a row into the audit table, nor allows the calling INSERT:

```
Shelf 'A' is closed for new inventory.
Msg 3609, Level 16, State 1, Line 2
The transaction ended in the trigger. The batch has been aborted.
```

In the previous example, the INSERT that caused the trigger to fire didn't use an explicit transaction. This next example demonstrates two deletions, one that is allowed (according to the rules of the trigger) and another that is not allowed. Both inserts are embedded within an explicit transaction:

```
BEGIN TRANSACTION

-- Deleting a row with a zero quantity
DELETE Production.ProductInventory
WHERE ProductID = 853 AND
   LocationID = 7

-- Deleting a row with a non-zero quantity
DELETE Production.ProductInventory
WHERE ProductID = 999 AND
   LocationID = 60

COMMIT TRANSACTION
```

This returns the following output:

```
(1 row(s) affected)
You cannot remove positive quantity rows!
Msg 3609, Level 16, State 1, Line 9
The transaction ended in the trigger. The batch has been aborted.
```

Because the trigger issued a rollback, the outer transaction is also invalidated (meaning that it doesn't remain open). Also, even though the first row was a valid deletion, because they were in the same calling transaction, neither row was deleted:

```
SELECT ProductID, LocationID
FROM Production.ProductInventory
WHERE (ProductID = 853 AND
   LocationID = 7) OR
(ProductID = 999 AND
   LocationID = 60)
```

This returns:

ProductID	LocationID
853	7
999	60

How It Works

This recipe demonstrated the interaction between triggers and transactions. In a nutshell, if your trigger issues a ROLLBACK command, any data modifications performed by the trigger or the rest of the statements in the transaction are undone. The Transact-SQL query or batch that invoked the trigger in the first place will also be cancelled and rolled back. If the invoking caller was embedded in an explicit transaction, the entire calling transaction is cancelled and rolled back. If you use explicit transactions within a trigger, SQL Server will treat it like a nested transaction. As I mentioned in Chapter 3, a ROLLBACK rolls back all transactions, no matter how may levels deep they may be nested.

Controlling DML Triggers Based on Modified Columns

When a trigger is fired, you can determine which columns have been modified by using the UPDATE function.

UPDATE, not to be confused with the DML command, returns a TRUE value if an INSERT or DML UPDATE has occurred against a column. For example, the following DML UPDATE trigger checks to see if a specific column has been modified, and if so, returns an error and rolls back the modification:

```
CREATE TRIGGER HumanResources.trg_U_Department
ON  HumanResources.Department
AFTER  UPDATE
AS

IF UPDATE(GroupName)
BEGIN
   PRINT 'Updates to GroupName require DBA involvement.'
   ROLLBACK
END
GO
```

An attempt is made to update a GroupName value in this next query:

```
UPDATE HumanResources.Department
SET GroupName = 'Research and Development'
WHERE DepartmentID = 10
```

This returns the warning message and error telling us that the batch has been aborted (no updates made):

```
Updates to GroupName require DBA involvement.
Msg 3609, Level 16, State 1, Line 1
The transaction ended in the trigger. The batch has been aborted.
```

How It Works

When your trigger logic is aimed at more granular, column-based changes, use the UPDATE function and conditional processing to ensure that code is only executed against specific columns. Embedding the logic in conditional processing can help reduce the overhead each time the trigger fires—at least for columns that may be unrelated to the purpose of the trigger.

Viewing DML Trigger Metadata

This next recipe demonstrates how to view information about the triggers in the current database.

The first example queries the sys.triggers catalog view, returning the name of the view or table, the associated trigger name, whether the trigger is INSTEAD OF, and whether the trigger is disabled:

```
-- Show the DML triggers in the current database
SELECT OBJECT_NAME(parent_id) Table_or_ViewNM,
name TriggerNM, is_instead_of_trigger, is_disabled
FROM sys.triggers
WHERE parent_class_desc = 'OBJECT_OR_COLUMN'
ORDER BY OBJECT_NAME(parent_id), name
```

This returns the following (abridged) results:

Table_or_ViewNM	TriggerNM	is_instead_of_trigger	is_disabled
Document	uDocument	0	0
Employee	dEmployee	1	0
Employee	uEmployee	0	0
EmployeeAddress	uEmployeeAddress	0	0
EmployeeDepartmentHistory	uEmployeeDepartmentHistory	0	0

To display a specific trigger's Transact-SQL definition, you can query the sys.sql_modules system catalog view:

```
-- Displays the trigger SQL definition
--(if the trigger is not encrypted)
SELECT o.name, m.definition
FROM sys.sql_modules m
INNER JOIN sys.objects o ON
    m.object_id = o.object_id
WHERE o.type = 'TR'
```

How It Works

The first query in this recipe queried the sys.triggers catalog view to show all the DML triggers in the current database. There are DDL triggers in the sys.triggers catalog view too, so to prevent them from being displayed in the results, the parent_class_desc was qualified to OBJECT_OR_COLUMN. This is because DDL triggers, as you'll see in the next section, are scoped at the database or SQL Server instance level—and not at the schema scope.

The second query showed the actual Transact-SQL trigger name and definition of each trigger in the database. If the trigger was encrypted (similar to an encrypted view or stored procedure, for example), the trigger definition will display a NULL value in this query.

DDL Triggers

Introduced in SQL Server 2005, DDL triggers respond to server or database events, rather than table data modifications. For example, you can create a DDL trigger that writes to an audit table whenever a database user issues the CREATE TABLE or DROP TABLE command. Or, at the server level, you can create a DDL trigger that responds to the creation of a new login (for example, preventing a certain login from being created).

Database DDL triggers are stored as objects within the database they were created in, whereas Server DDL triggers, which track changes at the server level, are stored in the master database.

The syntax for a DDL Trigger is as follows:

```
CREATE TRIGGER trigger_name
ON { ALL SERVER | DATABASE }
[ WITH <ddl_trigger_option> [ ...,n ] ]
FOR { event_type | event_group } [ ,...n ]
AS { sql_statement [ ...n ]}
```

Table 12-4 details the arguments of this command:

Table 12-4. *CREATE TRIGGER (DDL) Arguments*

Argument	Description
trigger_name	The user-defined name of the new DDL trigger (notice that a DDL trigger does not have an owning schema, since it isn't related to an actual database table or view).
ALL SERVER | DATABASE	Designates whether the DDL trigger will respond to server-scoped (ALL SERVER) or DATABASE-scoped events.
<ddl_trigger_option> [...,n]	Allows you to specify the ENCRYPTION and/or EXECUTE AS clause. ENCRYPTION will encrypt the Transact-SQL definition of the trigger. EXECUTE AS allows you to define the security context under which the trigger will be executed.
{ event_type | event_group } [,...n]	An event_type indicates a single DDL server or database event which can be reacted to by the trigger. For example CREATE_TABLE, ALTER_TABLE, DROP_INDEX, and more.
	An event_group is a logical grouping of event_type events. A single DDL trigger can be created to react against one or more event types or groups. For example the DDL_PARTITION_FUNCTION_EVENTS group reacts to the following individual events: CREATE_PARTITION_FUNCTION, ALTER_PARTITION_FUNCTION, and DROP_PARTITION_FUNCTION.
	You can find a complete list of trigger event types in the SQL Server 2005 Books Online topic "DDL Events for Use with DDL Triggers" and a complete list of trigger event groups in the SQL Server 2005 Books Online topic "Event Groups for Use with DDL Triggers."

(Continued)

Table 12-4. *Continued*

Argument	Description
`sql_statement [ ...n ]`	One or more Transact-SQL statements which can be used to carry out actions in response to the DDL database or server event.

Creating a DDL Trigger That Audits Database-Level Events

This recipe demonstrates creating an audit table that can contain information on any attempts at the creation, alteration, or dropping of indexes in the AdventureWorks database.

First, the audit table is created:

```
CREATE TABLE dbo.ChangeAttempt
    (EventData xml NOT NULL,
     AttemptDate datetime NOT NULL DEFAULT GETDATE(),
     DBUser char(50) NOT NULL)
GO
```

Next, a database DDL trigger is created to track index operations, inserting the event data to the newly created table:

```
CREATE TRIGGER db_trg_RestrictINDEXChanges
ON DATABASE
FOR CREATE_INDEX, ALTER_INDEX, DROP_INDEX
AS

SET NOCOUNT ON

INSERT dbo.ChangeAttempt
(EventData, DBUser)
VALUES (EVENTDATA(), USER)

GO
```

Now we'll attempt an actual index creation in the database:

```
CREATE NONCLUSTERED INDEX ni_ChangeAttempt_DBUser ON
    dbo.ChangeAttempt(DBUser)
GO
```

Next, we'll query the ChangeAttempt audit table to see if the new index creation event was captured by the trigger:

```
SELECT EventData
FROM dbo.ChangeAttempt
```

This returns the actual event information, stored in XML format (see Chapter 14, for more information on XML in SQL Server 2005):

```
<EVENT_INSTANCE>
  <EventType>CREATE_INDEX</EventType>
  <PostTime>2005-08-26T20:11:58.317</PostTime>
  <SPID>52</SPID>
  <ServerName>JOEPROD</ServerName>
  <LoginName>JOEPROD\Owner</LoginName>
  <UserName>dbo</UserName>
  <DatabaseName>AdventureWorks</DatabaseName>
  <SchemaName>dbo</SchemaName>
  <ObjectName>ni_ChangeAttempt_DBUser</ObjectName>
  <ObjectType>INDEX</ObjectType>
  <TargetObjectName>ChangeAttempt</TargetObjectName>
  <TargetObjectType>TABLE</TargetObjectType>
  <TSQLCommand>
    <SetOptions ANSI_NULLS="ON" ANSI_NULL_DEFAULT="ON" ANSI_PADDING="ON"
QUOTED_IDENTIFIER="ON" ENCRYPTED="FALSE" />
    <CommandText>CREATE NONCLUSTERED INDEX ni_ChangeAttempt_DBUser ON
    dbo.ChangeAttempt(DBUser)
</CommandText>
  </TSQLCommand>
</EVENT_INSTANCE>
```

How It Works

The recipe began with you creating a table that could contain audit information on index modification and login creation attempts. The EventData column uses SQL Server 2005's new xml data type, which was populated by the new EVENTDATA function (described later on in this recipe):

```
CREATE TABLE dbo.ChangeAttempt
   (EventData xml NOT NULL,
   AttemptDate datetime NOT NULL DEFAULT GETDATE(),
   DBUser char(50) NOT NULL)
GO
```

The first trigger created in the recipe applied to the current database. The new DDL trigger responded to CREATE INDEX, ALTER INDEX, or DROP INDEX commands:

```
CREATE TRIGGER db_trg_RestrictINDEXChanges
ON DATABASE
FOR CREATE_INDEX, ALTER_INDEX, DROP_INDEX
AS
```

The SET NOCOUNT command was used in the trigger to suppress the number of row-affected messages from SQL Server (otherwise every time you make an index modification, you'll see a "1 row affected" message:

```
SET NOCOUNT ON
```

An INSERT was then made to the new audit table, populating it with the event data and user:

```
INSERT dbo.ChangeAttempt
(EventData, DBUser)
VALUES (EVENTDATA(), USER)

GO
```

The EVENTDATA function returns server and data event information in an XML format, and is also used for SQL Server 2005's SQL Service Broker functionality.

■**Note** See Chapter 20 for more information on event notification.

The XML data captured by the EVENTDATA function included useful information such as the event, the login name that attempted the CREATE INDEX, the target object name, and the time that it occurred.

Creating a DDL Trigger That Audits Server-Level Events

In this recipe, I demonstrate using a server-level DDL trigger to restrict users from creating new logins on the SQL Server instance.

We'll start by creating the DDL trigger:

```
USE master
GO
-- Disallow new Logins on the SQL instance
CREATE TRIGGER srv_trg_RestrictNewLogins
ON ALL SERVER
FOR CREATE_LOGIN
AS
PRINT 'No login creations without DBA involvement.'

    ROLLBACK
GO
```

Next, an attempt is made to add a new SQL login:

```
CREATE LOGIN JoeS WITH PASSWORD = 'A235921'
GO
```

This returns:

```
No login creations without DBA involvement.
Msg 3609, Level 16, State 2, Line 1
The transaction ended in the trigger. The batch has been aborted.
```

How It Works

This recipe demonstrated using a server-level DDL trigger to restrict a SQL login from being created. The FOR statement of the trigger was set to the CREATE LOGIN event:

```
CREATE TRIGGER srv_trg_RestrictNewLogins
ON ALL SERVER
FOR CREATE_LOGIN
AS
```

The body of the trigger used a PRINT statement to warn the end-user that their attempt was not allowed:

```
PRINT 'No login creations without DBA involvement.'
```

This was followed by a ROLLBACK, which cancels the CREATE LOGIN attempt from the trigger:

```
    ROLLBACK
GO
```

Viewing DDL Trigger Metadata

In this recipe, I demonstrate the retrieval of DDL trigger metadata.

The first example queries the sys.triggers catalog view, returning the associated *database-scoped* trigger name and trigger enabled/disabled status:

```
USE AdventureWorks
GO

-- Show the DML triggers in the current database
SELECT name TriggerNM, is_disabled
FROM sys.triggers
WHERE parent_class_desc = 'DATABASE'
ORDER BY OBJECT_NAME(parent_id), name
```

This returns the following (abridged) results:

```
TriggerNM           is_disabled
db_trg_RestrictINDEXChanges      0
ddlDatabaseTriggerLog      1
```

This next example queries the sys.server_triggers and sys.server_trigger_events system catalog views to retrieve a list of server-scoped DDL triggers. This returns the name of the DDL trigger, the type of trigger (Transact-SQL or CLR), the disabled state of the trigger, and the events the trigger is fired off of (you'll see one row for each event a trigger is based on):

```
SELECT name, s.type_desc SQL_or_CLR,
is_disabled, e.type_desc FiringEvents
FROM sys.server_triggers s
INNER JOIN sys.server_trigger_events  e ON
   s.object_id = e.object_id
```

This returns data based on the previous sever-level trigger created earlier:

```
name                     SQL_or_CLR      is_disabled   FiringEvents
srv_trg_RestrictNewLogins   SQL_TRIGGER    0            CREATE_LOGIN
```

To display *database-scoped* DDL trigger Transact-SQL definitions, you can query the sys.sql_modules system catalog view:

```
SELECT t.name, m.Definition
FROM sys.triggers AS t
INNER JOIN sys.sql_modules m ON
t.object_id = m.object_id
WHERE t.parent_class_desc = 'DATABASE'
```

To display *server-scoped* DDL triggers, we query the sys.server_sql_modules and sys.server_triggers system catalog views:

```
SELECT t.name, m.definition
FROM sys.server_sql_modules m
INNER JOIN sys.server_triggers t ON
   m.object_id = t.object_id
```

How It Works

The first query in this recipe returns a list of database-scoped triggers using the sys.triggers system catalog view. In order to only display DDL database-scoped triggers, I had to qualify the parent_class_desc value to DATABASE. The second query was written to return a list of server-scoped triggers and their associated triggering events. In that situation, the sys.server_triggers and sys.server_trigger_events system catalogs were queried.

The third query was used to return the Transact-SQL definitions of database-scoped triggers by qualifying sys.triggers to sys.sql_modules. To return server-scoped trigger Transact-SQL definitions, the sys.server_sql_modules and sys.server_triggers system catalog views were queried.

Managing Triggers

The next set of recipes demonstrate how to modify, drop, enable, disable, and control trigger options. Some of the commands I'll be demonstrating include: ALTER TRIGGER to modify a trigger's definition, DROP TRIGGER to remove it from the database, ALTER DATABASE to set trigger recursion options, sp_configure to control trigger nesting, and sp_settriggerorder to set the firing order of a trigger.

Modifying a Trigger

You can modify an existing DDL or DML trigger by using the ALTER TRIGGER command. ALTER TRIGGER takes the same arguments as the associated DML or DDL CREATE TRIGGER syntax does.

In this example, I modify a trigger created in the previous recipe. Instead of restricting users from creating new logins, the login event will be allowed, followed by a warning and an INSERT into an auditing table:

```
ALTER TRIGGER srv_trg_RestrictNewLogins
ON ALL SERVER
FOR CREATE_LOGIN
AS

SET NOCOUNT ON

PRINT 'Your login creation is being monitored.'

INSERT AdventureWorks.dbo.ChangeAttempt
(EventData, DBUser)
VALUES (EVENTDATA(), USER)

GO
```

How It Works

ALTER TRIGGER allows you to modify existing DDL or DML triggers. The arguments for ALTER TRIGGER are the same as for CREATE TRIGGER. You can't use it to change the actual trigger name, however, so in this example, the trigger name is no longer applicable to the actual actions the DDL trigger will take (in this case just monitoring, no longer restricting new logins).

Enabling and Disabling Table Triggers

Sometimes triggers must be disabled if they are causing problems that you need to troubleshoot, or if you need to import or recover data that shouldn't fire the trigger. In this recipe, I demonstrate how to disable a trigger from firing using the new SQL Server 2005 DISABLE TRIGGER command, as well as how to re-enable a trigger using ENABLE TRIGGER.

The syntax for DISABLE TRIGGER is as follows:

```
DISABLE TRIGGER [ schema . ] trigger_name
ON { object_name | DATABASE | SERVER }
```

The syntax for enabling a trigger is as follows:

```
ENABLE TRIGGER [ schema_name . ] trigger_name
ON { object_name | DATABASE | SERVER }
```

Table 12-5 details the arguments of this command.

Table 12-5. *ENABLE and DISABLE Trigger Arguments*

Argument	Description
[schema_name .]trigger_name	The optional schema owner and required user-defined name of the trigger you want to disable.
object_name	DATABASE	SERVER	object_name is the table or view that the trigger was bound to (if it's a DML trigger). Use DATABASE if the trigger was a DDL database-scoped trigger and SERVER if the trigger was a DDL server-scoped trigger.

This example starts off by creating a trigger (which is enabled by default) that prints a message back to a connection that is performing an INSERT against the HumanResources.Department table:

```
CREATE TRIGGER HumanResources.trg_Department
ON  HumanResources.Department
AFTER  INSERT
AS

PRINT 'The trg_Department trigger was fired'

GO
```

The trigger is then disabled using the DISABLE TRIGGER command:

```
DISABLE TRIGGER HumanResources.trg_Department
ON HumanResources.Department
```

Because the trigger was disabled, no printed message will be returned when the following INSERT is executed:

```
INSERT HumanResources.Department
(Name, GroupName)
VALUES ('Construction', 'Building Services')

GO
```

This returns:

```
(1 row(s) affected)
```

Next, the trigger is enabled using the ENABLE TRIGGER command:

```
ENABLE TRIGGER HumanResources.trg_Department
ON HumanResources.Department
```

Now when another INSERT is attempted, the trigger will fire, returning a message back to the connection:

```
INSERT HumanResources.Department
(Name, GroupName)
VALUES ('Cleaning', 'Building Services')
```

This returns:

```
The trg_Department trigger was fired

(1 row(s) affected)
```

How It Works

This recipe started by creating a new trigger that printed a statement whenever a new row was inserted into the HumanResources.Department table.

After creating the trigger, the DISABLE TRIGGER command was used to keep it from firing (although the trigger's definition still stays in the database):

```
DISABLE TRIGGER HumanResources.trg_Department
ON HumanResources.Department
```

An insert was then performed that did not fire the trigger. The ENABLE TRIGGER command was then executed, and then another insert was attempted, this time firing off the trigger.

Limiting Trigger Nesting

Trigger nesting occurs when a trigger is fired, which performs an action (for example, inserting into a different table), which in turn fires another trigger, which then initiates the firing of other triggers. An infinite loop firing of triggers is prevented by SQL Server 2005's maximum level of nesting, which is 32 levels deep.

You can also modify the SQL Server instance to not allow trigger nesting at all. Disabling the 'nested triggers' option prevents any AFTER trigger from causing the firing of another trigger.

This example demonstrates how to disable or enable this behavior:

```
USE master
GO

-- Disable nesting
EXEC sp_configure 'nested triggers', 0
RECONFIGURE WITH OVERRIDE
GO

-- Enable nesting
EXEC sp_configure 'nested triggers', 1
RECONFIGURE WITH OVERRIDE
GO
```

This returns:

```
Configuration option 'nested triggers' changed from 1 to 0. Run the RECONFIGURE statement
to install.
Configuration option 'nested triggers' changed from 0 to 1. Run the RECONFIGURE statement
to install.
```

How It Works

This recipe used the `sp_configure` system stored procedure to change the nested trigger behavior at the server level. To disable nesting altogether, `sp_configure` was executed for the "nested trigger" server option, followed by the parameter 0, which disables nesting:

```
EXEC sp_configure 'nested triggers', 0
RECONFIGURE WITH OVERRIDE
GO
```

Because server options contain both a current configuration versus an actual runtime configuration value, the `RECONFIGURE WITH OVERRIDE` command was used to update the runtime value so that it takes effect right away.

In order to enable nesting again, this server option is set back to "1" in the second batch of the recipe.

■Note For more information on configuring server options, see Chapter 21.

Controlling Trigger Recursion

Trigger nesting is considered to be recursive if the action performed when a trigger fires causes the *same* table trigger to fire again. Recursion can also occur when a trigger's fire impacts a different table, which also has a trigger that impacts the original table, thus causing the trigger to fire again.

You can control whether recursion is allowed by configuring the `RECURSIVE_TRIGGERS` database option. If you allow recursion, your `AFTER` triggers will still be impacted by the 32-level nesting limit, preventing an infinite looping situation.

This example demonstrates enabling and disabling this option:

```
-- Allows recursion
ALTER DATABASE AdventureWorks
SET RECURSIVE_TRIGGERS ON

-- View the db setting
SELECT is_recursive_triggers_on
FROM sys.databases
WHERE name = 'AdventureWorks'

-- Prevents recursion
ALTER DATABASE AdventureWorks
SET RECURSIVE_TRIGGERS OFF

-- View the db setting
SELECT is_recursive_triggers_on
FROM sys.databases
WHERE name = 'AdventureWorks'
```

This returns:

```
is_recursive_triggers_on
------------------------
1

is_recursive_triggers_on
------------------------
0
```

How It Works

ALTER DATABASE was used to configure database-level options, including whether or not triggers were allowed to fire recursively within the database. The option was enabled by setting RECURSIVE_TRIGGERS ON:

```
ALTER DATABASE AdventureWorks
SET RECURSIVE_TRIGGERS ON
```

The option was then queried by using the sys.databases system catalog view, which showed the current database option in the is_recursive_triggers_on field (1 for on, 0 for off):

```
SELECT is_recursive_triggers_on
FROM sys.databases
WHERE name = 'AdventureWorks'
```

The recipe then disabled trigger recursion by setting the option OFF, and then confirming it again in a sys.databases query.

■**Note** For more information on ALTER DATABASE and database options, see Chapter 22.

Setting Trigger Firing Order

In general you should try to encapsulate triggers that react to the same events within a single trigger. This improves manageability and supportability of the triggers, because you'll have an easier time finding the code you are looking for, and be able to troubleshoot accordingly. You'll also avoid the issue of trying to figure out which trigger ran first. Instead, you can define multiple triggers on the same table, referencing the same DML types (for example multiple INSERT triggers). DDL triggers can also be set on the same database or server scope events or event groups.

If you find that you must have separate triggers referencing the same database objects (perhaps you've added triggers so as not to overlap a third party's code), and if the order in which they are fired is important to you, you should configure it using the sp_settriggerorder system stored procedure.

The syntax for sp_settriggerorder is as follows:

```
sp_settriggerorder [ @triggername = ] '[ triggerschema. ] triggername'
        , [ @order = ] 'value'
        , [ @stmttype = ] 'statement_type'
        [ , [ @namespace = ] { 'DATABASE' | 'SERVER' } ]
```

Table 12-6 details the arguments of this command.

Table 12-6. *sp_settriggerorder Arguments*

Argument	Description
'[triggerschema.] triggername'	The optional schema owner and required user-defined name of the trigger to be ordered.
[@order =] 'value'	This can be either "First," "None," or "Last." Any triggers in between these will be fired in an random order after the first and last firings.
[@stmttype =] 'statement_type'	Designates the type of trigger to be ordered, for example INSERT, UPDATE, DELETE, CREATE_INDEX, ALTER_INDEX...
[@namespace =] { 'DATABASE'	'SERVER' }	Designates if this is a DDL trigger, and if so, whether it is database- or server-scoped.

This recipe will create a test table and add three DML INSERT triggers to it. The sp_settriggerorder will then be used to define the firing order:

```
CREATE TABLE dbo.TestTriggerOrder
    (TestID int  NOT NULL)
GO

CREATE TRIGGER dbo.trg_i_TestTriggerOrder
ON dbo.TestTriggerOrder
AFTER INSERT
AS
PRINT 'I will be fired first.'
GO

CREATE TRIGGER dbo.trg_i_TestTriggerOrder2
ON dbo.TestTriggerOrder
AFTER INSERT
AS
PRINT 'I will be fired last.'
GO

CREATE TRIGGER dbo.trg_i_TestTriggerOrder3
ON dbo.TestTriggerOrder
AFTER INSERT
AS
PRINT 'I won't be first or last.'
GO

EXEC sp_settriggerorder 'trg_i_TestTriggerOrder', 'First', 'INSERT'
EXEC sp_settriggerorder 'trg_i_TestTriggerOrder2', 'Last', 'INSERT'

INSERT dbo.TestTriggerOrder
(TestID)
VALUES (1)
```

This returns:

```
I will be fired first.
I won't be first or last.
I will be fired last.
```

How It Works

This recipe started off by creating a single column test table. Three DML INSERT triggers were then added to it. Using sp_settriggerorder, the first and last triggers to fire were defined:

```
EXEC sp_settriggerorder 'trg_i_TestTriggerOrder', 'First', 'INSERT'
EXEC sp_settriggerorder 'trg_i_TestTriggerOrder2', 'Last', 'INSERT'
```

An INSERT was then performed against the table, and the trigger messages were returned in the expected order.

To reiterate this point, if you can, use a single trigger on a table when possible (when of the same type). If you must create multiple triggers of the same type, and your trigger contains ROLLBACK functionality if an error occurs, be sure to set the trigger that has the most likely chance of failing as the first trigger to execute. This way only the first-fired trigger need execute, preventing the other triggers from having to fire and roll back transactions unnecessarily.

Dropping a Trigger

The syntax for dropping a trigger differs by trigger type (DML or DDL).

The syntax for dropping a DML trigger is as follows:

```
DROP TRIGGER schema_name.trigger_name [ ,...n ]
```

Table 12-7 details the argument of this command.

Table 12-7. *DROP TRIGGER Argument (DML)*

Argument	Description
schema_name.trigger_name	The owning schema name of the trigger and the DML trigger name to be removed from the database.

The syntax for dropping a DDL trigger is as follows:

```
DROP TRIGGER trigger_name [ ,...n ]
ON { DATABASE | ALL SERVER }
```

Table 12-8 details the arguments of this command.

Table 12-8. *DROP TRIGGER Arguments (DDL)*

Argument	Description
trigger_name	The DDL trigger name to be removed from the database (for a database-level DDL trigger) or SQL Server instance (for a server-scoped trigger).
DATABASE	ALL SERVER	Defines whether you are removing a DATABASE-scoped DDL trigger or a server-scoped trigger (ALL SERVER).

In the case of both DDL and DML syntax statements, the [,...n] syntax block indicates that more than one trigger can be dropped at the same time.

This example demonstrates dropping a DML and a DDL trigger:

```
-- Drop a DML trigger
DROP TRIGGER dbo.trg_i_TestTriggerOrder

-- Drop multiple DML triggers
DROP TRIGGER dbo.trg_i_TestTriggerOrder2, dbo.trg_i_TestTriggerOrder3

-- Drop a DDL trigger
DROP TRIGGER db_trg_RestrictINDEXChanges
ON DATABASE
```

How It Works

In this recipe, DML and DDL triggers were explicitly dropped using the DROP TRIGGER command. You will also drop all DML triggers when you drop the table or view that they are bound to. You can also remove multiple triggers in the same DROP command if each of the triggers were created using the same ON clause.

CHAPTER 13

■ ■ ■

CLR Integration

In this chapter, you'll dip your foot into what is most definitely another book-sized topic. Although this book focuses on the Transact-SQL language, there are significant areas of overlap between Common Language Runtime (CLR) and Transact-SQL, which I'll discuss in this chapter, along with a few recipes to get you started.

In many people's eyes, the inclusion of the CLR within the database is the biggest advancement in SQL Server 2005. As a result of the inclusion, developers no longer have to use Transact-SQL to write procedural database objects such as stored procedures, functions, and triggers. They can now create these objects using any of the .NET languages (VB.NET, C#, C++ and so on) and compile them into .NET *assemblies*. These assemblies are deployed inside the database and run by the CLR, which in turn is hosted inside the SQL Server memory space.

T-SQL, the traditional programming language for the SQL Server database, is a powerful language for data-intensive operations, but is limited in its computational complexity. For these complex operations in the database, the developer traditionally had to resort to the notoriously difficult extended procedures written in C++, or create hideously long and awkward stored procedure code.

In theory, CLR integration offers the "best of both worlds." Your code can be hosted in the secure environment of the database, delegating memory management, garbage collection, and thread support to the robust database engine, while exploiting .NET's computational power, advanced data type support, and rich array of built-in classes.

Although this book is focused on Transact-SQL functionality, I'll still be introducing the basic methods for creating assemblies, importing them into the database, and then associating them to database objects. I'll start off by describing the basic end-to-end steps, and then going into the variations that exist for the different CLR database object types. Discussions and recipes in this chapter include:

- A discussion of both when and when not to use assemblies in SQL Server 2005
- Available SQL Server 2005 CLR database objects, and how to create them
- A recipe-by-recipe walkthrough on creating a CLR stored procedure
- Creating a CLR scalar user-defined function
- Creating a CLR trigger
- Viewing, modifying, and removing assemblies from the database

First, however, I'll begin the chapter with a brief overview of the Common Language Runtime (CLR).

CLR Overview

Before getting too far into the discussion of SQL Server integration, I need to cover some of the basics for those of you who are new to the *.NET framework*. First of all, the .NET framework is a programmatic platform that is used to build Microsoft Windows applications and services. This framework can be used to create Windows forms, web services, and ASP.NET applications (to name a few). The major parts of the framework include the CLR, the framework classes and libraries (containing reusable functionality and programming models for your applications to use), and ASP.NET (which allows the creation of web-based applications).

■Note Programming in .NET requires the actual Microsoft .NET Framework. This is why Microsoft Windows .NET Framework 2.0 is a software prerequisite to installing SQL Server 2005.

The *Common Language Runtime (CLR)* is the environment where .NET programs are actually executed and managed. The CLR is used to execute the .NET programs, manage memory, and maintain program metadata. As noted in the introduction, in SQL Server 2005, the CLR is hosted *within* the SQL Server 2005 process. This means that reserved space within the SQL Server process handles memory management, security, and execution context.

When you write managed .NET code (code that is executed and managed within the CLR), *assemblies* are the packaged DLL or executable file that is used to deploy the functionality. You can then associate this assembly with various database objects, such as triggers, procedures, user-defined functions and so on. Using CLR-based database objects opens up a wide range of functionality, allowing you to perform complex calculations, access data from external sources, integrate with other business applications, and solve problems that cannot be addressed using Transact-SQL.

You can write your assemblies in the .NET language with which you are most comfortable—the two most common being Visual Basic.NET and C# ("c-sharp"). One reason why you can choose your preferred .NET language is because the code is compiled into an *intermediate language* (IL) form first. It's the IL form that is read and executed by the CLR. Code written in C# or VB.NET (short for Visual Basic.NET) that performs the same tasks usually ends up with intermediate language instructions that look almost identical to one another.

Aside from the programming language, you also have your choice in how you actually develop your code. One obvious choice is Visual Studio 2005, which includes templates that can ease the creation of SQL Server database CLR objects. You don't have to use Visual Studio 2005, however, as there are other, free open source .NET development environments that you can download off the web. You can also hand-code your .NET applications in Windows Notepad. Although not ideal for development projects, this method requires no additional software, and is the method I'll use in this chapter. I'm using this low tech method in order to keep the focus on CLR integration with Transact-SQL and not get too deeply into the many features and considerations of Visual Studio.

When (and When Not) to Use Assemblies

The announcement of the CLR and .NET framework integration with SQL Server 2005 caused a great deal of conflicting emotions among seasoned users. At one extreme, people had the vision of an all .NET database environment usurping Transact-SQL entirely. At the other were the anxious, hardcore database administrators and developers, some without a .NET programming background, many of whom vowed early on to keep this feature locked away indefinitely.

The first and most obvious thing to note is that .NET-based database objects are not a replacement for T-SQL-created database objects. Transact-SQL is still very much alive. There are major units of functionality that would be impossible to implement without Transact-SQL, and several .NET constructs and programming models that end up using Transact-SQL under the covers anyway.

There are two main reasons to consider using CLR database objects:

- You have "data-specific" logic that was previously impossible to implement in the database, using existing functionality and T-SQL. Therefore you have created extended stored procedures or modules in the middle tier or client layers.

- You have forced T-SQL to perform a highly complex task, resulting in complex and inelegant/ inefficient Transact-SQL code.

In some ways, the replacement of extended stored procedures with .NET CLR counterparts is the most clear-cut case for using assemblies. In previous versions of SQL Server, if you needed to add functionality to SQL Server that didn't already exist, or needed to access external resources, a common option was to use *extended stored procedures*. Database users called extended stored procedures and optionally passed parameters to them, just as with regular stored procedures. Extended stored procedures could be written in the programming language (such as C++), resulting in a DLL file. The sp_addextendedproc system stored procedure was used to create a new procedure and bind it to the DLL file (which had to exist on the SQL Server instance). The DLL file was not imported into the SQL Server database, so it needed to exist on the SQL Server instance machine. Because a DLL was loaded and used within SQL Server without any special management or protection, there was an increased risk of memory leaks or performance issues, depending on how the DLL code was written. If the DLL misbehaved, SQL Server could crash.

CLR integration addresses several of the inherent issues of extended stored procedures. When using managed code, memory leaks are not possible and security is fully integrated with the SQL Server environment. In short, assemblies are safer to use than extended stored procedures. So if you have:

- A database application that must perform very complex calculations that cannot be performed (or are very difficult to perform) using Transact-SQL

- A database application that needs access to functionality that exists in the .NET framework, but not in Transact-SQL

- A database application that needs access to external data sources (web services, files, system settings), that you cannot access using Transact-SQL

Then you may well want to consider assemblies as a potential solution. If you have implanted such functionality in extended stored procedures in your system, then these should be the first assembly migration candidates.

If you have complex business logic that exists in other tiers of the system (whether client or middle tier), then you need to assess and test on a case-by-case basis whether it would be wise to move that functionality into an assembly in the database. Database applications, integration with other applications, and ad-hoc reporting against the same database are all common components of today's applications. If there are business rules/logic central to the data itself, then it may well make sense to encapsulate this logic within the database so that each different data consumer does not have to duplicate these rules.

One thing is for sure, though: CLR database objects should *not* be used to replace functionality that already exists in Transact-SQL. Set-based processing using SELECT/INSERT/UPDATE/DELETE will always be the preferred method for data-intensive retrieval and modification. If an action can be performed efficiently within the database using Transact-SQL, you should use Transact-SQL over CLR methods.

CLR Objects Overview

In order to use CLR support, you must create and compile an assembly into a DLL, and then import the new assembly (using CREATE ASSEMBLY) into a SQL Server database. Once integrated in the database, it is backed up along with your tables, data, and other database objects—since it is a database object just like any other. Once an assembly is added, you can then associate it to different database objects, including user-defined functions, stored procedures, triggers, user-defined types, and aggregate functions:

- *User-defined functions.* These create scalar or table-valued functions that can access .NET framework calculation classes and access external resources. Later on in the chapter you'll see an example of using regular expressions functionality within a scalar function (something you could not do using Transact-SQL).

- *Stored procedures.* This is probably the SQL Server 2005 database object with the most creative potential. You can use CLR-stored procedures to replace extended stored procedures, utilize .NET framework classes, and perform calculation-heavy or external resource activities that aren't possible using Transact-SQL.

- *Triggers.* These allow you to create .NET programmatic responses to data manipulation language (INSERT/UPDATE/DELETE) or data definition language (CREATE, ALTER, DROP).

- *User-defined types.* These allow you to create new complex data types (unlike Transact-SQL user-defined types which are based on predefined data types). CLR user-defined types include methods and properties along the lines of a .NET object/class. This may be one of the more controversial additions to SQL Server 2005, because the multiple properties for a single type can fly in the face of basic relation database design principals. CLR user-defined types do allow you to implement data verification and string formatting, which *isn't* possible for Transact-SQL user-defined types.

- *User-defined aggregate functions.* Unlike the other CLR object, you can't create aggregate functions using Transact-SQL, so this is the first you'll have heard of this functionality in this book. User-defined aggregate functions can be used to create your own complex statistical analysis aggregates not available in SQL Server 2005, or to collect multiple string values into a single business-defined result.

The rest of this chapter will focus on creating CLR stored procedures, user-defined functions, and triggers, as these are the most directly analogous to their T-SQL counterparts (in terms of the way that they are accessed and executed) and therefore are the most relevant for this book.

Creating CLR Database Objects

The recipes in this section walk through the creation of three CLR-based objects, namely a CLR stored procedure, a CLR UDF, and a CLR trigger. In the case of the *CLR stored procedure,* I'll actually present a series of four sub-recipes that describe each of the following steps:

1. Use the system stored procedure sp_configure to enable CLR functionality for the SQL Server instance. Set the database where you will be using CLR database objects to TRUSTWORTHY if you plan on using CLR database objects with EXTERNAL_ACCESS or UNSAFE permissions.

2. Create the Assembly code using your .NET language of choice, and your tool of choice. For example, you can use C# or VB.NET to create the assembly. Using Visual Studio 2005 makes the process of creating CLR assemblies easier, however you can use something as simple as Notepad and the vsc.exe compiler.

3. Compile the code into a DLL file.

4. Use the `CREATE ASSEMBLY` Transact-SQL command to load the new assembly into the database. Choose the safety level based on the functionality of the assembly. Try to build code that is covered by either `SAFE` or `EXTERNAL_ACCESS` safety levels. These levels offer more stability for the SQL Server instance, and help avoid the potential issues that unsafe code may incur.

After that, I'll demonstrate how to create a *CLR scalar user-defined function*, following the similar steps (in a single recipe), but with a new assembly and a few twists on the code. Finally, I'll take a look at a CLR trigger.

Enabling CLR Support in SQL Server 2005

When SQL Server 2005 is installed, CLR functionality is disabled by default. To enable the use of CLR database objects, the system stored procedure `sp_configure` must be used to configure the `'clr enabled'` option (see Chapter 21 for a full review of this system stored procedure):

```
EXEC sp_configure 'clr enabled', 1
RECONFIGURE WITH OVERRIDE
GO
```

This returns:

```
Configuration option 'clr enabled' changed from 0 to 1.
Run the RECONFIGURE statement to install.
```

If you plan on using CLR database objects that require `EXTERNAL_ACCESS` or `UNSAFE` security permissions (we review the meanings of these in more detail later on), you must enable the `TRUSTWORTHY` database option to `ON`. For example:

```
ALTER DATABASE BookStore
SET TRUSTWORTHY ON
```

How It Works

This example demonstrated enabling CLR functionality for the SQL Server instance. After executing the command, CLR functionality is enabled immediately without having to restart the SQL Server instance. We then enabled the `TRUSTWORTHY` option for the `BookStore` database, in order to allow `EXTERNAL_ACCESS` and `UNSAFE` security permissions later on (although we'll only be demonstrating a CLR database object that requires external access, and not demoing anything that is unsafe!)

In the next recipe, we'll demonstrate creating an assembly using VB.NET.

Writing an Assembly for a CLR Stored Procedure

In this recipe, I'll demonstrate creating the code for an assembly. Specifically, VB.NET code is used to read data from an external text file and then output the text file data in a result set.

Before getting to the actual code, I first need to discuss a few new concepts regarding assemblies themselves.

So far I've discussed CLR assemblies as though they are used on a one-for-one basis with database objects. Assemblies, however, can contain code for use by one or more CLR database objects. For example, the code I'll be using in this recipe is intended for a single stored procedure. You can, however, put several subroutines or types within a single assembly, for use in different CLR database objects. As a best practice, try to group related functionality within a single assembly. This is important (if not necessary) if your various functions or methods have dependencies on one another.

Take a situation where you have a set of functionalities that will all cross-reference with an external mapping application. For example, your assembly could contain code that can be used by a CLR stored procedure to return driving directions, a CLR user-defined function to return mapping coordinates based on address input information, and a new user-defined CLR type that contains the varying address details.

Another important concept to understand is assembly security. When you use managed code, you must consider how much access to specific resources that your code requires. Later on in the chapter you'll see that when an assembly is added to SQL Server 2005, you'll need to indicate the level of permissions that the assembly requires. You'll have three choices, SAFE, EXTERNAL_ACCESS, and UNSAFE, which I'll describe in more detail later on in the chapter.

This assembly example demonstrates creating a class and function using VB.NET, which then takes a file and path name as an input value, opens the file for reading, and, finally, returns the results back to the SQL Server connection context that made the call. I'll discuss the elements of this script in the "How It Works" section:

```vbnet
Imports System.Data
Imports System.Data.Sql
Imports System.Data.SqlTypes
Imports Microsoft.SqlServer.Server
Imports System.IO

Public Class ReadFiles

Public Shared Sub Main(ByVal sFile As SqlString)

    Dim sReader As StreamReader = New StreamReader(sFile)
    Dim sLine As String
    Dim sPipe As SqlPipe = SqlContext.Pipe

    Do
    sLine =  sReader.ReadLine()
 If Not sLine Is Nothing Then
  sPipe.Send(sLine)
End If
    Loop Until sLine Is Nothing

    sReader.Close()

    End Sub
End Class
```

How It Works

This current recipe's example contains a class and function that will be associated specifically to a CLR stored procedure. CLR database objects require specific namespaces to exist within the assembly so that SQL Server can reference built-in CLR assemblies in your assembly code. For example, the code included the following namespaces:

```vbnet
Imports System.Data
Imports System.Data.Sql
Imports System.Data.SqlTypes
Imports Microsoft.SqlServer.Server
```

You can also include other namespaces, depending on the required functionality of the assembly. For example, the System.IO namespace contains the functions needed to read and write from file system files:

```
Imports System.IO
```

The example continued declaring a public class called ReadFiles:

```
Public Class ReadFiles
```

Next, a public, shared subroutine included a single parameter string value (in this case expecting the name and path of the file to be read):

```
Public Shared Sub Main(ByVal sFile As SqlString)
```

Notice that the sFile input parameter was defined as the SqlString type. As you work with CLR assemblies, you'll need to understand the SQL Server data types that associate to specific SQL CLR .NET data types. Table 13-1 lists some of the available data types and their CLR versus SQL Server 2005 translations (notice that with some types you can pick and choose, due to overlap):

Table 13-1. *Converting SQL Server to CLR Data Types*

CLR Data Type(s)	SQL Server Data Type(s)
SqlBytes	varbinary, binary
SqlBinary	varbinary, binary
SqlChars (ideal for data access and retrieval)	nvarchar, nchar
SqlString (ideal for string operation)	nvarchar, nchar
SqlGuid	uniqueidentifier
SqlBoolean	bit
SqlByte	tinyint
SqlInt16	smallint
SqlInt32	int
SqlInt64	bigint
SqlMoney	smallmoney, money
SqlDecimal	decimal, numeric
SqlSingle	real
SqlDouble	float
SqlDateTime	smalldatetime, datetime
SqlXml	xml

Continuing the walk-through of the example, you'll note that a StreamReader object was declared and set to the passed file name and path. The StreamReader class is used to read text data from a file. Because it is not a Transact-SQL function, you would not normally be able to reference this function in your code. CLR assemblies allow you to use these .NET commands from your SQL Server database:

```
Dim sReader As StreamReader = New StreamReader(sFile)
```

A string variable is created to hold a single line of data from the file:

```
Dim sLine As String
```

Next, I use two classes, SqlPipe and SqlContext:

```
Dim sPipe As SqlPipe = SqlContext.Pipe
```

The SqlPipe object is used to send zero or more rows back to the connected caller's connection. So, if I execute a CLR stored procedure that I expect will return a list of results (similar to a SELECT query), the Send method of the SqlPipe object is used. This SqlContext class maintains and accesses the SQL Server caller's context, meaning if I execute a stored procedure, SqlContext knows that it is my action and that the results belong to my client. A SqlPipe is spawned based on the SqlContext of a user's connection using the Pipe method of SqlContext.

Next, a Do loop (similar to a Transact-SQL WHILE) is created to read through each line of the file until there are no longer any rows:

```
Do
```

The sLine variable is set to the first line of the file using the ReadLine method of the StreamReader object:

```
sLine = sReader.ReadLine()
```

If something exists in the line from the file, the values of that line are sent back to the SQL Server connection using the Send method of the SqlPipe object:

```
If Not sLine Is Nothing Then
  sPipe.Send(sLine)
End If
```

Once the file is complete, however, the Do loop is finished and the connection to the file is closed:

```
Loop Until sLine Is Nothing
```

```
sReader.Close()
```

Finishing off the assembly, I ended the sub, and then the class definition.

```
    End Sub
End Class
```

Now that you have written the assembly in VB.NET, you can move to the next step, which is compiling the assembly code into a DLL file which can then be imported into SQL Server. In preparation for this exercise, create a file directory called C:\Apress\Recipes\CLR\ and then save this file as ReadFiles.vb.

Compiling an Assembly into a DLL File

Use vbc.exe to compile the assembly file without the use of Visual Studio 2005. The vbc.exe compiler can be found on the SQL Server instance machine under the latest version of C:\WINDOWS\MICROSOFT.NET\framework\ directory.

In this example, the following command creates the DLL assembly file based on the ReadFiles.vb code by executing the vbc executable at the command prompt:

```
vbc /t:library /out:C:\Apress\Recipes\CLR\ReadFiles.DLL /r:"C:\Program
➥ Files\Microsoft SQL Server\MSSQL.1\MSSQL\Binn\sqlaccess.dll"
➥ C:\Apress\Recipes\CLR\ReadFiles.vb"
```

How It Works

Executing the vbc.exe executable in this recipe creates a DLL file under C:\Apress\Recipes\CLR directory which can then be used to create an assembly in SQL Server 2005. I'll review how to do that next.

Loading the Assembly Into SQL Server

To load the new assembly into a SQL Server 2005 database, use the `CREATE ASSEMBLY` command.
    The basic syntax, as used in this example, is as follows:

```
CREATE ASSEMBLY assembly_name
[ AUTHORIZATION owner_name ]
FROM { '[\\computer_name\]share_name\[path\]manifest_file_name'
  | '[local_path\]manifest_file_name'|
{ varbinary_literal | varbinary_expression }}
[ WITH PERMISSION_SET = { SAFE | EXTERNAL_ACCESS | UNSAFE } ]
```

    Table 13-2 describes this command's arguments:

Table 13-2. *CREATE ASSEMBLY Arguments*

Argument	Description
`assembly_name`	The name of the new database assembly.
`owner_name`	The user or role owner of the assembly.

`'[\\computer_name\]share_name\`
`[path\]manifest_file_name'`
`
	'[local_path\]manifest_file_name'`	The path and file name of the assembly to be loaded.

`varbinary_literal	varbinary_expression`	Instead of an actual file, the binary values that make up the assembly can be passed to the command.
`SAFE	EXTERNAL_ACCESS	UNSAFE`	This references the safety permission level for the assembly, per the discussion earlier in this section.

    The safety permission levels for the assembly require special consideration. `SAFE` permissions allow you to run code that only requires access to the local SQL Server instance. Using this default mode, your assembly won't be able to access the network, external files (even files on the same machine as the SQL Server instance), the registry, or environment variables. `EXTERNAL_ACCESS` permissions permit access to the network, external files, the registry, environment variables, and web services. Both the `SAFE` and `EXTERNAL_ACCESS` modes have a specific level of internal safety. These internal measures include the protection of the memory space of other applications, as well as a restriction from any action that could hurt the SQL Server instance.

    `UNSAFE` permissions are most similar to the extended stored procedures discussed earlier in the chapter. This level of permission doesn't put any restrictions on how the assembly accesses resources, allowing for the potential of memory space violations or performing actions that could hurt the stability of the SQL Server instance. As you may suspect, this is the permission level you should avoid unless necessary, and only under conditions where you can ensure the assembly is thoroughly tested and free of negative side-effects.

    Continuing with this section's example of creating a CLR stored procedure, a new assembly is created based on the `ReadFiles.DLL`, using the `EXTERNAL_ACCESS` option, since the assembly needs to read from the file system:

```
CREATE ASSEMBLY ReadFiles FROM 'C:\Apress\Recipes\CLR\ReadFiles.DLL'
WITH PERMISSION_SET = EXTERNAL_ACCESS
GO
```

How It Works

When creating a new assembly, the actual assembly contents are loaded into the database. This means that database backups will also backup the assemblies contained within. In our example, a new assembly called ReadFiles was created based on the assembly DLL file. The permission was set to EXTERNAL_ACCESS because the assembly is used to read data from a file and return it back as a result set to the SQL Server 2005 caller.

Importing an assembly into SQL Server 2005 isn't enough to start using its functionality. You must then associate that assembly to a CLR database object. The next recipe demonstrates how to do this.

Creating the CLR Stored Procedure

CLR database objects are created similarly to their regular Transact-SQL equivalents, only the procedural definition references an assembly instead. The following commands each have the CLR option of EXTERNAL NAME:

- CREATE PROCEDURE
- CREATE FUNCTION
- CREATE TRIGGER
- CREATE TYPE

As a side note, the CREATE AGGREGATE command, which creates a user-defined SQL Server aggregate function, can't be written in Transact-SQL and is only used in conjunction with a .NET assembly.

The specific extension syntax for creating a CLR-based stored procedure, user-defined function, or trigger is as follows:

```
EXTERNAL NAME assembly_name.class_name.method_name
```

For creating a new CLR data type or aggregate, only the assembly and class name are referenced:

```
EXTERNAL NAME assembly_name [ .class_name ]
```

This example demonstrates creating a new CLR stored procedure using the EXTERNAL NAME extension of the CREATE PROCEDURE command to map to your new assembly, created in the previous recipe:

```
CREATE PROCEDURE dbo.usp_FileReader
(@FileName nvarchar(1024))
AS EXTERNAL NAME ReadFiles.ReadFiles.Main
GO
```

ReadFiles appears twice because it is the CLR assembly name and the class within the VB.NET code block.

Once created, the CLR stored procedure is executed like a normal Transact-SQL defined stored procedure. Continuing this example, the contents of a SQL Server error log file are returned in the results of the stored procedure (looking at an error log that is not currently being used by the SQL Server instance):

```
EXEC dbo.usp_FileReader
N'C:\Program Files\Microsoft SQL Server\MSSQL.1\MSSQL\LOG\ERRORLOG.1'
```

This returns the contents of the ERRORLOG file as a result set (abridged here):

```
2005-07-02 07:50:11.10 Server     Microsoft SQL Server 2005 - 9.00.1187.07 (Intel X86)
May 24 2005 18:22:46
Copyright (c) 1988-2005 Microsoft Corporation
Beta Edition on Windows NT 5.1 (Build 2600: Service Pack 2)

2005-07-02 07:50:11.10 Server     (c) 2005 Microsoft Corporation.
2005-07-02 07:50:11.10 Server     All rights reserved.
2005-07-02 07:50:11.16 Server     Server process ID is 704.
...
```

Once created, database CLR objects can be altered or dropped using the normal ALTER or DROP commands for the database object type.

How It Works

This recipe demonstrated how to create a CLR stored procedure. The parameters required for the stored procedure depend on the parameters expected by the .NET assembly methods. In this case, the Main method of the ReadFiles assembly expected a string parameter for the file and path name to be read, so a @FileName nvarchar data type parameter is used in the stored procedure reference. In the EXTERNAL NAME clause, the ReadFiles assembly was referenced, followed by the ReadFiles class, and Main method.

Using the .NET framework, the procedure was able to access external resources and iterate through the contents of a file. With CLR integration, the functional scope of SQL Server now extends out to the capabilities of the .NET framework.

Creating a CLR Scalar User-Defined Function

You can create two different types of CLR user-defined functions: scalar and table-valued. It is most likely that the former will be more beneficial for performance in CLR than the latter. This is because table-valued functions are used to query database data, and they should therefore never be replaced by CLR equivalents. If your solution requires a table result set from an external file or resource, CLR UDFs may fit your needs well, particularly if you need to reference the external data in the FROM clause of your query (something that a CLR stored procedure would not allow).

Using CLR for scalar UDF functions that don't focus on data retrieval from SQL Server may often perform quite well over a Transact-SQL equivalent. As explained in the introduction at the beginning of the chapter, you'll benefit most from CLR when using it to execute high-complexity computational operations. CLR scalar UDFs are also useful for operations that simply aren't possible using Transact-SQL (for example, accessing external data or using .NET library functionality that doesn't exist in Transact-SQL).

In this example, an assembly is created that contains a class and method intended for use with a CLR user-defined scalar function. I'm going to take advantage of the System.Text.RegularExpressions .NET framework namespace. This contains a class called Regex, which will allow us to break apart a single string into an array of values based on a specific delimiter. Regular expression functionality, which is often used for pattern matching, isn't built into SQL Server 2005, but now, with CLR integration, you can safely and efficiently use the regular expression libraries written for VB.NET.

The goal of this example is to create a scalar UDF that takes three parameters. The first parameter is a delimited string of values. The second parameter is the delimiter character used to separate the string. The third parameter is the value from the array that I would like to select. I'll walk through the code in more detail in the "How It Works" section, but in the meantime, this example compiles the following code using vbc.exe:

```
Imports System.Data
Imports System.Data.Sql
Imports System.Data.SqlTypes
Imports Microsoft.SqlServer.Server
Imports System.Text.RegularExpressions

Public Class SQLArrayBuilder

Public Shared Function ChooseValueFromArray(ArrayString as String, ArrayDelimiter as
➥ String, ArrayItemSelection as SqlInt16) as SqlString

Dim NewArrayString as String() = Regex.Split(ArrayString, ArrayDelimiter)

Dim NewArrayItemSelection as SqlInt16=ArrayItemSelection-1

Dim ReturnString as SQLString = NewArrayString(NewArrayItemSelection)


Return ReturnString

End Function

End Class
```

After compiling this assembly, it can then be imported into the database. Because nothing in the assembly accesses external resources, I can use a SAFE permission level:

```
CREATE ASSEMBLY SQLArrayBuilder FROM 'C:\Apress\Recipes\CLR\SQLArrayBuilder.DLL'
WITH PERMISSION_SET = SAFE
GO
```

Next, the new assembly is associated to a scalar user-defined function. Notice that the syntax is the same as if it were a Transact-SQL command, except that after AS, the EXTERNAL NAME keywords are used to designate the assembly, class, and function:

```
CREATE FUNCTION dbo.CountSalesOrderHeader
(@ArrayString nvarchar(4000), @ArrayDelimiter nchar(1), @ArrayItemSelection smallint)
RETURNS nvarchar(4000)
AS
EXTERNAL NAME SQLArrayBuilder.SQLArrayBuilder.ChooseValueFromArray
GO
```

Now to test the function, the first parameter will include three comma-separated values. The second parameter designates a comma as the delimiter, and the third value indicates the value you would like to choose from the array:

```
SELECT dbo.CountSalesOrderHeader
('Brian,Steve,Boris', ',', 3) Choice
```

This returns:

```
Choice
Boris
```

This time the second value is selected from the array:

```
SELECT dbo.CountSalesOrderHeader
('Brian,Steve,Boris', ',', 2) Choice
```

This returns:

```
Choice
Steve
```

How It Works

This recipe shares the same general setup steps as the CLR stored procedure example. Once again, an assembly was created and then compiled. Next, the assembly was added to the database using CREATE ASSEMBLY. A new user-defined function was then created, using the expected three input parameters, and the appropriate output parameter data type. The UDF also included a reference to the assembly, class, and function name.

Walking through the code, you'll see that I included the core namespaces also seen in the stored procedure example:

```
Imports System.Data
Imports System.Data.Sql
Imports System.Data.SqlTypes
Imports Microsoft.SqlServer.Server
```

The reference to the regular expressions namespace was also included, so that you could use the functionality of the Regex object, which is a collection of library classes created and shipped with .NET:

```
Imports System.Text.RegularExpressions
```

Our class name was then declared, which will be the reference that is used during the creation of the CLR function:

```
Public Class SQLArrayBuilder
```

The function was declared, including the three input parameters in parentheses, followed by the expected return data type (SqlString) of the function:

```
Public Shared Function ChooseValueFromArray(ArrayString as String, ArrayDelimiter as
➥ String, ArrayItemSelection as SqlInt16) as SqlString
```

Next, a new string array variable was declared and populated with the array generated from the Regex.Split method, which is used to split an array of strings at the positions defined by a regular expression match (in this case, our delimiter):

```
Dim NewArrayString as String() =
Regex.Split(ArrayString, ArrayDelimiter)
```

VB.NET arrays are zero-based—meaning the first value in the array is indexed at "0," followed by "1," "2," and so on. Because the SQL Server caller of the scalar UDF will want to pass an array selection value based on a one-based value, I take the input array item selection and subtract "1" from it, so as to select the appropriate value from the array:

```
Dim NewArrayItemSelection as SqlInt16=ArrayItemSelection-1
```

After the array is populated, a new string variable is created to hold the selected value:

```
Dim ReturnString as SQLString = NewArrayString(NewArrayItemSelection)
```

This value is the passed back using the Return command, followed by the end of the function and class definition:

```
Return ReturnString

End Function

End Class
```

After that, the assembly was compiled, and then imported into the database using CREATE ASSEMBLY. The function was then created using CREATE FUNCTION referencing the assembly, class, and function:

```
SQLArrayBuilder.SQLArrayBuilder.ChooseValueFromArray
```

The function was then tested, parsing out a comma-delimited string and returning the desired scalar value.

■**Caution** The examples in this chapter are written in order to introduce the core concepts and functionality of CLR integration with SQL Server 2005. Although this function works properly when the appropriate values are passed to the function, it does not contain error trapping code to handle unexpected values. Using SAFE and EXTERNAL_ACCESS pads you from damage, although bad input values may cause rather unfriendly error messages returned to the end user. In your production .NET code, be sure to add error handling.

Creating a CLR Trigger

In this next recipe, I'll demonstrate creating a CLR trigger, which is used to generate an external "control file" that can in turn be used to notify an outside hypothetical application that a process is finished.

In this example scenario, I have a table called dbo.DataWarehouseLoadHistory. This table contains a row inserted whenever the daily data warehouse load finishes. When a row is inserted, the trigger will output a control file to an external directory, notifying the legacy system (and I'm assuming this is a system that cannot access SQL Server 2005 programmatically).

First, the new table is created in a user-defined database:

```
CREATE TABLE dbo.DataWarehouseLoadHistory
(DataWarehouseLoadHistoryID int
    NOT NULL IDENTITY(1,1) PRIMARY KEY ,
LoadDT datetime NOT NULL)
```

Next, the following assembly code is compiled using vbc.exe:

```
Imports System
Imports System.Data
Imports System.Data.Sql
Imports System.Data.SqlTypes
Imports System.Data.SqlClient
Imports Microsoft.SqlServer.Server
Imports System.IO


Public Class DW_Trigger

  Public Shared Sub ExportFile()

    Dim DWTrigger As SqlTriggerContext
    DWTrigger = SqlContext.TriggerContext
```

```
    If (DWTrigger.TriggerAction = _
     TriggerAction.Insert) Then

    Dim DWsw As StreamWriter = New _
     StreamWriter("C:\DataWarehouseLoadTrigger.txt")

    DWsw.WriteLine(Now())
    DWsw.Close()

    End If

  End Sub

End Class
```

After compiling the assembly into a DLL, it is then imported into SQL Server using CREATE ASSEMBLY:

```
CREATE ASSEMBLY DataWarehouseLoadNotification
FROM 'C:\Apress\Recipes\CLR\Trigger\
➥ DataWarehouseLoadNotification.dll'
WITH PERMISSION_SET = EXTERNAL_ACCESS
GO
```

Next, a trigger is created that is mapped to the assembly subroutine:

```
CREATE TRIGGER dbo.trg_i_DWNotify
ON dbo.DataWarehouseLoadHistory  AFTER INSERT
AS
EXTERNAL NAME
DataWarehouseLoadNotification.[DataWarehouseLoadNotification.DW_Trigger].ExportFile
```

A new row is then inserted into the DataWarehouseLoadHistory table:

```
INSERT dbo.DataWarehouseLoadHistory
(LoadDT)
VALUES(GETDATE())
```

This INSERT causes the CLR trigger to fire and then create a notification file under the C:\ drive of the SQL Server instance machine (of course in a production scenario, I'd be putting this file some place else for the legacy system to pick up). The file contains the current date and time that the trigger was fired:

9/5/2005 1:29:03 PM

How It Works

This recipe demonstrated creating a CLR trigger that created a text file in response to an INSERT into a table. Of course, this CLR database object would *not* have been a good idea to create for a table that receives numerous new rows each day (continually overlaying a file non-stop)! But in this scenario, I'm assuming that the data is only updated periodically, and that the external legacy application is monitoring any changes in the file.

The steps to creating this CLR trigger were similar to creating a user-defined function and stored procedure: a new assembly was compiled, added to SQL Server, and then associated to a database object using CREATE TRIGGER.

Something to point out, however, is the SqlTriggerContext class, which was used to define the context information for the trigger within SQL Server:

```
Dim DWTrigger As SqlTriggerContext
DWTrigger = SqlContext.TriggerContext
```

Once the object was created, it was then used to find out the actions that cause the trigger to fire or determine which columns were modified. In this example, the SqlTriggerContext object was used to determine if the trigger firing event was an INSERT, and if so, the external file would be written:

```
If (DWTrigger.TriggerAction = _
   TriggerAction.Insert) Then
...
```

Administering Assemblies

The next three recipes will demonstrate how to administer database assemblies. I'll demonstrate how to view assembly metadata, modify an assembly's permissions, and remove an assembly from the database.

Viewing Assembly Metadata

To view all assemblies in the current database, you can query the sys.assemblies system catalog view. For example:

```
SELECT name, permission_set_desc
FROM sys.assemblies
```

This returns:

name	permission_set_desc
ReadFiles	EXTERNAL_ACCESS

How It Works

The system catalog view sys.assemblies can be used to view the name of the assemblies and the security profile assigned to it.

Modifying an Assembly's Permissions

You can use the ALTER ASSEMBLY command (which uses many of the same options as CREATE ASSEMBLY) to modify specific configurations of an existing assembly permissions.

In this example, the permissions of an assembly are set from EXTERNAL_ACCESS to SAFE:

```
ALTER ASSEMBLY ReadFiles
WITH PERMISSION_SET = SAFE
```

After executing this command, an attempt is made to execute the stored procedure associated to this assembly:

```
EXEC dbo.usp_FileReader
N'C:\Program Files\Microsoft SQL Server\MSSQL.1\MSSQL\LOG\ERRORLOG'
```

This returns the following (abridged) error:

```
Msg 6522, Level 16, State 1, Procedure usp_FileReader, Line 0
A .NET Framework error occurred during execution of user defined routine or aggregate
'usp_FileReader':
System.Security.SecurityException: Request for the permission of type
'System.Security.Permissions.FileIOPermission, mscorlib, Version=2.0.0.0,
Culture=neutral, PublicKeyToken=b77a5c561934e089' failed.
```

How It Works

Although SQL Server 2005 allowed us to change the permission level of the assembly, external oper-ations (reading from a file) attempted by the assembly were no longer allowed. This means that when you write your assembly, you must think about what level of permissions it will need, and then set it upon creation. If you think it is SAFE, but it actually needs access to external resources, you can use ALTER ASSEMBLY to change the permissions.

Removing an Assembly from the Database

To remove an assembly from the database, use the DROP ASSEMBLY command. The abridged syntax is as follows:

```
DROP ASSEMBLY assembly_name [ ,...n ]
```

The first argument is the name or comma delimited list of assembly names to be dropped from the database. For example:

```
DROP ASSEMBLY ReadFiles
```

How It Works

This example demonstrated dropping an assembly. Any existing CLR object references (stored procedure, for example) must be dropped prior to removing the assembly from the database. If you don't drop referencing objects first, you'll see an error message like:

```
Msg 6590, Level 16, State 1, Line 1
DROP ASSEMBLY failed because 'ReadFiles' is referenced by object 'usp_FileReader'.
```

CHAPTER 14

■■■

XML

In this chapter, I'll present recipes discussing and demonstrating the various integration points between XML and SQL Server 2005. Before taking a look at what's new (and there's quite a bit that is), we should take a quick look back at the XML integration that existed in SQL Server 2000.

SQL Server 2000 included two built-in XML commands:

- OPENXML, which allowed you to use Transact-SQL extensions and system-stored procedures to load an XML document into the SQL Server memory space. The source XML document was stored in a char, nchar, varchar, nvarchar, text, or ntext data type column. Once the document was in memory, a relational rowset view could be made of the XML document.

- FOR XML, which allowed you to use Transact-SQL to output relational data into an XML hierarchical format.

Shortly after SQL Server 2000 was released, Microsoft also began offering free downloads of *SQLXML (XML for SQL Server)*, which further extended interoperability between XML and SQL Server 2000. Some of the SQLXML 3.0 features included a high-speed, bulk-load utility used to import XML data into SQL Server- and SQLXML-managed classes which consisted of .NET objects that allowed programmers to use XML technologies in order to query SQL Server. SQLXML also included Internet Information Services (IIS) integration, allowing for queries against SQL Server using predefined query templates, and direct URL SQL queries, which return XML data back to the client. SQLXML also included *Updategrams* and *Diffgrams*. Updategrams allowed you to modify data in SQL Server by using special XML tags in an XML message. Diffgrams were similar to Updategrams, but could be generated automatically from an ADO.NET Dataset object.

Another free download that could be used either independently or in conjunction with SQL Server 2000 was *Microsoft XML Core Services (MSXML)*, which included an XML parser and an array of other XML technologies.

Microsoft wanted to make XML more integrated with SQL Server 2000; however the only way to do this post-ship date was to offer free add-on downloads. Also, XML data was not actually stored in its native form in SQL Server 2000.

In SQL Server 2005, XML integration has taken a front seat, with several new features now built-in. This chapter will cover these new features, including:

- Storing XML in SQL Server 2005 using the new xml data type.

- Applying constraints to the stored XML documents by using the new XML Schema Collection database object.

- Modifying and retrieving data from the xml data type using XQuery and Microsoft-based Transact-SQL extensions.

- Improving query performance against the xml data type data by creating XML indexes.

- Covering OPENXML and FOR XML, which are still in use (with enhancements in SQL Server 2005).

Before diving into the specific enhancements and additions, in the next section I'll give a brief overview of XML and its related technologies (and there are many).

■**Note** The web service integration included in SQLXML can now be handled using SQL Server-hosted HTTP endpoints, which are reviewed in Chapter 15.

XML and Related Technologies

XML stands for Extensible Markup Language and is used to create self-describing documents. XML documents are transferred across the Internet, rendered via web pages, stored in files, and converted to various file types. XML has been a widely adopted interface standard because of its easy-to-understand, straightforward, text-based format. Because XML is easy to read, it is also easy to build programs around it for use in exchanging or storing data. The format is flexible, allowing you to separate the data from the presentation, as well as keep the data format platform-independent. For example, in HTML, you'll see tags that describe the page presentation intermingled with the data itself. In XML, tags describe the data, and not the presentation of that data to a web browser.

XML, similar to HTML, makes use of tags. Unlike HTML, however, you define your own tags, which are then used to describe the data instead of using pre-defined tags. Tags in HTML embed formatting, whereas XML tags describe the data itself. For example, in HTML, the following block means that the string Welcome is presented in bold characters:

```
<b>Welcome</b>
```

In XML, the tag <b> doesn't have a predefined meaning.

You'll also hear XML tags referred to as *elements* (which is the term I'll be using for the rest of the chapter). Data is contained within elements and these elements assist with describing the data held within. For example, the following open and close elements are used to self-describe the data in between them:

```
<FirstName>David</FirstName>
```

In XML documents, you'll also see the use of *attributes*. Attributes are normally used to further describe elements, or provide additional information about elements. There are no fixed rules on when to use attributes and elements for communicating information, but if an item needs to occur multiple times, it *must* be an element, because each attribute can only occur once for a single element.

Also, it is important to note that XML is *not* a programming language (and neither is HTML for that matter). XML is a data format that presents data in a hierarchy, and not in a relational format. To show how these two approaches are different, let's look at an example. The following query returns the result set in a relational format:

```
SELECT BookNM, ChapterNBR, ChapterNM
FROM dbo.RecipeChapter
```

The results of this query are:

```
BookNM                         ChapterNBR  ChapterNM
----------------------------   ----------  ----------------------------
SQL Server 2005 T-SQL Recipes  5           Indexes
SQL Server 2005 T-SQL Recipes  6           Full-text search
SQL Server 2005 T-SQL Recipes  7           Views
SQL Server 2005 T-SQL Recipes  8           SQL Server Functions
SQL Server 2005 T-SQL Recipes  9           Conditional processing...
```

Contrast this with the same results presented in a hierarchical XML document:

```
<Book name="SQL Server 2005 T-SQL Recipes">
 <Chapters>
   <Chapter chnbr="5" chname="Indexes"/>
   <Chapter chnbr="6" chname="Full-text search"/>
   <Chapter chnbr="7" chname="Views"/>
   <Chapter chnbr="8" chname="SQL Server Functions"/>
   <Chapter chnbr="9" chname="Conditional processing..."/>
 </Chapters>
</Book>
```

This XML fragment is presented as a hierarchy. At the top of the hierarchy is the `<Book>` element, which contains an attribute called `name`, which in turn describes the name of a specific book ("SQL Server 2005 T-SQL Recipes"). Nesting just one level in is the `<Chapters>` element. In the inner-most level of the hierarchy are the individual `<Chapter>` elements, each with self-describing attributes.

Tip I've only briefly covered a couple of the components that make up an XML document. There are other syntax rules that are required in order to make an XML document "well formed." One of the best, free, online tutorials on the subject can be found at the W3 Schools website, http://www.w3schools.com/xml/default.asp.

There are *numerous* technologies associated with XML, producing a plethora of "X" prefixed acronyms. A detailed review of each of these technologies is outside the scope of this book; however there are a few you should be aware of that are applicable to features reviewed in this chapter:

- *XML Schema Definition Language*. XML Schema Definition Language is written in XML and is used to describe the valid format of a particular XML document. SQL Server 2005 introduces the use of XML Schema Collections, which can be used to similarly constrain data stored in native `xml` data type columns.

- *XML Path Language (XPath)*. XPath is used to locate specific content and elements within an XML document. XPath is the precursor to XQuery, which is not integrated into SQL Server 2005.

- *XML Query Language (XQUERY)*: XML Query Language (XQuery) is based on XPath, and like XPath, is also used to query XML data. SQL Server 2005 integrates a subset of this language in order to allow querying of the native `xml` data type. This will be demonstrated later in the chapter.

The next section discusses and demonstrates how to use the new SQL Server `xml` native data type.

Working with Native XML

In SQL Server 2000, if you wanted to store XML data within the database, you had to store it in a character or binary format. This wasn't too troublesome if you just used SQL Server for XML document storage, but attempts to query or modify the stored document within SQL Server were not so straightforward. The new SQL Server 2005 native xml data type helps address this issue.

Relational database designers may be concerned about this new data type, and rightly so. The normalized database provides performance and data integrity benefits that put into question why we would need to store XML documents in the first place. Having an xml data type allows you to have your relational data stored alongside your hierarchical data. Microsoft isn't suggesting that you run your high-speed applications based on XML documents. Rather, you may find XML document storage is useful when data must be "somewhat" structured. For example, let's say your company's website offers an online contract. This contract is available over the web for your customer to fill out, and then submit. The submitted data is stored in an xml data type. You might choose this because your legal department changes the entries on the contract frequently, adding new fields and removing others. These contracts are only filled out a few times a day, so performance and throughput isn't an issue.

Another good reason to use native xml data type is for "state" storage. For example, if your .NET applications use XML configuration files, you can store them in a SQL Server 2005 database in order to maintain a history of changes, and as a backup/recovery option.

These next few recipes will demonstrate xml data type columns in action.

Creating XML Data Type Columns

Native xml data types can be used as a data type for columns in a table, local variables, or parameters. Data stored in the xml data type can contain an XML document or XML fragments. An XML fragment is an XML instance without a single top-level element for the contents to nest in. Creating an XML data type column is as easy as just using it in the table definition. For example, the ChapterDESC column uses an XML data type in the following table:

```
CREATE TABLE dbo.Book
(BookID int IDENTITY(1,1) PRIMARY KEY,
 ISBNNBR char(10) NOT NULL,
 BookNM varchar(250) NOT NULL,
 AuthorID int NOT NULL,
 ChapterDESC XML NULL)
```

In this second example, a local variable called @Book is given an XML data type and is set to an XML value (in the next recipe I'll demonstrate how that value can be used):

```
DECLARE @Book XML

SET @Book =
CAST('<Book name="SQL Server 2000 Fast Answers">
<Chapters>
<Chapter id="1"> Installation, Upgrades... </Chapter>
<Chapter id="2"> Configuring SQL Server </Chapter>
<Chapter id="3"> Creating and Configuring Databases </Chapter>
<Chapter id="4"> SQL Server Agent and SQL Logs </Chapter>
</Chapters>
</Book>' as XML)
```

In the third example, an xml data type input parameter is used for a stored procedure:

```
CREATE PROCEDURE dbo.usp_INS_Book
    @ISBNNBR char(10),
    @BookNM varchar(250),
    @AuthorID int,
    @ChapterDESC xml
AS

INSERT dbo.Book
(ISBNNBR, BookNM, AuthorID, ChapterDESC)
VALUES (@ISBNNBR, @BookNM, @AuthorID, @ChapterDESC)

GO
```

How It Works

This recipe demonstrated how to use the xml data type in the column definition of a table, a local variable, and the input parameter for a stored procedure. The syntax is not different from what you'd use with other SQL Server 2005 data types. The next recipe demonstrates how to INSERT XML data into a table using Transact-SQL.

Inserting XML Data into a Column

In this recipe, I'll demonstrate inserting an XML document into the table created in the previous recipe. The INSERT command is used, and the XML document is embedded in single quotes (as a string would be), but is also CAST explicitly into the xml data type:

```
INSERT dbo.Book
(ISBNNBR, BookNM, AuthorID, ChapterDESC)
VALUES ('570X000000',
       'SQL Server 2005 T-SQL Recipes',
       55,
CAST('<Book name="SQL Server 2005 T-SQL Recipes">
<Chapters>
<Chapter id="1"> SELECT </Chapter>
<Chapter id="2"> INSERT,UPDATE,DELETE </Chapter>
<Chapter id="3"> Transactions, Locking, Blocking, and Deadlocking </Chapter>
<Chapter id="4"> Tables </Chapter>
<Chapter id="5"> Indexes </Chapter>
<Chapter id="6"> Full-text search </Chapter>
</Chapters>
</Book>' as XML))
```

In this second example, a local variable called @Book is given an xml data type and is set to an XML value. That value is then used in a table INSERT:

```
DECLARE @Book XML

SET @Book =
CAST('<Book name="SQL Server 2000 Fast Answers">
<Chapters>
<Chapter id="1"> Installation, Upgrades... </Chapter>
<Chapter id="2"> Configuring SQL Server </Chapter>
<Chapter id="3"> Creating and Configuring Databases </Chapter>
<Chapter id="4"> SQL Server Agent and SQL Logs </Chapter>
</Chapters>
</Book>' as XML)
```

```
INSERT dbo.Book
(ISBNNBR, BookNM, AuthorID, ChapterDESC)
VALUES ('1590591615',
        'SQL Server 2000 Fast Answers',
        55,
        @Book)
```

How It Works

In both the INSERT examples, the XML data for the ChapterDESC column was converted explicitly to xml using the CAST function and was checked by SQL Server to ensure that it was "well formed" (well formed, in this case, means that it follows the general rules of an XML document). For example, if the document fragment had been missing the closing </Book> element, the following error would have been raised:

```
Msg 9400, Level 16, State 1, Line 1
XML parsing: line 9, character 12, unexpected end of input
```

The XML column defined in the example, however, was *untyped*. When an XML column is untyped, it means that the contents inserted into the column are not validated against an XML schema. An XML schema is used to define the allowed elements and attributes for an XML document, and is discussed in the next recipe.

Validating XML Data Using Schemas

As I mentioned at the beginning of the chapter, an XML Schema (also referred to as XML Schema Definition, or XSD) defines the elements, attributes, data types, and allowed values for an XML document. Using CREATE XML SCHEMA COLLECTION, you can add XML Schema definitions to SQL Server 2005 and use them in constraining XML data type columns, local variables, or parameters.

■**Tip** For a review of XML Schema fundamentals, visit the World Wide Web Consortium W3C standards site at http://www.w3.org/TR/XMLschema-0/.

The CREATE XML SCHEMA COLLECTION command is used to add new XML schemas, and uses the following syntax:

```
CREATE XML SCHEMA COLLECTION [ <relational_schema>. ]sql_identifier
AS Expression
```

The command takes two arguments, the first being the unique name of the new XML Schema, while the second is the body of the XML Schema or Schemas.

To add additional XML Schemas to an existing collection, you can use the ALTER XML SCHEMA COLLECTION. The syntax is as follows:

```
ALTER XML SCHEMA COLLECTION [ relational_schema. ]sql_identifier
ADD 'Schema Component'
```

To remove the entire XML Schema collection from the database, use the DROP XML SCHEMA command. The syntax is as follows:

```
DROP XML SCHEMA COLLECTION [ relational_schema. ]sql_identifier
```

The only argument for dropping an existing XML Schema collection is the name of the collection.

In this example, a new XML Schema collection is created called BookStoreCollection, which contains a single XML Schema defined within:

```
CREATE XML SCHEMA COLLECTION BookStoreCollection
AS
N'<xsd:schema targetNamespace="http://JOEPROD/BookStore"
xmlns:xsd="http://www.w3.org/2001/XMLSchema"
xmlns:sqltypes="http://schemas.microsoft.com/sqlserver
/2004/sqltypes" elementFormDefault="qualified">
<xsd:import namespace=
"http://schemas.microsoft.com/sqlserver/2004/sqltypes" />
<xsd:element name="Book">
    <xsd:complexType>
      <xsd:sequence>
        <xsd:element name="BookName" minOccurs="0">
          <xsd:simpleType>
            <xsd:restriction base="sqltypes:varchar">
              <xsd:maxLength value="50" />
            </xsd:restriction>
          </xsd:simpleType>
        </xsd:element>
<xsd:element name="ChapterID" type="sqltypes:int"
minOccurs="0" />
        <xsd:element name="ChapterNM" minOccurs="0">
          <xsd:simpleType>
            <xsd:restriction base="sqltypes:varchar">
              <xsd:maxLength value="50" />
            </xsd:restriction>
          </xsd:simpleType>
        </xsd:element>
      </xsd:sequence>
    </xsd:complexType>
  </xsd:element>
</xsd:schema>'
```

Once created, you can verify an XML Schema's existence using the system catalog views sys.XML_schema_collections and sys.XML_schema_namespaces. This first query shows all schema collections defined in the database:

```
SELECT name
FROM sys.XML_schema_collections
ORDER BY create_date
```

This second query shows namespaces found in a specific XML Schema collection (namespaces uniquely identify the scope of elements and attributes, helping uniquely identify these components):

```
SELECT n.name
FROM sys.XML_schema_namespaces n
INNER JOIN sys.XML_schema_collections  c ON
   c.XML_collection_id = n.XML_collection_id
WHERE c.name = 'BookStoreCollection'
```

This returns:

```
name
-----------------------------
http://JOEPROD.com/BookStore
```

Once a schema collection is available, you can bind it to an XML column in a table by referencing it in parentheses after the data type definition. For example, the ChapterDESC column is bound to the BookStoreCollection XML Schema collection:

```
CREATE TABLE dbo.BookInfoExport
(BookID int IDENTITY(1,1) PRIMARY KEY,
 ISBNNBR char(10) NOT NULL,
 BookNM varchar(250) NOT NULL,
 AuthorID int NOT NULL,
 ChapterDESC XML (BookStoreCollection) NULL)
```

This XML column will now only allow typed xml values (XML documents that conform to the defined XML Schema collection). Attempting to assign XML values that do not conform with the XSD specified for the column will raise an error (for example if expected elements or attributes are missing). Using the keyword DOCUMENT or CONTENT with the schema collection reference lets you determine whether the allowed XML will allow only a full XML document (DOCUMENT) or XML fragments (CONTENT) instead.

For example, the following local variable requires a full XML document that conforms to the XML Schema collection:

```
DECLARE @Book XML (DOCUMENT BookStoreCollection)
```

How It Works

This recipe provided a quick tour through the XML Schema functionality built into SQL Server 2005. Using an XML Schema collection, you can validate and constrain the content of XML data within the xml data type. Untyped XML data will still be validated for general XML structure, but by using XML Schema collections you can apply more sophisticated validation and constraints.

Retrieving XML Data

The xml data type column can be queried using XQuery methods. XQuery is a query language that is used to search XML documents. These XQuery methods described in Table 14-1 are integrated into SQL Server 2005 and can be used in regular Transact-SQL queries.

Table 14-1. *XQuery Methods*

Method	Description
exist	Returns "1" for an XQuery expression when it evaluates to TRUE, otherwise it returns "0" for FALSE.
nodes	Shreds XML data to relational data, identifying nodes-to-row mapping.
query	Returns XML results based on an XQuery expression.
value	Returns a scalar SQL data type value based on an XQuery expression.

■**Tip** For an in depth review of XQuery fundamentals, visit the World Wide Web Consortium W3C standards site at http://www.w3.org/TR/xquery/.

To demonstrate each of these methods, a new table is created with an XML data type column and three rows are inserted:

```
CREATE TABLE dbo.BookInvoice
(BookInvoiceID int IDENTITY(1,1) PRIMARY KEY,
 BookInvoiceXML XML NOT NULL)
GO

INSERT dbo.BookInvoice
(BookInvoiceXML)
VALUES ('<BookInvoice invoicenumber="1" customerid="22" orderdate="7/1/2005">
<OrderItems>
<Item id="22" qty="1" name="SQL Fun in the Sun"/>
<Item id="24" qty="1" name="T-SQL Crossword Puzzles"/>
</OrderItems>
</BookInvoice>')

INSERT dbo.BookInvoice
(BookInvoiceXML)
VALUES ('<BookInvoice invoicenumber="1" customerid="40" orderdate="7/11/2005">
<OrderItems>
<Item id="11" qty="1" name="MCDBA Cliff Notes"/>
</OrderItems>
</BookInvoice>')

INSERT dbo.BookInvoice
(BookInvoiceXML)
VALUES ('<BookInvoice invoicenumber="1" customerid="9" orderdate="7/22/2005">
<OrderItems>
<Item id="11" qty="1" name="MCDBA Cliff Notes"/>
<Item id="24" qty="1" name="T-SQL Crossword Puzzles"/>
</OrderItems>
</BookInvoice>')
```

In the first example, the exists method is used to find all rows from the table for purchases of the item with an ID of "11":

```
SELECT BookInvoiceID
FROM dbo.BookInvoice
WHERE BookInvoiceXML.exist
('/BookInvoice/OrderItems/Item[@id=11]') = 1
```

This returns:

```
BookInvoiceID
2
3
```

This next example demonstrates the nodes method, which shreds a document into a relational rowset. A local variable is used to populate a single XML document from the BookInvoice table, which is then referenced using the nodes method:

```
DECLARE @BookInvoiceXML XML

SELECT @BookInvoiceXML = BookInvoiceXML
FROM dbo.BookInvoice
WHERE BookInvoiceID = 2

SELECT BookID.value('@id','integer') BookID
FROM  @BookInvoiceXML.nodes('/BookInvoice/OrderItems/Item')
AS BookTable(BookID)
```

The last query returns the item ID values in the virtual BookTable table:

```
BookID
-----------
11
```

The next example demonstrates the query method, which is used to return the two item elements for a specific XML document:

DECLARE @BookInvoiceXML XML

```
SELECT @BookInvoiceXML = BookInvoiceXML
FROM dbo.BookInvoice
WHERE BookInvoiceID = 2

SELECT @BookInvoiceXML.query('/BookInvoice/OrderItems/Item')
```

This returns:

```
<Item id="11" qty="1" name="MCDBA Cliff Notes" />
```

The last example of this recipe demonstrates the value method, which is used to find the distinct book names from the first and second items within the BookInvoiceXML XML column:

```
SELECT DISTINCT
BookInvoiceXML.value
('(/BookInvoice/OrderItems/Item/@name)[1]', 'varchar(30)') as BookTitles
FROM dbo.BookInvoice
UNION
SELECT DISTINCT
BookInvoiceXML.value
('(/BookInvoice/OrderItems/Item/@name)[2]', 'varchar(30)')
FROM dbo.BookInvoice
```

Two result sets were combined together using UNION, as two levels of the /BookInvoice/OrderItems/Item node were explored in two separate queries (the NULL value is from the stored XML fragment that only had a single item):

```
BookTitles
NULL
MCDBA Cliff Notes
SQL Fun in the Sun
T-SQL Crossword Puzzles
```

How It Works

XQuery methods enable you to query and modify data within an XML data type. Most of the examples in this recipe used a similar format of `XMLColumn.MethodName`.

For example the `exist` method was used on the `BookInvoiceXML` XML column to show items with an ID of 11. The XQuery expression followed the method name in parentheses:

```
BookInvoiceXML.exist ('/BookInvoice/OrderItems/Item[@id=11]') = 1
```

The `query` method used a simple XQuery expression in order to return item elements in the results:

```
@BookInvoiceXML.query('/BookInvoice/OrderItems/Item')
```

The `value` method included the XQuery expression that returns a scalar value for each row, defined by the data type in the second parameter:

```
BookInvoiceXML.value
('(/BookInvoice/OrderItems/Item/@name)[2]', 'varchar(30)')
```

The `nodes` function example included an XQuery expression to define the results to return in a shredded format, followed by the name of the new result table and column name in parentheses:

```
@BookInvoiceXML.nodes('/BookInvoice/OrderItems/Item')
AS BookTable(BookID)
```

Modifying XML Data

The `xml` data type column can be modified using the new `modify` method in conjunction with `UPDATE`, allowing you to insert, update, or delete an XML node in the `xml` data type column.

This example demonstrates the `modify` method by inserting a new item into an existing XML document (specifically, a new item into the `/BookInvoice/OrderItems` node):

```
UPDATE dbo.BookInvoice
SET BookInvoiceXML.modify
('insert <Item id="920" qty="1" name="SQL Server 2005 T-SQL Recipes"/>
into (/BookInvoice/OrderItems)[1]')
WHERE BookInvoiceID = 2
```

Checking the `BookInvoice` XML document for this row confirms that the new item was added:

```
<BookInvoice invoicenumber="1" customerid="40" orderdate="7/11/2005">
  <OrderItems>
    <Item id="11" qty="1" name="MCDBA Cliff Notes" />
    <Item id="920" qty="1" name="SQL Server 2005 T-SQL Recipes" />
  </OrderItems>
</BookInvoice>
```

How It Works

The `modify` function also used the `XMLColumn.MethodName` format, and used an XQuery insert expression in parentheses to insert a new item element into an existing document:

```
BookInvoice.modify
('insert <Item id="920" qty="1" name="SQL Server 2005 T-SQL Recipes"/>
into (/BookInvoice/OrderItems)[1]')
```

The insert command is used to add a new item element is an extension to the XQuery language and is called *XML DML*. Other XML DML commands include the replace statement, used to update XML data, and the delete statement, used to remove a node from an XML document or fragment.

Using XML Indexes

You can improve performance of queries against XML data type columns by using XML indexes. To create an XML index, the table must first already have a clustered index defined on the primary key of the table.

XML columns can only have *one* primary XML index defined, and then up to *three* secondary indexes (of different types described below). The CREATE INDEX command is used to define XML indexes. The syntax is as follows:

```
CREATE [ PRIMARY ] XML INDEX index_name
  ON <object> ( XML_column_name )
[ USING XML INDEX XML_index_name
[ FOR { VALUE | PATH | PROPERTY } ]
[ WITH ( PAD_INDEX = { ON | OFF }
| FILLFACTOR = fillfactor
| SORT_IN_TEMPDB = { ON | OFF }
| STATISTICS_NORECOMPUTE = { ON | OFF }
| DROP_EXISTING = { ON | OFF }
| ALLOW_ROW_LOCKS = { ON | OFF }
| ALLOW_PAGE_LOCKS = { ON | OFF }
| MAXDOP = max_degree_of_parallelism
) ]
```

Creating an index for an XML column uses several of the same arguments as a regular table index (see Chapter 5 for more information). The XML-specific arguments of this command are described in Table 14-2.

Table 14-2. *CREATE XML INDEX Arguments*

Argument	Description
object	The name of the table the index is being added to.
XML_column_name	The name of the XML data type column.
XML_index_name	The unique name of the XML index.
VALUE | PATH | PROPERTY	These are arguments for secondary indexes only and relate to XQuery optimization. A VALUE secondary index is used for indexing based on imprecise paths. A PATH secondary index is used for indexing via a path and value. A PROPERTY secondary index is used for indexing based on a querying node values based on a path.

In this first example, a primary XML index is created on an XML data type column:

```
CREATE PRIMARY XML INDEX idx_XML_Primary_Book_ChapterDESC
    ON dbo.Book(ChapterDESC)
GO
```

Next, a secondary VALUE index is created on the same xml column, but with a different name. The USING clause is added for secondary indexes, specifying in the FOR clause that the xml data type column be given a VALUE index in addition to the existing primary index:

```
CREATE XML INDEX idx_XML_Value_Book_ChapterDESC
    ON dbo.Book(ChapterDESC)
```

```
      USING XML INDEX idx_XML_Primary_Book_ChapterDESC
FOR VALUE
GO
```

You can use the sys.XML_indexes system catalog view to view the XML indexes used in a database. In this query, all XML indexes are listed for a specific table:

```
SELECT   name, secondary_type_desc
FROM     sys.XML_indexes
WHERE object_id = OBJECT_ID('dbo.Book')
```

This query returns the name of the XML indexes, and if the index is a secondary index, the type:

name	secondary_type_desc
idx_XML_Primary_Book_Chap	NULL
idx_XML_Value_Book_Chapte	VALUE

Once created, XML indexes can be modified or removed just like regular indexes using the ALTER INDEX and DROP INDEX commands.

How It Works

Because XML documents can store up to 2GB for a single column and row, query performance can suffer when you are trying to query the data stored in the XML column. Make use of XML indexes if you plan on frequently querying XML data type data. Indexing xml data types internally persists the tabular form of the XML data, allowing for more efficient querying of hierarchical data.

XML indexes may look a little odd at first because you are adding secondary indexes to the same xml data type column. Adding the different types of secondary indexes helps benefit performance, based on the different types of XQuery queries you plan to execute. All in all you can have up to four indexes on a single xml data type column: one primary and three secondary. A primary XML index must be created prior to being able to create secondary indexes. A secondary PATH index is used to enhance performance for queries that specify a path and value from the xml column using XQuery. A secondary PROPERTY index is used to enhance performance of queries that retrieve specific node values by specifying a path using XQuery. The secondary VALUE index is used to enhance performance of queries that retrieve data using an imprecise path.

Converting Between XML Documents and Relational Data

In the next recipe, I'll demonstrate how to convert relational data sets into a hierarchical XML format using FOR XML. After that, in the final recipe of the chapter I'll demonstrate how to use OPENXML to convert an XML format into a relational data set.

Using FOR XML

Introduced in SQL Server 2000, FOR XML extends a SELECT statement by returning the relational query results in an XML format. FOR XML operates in four different modes: RAW, AUTO, EXPLICIT, and PATH.

In RAW mode, a single row element is generated for each row in the result set, with each column in the result converted to an attribute within the element.

The syntax for using RAW mode is as follows:

```
FOR XML { RAW [ ('ElementName') ] }
[ [ , BINARY BASE64 ] [ , TYPE ]
[ , ROOT [ ('RootName') ] ]
[ , { XMLDATA | XMLSCHEMA
[ ('TargetNameSpaceURI') ]} ]
[ , ELEMENTS [ XSINIL | ABSENT ]    ]
```

The arguments of this command are described in Table 14-3.

Table 14-3. *FOR XML Arguments*

Argument	Description
('ElementName')	Using ElementName, you can either explicitly define the element name instead of using the generic "row" name.
BINARY BASE64	When this option is selected, binary data is returned using Base64-encoded format.
TYPE	When TYPE is designated, the query returns results in the XML data type.
ROOT [('RootName')]	Specifies the top-level element for the XML results.
XMLDATA	When XMLDATA is used, XML-Data Reduced (XDR) schema is returned.
XMLSCHEMA [('TargetNameSpaceURI')]	When XMLSCHEMA is used, XSD in-line schema is returned with the data results. You can also designate an optional target namespace URI (Uniform Resource Identifier).
ELEMENTS	When ELEMENTS is used, columns are returned as sub-elements.
XSINIL	In conjunction with ELEMENTS, empty elements are returned for NULL values.
ABSENT	Specifies that in conjunction with ELEMENTS, elements are not created for NULL values (this behavior is the default).

In this example, FOR XML RAW is used to return the results of the HumanResources.Shift table in an XML format. The TYPE option is used to return the results in the XML data type, and ROOT is used to define a top-level element where the results will be nested:

```
SELECT ShiftID, Name
FROM HumanResources.Shift
FOR XML RAW('Shift'), ROOT('Shifts'), TYPE
```

This returns:

```
<Shifts>
   <Shift ShiftID="1" Name="Day" />
   <Shift ShiftID="2" Name="Evening" />
   <Shift ShiftID="3" Name="Night" />
</Shifts>
```

The FOR XML AUTO mode creates XML elements in the results of a SELECT statement, and also automatically nests the data, based on the columns in the SELECT clause. AUTO shares the same options as RAW.

In this example, Employee, Shift, and Department information is queried from AdventureWorks— with XML AUTO automatically arranging the hierarchy of the results:

```
SELECT  TOP 3  EmployeeID,
        Shift.Name,
        Department.Name
FROM    HumanResources.EmployeeDepartmentHistory Employee
INNER JOIN HumanResources.Shift Shift ON
    Employee.ShiftID = Shift.ShiftID
INNER JOIN HumanResources.Department Department ON
    Employee.DepartmentID = Department.DepartmentID
ORDER BY EmployeeID
FOR XML AUTO, TYPE
```

This returns:

```
<Employee EmployeeID="1">
   <Shift Name="Day">
      <Department Name="Production" />
   </Shift>
</Employee>
<Employee EmployeeID="2">
   <Shift Name="Day">
      <Department Name="Marketing" />
   </Shift>
</Employee>
<Employee EmployeeID="3">
   <Shift Name="Day">
      <Department Name="Engineering" />
   </Shift>
</Employee>
```

Notice that the third INNER JOIN caused the values from the Department table to be children of the Shift table's values. The Shift element was then included as a child of the Employee element. Rearranging the order of the columns in the SELECT clause, however, impacts how the hierarchy is returned. For example:

```
SELECT  TOP 3
        Shift.Name,
        Department.Name,
        EmployeeID
FROM    HumanResources.EmployeeDepartmentHistory Employee
INNER JOIN HumanResources.Shift Shift ON
    Employee.ShiftID = Shift.ShiftID
```

```
INNER JOIN HumanResources.Department Department ON
    Employee.DepartmentID = Department.DepartmentID
ORDER BY Shift.Name, Department.Name, EmployeeID
FOR XML AUTO, TYPE
```

This time the top of the hierarchy is the Shift, with the child element of Department, and Employees children of the Department elements:

```
<Shift Name="Day">
   <Department Name="Document Control">
      <Employee EmployeeID="90" />
      <Employee EmployeeID="127" />
      <Employee EmployeeID="161" />
   </Department>
</Shift>
```

The FOR XML EXPLICIT mode allows you more control over the XML results, letting you define whether columns are assigned to elements or attributes. The syntax for this is as follows:

```
EXPLICIT
[ , BINARY BASE64 ]  [ , TYPE ] [ , ROOT [ ('RootName') ]
 [ , XMLDATA ]     ]
```

The EXPLICIT parameters have the same use and meaning as for RAW and AUTO, however EXPLICIT also makes use of *directives* which are used to define the resulting elements and attributes. For example, the following query displays the VendorID and CreditRating columns as attributes, and the VendorName column as an element. The column is defined after the column alias using an element name, tag number, attribute, and directive:

```
SELECT TOP 3
   1 AS Tag,
   NULL AS Parent,
   VendorID AS [Vendor!1!VendorID],
   Name AS [Vendor!1!VendorName!ELEMENT],
   CreditRating AS [Vendor!1!CreditRating]
FROM Purchasing.Vendor
ORDER BY CreditRating
FOR XML EXPLICIT, TYPE
```

This returns:

```
<Vendor VendorID="4" CreditRating="1">
   <VendorName>Comfort Road Bicycles</VendorName>
</Vendor>
<Vendor VendorID="3" CreditRating="1">
   <VendorName>Premier Sport, Inc.</VendorName>
</Vendor>
<Vendor VendorID="2" CreditRating="1">
   <VendorName>Electronic Bike Repair &amp; Supplies</VendorName>
</Vendor>
```

The Tag column is required in EXPLICIT mode in order to produce the XML document output, and it returns an integer data type value for each element in the rowset. The Parent column alias is also required, providing the hierarchical information about any parent elements (in the previous query, there was no parent, so the value was NULL).

The TYPE directive in the FOR XML clause of the previous query was used to return the results as a true SQL Server 2005 native xml data type, allowing you to store the results in XML or query it using XQuery.

Next, the FOR XML PATH option defines column names and aliases as XPath expressions. As I mentioned at the beginning of this chapter, XPath is a language used for searching data within an XML document.

Tip For information on XPath, visit the World Wide Web Consortium W3C standards site at http://www.w3.org/TR/xpath.

The syntax for using FOR XML PATH is as follows:

```
PATH [ ('ElementName') ]
[[ , BINARY BASE64 ] [ , TYPE ] [ , ROOT [('RootName') ]]
 [ , ELEMENTS [ XSINIL | ABSENT ] ]     }
```

FOR XML PATH uses some of the same arguments and keywords as other FOR XML variations. Where it differs, however, is in the SELECT clause, where XPath syntax is used to define elements, sub elements, attributes, and data values.

For example:

```
SELECT Name as "@Territory",
       CountryRegionCode as "@Region",
       SalesYTD
FROM Sales.SalesTerritory
WHERE SalesYTD > 6000000
ORDER BY SalesYTD DESC
FOR XML PATH('TerritorySales'), ROOT('CompanySales'), TYPE
```

This returns:

```
<CompanySales>
    <TerritorySales Territory="Southwest" Region="US">
        <SalesYTD>8351296.7411</SalesYTD>
    </TerritorySales>
    <TerritorySales Territory="Canada" Region="CA">
        <SalesYTD>6917270.8842</SalesYTD>
    </TerritorySales>
</CompanySales>
```

This query returned results with a root element of CompanySales and a sub element of TerritorySales. The TerritorySales element was then attributed based on the territory and region code (both prefaced with ampersands (@)in the SELECT clause). The SalesYTD, which was unmarked with XPath directives, became a sub-element to TerritorySales.

How It Works

The FOR XML command is included at the end of a SELECT query in order to return data in an XML format. The AUTO and RAW modes allow for a quick and semi-automated formatting of the results, whereas EXPLICIT and PATH provide more control over the hierarchy of data and the assignment of elements versus attributes. FOR XML PATH, on the other hand, is an easier alternative to EXPLICIT mode for those developers who are more familiar with the XPath language.

The FOR XML options I demonstrated in this recipe were the most common variations you will see when trying to create XML from a result set. Generating XML document fragments using FOR XML eases the process of having to create the hierarchy using other manual methods in Transact-SQL. Keep in mind that you always have the option of falling back on programmatic XML document creation too (using .NET, for example).

Using OPENXML

Whereas FOR XML converts relational query results to an XML format, OPENXML converts XML format to a relational form. To perform this conversion, the sp_XML_preparedocument system stored procedure is used to create an internal pointer to the XML document, which is then used with OPENXML in order to return the rowset data.

The syntax for the OPENXML command is as follows:

```
OPENXML(idoc ,rowpattern, flags)
[WITH (SchemaDeclaration | TableName)]
```

The arguments for this command are described in Table 14-4.

Table 14-4. *OPENXML Arguments*

Argument	Description
idoc	The internal representation of the XML document as represented by the sp_XML_preparedocument system stored procedure.
rowpattern	The XPath pattern used to return nodes from the XML document.
flags	When the flag 0 is used, results default to attribute-centric mappings.
	When flag 1 is used, attribute-centric mapping is applied first, and then element-centric mapping for columns that are not processed.
	Flag 2 uses element-centric mapping.
	Flag 8 specifies that consumed data should not be copied to the overflow property.
SchemaDeclaration	TableName	SchemaDeclaration defines the output of the column name (rowset name), column type (valid data type), column pattern (optional XPath pattern), and optional meta data properties (about the XML nodes). If Tablename is used instead, a table must already exist for holding the rowset data.

In this example, an XML document is stored in a local variable and is then passed to a stored procedure which uses OPENXML in order to convert it into a relational rowset. First, the stored procedure is created:

```
CREATE PROCEDURE dbo.usp_SEL_BookXML_Convert_To_Relational
    @XMLDoc xml
AS

DECLARE @docpointer int
```

```
EXEC sp_XML_preparedocument @docpointer OUTPUT, @XMLdoc

SELECT    Chapter, ChapterNM
FROM      OPENXML (@docpointer, '/Book/Chapters/Chapter',0)
          WITH (Chapter int '@id',
            ChapterNM varchar(50) '@name' )
GO
```

Next, a local xml data type variable is populated and sent to the new stored procedure:

```
DECLARE @XMLdoc XML
SET @XMLdoc =
'<Book name="SQL Server 2000 Fast Answers">
   <Chapters>
       <Chapter id="1" name="Installation, Upgrades"/>
       <Chapter id="2" name="Configuring SQL Server"/>
       <Chapter id="3" name="Creating and Configuring Databases"/>
       <Chapter id="4" name="SQL Server Agent and SQL Logs"/>
   </Chapters>
   </Book>'

EXEC dbo.usp_SEL_BookXML_Convert_To_Relational @XMLdoc
```

This returns:

Chapter	ChapterNM
1	Installation, Upgrades
2	Configuring SQL Server
3	Creating and Configuring Databases
4	SQL Server Agent and SQL Logs

How It Works

The example started off by creating a stored procedure that would be used to convert an XML document fragment into a relational data set. The procedure had a single input parameter defined of an xml data type:

```
CREATE PROCEDURE dbo.usp_SEL_BookXML_Convert_To_Relational
    @XMLDoc xml
AS
```

A local variable was declared for use as an output parameter in the sp_XML_preparedocument system stored procedure to hold the value of the internal document pointer:

```
DECLARE @docpointer int
```

Next, the system stored procedure is called with the OUTPUT parameter and the second argument being the input xml data type parameter:

```
EXEC sp_XML_preparedocument @docpointer OUTPUT, @XMLdoc
```

Next, a SELECT statement referenced the OPENXML function in the FROM clause, with the name of the two columns to be returned in the results:

```
SELECT    Chapter, ChapterNM
FROM      OPENXML
```

The first argument in the OPENXML command was the internal pointer variable. The second argument was the XPATH expression of the node to be used in the XML document. The third argument was the flag, which designated an attribute-centric mapping:

```
(@docpointer, '/Book/Chapters/Chapter',0)
```

The WITH clause defined the actual result output. Two columns were defined, one for the Chapter and the other for the ChapterNM. The @id designated the id attribute to be mapped to the Chapter column and the @name attribute mapped to the ChapterNM column:

```
WITH (Chapter int '@id',
  ChapterNM varchar(50) '@name' )
```

After creating the stored procedure, a local variable was then populated with an XML fragment, and then passed to the stored procedure, returning two columns and four rows.

CHAPTER 15

■ ■ ■

Web Services

SQL Server 2005 introduces integrated native HTTP and SOAP (Simple Object Access Protocol) support within the database engine. Web services, in a nutshell, are applications made accessible via the Internet or intranet. Web services provide interfaces through HTTP and SOAP, allowing an easy and common interface across varying technologies

For example, an ASP.NET or Java web application can both use a common web service to perform activities such as retrieving data from a database, submitting an order, or other data-exchange tasks. HTTP is a very common network protocol. SOAP is a language-independent XML-based protocol used for communication between web services. SOAP is a message format which can be communicated over HTTP.

For example, leading web site search companies make their search functionality available to developers as a set of web services that can be accessed using SOAP. Developers can build calls to the web services in their own applications, submitting search requests to the web services and receiving results back from them in the form of structured data sets.

Using Transact-SQL, you can now create and manage your own custom database-oriented web services in SQL Server. SQL Server 2005's native HTTP support allows a developer to provide access to your database over the internet. Using a web service, you can invoke Transact-SQL statements, stored procedures, and user-defined functions. Native HTTP support in SQL Server 2005 doesn't require the installation of other web applications, such as Internet Information Services (IIS) on the SQL Server machine. SQL Server processes HTTP itself, and communicates its available web services to potential callers using a specific set of XML messages called *WSDL (Web Services Description Language)*.

In this chapter, I'll take you through the creation of a SQL Server 2005 web service using an HTTP endpoint, and then I'll show you how to create a simple .NET Web application to consume the data from it.

■Note Endpoints are also used in creating Database Mirroring sessions and Service Broker processing. For more information on this, see Chapters 20 and 25.

Web Service Technologies

Before launching into the specific steps needed to establish a SQL Server 2005 hosted web service, I'll elaborate a little more about exactly what a web service *is* and the technologies that are commonly used in conjunction with it.

Web services allow for the creation of distributed applications. Specifically, web services can be built to expose data and perform programmatic actions—all triggered in response to calls from a remote application. This calling application can be another web site, desktop application, or Windows service (to name a few). The application can exist on non-Windows operating systems and be built using non-Microsoft programming languages. The only requirement is that the caller of the web service be able to communicate using HTTP, XML, and SOAP. Given the broad exposure to both these protocols and formats, your web service can have a much wider audience than it would, had your web service application been written for proprietary software instead. The main benefit for distributed applications is that these applications can access and utilize a significant amount of functionality without having to house, store, maintain, or synchronize large amounts of data and code on a single application server. Instead, the application code can develop lightweight interfaces to consume and serve one or more web services to the end-user or process.

When we get into the realm of web and XML technologies, the large number of acronyms can be intimidating to the uninitiated SQL Server professional. Table 15-1 reviews some of the major technologies used in conjunction with XML and web services. Some of these terms were also referenced in Chapter 14.

Table 15-1. *Web and XML Technologies*

Term	Description
XML	XML stands for Extensible Markup Language, and is used to create self-describing documents. XML documents are transferred across the Internet, rendered via web pages, stored in files, and converted to various file types.
HTTP	Something that most people are quite familiar with, but is included here nonetheless, HTTP stands for Hypertext Transfer Protocol and is the main protocol used for the World Wide Web to transfer HTML documents.
SOAP	SOAP stands for Simple Object Access Protocol, and is a message protocol used for communicating with web services. The message is actually an XML document that contains a specific body and header. Messages are sent from the sending application to the web service using HTTP.
WSDL	WSDL stands for Web Services Description Language, and is used to describe web services provided by a specific machine. A .NET application, for example, can use a WSDL document to determine the web services that are available and the functionality that they expose.
Clear Port	This refers to unencrypted transmission of information over the Internet. When setting up your web service endpoint, you'll have the choice of using a clear port (no encryption) or SSL (described next). Clear port communication uses the "http" URL prefix.
SSL	SSL stands for Secure Sockets Layer, and is used to transmit private information over the Internet. SSL configuration on your server requires the procurement of an SSL certificate, which is installed on the server and then used to encrypt the data. SSL requires the use of the "https" URL prefix.
Endpoint	An endpoint in SQL Server 2005 is a service that listens in on either a clear or SSL port external request. Specifically, this chapter discusses using endpoints with the SOAP payload (message) over the HTTP protocol (communication and transport method). An endpoint listens in on a specific port (either a clear or SSL), and responds according to the web service functionality and the client request.

In the next section, I'll go into more detail on how to create and manage HTTP endpoints.

HTTP Endpoints

In order to use SQL Server 2005's web service functionality, you need to first create an HTTP endpoint. An HTTP endpoint is a service that listens for requests on the SQL Server 2005 machine. Internet Information Services (IIS) and other web application server products are often used to host web services. In SQL Server 2005, however, IIS doesn't need to be installed on the SQL Server 2005 machine because an HTTP endpoint registers with the Windows 2003 operating system's HTTP listener process (called Http.sys). The CREATE ENDPOINT command reserves the listener port and defines the methods that will be exposed in the web service.

The syntax for creating an HTTP endpoint can be broken down into two parts (and when first encountering the full syntax of this command, probably *should* be broken down for clarity's sake). The first part of the CREATE ENDPOINT syntax defines the HTTP settings:

```
CREATE ENDPOINT endPointName [ AUTHORIZATION login ]
STATE = { STARTED | STOPPED | DISABLED }
AS HTTP (
  PATH = 'url'
, AUTHENTICATION =( { BASIC | DIGEST | INTEGRATED |
NTLM | KERBEROS } [ ,...n ] )
     , PORTS = ( { CLEAR | SSL} [ ,... n ] )
  [ SITE = {'*' | '+' | 'webSite' },]
  [, CLEAR_PORT = clearPort ]
  [, SSL_PORT = SSLPort ]
  [, AUTH_REALM = { 'realm' | NONE } ]
  [, DEFAULT_LOGON_DOMAIN = { 'domain' | NONE } ]
  [, COMPRESSION = { ENABLED | DISABLED } ]
  )
)
```

The starting state of the endpoint is defined right after the definition of the endpoint name and login. The actual web site and path configurations are then configured after the AS HTTP keywords. The arguments of the first part of this command are described in Table 15-2.

Table 15-2. *CREATE ENDPOINT Arguments*

Argument	Description
endPointName	The name of the new endpoint.
login	The Windows or SQL Server login that owns the endpoint, defaulting to the caller of this command.
STATE = { STARTED	STOPPED	DISABLED }	The endpoint's state, once it is created, with STOPPED as the default, which means that the endpoint is listening to requests, but returns errors to clients. STARTED means the endpoint is started and listening for connections, and DISABLED means the server is neither listening to the endpoint nor responding to requests.
PATH = 'url'	The URL path that the application client sends HTTP SOAP requests to.
AUTHENTICATION = ({ BASIC | DIGEST | INTEGRATED | NTLM | KERBEROS } [,...n])	This option defines how endpoint users connect to SQL Server.
PORTS = ({ CLEAR | SSL} [,... n])	This option specifies the listening port. CLEAR is used for HTTP requests. SSL assumes a secure, https:// request.

(Continued)

Table 15-2. *Continued*

Argument	Description
SITE = {'*' | '+' | 'webSite' },	This option defines the name of the host computer. The * (asterisk) directs the command to use the default host computer name(s). The + (plus sign) directs the endpoint to listen for all possible host names. webSite is the specific host name to listen for.
CLEAR_PORT = clearPort	The clear port number, which by default is port 80.
SSL_PORT = SSLPort	The SSL port number, which by default is port 443.
AUTH_REALM = { 'realm' | NONE }	Used in conjunction with DIGEST authentication, this returns a hint to the client.
DEFAULT_LOGON_DOMAIN = { 'domain' | NONE }	Used in conjunction with BASIC authentication, specifying the default login domain.
COMPRESSION = { ENABLED | DISABLED }	When enabled, SQL Server responds to gzip requests, returning compressed responses.

The second part of the CREATE ENDPOINT command syntax for creating an HTTP endpoint follows after the FOR SOAP keywords:

```
FOR SOAP(
  [ { WEBMETHOD [ 'namespace' .] 'method_alias'
  (    NAME = 'database.owner.name'
    [ , SCHEMA = { NONE | STANDARD | DEFAULT } ]
    [ , FORMAT = { ALL_RESULTS | ROWSETS_ONLY } ]
  )
  } [ ,...n ] ]
  [    BATCHES = { ENABLED | DISABLED } ]
  [ , WSDL = { NONE | DEFAULT | 'sp_name' } ]
  [ , SESSIONS = { ENABLED | DISABLED } ]
  [ , LOGIN_TYPE = { MIXED | WINDOWS } ]
  [ , SESSION_TIMEOUT = timeoutInterval | NEVER ]
  [ , DATABASE = { 'database_name' | DEFAULT } ]
  [ , NAMESPACE = { 'namespace' | DEFAULT } ]
  [ , SCHEMA = { NONE | STANDARD } ]
  [ , CHARACTER_SET = { SQL | XML }]
  [ , HEADER_LIMIT = int ]
```

The arguments of this command are described in Table 15-3.

Table 15-3. *FOR SOAP Arguments*

Argument	Description
WEBMETHOD ['namespace' .] 'method_alias'	This is the unique method name to be exposed in the HTTP SOAP request. You can define multiple methods for a single endpoint.
(NAME = 'database.owner.name'	The three-part name of the stored procedure or user-defined function for the method.
SCHEMA = { NONE | STANDARD | DEFAULT }	When STANDARD is specified, XSD schema is not returned with the SOAP results. When NONE is specified, the web method is omitted from the schema. When DEFAULT is designated, the SCHEMA option setting defaults to the SCHEMA argument (see later on in this table).

Argument	Description
FORMAT = { ALL_RESULTS | ROWSETS_ONLY }	When ALL_RESULTS is designated, the result set, row count, and any error messages or warnings are returned in the SOAP response to an application call. When ROWSETS_ONLY is designated, only the result set is returned.
BATCHES = { ENABLED | DISABLED }	When ENABLED, SQL Server allows ad hoc Transact-SQL sqlbatch methods (this option is DISABLED by default).
WSDL = { NONE | DEFAULT | 'sp_name' }	Disabled by default, this option determines whether a WSDL document is created automatically for an endpoint. If NONE, a document is not created. If DEFAULT, a system-stored procedure creates the WSDL automatically. Otherwise, you can designate a specific stored procedure name.
SESSIONS = { ENABLED | DISABLED }	When ENABLED, SOAP request/response message pairs can be grouped as a part of a single SOAP session (this option is DISABLED by default).
LOGIN_TYPE = { MIXED | WINDOWS }	Specifies the SQL Server authentication mode (WINDOWS is the default).
SESSION_TIMEOUT = timeoutInterval | NEVER	The number of seconds before the SOAP session expires after a period of request inactivity.
DATABASE = { 'database_name' | DEFAULT }	The database context of the method. DEFAULT uses the login's default database.
NAMESPACE = { 'namespace' | DEFAULT }	The namespace of the endpoint, with http://tempuri.org as the default.
SCHEMA = { NONE | STANDARD }	If STANDARD, an XSD schema is returned with the results of the method. Otherwise NONE means the XSD schema is not returned.
CHARACTER_SET = { SQL | XML }	This option defines how invalid characters are handled in XML. The SQL option escapes invalid XML characters from parsing. For example "<" becomes "<".
HEADER_LIMIT = int	Defines the maximum byte size of the SOAP header, with a default value of 8192 bytes.

Creating an HTTP Endpoint

In this recipe, I'll create a stored procedure that will be used as a method in a web service. The following stored procedure returns special offer discount information for products:

```
CREATE PROCEDURE dbo.usp_SEL_SpecialOffer
AS

SELECT p.Name,
       o.Description,
       o.StartDate,
       o.EndDate,
       o.MinQty,
       o.MaxQty
FROM    Sales.SpecialOffer o
INNER JOIN Sales.SpecialOfferProduct op ON
    o.SpecialOfferID = op.SpecialOfferID
```

```
INNER JOIN Production.Product p ON
    op.ProductID = p.ProductID
WHERE Description NOT IN ('No Discount')
ORDER BY p.Name

GO
```

Next, an HTTP endpoint will be created that uses the usp_SEL_SpecialOffer stored procedure as a web method:

```
CREATE ENDPOINT AW_SpecialOffers
    STATE = STARTED
  AS HTTP
  (
      PATH = '/ProductOffers',
      AUTHENTICATION = (INTEGRATED),
      PORTS = (CLEAR),
      SITE = 'JOEPROD'
  )
  FOR SOAP
  (
      WEBMETHOD 'ProductSpecialOffer'
          (NAME='AdventureWorks.dbo.usp_SEL_SpecialOffer'),
      WSDL = DEFAULT,
      DATABASE = 'AdventureWorks',
      NAMESPACE = DEFAULT
  )
```

Once the HTTP endpoint is created, it can then be accessed using an external programmatic client. At the end of this chapter, I'll demonstrate how to do this using a simple VB.NET application. In the meantime, once the endpoint is created, you can view information about its current status by querying the sys.endpoints system catalog view:

```
SELECT endpoint_id, protocol_desc, type_desc, state_desc
FROM sys.endpoints
WHERE name = 'AW_SpecialOffers'
```

This returns:

endpoint_id	protocol_desc	type_desc	state_desc
65538	HTTP	SOAP	STARTED

The sys.http_endpoints system catalog view can be queried for information on the HTTP settings (for settings configured in the AS HTTP section of the CREATE ENDPOINT command), such as the path, port, and security settings:

```
SELECT site, url_path, clear_port, is_integrated_auth_enabled
FROM sys.http_endpoints
WHERE name = 'AW_SpecialOffers'
```

This returns:

site	url_path	clear_port	is_integrated_auth_enabled
localhost	/ProductOffers	80	1

The sys.soap_endpoints system catalog view can be queried for the SOAP configurations of an endpoint (settings chosen in the FOR SOAP in the CREATE ENDPOINT command), for example the default namespace, session timeout, and character set validation type:

```
SELECT default_namespace, session_timeout, is_xml_charset_enforced
FROM sys.soap_endpoints
WHERE name = 'AW_SpecialOffers'
```

This returns:

default_namespace	session_timeout	is_xml_charset_enforced
http://tempuri.org	60	1

The sys.endpoint_webmethods system catalog view can be queried to see what web methods are available from the specific endpoint, including the method name, database object associated to it, and result format (this query joins sys.endpoints and sys.endpoint_webmethods on the endpoint_id):

```
SELECT method_alias, object_name
FROM sys.endpoint_webmethods w
INNER JOIN sys.endpoints e ON
   w.endpoint_id = e.endpoint_id
WHERE e.name = 'AW_SpecialOffers'
```

This returns:

method_alias	object_name
ProductSpecialOffer	[AdventureWorks].[dbo].[usp_SEL_SpecialOffer]

How It Works

In this example, a stored procedure was created to return product "special offer" information. An endpoint was then created using CREATE ENDPOINT. This endpoint can then be used as a web service, providing data to external client applications (other web sites, .NET desktop applications, Java applications).

The first line of code designated the name of the new endpoint, followed by the initial status of the endpoint (in this case STARTED):

```
CREATE ENDPOINT AW_SpecialOffers
     STATE = STARTED
```

The next code section defined the HTTP settings, including the path, method of authentication, server port to use, and name of the web site:

```
AS HTTP
   (
      PATH = '/ProductOffers',
      AUTHENTICATION = (INTEGRATED),
      PORTS = (CLEAR),
      SITE = 'JOEPROD'
   )
```

The SOAP information (also referred to as the *payload* information) was defined in the FOR SOAP section of the code. This included the name of the method, the stored procedure to be executed, and the default database connection:

```
FOR SOAP
  (
      WEBMETHOD 'ProductSpecialOffer'
          (NAME='AdventureWorks.dbo.usp_SEL_SpecialOffer'),
      WSDL = DEFAULT,
      DATABASE = 'AdventureWorks',
      NAMESPACE = DEFAULT
  )
```

Once the endpoint was created and was in STARTED mode, it could be accessed by a web service client application once security is defined for it (managing HTTP endpoint security is reviewed in the next recipe). A simple .NET client used to consume this information will be demonstrated at the end of the chapter.

Endpoint information was then queried in this example using sys.endpoints to view general endpoint information, sys.http_endpoints to view the HTTP settings, sys.soap_endpoints to view the SOAP configurations, and sys.endpoint_webmethods to view the methods defined for the specific endpoint.

Managing HTTP Endpoint Security

In order to permit users to access the endpoint, security access must be granted both to the endpoint itself and to any database objects exposed as methods within it. Securing the endpoint involves the following steps:

- Creating the SQL Server login(s), whether Windows or SQL, which need to have access to the endpoint. Grant the login(s) access.

- Mapping the login(s) to a user in the appropriate database (where the method database objects are invoked).

- Granting the user execution permissions to the stored procedure and/or user-defined function exposed as a method in the endpoint.

■**Note** This recipe touches on several security commands which are covered in more detail in Chapters 17 and 18. These chapters will demonstrate the commands used within the example, including CREATE LOGIN, CREATE USER, and GRANT.

In the first part of this example, a Windows login is created in SQL Server:

```
USE master
GO

CREATE LOGIN [JOEPROD\TestUser]
FROM WINDOWS
WITH DEFAULT_DATABASE=AdventureWorks
GO
```

Next, that login is mapped to a new database user in the AdventureWorks database:

```
USE AdventureWorks
GO
CREATE USER TestUser
FOR LOGIN [JOEPROD\TestUser]
GO
```

The database user `TestUser` is then granted execute permissions on the stored procedure used in the web method definition of the HTTP endpoint:

```
USE AdventureWorks
GO
GRANT EXECUTE ON dbo.usp_SEL_SpecialOffer
TO TestUser
GO
```

Lastly, the login [JOEPROD\TestUser] is granted access to connect to the HTTP endpoint:

```
USE master
GO
GRANT CONNECT ON ENDPOINT:: AW_SpecialOffers
TO [JOEPROD\TestUser]
```

How It Works

This example used several commands that haven't been reviewed yet, but will be reviewed in Chapters 17 and 18. The key concepts to take away from this recipe are that in order to connect to an endpoint you need a SQL Server login (Windows or SQL), and that login needs CONNECT permissions on the endpoint. The login also needs to be mapped to a database user in the database containing the method objects (stored procedure or user-defined functions). That database user must be granted EXECUTE permissions on the objects used as web methods in the HTPP endpoint. For sysadmin level connections, these steps may not be necessary, however for regular application access by low-level permissions users, these security steps apply.

Modifying an HTTP Endpoint

Using ALTER ENDPOINT you can modify the settings and web methods of an existing endpoint. ALTER ENDPOINT uses the same options that are available in CREATE ENDPOINT, and includes a few extra sub-commands used for specific web method changes.

The general syntax for modifying endpoint configurations is as follows:

```
ALTER ENDPOINT endPointName
    <endpoint_options>
AS HTTP
    (<HTTP options>)
FOR SOAP
([ADD WEBMETHOD | ALTER WEBMETHOD | DROP WEBMETHOD ]
[ 'namespace' .] 'method_alias' (<web method options>)
)
```

The arguments for this command are described in Table 15-4.

Table 15-4. *ALTER ENDPOINT Arguments*

Argument	Description
endPointName	The name of the endpoint you want to modify.
endpoint options	The endpoint options you want to modify (see CREATE ENDPOINT). You should only reference options that will be updated—remaining options not referenced in the command will be left unchanged.
http options	HTTP options to modify (see the AS HTTP clause in CREATE ENDPOINT).

(Continued)

Table 15-4. *Continued*

Argument	Description
ADD WEBMETHOD | ALTER WEBMETHOD | DROP WEBMETHOD	Specify ADD WEBMETHOD to add a new web method to the endpoint, ALTER WEBMETHOD to modify web method options, or DROP WEBMETHOD to remove a web method from the endpoint.
['namespace' .] 'method_alias'	The name of the web method you want to add, alter, or drop.
web method options	Web method options for the new or modified web method.

In this first example, the AW_SpecialOffers endpoint's web site is changed from "JOEPROD" to a new value:

```
-- HTTP change
ALTER ENDPOINT AW_SpecialOffers
AS HTTP
(SITE = 'TESTSRV')
```

In this second example, a new web method is added to an existing endpoint, referencing a stored procedure in the AdventureWorks database. This allows you to add new functionality for use by applications that utilize the web service:

```
-- Add a new web method
ALTER ENDPOINT AW_SpecialOffers
FOR SOAP
(ADD WEBMETHOD 'TransactionHistory'
(name='AdventureWorks.dbo.usp_SEL_Production_TransactionHistory'))
```

In this third example, an endpoint is disabled (meaning that the server will neither listen to the endpoint nor respond to requests):

```
-- Endpoint change
ALTER ENDPOINT AW_SpecialOffers
STATE = DISABLED
```

How It Works

ALTER ENDPOINT allows you to modify an existing endpoint and uses the same options that were configurable in CREATE ENDPOINT, letting you modify HTTP and SOAP settings, add web methods, modify existing web methods, or drop web methods.

In the first example, changing the HTTP web site of an endpoint involved using the AS HTTP keyword, followed by the new site name in parentheses:

```
ALTER ENDPOINT AW_SpecialOffers
AS HTTP
(SITE = 'TESTSRV')
```

The second recipe demonstrated adding a new web method to an existing endpoint. For this, the keywords FOR SOAP followed the ALTER ENDPOINT and endpoint name. The ADD METHOD command was put in parentheses, followed by the name of the new web method:

```
ALTER ENDPOINT AW_SpecialOffers
FOR SOAP
(ADD WEBMETHOD 'TransactionHistory'
```

Continued in parentheses after the web method name was the name of the database object that will be invoked by the new web method (in this case a stored procedure in the AdventureWorks database):

```
(name='AdventureWorks.dbo.usp_SEL_Production_TransactionHistory'))
```

The third example demonstrated disabling an endpoint. Notice that no other keywords or parentheses were needed—only the name of the endpoint, and the state assignment:

```
ALTER ENDPOINT AW_SpecialOffers
STATE = DISABLED
```

Removing an HTTP Endpoint

In this recipe, I demonstrate dropping an HTTP endpoint from the server. To do this, use the `DROP ENDPOINT` command.

The syntax is as follows:

```
DROP ENDPOINT endPointName
```

The only argument for this command is the endpoint name to be dropped.

In this example, the endpoint is dropped from the SQL Server instance:

```
DROP ENDPOINT AW_SpecialOffers
```

How It Works

In this recipe's example, the endpoint was dropped using the `DROP ENDPOINT` command:

```
DROP ENDPOINT AW_SpecialOffers
```

This command can be used to drop endpoints of all types, including those used for database mirroring (see Chapter 25) and SQL Server Broker functionality (see Chapter 20).

Reserving Namespaces

After creating an endpoint, the namespace is only reserved by the endpoint while the SQL Server 2005 service is running. When the service is *not* running, there is a chance that this namespace can be taken by other non-SQL Server processes on the same machine (however, as a best practice, SQL Server 2005 should be on its own machine).

In order to reserve an HTTP namespace so that it cannot be used by a non-SQL Server process (even when the SQL Server service is not running) you can use the `sp_reserve_http_namespace` system stored procedure.

The syntax for this stored procedure is as follows:

```
sp_reserve_http_namespace N'<scheme>://<hostpart>:<port>/<RelativeURI>'
```

The arguments of this command are described in Table 15-5.

Table 15-5. *sp_reserve_http_namespace Parameters*

Argument	Description
`<scheme>://`	The scheme is either HTTP or HTTPS (secure SSL site).
`hostpart`	The host name or wildcard characters. * (asterisk) designates the default host computer name(s). + (plus sign) directs the listening operation to listen for all possible host names.
`port`	The TCP port number.
`RelativeURI`	The path that the application client uses to send HTTP SOAP requests.

To *remove* a namespace reservation, use the sp_delete_http_namespace_reservation system stored procedure. The syntax is as follows:

```
sp_delete_http_namespace_reservation N<scheme>://<hostpart>:<port>/<RelativeURI>'
```

The system stored procedure takes the same parameter information as sp_reserve_http_ namespace.

This first example demonstrates reserving a namespace:

```
EXEC sp_reserve_http_namespace N'http://JOEPROD:80/MyNewEndpoint'
```

This returns:

```
Command(s) completed successfully.
```

This second example demonstrates removing the reserved namespace:

```
EXEC sp_delete_http_namespace_reservation  N'http://JOEPROD:80/MyNewEndpoint'
```

This returns:

```
The reservation for the HTTP namespace (http://JOEPROD:80/MyNewEndpoint) has been
deleted. If there are any endpoints associated with this namespace, they will continue to
receive and process requests until the server is restarted.
```

How It Works

This recipe reviewed how to reserve a namespace for SQL Server, even when the SQL Server instance isn't running. Removing a reservation was also reviewed. Both system stored procedures use a syntax of the procedure name, followed by the namespace information to reserve. This technique is useful if the SQL Server instance is being shared with other applications such, as IIS.

■**Tip** As a best practice, however, the SQL Server instance should be completely "dedicated," meaning that no other major applications are running on the operating system. This is because SQL Server can require significant resources (such as memory), and other applications may force SQL Server to compete for resources.

Creating a .NET Client That Uses a Web Service

The bulk of this chapter has been spent setting the stage for this final recipe. Web services are useless without an audience, and in this recipe I'll demonstrate a simple VB.NET client, which will be used to consume data from the HTTP endpoint we created in the "Create an HTTP Endpoint" recipe.

■**Note** Unlike in the CLR chapter of this book, we're going to use Visual Studio 2005 to create this .NET client. This recipe assumes you have some background using Visual Studio 2005, as well as a .NET programming language.

This example demonstrates creating a .NET client application to consume the data of our web service. Specifically, a Windows form will be created with a button and a data grid view. When the button is clicked, the data grid view will show the results of the AdventureWorks.dbo.usp_SEL_SpecialOffer stored procedure exposed by the web service, using the following steps:

1. In Visual Studio 2005, a new Visual Basic Windows Application is created. It is named "MyFirstWebServiceClient" under the C:\Apress\Recipes\WebService folder.

2. A web reference must be created in order for this application to utilize the web service. To do so, the Add Web Reference dialog box is opened from the Project menu. In the URL text box, the URL of the WSDL definition describing the web service is http://localhost/ProductOffers?wsdl (where localhost is the name of the SQL Server 2005 machine). The Go button is pressed in order to return the details of the AW_SpecialOffers web service. Figure 15-1 shows the single method defined in the earlier recipe based on the stored procedure:

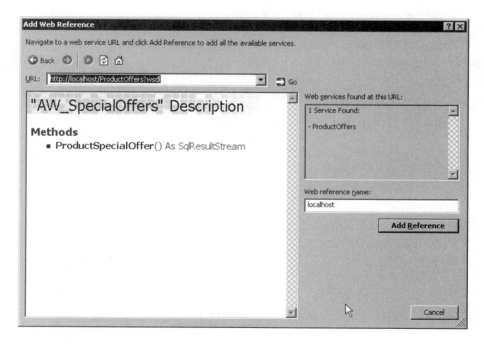

Figure 15-1. *Add Web Reference dialog box*

3. In the Add Web Reference dialog box, the Add Reference button is clicked to add a reference to the project. Figure 15-2 shows that the new Web Reference appears in the Solution Explorer. It is called `localhost` and will be used in the VB.NET code later on.

Figure 15-2. *Solution Explorer after adding a new Web Reference*

4. Next, a Button and a DataGridView are added to the form. The Button is renamed btnShowOffers with a caption of "Show Special Offers!" The DataGridView is renamed to dgvOfferResults, arranged per Figure 15-3:

Figure 15-3. *New Form with DataGridView and button*

5. Next, the button is double-clicked in order to program the VB.NET Click response. The following code is placed within the subroutine and header information (I'll describe this in more detail in the "How It Works" section):

```
Imports System.Data

Public Class Form1

Private Sub Button1_Click(ByVal sender As System.Object, _
ByVal e As System.EventArgs) Handles btnShowOffers.Click

Dim MyWebReference As localhost.AW_SpecialOffers = _
New localhost.AW_SpecialOffers

MyWebReference.Credentials = _
System.Net.CredentialCache.DefaultCredentials

Dim MyDataSet As DataSet = New DataSet
Dim MyObject As Object() = _
MyWebReference.ProductSpecialOffer()

For Each NewObj As Object In MyObject
   If TypeOf NewObj Is DataSet Then
      MyDataSet = CType(NewObj, DataSet)
   End If
Next
```

```
dgvOfferResults.DataSource = MyDataSet.Tables(0)

End Sub
End Class
```

6. Next, the application is ready to be tested. From the Debug menu, Start Debugging is selected. This brings up the active form. The button is clicked, which then returns the result set from the web service into the data grid view as shown in Figure 15-4:

Figure 15-4. *The DataGridView populated with web service data*

How It Works

In this recipe's example I demonstrated creating a .NET Windows form application that was used to retrieve special product offer information from the AdventureWorks database. The example started off by creating a new Windows Visual Basic project, and then adding a reference to the WSDL page in order to add a reference to the web service (recall earlier that I described WSDL as containing a registry of web services on a specified machine, along with any methods and functionality).

After adding a reference, I added a button and a data grid view to the form. Since the data grid view was to be populated based on the click of a button, I double-clicked it in order to enter the code window.

Walking through the code, the first line imported a reference to the System.Data namespace:

```
Imports System.Data
```

This namespace contains classes for ADO.NET, which is used in the management of data from various data sources. Specifically, this example used the DataSet and DataTable ADO.NET objects. DataSet is used to hold one or more DataTable objects. A DataTable object contains data from a single data source.

Next, the form class is declared, followed by the declaration of the button-click subroutine:

```
Public Class Form1

Private Sub Button1_Click(ByVal sender As System.Object, _
ByVal e As System.EventArgs) Handles btnShowOffers.Click
```

We now declare a web reference variable which points to the web reference added earlier in the example:

```
Dim MyWebReference As localhost.AW_SpecialOffers = _
New localhost.AW_SpecialOffers
```

After that, the security credentials under which the application will connect to the web service are defined. In this case, we are using the Windows account of the user executing the Windows application:

```
MyWebReference.Credentials = _
System.Net.CredentialCache.DefaultCredentials
```

Next, a new DataSet object is declared followed by an object declaration which references the web service method (which is hooked in our endpoint to the AdventureWorks.dbo.usp_SEL_SpecialOffer stored procedure):

```
Dim MyDataSet As DataSet = New DataSet
Dim MyObject As Object() = _
MyWebReference.ProductSpecialOffer()
```

For each object in the web service's method, if the value is a DataSet, it is converted into the DataSet object declared previously:

```
For Each NewObj As Object In MyObject
   If TypeOf NewObj Is DataSet Then
      MyDataSet = CType(NewObj, DataSet)
   End If
Next
```

Lastly, the data source of the data grid view is set to the first populated table of the declared MyDataSet DataSet object (thus populating the stored procedure results to the data grid view):

```
dgvOfferResults.DataSource = MyDataSet.Tables(0)

End Sub
End Class
```

Error Handling

In this chapter, I'll present recipes for creating, raising, and handling SQL Server errors using Transact-SQL. The most notable feature in the error handling arena, TRY...CATCH, was added in SQL Server 2005. The TRY...CATCH command allows you to implement more sophisticated error handling than what was available in previous versions of SQL Server. In the last recipe of this chapter, error trapping methods will be compared with the new TRY...CATCH method.

System-Defined and User-Defined Error Messages

This first batch of recipes is concerned with the viewing and raising of system and user-defined error messages. The sys.messages table contains one row for each user-defined and built-in error message on the SQL Server instance. *Built-in error messages* are those that are raised in response to standard SQL Server errors. *User-defined error messages* are often used in third party applications that define a set of error messages for use within an application. User-defined error messages allow for *parameterization*, meaning that you can create custom messages that allow for customizable messages based on parameters (as you'll see demonstrated later on in the chapter when I discuss RAISERROR).

Viewing System Error Information

You can use the sys.messages system catalog view to see all system and user-defined error messages in the SQL Server instance, as this example demonstrates:

```
SELECT message_id, severity, is_event_logged, text
FROM sys.messages
ORDER BY severity DESC, text
```

This returns the following results (the output has been truncated and formatted for clarity):

message_id	severity	is_event_logged	text
832	24	1A	page that should have been constant has changed (expected checksum: %08x, actual checksum: %08x, database %d, file '%ls', page %S_PGID). This usually indicates a memory failure or other hardware or OS corruption.
1459	24	1	An error occurred while accessing the database mirroring metadata. Drop mirroring (ALTER DATABASE database_name SET PARTNER OFF) and reconfigure it.
17405	24	1	An image corruption/hotpatch detected while reporting exceptional situation. This may be a sign of a hardware problem. Check SQLDUMPER_ERRORLOG.log for details.

How It Works

In this recipe, a simple `SELECT` query returned the following information about both SQL Server built-in error messages, and the custom error messages defined for this particular instance of SQL Server:

- `message_id`. This is the error message identifier
- `severity`. This is the severity level
- `is_event_logged`. This is used if the error writes to the Windows event log
- `text`. This is the text of the message.

The severity level ranges from 1 to 25, with the following implied categorizations:

- Severity levels 0 through 10 denote informational messages.
- Severity levels 11 through 16 are database engine errors that can be corrected by the user (database objects that are missing when the query is executed, incompatible locking hints, transaction deadlocks, denied permissions, and syntax errors). For example, a `PRIMARY KEY` violation will return a level 14 severity level error. A divide-by-zero error returns a severity 16 level error.
- Severity levels 17 through 19 are for errors needing sysadmin attention (for instance if SQL Server has run out of memory resources, or if database engine limits have been reached).
- Severity levels 20 through 25 are fatal errors and system issues (hardware or software damage which impacts the database, integrity problems, and media failures).

The text column in `sys.messages` contains the actual error message to be presented to the user from the database engine. Notice that the first message in the recipe's results had percentage signs and other symbols combined within it:

```
A page that should have been constant has changed (expected checksum: %08x, actual
checksum: %08x, database %d, file '%ls', page %S_PGID). This usually indicates a memory
failure or other hardware or OS corruption.
```

The `%` sign is a substitution parameter which allows the database engine to customize error message output based on the current database context and error event. The values concatenated to the `%` sign indicate the data type and length of the substitution parameter.

Creating a User-Defined Error Message

In this recipe, I demonstrate how to create a new user-defined error message using the `sp_addmessage` system stored procedure. You may wish to create user-defined, custom messages for your application to use, ensuring consistency across your application-specific error handling routines. Creating a new error message adds it to the `sys.messages` system catalog view and allows you to invoke it with the `RAISERROR` command (reviewed in the next recipe).

The syntax for this system stored procedure is as follows:

```
sp_addmessage [ @msgnum = ] msg_id ,
    [ @severity = ] severity ,
    [ @msgtext = ] 'msg'
    [ , [ @lang = ] 'language' ]
    [ , [ @with_log = ] 'with_log' ]
    [ , [ @replace = ] 'replace' ]
```

The parameters are briefly described in Table 16-1.

Table 16-1. *sp_addmessage Arguments*

Parameter	Description
msg_id	This is the user supplied error id which can be between 50,001 and 2,147,483,647. The message id is not the unique key or primary key of this table; rather, the unique composite key is the combination of the message id and the language id.
severity	Defines the severity level of your message (1 through 25).
msg	The actual error message, which uses a data type of nvarchar(255).
language	The language in which the error message is written.
with_log	Whether or not the message will be written to the Windows application log when the error is invoked.
replace	When specified, the existing user-defined error (based on message ID and language) is overwritten with the new parameters passed to the system stored procedure.

In this recipe, a new error message will be created to warn the user that their group can't update a specific table (which you might use if you were building your own application-based security system in a database, for example):

```
-- Creating the new message
USE master
GO
EXEC sp_addmessage
      100001,
      14,
   N'The current table %s is not updateable by your group!'
GO

-- Using the new message (RAISERROR reviewed in the next recipe)
RAISERROR (100001, 14, 1, N'HumanResources.Employee')
```

This returns:

```
Msg 100001, Level 14, State 1, Line 3
The current table HumanResources.Employee is not updateable by your group!
```

How It Works

In this recipe, a new message was created using sp_addmessage:

```
EXEC sp_addmessage
      100001,
      14,
   N'The current table %s is not updateable by your group!'
```

The first parameter, 100001, was the new message ID. You can use an integer value between 50,001 and 2,147,483,647. The second parameter value of 14 indicated the severity level, and the third parameter was the actual error message.

A substitution parameter value was included within the body of the message, %s, where the s tells us that the parameter is a string value. You can also designate a parameter as a signed integer (d or i), unsigned octal (o), unsigned integer (u), or unsigned hexadecimal (x or X).

The other optional parameters such as language, with_log, and replace were not used.

The last command in this recipe, RAISERROR, was used to raise an instance of the newly created error:

```
RAISERROR (100001, 14, 1, N'HumanResources.Employee')
```

RAISERROR is often used to return errors related to application or business logic, for example the returning of errors based on conditions that are syntactically correct, yet violate some condition or requirement of the application or business.

In this example, the first parameter was the new error message ID, the second parameter was the severity level, the third parameter was the state (a number you can use to identify which part of your code throws the error), and the fourth is the Unicode substitution parameter that passes to the error message. The argument can take substitution parameters for the int, tinyint, smallint, varchar, char, nchar, nvarchar, varbinary, and binary data types. The new error message was then returned to the SQL user with the value "HumanResources.Employee" plugged into the substitution parameter value.

Dropping a User-Defined Error Message

In this recipe, I demonstrate how to remove a user-defined error message from the sys.messages table. The syntax is as follows:

```
sp_dropmessage [ @msgnum = ] message_number
[ , [ @lang = ] 'language' ]
```

The parameters are briefly described in Table 16-2.

Table 16-2. *sp_dropmessage Arguments*

Parameter	Description
message_number	This is the message number of the user-defined error message.
language	This is the language of the message to drop. If you designate ALL and a message exists with the same message number but in different languages, all messages for that number will be dropped.

This recipe drops the user-defined error message created in the previous recipe:

```
EXEC sp_dropmessage 100001
```

How It Works

This recipe dropped the user-defined error message created in the previous recipe by using the system stored procedure sp_dropmessage. This system stored procedure can only be used to drop user-added messages, which have a message ID greater than 49,999.

Using RAISERROR

The RAISERROR command allows you to invoke either a user-defined error message from the sys.messages system catalog view or an error message produced from a string or string variable. The syntax of RAISERROR is:

```
RAISERROR ( { msg_id | msg_str | @local_variable }
    { ,severity ,state }
    [ ,argument [ ,...n ] ] )
    [ WITH option [ ,...n ] ]
```

The parameters are briefly described in Table 16-3.

Table 16-3. *RAISERROR Arguments*

Parameter	Description
msg_id | msg_str | @local_variable	When using RAISERROR, you can choose one of three options for this parameter. The msg_id option is a user-defined error message number from the sys.messages table. The msg_str is a user-defined message with up to 2,047 characters. The @local_variable is a string variable used to pass this message string.
severity	Defines the severity level of your message (1 through 25).
state	A user-defined number between 1 and 127 that can be used for identifying the location of the failing code (if your code is divided into multiple sections, for example).
argument [,...n]	This is one or more substitution parameters to be used within the error message.
WITH option [,...n]	Three options are allowed in the WITH clause including LOG, NOWAIT, and SETERROR. LOG writes to the SQL Server error and Windows application log. NOWAIT sends the messages immediately to the client. SETERROR sets the @@ERROR and ERROR_NUMBER values to the error message id (or 50,000 if not using an error from sys.messages).

Invoking an Error Message Using RAISERROR

In this recipe, I create a stored procedure to INSERT a new row into the HumanResources.Department table. When an attempt is made to insert a new department into the HumanResources.Department table, the group name will be evaluated first to see if it is the "Research and Development." If it isn't, the insert will not occur, and an error using RAISERROR will be invoked:

```
CREATE PROCEDURE usp_INS_Department
    @DepartmentName nvarchar(50),
     @GroupName nvarchar(50)
AS
IF  @GroupName = 'Research and Development'
BEGIN
    INSERT HumanResources.Department
    (Name, GroupName)
    VALUES (@DepartmentName, @GroupName)
END
ELSE
BEGIN
RAISERROR('%s group is being audited
for the next %i days.
No new departments for this group can be added
during this time.',
        16,
        1,
        @GroupName,
        23)
END

GO
```

Next, the new procedure is executed:

```
EXEC dbo.usp_INS_Department 'Mainframe Accountant', 'Accounting'
```

This returns:

```
Msg 50000, Level 16, State 1, Line 16
Mainframe Accountant dept is being audited for the next 23 days. No new departments can
be added during this time.
```

An alternative to creating the error message within the stored procedure is to create it as a user-defined message (as discussed earlier in the chapter). For example:

```
EXEC sp_addmessage
    100002,
    14,
  N'%s group is being audited for the next %i
days. No new departments for this group can be added
during this time.'
GO
```

Then, by rewriting the previous RAISERROR example, you can reference the user-defined error message number instead:

```
...
ELSE
BEGIN
   RAISERROR(100002,
          16,
          1,
          @GroupName,
          23)
END
```

How It Works

This recipe used RAISERROR to return an error if a specific IF condition was not met. RAISERROR is often used to send errors to the calling application from Transact-SQL batches, stored procedures, and triggers—especially for data or logical conditions that wouldn't normally cause a syntactic error to be raised.

Within the body of the stored procedure, the value of the group name was evaluated. If it had been equal to "Research and Development," the insert would have happened:

```
IF  @GroupName = 'Research and Development'
BEGIN
   INSERT HumanResources.Department
   (Name, GroupName)
   VALUES (@DepartmentName, @GroupName)
END
```

Because the group was *not* equal to Research and Development, the ELSE clause initiates the RAISERROR command instead:

```
ELSE
BEGIN
   RAISERROR('%s group is being audited for the next %i
days. No new departments for this group can be added
during this time.',
          16,
          1,
          @GroupName,
          23)
END
```

The first parameter of the RAISERROR command was the error message text, which used two substitution parameters: one for the group name, and the second for the number of days the group will be audited. The second parameter, 16, was the severity level. The third parameter, 1, was the state. The last two parameters, @GroupName and 23, were the substitution parameters to be plugged into the error message when it was invoked.

This recipe also demonstrated adding a user-defined message and then invoking it with RAISERROR, instead of creating the text on-the-fly. This technique is useful for error messages that must be used in multiple areas of your database, and it prevents you from having to re-type the message in each referencing procedure or script. It also ensures the consistency of the error message.

Using TRY...CATCH

Prior to SQL Server 2005, catching errors within a multi-batch procedure, trigger, or ad hoc script involved additional, repetitive code for capturing the potential error value after each executing statement.

Now in SQL Server 2005, the TRY...CATCH command can be used to capture execution errors within your Transact-SQL code. TRY...CATCH can catch any execution error with a severity level greater than 10 (so long as the raised error doesn't forcefully terminate the Transact-SQL user session). TRY...CATCH can also handle severity level errors (greater than 10) invoked using RAISERROR.

The syntax for TRY...CATCH is as follows:

```
BEGIN TRY
     { sql_statement | statement_block }
END TRY
BEGIN CATCH
     { sql_statement | statement_block }
END CATCH
```

The arguments, used in both the TRY and CATCH sections are sql_statement and statement_block. In a nutshell, statements within the TRY block are those you wish to execute. If errors are raised within the TRY block, then the CATCH block of code is executed. The CATCH block is then used to handle the error. Handling just means that you wish to take some action in response to the error: whether it's to report the error's information, log information in an error table, or roll back an open transaction.

The benefit of TRY...CATCH is in the ability to nest error handling inside code blocks, allowing you to handle errors more gracefully and with less code than non-TRY...CATCH methods. TRY...CATCH also allows you to use new SQL Server 2005 error logging and transaction state functions which capture granular error information about an error event. Table 16-4 details the use of each.

Table 16-4. *Error and Transaction State Functions*

Function	Description
ERROR_LINE	The error line number in the SQL statement or block where the error was raised.
ERROR_MESSAGE	The error message raised in the SQL statement or block.
ERROR_NUMBER	The error number raised in the SQL statement or block.
ERROR_PROCEDURE	Name of the trigger or stored procedure where the error was raised (assuming TRY...CATCH was used in a procedure or trigger).
ERROR_SEVERITY	The severity level of the error raised in the SQL statement or block.
ERROR_STATE	The state of the error raised in the SQL statement or block.
XACT_STATE	In the CATCH block, XACT_STATE reports on the state of open transactions from the TRY block. If "0" is returned, there are no open transactions from the TRY block. If "1" is returned, it means that no errors were raised in the TRY block. If "-1" is returned, an error occurred in the TRY block, and the transaction must be rolled back. XACT_STATE can also be used outside of a TRY...CATCH command.

If an error is encountered in a TRY batch, SQL Server will exit at the point of the error and move to the CATCH block, without processing any of the other statements in the TRY batch (the exception to the rule is if you're using nested TRY...CATCH blocks, which I'll demonstrate later on in the chapter).

TRY...CATCH can be used within a trigger or stored procedure, or used to encapsulate the actual execution of a stored procedure (capturing any errors that "bubble up" from the procedure execution and then handling them accordingly).

Warnings and most informational attention messages (severity level less than 10 or lower), are *not* caught by TRY...CATCH, and neither are syntax and object name resolution errors. Nonetheless, this new construct is now an ideal choice for capturing many other common error messages that in previous versions required bloated and inelegant Transact-SQL code.

In general, you'll want to make sure that every block of non-anonymous Transact-SQL code that modifies data in some way or participates in a transaction has an error handler. I'm not part of the group that believes in going overboard with error handling, however. I've seen some coders put error handling around each and every SELECT statement they write. I personally think this is overkill, as any issues that would cause a SELECT statement to "break" will require manual intervention of some sort. Also, with the progresses in .NET error handling, putting wrappers around your SELECT queries often redundantly handle errors that may already be handled in the application tier.

In the next two recipes, I demonstrate two different scripts: one that uses a pre-2005 method of trapping error messages, and one which demonstrates the new TRY...CATCH syntax method for doing the same thing. After those recipes, I'll demonstrate how to apply TRY...CATCH to a stored procedure and then how to use nested TRY...CATCH calls.

Old Style Error Handling

Pre-SQL Server 2005, error handling generally involved checking the T-SQL @@ERROR function after every statement was executed. You would then use GOTO statements to point to a centralized error-handling block where, if an error had occurred, the process would be terminated and the transaction rolled back.

This is demonstrated by the following code:

```
-- Pre SQL Server 2005, capturing errors if they occur

DECLARE @ErrorNBR int
```

```
BEGIN TRAN

    INSERT Production.Location
    (Name, CostRate, Availability)
    VALUES
    ('Tool Verification', 0.00, 0.00)

    SELECT @ErrorNBR = @@ERROR
    IF @ErrorNBR <> 0
    GOTO UndoTran

    INSERT Production.Location
    (Name, CostRate, Availability)
    VALUES
    ('Frame Forming', 0.00, 0.00)

    SELECT @ErrorNBR = @@ERROR
    IF @ErrorNBR <> 0
    GOTO UndoTran

COMMIT TRAN

UndoTran:
IF @ErrorNBR <> 0
BEGIN
PRINT CAST(@ErrorNBR as varchar(6)) +
' occurred after an attempt to insert into Production.Location'
ROLLBACK TRAN
END
```

This returns:

```
(1 row(s) affected)
Msg 2601, Level 14, State 1, Line 17
Cannot insert duplicate key row in object 'Production.Location' with unique index
'AK_Location_Name'.
The statement has been terminated.
2601 occurred after an attempt to insert into Production.Location
```

How It Works

The first example in this recipe demonstrated an error trapping method used pre-SQL Server 2005. The first line of code created an integer variable to hold the value of @@ERRORNBR after each statement was executed. @@ERRORNBR's value changes after each statement's execution, so a local variable will allow you to retain the original value of the error number:

```
DECLARE @ErrorNBR int
```

Next, a transaction was begun:

```
BEGIN TRAN
```

Two inserts were attempted against the Production.Location table. The first inserted a value that doesn't already exist in the table, and therefore succeeds:

```
INSERT Production.Location
(Name, CostRate, Availability)
VALUES
('Tool Verification', 0.00, 0.00)
```

Immediately after this insert, the value of @@ERROR is captured and stored in @ErrorNBR:

```
SELECT @ErrorNBR = @@ERROR
```

Since the insert succeeded, the value is "0." Had the insert failed, the value would have been equal to the appropriate error message ID as found in sys.messages.

Next, an IF statement evaluates the local variable value, and since it is "0," it does not invoke the IF condition:

```
IF @ErrorNBR <> 0
GOTO UndoTran
```

Another insert is then attempted, this time using a location name that already exists in the table. This insert fails this time, due to a unique constraint on the location name:

```
INSERT Production.Location
(Name, CostRate, Availability)
VALUES
('Frame Forming', 0.00, 0.00)
```

The error trapping logic from the first insert is repeated for the second insert, and when executed, the GOTO section was invoked since the value of @ErrorNBR is no longer equal to 0:

```
SELECT @ErrorNBR = @@ERROR
IF @ErrorNBR <> 0
GOTO UndoTran
```

Because the GOTO command is invoked, the COMMIT TRAN was skipped:

```
COMMIT TRAN
```

The UndoTran label code prints the error number and a message and rolls back the transaction:

```
UndoTran:
IF @ErrorNBR <> 0
BEGIN
PRINT CAST(@ErrorNBR as varchar(6)) + ' occurred after an
attempt to insert into Production.Location'
ROLLBACK TRAN
END
```

It's clear from this example that this method requires repetitive code to trap possible errors for each and every statement. For larger procedures or batch scripts, this can significantly increase the amount of Transact-SQL code required in order to achieve statement-level error trapping.

Error Handling with TRY...CATCH

In this recipe, I'll demonstrate the same error handling functionality, this time using TRY...CATCH:

```
BEGIN TRY

    BEGIN TRAN

    INSERT Production.Location
    (Name, CostRate, Availability)
    VALUES
    ('Tool Verification', 0.00, 0.00)

    INSERT Production.Location
    (Name, CostRate, Availability)
    VALUES
    ('Frame Forming', 0.00, 0.00)
```

```
COMMIT TRANSACTION

END TRY
BEGIN CATCH
    SELECT   ERROR_NUMBER() ErrorNBR, ERROR_SEVERITY() Severity,
          ERROR_LINE () ErrorLine, ERROR_MESSAGE() Msg

        ROLLBACK TRANSACTION

END CATCH
```

This returns the following results:

```
ErrorNBR Severity ErrorLine       Msg
2601    14      5         Cannot insert duplicate key row in object 'Production.Location'
with unique index 'AK_Location_Name'.
```

How It Works

This recipe duplicates the previous recipe's results, only this time using TRY...CATCH. The batch started with the BEGIN TRY command, and the starting of a new transaction:

```
BEGIN TRY

    BEGIN TRAN
```

Next, the two inserts used in the previous example were attempted again, this time *without* individual error trapping blocks following each statement:

```
INSERT Production.Location
(Name, CostRate, Availability)
VALUES
('Tool Verification', 0.00, 0.00)

INSERT Production.Location
(Name, CostRate, Availability)
VALUES
('Frame Forming', 0.00, 0.00)
```

The TRY batch, which included the statements I wished to error-check, is completed with the END TRY keywords:

```
END TRY
```

The BEGIN CATCH marked the beginning of the error handling code block:

```
BEGIN CATCH
```

Using some of the error functions described at the beginning of this recipe, information on the *first* error that occurred within the TRY block is reported:

```
SELECT   ERROR_NUMBER() ErrorNBR, ERROR_SEVERITY() Severity,
          ERROR_LINE () ErrorLine, ERROR_MESSAGE() Msg
```

Next, the open transaction declared earlier in the batch is then rolled back:

```
    ROLLBACK TRANSACTION
```

The END CATCH command was used to mark the ending of the error handling CATCH block.

Applying TRY...CATCH Error Handling Without Recoding a Stored Procedure

You don't have recode each of your database's stored procedures in order to start benefiting from the new TRY...CATCH construct. Instead, you can use TRY...CATCH to capture and handle errors from outside a procedure's code.

To demonstrate, a stored procedure is created that will return an error when executed:

```
CREATE PROCEDURE usp_SEL_DivideByZero
AS

SELECT 1/0

GO
```

The stored procedure included no error handling whatsoever, but this doesn't pose a problem if I use TRY...CATCH as follows:

```
BEGIN TRY
    EXEC dbo.usp_SEL_DivideByZero
END TRY
BEGIN CATCH
    SELECT   ERROR_NUMBER() ErrorNBR, ERROR_SEVERITY() Severity,
         ERROR_LINE () ErrorLine, ERROR_MESSAGE() Msg
    PRINT 'This stored procedure did not execute properly.'
END CATCH
```

This returns:

ErrorNBR	Severity	ErrorLine	Msg
8134	16	4	Divide by zero error encountered.

```
(1 row(s) affected)
```

```
This stored procedure did not execute properly.
```

How It Works

Although the stored procedure created in this exercise didn't include error handling, I was still able to add a programmatic response to errors by using TRY...CATCH to execute the stored procedure. The procedure was called from within the TRY block, and the error information and message caught and handled by the CATCH block.

```
BEGIN TRY
    EXEC dbo.usp_SEL_DivideByZero
END TRY
BEGIN CATCH
    SELECT   ERROR_NUMBER() ErrorNBR, ERROR_SEVERITY() Severity,
         ERROR_LINE () ErrorLine, ERROR_MESSAGE() Msg
    PRINT 'This stored procedure did not execute properly.'
END CATCH
```

Nesting TRY...CATCH Calls

TRY...CATCH statements can be nested, which means you can use the TRY...CATCH statements within other TRY...CATCH blocks. This allows you to handle errors that may happen, even in your error handling.

In this example, a new stored procedure is created to handle INSERTs into the HumanResources. Department table. This procedure includes two levels of error handling. If an error occurs when attempting the first INSERT, a second attempt is made with a different department name:

```
CREATE PROCEDURE dbo.usp_INS_Department
    @Name nvarchar(50),
    @GroupName nvarchar(50)
AS


BEGIN TRY

    INSERT HumanResources.Department (Name, GroupName)
    VALUES (@Name, @GroupName)

END TRY
BEGIN CATCH

    BEGIN TRY

    PRINT 'The first department attempt failed.'

    INSERT HumanResources.Department (Name, GroupName)
    VALUES ('Misc', @GroupName)

    END TRY
    BEGIN CATCH
        PRINT 'A Misc department for that group already exists.'
    END CATCH

END CATCH

GO
```

Executing the code for the existing department "Engineering" causes the first INSERT to fail, but the second INSERT of the "misc" department for the "Research and Development" department succeeds:

```
EXEC dbo.usp_INS_Department 'Engineering', 'Research and Development'
```

This returns:

```
(0 row(s) affected)
The first department attempt failed.
(1 row(s) affected)
```

If this same exact department and group INSERT is attempted again, both INSERTs will fail, causing the second nested CATCH to return a printed error too:

```
EXEC dbo.usp_INS_Department 'Engineering', 'Research and Development'
```

This returns:

```
(0 row(s) affected)
The first department attempt failed.

(0 row(s) affected)
A Misc department for that group already exists.
```

How It Works

This recipe demonstrated nesting a TRY...CATCH within another TRY...CATCH. This allows you to add error handling around your error handling, in cases where you anticipate that this is necessary.

Walking through the code, the first few lines of the stored procedure defined the input parameters for use with inserting into the HumanResources.Department table:

```
CREATE PROCEDURE dbo.usp_INS_Department
    @Name nvarchar(50),
    @GroupName nvarchar(50)
AS
```

Next, the first level TRY block is begun with an attempt to INSERT the new row into the table:

```
BEGIN TRY

    INSERT HumanResources.Department (Name, GroupName)
    VALUES (@Name, @GroupName)

END TRY
```

If this fails, the CATCH block contains another TRY block:

```
BEGIN CATCH

    BEGIN TRY
```

A statement is printed, and then another attempt is made to INSERT into the table, this time using a generic name of "Misc" instead of the original department name sent by the input parameter:

```
    PRINT 'The first department attempt failed.'

    INSERT HumanResources.Department (Name, GroupName)
    VALUES ('Misc', @GroupName)

    END TRY
```

If this fails, the nested CATCH will print a second message telling the user that the "Misc" department for the specified group already exists:

```
    BEGIN CATCH
        PRINT 'A Misc department for that group already exists.'
    END CATCH

END CATCH

GO
```

The stored procedure was then tested, using a department that already existed in the table. Because there is a UNIQUE constraint on the department name, the first INSERT failed, and control was passed to the CATCH block. The TRY block within the CATCH then successfully inserted into the table using the "Misc" department name.

On a second execution of the stored procedure, both INSERTs failed, but were handled by returning a PRINT statement warning you about it.

CHAPTER 17

■ ■ ■

Principals

Beginning with SQL Server 2005, Microsoft uses a new set of terminology to describe SQL Server security functionality, which separates the architecture into:

- *Principals.* These are objects (for example a user login, a role, or an application) that may be granted permission to access particular database objects.
- *Securables.* These are objects (a table or view, for example) to which access can be controlled
- *Permissions.* These are individual rights, granted (or denied) to a principal, to access a securable object

Principals are the topic of this chapter, and securable and permissions are discussed in the next chapter.

Principals fall into three different scopes:

- *Windows principals* are principals based on Windows domain user accounts, domain groups, local user accounts, and local groups. Once added to SQL Server and given permissions to access objects, these types of principals gain access to SQL Server based on Windows authentication.
- *SQL Server principals* are SQL Server-level logins and fixed server roles. SQL logins are created within SQL Server and have a login name and password independent of any Windows entity. Server roles are groupings of SQL Server instance-level permissions that other principals can become members of, inheriting that server role's permissions.
- *Database principals* are database users, database roles (fixed and user-defined), and application roles—all of which I'll cover in this chapter.

I'll start this chapter off with a discussion of Windows principals.

Windows Principals

Windows principals allow access to a SQL Server instance using Windows authentication. SQL Server allows us to create Windows logins based on Windows user accounts or groups, which can belong either to the local machine or to a domain. A Windows login can be associated with a domain user, local user, or Windows group. When adding a Windows login to SQL Server, the name of the user or group is bound to the Windows account. Windows logins added to SQL Server don't require separate password logins; in that case, Windows handles the login authentication process.

When users log on to SQL Server using Windows authentication, their current user account must either be identified as a login to the SQL Server instance, or they must belong to a Windows user group that exists as a login.

Windows logins apply only at the server operating system level: you can't grant permissions on Windows logins to specific database objects. To grant permissions based on Windows logins, you need to create a database user and associate it with the login. We'll see how to do this when we look at database principals.

When installing SQL Server, you are asked to decide between Windows-only and mixed authentication modes. Whichever authentication method you choose, you can always change your mind later. Microsoft Windows authentication allows for tighter security than SQL Server logins (described later), because security is integrated with the Windows operating system, local machine, and domain, and because no passwords are ever transmitted over the network. When using mixed authentication mode, you can create your own database logins and passwords within SQL Server, as we will discuss later.

In SQL Server 2000, the system stored procedure sp_grantlogin was used to add a Windows group or user login. In SQL Server 2005, the new CREATE LOGIN command is used instead.

The syntax for creating a database login from a Windows group or user login is as follows:

```
CREATE LOGIN login_name
FROM    WINDOWS
[ WITH DEFAULT_DATABASE = database
    | DEFAULT_LANGUAGE = language
]
    | CERTIFICATE certname
    | ASYMMETRIC KEY asym_key_name
```

The arguments of this command are described in Table 17-1.

Table 17-1. *CREATE LOGIN Arguments*

Argument	Description
login_name	The name of the Windows user or group.
DEFAULT_DATABASE = database	This option specifies the default database context of the Windows login, with the master system database being the default.
DEFAULT_LANGUAGE = language	This option specifies the default language of the Windows login, with the server default language being the login default if this option isn't specified.
CERTIFICATE certname	This option allows you to bind a certificate to a Windows login. See Chapter 19 for more information on certificates, and Chapter 20 for an example of doing so.
ASYMMETRIC KEY asym_key_name	This option binds a key to a Windows login. See Chapter 19 for more information on keys.

Creating a Windows Login

In this recipe, I assume that you already have certain Windows accounts and groups on the local machine or in your domain. This example creates a Windows *login* on the SQL Server instance, which is internally mapped to a Windows user:

```
CREATE LOGIN [JOEPROD\Danny]
FROM WINDOWS
WITH DEFAULT_DATABASE = AdventureWorks,
DEFAULT_LANGUAGE = English
```

In the second example, a new Windows login is created, based on a Windows group. This is identical to the previous example, except that you are mapping to a Windows group instead of a Windows user:

```
CREATE LOGIN [JOEPROD\DBAs]
FROM WINDOWS
WITH DEFAULT_DATABASE= AdventureWorks
```

How It Works

This recipe demonstrated adding access for a Windows user and Windows group to the SQL Server instance. In the first example, the CREATE LOGIN designated the Windows user in square brackets:

```
CREATE LOGIN [JOEPROD\Danny]
```

On the next line, the WINDOWS keyword was used to designate that this is a new login associated to a Windows account:

```
FROM WINDOWS
```

Next, the default database and languages were designated in the WITH clause:

```
WITH DEFAULT_DATABASE = AdventureWorks,
DEFAULT_LANGUAGE = English
```

In the second example, I demonstrated how to add a Windows group to SQL Server, which again requires square brackets in the CREATE LOGIN command:

```
CREATE LOGIN [JOEPROD\DBAs]
```

The FROM WINDOWS clause designated that this was a Windows group, followed by the default database:

```
FROM WINDOWS
WITH DEFAULT_DATABASE= AdventureWorks
```

When a Windows group is associated to a SQL Server login, it enables any member of the Windows group to inherit the access and permissions of the Windows login. So, for example, the BUILTIN\Administrators local Windows group is installed by default with a SQL Server instance with sysadmin server role permissions. Therefore, any members of this group will also have access to the SQL Server instance without explicitly having to add each Windows account to the SQL Server instance separately.

Viewing Windows Logins

You can view Windows logins and groups by querying the sys.server_principals system catalog view. This example shows the name of each Windows login and group with access to SQL Server, along with the security-identifier (sid). Each principal in the system catalog view has a sid, which helps uniquely identify it on the SQL Server instance:

```
SELECT name, sid
FROM sys.server_principals
WHERE type_desc IN ('WINDOWS_LOGIN', 'WINDOWS_GROUP')
ORDER BY type_desc
```

This returns the following results:

name	sid
BUILTIN\Administrators	0x01020000000000052000000020020000
JOEPROD\DBAs	0x0105000000000005150000000527A777BF094B3850FF83D06FF030000
NT AUTHORITY\SYSTEM	0x010100000000000512000000
JOEPROD\Owner	0x0105000000000005150000000527A777BF094B3850FF83D06EB030000
JOEPROD\TestUser	0x0105000000000005150000000527A777BF094B3850FF83D0600040000
JOEPROD\Danny	0x0105000000000005150000000527A777BF094B3850FF83D0608040000

How It Works

In this recipe, I demonstrated how to query Windows logins on the SQL Server instance using the
sys.server_principals system catalog view. This view actually allows you to see other principal
types too, which will be reviewed later in the chapter.

Altering a Windows Login

SQL Server 2000 required several different stored procedures in order to modify the attributes of
a SQL or Windows login. For example, sp_defaultdb was used to change the login's default database
and sp_defaultlanguage was used to change the login's default language. Now, in SQL Sever 2005,
you can perform several login changes just by using the ALTER LOGIN command. Another benefit of
this change is that we can now use the standard Transact-SQL CREATE, ALTER, and DROP to modify the
login instead of resorting to system stored procedures.

Once a Windows login is added to SQL Server, it can be modified using the ALTER LOGIN command (this command has several more options which are applicable to SQL Logins, as you'll see
reviewed later in the chapter). Using this command, you can perform tasks such as:

- Changing the default database of the login

- Changing the default language of the login

- Enabling or disabling a login from being used

The syntax is as follows:

```
ALTER LOGIN login_name
    {
    ENABLE | DISABLE
    |
WITH
    | DEFAULT_DATABASE = database
    | DEFAULT_LANGUAGE = language    }
```

The arguments of this command are described in Table 17-2.

Table 17-2. *ALTER LOGIN Arguments*

Argument	Description
login_name	The name of the Windows or SQL login.
ENABLE	DISABLE	Enables or disables a login from being used in SQL Server (disabling is an alternative to dropping a login).
DEFAULT_DATABASE = database	This option specifies the default database context of the SQL login, with the master system database being the default.
DEFAULT_LANGUAGE = language	This option specifies the default language of the login, with the server default language being the login default if this option isn't specified.

In the first example, a Windows login (associated with a Windows user) is disabled from use in SQL Server. This prevents the login from accessing SQL Server, and if connected, ceases any further activity on the SQL Server instance:

```
ALTER LOGIN [JOEPROD\Danny]
DISABLE
```

This next example demonstrates enabling this account again:

```
ALTER LOGIN [JOEPROD\Danny]
ENABLE
```

In this example, the default database is changed for a Windows group:

```
ALTER LOGIN [JOEPROD\DBAs]
WITH DEFAULT_DATABASE = master
```

How It Works

In the first example, a Windows login was disabled using ALTER LOGIN and the login name:

```
ALTER LOGIN [JOEPROD\Danny]
```

Following this was the DISABLE keyword, which removes this account's access to the SQL Server instance (it removes the account's access, but still keeps the login in the SQL Server instance for the later option of re-enabling access):

```
DISABLE
```

The second example demonstrated re-enabling access to the login by using the ENABLE keyword.

The third example changed the default database for a Windows group. The syntax for referencing Windows logins and groups is the same—both principal types are designated within square brackets:

```
ALTER LOGIN [JOEPROD\DBAs]
```

The second line then designated the new default database context for the Windows group:

```
WITH DEFAULT_DATABASE = master
```

Dropping a Windows Login

In this recipe, I'll demonstrate dropping a login from the SQL Server instance entirely by using the DROP LOGIN command. This removes the login's permission to access the SQL Server instance. If the login is currently connected to the SQL Server instance when the login is dropped, any actions attempted by the connected login will no longer be allowed.

The syntax is as follows:

```
DROP LOGIN login_name
```

The only parameter is the login name—which can be a Windows or SQL login (demonstrated later in the chapter), as this recipe demonstrates:

```
-- Windows Group login
DROP LOGIN [JOEPROD\DBAs]

-- Windows user login
DROP LOGIN [JOEPROD\Danny]
```

How It Works

This recipe demonstrated the simple DROP LOGIN command, which removes a login from SQL Server. If a login owns any securables (see the next chapter for more information on securables), the DROP attempt will fail. For example if the JOEPROD\Danny login had been a database owner, an error like the following would have been raised:

```
Msg 15174, Level 16, State 1, Line 3
Login 'JOEPROD\Danny' owns one or more database(s). Change the owner of the database(s)
before dropping the login.
```

Denying SQL Server Access to a Windows User or Group

In SQL Server 2000, the system stored procedure sp_denylogin was used to deny a Windows user or group access to SQL Server. This included domain users, domain groups, local users, and local groups. In SQL Server 2005, you can use the DENY CONNECT SQL command. For example:

```
USE [master]
GO
DENY CONNECT SQL TO [JOEPROD\TestUser]
GO
```

To allow access again, you can use GRANT:

```
USE [master]
GO
GRANT CONNECT SQL TO [JOEPROD\TestUser]
GO
```

How It Works

This section is a sneak preview of Chapter 18, where GRANT and DENY will be explained in more detail. In a nutshell, the GRANT command grants permissions to securables, and DENY denies permissions to them. Use DENY CONNECT to restrict the Windows User or Group login from accessing a SQL Server instance the next time a login attempt is made. In both GRANT CONNECT and DENY CONNECT, it is assumed that the Windows user or group already has a login in SQL Server. Keep in mind that there are limitations to which logins you can deny permissions to. For example, if you try to DENY CONNECT to your own login with the following code:

```
DENY CONNECT SQL TO [JOEPROD\Owner]
```

It returns the following warning:

```
Cannot grant, deny, or revoke permissions to sa, dbo, information_schema,
sys, or yourself.
```

SQL Server Principals

Windows authentication relies on the underlying operating system to perform authentication (determining who a particular user is), and means that SQL Server performs the necessary authorization (determining what actions an authenticated user is entitled to perform). When working with SQL Server principals and SQL Server authentication, SQL Server itself performs both authentication and authorization.

As noted earlier, when using mixed authentication mode, you can create your own login and passwords within SQL Server. These SQL logins only exist in SQL Server and do not have an outside Windows user/group mapping. With SQL logins, the passwords are stored within SQL Server. These user credentials are stored in SQL Server and are used to authenticate the user in question and to determine his or her appropriate access rights.

Because the security method involves explicit passwords, it is inherently less secure than using Windows Authentication alone. However, SQL Server logins are still commonly used with third-party and non-Windows operating system applications. SQL Server 2005 *has* improved the password protection capabilities by enabling Windows-like password functionality, such as forced password changes, expiration dates, and other password policies (e.g. password complexity), with Windows 2003 Server and higher.

As with Windows logins, SQL Server logins apply only at the server level; you can't grant permissions on these to specific database objects. Unless you are granted membership to a fixed-server role such as sysadmin, you must create database users associated to the login before you can begin working with database objects.

As in previous versions of SQL Server, SQL Server 2005 supports principals based on both individual logins and server roles, which multiple individual users can be assigned to.

In SQL Server 2000, the system stored procedure sp_addlogin was used to create a new SQL Server login but, again, this has now been replaced by use of the CREATE LOGIN command:

```
CREATE LOGIN login_name
[WITH PASSWORD = ' password ' [ HASHED ] [ MUST_CHANGE ],
    SID = sid],
    DEFAULT_DATABASE = database,
    DEFAULT_LANGUAGE = language,
    CHECK_EXPIRATION = { ON | OFF},
    CHECK_POLICY = { ON | OFF},
    CREDENTIAL = credential_name ]h
```

The arguments of this command are described in Table 17-3.

Table 17-3. *CREATE LOGIN Arguments*

Argument	Description
login_name	This is the login name.
' password ' [HASHED] [MUST_CHANGE]	This is the login's password. Specifying the HASHED option means that the provided password is already hashed (made into an unreadable and secured format). If MUST_CHANGE is specified, the user is prompted to change the password the first time the user logs in.
SID = sid	This explicitly specifies the sid which will be used in the system tables of the SQL Server instance. This can be based on a login from a different SQL Server instance (if you're migrating logins). If this isn't specified, SQL Server generates its own sid in the system tables.
DEFAULT_DATABASE = database	This option specifies the default database context of the SQL login, with the master system database being the default.
DEFAULT_LANGUAGE = language	This option specifies the default language of the login, with the server default language being the login default if this option isn't specified.

(Continued)

Table 17-3. *Continued*

Argument	Description
CHECK_EXPIRATION = { ON | OFF },	When set to ON (the default), the SQL login will be subject to a password expiration policy. A password expiration policy effects how long a password will remain valid before it must be changed. This functionality requires Windows 2003 Server or higher versions.
CHECK_POLICY = { ON | OFF },	When set to ON (the default), Windows password policies are applied to the SQL login (for example, policies regarding the password's length, complexity, and inclusion of non-alphanumeric characters).This functionality requires Windows 2003 Server or higher versions.
CREDENTIAL = credential_name	Allows a server credential to be mapped to the SQL login. See Chapter 18, "Securables and Permissions" for more information on credentials.

Creating a SQL Server Login

This example first demonstrates how to create a SQL Server login with a password and a default database designated:

```
CREATE LOGIN Veronica
WITH PASSWORD = 'InfernoII',
DEFAULT_DATABASE = AdventureWorks
```

Assuming you are using Windows 2003 Server or higher, as well as mixed authentication, the recipe goes on to create a SQL login with a password that must be changed the first time the user logs in. This login also is created with the CHECK_POLICY option ON, requiring it to comply with Windows password policies:

```
CREATE LOGIN Trishelle
WITH PASSWORD = 'ChangeMe' MUST_CHANGE ,
    CHECK_EXPIRATION = ON,
        CHECK_POLICY = ON
```

How It Works

The first example in this recipe demonstrated creating a SQL login named Veronica. The login name was designated after CREATE LOGIN:

```
CREATE LOGIN Veronica
```

The second line designated the login's password:

```
WITH PASSWORD = 'InfernoII',
```

The last line of code designated the default database that the login's context would first enter after logging into SQL Server:

```
DEFAULT_DATABASE = AdventureWorks
```

The second SQL login example demonstrated how to force a password to be changed on the first login by designating the MUST CHANGE token after the password:

```
CREATE LOGIN Trishelle
WITH PASSWORD = 'ChangeMe' MUST_CHANGE ,
```

This password policy integration requires Windows 2003 Server, as did the password expiration and password policy options also designated for this login:

```
CHECK_EXPIRATION = ON,
    CHECK_POLICY = ON
```

Viewing SQL Server Logins

Again, you can view SQL Server logins (and other principals) by querying the sys.server_principals system catalog view:

```
SELECT name, sid
FROM sys.server_principals
WHERE type_desc IN ('SQL_LOGIN')
ORDER BY name
```

This returns the following results:

name	sid
Boris	0xC2692B07894DFD45913C5595C87936B9
BrianG	0x4EC3966D4E33844F89680AFD87D2D5BD
JoeSa	0xB64D3C39533CC648B581884EC143F2D4
Prageeta	0x00CACEF1F0E0CE429B7C808B11A624E7
sa	0x01
SteveP	0xAAA2CD258750C641BBE9584627CAA11F
Veronica	0xE08E462A75D8C047A4561D4E9292296D

How It Works

This recipe's query returned the name and sid of each SQL login on the SQL Server instance.

Altering a SQL Server Login

Once a login is added to SQL Server it can be modified using the ALTER LOGIN command. Using this command, you can perform several tasks:

- Change the login's password.
- Change the default database or language.
- Change the name of the existing login without disrupting the login's currently assigned permissions.
- Change the password policy settings (enabling or disabling them).
- Map or remove mapping from a SQL login credential.
- Enable or disable a login from being used.
- Unlock a locked login.

The syntax is as follows:

```
ALTER LOGIN login_name
    {
    ENABLE | DISABLE
    |
WITH  PASSWORD = ' password '
    [ OLD_PASSWORD = ' oldpassword '
      | [ MUST_CHANGE | UNLOCK ] ]
```

```
| DEFAULT_DATABASE = database
| DEFAULT_LANGUAGE = language
| NAME = login_name
| CHECK_POLICY = { ON | OFF }
| CHECK_EXPIRATION = { ON | OFF }
| CREDENTIAL = credential_name
| NO CREDENTIAL
}
```

The arguments of this command are described in Table 17-4.

Table 17-4. *ALTER LOGIN Arguments*

Argument	Description
`login_name`	The name of the SQL login.
`ENABLE	DISABLE`	Enables or disables a login from being used in SQL Server (disabling is an alternative to dropping a login).
`PASSWORD = ' password '` `[ OLD_PASSWORD = 'oldpassword ' |` `[MUST_CHANGE	UNLOCK]]`	The PASSWORD argument specifies the new password name and the OLD_PASSWORD is the current password which is being changed (although when logged in as the sysadmin fixed server role, the OLD_PASSWORD is not required). If MUST_CHANGE is specified, the user is prompted to change the password the first time the password is used. UNLOCK unlocks a locked login (a login can become locked due to too many unsuccessful login attempts, or exceeding expiration limits).
`DEFAULT_DATABASE = database`	This option specifies the default database context of the SQL login, with the master system database being the default.
`DEFAULT_LANGUAGE = language`	This option specifies the default language of the login, with the server default language being the login default if this option isn't specified.
`NAME = login_name`	Specifies the new login name.
`CHECK_POLICY = { ON	OFF }`	When set to ON (the default), the SQL login will be subject to a password expiration policy (this functionality requires Windows 2003 Server or higher versions).
`CHECK_EXPIRATION = { ON	OFF }`	When set to ON (the default), Windows password policies are applied to the SQL login (this functionality requires Windows 2003 Server or higher versions).
`CREDENTIAL = credential_name`	Allows a server credential to be mapped to the SQL login. See Chapter 18 for more information on credentials.
`NO CREDENTIAL`	This option removes a credential mapping from the SQL login.

In the first example of this recipe, a SQL login's password is changed from "InfernoII" to "InfernoIII":

```
ALTER LOGIN Veronica
WITH  PASSWORD = 'InfernoIII'
OLD_PASSWORD = 'InfernoII'
```

The OLD_PASSWORD is the current password which is being changed, however sysadmin fixed server role members don't have to know the old password in order to change it.

This second example demonstrates changing the default database of the Veronica SQL login:

```
ALTER LOGIN Veronica
WITH DEFAULT DATABASE = [AdventureWorks]
```

This third example in this recipe demonstrates changing both the name and password of a SQL login:

```
ALTER LOGIN Veronica
WITH NAME = Angela,
PASSWORD = 'BOS2004'
```

Changing the login name instead of just dropping and creating a new one offers one major benefit—the permissions associated to the original login are not disrupted when the login is renamed. In this case, the Veronica login is renamed to Angela, but the permissions remain the same.

How It Works

In the first example of this recipe, ALTER LOGIN was used to change a password designating the old password and the new password. If you have sysadmin fixed server role permissions, you only need to designate the new password. The second example demonstrated how to change the default database of a SQL login. The last example demonstrated how to change a login's name from "Veronica" to "Angela," as well as change the login's password.

Dropping a SQL Login

This recipe demonstrates dropping a SQL login from a SQL Server instance by using the DROP LOGIN command.

The syntax is as follows:

```
DROP LOGIN login_name
```

The only parameter is the login name—which can be a Windows or SQL login, as this recipe demonstrates:

```
-- SQL Login
DROP LOGIN Angela
```

How It Works

This recipe demonstrated the simple DROP LOGIN command, which removes a login from SQL Server. The process is simple, however if a login owns any securables (see the next chapter for information on securables), the DROP attempt will fail. For example, if the Angela login had been a database owner, an error like the following would have been raised:

```
Msg 15174, Level 16, State 1, Line 3
Login 'Angela' owns one or more database(s). Change the owner of the database(s) before
dropping the login.
```

Managing Server Role Members

Fixed server roles are pre-defined SQL groups that have specific SQL Server-scoped (as opposed to database- or schema-scoped) permissions assigned to them. You cannot create new fixed server roles, you can only add or remove membership to that role from other SQL or Windows logins.

The sysadmin fixed server role is the role with the highest level of permissions in a SQL Server instance. Although server roles are permissions-based, they have members (SQL or Windows logins/groups) and are categorized by Microsoft as principals.

To add a login to a fixed server role, use the sp_addsrvrolemember system stored procedure.

The syntax is as follows:

```
sp_addsrvrolemember [ @loginame= ] 'login',
[ @rolename = ] 'role'
```

The first parameter of the system stored procedure is the login name to add to the fixed server role. The second parameter is the fixed server role you are adding the login to.

In this example, the login Veronica is created and then added to the sysadmin fixed server role:

```
CREATE LOGIN Veronica
WITH PASSWORD = 'PalmTree1'
GO

EXEC master..sp_addsrvrolemember
'Veronica',
'sysadmin'
GO
```

To remove a login from a fixed server role, the system stored procedure sp_dropsrvrolemember is used. The syntax is almost identical to sp_addsrvrolemember:

```
sp_dropsrvrolemember [ @loginame= ] 'login' ,
[ @rolename= ] 'role'
```

This example *removes* the Veronica login from the sysadmin fixed role membership:

```
EXEC master..sp_dropsrvrolemember
'Veronica',
'sysadmin'
GO
```

How It Works

Once a login is added to a fixed server role, that login receives the permissions associated with the fixed server role. The sp_addsrvrolemember system stored procedure was used to add a new login to a fixed role membership, and sp_dropsrvrolemember was used to remove a login from a fixed role membership.

Adding SQL or Windows logins to a fixed server role should never be done lightly. Fixed server roles contain far-reaching permissions—so as a rule of thumb, seek to grant only those permissions that are absolutely necessary for the job at hand. For example, don't give sysadmin membership to someone who just needs SELECT permission on a table.

■**Note** In the next chapter you'll learn more about the granularity of permissions, and how in SQL Server 2005 it is easier to assign "least permissions" instead of having to add logins to fixed server roles.

Reporting Fixed Server Role Information

Fixed server roles define a grouping of SQL Server-scoped permissions (such as backing up a database or creating new logins). Like SQL or Windows logins, fixed server roles have a security-identifier (sid) and can be viewed in the sys.server_principals system catalog view. Unlike SQL or Windows logins, fixed server roles can have members (SQL and Windows logins) defined within them which inherit the permissions of the fixed server role.

To view fixed server roles, query the sys.server_principals system catalog view:

```
SELECT name
FROM sys.server_principals
WHERE type_desc = 'SERVER_ROLE'
```

This returns:

```
name
------------------------------------------------------------------------
public
sysadmin
securityadmin
serveradmin
setupadmin
processadmin
diskadmin
dbcreator
bulkadmin

(9 row(s) affected)
```

You can also view a list of fixed server roles by executing the sp_helpserverrole system stored procedure:

```
EXEC sp_helpsrvrole
```

This returns:

```
ServerRole                          Description
----------------------------------  ---------------------------------
sysadmin                            System Administrators
securityadmin                       Security Administrators
serveradmin                         Server Administrators
setupadmin                          Setup Administrators
processadmin                        Process Administrators
diskadmin                           Disk Administrators
dbcreator                           Database Creators
bulkadmin                           Bulk Insert Administrators

(8 row(s) affected)
```

Table 17-5 details the permissions granted to each fixed server role.

Table 17-5. *Server Role Permissions*

Server Role	Granted Permissions
sysadmin	GRANT option (can GRANT permissions to others), CONTROL SERVER
setupadmin	ALTER ANY LINKED SERVER
serveradmin	ALTER SETTINGS, SHUTDOWN, CREATE ENDPOINT, ALTER SERVER STATE, ALTER ANY ENDPOINT, ALTER RESOURCES
securityadmin	ALTER ANY LOGIN
processadmin	ALTER SERVER STATE, ALTER ANY CONNECTION
diskadmin	ALTER RESOURCES
dbcreator	CREATE DATABASE
bulkadmin	ADMINISTER BULK OPERATIONS

To see the members of a fixed server role, you can execute the sp_helpsrvrolemember system stored procedure:

```
EXEC sp_helpsrvrolemember 'sysadmin'
```

This returns the following results:

ServerRole	MemberName	MemberSid
sysadmin	sa	0x01
sysadmin	BUILTIN\Administrators	0x01020000000000052000000020020000
sysadmin	NT AUTHORITY\SYSTEM	0x010100000000000512000000
sysadmin	Veronica	0xEC5C372109E10344BC6CE7B04514EC8D
sysadmin	JOEPROD\Owner	0x0105000000000000515000000527A777BF094B3
sysadmin	sa	0x01

How It Works

You can query the system catalog view sys.server_principals in order to view fixed server roles, or you can use the sp_helpsrvrole system stored procedure to view descriptions for each of the roles. To view members of a role (other principals), use the sp_helpsrvrolemember system stored procedure.

The next recipe will show you how to *add* or *remove* other principals to a fixed server role.

Database Principals

Database principals are the objects that represent users to which we can assign permissions to access databases or particular objects within a database. Whereas logins operate at the server level and allow us to perform actions such as connecting to a SQL Server, database principals operate at the database level, and allow us to select or manipulate data, to perform DDL statements on objects within the database, or to manage users' permissions at the database level.

SQL Server 2005 recognizes four different types of database principals:

- *Database users*. Database user principals are the database-level security context under which requests within the database are executed, and are associated with either SQL Server or Windows logins.

- *Database roles*. Database roles come in two flavors, fixed and user-defined. Fixed database roles are found in each database of a SQL Server instance, and have database scoped permissions assigned to them (such as SELECT permission on all tables or the ability to CREATE tables). User defined database roles are those that you can create yourself, allowing you to manage permissions to securables more easily than if you had to individually grant similar permissions to multiple database users.

- *Application roles*. Application roles are groupings of permissions that don't allow members. Instead, you can "log in" as the application role. When you use an application role, it overrides all of the other permissions your login would otherwise have, giving you only those permissions granted to the application role.

In this section, I'll review how to create, modify, report on, and drop database users. We'll also cover how to work with database roles (fixed and user-defined) and application roles.

Creating Database Users

Once a login is created, it can then be mapped to a database user. A login can be mapped to multiple databases on a single SQL Server instance—but only one user for each database it has access to.

In SQL Server 2000, users were granted access with the sp_grantdbaccess system stored procedure. In SQL Server 2005, the CREATE USER command is used instead.

The syntax is as follows:

```
CREATE USER user_name
    [ FOR
        { LOGIN login_name
        | CERTIFICATE cert_name
        | ASYMMETRIC KEY asym_key_name
        }
    ]
    [ WITH DEFAULT_SCHEMA = schema_name ]
```

The arguments of this command are described in Table 17-6.

Table 17-6. *CREATE USER Arguments*

Argument	Description
user_name	The name of the user in the database.
login_name	The name of the SQL or Windows login that is mapping to the database user.
cert_name	When designated, this specifies a certificate that is bound to the database user. See Chapter 19 for more information on certificates.
asym_key_name	When designated, this specifies an asymmetric key that is bound to the database user. See Chapter 19 for more information on keys.
schema_name	The default schema that the user will belong to, which will determine what schema is checked first when the user references database objects. If this option is unspecified, the dbo schema will be used. This schema name can also be designated for a schema not yet created in the database.

In this first example of the recipe, a new user called Veronica is created in the TestDB database:

```
USE TestDB
GO
CREATE USER Veronica
```

In the second example, a Windows login is mapped to a database user called Joe with a default schema specified:

```
USE AdventureWorks
GO
CREATE USER Joe
FOR LOGIN [JOEPROD\TestUser]
WITH DEFAULT_SCHEMA = HumanResources
```

How It Works

In the first example of the recipe, a user named Veronica was created in the TestDB database. If you don't designate the FOR LOGIN clause of CREATE USER, it is assumed that the user maps to a login with the same name (in this case, a login named Veronica). Notice that the default schema was not designated, which means Veronica's default schema will be dbo.

In the second example, a new user named Joe was created in the AdventureWorks database, mapped to a Windows login named [JOEPROD\TestUser] (notice the square brackets). The default schema was also set for the Joe login to HumanResources. For any unqualified object references in queries performed by Joe, SQL Server will first search for objects in the HumanResources schema.

Reporting Database User Information

You can report database user (and role) information for the current database connection by using the sp_helpuser system stored procedure.

The syntax is as follows:

```
sp_helpuser [ [ @name_in_db= ] ' security_account ' ]
```

The single, optional parameter is the name of the database user for which you wish to return information. For example:

```
EXEC sp_helpuser 'Veronica'
```

This returns the following results:

UserName	GroupName	LoginName	DefDBName	DefSchemaName	UserID	SID
Veronica	public	Veronica	NewDB	dbo	8	0xEC5C372109E10344BC6CE7B04514EC8D

How It Works

The sp_helpuser system stored procedure returns the database users defined in the current database. From the results, you can determine important information such as the user name, login name, default database and schema, and the user's security-identifier (sid). If a specific user isn't designated, sp_helpuser returns information on all users in the current database you are connected to.

Modifying a Database User

In SQL Server 2005 you can rename a database user or change the user's default schema by using the ALTER USER command.

The syntax is as follows:

```
ALTER USER user_name
    WITH  NAME = new_user_name
    | DEFAULT_SCHEMA = schema_name
```

The arguments of this command are described in Table 17-7.

Table 17-7. *ALTER USER Arguments*

Argument	Description
User_name	The name of the user in the database.
New_user_name	The new name of the database user.
schema_name	The new default schema of the database user.

In this first example of this recipe, the default schema of the Joe database user is changed:

```
USE AdventureWorks
GO

ALTER USER Joe
WITH DEFAULT_SCHEMA = Production
```

In the second example of this recipe, a database user name is changed:

```
USE TestDB
GO

ALTER USER Veronica
WITH NAME = VSanders
```

How It Works

The ALTER USER command allows you to perform one of two changes: renaming a database user or changing a database user's default schema. The first example changed the default schema of the Joe login to the Production schema. The second example renamed the database user Veronica to VSanders.

Removing a Database User from the Database

In SQL Server 2000, the sp_dropuser system stored procedure was used to drop a user from a database. In SQL Server 2005, the DROP USER command is used instead.

The syntax is as follows:

```
DROP USER user_name
```

The user_name is the name of the database user, as this example demonstrates:

```
USE TestDB
GO

DROP USER VSanders
```

How It Works

The DROP USER command removes a user from the database, but does not impact the Windows or SQL login that is associated to it. Like DROP LOGIN, you can't drop a user that is the owner of database objects. For example, if the database user Joe is the schema owner for a schema called Test, you'll get an error like the following:

```
Msg 15138, Level 16, State 1, Line 2
The database principal owns a schema in the database, and cannot be dropped.
```

Fixing Orphaned Database Users

When you migrate a database to a new server (by using BACKUP/RESTORE, for example) the relationship between logins and database users can break. A login has a security-identifier (sid) which uniquely identifies it on the SQL Server instance. This sid is stored for the login's associated database user in each database that the login has access to. Creating another login on a different SQL Server instance with the same name will not recreate the same sid.

The following query demonstrates this link by joining the sys.database_principals system catalog view to the sys.server_principals catalog view on the sid column:

```
SELECT s.name LoginName, d.name DbName, d.sid
FROM sys.database_principals d
INNER JOIN  sys.server_principals s ON
d.sid = s.sid
WHERE s.name = 'Veronica'
```

This returns:

```
LoginName        DbUserName      sid
--------------   --------------  ---------------------------------
Veronica         Veronica        0xEC5C372109E10344BC6CE7B04514EC8D

(1 row(s) affected)
```

If you RESTORE a database from a different SQL Server instance onto a new SQL Server instance—and the database users don't have associated logins on the new SQL Server instance—the database users can become "orphaned." If there are logins with the same name on the new SQL Server instance that match the name of the database users, the database users still may be orphaned in the database if the login sid doesn't match the restored database user sid.

To fix this for SQL logins, you can use the sp_change_users_login system stored procedure, which uses the following syntax:

```
sp_change_users_login [ @Action = ] 'action'
    [ , [ @UserNamePattern = ] 'user' ]
    [ , [ @LoginName = ] 'login' ]
        [ , [ @Password = ] 'password' ]
```

The parameters of the command are described in Table 17-8.

Table 17-8. *sp_change_users_login Parameters*

Parameter	Description
Action	If selecting auto_fix, database users and logins will automatically be linked if they have the same name. The report option lists orphaned users in the current database. The update_one option explicitly links a user in the current database to an existing SQL Server login.
User	The database user name.
Login	The SQL Server login name.
Password	This is the password that the new SQL Server login will use if there is no matching login name on the SQL Server instance. This system stored procedure will link those names that match, and create new SQL logins for those orphaned database users that don't match.

In this example, a database called TestDB was restored to a new SQL Server instance. TestDB has a user named Danny. There isn't a login named Danny on the *new* SQL Server instance, so the database user is orphaned. To detect this, sp_change_users_login with the report action is used:

```
EXEC sp_change_users_login 'Report'
```

This returns:

```
UserName        UserSID
--------------  ---------------------------------
Danny           0x87424DA9CF8EF548AE58E19BD04A798D
```

Next, the sp_change_users_login is executed with the auto_fix action to fix the orphaned database user:

```
EXEC sp_change_users_login 'Auto_Fix', 'Danny', NULL, 'newDannypassword!#@'
```

This returns:

```
Barring a conflict, the row for user 'Danny' will be fixed by updating its link to a new
login.
The number of orphaned users fixed by updating users was 0.
The number of orphaned users fixed by adding new logins and then updating users was 1.
```

How It Works

This recipe demonstrated how to use sp_change_users_login to fix orphaned database users. The first query executed the procedure with the Report option in order to show any orphaned users:

```
EXEC sp_change_users_login 'Report'
```

After that, the stored procedure used the Auto_Fix option to link a specific database user (Danny):

```
EXEC sp_change_users_login 'Auto_Fix', 'Danny', NULL, 'newDannypassword!#@'
```

A password was provided in the fourth parameter so that if an existing login named Danny isn't found, it will be created and will use the provided password. The results of that operation tell us that no existing logins were found ("the number of orphaned users fixed by updating users was 0"). Instead, a new login was created ("the number of orphaned users fixed by adding new logins and then updating users was 1").

Reporting Fixed Database Roles Information

Fixed database roles are found in each database of a SQL Server instance, and have database scoped permissions assigned to them (such as SELECT permission on all tables or the ability to CREATE tables). Like fixed server roles, fixed database roles have members (database users) which inherit the permissions of the role.

A list of fixed database roles can be viewed by executing the sp_helpdbfixedrole system stored procedure:

```
EXEC sp_helpdbfixedrole
```

This returns the following results:

```
DBFixedRole            Description
db_owner               DB Owners
db_accessadmin         DB Access Administrators
db_securityadmin       DB Security Administrators
db_ddladmin            DB DDL Administrators
db_backupoperator      DB Backup Operator
db_datareader          DB Data Reader
db_datawriter          DB Data Writer
db_denydatareader      DB Deny Data Reader
db_denydatawriter      DB Deny Data Writer
```

Table 17-9 details the permissions granted to each fixed database roles:

Table 17-9. *Fixed Database Role Permissions*

Server Role	Granted Permissions
db_owner	Granted CONTROL (with GRANT option)
db_accessadmin	Granted CONNECT (with GRANT option), CREATE SCHEMA
db_securityadmin	Granted ALTER ANY APPLICATION ROLE, ALTER ANY ROLE, CREATE SCHEMA, granted VIEW DEFINITION
db_ddladmin	Granted ALTER ANY (ASSEMBLY, CERTIFICATE, CONTRACT, EVENT NOTIFICATION, DATASPACE, FULLTEXT CATALOG, MESSAGE TYPE, REMOTE SERVICE BINDING, ROUTE, SCHEMA, SERVICE, SYMMETRIC KEY, TRIGGER, XML SCHEMA COLLECTION), CHECKPOINT, CREATE (AGGREGATE, ASSEMBLY, CONTRACT, DEFAULT, FUNCTION, MESSAGE TYPE, PROCEDURE, QUEUE, REMOTE SERVICE BINDING, ROUTE, RULE, SCHEMA, SERVICE, SYMMETRIC KEY, SYNONYM, TABLE, TYPE, VIEW, XML SCHEMA COLLECTION), REFERENCES
db_backupoperator	Granted BACKUP DATABASE, BACKUP LOG, CHECKPOINT
db_datareader	Granted SELECT
db_datawriter	Granted DELETE, INSERT, UPDATE
db_denydatareader	Denied SELECT
db_denydatawriter	Denied INSERT, UPDATE, DELETE

To see the database members of a fixed database role (or any user-defined or application role), you can execute the sp_helprolemember system stored procedure:

```
EXEC sp_helprolemember
```

This returns the following results (the member sid refers to the sid of the login mapped to the database user):

```
DbRole                MemberName    MemberSid
db_backupoperator     Joe           0x0105000000000000515000000527A777BF094B3850F
db_datawriter         Joe           0x0105000000000000515000000527A777BF094B3850FF83D0
db_owner              dbo           0x0105000000000000515000000527A777BF094B3850FF8
```

How It Works

Fixed database roles are found in each database on a SQL Server instance. A fixed database role groups important database permissions together. These permissions can't be modified or removed.

In this recipe, we used sp_helpdbfixedrole to list the available fixed database roles:

```
EXEC sp_helpdbfixedrole
```

After that, the sp_helprolemember system stored procedure was used to list the members of each fixed database role (database users), showing the role name, database user name, and login sid:

```
EXEC sp_helprolemember
```

As with fixed server roles, it's best not to grant membership to them without assurance that all permissions are absolutely necessary for the database user. Do not, for example, grant a user db_owner membership when only SELECT permissions on a table are needed.

The next recipe shows you how to add or remove database users to a fixed database role.

Managing Fixed Database Role Membership

To associate a database user or role with a database role (user defined or application role), use the sp_addrolemember system stored procedure.

The syntax is as follows:

```
sp_addrolemember [ @rolename = ] 'role',
    [ @membername = ] 'security_account'
```

The first parameter of the system stored procedure takes the role name, and the second parameter the name of the database user.

To remove the association between a database user and role, use the sp_droprolemember system stored procedure:

```
sp_droprolemember [ @rolename= ] 'role' ,
        [ @membername= ] 'security_account'
```

Like sp_addrolemember, the first parameter of the system stored procedure takes the role name, and the second parameter takes the name of the database user.

This first example demonstrates adding the database user Veronica to the fixed db_datawriter and db_datareader roles:

```
USE AdventureWorks
GO
EXEC sp_addrolemember 'db_datawriter', 'Veronica'
EXEC sp_addrolemember 'db_datareader', 'Veronica'
```

This second example demonstrates how to *remove* the database user Veronica from the db_datawriter role:

```
USE AdventureWorks
GO
EXEC sp_droprolemember 'db_datawriter', 'Veronica'
```

How It Works

This recipe began by discussing sp_addrolemember, which allows you to add a database user to an existing database role. The database user Veronica was added to db_datawriter and db_datareader, which gives her cumulative permissions to SELECT, INSERT, UPDATE, or DELETE from any table or view in the AdventureWorks database:

```
EXEC sp_addrolemember 'db_datawriter', 'Veronica'
EXEC sp_addrolemember 'db_datareader', 'Veronica'
```

The first parameter of the stored procedure was the database role, and the second parameter was the name of the database user (or role) that the database role is associated to.

After that, the sp_droprolemember was used to remove Veronica's membership from the db_datawriter role:

```
EXEC sp_droprolemember 'db_datawriter', 'Veronica'
```

Managing User-Defined Database Roles

User defined database roles allow you to manage permissions to securables more easily than if you had to individually grant the same permissions to multiple database users over and over again. Instead, you can create a database role, grant it permissions to securables, and then add one or more database users as members to that database role. When permission changes are needed, you only have to modify the permissions of the single database role and the members of the role will then automatically inherit those permission changes.

In SQL Server 2000, the sp_addrole system-stored procedure was used to create a new database role. In SQL Server 2005, the CREATE ROLE command is used instead.

The syntax is as follows:

```
CREATE ROLE role_name [ AUTHORIZATION owner_name ]
```

The command takes the name of the new role, and an optional role owner name. The owner name is the name of the user or database role that owns the new database role (and thus can manage it).

You can list all database roles (fixed, user-defined, and application) by executing the sp_helprole system stored procedure:

```
EXEC sp_helprole
```

This returns the following abridged results (the IsAppRole column shows as a "1" if the role is an application role, and "0" if not):

RoleName	RoleId	IsAppRole
public	0	0
HR_ReportSpecialist	7	0
db_owner	16384	0
...	...	...

Once a database role is created in a database, you can grant or deny it permissions as you would a regular database user (see the next chapter for more on permissions). I'll also demonstrate granting permissions to a database role in a moment.

If you wish to change the name of the database role, *without* also disrupting the role's current permissions and membership, you can use the ALTER ROLE command, which has the following syntax:

```
ALTER ROLE role_name WITH NAME = new_name
```

The command takes the name of the original role as the first argument, and the new role name in the second argument.

To drop a role, use the DROP ROLE command. The syntax is as follows:

```
DROP ROLE role_name
```

If a role owns any securables, you'll need to transfer ownership to a new owner before you can drop the role.

In this example, a new role is created in the AdventureWorks database:

```
USE AdventureWorks
GO
CREATE ROLE HR_ReportSpecialist AUTHORIZATION db_owner
```

After being created, this new role doesn't have any database permissions yet. In this query, the HR_ReportSpecialist database role is granted permission to SELECT from the HumanResources.Employee table:

```
GRANT SELECT ON HumanResources.Employee TO HR_ReportSpecialist
```

If you want the login Veronica to have permissions to read from the HumanResources.Employee table, along with any other permissions this role may be granted in the future, you must execute sp_droprolemember:

```
EXEC sp_addrolemember 'HR_ReportSpecialist',
        'Veronica'
GO
```

If, later on, we decide that the name of the role doesn't match its purpose, we can change its name using ALTER ROLE:

```
ALTER ROLE HR_ReportSpecialist WITH NAME = HumanResources_RS
```

Even though the role name was changed, Veronica remains a member of the role.
This last example demonstrates dropping a database role:

```
DROP ROLE HumanResources_RS
```

This returns an error message, because the role must be emptied of members before it can be dropped:

```
Msg 15144, Level 16, State 1, Line 1
The role has members. It must be empty before it can be dropped.
```

So, the single member of this role is then dropped, prior to dropping the role:

```
EXEC sp_droprolemember 'HumanResources_RS',
        'Veronica'
GO

DROP ROLE HumanResources_RS
```

How It Works

The CREATE ROLE command creates a new database role in a database. Once created, you can apply permissions to the role as you would a regular database user. Roles allow you to administer permissions at a group level—allowing individual role members to inherit permissions in a consistent manner instead of applying permissions to individual users, which may or may not be identical.

This recipe demonstrated several commands related to managing user-defined database roles. The sp_helprole system stored procedure was used to list all database roles in the current database. CREATE ROLE was used to create a new user-defined role owned by the db_owner fixed database role:

```
CREATE ROLE HR_ReportSpecialist AUTHORIZATION db_owner
```

We then granted permissions to the new role to SELECT from a table:

```
GRANT SELECT ON HumanResources.Employee TO HR_ReportSpecialist
```

The Veronica user was then added as a member of the new role:

```
EXEC sp_addrolemember 'HR_ReportSpecialist',
        'Veronica'
```

The name of the role was changed using ALTER ROLE (still leaving membership and permissions intact):

```
ALTER ROLE HR_ReportSpecialist WITH NAME = HumanResources_RS
```

The Veronica user was then dropped from the role (so that we could drop the user-defined role):

```
EXEC sp_droprolemember 'HumanResources_RS',
        'Veronica'
```

Once emptied of members, the user-defined database role was then dropped:

```
DROP ROLE HumanResources_RS
```

Managing Application Roles

An application role is a hybrid between a login and a database role. You can assign permissions to application roles in the same way that you can assign permissions to user-defined roles. Application roles differ from database and server roles, however, in that application roles *do not allow members*. Instead, an application role is *activated* using a password enabled system stored procedure. When you use an application role, it overrides all of the other permissions your login would otherwise have.

Because an application role has no members, it requires a password for the permissions to be enabled. In addition to this, once a session's context is set to use an application role, any existing user or login permissions are nullified. Only the application role's permissions apply.

To create an application role, use the CREATE APPLICATION ROLE, which has the following syntax:

```
CREATE APPLICATION ROLE application_role_name
    WITH PASSWORD = ' password ' [ , DEFAULT_SCHEMA = schema_name ]
```

The arguments of this command are described in Table 17-10.

Table 17-10. *CREATE APPLICATON ROLE Arguments*

Argument	Description
application_role_name	The name of the application role.
password	The password to enable access to the application role's permissions.
schema_name	The default database schema of the application role that defines which schema is checked for unqualified object names in a query.

In this example, a new application role name, DataWareHouseApp, is created and granted permissions to a view in the AdventureWorks database:

```
CREATE APPLICATION ROLE DataWareHouseApp
WITH PASSWORD =  'mywarehouse123!',
 DEFAULT_SCHEMA = dbo
```

An application role by itself is useless without first granting it permissions to do something. So, in this example, the application role is given SELECT permissions on a specific database view:

```
-- Now grant this application role permissions
GRANT SELECT ON  Sales.vSalesPersonSalesByFiscalYears
TO DataWareHouseApp
```

The system stored procedure sp_setapprole is used to enable the permissions of the application role for the current user session.

The syntax is as follows:

```
sp_setapprole [@rolename=] 'role', [@password=]
{Encrypt N'password'} | 'password' [,[@encrypt =] 'encrypt_style']
```

The parameters of this stored procedure are described in Table 17-11.

Table 17-11. *sp_setapprole Parameters*

Parameter	Description
role	The application role name.
password	The application role password designated in CREATE ROLE.
encrypt_style	When designated, you can choose "none" for no encryption of the password, or "odbc" when the password is encrypted using the ODBC encryption functionality.

In this next example, I activate an application role and query two tables:

```
EXEC sp_setapprole 'DataWareHouseApp', -- App role name
    'mywarehouse123!' -- Password

-- Works
SELECT COUNT(*)
FROM Sales.vSalesPersonSalesByFiscalYears

-- Doesn't work
SELECT COUNT(*)
FROM HumanResources.vJobCandidate
```

This returns:

```
-----------
14

(1 row(s) affected)

Msg 229, Level 14, State 5, Line 7
SELECT permission denied on object 'vJobCandidate', database 'AdventureWorks', schema
'HumanResources'.
```

Even though the original connection login was for a login with sysadmin permissions, using sp_setapprole to enter the application permissions means that only that role's permissions apply. So, in this case, the application role had SELECT permission for the Sales.vSalesPersonSalesByFiscalYears view, but not the HumanResources.vJobCandidate view queried in the example.

To revert back to the original login's permissions, you must close out the connection and open a new connection.

You can modify the name, password, or default database of an application role using the ALTER APPLICATION ROLE command.

The syntax is as follows:

```
ALTER APPLICATION ROLE application_role_name
WITH  NAME = new_application_role_name
    | PASSWORD = ' password '
    | DEFAULT_SCHEMA = schema_name
```

The arguments of the command are described in Table 17-12.

Table 17-12. *ALTER APPLICATION ROLE Arguments*

Parameter	Description
new_application_role_name	The new application role name.
password	The new application role password.
schema_name	The new default schema.

In this example, the application role name and password are changed:

```
ALTER APPLICATION ROLE DataWareHouseApp
WITH  NAME = DW_App, PASSWORD = 'newsecret!123'
```

To remove an application role from the database, use DROP APPLICATION ROLE, which has the following syntax:

```
DROP APPLICATION ROLE rolename
```

This command takes only one argument, the name of the application role to be dropped. For example:

```
DROP APPLICATION ROLE DW_App
```

How It Works

This recipe demonstrated how to:

- Create a new application role using CREATE APPLICATION ROLE.
- Activate the role permissions using sp_setapprole.
- Modify an application role using ALTER APPLICATION ROLE.
- Remove an application role from a database using DROP APPLICATION ROLE.

Application roles are a convenient solution for application developers who wish to grant users access *only through an application*. Perceptive end-users often figure out that their SQL login can also be used to connect to SQL Server with other applications such as Microsoft Access or SQL Server Management Studio. To prevent this, you can change the login account to have minimal permissions for the databases, and then use an application role for the required permissions. This way, the user can only access the data through the application, which is then programmed to use the application role.

CHAPTER 18

■■■

Securables and Permissions

In the previous chapter, I discussed principals, which are security accounts that can access SQL Server. In this chapter, I'll discuss and demonstrate *securables* and *permissions*. Securables are resources that SQL Server controls access to through permissions. Securables in SQL Server 2005 fall into three nested hierarchical scopes. The top level of the hierarchy is the *server* scope, which contains logins, databases, and endpoints. The *database* scope, which is contained within the server scope, controls securables such as database users, roles, certificates, and schemas. The third and innermost scope is the *schema* scope, which controls securables such as the schema itself, and objects within the schema such as tables, views, functions, and procedures.

Permissions enable a principal to perform actions on securables. SQL Server 2005 has expanded the permission model, providing finer-grained control of specific SQL Server resources. Across all securable scopes, the primary commands used to control a principal's access to a securable are GRANT, DENY, and REVOKE. These commands are applied in similar ways, depending on the scope of the securable that you are targeting. GRANT is used to enable access to securables. DENY explicitly restricts access, trumping other permissions that would normally allow a principal access to a securable. REVOKE removes a specific permission on a securable altogether, whether it was a GRANT or DENY permission.

In this chapter, I'll discuss how permissions are granted to principals at all three securable scopes. In addition to permissions, this chapter also presents the following related securable and permissions recipes:

- How to manage schemas using CREATE, ALTER, and DROP SCHEMA.

- How to report allocated permissions for a specific principal by using the fn_my_permissions function.

- How to determine a connection's permissions to a securable using the new system function Has_perms_by_name, as well as using EXECUTE AS to define your connection's security context to a different login or user to see their permissions too.

- How to change a securable's ownership using ALTER AUTHORIZATION.

- How to provide Windows external resource permissions to a SQL login using CREATE CREDENTIAL and ALTER LOGIN.

This chapter starts off with a general discussion of SQL Server 2005 permissions.

Permissions Overview

Microsoft has greatly expanded the number of permissions that can be managed in SQL Server 2005. These permissions apply to SQL Server objects within the three securable scopes (server, database, and schema).

SQL Server 2005 uses a set of common permission names that are applied to different securables (and at different scopes), and imply different levels of authorization against a securable. Table 18-1 shows those permissions that are used for multiple securables (however this isn't the exhaustive list).

Table 18-1. *Major Permissions*

Permission	Description
ALTER	Enables the grantee the use of ALTER, CREATE, or DROP commands for the securable. For example, using ALTER TABLE requires ALTER permissions on that specific table.
AUTHENTICATE	Enables the grantee to be trusted across database or SQL Server scopes.
CONNECT	Enables a grantee the permission to connect to a SQL Server resources (such as an endpoint, or the SQL Server instance).
CONTROL	Enables all available permissions on the specific securable to the grantee, as well as any nested or implied permissions within (so if you CONTROL a schema, for example, you also control any tables, views, or other database objects within that schema).
CREATE	Enables the grantee to create a securable (which can be at the server, database, or schema scope).
IMPERSONATE	Enables the grantee to impersonate another principal (login or user). For example, using the EXECUTE AS command for a login requires IMPERSONATE permissions. I demonstrated using EXECUTE AS in Chapter 10's recipe, "Using EXECUTE AS to Specify the Procedure's Security Context." In this chapter, I'll also go over how to use EXECUTE AS to set your security context outside of a module.
TAKE OWNERSHIP	Enables the grantee to take ownership of a granted securable.
VIEW	Enables the grantee to see system metadata regarding a specific securable.

To report available permissions in SQL Server 2005, as well as view that specific permission's place in the permission hierarchy, use the sys.fn_builtin_permissions system catalog table function.

The syntax is as follows:

```
Sys.fn_builtin_permissions
( [ DEFAULT | NULL  | empty_string |
APPLICATION ROLE | ASSEMBLY | ASYMMETRIC KEY |
CERTIFICATE | CONTRACT | DATABASE |
ENDPOINT | FULLTEXT CATALOG| LOGIN |
MESSAGE TYPE | OBJECT | REMOTE SERVICE BINDING |
ROLE | ROUTE | SCHEMA | SERVER | SERVICE |
SYMMETRIC KEY | TYPE  | USER | XML SCHEMA COLLECTION )
```

The arguments of this command are described in Table 18-2.

Table 18-2. *fn_builtin_permissions Arguments*

Argument	Description
`DEFAULT | NULL | empty_string`	Designating any of these first three arguments results in all permissions being listed in the result set.
`APPLICATION ROLE | ASSEMBLY | ASYMMETRIC KEY | CERTIFICATE | CONTRACT | DATABASE | ENDPOINT | FULLTEXT CATALOG| LOGIN | MESSAGE TYPE | OBJECT | REMOTE SERVICE BINDING |ROLE | ROUTE | SCHEMA | SERVER | SERVICE | SYMMETRIC KEY | TYPE | USER | XML SCHEMA COLLECTION`	Specify any one of these securable types in order to return permissions for that type.

In addition to the permission name, you can determine the nested hierarchy of permissions by looking at the `covering_permission_name` (a permission within the same class that is the superset of the more granular permission), `parent_class_desc` (the parent class of the permission—if any), and `parent_covering_permission_name` (the parent covering permission—if any) columns in the result set, which you'll see demonstrated in the next recipe.

Reporting SQL Server 2005 Assignable Permissions

In this recipe, I show you how to view the available permissions within SQL Server 2005 and explain their place within the permissions hierarchy. In the first example, all permissions will be returned, regardless of securable scope:

```
SELECT class_desc, permission_name, covering_permission_name,
parent_class_desc, parent_covering_permission_name
FROM sys.fn_builtin_permissions(DEFAULT)
ORDER BY class_desc, permission_name
```

This returns the following (abridged) result set:

class_desc	permission_name	covering_permission_name	parent_class_desc	parent_covering_permission_name
APPLICATION ROLE	ALTER	CONTROL	DATABASE	ALTER ANY APPLICATION ROLE
APPLICATION ROLE	CONTROL		DATABASE	CONTROL
APPLICATION ROLE	VIEW DEFINITION	CONTROL	DATABASE	VIEW DEFINITION
...				
OBJECT	ALTER	CONTROL	SCHEMA	ALTER
OBJECT	CONTROL		SCHEMA	CONTROL
OBJECT	DELETE	CONTROL	SCHEMA	DELETE
OBJECT	EXECUTE	CONTROL	SCHEMA	EXECUTE
...				
SERVER	ADMINISTER BULK ➥ OPERATIONS	CONTROL SERVER		
SERVER	ALTER ANY CONNECTION	CONTROL SERVER		
SERVER	ALTER ANY CREDENTIAL	CONTROL SERVER		
SERVER	ALTER ANY DATABASE	CONTROL SERVER		

This next example only shows permissions for the schema securable scope:

```
SELECT permission_name, covering_permission_name, parent_class_desc
FROM sys.fn_builtin_permissions('schema')
ORDER BY permission_name
```

This returns the following abridged result set:

permission_name	covering_permission_name	parent_class_desc
ALTER	CONTROL	DATABASE
CONTROL		DATABASE
DELETE	CONTROL	DATABASE
EXECUTE	CONTROL	DATABASE
...		

How It Works

The sys.fn_builtin_permissions system catalog function allows you to view available permissions in SQL Server 2005.

The first example in this recipe, sys.fn_builtin_permissions, was used to display all permissions by using the DEFAULT option. The first line of code referenced the column names to be returned from the function:

```
SELECT class_desc, permission_name, covering_permission_name,
parent_class_desc, parent_covering_permission_name
```

The second line referenced the function in the FROM clause, using the DEFAULT option to display all permissions:

```
FROM sys.fn_builtin_permissions(DEFAULT)
```

The last line of code allowed us to order by the permission's class and name:

```
ORDER BY class_desc, permission_name
```

The results displayed the securable class description, permission name, and covering permission name (the covering permission name is the name of a permission class that is higher in the nested permission hierarchy). For example, for the APPLICATION ROLE class, you saw that the CONTROL permission was a child of the DATABASE class and ALTER ANY APPLICATION permission, but was not subject to any covering permission in the APPLICATION ROLE class (because CONTROL enables all available permissions on the specific securable to the grantee, as well as any nested or implied permissions within):

class_desc	permission_name	covering_permission_name	parent_class_desc	parent_covering_permission_name
...				
APPLICATION ROLE	CONTROL	DATABASE	CONTROL	
...				

For the OBJECT class, we saw that the ALTER permission was a child of the SCHEMA parent class and ALTER permission. Within the OBJECT class the ALTER permissions was also a child of the covering CONTROL permission (as seen in the covering_permission_name column):

class_desc	permission_name	covering_permission_name	parent_class_desc	parent_covering_permission_name
...				
OBJECT	ALTER	CONTROL	SCHEMA	ALTER
...				

For the SERVER class and ALTER ANY DATABASE permission, the covering permission for the SERVER class was CONTROL SERVER. Notice that the SERVER class does *not* have a parent class and permission:

class_desc	permission_name	covering_permission_name	parent_class_desc	parent_covering_permission_name
...				
SERVER	ALTER ANY DATABASE	CONTROL SERVER		
...				

The second example in this recipe returned permissions for just the schema-securable class. The first line of code included just three of the columns this time:

```
SELECT permission_name, covering_permission_name, parent_class_desc
```

The second line included the word 'schema' in order to show permissions for the schema-securable class:

```
FROM sys.fn_builtin_permissions('schema')
```

The results were then ordered by the permission name:

```
ORDER BY permission_name
```

Permissions that control database objects contained within a schema (such as views, tables, etc.) were returned. For example, you saw that the DELETE permission is found within the schema scope, and is covered by the CONTROL permission. Its parent class is the DATABASE securable:

permission_name	covering_permission_name	parent_class_desc
...		
DELETE	CONTROL	DATABASE
...		

Server-Scoped Securables and Permissions

Server-scoped securables are objects that are unique within a SQL Server instance, including endpoints, logins, and databases. Permissions on server-scoped securables can be granted only to server-level principals (SQL Server logins or Windows logins), and not to database-level principals such as users or database roles.

At the top of the permissions hierarchy, server permissions allow a grantee to perform activities such as creating databases, logins, or linked servers. Server permissions also give you the ability to shut down the SQL Server instance (using SHUTDOWN) or use SQL Profiler (using the ALTER TRACE permission). When allocating permissions on a securable to a principal, the person doing the allocating is the *grantor*, and the principal receiving the permission is the *grantee*.

The syntax for granting server permissions is as follows:

```
GRANT
ADMINISTER BULK OPERATIONS | ALTER ANY CONNECTION|
ALTER ANY CREDENTIAL | ALTER ANY DATABASE |
ALTER ANY ENDPOINT | ALTER ANY EVENT NOTIFICATION |
ALTER ANY LINKED SERVER | ALTER ANY LOGIN |
ALTER RESOURCES | ALTER SERVER STATE |
ALTER SETTINGS | ALTER TRACE |
AUTHENTICATE SERVER | CONNECT SQL |
CONTROL SERVER | CREATE ANY DATABASE |
CREATE DDL EVENT NOTIFICATION | CREATE ENDPOINT |
CREATE TRACE EVENT NOTIFICATION | EXTERNAL ACCESS |
```

```
SHUTDOWN | VIEW ANY DATABASE |
VIEW ANY DEFINITION | VIEW SERVER STATE
[ ,...n ]
TO  SQL_Server_login [ ,...n ]
[ WITH GRANT OPTION ]
[ AS SQL_Server_login ]
```

The arguments of this command are described in Table 18-3.

Table 18-3. *GRANT Arguments*

Argument	Description
ADMINISTER BULK OPERATIONS | ALTER ANY CONNECTION... [,...n]	You can grant one or more server permissions in a single GRANT statement.
TO SQL_Server_login [,...n]	This is the grantee, also known as the principal (SQL Server login or logins), who you are granting permissions to.
WITH GRANT OPTION	When designating this option, the grantee will then have permission to grant the permission(s) to other grantees.
AS SQL_Server_login	This optional clause specifies where the grantor derives its right to grant the permission to the grantee.

To explicitly *deny* permissions on a securable to a server-level principal, use the DENY command.

The syntax is as follows:

```
DENY { server_permission  [ ,...n ] }
      TO < server_principal > [ ,...n ]
  [ CASCADE ]
  [ AS SQL_Server_login ]
```

The arguments of this command are described in Table 18-4.

Table 18-4. *DENY Arguments*

Argument	Description
server_permission [,...n]	One or more server-scoped permissions to deny.
< server_principal > [,...n]	One or more logins (Windows or SQL) that you can deny permissions to.
CASCADE	When this option is designated, if the grantee principal granted any of these permissions to others, those grantees will also have their permissions denied.
AS SQL_Server_login	This optional clause specifies where the grantor derives its right to deny the permission to the grantee.

To *revoke* permissions on a securable to a principal, use the REVOKE command. Revoking a permission means you'll neither be granting nor denying that permission—revoke *removes* the specified permission(s) that had previously been either granted or denied permission.

The syntax is as follows:

```
REVOKE [ GRANT OPTION FOR ] { server_permission  [ ,...n ] }
    FROM < server_principal > [ ,...n ]
    [ CASCADE ]
    [ AS SQL_Server_login ]
```

The arguments of this command are described in Table 18-5.

Table 18-5. *REVOKE Arguments*

Argument	Description
GRANT OPTION FOR	When specified, the right for the grantee to grant the permission to other grantees is revoked.
server_permission [,...n]	One or more server-scoped permissions to revoke.
< server_principal > [,...n]	One or more logins (Windows or SQL) to revoke permissions from.
CASCADE	When this option is designated, if the grantee principal granted any of these permissions to others, those grantees will also have their permissions revoked.
AS SQL_Server_login	This optional clause specifies where the grantor derives its right to revoke the permission to the grantee.

Managing Server Permissions

In this first example of this recipe, the SQL login Veronica is granted the ability to use the SQL Profiler tool to monitor SQL Server activity. This permission is given with the WITH GRANT OPTION, so Veronica can also GRANT the permission to others. Keep in mind that permissions at the server scope can only be granted when the current database is master, so we start off the batch by switching database context:

```
USE master
GO

GRANT ALTER TRACE  TO Veronica
WITH GRANT OPTION
```

In this second example, the Windows login [JOEPROD\TestUser] is granted the permissions to create and view databases on the SQL Server instance:

```
USE master
GO

GRANT CREATE ANY DATABASE, VIEW ANY DATABASE TO [JOEPROD\TestUser]
```

In this next example, the right to execute the SHUTDOWN command is denied the Windows login [JOEPROD\TestUser]:

```
DENY SHUTDOWN TO [JOEPROD\TestUser]
```

In the last example, the permission to use SQL Profiler is revoked from Veronica, including any other grantees she may have given this permission to as well:

```
USE master
GO
REVOKE ALTER TRACE FROM Veronica CASCADE
```

How It Works

Permissions on server-scoped securables are granted using GRANT, denied with DENY, and removed with REVOKE. Using these commands, one or more permissions can be assigned in the same command, as well as allocated to one or more logins (Windows or SQL).

This recipe dealt with assigning permissions at the server scope, although you'll see in future recipes that the syntax for assigning database and schema permissions are very similar.

Database-Scoped Securables and Permissions

Database-level securables are unique to a specific database, and include the following SQL Server 2005 objects:

- Roles, both user-defined and application varieties
- Assemblies
- Cryptography objects, including asymmetric and symmetric keys, certificates, and symmetric keys
- Service Broker objects, including contracts, message types, routes, services, and remote service bindings
- Fulltext catalogs
- Database users
- Schemas

You can grant permissions on these securables to database principals (database users, roles). The abridged syntax for granting database permissions is as follows:

```
GRANT { database_permission [ ,...n ] }
TO
Database_user | Database_role | Application_role [ ,...n ]
[ WITH GRANT OPTION ]
    [ AS { Database_user | Database_role | Application_role } ]
```

The arguments of this command are described in Table 18-6.

Table 18-6. *GRANT Arguments*

Argument	Description
database_permission	One or more database permissions to be granted to the principal(s).
Database_user | Database_role | Application_role [,...n]	One or more database principals that will be the grantees of the new permissions.
WITH GRANT OPTION	When designating this option, the grantee has permissions to grant the permission(s) to other grantees.
AS { Database_user | Database_role | Application_role }	This optional clause specifies where the grantor derives its right to grant the permission to the grantee. For example, if your current database user context does not have permission to GRANT a specific permission, but you have an IMPERSONATE permission on a database user that does, you can designate that user in the AS clause.

To *deny* database-scoped permissions to a grantee, the DENY command is used. The syntax is as follows:

```
DENY { database_permission [ ,...n ] }
TO < database_principal > [ ,...n ] [ CASCADE ]
    [ AS { Windows_group | database_role | application_role } ]
```

The arguments of this command are described in Table 18-7.

Table 18-7. *DENY Arguments*

Argument	Description
database_permission [,...n]	One or more database-scoped permissions to deny.
< database_principal > [,...n]	One or more database principals to deny permissions for.
CASCADE	When this option is designated, if the grantee principal granted any of these permissions to others, those grantees will also have their permissions denied.
AS { Windows_group	database_role	application_role }	This optional clause specifies where the grantor derives its right to deny the permission to the grantee.

To *revoke* database-scoped permissions to the grantee, the REVOKE command is used. The syntax is as follows:

```
REVOKE { database_permission [ ,...n ] }
FROM  < database_principal > [ ,...n ]
[ CASCADE ]
[ AS { Windows_group | database_role | application_role } ]
```

The arguments of this command are described in this Table 18-8.

Table 18-8. *REVOKE Arguments*

Argument	Description
database_permission [,...n]	One or more database-scoped permissions to revoke.
< database_principal > [,...n]	One or more database principals to revoke permissions from.
CASCADE	When this option is designated, if the grantee principal granted any of these permissions to others, those grantees will also have their permissions revoked.
AS { Windows_group	database_role	application_role }	This optional clause specifies where the grantor derives its right to revoke the permission to the grantee.

Managing Database Permissions

This first example demonstrates granting database permissions to the Veronica database user in the TestDB database:

```
USE TestDB
GO
GRANT ALTER ANY ASSEMBLY, ALTER ANY CERTIFICATE
TO VERONICA
```

This second example demonstrates denying permissions to the Danny database user:

```
USE TestDB
GO
DENY ALTER ANY DATABASE DDL TRIGGER TO Danny
GO
```

The last example demonstrates revoking database permissions to connect to the TestDB database from the Joe user:

```
USE TestDB
GO
REVOKE CONNECT FROM Joe
GO
```

How It Works

This recipe demonstrated how to grant, revoke, or deny database-scoped permissions to database principals. As you may have noticed, the syntax for granting database-scoped permissions is almost identical to server-scoped permissions. Schema-scoped permissions are also managed with the same commands, but with slight variations.

Before reviewing how to manage schema permissions, in this next recipe I'll demonstrate how to manage schemas in general.

Schema-Scoped Securables and Permissions

Schema-scoped securables are contained within the database securable scope and include user-defined data types, XML schema collections, and objects. The object securable also has other securable object types within it, but I'll review this later in the chapter.

In SQL Server 2000, the first part of the two-part object name was the object owner. Now with SQL Server 2005, users are separated from direct ownership of a database object (such as tables, views, and stored procedures). This separation is achieved by the use of schemas, which are basically containers for database objects. Instead of having a direct object owner, the object is contained within a schema, and that schema is then owned by a user.

For example, in SQL Server 2000, if you have an object called Customers, which is owned by the Jane user, this would result in the object Jane.Customers. If Jane left the company, you would not be able to drop her login and associated database users until you gave the ownership of her objects to someone else. Changing the ownership also changed the fully qualified name of the object, for example Joe.Customers instead of Jane.Customers. Of course this also forces you to rewrite any code that referenced the original name. Now in SQL Server 2005, with users owning a schema instead of the objects within a schema, you can change the owner of the schema and then drop Jane's login without having to modify the object owner itself or any of the code that referenced it.

Schemas offer a few other benefits. In the Jane.Customers example, only Jane "owned" the Customers table. In SQL Server 2005, one or more users can own a schema or use it as their default schema for creating objects. What's more, you can apply security at the schema level. This means any objects within the schema can be managed as a unit, instead of at the individual object level.

Every database comes with a dbo schema, which is where your objects go if you don't specify a default schema. But if you wish to create your own schemas, you can use the CREATE SCHEMA command.

The syntax is as follows:

```
CREATE SCHEMA
schema_name [AUTHORIZATION owner_name ]
{ table_definition | view_definition | grant_statement
    revoke_statement | deny_statement }
```

The arguments of this command are described in Table 18-9.

Table 18-9. *CREATE SCHEMA Arguments*

Argument	Description
`schema_name` | `schema_name AUTHORIZATION owner_name`	The name of the schema and the schema owner. The schema owner is a database principal which can own one or more schemas in the database.
`table_definition` | `view_definition` | `grant_statement revoke_statement` | `deny_statement`	The CREATE SCHEMA command lets you create tables, views, and permissions within the schema as part of a single schema creation transaction.

To remove an existing schema, use the DROP SCHEMA command. The syntax is as follows:

```
DROP SCHEMA schema_name
```

The command only takes a single argument: the name of the schema to drop from the database. Also, you can't drop a schema that contains objects, so the objects must either be dropped or transferred to a new schema.

> ■**Note** See the topic "Change an Object's Schema" in Chapter 24 for a review of using ALTER SCHEMA to transfer schema ownership of an object.

Like with server- and database-scoped permissions, permissions for schemas are managed using the GRANT, DENY, and REVOKE commands.

The specific syntax for granting permissions on a schema is as follows:

```
GRANT { schema_permission  [ ,...n ] } ON SCHEMA :: schema_name
    TO < database_principal > [ ,...n ]
    [ WITH GRANT OPTION ]
    [ AS { Windows_group | database_role | application_role } ]
```

The arguments of this command are described in Table 18-10.

Table 18-10. *GRANT Arguments*

Argument	Description
`schema_permission  [ ,...n ]`	One or more schema permissions to be granted to the grantee.
`schema_name`	The name of the schema the grantee is receiving permissions to.
`database_principal`	The database principal permissions recipient.
`WITH GRANT OPTION`	When designating this option, the grantee has permissions to grant the schema permission(s) to other grantees.
`AS { Windows_group	database_role	application_role }`	This optional clause specifies where the grantor derives its right to grant the schema-scoped permission to the grantee.

To deny schema-scoped permissions to a grantee, the DENY command is used. The syntax is as follows:

```
DENY { schema_permission  [ ,...n ] } ON SCHEMA :: schema_name
    TO < database_principal > [ ,...n ]
    [ CASCADE ]
    [ AS { Windows_group | database_role | application_role } ]
```

The arguments of this command are described in Table 18-11.

Table 18-11. *DENY Arguments*

Argument	Description
schema_permission [,...n]	One or more schema-scoped permissions to deny.
schema_name	The name of the schema where permissions will be denied.
< database_principal > [,...n]	One or more database principals to deny permissions for.
CASCADE	When this option is designated, if the grantee principal granted any of these permissions to others, those grantees will also have their permissions denied.
AS { Windows_group	database_role	application_role }	This optional clause specifies where the grantor derives its right to deny the permission to the grantee.

To revoke schema-scoped permissions to the grantee, the REVOKE command is used. The syntax is as follows:

```
REVOKE [ GRANT OPTION FOR ] { schema_permission  [ ,...n ] }
    ON SCHEMA :: schema_name
    { TO | FROM } < database_principal > [ ,...n ]
    [ CASCADE ]
    [ AS { Windows_group | database_role | application_role } ]
```

The arguments of this command are described in Table 18-12.

Table 18-12. *REVOKE Arguments*

Argument	Description
schema_permission [,...n]	One or more schema-scoped permissions to revoke.
schema_name	The name of the schema of which the permissions will be revoked.
< database_principal > [,...n]	One or more database principals to revoke permissions for.
CASCADE	When this option is designated, if the grantee principal granted any of these permissions to others, those grantees will also have their permissions revoked.
AS { Windows_group	database_role	application_role }	This optional clause specifies where the grantor derives its right to revoke the permission to the grantee.

Managing Schemas

In this recipe, I'll create a new schema in the TestDB database called Publishers:

```
USE TestDB
GO
CREATE SCHEMA Publishers AUTHORIZATION db_owner
```

We now have a schema called `Publishers`, which can be used to contain other database objects. It can be used to hold all objects related to publication functionality, for example, or used to hold objects for database users associated to publication activities.

To start using the new schema, use the `schema.object_name` two-part naming format, just as you did in SQL Server 2000, only this time the first part of the two-part name is the schema name:

```
CREATE TABLE Publishers.ISBN
(ISBN char(13) NOT NULL PRIMARY KEY,
 CreateDT datetime NOT NULL DEFAULT GETDATE())
```

This next example demonstrates making the `Publishers` schema a database user's default schema. For this example, a new SQL login in the master database:

```
USE master
GO
CREATE LOGIN Veronica
WITH PASSWORD=N'test123',
    DEFAULT_DATABASE=TestDB,
    CHECK_EXPIRATION=OFF,
    CHECK_POLICY=OFF
GO
```

Next, a new database user is mapped to the login in the `TestDB` database:

```
USE TestDB
GO
CREATE USER Veronica
FOR LOGIN Veronica
GO
```

Now the default schema of the existing database user will be changed to the `Publishers` schema. Any objects this database user creates by default will belong to this schema (unless the database user explicitly uses a different schema in the object creation statement):

```
USE TestDB
GO
ALTER USER Veronica
WITH DEFAULT_SCHEMA=Publishers
GO
```

Chapter 24 reviews how to transfer the ownership of an object from one schema to another using `ALTER SCHEMA`. You'll need to use this in situations where you wish to drop a schema. For example, if we tried to drop the `Publishers` schema right now, with the `Publishers.ISBN` table still in it, we would get an error warning us that there are objects referencing that schema. This example demonstrates using `ALTER SCHEMA` to transfer the table to the dbo schema prior to dropping the Publishers schema from the database:

```
ALTER SCHEMA dbo TRANSFER Publishers.ISBN
GO

DROP SCHEMA Publishers
```

How It Works

Schemas act as a container for database objects. Unlike when a database user owns objects directly, a database user now can own a schema (or, in other words, have permissions to use the objects within it).

In this recipe, CREATE SCHEMA was used to create a new schema called Publishers. A new table was created in the new schema called Publishers.ISBN. After that, a new login and database user was created for the TestDB database. ALTER USER was used to make that new schema the default schema for the new user.

Since a schema cannot be dropped until all objects are dropped or transferred from it, ALTER SCHEMA was used to transfer Publishers.ISBN into the dbo schema. DROP SCHEMA was used to remove the Publishers schema from the database.

Managing Schema Permissions

In this next set of examples, I'll show you how to manage schema permissions. Before showing you this though, I would like to quickly point out how you can identify which schemas exist for a particular database. To view the schemas for a database, you can query the sys.schemas system catalog view. This example demonstrates listing the schemas that exist within the AdventureWorks database:

```
USE AdventureWorks
GO
SELECT s.name SchemaName, d.name SchemaOwnerName
FROM sys.schemas s
INNER JOIN sys.database_principals d ON
   s.principal_id= d.principal_id
ORDER BY s.name
```

This returns a list of built-in database schemas (the fixed database roles, dbo, guest, sys, and INFORMATION_SCHEMA) along with user-defined schemas (Person, Production, Purchasing, Sales, HumanResources):

```
SchemaName              SchemaOwnerName
db_accessadmin          db_accessadmin
db_backupoperator       db_backupoperator
db_datareader           db_datareader
db_datawriter           db_datawriter
db_ddladmin             db_ddladmin
db_denydatareader       db_denydatareader
db_denydatawriter       db_denydatawriter
db_owner                db_owner
db_securityadmin        db_securityadmin
dbo                     dbo
guest                   guest
HumanResources          dbo
INFORMATION_SCHEMA      INFORMATION_SCHEMA
Person                  dbo
Production              dbo
Purchasing              dbo
Sales                   dbo
sys                     sys
```

Within the AdventureWorks database, I'll now demonstrate assigning permissions on schemas to database principals. In this example, the database user Angela is granted TAKE OWNERSHIP permissions to the Person schema, which enables the grantee to take ownership of a granted securable:

```
GRANT TAKE OWNERSHIP
ON SCHEMA ::Person
TO Angela
```

In the next example, the database user Veronica is granted multiple permissions in the same statement, including the ability to ALTER a schema, EXECUTE stored procedures within the schema, or SELECT from tables or views in the schema. Using the WITH GRANT OPTION, Veronica can also grant other database principals these permissions too:

```
GRANT ALTER, EXECUTE, SELECT
ON SCHEMA  ::Production
TO Veronica
WITH GRANT OPTION
```

In this next example, the database user Veronica is denied the ability to INSERT, UPDATE, or DELETE data from any tables within the Production schema:

```
DENY INSERT, UPDATE, DELETE
ON SCHEMA ::Production
TO Veronica
```

In the last example of this recipe, Veronica's right to ALTER the Production schema or SELECT from objects within the production schema is revoked along with the permissions she may have granted to others (using CASCADE):

```
REVOKE ALTER, SELECT
ON SCHEMA ::Production
TO Veronica
CASCADE
```

How It Works

Granting, denying, or revoking permissions occurs with the same commands that are used with database- and server-level scoped permissions. One difference, however, is the reference to ON SCHEMA, where a specific schema name is the target of granted, denied, or revoked permissions. Notice, also, that the name of the schema was prefixed with two colons (called a "scope qualifier"). A scope qualifier is used to scope permissions to a specific object type.

Object Permissions

Objects are nested within the schema scope and include objects such as tables, views, stored procedures, functions, aggregates, constraints, queues, statistics, and synonyms. Defining permissions at the schema scope (such as SELECT or EXECUTE) can allow you to define permissions for a grantee on all objects within a schema. You can also define permissions at the object level. Object permissions are nested within schema permissions, schema permissions within database-scoped permissions, and database-scoped permissions within server-level permissions.

Like server-level, database-scoped, and schema-scoped permissions, you can use GRANT, DENY, and REVOKE to define permissions on specific database objects.

The syntax for granting object permissions is as follows:

```
GRANT
    { ALL [ PRIVILEGES ] |
      object_permission [ ,...n ] }
    { [ ( column [ ,...n ] ) ] ON { table | view | table_function }
      | ON { table | view | table_function } [ ( column [ ,...n ] ) ]
      | ON { stored_procedure | extended_procedure }
      | ON { scalar_function | aggregate_function }
      | ON service_queue
      | ON synonym
    }
```

```
TO < database_principal > [ ,...n ]
[ WITH GRANT OPTION ]
[ AS { Windows_group | database_role | application_role } ]
```

The arguments of this command are described in Table 18-13.

Table 18-13. *GRANT Arguments*

Argument	Description
ALL [PRIVILEGES]	The ALL keyword is used to grant all permissions applicable to the selected object. The permissions actually granted depend on the object. For example, if you choose to grant ALL for a table, you'll be granting INSERT, UPDATE, DELETE, SELECT, and REFERENCES permissions on the table.
object_permission [,...n]	One or more object permissions to be granted to the grantee.
[(column [,...n])] ON { table | view | table_function }	Syntax used to grant permissions on a specific column or columns on a table, view, or table function.
stored_procedure | extended_procedure	Permission granted on a specific stored procedure or extended stored procedure.
scalar_function | aggregate_function	Permission granted on a specific scalar or aggregate function.
service_queue	Permission granted on a Service Broker service queue.
synonym	Permission granted on a synonym.
database_principal	The database principal permissions recipient.
WITH GRANT OPTION	When designating this option, the grantee has permissions to grant the permission(s) to other grantees.
AS { Windows_group | database_role | application_role }	This optional clause specifies where the grantor derives its right to grant the permission to the grantee.

To deny object permissions to a grantee, the DENY command is used. The syntax is as follows:

```
DENY [ GRANT OPTION FOR ]
    { ALL [ PRIVILEGES ] |
      object_permission [ ,...n ] }
    { [ ( column [ ,...n ] ) ] ON { table | view | table_function }
      | ON { table | view | table_function } [ ( column [ ,...n ] ) ]
      | ON { stored_procedure | extended_procedure }
      | ON { scalar_function | aggregate_function }
          | ON service_queue
      | ON synonym
    }
      TO < database_principal > [ ,...n ] [ CASCADE ]
    [ AS { Windows_group | database_role | application_role } ]
```

The arguments of this command are described in Table 18-14.

Table 18-14. *DENY Arguments*

Argument	Description
GRANT OPTION FOR	When this option is used, the right to grant the permission to other database principals is denied.
ALL [PRIVILEGES]	Denies all permissions based on the object selected. For example if denying ALL permissions to a view, you'll be denying INSERT, UPDATE, DELETE, SELECT, and REFERENCES permissions in one operation.
object_permission [,...n]	One or more object permissions to be denied to the grantee.
[(column [,...n])] ON { table | view | table_function }	Syntax used to deny permissions on a specific column or columns on a table, view, or table function.
stored_procedure | extended_procedure	Permission denied on a specific stored procedure or extended stored procedure.
scalar_function | aggregate_function	Permission denied on a specific scalar or aggregate function.
service_queue	Permission denied on a Service Broker service queue.
synonym	Permission denied on a synonym.
< database_principal > [,...n]	One or more database principals to deny permissions for.
CASCADE	When this option is designated, if the grantee principal granted any of these permissions to others, those grantees will also have their permissions denied.
AS { Windows_group | database_role | application_role }	This optional clause specifies where the grantor derives its right to deny the permission to the grantee.

To revoke object permissions to the grantee, the REVOKE command is used. The syntax is as follows:

```
REVOKE [ GRANT OPTION FOR ]
    { ALL [ PRIVILEGES ] |
      object_permission [ ,...n ] }
    { [ ( column [ ,...n ] ) ] ON { table | view | table_function }
      | ON { table | view | table_function } [ ( column [ ,...n ] ) ]
      | ON { stored_procedure | extended_procedure }
      | ON { scalar_function | aggregate_function }
            | ON service_queue
      | ON synonym
    }
    { TO | FROM } < database_principal > [ ,...n ]
    [ CASCADE ]
    [ AS { Windows_group | database_role | application_role } ]
```

The arguments of this command are described in Table 18-15.

Table 18-15. *REVOKE Arguments*

Argument	Description
GRANT OPTION FOR	When this option is used, the right to grant the permission to other database principals is revoked.
ALL [PRIVILEGES]	Revokes all permissions based on the specified securable (based on the permissions that are available for that object type).
object_permission [,...n]	One or more object permissions to be revoked from the grantee.
[(column [,...n])] ON { table | view | table_function }	Syntax used to revoke permissions on a specific column or columns on a table, view, or table function.
stored_procedure | extended_procedure	Permission revoked on a specific stored procedure or extended stored procedure.
scalar_function | aggregate_function	Permission revoked on a specific scalar or aggregate function.
service_queue	Permission revoked on a Service Broker service queue.
synonym	Permission revoked on a synonym.
< database_principal > [,...n]	One or more database principals to revoke permissions from.
CASCADE	When this option is designated, if the grantee principal granted any of these permissions to others, those grantees will also have their permissions revoked.
AS { Windows_group | database_role | application_role }	This optional clause specifies where the grantor derives its right to revoke the permission to the grantee.

Managing Object Permissions

In this recipe, I grant the database user Joe the permission to SELECT, INSERT, DELETE, and UPDATE data in the HumanResources.Department table:

```
GRANT DELETE, INSERT, SELECT, UPDATE
ON HumanResources.Department
TO Joe
```

Here, the database role called ReportViewers is granted the ability to execute a procedure, as well as view metadata regarding that specific object in the system catalog views:

```
GRANT EXECUTE, VIEW DEFINITION
ON dbo.uspGetManagerEmployees
TO ReportViewers
```

In this next example, ALTER permission is denied to the database user Joe for the HumanResources.Department table:

```
DENY ALTER ON HumanResources.Department TO Joe
```

In this last example, INSERT, UPDATE, and DELETE permissions are revoked from Joe on the HumanResources.Department table:

```
REVOKE INSERT, UPDATE, DELETE
ON HumanResources.Department
TO Joe
```

How It Works

This recipe demonstrated granting object permissions to specific database securables. Object permissions are granted by designating the specific object name and the permissions that are applicable to the object. For example, EXECUTE permissions can be granted to a stored procedure, but not SELECT.

■**Note** For a complete list of permissions by object type, see the SQL Server Books Online topic "Permissions," and sub-topic "Permissions Applicable to Specific Securables."

Permissions can be superseded by other types of permissions. For example, if the database user Veronica has been granted SELECT permissions on the HumanResources.Department table, but has been denied permissions on the HumanResources schema itself, she will receive the following error message when she attempts to SELECT from that table, as the DENY overrides any GRANT SELECT permissions:

```
Msg 229, Level 14, State 5, Line 2
SELECT permission denied on object 'Department', database 'AdventureWorks', schema
'HumanResources'.
```

Managing Permissions Across Securable Scopes

Now that I've reviewed the various securable scopes and the methods by which permissions can be granted to principals, in the next set of recipes I'll show you how to report and manage the permissions a principal has on securables across the different scopes.

Determining a Current Connection's Permissions to a Securable

With SQL Server 2005's nested hierarchy of securable permissions (server, database, and schema), permissions can be inherited by higher level scopes. Figuring out what permissions your current login/database connection has to a securable can become tricky, especially when you add server or database roles to the equation.

Understanding what permissions your database connection has added to a securable can be determined by using the Has_perms_by_name function. This system scalar function returns a "1" if the current user has granted permissions to the securable and "0" if not.

The syntax for this function is as follows:

```
Has_perms_by_name (
                securable ,
                securable_class ,
                permission
                [, sub-securable ]
                [, sub-securable_class ]
                )
```

The arguments for this function are described in Table 18-16.

Table 18-16. *Has_perms_by_name Arguments*

Parameter	Description
securable	The name of the securable that you want to verify permissions for.
securable_class	The name of the securable class that you want to check. Class names (for example DATABASE or SCHEMA) can be retrieved from the class_desc column in the sys.fn_builtin_permissions function (see the beginning of this chapter).
permission	The name of the permission to check.
sub-securable	The name of the securable sub-entity.
sub-securable_class	The name of the securable sub-entity class.

This example demonstrates how to check if the current connected user has permissions to ALTER the AdventureWorks database:

```
SELECT Has_perms_by_name ('AdventureWorks', 'DATABASE', 'ALTER')
```

This returns "0," which means the current connection *does not* have permission to ALTER the AdventureWorks database:

```
-----------
0

(1 row(s) affected)
```

The following query tests the current connection to see if the Person.Address table can be updated or selected from:

```
SELECT  CASE Has_perms_by_name ('Person.Address', 'OBJECT', 'UPDATE')
           WHEN 1 THEN 'Yes'
           ELSE 'No'
        END UpdateTable,
         CASE Has_perms_by_name ('Person.Address', 'OBJECT', 'SELECT')
           WHEN 1 THEN 'Yes'
           ELSE 'No'
        END SelectFromTable
```

This returns:

```
UpdateTable SelectFromTable
----------- ---------------
Yes         No

(1 row(s) affected)
```

How It Works

The Has_perms_by_name system function evaluates whether or not the current connection has granted permissions to access a specific securable (granted permissions either explicitly, or inherently through a higher-scoped securable). In both examples in this recipe, the first parameter used was the securable name (the database name or table name). The second parameter was the securable class, for example OBJECT or DATABASE. The third parameter used was the actual permission to be validated, for example ALTER, UPDATE, or SELECT (depending on which permissions are applicable to the securable being checked).

Reporting the Permissions For a Principal by Securable Scope

In this recipe, I'll demonstrate using the fn_my_permissions function to return the assigned permissions for the currently connected principal. The syntax for this function is as follows:

```
fn_my_permissions ( securable , 'securable_class')
```

The arguments for this command are described in Table 18-17.

Table 18-17. *fn_my_permissions Arguments*

Argument	Description
securable	The name of the securable to verify. Use NULL if you are checking permissions at the server or database scope.
securable_class	The securable class that you are listing permissions for.

This first example demonstrates checking the server-scoped permissions for the current connection:

```
SELECT permission_name
FROM fn_my_permissions(NULL, N'SERVER')
ORDER BY permission_name
```

This returns the following results (this query example was executed under the context of sysadmin, so in this case every available server-scoped permission is returned):

```
ADMINISTER BULK OPERATIONS
ALTER ANY CONNECTION
ALTER ANY CREDENTIAL
ALTER ANY DATABASE
ALTER ANY ENDPOINT
ALTER ANY EVENT NOTIFICATION
ALTER ANY LINKED SERVER
ALTER ANY LOGIN
ALTER RESOURCES
ALTER SERVER STATE
ALTER SETTINGS
ALTER TRACE
AUTHENTICATE SERVER
CONNECT SQL
CONTROL SERVER
CREATE ANY DATABASE
CREATE DDL EVENT NOTIFICATION
CREATE ENDPOINT
CREATE TRACE EVENT NOTIFICATION
EXTERNAL ACCESS ASSEMBLY
SHUTDOWN
UNSAFE ASSEMBLY
VIEW ANY DATABASE
VIEW ANY DEFINITION
VIEW SERVER STATE
```

If you have IMPERSONATE permissions on the login or database user, you can also check the permissions of another principal other than your own by using the EXECUTE AS command. In Chapter 10 I demonstrated how to use EXECUTE AS to specify a stored procedure's security context. You can also use EXECUTE AS in a stand-alone fashion, using it to switch the security context of the current database session. You can then switch back to your original security context by issuing the REVERT command.

The abridged syntax for EXECUTE AS is as follows (the advanced cookie and CALLER options of this command are not discussed here—but can be referenced in SQL Server 2005 Books Online under the "EXECUTE AS" topic):

```
EXECUTE AS { LOGIN | USER } = 'name'
[ WITH { NO REVERT } ]
```

The arguments of this command are described in Table 18-18.

Table 18-18. *EXECUTE AS Abridged Syntax Arguments*

Argument	Description
{ LOGIN	USER } = 'name'	Select LOGIN to impersonate a SQL or Windows login or USER to impersonate a database user. The name value is the actual login or user name.
NO REVERT	If NO REVERT is designated, you cannot use the REVERT command to switch back to your original security context.

To demonstrate EXECUTE AS's power, the previous query is re-executed, this time by using the security context of the Veronica login:

```
EXECUTE AS LOGIN = N'Veronica'
GO

SELECT permission_name
FROM fn_my_permissions(NULL, N'SERVER')
ORDER BY permission_name
GO

REVERT
GO
```

This returns a much smaller list of server permissions, as you are no longer executing the call under a login with sysadmin permissions:

```
CONNECT SQL
VIEW ANY DATABASE
```

This next example demonstrates returning database-scoped permissions for the Veronica database user:

```
EXECUTE AS USER = N'Veronica'
GO

SELECT permission_name
FROM fn_my_permissions(N'AdventureWorks', N'DATABASE')
ORDER BY permission_name
GO

REVERT
GO
```

This returns:

```
CONNECT
CREATE TABLE
CREATE VIEW
```

In this next example, permissions are checked for the current connection on the Production. Culture table, this time showing any sub-entities of the table (meaning any explicit permissions on table columns):

```
SELECT subentity_name, permission_name
FROM fn_my_permissions(N'Production.Culture', N'OBJECT')
ORDER BY permission_name, subentity_name
```

This returns the following results (when the subentity_name is populated, this is a column reference):

subentity_name	permission_name
	ALTER
	CONTROL
	DELETE
	EXECUTE
	INSERT
	RECEIVE
	REFERENCES
CultureID	REFERENCES
ModifiedDate	REFERENCES
Name	REFERENCES
	SELECT
CultureID	SELECT
ModifiedDate	SELECT
Name	SELECT
	TAKE OWNERSHIP
	UPDATE
CultureID	UPDATE
ModifiedDate	UPDATE
Name	UPDATE
	VIEW DEFINITION

How It Works

This recipe demonstrated how to return permissions for the current connection using the fn_my_permissions function. The first example used a NULL in the first parameter and SERVER in the second parameter in order to return the server-scoped permissions of the current connection:

```
...
FROM fn_my_permissions(NULL, N'SERVER')
```

We then used EXECUTE AS to execute the same query, this time under the Veronica login's context, which returned server-scoped permissions for her login:

```
EXECUTE AS LOGIN = N'Veronica'
GO
...

REVERT
GO
```

The next example showed database-scoped permissions by designating the database name in the first parameter, and DATABASE in the second parameter:

```
FROM fn_my_permissions(N'AdventureWorks', N'DATABASE')
```

The last example checked the current connection's permissions to a specific table:

```
...
FROM fn_my_permissions(N'Production.Culture', N'OBJECT')
```

This returned information at the table level *and* column level. For example the ALTER and CONTROL permissions applied to the table level, while those rows with a populated entity_name (for example CultureID and ModifiedDate) refer to permissions at the table's column level.

Changing Securable Ownership

As described earlier, in SQL Server 2005, objects are contained within schemas and schemas are then owned by a database user or role. Changing a schema's owner no longer means having to rename the objects held within that schema. Aside from schemas, however, other securables on a SQL Server instance still *do* have direct ownership by either a server or database level principal.

For example, schemas have database principal owners (such as database user) and endpoints have server level owners, such as a SQL login.

Assuming that the login performing the operation has the appropriate TAKE OWNERSHIP permission, you can use the ALTER AUTHORIZATION command to change the owner of a securable.

The syntax for ALTER AUTHORIZATION is as follows:

```
ALTER AUTHORIZATION
    ON [ {Object | Type | XML Schema Collection | Fulltext Catalog | Schema
       | Assembly | Role | Message Type | Contract | Service | Remote
       | Binding | Route | Symmetric Key | Endpoint | Certificate}
 :: ] entity_name
    TO { SCHEMA OWNER | principal_name }
```

The arguments for this command are described in Table 18-19.

Table 18-19. *ALTER AUTHORIZATION Arguments*

Argument	Description
Object | Type | XML Schema Collection | Fulltext Catalog | Schema | Assembly | Role | Message Type | Contract | Service | Remote | Binding | Route | Symmetric Key | Endpoint | Certificate	This designates the type of securable being given a new owner.
entity_name	The name of the securable.
SCHEMA OWNER | principal_name	The name of the new schema owner, or the name of the database or server principal taking ownership of the securable.

In this example, the owner of the HumanResources schema is changed to the database user Veronica:

```
ALTER AUTHORIZATION ON Schema::HumanResources
TO Veronica
```

In this second example, the owner of an endpoint (for more on endpoints, see Chapter 15) is changed to a SQL login. Before doing so, the existing owner of the endpoint is verified using the sys.endpoints and sys.server_principals system catalog views:

```
SELECT p.name OwnerName
FROM sys.endpoints e
INNER JOIN sys.server_principals p ON
    e.principal_id = p.principal_id
WHERE e.name = 'ProductWebsite'
```

This returns:

```
OwnerName
-------------------------
JOEPROD\Owner

(1 row(s) affected)
```

Next, the owner is changed to a different SQL login:

```
ALTER AUTHORIZATION ON Endpoint::ProductWebSite
TO Veronica
```

Re-executing the query against sys.server_principals and sys.endpoints, the new owner is displayed:

```
OwnerName
------------------
Veronica

(1 row(s) affected)
```

How It Works

This recipe demonstrated how to change object ownership. You may wish to change ownership when a login or database user needs to be removed. If that login or database user owns securables, you can use ALTER AUTHORIZATION to change that securables owner prior to dropping the SQL login or database user.

In this recipe, ALTER AUTHORIZATION was used to change the owner of a schema to a different database user, and the owner of an endpoint to a different SQL login (associated to a Windows account). In both cases, the securable name was prefixed by the "::" scope qualifier, which designates the type of object you are changing ownership of.

Allowing SQL Logins to Access Non-SQL Server Resources

In this chapter, I've discussed permissions and securables within a SQL Server instance, however sometimes a SQL login (not associated to a Windows user or group) may need permissions outside of the SQL Server instance. A Windows principal (a Windows user or group) has implied permissions outside of the SQL Server instance, but a SQL login does not, because a SQL login and password is created inside SQL Server. New in SQL Server 2005, you can now bind a SQL login to a Windows credential, giving the SQL login the implied Windows permissions of that credential. This SQL login can then use more advanced SQL Server functionality, where outside resource access may be required. This credential can be bound to more than one SQL login (although one SQL login can only be bound to a single credential).

To create a credential, use the CREATE CREDENTIAL command.

The syntax is as follows:

```
CREATE CREDENTIAL credential_name WITH IDENTITY = ' identity_name '
    [ , SECRET = ' secret ' ]
```

The arguments for this command are described in Table 18-20.

Table 18-20. *CREATE CREDENTIAL Arguments*

Argument	Description
credential_name	The name of the new credential.
identity_name	The external account name (a Windows user, for example).
secret	The credential's password.

In this example, a new credential is created that is mapped to the JOEPROD\Owner Windows user account:

```
USE master
GO

CREATE CREDENTIAL AccountingGroup
WITH IDENTITY = N'JOEPROD\AccountUser1',
SECRET = N'mypassword!'
```

Once created, the credential can be bound to existing or new SQL logins using the CREDENTIAL keyword in CREATE LOGIN and ALTER LOGIN:

```
USE master
GO
ALTER LOGIN Veronica
WITH CREDENTIAL = AccountingGroup
GO
```

How It Works

A credential allows SQL authentication logins to be bound to Windows external permissions. This builds on the limited proxy account functionality that was available in SQL Server 2000. Unlike SQL Server 2000 proxy functionality, SQL Server 2005 credential abilities allow SQL logins to access external resources using more than one account (you can create multiple credentials, but in 2000, only one proxy).

In this recipe, a new credential was created called AccountingGroup. It was mapped to the Windows user JOEPROD\Owner, and given a password in the SECRET argument of the command. After creating the credential, it was then bound to the SQL login Veronica by using ALTER LOGIN and WITH CREDENTIAL. The Veronica login can only have a single credential bound to it; however, the AccountingGroup credential can be bound to more than one login. Now the Veronica login, using credentials, has outside-SQL Server permissions equivalent to the JOEPROD\AccountUser1 Windows account.

CHAPTER 19

■ ■ ■

Encryption

In previous versions of SQL Server, if you wanted to encrypt sensitive data such as financial information, salary, or personal identification numbers, you were forced to rely on outside application programs and algorithms. In a most welcome addition to the SQL Server 2005 functionality set, Microsoft introduces built-in data encryption support using a combination of certificates, keys, and system functions.

Similar to a digital certificate that is issued by certificate authority, a SQL Server 2005 certificate contains a pair of keys: a public key as well as a private key, which is used to encrypt and decrypt data. SQL Server 2005 also has the ability to create asymmetric and symmetric key objects. An *asymmetric key object* is similar to a certificate, in that a public key is used to encrypt data and the private key is used to decrypt data. Both asymmetric keys and certificates provide powerful encryption strength, but with more performance overhead due to the complexity of the encryption/decryption process. A lower overhead solution, which is more appropriate for the encryption of large amounts of data, is a *symmetric key*, which is a single key that is used to both encrypt and decrypt the same data.

SQL Server 2005 allows you to layer these encryption capabilities into an encryption hierarchy. When SQL Server 2005 is installed, a server-level certificate called the Service Master Key is created in the master database and is bound to the SQL Server service account login by default. The Service Master Key is used to encrypt all other database certificates and keys created within the SQL Server instance. Additionally, you can also create a Database Master Key in a user database, which you can use to encrypt database certificates and keys.

I'll start the chapter slowly by first discussing and then demonstrating how to encrypt data without the use of certificates and keys.

Encryption by Passphrase

For a quick-and-dirty encryption of data that doesn't involve certificates or keys, you can simply encrypt/decrypt data based on a password supplied by the user. A passphrase is simply a password that allows spaces in it. This passphrase is not stored in the database, which can be advantageous because it means that internal passwords cannot be "cracked" using stored system data. Because the password can include spaces, you can create a long, easy-to-remember sentence that can be used to encrypt and decrypt sensitive data.

In the next recipe I'll demonstrate how to encrypt and decrypt data using passphrase functions.

Using a Function to Encrypt by Passphrase

To encrypt data with a user-supplied passphrase, you can call the EncryptByPassPhrase function. The syntax is as follows:

```
EncryptByPassPhrase(
{ ' passphrase ' | @passphrase }
, { ' cleartext ' | @cleartext }
[ , { add_authenticator | @add_authenticator }
, { authenticator | @authenticator } ]     )
```

The arguments of this command are described in Table 19-1.

Table 19-1. *EncryptByPassPhrase Arguments*

Argument	Description
' passphrase '	@passphrase	The passphrase that is used to encrypt the data.
' cleartext '	@cleartext	The text to be encrypted.
add_authenticator	@add_authenticator	A Boolean value (1 or 0) determining whether an authenticator will be used with the encrypted value.
authenticator	@authenticator	The data used for the authenticator.

To decrypt the encrypted value, the DecryptByPassPhrase function is used, which includes the same arguments as EncryptByPassPhrase except that it takes encrypted text instead of clear text:

```
DecryptByPassPhrase(
{ ' passphrase ' | @passphrase }
, { ' ciphertext ' | @ciphertext }
[ , { add_authenticator | @add_authenticator }
, { authenticator | @authenticator } ]   )
```

In this recipe, the "my secure secret text" string is encrypted using a passphrase:

```
-- Table used to store the encrypted data
-- for the purposes of this recipe
CREATE TABLE #SecretInfo
(Secret varbinary(8000) NOT NULL)
GO

INSERT #SecretInfo
(Secret)
SELECT   EncryptByPassPhrase(
         'My Password Used To Encrypt This String in 2005.',
         'This is the text I need to secure.')

SELECT Secret
FROM #SecretInfo
```

This returns:

```
0x0100000031AF7E0656FB1C3253AE708B4DB5F3F1EDEA48C832E5BE493E01655D8E7783D6C21E
2B94817636EAD39328D940B8BD4F9718081E6EB837BE
```

Taking the returned varbinary value from the #SecretInfo table, the text is decrypted using the same passphrase:

```
SELECT CAST(DecryptByPassPhrase(
'My Password Used To Encrypt This String in 2005.',
Secret) as varchar(50))
FROM #SecretInfo
```

This returns:

```
This is the text I need to secure.
```

How It Works

In this recipe, a temporary table was used to hold the encrypted output of the EncryptByPassPhrase function. The column was defined with a varbinary(8000) data type (8000 is the maximum size allowed to be encrypted by this function):

```
CREATE TABLE #SecretInfo
(Secret varbinary(8000) NOT NULL)
GO
```

Next, a new row was inserted into the temporary table, using INSERT...SELECT:

```
INSERT #SecretInfo
(Secret)
```

The SELECT references the EncryptByPassPhrase function. The first parameter was the actual password (in this case an entire sentence) that was used to encrypt the string. The second parameter was the string to be encrypted:

```
SELECT   EncryptByPassPhrase('My Password Used To Encrypt This String in 2005.',
         'This is the text I need to secure.')
```

The next step queried the varbinary(8000) value that was inserted, returning an unintelligble value:

```
SELECT Secret
FROM #SecretInfo
```

The data was then decrypted using the DecryptByPassPhrase function, which took the password as the first parameter (the one originally used to encrypt the data in the first place), and a reference to the encrypted data in the Secret column of the #SecretInfo temporary table:

```
SELECT CAST(DecryptByPassPhrase(
'My Password Used To Encrypt This String in 2005.',
Secret) as varchar(50))
FROM #SecretInfo
```

Passphrase encryption functions allow you to encrypt data without fear of even sysadmin server role members reading the data (sysadmin server role members, as you'll see in this chapter, have inherent permissions to read other forms of encrypted data).

The encrypted data will be protected from database backup theft or even the infiltration of the database while on the SQL Server instance, assuming that you haven't stored the password in a table or used the password in any of your modules (stored procedures, triggers, and so on).

Master Keys

Encryption in SQL Server 2005 is handled in a hierarchical manner. SQL Server 2005 includes two key types that are used to encrypt SQL Server 2005 data. The *Service Master Key* is at the top of the hierarchy and is automatically created when SQL Server is installed. The Service Master Key is also used to encrypt Database Master Keys below it. *Database Master Keys* are then used to encrypt certificates, and both asymmetric and symmetric keys. This layering of keys and certificates provides stronger encryption. In this section, I'll discuss these two different types of keys: the Service Master Key and Database Master Key.

As stated before, the Service Master Key is at the top of the encryption hierarchy in SQL Server 2005 and is responsible for encrypting system data, linked server logins, and Database Master Keys. is the Service Master Key is automatically generated the first time it is used by SQL Server to encrypt a credential, Database Master Key, or linked server password, and it's generated using the Windows credentials of the SQL Server service account. If you have to change the SQL Server service account, Microsoft recommends that you use SQL Server Configuration Manager, because this tool will perform the appropriate decryptions and encryptions required to generate a new Service Master Key, while keeping the encryption hierarchy intact.

The Database Master Key is an additional layer of SQL Server 2005 security in the encryption hierarchy, which allows you to encrypt database certificates and asymmetric keys. Each database can contain only a single database master key, which, when created, is encrypted by the Service Master Key.

When you're creating an asymmetric key (reviewed later in the chapter), you can decide whether or not to include a password for encrypting the private key of the asymmetric key pair. If a password is not included, however, the database master key is then used to encrypt the private key instead. This is a good example of using the Database Master Key to encrypt other objects.

In this next group of recipes, I'll demonstrate how to manage these two different key types.

Backing Up and Restoring a Service Master Key

Because of the Service Master Key's critical role in SQL Server, it is very important for you to back up this key to a safe location in the event that it is damaged or modified. This is performed by using the BACKUP SERVICE MASTER KEY command.

The syntax is as follows:

```
BACKUP SERVICE MASTER KEY TO FILE = 'path_to_file'
    ENCRYPTION BY PASSWORD = 'Password'
```

This command takes two arguments; the first argument is the name of the path and filename where the key backup will be exported. The second argument is the password used to encrypt the file containing the key backup. After backing up a Service Master Key, the backup file should then be backed up to tape or copied off the server to a safe location.

In the event that a Service Master Key must be recovered from backup on the SQL Server instance, the RESTORE SERVICE MASTER KEY command is used.

The syntax is as follows:

```
RESTORE SERVICE MASTER KEY FROM FILE = 'path_to_file'
    DECRYPTION BY PASSWORD = 'password' [FORCE]
```

This command takes the name of the backup file and the encryption password. The FORCE argument is used to force a replacement of the existing Service Master Key even in the event of data loss (so it should only be used under dire circumstances and if you can afford to lose the encrypted data that cannot be encrypted).

This recipe demonstrates backing up and then restoring the Service Master Key.

In the first example, BACKUP SERVICE MASTER KEY is used to back up to a file on the C:\Apress\Recipes directory:

```
BACKUP SERVICE MASTER KEY
TO FILE = 'C:\Apress\Recipes\SMK.bak'
ENCRYPTION BY PASSWORD = 'MakeItAGoodOne!1AB'
```

The following code demonstrates recovering the Service Master Key from a backup file:

```
RESTORE SERVICE MASTER KEY
FROM FILE = 'C:\Apress\Recipes\SMK.bak'
DECRYPTION BY PASSWORD = 'MakeItAGoodOne!1AB'
```

How It Works

In the first example, the Service Master Key was backed up to a file. The second line of code designated the filename to back up the file to:

```
BACKUP SERVICE MASTER KEY
TO FILE = 'C:\Apress\Recipes\SMK.bak'
```

The third line of code designated the password used to protect the file (and is required in order to initiate a restore):

```
ENCRYPTION BY PASSWORD = 'MakeItAGoodOne!1AB'
```

In the second example, a Service Master Key restore was initiated. The second line of code designated the filename to restore the Service Master Key from:

```
RESTORE SERVICE MASTER KEY
FROM FILE = 'C:\Apress\Recipes\SMK.bak'
```

The third line of code designated the password which was used to protect and generate the Service Master Key backup:

```
DECRYPTION BY PASSWORD = 'MakeItAGoodOne!1AB'
```

If you are testing this example out yourself, you'll see that if you perform a backup and restore without any actual change in the Service Master Key, you'll see the following message during a RESTORE operation:

```
The old and new master keys are identical. No data re-encryption is required.
```

Creating, Regenerating, and Dropping a Database Master Key

The database master key, when explicitly created, adds an extra layer of security by automatically encrypting new certificates or asymmetric keys in the database, serving to further protect encrypted data.

To create a database master key, the CREATE MASTER KEY command is used. The syntax is as follows:

```
CREATE MASTER KEY ENCRYPTION BY PASSWORD = 'password'
```

Like the Service Master Key, the database master key doesn't have an explicit name, and uses a single argument, the database master key's password.

The database master key can be regenerated by using the ALTER MASTER KEY command. The syntax for regenerating the database master key is as follows:

```
ALTER MASTER KEY
[FORCE] REGENERATE WITH ENCRYPTION BY PASSWORD = 'password'
```

This command only takes a single argument, the password of the regenerated key. Regenerating the key decrypts all objects encrypted by the key and re-encrypts them using the newly regenerated key. If there is an error during the decryption (for data that cannot be decrypted for various reasons), the FORCE option forces the regeneration process, but, and this is important, *with the danger of rendering some encrypted data inaccessible*.

To remove the database master key entirely, the DROP MASTER KEY command is used (no additional arguments needed).

For example:

```
USE BookStore
GO
DROP MASTER KEY
```

The database master key can't be dropped, however, if it was used to encrypt other database objects.

In this first example, a Database Master Key is created for the BookStore database:

```
USE BookStore
GO
CREATE MASTER KEY ENCRYPTION BY PASSWORD = 'keepitsecretkeepitsafe!'
```

This recipe demonstrates regenerating the Database Master Key with a new password:

```
Use BookStore
GO
ALTER MASTER KEY
REGENERATE WITH ENCRYPTION BY PASSWORD = 'uglypassword1C3ED8CF'
```

How It Works

This example demonstrated creating a Database Master Key for the BookStore database. The only user-provided information was the password used to encrypt the Database Master Key:

```
CREATE MASTER KEY ENCRYPTION BY PASSWORD = 'keepitsecretkeepitsafe!'
```

The second example also only required a single user-provided argument; the password used to regenerate the new Database Master Key:

```
ALTER MASTER KEY
REGENERATE WITH ENCRYPTION BY PASSWORD = 'uglypassword1C3ED8CF'
```

The Database Master Key was then dropped using the following command:

```
DROP MASTER KEY
```

Backing Up and Restoring a Database Master Key

Like a Service Master Key , the Database Master Key can also be backed up to disk using the BACKUP MASTER KEY command. The syntax is as follows:

```
BACKUP MASTER KEY TO FILE = 'path_to_file'
    ENCRYPTION BY PASSWORD = 'Password'
```

The command takes two arguments, the first being the path and filename (that the Database Master Key is backed up to), and the second being the password used to protect the backup file.

To restore a Database Master Key from the file backup, the RESTORE MASTER KEY command is used. The syntax is as follows:

```
RESTORE MASTER KEY FROM FILE = 'path_to_file'
    DECRYPTION BY PASSWORD = 'password'
    ENCRYPTION BY PASSWORD = 'password'
    [FORCE]
```

This command takes the filename and path, the password used to decrypt the backup file, and the new password to encrypt the new Database Master Key. The FORCE option forces the Database Master Key restore even if all dependent encrypted data in the database cannot be re-encrypted using the new key. This means dependent encrypted data would be unavailable because it cannot be decrypted—so use this option with caution and as a last resort!

In this first example, the Database Master Key is backed up to file:

```
BACKUP MASTER KEY TO FILE = 'C:\Apress\Recipes\BookStore_Master_Key.BAK'
    ENCRYPTION BY PASSWORD = '4D280837'
```

In the following code, the Database Master Key is restored from file:

```
RESTORE MASTER KEY FROM FILE = 'C:\Apress\Recipes\BookStore_Master_Key.BAK'
DECRYPTION BY PASSWORD = '4D280837'
ENCRYPTION BY PASSWORD = '641076B0'
```

How It Works

As you'll see in upcoming recipes, the Database Master Key is used to encrypt other subordinate encryption objects. Therefore, it's a good idea for you to back up the Database Master Key immediately after it is first created.

In this recipe, a Database Master Key was backed up to file, which was designated in the first argument of the BACKUP MASTER KEY command:

```
BACKUP MASTER KEY TO FILE = 'C:\Apress\Recipes\BookStore_Master_Key.BAK'
```

The second line of code designated the password used to encrypt the backup file:

```
ENCRYPTION BY PASSWORD = '4D280837'
```

The second example demonstrated restoring the Database Master Key from file. The first line of code designated the name of the backup file:

```
RESTORE MASTER KEY FROM FILE = 'C:\Apress\Recipes\BookStore_Master_Key.BAK'
```

The second line designated the password used to originally encrypt the backup file:

```
DECRYPTION BY PASSWORD = '4D280837'
```

The third line of code designated the password used to encrypt the Database Master Key once it is restored:

```
ENCRYPTION BY PASSWORD = '641076B0'
```

If you tested this example out on your own SQL Server instance, and your Database Master Key hadn't changed between the backup and restore, you would see the following message:

```
The old and new master keys are identical. No data re-encryption is required.
```

Removing Service Master Key Encryption from the Database Master Key

When a Database Master Key is created, it is encrypted using two methods by default: the Service Master Key and the password used in the CREATE MASTER KEY command. If you don't wish to have the Database Master Key encrypted by the Service Master Key (so that SQL Server logins with sysadmin permissions can't access the encrypted data without knowing the Database Master Key password), you can drop it using a variation of the ALTER MASTER KEY command.

The syntax is as follows:

```
ALTER MASTER KEY
ADD ENCRYPTION BY SERVICE MASTER KEY |
DROP ENCRYPTION BY SERVICE MASTER KEY
```

Since the Service Master Key allows for automatic decryption of the Database Master Key by users with appropriate permissions (sysadmin, for example), once you drop encryption by the Service Master Key you must use a new command to access the Database Master Key if you wish to modify it. This command is OPEN MASTER KEY, which has the following syntax:

```
OPEN MASTER KEY DECRYPTION BY PASSWORD = 'password'
```

The CLOSE MASTER KEY command is used once the example is finished using the Database Master Key (with no additional arguments).

In this example, encryption by the Service Master Key is dropped for the BookStore database:

```
ALTER MASTER KEY DROP ENCRYPTION BY SERVICE MASTER KEY
```

To re-enable encryption by the Service Master Key, we must first open access to the Database Master Key, Service Master Key encryption is re-added to the Database Master Key, and then the Database Master Key is closed again:

```
OPEN MASTER KEY DECRYPTION BY PASSWORD = '641076B0'
```

```
ALTER MASTER KEY ADD ENCRYPTION BY SERVICE MASTER KEY
```

```
CLOSE MASTER KEY
```

Once the Service Master Key is used to encrypt the Database Master Key, the Database Master Key no longer needs to be explicitly opened or closed.

How It Works

This recipe demonstrated removing encryption of the Database Master Key by the Service Master Key using the ALTER MASTER KEY command:

```
ALTER MASTER KEY DROP ENCRYPTION BY SERVICE MASTER KEY
```

Once this is done, any modification of the Database Master Key requires password access using OPEN MASTER KEY. This was used in order to reapply encryption by the Service Master Key:

```
OPEN MASTER KEY DECRYPTION BY PASSWORD = '641076B0'
```

The ALTER MASTER KEY was used then to add Service Master Key encryption back again:

```
ALTER MASTER KEY ADD ENCRYPTION BY SERVICE MASTER KEY
```

After finishing the ALTER MASTER KEY operation, the Database Master Key was closed:

```
CLOSE MASTER KEY
```

Asymmetric Key Encryption

An asymmetric key contains a database-side internal public and private key, which can be used to encrypt and decrypt data in the SQL Server 2005 database. Asymmetric keys can be imported from an external file or assembly, and can also be generated within the SQL Server 2005 database.

Unlike a certificate (which is discussed later in the chapter), asymmetric keys cannot be backed up to a file. This means that if an asymmetric key is created within SQL Server 2005, there isn't an easy mechanism for reusing that same key in other user databases.

Asymmetric keys are a highly secure option for data encryption, but they also require more SQL Server resources when in use. In the next set of recipes, I'll demonstrate how to create, manage, and use asymmetric key encryption.

Creating an Asymmetric Key

In this recipe, I'll demonstrate creating an asymmetric key, which will then be used for encrypting and decrypting data. The syntax for creating an asymmetric key is as follows:

```
CREATE ASYMMETRIC KEY Asym_Key_Name
   [ AUTHORIZATION database_principal_name ]
   {  FROM    {FILE = ' path_to_strong_name_file     |
   EXECUTABLE FILE = ' path_to_executable_file ' |
   ASSEMBLY Assembly_Name}   |
      WITH ALGORITHM = { RSA_512 | RSA_1024 | RSA_2048 } }
   ENCRYPTION BY PASSWORD = ' password '
```

The arguments of this command are described in Table 19-2.

Table 19-2. *CREATE ASYMMETRIC KEY Arguments*

Argument	Description
Asym_Key_Name	The name of the asymmetric key.
database_principal_name	The owner of the asymmetric key.
path_to_strong_name_file	The existing file and path of the strong-name file containing the key pair.
path_to_executable_file	The existing executable key pair file.
Assembly_Name	The existing assembly filename and path containing the public key.
RSA_512 | RSA_1024 | RSA_2048	Used for generating a new key, this option selects the security type. Each designates the number of bits long the private key will be (512, 1024, 2048 bits).
Password	The password used to encrypt the private key. When not used, the private key is automatically encrypted by the Database Master Key.

In this example, a new asymmetric key is created in the BookStore database:

```
USE BookStore
GO

CREATE ASYMMETRIC KEY asymBookSellerKey
WITH ALGORITHM = RSA_512
ENCRYPTION BY PASSWORD = 'EEB0B4DD'
```

How It Works

This example demonstrated creating an asymmetric key in the BookStore database. The first line of code designated the name of the new key:

```
CREATE ASYMMETRIC KEY asymBookSellerKey
```

The second line of code designated the encryption security type:

```
WITH ALGORITHM = RSA_512
```

The third line of code designated the password used to encrypt the asymmetric key:

```
ENCRYPTION BY PASSWORD = 'EEB0B4DD'
```

Viewing Asymmetric Keys in the Current Database

You can view all asymmetric keys in the current database by querying the sys.asymmetric_keys system catalog view. For example:

```
SELECT name, algorithm_desc, pvt_key_encryption_type_desc
FROM sys.asymmetric_keys
```

This returns:

name	algorithm_desc	pvt_key_encryption_type_desc
asymBookSellerKey	RSA_512	ENCRYPTED_BY_PASSWORD

How It Works

The `sys.asymmetric_keys` system catalog view was used to see asymmetric keys in the current database. The first line of code designated the name, security type, and method by which the private key was encrypted:

```
SELECT name, algorithm_desc, pvt_key_encryption_type_desc
```

The second line designated the system catalog view in the FROM clause:

```
FROM sys.asymmetric_keys
```

Modifying the Asymmetric Key's Private Key Password

You can also modify the password of the private key by using the ALTER ASYMMETRIC KEY command with the ENCRYPTION BY PASSWORD and DECRYPTION BY PASSWORD options.

This example demonstrates giving the asymmetric key a new password:

```
ALTER ASYMMETRIC KEY asymBookSellerKey
WITH PRIVATE KEY
(ENCRYPTION BY PASSWORD = 'newpasswordE4D352F280E0',
DECRYPTION BY PASSWORD = 'EEB0B4DD')
```

How It Works

In this recipe, we used ALTER ASYMMETRIC KEY to change the private key password. The first line of code designated the asymmetric key name:

```
ALTER ASYMMETRIC KEY asymBookSellerKey
```

The new password was designated in the ENCRYPTION BY PASSWORD argument:

```
WITH PRIVATE KEY
(ENCRYPTION BY PASSWORD = 'newpasswordE4D352F280E0',
```

The old private key password was designated in the DECRYPTION BY PASSWORD argument:

```
DECRYPTION BY PASSWORD = 'EEB0B4DD')
```

Encrypting and Decrypting Data Using an Asymmetric Key

Using an asymmetric key to encrypt data is a very secure method of maintaining the secrecy of the data, because both a public and private key pair are required. Encryption by asymmetric key is a more costly operation when used in conjunction with large data sets, though, compared to the faster option of encrypting symmetric keys, which use a single key to encrypt and decrypt data.

Once an asymmetric key is added to the database, it can be used to encrypt and decrypt data. To encrypt data, the `EncryptByAsmKey` function is used.

The syntax is as follows:

```
EncryptByAsmKey ( Asym_Key_ID , { 'cleartext' | @cleartext } )
```

The arguments of this command are described in Table 19-3.

Table 19-3. *EncryptByAsymKey Arguments*

Argument	Description
Asym_Key_ID	The ID of the asymmetric key to be used to encrypt the data. The AsymKey_ID function can be used to return the ID of the asymmetric key.
' cleartext ' | @cleartext	The unencrypted text to be encrypted (from a string or a local variable).

As with encrypting data via a certificate, the EncryptByAsymKey function returns varbinary encrypted data.

To decrypt data encrypted by a specific asymmetric key, the DecryptByAsymKey function is used. The syntax is as follows:

```
DecryptByAsymKey ( Asym_Key_ID ,
                 { ' ciphertext ' | @ciphertext }
                 [ , ' Asym_Key_Password ' ] )
```

The arguments of this command are described in Table 19-4.

Table 19-4. *DecryptByAsymKey Arguments*

Argument	Description
Asym_Key_ID	The ID of the asymmetric key to be used to decrypt the data. The Asym_Key_ID system function can be used to return the ID of the asymmetric key.
' ciphertext ' | @ciphertext	The encrypted text to be decrypted.
' Asym_Key_Password '	The password of the asymmetric key's private key (password used when the asymmetric key was created).

In this example, a table containing bank routing information for specific booksellers is created:

```
CREATE TABLE dbo.BookSellerBankRouting
(BookSellerID int NOT NULL PRIMARY KEY,
 BankRoutingNBR varbinary(300) NOT NULL)
GO
```

Next, a new row is inserted into the table using the EncryptByAsumKey, on the yet-to-be-encrypted bank routing number:

```
INSERT dbo.BookSellerBankRouting
(BookSellerID, BankRoutingNBR)
VALUES (22,
EncryptByAsymKey(AsymKey_ID('asymBookSellerKey'),
          '137492837583249ABR'))
```

Querying the value of BankRoutingNBR for the newly inserted row returns cipher text:

```
SELECT CAST(BankRoutingNBR as varchar(100)) BankRoutingNBR
FROM dbo.BookSellerBankRouting
WHERE BookSellerID = 22
```

This returns:

```
BankRoutingNBR
----------------------------------------------------------------------
m(Ì_'dc`Ó«·"ÆöÖï2ö]Œ¡ìåßO'a8___.§6øovPgîÎwñ@lÈ__µq-@'cda_?Lÿ<_3p'85íàj_{
```

Next, the DecryptByAsymKey function is used to decrypt the BankRoutingNBR column value. CAST is also used to convert the varbinary data into varchar data:

```
SELECT CAST(DecryptByAsymKey
      ( AsymKey_ID('asymBookSellerKey'),
              BankRoutingNBR,
              N'newpasswordE4D352F280E0') as varchar(100)) BankRoutingNBR
FROM dbo.BookSellerBankRouting
WHERE BookSellerID = 22
```

This returns:

```
BankRoutingNBR
----------------------------------------------------------------------
137492837583249ABR
```

How It Works

This recipe started off by creating a table to store encrypted bank routing numbers. The BankRoutingNBR column was given a varbinary data type in order to stored the encrypted data. An INSERT was then performed on the table. The two columns to be inserted into were designated:

```
INSERT dbo.BookSellerBankRouting
(BookSellerID, BankRoutingNBR)
```

The BookSellerID was set to a value of 22:

```
VALUES (22,
```

The BankRoutingNBR was populated using the EncryptByAsymKey function:

```
EncryptByAsymKey(
```

This function took a first parameter of the asymmetric key's system ID, using the AsymKey_ID function to convert the

```
AsymKey_ID('asymBookSellerKey'),
```

The second parameter contained the bank routing number to be encrypted:

```
        '137492837583249ABR'))
```

The data was then stored in the table in encrypted cipher text. To decrypt the data, the DecryptByAsymKey function was used. The CAST function was wrapped around it in order to convert the varbinary value into varchar:

```
SELECT CAST(
```

The first parameter of the DecryptByAsymKey function was the asymmetric key's system ID, again using the AsymKey_ID to convert the asymmetric key name into the ID:

```
DecryptByAsymKey
      ( AsymKey_ID('asymBookSellerKey'),
```

The second parameter was the `BankRoutingNBR` column from the `dbo.BookSellerBankRouting` table:

```
BankRoutingNBR,
```

The third parameter was the password of the asymmetric key's private key:

```
N'newpasswordE4D352F280E0')
```

The data type was then converted to varchar(100) :

```
as varchar(100)) BankRoutingNBR
FROM dbo.BookSellerBankRouting
WHERE BookSellerID = 22
```

Dropping an Asymmetric Key

To drop an asymmetric key, use the `DROP ASYMMETRIC KEY` command. This command takes just one argument—the name of the asymmetric key.

For example:

```
DROP ASYMMETRIC KEY asymBookSellerKey
```

How It Works

This example demonstrated the simple method of dropping an asymmetric key. Keep in mind that an asymmetric key can't be dropped if it was used to encrypt other keys or is mapped to a login.

Symmetric Key Encryption

Certificates (reviewed later in the chapter) and asymmetric keys encrypt data using a database-side internal public key and decrypt data using a database-side internal private key. Symmetric keys are simpler. They contain a key that is used for *both* encryption and decryption. Consequently, symmetric keys encrypt data faster, and are more suitable for use against large data sets. Although a trade-off in terms of encryption complexity, symmetric keys are still considered to be a good option for encrypting secret data within the database.

In the next set of recipes, I'll demonstrate how to create, manage, and use symmetric key encryption.

Creating a Symmetric Key

A symmetric key is a less resource-intensive method of encrypting large amounts of data. Unlike certificates or asymmetric keys, a symmetric key both encrypts and decrypts the data with a single internal key. The distinguishing feature of symmetric keys is that the key must be opened for use within a database session, prior to the encrypting or decrypting of data.

To create a symmetric key, the `CREATE SYMMETRIC KEY` command is used. The syntax is as follows:

```
CREATE SYMMETRIC KEY key_name
[ AUTHORIZATION owner_name ]
    WITH  KEY_SOURCE = ' pass_phrase '   |
    ALGORITHM =
{DES | TRIPLE_DES | RC2 | RC4 | DESX | AES_128 | AES_192 | AES_256} |
    IDENTITY_VALUE = ' identity_phrase '
    ENCRYPTION BY
    CERTIFICATE Certificate_Name |
```

```
PASSWORD = ' password ' |
SYMMETRIC KEY Symmetric_Key_Name   |
ASYMMETRIC KEY Asym_Key_Name
```

The arguments of this command are described in Table 19-5.

Table 19-5. *CREATE SYMMETRIC KEY Arguments*

Argument	Description
key_name	The name of the new symmetric key. If prefixed with a # sign, a temporary key can be created for the current session and user.
owner_name	The databhase user that owns the key.
pass_phrase	A passphrase used to derive the symmetric key.
DES | TRIPLE_DES | RC2 | RC4 | DESX | AES_128 | AES_192 | AES_256	The encryption algorithm used to create the key.
IDENTITY_VALUE = ' identity_phrase '	This character-based phrase is used to generate a GUID that tags data with a temporary key (when a temporary key is used).
ENCRYPTION BY CERTIFICATE Certificate_Name	The symmetric key can be encrypted by using an existing certificate.
PASSWORD = ' password '	The symmetric key can be encrypted by using a password.
SYMMETRIC KEY Symmetric_Key_Name	The symmetric key can be encrypted by using another symmetric key.
ASYMMETRIC KEY Asym_Key_Name	The symmetric key can be encrypted by using an asymmetric key.

In this recipe, a new symmetric key is created that is encrypted by an existing database asymmetric key:

```
CREATE SYMMETRIC KEY sym_BookStore
WITH ALGORITHM = TRIPLE_DES
ENCRYPTION BY ASYMMETRIC KEY asymBookSellerKey
```

How It Works

In this recipe I demonstrated the creation of a symmetric key, which will then be used to encrypt data. It must be encrypted using a certificate, password, asymmetric key, or another symmetric key. In this case, we used an asymmetric key to encrypt it.

The first line of code designated the symmetric key name:

```
CREATE SYMMETRIC KEY sym_BookStore
```

The second line of code designated the encryption algorithm used to create the encrypting key:

```
WITH ALGORITHM = TRIPLE_DES
```

The last line of code defined the asymmetric key in the current database that would be used to encrypt the symmetric key:

```
ENCRYPTION BY ASYMMETRIC KEY asymBookSellerKey
```

Viewing Symmetric Keys in the Current Database

You can see the symmetric keys in the current database by querying the `sys.symmetric_keys` system catalog view:

```
SELECT name, algorithm_desc
FROM sys.symmetric_keys
```

This returns:

```
name                                  algorithm_desc
------------------------------------  -----------------------------------
##MS_DatabaseMasterKey##              TRIPLE_DES
sym_BookStore                         TRIPLE_DES
```

How It Works

The `sys.symmetric_keys` system catalog view was used to return the name and encryption algorithm of symmetric keys in the current database. Notice that this query against `sys.symmetric_keys` also returned a row for the Database Master Key.

Changing How a Symmetric Key Is Encrypted

In this recipe, I'll demonstrate how to change the way a symmetric key is encrypted using `ALTER SYMMETRIC KEY`. Before doing this, however, I must first open it using the `OPEN SYMMETRIC KEY` command.

The syntax for `OPEN SYMMETRIC KEY` is as follows:

```
OPEN SYMMETRIC KEY Key_name DECRYPTION BY < decryption_mechanism >
```

The decryption mechanism for opening the key depends on how the key was originally encrypted:

```
< decryption_mechanism >::=
CERTIFICATE certificate_name
   [ WITH PASSWORD = ' password ' ] |
ASYMMETRIC KEY asym_key_name
   [ WITH PASSWORD = ' password ' ]|
SYMMETRIC KEY decrypting_Key_name
| PASSWORD = ' decryption_password '
```

For example, the following symmetric key is opened using the private key password of an encryption key:

```
OPEN SYMMETRIC KEY sym_BookStore
DECRYPTION BY ASYMMETRIC KEY asymBookSellerKey
WITH PASSWORD = 'newpasswordE4D352F280E0'
```

Once opened for use, the key can be changed to use encryption by a password instead (adding the password encryption first, *then* removing the asymmetric key encryption):

```
ALTER SYMMETRIC KEY sym_BookStore
ADD ENCRYPTION BY PASSWORD = 'hushhush!123'

ALTER SYMMETRIC KEY sym_BookStore
DROP ENCRYPTION BY ASYMMETRIC KEY asymBookSellerKey
```

Once finished with the operations, the CLOSE SYMMETRIC KEY command closes the key for use in the database session:

```
CLOSE SYMMETRIC KEY sym_BookStore
```

How It Works

This example demonstrated ways to change how a symmetric key is encrypted, in this case from using a asymmetric key to using a password instead.

First, OPEN SYMMETRIC KEY was used to open the key up for modification. The first line of code designated the symmetric key name:

```
OPEN SYMMETRIC KEY sym_BookStore
```

The second line of code designated the name of the asymmetric key used to encrypt the symmetric key:

```
DECRYPTION BY ASYMMETRIC KEY asymBookSellerKey
```

The third line of code designated the private key password of the asymmetric key:

```
WITH PASSWORD = 'newpasswordE4D352F280E0'
```

Once opened for use, the key was changed to use encryption by a password. The first line of code designated the symmetric key to modify:

```
ALTER SYMMETRIC KEY sym_BookStore
```

The second line of code designated that the symmetric key would be encrypted by a password:

```
ADD ENCRYPTION BY PASSWORD = 'hushhush!123'
```

After that, ALTER SYMMETRIC KEY was called again to drop the asymmetric key encryption. The first line of code designated the symmetric key to be modified:

```
ALTER SYMMETRIC KEY sym_BookStore
```

The second line of code designated the asymmetric key encryption to be dropped:

```
DROP ENCRYPTION BY ASYMMETRIC KEY asymBookSellerKey
```

Once we finished, the CLOSE SYMMETRIC KEY command was used to close the key for use in the database session:

```
CLOSE SYMMETRIC KEY sym_BookStore
```

Using Symmetric Key Encryption and Decryption

To encrypt data using a symmetric key, the symmetric key must first be opened, and then the EncryptByKey function used.

The syntax for this function is as follows:

```
EncryptByKey( key_GUID , { ' cleartext ' | @cleartext }
[ , { add_authenticator | @add_authenticator }
, { authenticator | @authenticator } ])
```

The arguments of this command are described in Table 19-6.

Table 19-6. *EncryptByKey Arguments*

Argument	Description
key_GUID	The symmetric key global unique identifier (GUID), which can be derived by using the Key_GUID system function.
' cleartext ' | @cleartext	The text to be encrypted.
add_authenticator | @add_authenticator	A Boolean value (1 or 0) determining whether an authenticator will be used with the encrypted value. The data being encrypted can be further encrypted by using an additional binding value—for example the table's primary key. If the authenticator is modified (or tampered with) the encrypted data will not be able to be decrypted.
authenticator | @authenticator	Data column used for the authenticator. For example, you can bind the encrypted data along with the primary key of the table.

In this example, a new table is created to hold password hints for customers. The answer to the password hint is to be encrypted in the table:

```
CREATE TABLE dbo.PasswordHint
(CustomerID int NOT NULL PRIMARY KEY,
 PasswordHintQuestion varchar(300) NOT NULL,
 PasswordHintAnswer varbinary(200) NOT NULL)
GO
```

In this example, a new row is inserted into the dbo.PasswordHint table that encrypts the PasswordHintAnswer column using a symmetric key:

```
OPEN SYMMETRIC KEY sym_BookStore
DECRYPTION BY PASSWORD = 'hushhush!123'

INSERT dbo.PasswordHint
(CustomerID, PasswordHintQuestion, PasswordHintAnswer)
VALUES
(23, 'What is the name of the hospital you were born in?',
EncryptByKey(Key_GUID('sym_BookStore '), 'Mount Marie'))

CLOSE SYMMETRIC KEY sym_BookStore
```

To decrypt data that was encrypted by a symmetric key, the DecryptByKey command is used. Notice that unlike the EncryptByKey command, DecryptByKey doesn't use the symmetric key GUID, so the correct symmetric key session must be opened in order to decrypt the data:

```
OPEN SYMMETRIC KEY sym_BookStore
DECRYPTION BY PASSWORD = 'hushhush!123'

SELECT CAST(DecryptByKey(PasswordHintAnswer) as varchar(200)) PasswordHintAnswer
FROM dbo.PasswordHint
WHERE CustomerID = 23

CLOSE SYMMETRIC KEY sym_BookStore
```

This returns:

```
PasswordHintAnswer
-------------------------------------------------------------------------
Mount Marie
```

If you attempted to query the value with the previous query without first opening the symmetric key that was used to encrypt the data, a NULL value would have been returned instead:

```
PasswordHintAnswer
-------------------------------------------------------------------------
NULL
```

As was shown in the EncryptByKey syntax shown earlier, you can also include an extra authenticator column value to be used in the encryption of the text data. This additional information helps further obscure the cipher text from any meaningful value that could potentially be derived from the cipher text and other non-encrypted columns in the table.

In this example, the primary key value of the dbo.PasswordHint table is used in the encryption of the data. First, a new table is created and an un-encrypted row added to it:

```
CREATE TABLE dbo.BookSellerLogins
(LoginID int NOT NULL PRIMARY KEY,
 Password varbinary(256) NOT NULL)
GO

INSERT dbo.BookSellerLogins
(LoginID, Password)
VALUES(22, CAST('myeasypassword' as varbinary))
```

Next, the symmetric key is opened, and the values of the password column are encrypted in an UPDATE statement, using the symmetric key and the LoginID of the row:

```
OPEN SYMMETRIC KEY sym_BookStore
DECRYPTION BY PASSWORD = 'hushhush!123'

UPDATE dbo.BookSellerLogins
SET Password =
   EncryptByKey(Key_GUID('sym_BookStore'),
           Password,
           1,
           CAST(LoginID as varbinary))

CLOSE SYMMETRIC KEY sym_BookStore
```

To decrypt the value of this updated row, the DecryptByKey must also include the authenticator column in the function call:

```
OPEN SYMMETRIC KEY sym_BookStore
DECRYPTION BY PASSWORD = 'hushhush!123'

SELECT LoginID,
CAST(DecryptByKey(Password, 1,
CAST(LoginID as varbinary)) as varchar(30)) Password
FROM dbo.BookSellerLogins

CLOSE SYMMETRIC KEY sym_BookStore
```

This returns:

```
LoginID      Password
-----------  ------------------------------
22           myeasypassword
```

How It Works

In this recipe, I demonstrated how to encrypt data using EncryptByKey and decrypt it using DecryptByKey. Before using the function, the symmetric key first had to be opened. The first line of OPEN SYMMETRIC KEY referenced the symmetric key name:

```
OPEN SYMMETRIC KEY sym_BookStore
```

The second line included the password used to access the symmetric key for use:

```
DECRYPTION BY PASSWORD = 'hushhush!123'
```

A new row was then inserted, with an encrypted value using EncryptByKey. The first argument used the Key_GUID function to return the system ID of the symmetric key to be used. The second argument was the text to be encrypted by the symmetric key:

```
...
EncryptByKey(Key_GUID('sym_BookStore '), 'Mount Marie'))
```

The key was then closed after finishing the encryption, referencing the symmetric key for the argument:

```
CLOSE SYMMETRIC KEY sym_BookStore
```

To decrypt the data, the symmetric key was reopened:

```
OPEN SYMMETRIC KEY sym_BookStore
DECRYPTION BY PASSWORD = 'hushhush!123'
```

The DecryptByKey function was used, taking just the table column where the encrypted data was stored as an argument:

```
SELECT CAST(DecryptByKey(PasswordHintAnswer) as varchar(200)) PasswordHintAnswer
FROM dbo.PasswordHint
WHERE CustomerID = 23
```

After returning the decrypted data, the symmetric key was then closed:

```
CLOSE SYMMETRIC KEY sym_BookStore
```

Encrypting data using an authenticator was also demonstrated. In the example, the third parameter was a flag indicating that an authenticator value would be used (1 for "True"), followed by the column authenticator (LoginID):

```
EncryptByKey(Key_GUID('sym_BookStore'),
             Password,
             1,
             CAST(LoginID as varbinary)
```

The LoginID was converted to varbinary prior to being included in the encrypted data. Using an authenticator further secures the encrypted data. However if the accompanying authenticator LoginID value was changed for the specific row, the encrypted data can no longer be decrypted with the modified LoginID value.

In the example, the symmetric key was opened, and the `DecryptByKey` function was used, including the encrypted column in the first argument, authenticator flag in the second argument, and the authenticator column in the third argument (CAST as a `varbinary` data type):

```
SELECT LoginID,
CAST(DecryptByKey(Password, 1,
CAST(LoginID as varbinary)) as varchar(30)) Password
FROM dbo.BookSellerLogins
```

After returning the decrypted data, the symmetric key was then closed.

Dropping a Symmetric Key

You can remove a symmetric key from the database by using the `DROP SYMMETRIC KEY` command, which takes the name of the symmetric key as its single argument.

For example:

```
DROP SYMMETRIC KEY sym_BookStore
```

How It Works

In this recipe, I demonstrated dropping a symmetric key from the database. It took a single argument—the name of the symmetric key. Keep in mind that if the key was open, the `DROP` command would fail with an error.

Certificate Encryption

Certificates can be used to encrypt and decrypt data within the database. A certificate contains a key pair, information about the owner of the certificate, and the valid start and end expiration dates for the certificate in question. A certificate contains both a public and a private key. As you'll see in later recipes, the public key of the certificate is used to *en*crypt data, and the private key is used to *de*crypt data. SQL Server can generate its own certificates, or, if you like, you can load one from an external file or assembly. Certificates are more portable than asymmetric keys, because they can be backed up and then loaded from files, whereas asymmetric keys cannot. This means that the same certificate can easily be reused in multiple user databases. Once a certificate is created, certificate encryption and decryption functions can then be used against database data.

Both certificates *and* asymmetric key database objects provide a very secure method for encrypting data. This strong method of encryption comes with a performance cost, however. Encrypting very large data sets with a certificate or asymmetric key may incur too much overhead for your environment. A lower overhead option (but a less secure one as well) is using a symmetric key, which was reviewed earlier.

In the next set of recipes I'll demonstrate how to create, manage, and use certificate-based encryption.

Creating a Database Certificate

To create a new database certificate, the `CREATE CERTIFICATE` command is used. The abridged syntax for creating a new certificate in the database is as follows:

```
CREATE CERTIFICATE certificate_name [ AUTHORIZATION user_name ]
    [ ENCRYPTION BY PASSWORD = ' password ']
    WITH SUBJECT = ' certificate_subject_name '
    START_DATE = ' mm/dd/yyyy ' | EXPIRY_DATE = ' mm/dd/yyyy '
```

The arguments of this command are described in Table 19-7.

Table 19-7. *CREATE CERTIFICATE Arguments*

Argument	Description
certificate_name	The name of the new database certificate.
user_name	The database user who owns the certificate.
Password	The password used to encrypt the certificate.
certificate_subject_name	The certificate metadata description.
START_DATE = ' mm/dd/yyyy '	The start date of the certificate, defaulting to the current date. System functions don't actually check these dates, so it will be up to your Transact-SQL code to validate the certificate period.
EXPIRY_DATE = ' mm/dd/yyyy '	The expiration date of the certificate, defaulting to one year after the start date.

In this example, a new certificate is created in the BookStore database:

```
USE BookStore
GO

CREATE CERTIFICATE cert_BookStore
ENCRYPTION BY PASSWORD = 'AA5FA6AC'
WITH SUBJECT = 'BookStore Database Encryption Certificate',
START_DATE = '7/15/2005', EXPIRY_DATE = '8/15/2006'
```

How It Works

In this recipe I created a new certificate that will be used to encrypt and decrypt data. The first line of code included the name of the new certificate:

```
CREATE CERTIFICATE cert_BookStore
```

The second line included the password used to encrypt the certificate:

```
ENCRYPTION BY PASSWORD = 'AA5FA6AC'
```

The third line designated the subject of the certificate, followed by the start and expiration date for the certificate:

```
WITH SUBJECT = 'BookStore Database Encryption Certificate',
START_DATE = '7/15/2005', EXPIRY_DATE = '8/15/2006'
```

Viewing Certificates in the Database

Once the certificate is created in the database, you can view it by querying the sys.certificates system catalog view:

```
SELECT name, pvt_key_encryption_type_desc, issuer_name
FROM sys.certificates
```

This returns:

```
name              pvt_key_encryption_type_desc  issuer_name
--------------    ----------------------------  ---------------------
cert_BookStore    ENCRYPTED_BY_PASSWORD             BookStore Database...
```

How It Works

Query the sys.certificates system catalog view to see certificates in the current database. The name column returned the name of the certificate. The pvt_key_encryption_type_desc column in the result set describes how the private key of the certificate was encrypted. The issuer_name returned the certificate subject.

Backing Up and Restoring a Certificate

Once a certificate is created it can also be backed up to file for safe keeping or for use in restoring in other databases using the BACKUP CERTIFICATE command.

The syntax is as follows:

```
BACKUP CERTIFICATE certname TO FILE = 'path_to_file'
    [ WITH PRIVATE KEY
        ( FILE = 'path_to_private_key_file' ,
            ENCRYPTION BY PASSWORD = 'encryption_password'
[ , DECRYPTION BY PASSWORD = 'decryption_password' ]   ) ]
```

The arguments of this command are described in Table 19-8.

Table 19-8. *BACKUP CERTIFICATE Arguments*

Argument	Description
path_to_file	The filename and path that the certificate backup is written to.
path_to_private_key_file	Specifies a path and filename to the private key file.
encryption_password	The private key password used when the certificate was created.
decryption_password	The private key password used to decrypt the key prior to backup.

This example demonstrates backing up the certificate:

```
BACKUP CERTIFICATE cert_BookStore
TO FILE = 'C:\Apress\Recipes\Certificates\certBookStore.BAK'
WITH PRIVATE KEY ( FILE = 'C:\Apress\Recipes\Certificates\certBookStorePK.BAK' ,
ENCRYPTION BY PASSWORD = '3439F6A',
DECRYPTION BY PASSWORD = 'AA5FA6AC' )
```

This backup creates two files, one for the certificate containing the public key (used to encrypt data), and another containing the password-protected private key (used to decrypt data).

Once backed up, you can use the certificate in other databases, or drop the existing certificate using the DROP CERTIFICATE command (which uses the certificate name as its argument) and restore it from backup, as this example demonstrates:

```
DROP CERTIFICATE cert_BookStore
GO

CREATE CERTIFICATE cert_BookStore
FROM FILE = 'C:\Apress\Recipes\Certificates\certBookStore.BAK'
WITH PRIVATE KEY (FILE = 'C:\Apress\Recipes\Certificates\certBookStorePK.BAK',
            DECRYPTION BY PASSWORD = '3439F6A',
            ENCRYPTION BY PASSWORD = 'AA5FA6AC')
```

How It Works

This recipe demonstrated backing up a certificate to external files using BACKUP CERTIFICATE, dropping it using DROP CERTIFICATE, and then recreating it from file using CREATE CERTIFICATE.

Walking through the code, the first line of the backup referenced the certificate name:

```
BACKUP CERTIFICATE cert_BookStore
```

The TO FILE clause included the filename where the public key of the certificate would be backed up to:

```
TO FILE = 'C:\Apress\Recipes\Certificates\certBookStore.BAK'
```

The WITH PRIVATE KEY clause designated the file where the private key backup would be output to, along with the encryption (the private key password used when the certificate was created) and decryption (the private key password used to decrypt the key prior to back up) passwords:

```
WITH PRIVATE KEY ( FILE = 'C:\Apress\Recipes\Certificates\certBookStorePK.BAK' ,
ENCRYPTION BY PASSWORD = '3439F6A',
DECRYPTION BY PASSWORD = 'AA5FA6AC' )
```

After removing the existing certificate using DROP CERTIFICATE, the certificate was then recreated from the backup files. The first line of CREATE CERTIFICATE referenced the certificate name:

```
CREATE CERTIFICATE cert_BookStore
```

The FROM FILE clause designated the location of the public key backup file:

```
FROM FILE =
'C:\Apress\Recipes\Certificates\certBookStore.BAK'
```

The WITH PRIVATE KEY clause designated the location of the private key file, followed by the decryption and encryption passwords:

```
WITH PRIVATE KEY (FILE = 'C:\Apress\Recipes\Certificates\certBookStorePK.BAK',
         DECRYPTION BY PASSWORD = '3439F6A',
         ENCRYPTION BY PASSWORD = 'AA5FA6AC')
```

Managing a Certificate's Private Key

You can add or remove the private key of a certificate by using the ALTER CERTIFICATE command. This command allows you to remove the private key (defaulting to encryption by the Database Master Key), add the private key, or change the private key password.

The following example drops the private key from the certificate:

```
ALTER CERTIFICATE cert_BookStore
REMOVE PRIVATE KEY
```

As with CREATE CERTIFICATE, you can also re-add a private key from a backup file to an existing certificate using ALTER CERTIFICATE:

```
ALTER CERTIFICATE cert_BookStore
WITH PRIVATE KEY
(FILE = 'C:\Apress\Recipes\Certificates\certBookStorePK.BAK',
     DECRYPTION BY PASSWORD = '3439F6A',
         ENCRYPTION BY PASSWORD = 'AA5FA6AC')
```

ALTER CERTIFICATE can also be used to change the password of an existing private key:

```
ALTER CERTIFICATE cert_BookStore
WITH PRIVATE KEY (DECRYPTION BY PASSWORD = 'AA5FA6AC',
ENCRYPTION BY PASSWORD = 'mynewpassword!!!Efsj')
```

The DECRYPTION BY PASSWORD was the old private key password, and the ENCRYPTION BY PASSWORD the new private key password.

How It Works

This recipe demonstrated how to modify the way that a certificate is encrypted. The private key was removed from the certificate using ALTER CERTIFICATE and REMOVE PRIVATE KEY:

```
ALTER CERTIFICATE cert_BookStore
REMOVE PRIVATE KEY
```

To add it back again, we also used ALTER CERTIFICATE. The first line referenced the certificate name:

```
ALTER CERTIFICATE cert_BookStore
```

The WITH PRIVATE KEY clause designated the location of the private key file, along with the decryption and encryption passwords:

```
WITH PRIVATE KEY
(FILE = 'C:\Apress\Recipes\Certificates\certBookStorePK.BAK',
        DECRYPTION BY PASSWORD = '3439F6A',
            ENCRYPTION BY PASSWORD = 'AA5FA6AC')
```

Finally, I modified the certificate's private key password. The first line referenced the certificate name:

```
ALTER CERTIFICATE cert_BookStore
```

The WITH PRIVATE KEY clause designated the decryption password, and the new encryption password:

```
WITH PRIVATE KEY (DECRYPTION BY PASSWORD = 'AA5FA6AC',
ENCRYPTION BY PASSWORD = 'mynewpassword!!!Efsj')
```

Using Certificate Encryption and Decryption

Once you have a certificate in the database, you can use the EncryptByCert system function to encrypt data using the certificate's public key. Encryption allows you to protect sensitive table data. Without the associated private key, the data will be unreadable.

The syntax for EncryptByCert is as follows:

```
EncryptByCert ( certificate_ID , { ' cleartext ' | @cleartext } )
```

The arguments of this command are described in Table 19-9.

Table 19-9. *EncryptByCert Arguments*

Argument	Description
certificate_ID	The certificateID of the certificate used to encrypt the data.
' cleartext ' | @cleartext	The unencrypted text to be encrypted.

In order to retrieve the certificate ID of a specific database certificate, you can use the Cert_ID function, which takes the certificate name as its single argument:

```
Cert_ID ( ' cert_name ' )
```

To decrypt data that has been encrypted by a certificate, use the DecryptByCert function. This function uses the internal private key of the certificate to decrypt the data (the private key requires the private key password defined when the certificate was created):

```
DecryptByCert (
            certificate_ID ,
            { ' ciphertext ' | @ciphertext }
            [ , { ' cert_password ' | @cert_password } ]
            )
```

The arguments of this command are described in Table 19-10.

Table 19-10. *DecryptByCert Arguments*

Argument	Description
certificate_ID	The certificate ID of the certificate used to decrypt the data.
' ciphertext '	@ciphertext	The encrypted text to be decrypted.
' cert_password '	@cert_password	The private key password of the certificate used to decrypt the data.

In this example, an INSERT is made into the PasswordHintAnswer table that is encrypted by the public key of the certificate:

```
INSERT dbo.PasswordHint
(CustomerID, PasswordHintQuestion, PasswordHintAnswer)
VALUES
(1, 'What is the name of the hospital you were born in?',
   EncryptByCert(Cert_ID('cert_BookStore'), 'Hickman Hospital'))
```

The next query shows the newly inserted row:

```
SELECT CAST(PasswordHintAnswer as varchar(200)) PasswordHintAnswer
FROM dbo.PasswordHint
WHERE CustomerID = 1
```

This returns unintelligible cipher text instead of the original text value:

```
PasswordHintAnswer
--------------------------------------------------------------------------------
o‹_*_1/2bYy-X-_Î`'5BuÄ*n«ßR_.´jõÑ†£sÙ_"ùüÔ_ÄÆ7(c) ±w__Àa_3U_'c9_›¨
‰@KsïÃ_â>J`¶ºp__:_Ä&ˆää_+c_4$£,_}Zj6;Ç›
```

This next example demonstrates querying the PasswordHintAnswer column; this time using the private key of the certificate to view the decrypted results:

```
SELECT CAST(DecryptByCert(Cert_ID('cert_BookStore'),
PasswordHintAnswer, N'mynewpassword!!!Efsj') as varchar(200)) PasswordHintAnswer
FROM dbo.PasswordHint
WHERE CustomerID = 1
```

This returns:

```
PasswordHintAnswer
-----------------------------------
Hickman Hospital
```

How It Works

In this recipe's example, a table was created with a varbinary data type column that was used to hold encrypted information. This data type was chosen because the EncryptByCert function returns varbinary, encrypted data. The first parameter of the EncryptByCert function took the certificate ID, followed by the text to be encrypted:

```
EncryptByCert(Cert_ID('cert_BookStore'), 'Hickman Hospital')
```

This text to be encrypted can be of the nvarchar, varchar, char, or nchar data types. The data is actually stored, however, in varbinary. If you attempt to convert the varbinary data to the original text data type, without the DecryptByCert function and the appropriate certificate and password, only encrypted garble is returned.

The encrypted string was then decrypted using the private key of the same certificate. The function's first parameter was the certificate ID, followed by the encrypted text in the second parameter. The third parameter was the private key password used when the certificate was created:

```
DecryptByCert(Cert_ID('cert_BookStore'), PasswordHintAnswer,
 N'mynewpassword!!!Efsj') PasswordHintAnswer
```

The results of the function were also CAST back into the varchar data type, in order to display the original text.

CHAPTER 20

■■■

Service Broker

Microsoft introduces the new Service Broker functionality to SQL Server 2005, allowing you to build asynchronous, database-driven messaging applications. *Asynchronous* in this context means that a task, such as placing an order, can be initiated and then completed over time without forming a bottleneck with other tasks. In contrast, *synchronous processing* means that one unit of work is dependent on another unit of work before it can proceed. For example, an order process is synchronous if it submits an order request to a destination service, but cannot proceed with other tasks until that submitted order request is accepted by the receiving service. Using the Service Broker, application tasks can keep moving forward while messages are handled in their own required timeframe. The Service Broker allows one database to send a message to another without waiting for a response, so the sending database will continue to function, even if the remote database cannot process the message immediately. The Service Broker is reviewed in this book because it can be managed entirely by using SQL Server 2005 Transact-SQL objects and commands.

The Service Broker provides message-queuing for SQL Server. It provides a means for you to send an asynchronous, transactional message from within a database to a queue, where it will be picked up and processed by another service, possibly running on another database or server. Again, with asynchronous programs, a message is sent, and the application can proceed with other related tasks without waiting for confirmation that the original message was received or processed. Once the specific task is finished, the conversation between the two Service Broker services is explicitly ended by both sides.

Service Broker includes several out-of-the-box features that address complex factors you may often encounter when trying to build your own asynchronous messaging system. For example, Service Broker messages are guaranteed to be received in the *proper order,* or in the order in which they were initially sent. These messages are also only received *once* (the broker guarantees that there will be no duplicate reads) and can be sent as part of the same conversation, correlated to the same instance of a task. Another benefit of Service Broker is the guaranteed *delivery* of messages. If the target database (the recipient of the first message) isn't available when the first message transmission is attempted, the message will be queued on the initiator database (the sender of the first message) and an attempt will be made to send the message when the receiving database becomes available. These messages are also recoverable in the event of a database failure, as the Service Broker is built within a SQL Server 2005 database, and can be backed up along with the rest of the database.

This chapter will provide a high-level overview of the new Service Broker objects and commands by setting up the `BookStore/BookDistribution` Service Broker application, using a stored procedure to automatically process messages in a Service Broker queue, and enabling Service Broker applications to communicate remotely across SQL Server instances. I'll finish the chapter with a review and demonstration of the new event notification functionality. Event notifications work with Service Broker to allow you to track database and SQL Server instance events (similar to SQL Trace)—only the event notifications are asynchronous and have a minimal impact on overall SQL Server instance performance.

Example Scenario: Online Bookstore

In a hypothetical online bookstore, an order is placed by a customer for a book. The purchase is made to the BookStore database, which uses built-in Service Broker functionality to send a message to the BookDistribution database. The BookDistribution database is used by a separate application that handles warehouse stocking and distribution delivery. These two separate databases can exist on the same or different SQL Server 2005 instances.

Continuing with the hypothetical example, the BookStore database starts a *conversation* with the other database by submitting a book order message. This book order is sent to a *queue* on the BookDistribution database, where the receiving service program can either pick up the message right away, or defer processing for a later time. The original transaction on the BookStore database is not held up because the communication is being conducted asynchronously. For example, the application can proceed with other tasks, such as sending an order confirmation to the customer or updating other dependent tables used within the hypothetical application. When the BookDistribution database is ready to process the order, the Service Broker allows it to pluck the message from the queue, extract the message information, and process it accordingly. The BookDistribution program can then send a message back to the BookStore database confirming that the order was received, and then take its own actions to get the book sent to the customer.

Creating a Basic Service Broker Application

In this next set of recipes, I'll demonstrate setting up an application which places a book order on the BookStore database. This book order is sent asynchronously to the BookDistribution database on the same SQL Server instance. Once the BookDistribution database gets a chance to process it, BookDistribution will send an order confirmation response. The task is then finished, and the conversation between Service Broker services is ended.

The following is a general list of steps used to put together a Service Broker application when both databases reside on the same SQL Server instance:

1. Define the asynchronous tasks that you want your application to perform. Service Broker is ideal for applications that perform loosely coupled actions, such as triggering messages and responses that can span over several minutes, hours, or days, while still letting other application tasks move ahead with other actions.

2. Determine whether the Service Broker initiator and target services will be created on the same SQL Server instance, or span two SQL Server instances. Multi-instance communication requires extra steps to establish authentication via certificates or NT security, and to create endpoints, routes, and dialog security. This is demonstrated later in the chapter.

3. If not already enabled, set the ENABLE_BROKER and TRUSTWORTHY database options for the participating databases using ALTER DATABASE.

4. Create a Database Master Key for each participating database (see Chapter 19 for more on the Database Master Key).

5. Create the message types that you wish to be sent between services. Message types define the type of data contained within a message that is sent from a Service Broker endpoint (initiator service or target service). These should be added on *both* databases participating in the Service Broker application.

6. Create a contract to define the kinds of message types that can be sent by the initiator and the message types that can be sent by the target. Contracts define which message types can be sent or received at a task level. This contract should be added to *both* participating databases.

7. Create a queue on both participating databases to hold messages. A queue stores messages. You can query a queue with the SELECT statement or use the RECEIVE command to retrieve one or more messages from the queue. Each queue can also be defined with an activation stored procedure or application which will automatically handle messages when they are received in the queue.

8. Create a service on both participating databases that binds the specific contract to a specific queue. A service defines the endpoint, which is used to bind a message queue to one or more contracts.

Once these steps are followed, you are ready to create new dialog conversations (a dialog conversation is the act of exchanging messages between services) and send/receive messages between the Service Broker services. The first recipe in this section will demonstrate how to enable SQL Server databases for Service Broker activity.

■**Tip** As you'll see in this chapter, several Service Broker commands require that if the statement isn't the first statement in the batch, the preceding statement must be terminated with a semicolon statement terminator.

Enabling Databases for Service Broker Activity

The demonstration starts in the master database, where ALTER DATABASE is used to ensure that both the ENABLE_BROKER and TRUSTWORTHY database setting are enabled for both participating databases:

```
USE master

ALTER DATABASE BookStore SET ENABLE_BROKER
GO
ALTER DATABASE BookStore SET TRUSTWORTHY ON
GO


ALTER DATABASE BookDistribution SET ENABLE_BROKER
GO
ALTER DATABASE BookDistribution SET TRUSTWORTHY ON
GO
```

How It Works

This recipe used ALTER DATABASE to enable Service Broker activity for the database. To disable Service Broker you can use the DISABLE_BROKER database option.

Creating the Database Master Key for Encryption

Service Broker uses dialog security when conversations span databases. In order for this security to take effect, each participating database must have a Database Master Key.

In the BookStore database, a Database Master Key is created, in order to allow for encrypted messages between the two local databases:

```
USE BookStore
GO
```

```
CREATE MASTER KEY
ENCRYPTION BY PASSWORD = 'D4C86597'
GO
```

Now the same is done for the BookDistribution database:

```
USE BookDistribution
GO

CREATE MASTER KEY
ENCRYPTION BY PASSWORD = '50255686DDC5'
GO
```

How It Works

See Chapter 19 for details on how to create Database Master Keys for a database. In this case, I created one for each database participating in the Service Broker application.

Managing Message Types

Message types define the type of data contained within a message sent from a Service Broker endpoint (initiator or target). Think of a message type as the message template (but not the actual message), defining the name, owner, and type of message content.

The CREATE MESSAGE TYPE command is used to create a new message type. Its syntax is as follows:

```
CREATE MESSAGE TYPE message_type_name
[ AUTHORIZATION owner_name ]
[ VALIDATION =
{ NONE | EMPTY    |
WELL_FORMED_XML  |
VALID_XML WITH SCHEMA COLLECTION  schema_collection_name } ]
```

The arguments of this command are described in Table 20-1.

Table 20-1. *CREATE MESSAGE TYPE Arguments*

Argument	Description
message_type_name	The name of the message type.
owner_name	The database owner of the message type.
NONE |EMPTY |WELL FORMED XML | VALID XML WITH SCHEMA COLLECTION schema_collection_name	These settings define the message validation. When NONE, no validation is performed. When EMPTY, the message body has to be NULL. When WELL FORMED XML is chosen, the body has to contain well formed XML. When VALID XML WITH SCHEMA COLLECTION is chosen, the message body must conform to a specific XML schema.

Continuing with the online bookstore example, the first Service Broker objects created are the two message types that will be exchanged between the databases. The first is a message type that is used to send the book order:

```
Use BookStore
GO
```

```
CREATE MESSAGE TYPE [//SackConsulting/SendBookOrder]
VALIDATION = WELL_FORMED_XML
GO
```

The second message type will be sent by the target database to confirm that it has received the book order. Both message types will use a well-formed XML message body, which means that valid XML must be supplied as message content, but no schema-based validation will be performed on the message content:

```
CREATE MESSAGE TYPE [//SackConsulting/BookOrderReceived]
VALIDATION = WELL_FORMED_XML
GO
```

Now the context is switched to the BookDistribution database and the same message types and contract that were created in the BookStore database are also created in the BookDistribution database. Without creating the same message types, the receiving database would not be able to accept the incoming message. Communication structures are a two-way street, with each side having to understand the messages to be exchanged in the dialog conversation:

```
USE BookDistribution
GO

CREATE MESSAGE TYPE [//SackConsulting/SendBookOrder]
VALIDATION = WELL_FORMED_XML
GO

CREATE MESSAGE TYPE [//SackConsulting/BookOrderReceived]
VALIDATION = WELL_FORMED_XML
GO
```

How It Works

In this recipe, two different recipe types were created in both databases that will participate in the online bookstore example. In the first line of code in the CREATE MESSAGE TYPE, the name was designated in square brackets. This is the name of the message type that will be used to send a book order message:

```
CREATE MESSAGE TYPE [//SackConsulting/SendBookOrder]
```

The message validation type was designated as well-formed XML:

```
VALIDATION = WELL_FORMED_XML
GO
```

Another message was created using the same validation type, this time with a different message type name. This is the message type that will be used to respond to book order messages:

```
CREATE MESSAGE TYPE [//SackConsulting/BookOrderReceived]
VALIDATION = WELL_FORMED_XML
GO
```

Notice that I don't actually define the contents of the message. The actual message is an instance of the message type, and will be demonstrated later on in the chapter.

Creating Contracts

Contracts define which message types can be sent or received at a task level. An example of a task could be "place a book order to the distribution center." Each task in your application should define a separate contract, based on the type of messages exchanged between the initiator of the conversation and the target. Contracts also define the intended direction of the message types (initiator to target, target to initiator).

To create a new contract, use the CREATE CONTRACT command. The abridged syntax is as follows:

```
CREATE CONTRACT contract_name
    [ AUTHORIZATION owner_name ]
(  {   message_type_name SENT BY
{ INITIATOR | TARGET | ANY }
} [ ,...n] )
```

The arguments of this command are described in Table 20-2.

Table 20-2. *CREATE CONTRACT Arguments*

Argument	Description
contract_name	The name of the new contract.
owner_name	The database owner of the contract.
message_type_name	The name of the message type included in the contract.
INITIATOR | TARGET | ANY	The SENT BY options define which directions a message type can be sent. When INITIATOR, only the service that starts the conversation can send the specific message type. When TARGET, only the target of the conversation can send the specific message type. ANY allows the message to be sent by both the initiator and target.
[,...n]	More than one message type can be defined within the contract definition.

Continuing with the online bookstore example, a contract is created on the BookStore database that defines which messages can be sent by the initiator (BookStore database) or the target (BookDistribution database):

```
Use BookStore
GO
CREATE CONTRACT
    [//SackConsulting/BookOrderContract]
    ( [//SackConsulting/SendBookOrder]
        SENT BY INITIATOR,
      [//SackConsulting/BookOrderReceived]
        SENT BY TARGET
    )
GO
```

Now context is switched to the BookDistribution database and a contract is also created:

```
USE BookDistribution
GO
```

```
CREATE CONTRACT
    [//SackConsulting/BookOrderContract]
    ( [//SackConsulting/SendBookOrder]
          SENT BY INITIATOR,
      [//SackConsulting/BookOrderReceived]
          SENT BY TARGET
    )
GO
```

How It Works

This recipe demonstrated creating a new contract in both the BookStore and BookDistribution
databases. In order for the conversation to be successful, the contract definition must be identical
for both the initiator and the target. The first argument of the CREATE CONTRACT command included
the contract name:

```
CREATE CONTRACT
    [//SackConsulting/BookOrderContract]
```

In parentheses, the allowed message types created in the previous recipe are designated, along
with a definition of which role can use a message type:

```
    ( [//SackConsulting/SendBookOrder]
          SENT BY INITIATOR,
      [//SackConsulting/BookOrderReceived]
          SENT BY TARGET
    )
GO
```

The BookStore database is where the [//SackConsulting/SendBookOrder] message will be sent
from (the INITIATOR) and the BookDistribution database is from where the
[//SackConsulting/BookOrderReceived] will be sent (the TARGET).

Creating Queues

A queue stores messages. You can query a queue with a SELECT statement or use the RECEIVE command to retrieve one or more messages from the queue.

Upon creation, a queue can be bound to a stored procedure which will handle messages when
they arrive (see the recipe, "Creating a Stored Procedure to Process Messages," found later in the chapter). Retrieval programs can also be external to SQL Server (such as .NET-based
programs)—however stored procedures provide an easy-to-implement solution.

To create a new queue, the CREATE QUEUE command is used. The syntax is as follows:

```
CREATE QUEUE [ database_name. [ schema_name ] .queue_name
[ WITH
  [ STATUS = { ON | OFF } [ , ] ]
  [ RETENTION = { ON | OFF } [ , ] ]
  [ ACTIVATION (
      [ STATUS = { ON|OFF } , ]
      PROCEDURE_NAME = [ database_name. [ schema_name ]➡
.stored_procedure_name,
      MAX_QUEUE_READERS = max_readers ,
      EXECUTE AS { SELF 'user_name' OWNER }    ) ]
  ]   [ ON { filegroup [ DEFAULT ] } ]
```

The arguments of this command are described in Table 20-3.

Table 20-3. *CREATE QUEUE Arguments*

Argument	Description
[database_name. [schema_name] .queue_name	The name of the new queue, which can be defined using the fully qualified database name, schema name, and queue name.
STATUS = { ON | OFF }	When STATUS is ON, the queue is available for use. When OFF, messages can't be added or removed from the queue.
RETENTION = { ON | OFF }	When RETENTION is ON, received or sent messages for the queue are kept until the conversation is done (allowing a prolonged view of in-progress messages in the conversation). When OFF (which is the default), messages are not retained after being either sent or received (and retrieved). Retained messages are available for reporting within the queue, but without risk of duplicate sending or receiving.
(ACTIVATION) STATUS = { ON|OFF }	When ON, the designated stored procedure will be activated to receive messages (up to the number designated in the max_readers argument). When OFF, the stored procedure isn't activated for the queue.
[database_name. [schema_name] .stored_procedure_name	The name of the stored procedure that will process messages for the queue. This can be fully qualified, using the database name, schema, and stored procedure name.
MAX_QUEUE_READERS = max_readers	Multiple instances of the queue reader stored procedure can be activated at the same time, from 0 to 32767 instances.
EXECUTE AS { SELF 'user_name' OWNER }	EXECUTE AS defines what database user account the stored procedure runs under. When SELF, it runs under the context of the current user. Otherwise a specific user name can be designated.
ON { filegroup [DEFAULT] }	Like a table, a queue can be placed on a specific filegroup. If not explicitly designated, the queue is placed on the DEFAULT filegroup.

Continuing with the online bookstore application example, a queue is created in the BookStore database to hold incoming messages from the BookDistribution database. It is created with a status of enabled:

```
Use BookStore
GO

CREATE QUEUE BookStoreQueue
WITH STATUS=ON
GO
```

The CREATE QUEUE command also has activation options which allow you to bind a program to it for automatically processing messages. This will be demonstrated later on in the chapter. But in the meantime, message exchanges from queues will be handled manually in this example.

Next, a new queue is added to the BookDistribution database for messages that will be received from the BookStore database:

```
USE BookDistribution
GO

CREATE QUEUE BookDistributionQueue
WITH STATUS=ON
GO
```

How It Works

In this example, a queue was created in both databases. The first queue created in BookStore was called BookStoreQueue:

```
CREATE QUEUE BookStoreQueue
```

The second line of code designated that the queue is created in an enabled state:

```
WITH STATUS=ON
```

The second queue was created in the BookDistribution database and used a different name, BookDistributionQueue. It too was created in an enabled state.

Creating Services

A service defines the endpoint, which is then used to bind a message queue to one or more contracts. Services make use of queues and contracts to define a task or set of tasks.

A service is both the initiator and the receiver of messages, enforcing the rules of the contract and routing the messages to the proper queue.

To create a new service, the CREATE SERVICE command is used. The abridged syntax is as follows:

```
CREATE SERVICE service_name
    [ AUTHORIZATION owner_name ]
    ON QUEUE [ schema_name. ]queue_name
    [ ( contract_name [ ,...n ] ) ]
```

The arguments of this command are described in Table 20-4.

Table 20-4. *CREATE SERVICE Arguments*

Argument	Description
service_name	The name of the new service.
owner_name	The owning database user or role of the service.
[schema_name.]queue_name	The name of the queue that receives messages.
contract_name [,...n]	The name of the contract(s) that can send messages to the new service. If none is designated, the new service can only initiate (and not receive) messages. If only an initiator, any contract can be used to send messages.

Continuing with the online bookstore example, a service is created in the BookStore database to bind the queue to a specific contract:

```
Use BookStore
GO

CREATE SERVICE [//SackConsulting/BookOrderService]
    ON QUEUE dbo.BookStoreQueue
    ([//SackConsulting/BookOrderContract])
GO
```

Now context is switched to the BookDistribution database and a service is created to bind the queue to the contract:

```
USE BookDistribution
GO

CREATE SERVICE [//SackConsulting/BookDistributionService]
    ON QUEUE dbo.BookDistributionQueue
    ([//SackConsulting/BookOrderContract])
GO
```

How It Works

In this recipe, I created a service in both the BookStore and BookDistribution databases. The CREATE SERVICE command was used to bind a specific queue to a contract.

The first argument used in CREATE SERVICE for the BookStore service was the service name:

```
CREATE SERVICE [//SackConsulting/BookOrderService]
```

The second line of code designated the queue for which the contract will be bound (will accept messages from):

```
ON QUEUE dbo.BookStoreQueue
```

The third argument was the name of the contract bound to the queue and exposed by the service:

```
([//SackConsulting/BookOrderContract])
```

In the BookDistribution database, a service was created with a different service name and queue name, but was bound to the same contract as the service in the BookStore database:

```
CREATE SERVICE [//SackConsulting/BookDistributionService]
    ON QUEUE dbo.BookDistributionQueue
    ([//SackConsulting/BookOrderContract])
GO
```

Now that the messages, queues, contracts, and services have been created, you are ready to start communication between the two databases using Service Broker commands.

Initiating a Dialog

A *dialog conversation* is the act of exchanging messages between services. A new conversation is created using the BEGIN DIALOG CONVERSATION. Each new conversation generates a unique conversation handle of the uniqueidentifier data type.

The syntax is as follows:

```
BEGIN DIALOG [ CONVERSATION ] @dialog_handle
   FROM SERVICE initiator_service_name
   TO SERVICE 'target_service_name'
       [ , { 'service_broker_guid' | 'CURRENT DATABASE' } ]
   [ ON CONTRACT contract_name ]
   [ WITH
   [ { RELATED_CONVERSATION = related_conversation_handle
     | RELATED_CONVERSATION_GROUP = related_conversation_group_id } ]
   [ [ , ] LIFETIME = dialog_lifetime ]
   [ [ , ] ENCRYPTION = { ON | OFF }  ] ]
```

The arguments of this command are described in Table 20-5.

Table 20-5. *BEGIN DIALOG Arguments*

Argument	Description
@dialog_handle	The uniqueidentifier data type local variable that is used to hold the new dialog handle.
initiator_service_name	The service that initiates the conversation.
'target_service_name'	The target service that the initiating service will exchange messages with.
'service_broker_guid' | 'CURRENT DATABASE'	The service_broker_guid as retrieved for the target service database from sys.databases. If CURRENT DATABASE is designated, the service_broker_guid is used from the current database.
contract_name	The name of the contract that the conversation is based on.
related_conversation_handle	The uniqueidentifier value of the existing conversation group that the dialog belongs to.
related_conversation_group_id	The uniqueidentifier value of the existing conversation group that the new dialog is added to.
dialog_lifetime	The number of seconds that the dialog is kept open.
ENCRYPTION = { ON | OFF }	When set to ON, encryption is used for messages sent outside of the initiator SQL Server instance.

The END CONVERSATION command finishes one side of the conversation. Messages can no longer be sent or received for the service that ends the conversation. Both services (initiator and target) must end the conversation in order for it to be completed.

The SEND command is used to send a message on a specific open conversation. In this command, the message type and message contents are also defined.

Continuing with the online bookstore example, and with the required objects established, you are now ready to initiate a dialog between the two Service Broker services.

On the BookStore database, the following commands are executed in a batch:

```
Use BookStore
GO

DECLARE @Conv_Handler uniqueidentifier
DECLARE @OrderMsg xml;

BEGIN DIALOG CONVERSATION @Conv_Handler
FROM SERVICE [//SackConsulting/BookOrderService]
TO SERVICE '//SackConsulting/BookDistributionService'
ON CONTRACT [//SackConsulting/BookOrderContract];

SET @OrderMsg =
'<order id="3439" customer="22" orderdate="7/15/2005">
<LineItem ItemNumber="1" ISBN="1-59059-592-0" Quantity="1" />
</order>';

SEND ON CONVERSATION @Conv_Handler
MESSAGE TYPE [//SackConsulting/SendBookOrder]
(@OrderMsg);
```

How It Works

In the previous batch of statements, two local variables were used to hold the dialog conversation handle and the order message XML document:

```
DECLARE @Conv_Handler uniqueidentifier
DECLARE @OrderMsg xml;
```

The BEGIN DIALOG CONVERSATION command was used to create a conversation between the two services, based on the established contract. The first argument passed was the @Conv_Handler local variable:

```
BEGIN DIALOG CONVERSATION @conv_handler
```

The initiator used to begin the dialog was designated in the second line and the target service in the third:

```
FROM SERVICE [//SackConsulting/BookOrderService]
TO SERVICE '//SackConsulting/BookDistributionService'
```

The contract name was then designated:

```
ON CONTRACT [//SackConsulting/BookOrderContract];
```

The @OrderMsg local variable was set to an XML document containing order and line item information:

```
SET @OrderMsg =
'<order id="3439" customer="22" orderdate="7/15/2005">
<LineItem ItemNumber="1" ISBN="1-59059-592-0" Quantity="1" />
</order>';
```

The SEND ON CONVERSATION command used the conversation handler local variable to send a message using the specified (and allowed) message type and the actual XML message content. The first argument in the command was the @Conv_Handler value populated from the BEGIN DIALOG CONVERSATION command:

```
SEND ON CONVERSATION @Conv_Handler
```

The second argument was the message type to be used, followed by the XML message in the local variable:

```
MESSAGE TYPE [//SackConsulting/SendBookOrder]
(@OrderMsg);
```

This message was then sent to the queue in the BookDistribution database.

Querying the Queue for Incoming Messages

Continuing with the online bookstore example, on the BookDistribution database, the queue is queried to view incoming messages using SELECT:

```
USE BookDistribution
GO

SELECT message_type_name, CAST(message_body as xml) message,
queuing_order, conversation_handle, conversation_group_id
FROM dbo.BookDistributionQueue
```

This returns the following result set:

message_type_name	message	queuing_order	conversation_handle	conversation_group_id
//SackConsulting/SendBookOrder	\<order id="3439" customer="22" orderdate="7/15/2005"\>\<LineItem ItemNumber="1" ISBN="1-59059-592-0" Quantity="1" /\>\</order\>	0	A34967B2-D62B-DA11-AB5D-000FB522BF5A	A24967B2-D62B-DA11-AB5D-000FB522BF5A

How It Works

In this recipe, I demonstrated that you can SELECT from a queue the same way you would from a table. The data returned showed the message type, message contents, queuing order, and the uniqueidentifier values that designate the conversation's handle and group.

Receiving and Responding to a Message

The RECEIVE statement is used to read rows (messages) from the queue. Unlike a SELECT statement, RECEIVE can be used to remove the rows that have been read. The results of the RECEIVE can be populated into regular tables or used in local variables to perform other actions or send other Service Broker messages.

If the message is an xml data type message, Transact-SQL XQuery methods can be used to query the message contents by acting on the data according to your application needs (for example, by extracting the Order ID or quantity of the product ordered).

Continuing with the online bookstore example in the BookDistribution database, a new table is created to hold information about received book orders:

```
USE BookDistribution
GO

CREATE TABLE dbo.BookOrderReceived
   (BookOrderReceivedID int IDENTITY (1,1) NOT NULL,
    conversation_handle uniqueidentifier NOT NULL,
    conversation_group_id uniqueidentifier NOT NULL,
    message_body xml NOT NULL)
GO
```

To process the received message in the BookDistribution database, the RECEIVE command is used. This batch of statements (which are executed together) performs several actions:

```
-- Declare the local variables needed to hold the incoming message data
DECLARE @Conv_Handler uniqueidentifier
DECLARE @Conv_Group uniqueidentifier
DECLARE @OrderMsg xml
DECLARE @TextResponseMsg varchar(8000)
DECLARE @ResponseMsg xml
DECLARE @OrderID int;

-- Take the message from the queue, retrieving its values into the local variables
RECEIVE TOP(1)   @OrderMsg = message_body,
         @Conv_Handler = conversation_handle,
         @Conv_Group = conversation_group_id
FROM dbo.BookDistributionQueue;
```

```
-- Insert the local variable values into the new table
INSERT dbo.BookOrderReceived
(conversation_handle, conversation_group_id, message_body)
VALUES
(@Conv_Handler,@Conv_Group, @OrderMsg  )

-- Use XQuery against the received message to extract
-- the order id, for use in the response message

SELECT @OrderID = @OrderMsg.value('(/order/@id)[1]', 'int' )

SELECT @TextResponseMsg =
    '<orderreceived id= "' +
    CAST(@OrderID as varchar(10)) +
    '"/>';

SELECT @ResponseMsg = CAST(@TextResponseMsg as xml);

-- Send the response message back to the initiator, using
-- the existing conversation handle
SEND ON CONVERSATION @Conv_Handler
MESSAGE TYPE [//SackConsulting/BookOrderReceived]
(@ResponseMsg );
```

How It Works

This recipe started off by creating a table to store the contents of the incoming Service Broker message. After that, six local variables were created to hold the incoming message data:

```
DECLARE @Conv_Handler uniqueidentifier
DECLARE @Conv_Group uniqueidentifier
DECLARE @OrderMsg xml
DECLARE @TextResponseMsg varchar(8000)
DECLARE @ResponseMsg xml
DECLARE @OrderID int;
```

The RECEIVE command was then used to return the message from the queue. The TOP clause in the first line designated the maximum number of messages to be returned, which in this case was 1:

```
RECEIVE TOP(1)
```

The next few lines populated the local variables with data from the message, similar to the way that you would perform a variable population using SELECT:

```
    @OrderMsg = message_body,
@Conv_Handler = conversation_handle,
   @Conv_Group = conversation_group_id
```

The last line of the RECEIVE command was the FROM clause referencing the queue where the message is found:

```
FROM dbo.BookDistributionQueue;
```

After that, an INSERT was performed, inserting a row containing values from the message body into a new table:

```
INSERT dbo.BookOrderReceived
(conversation_handle, conversation_group_id, message_body)
VALUES
(@Conv_Handler,@Conv_Group, @OrderMsg  )
```

An XQuery value method was used to retrieve the Order ID from the stored xml data type data:

```
SELECT @OrderID = @OrderMsg.value
('(/order/@id)[1]', 'int' )
```

The value taken from the XQuery was then used to populate a local variable, embedding the value in an <orderreceived> XML element:

```
SELECT @TextResponseMsg =
    '<orderreceived id= "' +
    CAST(@OrderID as varchar(10)) +
    '"/>';
```

This variable was then converted to an xml data type in preparation for sending a response to the BookStore database:

```
SELECT @ResponseMsg = CAST(@TextResponseMsg as xml);
```

Using the existing conversation uniqueidentifier handle in the first line, a message is sent using SEND ON CONVERSATION. The second line includes the message type to send, and the local variable in parenthesis the actual payload of the message:

```
SEND ON CONVERSATION @Conv_Handler
MESSAGE TYPE [//SackConsulting/BookOrderReceived]
(@ResponseMsg );
```

Ending a Conversation

A conversation involves both the sending and receiving of messages. This communication can continue for however many iterations are required by your application. Once a side is finished (initiator or target), you can notify the other side that you are done with the conversation by using the END CONVERSATION command.

In the previous recipe, an order confirmation was sent to BookStore based on an order message BookStore had sent. Continuing with the online bookstore example, a new table is created to store order confirmation information from the target service:

```
USE BookStore
GO

-- Create an order confirmation table
CREATE TABLE dbo.BookOrderConfirmation
    (BookOrderConfirmationID int IDENTITY (1,1) NOT NULL,
     conversation_handle uniqueidentifier NOT NULL,
     DateReceived datetime NOT NULL DEFAULT GETDATE(),
     message_body xml NOT NULL)
```

In the BookStore database, RECEIVE TOP is used to receive the response message and store it in the new table. Since the conversation for this particular BookOrder is complete once a response is received (when a dialog conversation should end depends on your own real-world task requirements), the END CONVERSATION command is used to notify the target database that it is done with its side of the conversation:

```
DECLARE @Conv_Handler uniqueidentifier
DECLARE @Conv_Group uniqueidentifier
DECLARE @OrderMsg xml
DECLARE @TextResponseMsg varchar(8000);

RECEIVE TOP(1)    @Conv_Handler = conversation_handle,
          @OrderMsg = message_body
FROM dbo.BookStoreQueue
```

```
INSERT dbo.BookOrderConfirmation
(conversation_handle, message_body)
VALUES (@Conv_Handler,@OrderMsg );

END CONVERSATION @Conv_Handler;
GO
```

On the BookDistribution database, the queue is checked again for new messages. When a conversation dialog is ended, an empty message with a message type name of http://schemas.microsoft.com/SQL/ServiceBroker/EndDialog is sent. This next batch of statements receives this message, and ends the conversation on its side if the message type is a dialog-ending message type:

```
USE BookDistribution
GO

DECLARE @Conv_Handler uniqueidentifier
DECLARE @Conv_Group uniqueidentifier
DECLARE @OrderMsg xml
DECLARE @message_type_name nvarchar(256);

RECEIVE TOP(1)    @Conv_Handler = conversation_handle,
            @OrderMsg = message_body,
            @message_type_name = message_type_name
FROM dbo.BookDistributionQueue

-- Both sides (initiator and target) must end the conversation

IF
@message_type_name = 'http://schemas.microsoft.com/SQL/ServiceBroker/EndDialog'
BEGIN
    END CONVERSATION @Conv_Handler;
END
```

The status of conversations is checked by querying the sys.conversation_endpoints view:

```
SELECT state_desc, conversation_handle
FROM sys.conversation_endpoints
```

This returns:

state_desc	conversation_handle
CLOSED	237A7DD6-86FB-D911-AAF4-000FB522BF5A

How It Works

In this recipe, I demonstrated how to end an open conversation dialog. I began by creating a table to hold order confirmations in the BookStore database received by the BookDistribution database. After that, RECEIVE TOP(1) was used to grab the latest message from BookDistribution from the BookStoreQueue. The contents of the message were then inserted into the BookOrderConfirmation table. The conversation was then ended using END CONVERSATION and the uniqueidentifier value for the specific conversation:

```
END CONVERSATION @Conv_Handler;
```

Ending a conversation automatically sends a message type of http://schemas.microsoft.com/SQL/ServiceBroker/EndDialog to the target database. Back on the BookDistribution database, the queue was checked again for new messages. RECEIVE TOP(1) was used to retrieve the latest response from the BookStore database. An IF statement was used to verify if the message received was an END DIALOG request:

```
IF
@message_type_name =
'http://schemas.microsoft.com/SQL/ServiceBroker/EndDialog'
```

If it was, the conversation was also ended on the target database (BookDistribution):

```
BEGIN
    END CONVERSATION @Conv_Handler;
END
```

The status of conversations was then checked by querying the sys.conversation_endpoints view, which confirmed that the conversation was indeed CLOSED.

This entire section of recipes demonstrated a simple message exchange application used to send a book order message to a book distribution handling database. A book order was sent from the initiator, a response was sent back, and the conversation was ended using END CONVERSATION on both databases. Of course, a real world scenario will involve more tasks, which may in turn translate to additional message types, contracts, services, and queues. Ideal tasks for Service Broker are those that can benefit from the asynchronous capabilities that prevent application hold-ups and bottlenecks.

Creating a Stored Procedure to Process Messages

In the previous block of recipes, ad hoc Transact-SQL batches were used to process incoming messages from the queue. You can, however, create service programs using stored procedures or external applications to *automatically* activate and process messages in the queue. Using the CREATE QUEUE and ALTER QUEUE options, you can also designate the number of simultaneous and identical service programs which can be activated to process incoming messages on the same queue.

Creating the Bookstore Stored Procedure

Using the previous recipe's existing objects for setting up the stored procedure application, this example creates a stored procedure used to process incoming messages on the dbo.BookDistributionQueue. This procedure uses several of the RECEIVE and SEND commands used in the previous recipe, only tailored to a stored procedure implementation:

```
USE BookDistribution
GO

CREATE PROCEDURE dbo.usp_SB_ReceiveOrders
AS

DECLARE @Conv_Handler uniqueidentifier
DECLARE @Conv_Group uniqueidentifier
DECLARE @OrderMsg xml
DECLARE @TextResponseMsg varchar(8000)
DECLARE @ResponseMsg xml
DECLARE @Message_Type_Name nvarchar(256);
DECLARE @OrderID int;

-- XACT_ABORT automatically rolls back the transaction when a run-time error occurs
SET XACT_ABORT ON

BEGIN TRAN;
```

```
    RECEIVE TOP(1)   @OrderMsg = message_body,
              @Conv_Handler = conversation_handle,
              @Conv_Group = conversation_group_id,
              @Message_Type_Name = message_type_name
    FROM dbo.BookDistributionQueue;

IF @Message_Type_Name = '//SackConsulting/SendBookOrder'
BEGIN
    INSERT dbo.BookOrderReceived
    (conversation_handle, conversation_group_id, message_body)
    VALUES
    (@Conv_Handler,@Conv_Group, @OrderMsg  )

    SELECT @OrderID = @OrderMsg.value('(/order/@id)[1]', 'int' )

    SELECT @TextResponseMsg =
        '<orderreceived id= "' +
        CAST(@OrderID as varchar(10)) +
        '"/>';

    SELECT @ResponseMsg = CAST(@TextResponseMsg as xml);

    SEND ON CONVERSATION @Conv_Handler
    MESSAGE TYPE [//SackConsulting/BookOrderReceived]
    (@ResponseMsg );
END

IF @Message_Type_Name = 'http://schemas.microsoft.com/SQL/ServiceBroker/EndDialog'
BEGIN
    END CONVERSATION @Conv_Handler;
END

COMMIT TRAN

GO
```

The procedure contains logic for processing the //SackConsulting/SendBookOrder and http://
schemas.microsoft.com/SQL/ServiceBroker/EndDialog message types. If the latter is sent, the specific
conversation for the specific conversation handle is ended. If a book order message type is received,
its information is inserted into a table, and an order confirmation is returned.

You can modify an existing queue by using the ALTER QUEUE command. This command uses the
same options as CREATE QUEUE, which allows you to change the status and retention of the queue,
the stored procedure to be activated, the maximum number of queue reader stored procedure instances,
and the security contact of the procedure. The syntax is as follows:

```
ALTER QUEUE [ database_name. [ schema_name ] .queue_name
WITH
    [ STATUS = { ON | OFF } [ , ] ]
    [ RETENTION = { ON | OFF } [ , ] ]
    [ ACTIVATION (
        { [ STATUS = { ON | OFF } [ , ] ]
        [ PROCEDURE_NAME =
[ database_name. [ schema_name ] .stored_procedure_name,[ , ] ]
        [ MAX_QUEUE_READERS = max_readers [ , ] ]
        [ EXECUTE AS { SELF | 'user_name'  | OWNER } ]
      | DROP }
        ) ]
```

ALTER QUEUE includes one additional parameter, DROP, which is used to drop all stored procedure activation settings for the queue.

To bind our stored procedure to an existing queue, the ALTER QUEUE command is used:

```
ALTER QUEUE dbo.BookDistributionQueue
WITH ACTIVATION (STATUS = ON,
                PROCEDURE_NAME = dbo.usp_SB_ReceiveOrders,
                MAX_QUEUE_READERS = 2,
                EXECUTE AS SELF)
```

The procedure name was designated, followed by the maximum number of simultaneous implementations of the same stored procedure that can independently process distinct messages from the queue.

To test the new service program on the BookStore database, a new conversation is started and a new order placed:

```
Use BookStore
GO

DECLARE @Conv_Handler uniqueidentifier
DECLARE @OrderMsg xml;

BEGIN DIALOG CONVERSATION @conv_handler
FROM SERVICE [//SackConsulting/BookOrderService]
TO SERVICE '//SackConsulting/BookDistributionService'
ON CONTRACT [//SackConsulting/BookOrderContract];

SET @OrderMsg =
'<order id="3490" customer="29" orderdate="7/22/2005">
<LineItem ItemNumber="1" ISBN="1-59059-592-0" Quantity="2" />
</order>';

SEND ON CONVERSATION @Conv_Handler
MESSAGE TYPE [//SackConsulting/SendBookOrder]
(@OrderMsg);
```

If the stored procedure on the target queue did its job and activated upon receipt of the new message, there should already be an order confirmation returned back into the dbo.BookStoreQueue:

```
SELECT conversation_handle, CAST(message_body as xml) message
FROM dbo.BookStoreQueue
```

This returns the following results:

conversation_handle	message
20E768EB-8EFB-D911-AAF4-000FB522BF5A	<orderreceived id="3490" />

How It Works

In this recipe, a stored procedure was created to handle messages in the queue. That stored procedure was bound to the queue using ALTER QUEUE. The first argument of this command was the name of the queue to be modified:

```
ALTER QUEUE dbo.BookDistributionQueue
```

The WITH ACTIVATION clause first designated that the status of the new application (the stored procedure) program is available to receive new messages:

```
WITH ACTIVATION (STATUS = ON,
```

Next, the name of the stored procedure bound to the queue is designated:

```
PROCEDURE_NAME = dbo.usp_SB_ReceiveOrders,
```

The MAX QUEUE READERS option is used to designate a maximum of two stored procedure applications executing simultaneously:

```
MAX_QUEUE_READERS = 2,
```

The EXECUTE AS argument was designated as SELF, meaning that the stored procedure will execute with the same permissions as the principal who executed the ALTER QUEUE command:

```
EXECUTE AS SELF)
```

When the queue STATUS = ON and a new message arrives in the queue, the stored procedure is executed to handle the incoming message(s). You can use internal stored procedures or external applications to handle incoming messages to a queue. The benefit of using stored procedures, however, is that they provide an out-of-the-box solution for handling messages and automatically performing any required responses and associated business tasks.

Remote-Server Service Broker Implementations

To demonstrate the basics of setting up a Service Broker program, the examples in this chapter have involved two databases on the same SQL Server instance. In most cases, however, you'll be setting up Service Broker to work with databases that exist on two or more SQL Server instances. The core components from this chapter remain the same, but to achieve cross-server communication, a few extra steps are required. Cross-server communication can be achieved either through using Windows authentication, or certificate-based authentication (which is what you'll see demonstrated here in this chapter). These steps will be demonstrated in this next batch of recipes.

The following is a general list of tasks that I'll go through in this section to enable Service Broker communication across SQL Server instances:

1. *Enable transport security.* Transport security in Service Broker refers to the network connections between two SQL Server instances, enabling or restricting encrypted communication between them. This is set up in the master system databases of both SQL Server instances, and as you'll see, involves creating endpoints, certificates, logins, and users.

2. *Enable dialog security.* Dialog security for Service Broker provides authentication, authorization, and encryption for dialog conversations. On the actual databases used for the Service Broker implementation, certificates are created and their public keys exchanged between SQL Server instances. Users are created that are not associated to a login, but are instead given authorization to the certificate created from the public key of the other SQL Server instance.

3. *Create routes.* A route is used by Service Broker to determine where a service is located, be it local or remote.

4. *Create remote service bindings.* A remote service binding is used to map the security credentials used to open a conversation with a remote Service Broker service.

In this cross-server scenario, the online bookstore Service Broker program will use the BookStore database on the JOEPROD SQL Server instance, and the BookDistribution database on the JOEPROD\ NODE2 SQL Server instance. Objects from the previous set of recipes will be used to demonstrate this functionality. Starting from scratch (if you happen to be following along), the example database is dropped and recreated with the BookStore database on JOEPROD and BookDistribution on JOEPROD\ NODE2. The following objects and settings are then created and configured on the BookStore database of the JOEPROD instance:

```
USE master
GO

-- Enable Service Broker for the database

ALTER DATABASE BookStore SET ENABLE_BROKER
GO

ALTER DATABASE BookStore SET TRUSTWORTHY ON
GO

USE BookStore
GO

-- Create the messages

CREATE MESSAGE TYPE [//SackConsulting/SendBookOrder]
VALIDATION = WELL_FORMED_XML
GO

CREATE MESSAGE TYPE [//SackConsulting/BookOrderReceived]
VALIDATION = WELL_FORMED_XML
GO

-- Create the contract

CREATE CONTRACT
    [//SackConsulting/BookOrderContract]
    ( [//SackConsulting/SendBookOrder]
        SENT BY INITIATOR,
      [//SackConsulting/BookOrderReceived]
        SENT BY TARGET
    )
GO

-- Create the queue

CREATE QUEUE BookStoreQueue
WITH STATUS=ON
GO

-- Create the service

CREATE SERVICE [//SackConsulting/BookOrderService]
    ON QUEUE dbo.BookStoreQueue
    ([//SackConsulting/BookOrderContract])
GO
```

On the BookDistribution database of the JOEPROD\NODE2 instance, the following objects are set up:

```
USE master
GO

-- Enable Service Broker for the database

ALTER DATABASE BookDistribution SET ENABLE_BROKER
GO
```

```
ALTER DATABASE BookDistribution SET TRUSTWORTHY ON
GO

USE BookDistribution
GO

-- Create the messages

CREATE MESSAGE TYPE [//SackConsulting/SendBookOrder]
VALIDATION = WELL_FORMED_XML
GO

CREATE MESSAGE TYPE [//SackConsulting/BookOrderReceived]
VALIDATION = WELL_FORMED_XML
GO

-- Create the contract

CREATE CONTRACT
    [//SackConsulting/BookOrderContract]
    ( [//SackConsulting/SendBookOrder]
         SENT BY INITIATOR,
     [//SackConsulting/BookOrderReceived]
         SENT BY TARGET
    )
GO

-- Create the queue

CREATE QUEUE BookDistributionQueue
WITH STATUS=ON
GO

-- Create the service

CREATE SERVICE [//SackConsulting/BookDistributionService]
    ON QUEUE dbo.BookDistributionQueue
    ([//SackConsulting/BookOrderContract])
GO
```

Enabling Transport Security

Transport security in Service Broker refers to the network connections between two SQL Server instances, and the enabling or restricting of encrypted communication between them. Transport security is at the SQL Server instance level, and therefore this recipe demonstrates creating objects in the master database of both SQL Server instances. You can choose from two forms of transport security: Windows authentication or certificate-based security.

This recipe includes several steps that involve working with objects that should be familiar to you from the previous chapters. Each of these steps requires activities on both SQL Server instances (this example includes JOEPROD and JOEPROD\NODE2). For this recipe, you'll only use the master system database, not the actual user databases for this recipe, because transport security applies to the SQL Server instance itself.

I begin this recipe by creating a Database Master Key in the master system database of each of the SQL Server instances. This is created in order to encrypt the certificate used for certificate-based transport security:

```
-- Executed on JOEPROD
USE master
GO

CREATE MASTER KEY ENCRYPTION BY PASSWORD = '1294934A!'

-- Executed on JOEPROD\NODE2
USE master
GO

CREATE MASTER KEY ENCRYPTION BY PASSWORD = '1294934B!'
```

Next, a new certificate is created in the master system database of each of the SQL Server instances:

```
-- Executed on JOEPROD
CREATE CERTIFICATE JOEPRODMasterCert
   WITH SUBJECT = 'JOEPROD Transport Security SB',
   EXPIRY_DATE = '10/1/2010'
GO

-- Executed on JOEPROD\NODE2
CREATE CERTIFICATE Node2MasterCert
   WITH SUBJECT = 'Node 2 Transport Security SB',
   EXPIRY_DATE = '10/1/2010'
GO
```

Next, each of these certificates is backed up to a file. The public key backup files will then be copied over for use in creating a certificate in the master database of the other SQL Server instance (this happens later in the recipe):

```
-- Executed on JOEPROD
BACKUP CERTIFICATE JOEPRODMasterCert
TO FILE = 'C:\Temp\JOEPRODMasterCert.cer'
GO

-- Executed on JOEPROD\NODE2
BACKUP CERTIFICATE Node2MasterCert
TO FILE = 'C:\Temp\Node2MasterCert.cer'
GO
```

On each SQL Server instance, a Service Broker endpoint is created, which both uses certificate based authentication and requires encrypted communication.

```
-- Executed on JOEPROD

CREATE ENDPOINT SB_JOEPROD_Endpoint
STATE = STARTED
AS TCP
(LISTENER_PORT = 4020)
FOR SERVICE_BROKER
(AUTHENTICATION = CERTIFICATE JOEPRODMasterCert,
  ENCRYPTION = REQUIRED)
GO
```

```
-- Executed on JOEPROD\NODE2

CREATE ENDPOINT SB_NODE2_Endpoint
STATE = STARTED
AS TCP
(LISTENER_PORT = 4021)
FOR SERVICE_BROKER
(AUTHENTICATION = CERTIFICATE Node2MasterCert,
  ENCRYPTION = REQUIRED)
GO
```

On each SQL Server instance, a new login and user are created in the master system database that will be used for remote connections from the other SQL Server instance:

```
-- Executed on JOEPROD
CREATE LOGIN SBLogin
    WITH PASSWORD = 'Used4TransSec'
GO

CREATE USER SBUser
    FOR LOGIN SBLogin
GO

-- Executed on JOEPROD\NODE2

CREATE LOGIN SBLogin
    WITH PASSWORD = 'Used4TransSec'
GO

CREATE USER SBUser
    FOR LOGIN SBLogin
GO
```

Next, each SQL Server instance's login is granted CONNECT permissions to the associated endpoint:

```
-- Executed on JOEPROD

GRANT CONNECT ON Endpoint::SB_JOEPROD_Endpoint TO SBLogin
GO

-- Executed on JOEPROD\NODE2

GRANT CONNECT ON Endpoint::SB_NODE2_Endpoint TO SBLogin
GO
```

On each SQL Server instance, a new certificate is created based on the certificate backup created in the other SQL Server instance. The newly created login and user created in the previous step is given authorization permissions over this certificate:

```
-- Executed on JOEPROD

CREATE CERTIFICATE Node2MasterCert
AUTHORIZATION SBUser
FROM FILE = 'C:\Temp\Node2MasterCert.cer'
GO

-- Executed on JOEPROD\NODE2
```

```
CREATE CERTIFICATE JOEPRODMasterCert
AUTHORIZATION SBUser
FROM FILE = 'C:\Temp\JOEPRODMasterCert.cer'
GO
```

How It Works

In this recipe, I walked through the various steps required to establish transport security through certificates. The recipe started off by creating a Database Master Key which would be used to encrypt the certificates (as a requirement for Service Broker endpoints—if using certificate-based security, the certificate can't be password encrypted).

A certificate was created on each SQL Server instance and was then backed up and copied to the other SQL Server instance. This exchange of public keys will be used later on in this section. In the meantime, Service Broker endpoints were created on each SQL Server instance, and were configured to allow access from other servers based on certificate security.

After that, a login and user were created on both SQL Server instances. The login was granted CONNECT permissions to the endpoint. This is not enough to enable connectivity though, because that user must also have access to the public key of the certificate used on the other SQL Server instance. This permission was granted in order to exchange the keys with the other server. The new certificates were then bound to the newly created user on each instance. Because the user has permissions to the certificate of the other SQL Server instance, and because the endpoint is based on that certificate, the SQL Server instances will have encrypted transport security access to one another.

This is only half the requirement for allowing cross-server communication with Service Broker. The next step is dialog security at the user database level, which I demonstrate in the next recipe.

Enabling Dialog Security

Whereas transport security handles communication at the SQL Server instance level, dialog security for Service Broker provides authentication, authorization, and encryption for dialog conversations. Like the previous recipe, setting up dialog security involves several small steps, many of which involve commands which have been covered in previous chapters of this book.

These recipes will take place in the BookStore database on the JOEPROD SQL Server instance and in the BookDistribution database on the NODE2 SQL Server instance. A certificate is created on each SQL Server instance (which requires a Database Master Key in each database, which you created at the beginning of this section). Later on, the certificates will be exchanged across SQL Server instances similarly to the previous transport security recipe:

```
-- Executed on JOEPROD
CREATE CERTIFICATE BookStoreCert
    WITH SUBJECT = 'BookStore SB cert',
    EXPIRY_DATE = '10/1/2010'
GO

-- Executed on NODE2
CREATE CERTIFICATE BookDistributionCert
    WITH SUBJECT = 'BookDistributionCert SB cert',
    EXPIRY_DATE = '10/1/2010'
GO
```

Next, the certificates from each of the databases are backed up to file:

```
-- Executed on JOEPROD
BACKUP CERTIFICATE BookStoreCert
TO FILE = 'C:\Temp\BookStoreCert.cer'
GO
```

```
-- Executed on NODE2
BACKUP CERTIFICATE BookDistributionCert
TO FILE = 'C:\Temp\BookDistributionCert.cer'
GO
```

After that, a user will be created in each database. Neither user will be associated to a login. Instead, later on, that user will be mapped to the public certificate of the other SQL Server instance:

```
-- Executed on JOEPROD
CREATE USER BookDistributionUser
WITHOUT LOGIN
GO
```

```
-- Executed on NODE2
CREATE USER BookStoreUser
WITHOUT LOGIN
GO
```

Next, a new certificate is created in each database based on the other database's certificate public key. The newly created user in each database is given authorization to this certificate:

```
-- Executed on JOEPROD
CREATE CERTIFICATE BookDistributionCert
AUTHORIZATION BookDistributionUser
FROM FILE = 'C:\Temp\BookDistributionCert.cer'
GO
```

```
-- Executed on NODE2
CREATE CERTIFICATE BookStoreCert
AUTHORIZATION BookStoreUser
FROM FILE = 'C:\Temp\BookStoreCert.cer'
GO
```

Lastly, the users for both databases need permissions to SEND rights on the associated Service Broker services and RECEIVE rights on the associated queues:

```
-- Executed on JOEPROD
GRANT SEND ON
SERVICE::[//SackConsulting/BookOrderService] TO BookDistributionUser
GO
```

```
-- Executed on NODE2
GRANT SEND ON
SERVICE::[//SackConsulting/BookDistributionService]
TO BookStoreUser
```

How It Works

In this recipe, I demonstrated setting up dialog security, which handles authentication, authorization, and encryption between the two user-defined databases in a Service Broker application.

The first step included creating a Database Master Key in each database which was then used to implicitly encrypt the certificates created in the BookStore and BookDistribution databases. After creating the certificates, a backup was made of each one, and the associated file was then copied to the other server.

After that, a new user was created in each database without an associated login. A new certificate was then created in each database based on the other database's certificate. The certificate creation included an AUTHORIZATION clause which designated the new user in each database.

Lastly, the two users were each granted permissions to SEND messages to their associated Service Broker services.

This leaves us with only a couple more steps before the Service Broker application can begin communicating across SQL Server instances.

Creating Routes and Remote Service Bindings

Once the transport and dialog security objects are taken care of, the next step in this distributed online bookstore example is to set up routes and remote service bindings.

A route is used by Service Broker to determine where a service is located, be it local or remote. A route is created using the CREATE ROUTE command. The syntax is as follows:

```
CREATE ROUTE route_name
[ AUTHORIZATION owner_name ]
WITH
    [ SERVICE_NAME = 'service_name', ]
    [ BROKER_INSTANCE = 'broker_instance_identifier' , ]
    [ LIFETIME = route_lifetime , ]
    ADDRESS =  'next_hop_address'
    [ , MIRROR_ADDRESS = 'next_hop_mirror_address' ]
```

The arguments for this command are described in Table 20-6.

Table 20-6. *CREATE ROUTE Arguments*

Argument	Description
route_name	The new route name.
AUTHORIZATION owner_name	The database principal owner of the route.
SERVICE_NAME = 'service_name'	The name of the remote service to be routed to.
BROKER_INSTANCE = 'broker_instance_identifier'	The service_broker_guid (from sys.databases) of the database hosting the target service.
LIFETIME = route_lifetime	This option allows you to designates for how many seconds a route is considered by SQL Server before it expires.
ADDRESS = 'next_hop_address'	The DNS, NetBios, or TCP/IP address of SQL Server instance housing the service. Also includes the port number of the Service Broker endpoint using a syntax of TCP://{ dns_name | netbios_name | ip_address } : port_number.
MIRROR_ADDRESS = 'next_hop_mirror_address'	If using database mirroring, this option allows you to specify the address for the mirrored database using the syntax of TCP:// { dns_name | netbios_name | ip_address } : port_number.

In this recipe's example, a route is created on JOEPROD that points to the NODE2 Service Broker endpoint (listening on port 4021), and referencing the BookDistribution database's //SackConsulting/BookDistributionService service:

```
-- Executed on JOEPROD
USE BookStore
GO

CREATE ROUTE Route_BookDistribution
WITH SERVICE_NAME = '//SackConsulting/BookDistributionService',
ADDRESS = 'TCP://192.168.0.101:4021'
GO
```

On NODE2, a route is created that points to the JOEPROD Service Broker endpoint (listening on port 4020), and referencing the BookStore database's //SackConsulting/BookStoreService service:

```
-- Executed on NODE2
USE BookDistribution
GO

CREATE ROUTE Route_BookStore
WITH SERVICE_NAME = '//SackConsulting/BookOrderService',
ADDRESS = 'TCP://192.168.0.101:4020'
GO
```

A remote service binding is used to map the security credentials used to open a conversation with a remote Service Broker service. Specifically, you use a remote service binding with the user that you created in the previous recipe (the one mapped to a certificate). A remote service binding is created using the CREATE REMOTE SERVICE BINDING command. The syntax is as follows:

```
CREATE REMOTE SERVICE BINDING binding_name
    [ AUTHORIZATION owner_name ]
    TO SERVICE 'service_name'
    WITH  USER = user_name [ , ANONYMOUS = { ON | OFF } ]
```

The arguments for this command are described in Table 20-7.

Table 20-7. *CREATE REMOTE SERVICE BINDING Arguments*

Argument	Description
binding_name	The name of the new remote service binding.
AUTHORIZATION owner_name	The database principal owner of the binding.
service_name	The name of the remote service to bind to.
USER = user_name	Designates the database user that is mapped to the remote service's certificate.
ANONYMOUS = { ON	OFF }	When this option is ON, anonymous authentication under the context of the public fixed database role is used to connect to the remote database.

In this example on JOEPROD, a binding is made on BookStore to the //SackConsulting/BookDistributionService service, using the BookStore user that was mapped to the BookDistribution database's public certificate:

```
USE BookStore
GO

CREATE REMOTE SERVICE BINDING BookDistributionBinding
    TO SERVICE '//SackConsulting/BookDistributionService'
    WITH USER =  BookDistributionUser
GO
```

On NODE2, a similar binding is made in the BookDistribution database, only this time pointing to the //SackConsulting/BookOrderService service:

```
USE BookDistribution
GO

CREATE REMOTE SERVICE BINDING BookStoreBinding
    TO SERVICE '//SackConsulting/BookOrderService'
```

```
       WITH USER =  BookStoreUser
GO
```

With the routes and bindings set up, you are now ready to test sending a remote message from the JOEPROD server's BookStore database to the NODE2 server's BookDistribution database:

```
Use BookStore
GO

DECLARE @Conv_Handler uniqueidentifier
DECLARE @OrderMsg xml;

BEGIN DIALOG CONVERSATION @Conv_Handler
FROM SERVICE [//SackConsulting/BookOrderService]
TO SERVICE '//SackConsulting/BookDistributionService'
ON CONTRACT [//SackConsulting/BookOrderContract];

SET @OrderMsg =
'<order id="3439" customer="22" orderdate="9/25/2005">
<LineItem ItemNumber="22" ISBN="1-59059-592-0" Quantity="10" />
</order>';

SEND ON CONVERSATION @Conv_Handler
MESSAGE TYPE [//SackConsulting/SendBookOrder]
(@OrderMsg);
```

Moving over to the NODE2 server and the BookDistribution database, the queue is checked for the incoming message:

```
USE BookDistribution
GO

SELECT message_type_name, CAST(message_body as xml) message,
queuing_order, conversation_handle, conversation_group_id
FROM dbo.BookDistributionQueue
```

This returns the following result set:

message_type_name	message	queuing_order	conversation_handle	conversation_group_id
//SackConsulting/SendBookOrder	<order id="3439" customer="22" orderdate="9/25/2005"><LineItem ItemNumber="22" ISBN="1-59059-592-0" Quantity="10" /></order>	0	01D3472E-E02D-DA11-AB61-000FB522BF5A	00D3472E-E02D-DA11-AB61-000FB522BF5A

How It Works

This recipe started off by creating routes on both SQL Server instances. Each route included the service name of the other SQL Server instance, the address for which to connect to it, and the port number of the Service Broker endpoint.

After that, a remote service binding was created on both SQL Server instances that was used to map the local database user (the one associated to the public key certificate of the other SQL Server instance) to the remote service.

Once this was completed, a message was sent from the BookStore database which then arrived at the remote NODE2 server's BookDistribution database.

Event Notifications

Event notification is a tie-in to the new SQL Server 2005 Service Broker functionality, allowing you to asynchronously capture SQL events on a SQL Server instance, routing the event information into a specified queue. With a minimal of system overhead, you can track events that occur on the SQL Server instance such as user logins, stored procedure recompiles, permission changes, object manipulation (for example CREATE/ALTER/DROP events on databases, assemblies, roles, or tables).

Unlike creating your own Service Broker applications, with event notification you need only create the queue and Service Broker components, because the initiator components are handled for you. The initiator components (message type and contract) that are used to capture and send the event notifications are already built in to SQL Server.

The next recipe will demonstrate this functionality in action.

Capturing Login Commands

In this recipe, I demonstrate how to capture any CREATE LOGIN, ALTER LOGIN, or DROP LOGIN commands that are executed on the SQL Server instance using event notifications. The command for creating an event notification is as follows:

```
CREATE EVENT NOTIFICATION event_notification_name
ON { SERVER | DATABASE | QUEUE queue_name }
[ WITH FAN_IN ]
FOR { event_type | event_group } [ ,...n ]
TO SERVICE 'broker_service' , { 'broker_instance_specifier' | 'current database' }
```

The arguments of this command are described in Table 20-8.

Table 20-8. *CREATE EVENT NOTIFICATION Arguments*

Argument	Description
event_notification_name	The name of the new event notification.
SERVER | DATABASE | QUEUE queue_name	These three arguments define the event notification scope, causing notifications to fire when an event occurs for the specific SQL Server instance (SERVER), current database (DATABASE), or specific queue (QUEUE queue_name).
WITH FAN_IN	Configures SQL Server to only send one message per event for event notifications that are created on the same event with the same principal and the same service and broker_instance_specifier.
{ event_type | event_group } [,...n]	The event_type is a Transact-SQL DDL, Service Broker, or SQL Trace event type to be monitored. The event_group is a predefined group of event types—and when designated, any member of the group will cause an event notification to be fired. An example of an event group is DDL_LOGIN_EVENTS, which contains the CREATE LOGIN, ALTER LOGIN, and DROP LOGIN events.
'broker_service' , { 'broker_instance_specifier' | 'current database' }	The broker_service argument is the name of the broker service receiving event notification data. The broker_instance_specifier is the service_broker_guid (from sys.databases) of the destination database, with 'current database' used to specify the current database guid.

The example starts off in a database called EventTracking, where a new queue is created to hold the event information:

```
USE EventTracking
GO

CREATE QUEUE SQLEventQueue
WITH STATUS=ON;
GO
```

Next, a new service is created on the queue, associated to the built-in event notification contract:

```
CREATE SERVICE [//JOEPROD/TrackLoginModificationService]
ON QUEUE SQLEventQueue
([http://schemas.microsoft.com/SQL/Notifications/PostEventNotification]);
GO
```

Next, a query is executed against the sys.databases system catalog view in order to retrieve the EventTracking database service_broker_guid (which will be used in the CREATE EVENT NOTIFICATION command):

```
select service_broker_guid
from sys.databases
WHERE name = 'EventTracking'
```

This returns:

```
service_broker_guid
-------------------------------------
C72069CD-ACBA-4EA8-80BB-5CC6FF3A40AA
```

Next, an event notification is created using the SERVER scope to track any login creation, modification, or drop from the SQL Server instance:

```
CREATE EVENT NOTIFICATION EN_LoginEvents
ON SERVER
FOR CREATE_LOGIN, ALTER_LOGIN, DROP_LOGIN
TO SERVICE '//JOEPROD/TrackLoginModificationService',
'C72069CD-ACBA-4EA8-80BB-5CC6FF3A40AA';
```

Testing the new event notification, a new login is created:

```
CREATE LOGIN Trishelle WITH PASSWORD = 'AR!3i2ou4'
GO
```

Next, you can query the queue using SELECT or RECEIVE (RECEIVE, unlike SELECT will also remove the event message from the queue):

```
SELECT CAST(message_body as xml) EventInfo
FROM dbo.SQLEventQueue
```

This returns XML-based information about the login event, including the added login name and the login that added it:

```
<EVENT_INSTANCE>
  <EventType>CREATE_LOGIN</EventType>
  <PostTime>2005-07-23T15:11:14.703</PostTime>
  <SPID>53</SPID>
  <ServerName>JOEPROD</ServerName>
  <LoginName>JOEPROD\Owner</LoginName>
  <ObjectName>Trishelle</ObjectName>
  <ObjectType>LOGIN</ObjectType>
  <DefaultLanguage>us_english</DefaultLanguage>
  <DefaultDatabase>master</DefaultDatabase>
  <LoginType>SQL Login</LoginType>
  <SID>5HDVhho4xkmFGVKTCcb3Bw==</SID>
</EVENT_INSTANCE>
```

How It Works

In this recipe, event notification was set up by performing the following steps:

1. Creating a new queue in an existing database.

2. Creating a new service that is bound to the new queue and the built-in event notification contract.

3. Using CREATE EVENT NOTIFICATION to track one or more events or event groups.

Event notification functionality provides a low-overhead method of tracking activities at the SQL Server instance, database, or Service Broker application level. As you saw in the example, very little coding was necessary in order to begin tracking events. This new functionality will be particularly useful for IT security or business-level auditing requirements. For example, when capturing the login creation event, the user that created it was also captured, along with the type of login (SQL login), default database, language, and security identifier of the new login.

CHAPTER 21

■ ■ ■

Configuring and Viewing SQL Server Options

Although SQL Server 2005 automatically maintains and adjusts many settings and configurations behind-the-scenes, there are still several options that the database administrator can configure. In SQL Server 2005, Microsoft added several new configurable options, and removed some of the older options. In an effort to improve total SQL Server instance availability, many options that once wouldn't have taken effect without requiring the database administrator to restart the SQL Server service, now take effect immediately (although there are still some options that require a service restart).

In this brief chapter, I'll show you recipes for viewing and configuring SQL Server settings using Transact-SQL.

■Note For a review of the SERVERPROPERTY, @@SERVERNAME, and other SQL Server instance-level functions, see Chapter 8.

Viewing SQL Server Configurations

SQL Server configurations control an array of behaviors, from the way memory is managed to the default fill factor of your indexes. Although the valid configuration values vary, based on the option you are modifying, you can use the sp_configure system-stored procedure to view or make changes:

The syntax for sp_configure is as follows:

```
sp_configure [ [ @configname = ] 'option_name'
    [ , [ @configvalue = ] 'value' ] ]
```

The parameters are briefly described in Table 21-1.

Table 21-1. *sp_configure Parameters*

Parameter	Description
[@configname =] 'option_name'	The name of the SQL Server option to be configured.
[@configvalue =] 'value']	The desired new value to be set for the SQL Server option.

In SQL Server 2000, sp_configure was used to return the SQL Server instance configuration settings. Beginning in SQL Server 2005, you can also query configuration settings using the new sys.configurations system catalog view. The sys.configurations view can be queried like any normal view, and it returns each configuration name, the value in use by the SQL Server instance, the configuration setting's description, whether the configuration requires a SQL Server instance restart, and whether the configuration is an advanced option.

This recipe demonstrates three methods for viewing SQL Server configurations. The first method shows basic options (those which Microsoft has deemed to be mostly harmless to configure). The second method displays "advanced" options, or those which require extra consideration by an experienced database administrator before modification. The third and last method shows how to query the sys.configurations system catalog view:

```
-- Display basic options
EXEC sp_configure
GO
```

This returns basic configurations and their current values (not all rows are displayed):

Name	Minimum	Maximum	config_value	run_value
allow updates	0	1	0	0
CLR enabled				
0	1	0	0	
cross db ownership chaining	0	1	0	0
...	...	...	...	...

The next query shows advanced options (in addition to the basic options):

```
-- Display advanced options
EXEC sp_configure 'show advanced option', 1
RECONFIGURE
GO

EXEC sp_configure
GO
```

This returns both basic and advanced options (not all rows displayed):

Name	Minimum	Maximum	config_value	run_value
Ad Hoc Distributed Queries	0	1	0	0
affinity I/O mask	-2147483648	2147483647	0	0
affinity mask	-2147483648	2147483647	0	0
Agent XPs	0	1	0	0
allow updates	0	1	0	0
awe enabled	0	1	0	0
...	...	...	...	...

Finally, the sys.configurations view is queried to show SQL Server configurations, ordered by configuration name:

```
SELECT name, value, minimum, maximum, value_in_use, is_dynamic, is_advanced
FROM sys.configurations
ORDER BY name
```

This returns all options, in addition to other useful information such as whether the option is advanced and whether it's dynamic. If the option has an is_dynamic value of "1," the configuration change will take effect after the RECONFIGURE command is executed:

Name is_advanced	Value	Minimum	Maximum	value_in_use	is_dynamic	
Ad Hoc Distributed Queries	0	0	1	0	1	1
affinity I/O mask	0	-2147483648	2147483647	0	0	1
affinity mask	0	-2147483648	2147483647	0	1	1
Agent XPs	0	0	1	0	1	1
allow updates	0	0	1	0	1	0
awe enabled	0	0	1	0	0	1

How It Works

In the first part of the recipe, basic options are returned using the system stored procedure sp_configure. Examples of basic options include the clr enabled and nested triggers configurations. The clr enabled option shows you whether or not CLR-based objects are allowed in the SQL Server instance. The nested triggers configuration determines whether or not triggers can be fired that fire other triggers. These are basic settings that all SQL Server users can see by default.

The second part of the recipe demonstrated how to view *all* server options, including advanced options. To do this, an actual SQL Server configuration change was necessary. The "show advanced option" setting was configured from 0 (false) to 1 (true):

```
EXEC sp_configure 'show advanced option', 1
RECONFIGURE
GO
```

After executing sp_configure, the RECONFIGURE command was used. For those SQL Server options that don't require reboots, the RECONFIGURE command forces an update to the currently configured value. If an invalid or not recommended value is used, RECONFIGURE will reject it. Using RECONFIGURE WITH OVERRIDE will override this validation, in most cases. Take, for example, the recovery interval option, which designates the maximum database recovery time (in minutes). Setting the value of this option *above* 60 minutes using RECONFIGURE would raise a warning indicating that the value is not recommended. The warning, however, doesn't stop you from making the change. Using RECONFIGURE WITH OVERRIDE would force this option's value to be changed.

After changing the 'show advanced option' value to 1, all options were returned by sp_configure:

```
EXEC sp_configure
GO
```

Last in the recipe, the sys.configurations system catalog view was queried to return all SQL Server options. It returned additional information for each setting, including whether the setting was dynamic and if it was an advanced option.

Changing SQL Server Configurations

SQL Server does a remarkable job of maintaining itself out-of-the-box, and for most small or medium-sized implementations, the default settings will suffice. When you must change a default configuration value, you need to do so with care, making sure that you understand exactly what it is you are changing. For example, the locks configuration, which determines the maximum number of available locks SQL Server can issue, should be left to SQL Server to manage, allowing SQL Server to allocate, de-allocate, and escalate lock types as it sees fit.

■**Note** This book doesn't discuss each of the available server options. For a complete list, see SQL Server 2005 Books Online's topic "Setting Server Configuration Options."

In this recipe, I'll demonstrate using sp_configure to disable query parallelism, as well as to set a cap on the maximum amount of memory (in MBs) that the SQL Server instance is permitted to use.

The max degree of parallelism option sets the limit on the number of processors used in a parallel plan execution. The default value for this option is to use all available processors (with the option equal to 0):

```
SELECT name, value_in_use
FROM sys.configurations
WHERE name IN ('max degree of parallelism')
```

This returns:

name	value_in_use
max degree of parallelism	0

In this example, the maximum degree of parallelism is set to a single CPU:

```
EXEC sp_configure 'max degree of parallelism', 1
RECONFIGURE
GO
```

This returns:

```
Configuration option 'max degree of parallelism' changed from 0 to 1.
Run the RECONFIGURE statement to install.
```

Now the value is checked again:

```
SELECT name, value_in_use
FROM sys.configurations
WHERE name IN ('max degree of parallelism')
```

This returns:

name	value_in_use
max degree of parallelism	1

The max server memory option designates the maximum amount of memory SQL Server is allowed to use, measured in megabytes. The default value for this setting is no set maximum, as this query will show:

```
SELECT name, value_in_use
FROM sys.configurations
WHERE name IN ('max server memory (MB)')
```

This returns the default memory value (which is very large):

name	value_in_use
max server memory (MB)	2147483647

In this example, a cap of 250MB is put on the SQL Server instance:

```
EXEC sp_configure 'max server memory', 250
RECONFIGURE
GO
```

This returns:

```
Configuration option 'max server memory (MB)' changed from 2147483647 to 250.
Run the RECONFIGURE statement to install.
```

The new value is then verified:

```
SELECT name, value_in_use
FROM sys.configurations
WHERE name IN ('max degree of parallelism', 'max server memory (MB)')
```

This returns:

```
name                      value_in_use
max server memory (MB)    250
```

How It Works

In this recipe, I demonstrated setting the max degree of parallelism to "1," which means that only a single processor will be used on a single query (disabling SQL Server's ability to use multiple CPUs for executing a single query). This recipe also demonstrated limiting the maximum server memory to 250 megabytes. As long as other options have not been configured to constrain SQL Server any further, SQL Server will still dynamically manage memory, but only up to the limit specified using sp_configure. Neither change in setting required a restart of the SQL Server instance, so the RECONFIGURE command was enough to set the value during execution time.

■ ■ ■

Creating and Configuring Databases

In this chapter, you'll see an assortment of recipes that revolve around creating and configuring a SQL Server database. Some of the things you'll learn to do with Transact-SQL include:

- Creating a new database.
- Adding or removing files or filegroups from a database.
- Viewing and modifying database settings (including several new settings introduced in SQL Server 2005).
- Increasing or decreasing a database or database file size.
- Removing a database from the SQL Server instance.
- Detaching and reattaching a database from a SQL Server instance.

I'll also review the various "state" settings, such as configuring the database to be read-only, or putting the database into single-user mode.

■Note SQL Server 2005's new database mirroring functionality is reviewed in Chapter 25 and database snapshots in Chapter 26.

Creating, Altering, and Dropping Databases

In this first set of recipes, I cover how to create, modify, and drop databases in a SQL Server instance. Specifically, I'll be showing you how to:

- Create a database based on the default configuration of the model system database.
- View information about a database's configuration.
- Create a database using explicit file options (instead of depending on the model system database).
- Create a database that uses a user-defined filegroup.
- Change the name of an existing database.
- Drop a database from the SQL Server instance.
- Detach a database from the SQL Server instance so that only the underlying data and log files remain. Reattach the database using those same files.

The primary commands you'll be using to create and modify databases are CREATE DATABASE and ALTER DATABASE. Similar to my discussion in Chapter 1 about the SELECT statement, in this chapter, each recipe will slice off the relevant components used to perform the specified task, instead of presenting the syntax in one large block.

Creating a Database with a Default Configuration

This recipe demonstrates how to create a database in its simplest form, by using the default configuration based on the model system database. The model database is a system database installed with SQL Server and defines the template for all other databases created on the SQL Server instance. If you create a database without specifying any options other than the database name, the options will be based on the model system database.

The syntax for creating a database based on model is as follows:

```
CREATE DATABASE database_name
```

The CREATE DATABASE command, in its simplest form, can take just a single argument: the new database name.

This recipe creates a new database called BookStore:

```
USE master
GO

CREATE DATABASE BookStore
GO
```

How It Works

In this recipe, a new database called BookStore was created, without any other options but the database name. By omitting details such as file locations, size, and file growth options, the new database is created based on the model system database. The database will include any user-defined objects that you've placed in the model database and will use a file-naming convention based on the new database name.

Although this is a quick way to create a new database, it doesn't give you much control over several of the options that I'll describe throughout this chapter.

Viewing Database Information

This recipe demonstrates how to view database properties and file information using the system-stored procedure sp_helpdb:

```
EXEC sp_helpdb 'BookStore'
GO
```

This returns the following two result sets (albeit a bit packed due to the constraints of the printed page):

name	db_size	owner	dbid	created	status	compatibility_level
BookStore	1.68 MB	JOEPROD\Owner	8	Sep 30 2005	Status=ONLINE, Updateability=READ_WRITE, UserAccess=MULTI_USER, Recovery=FULL, Version=611, Collation=SQL_Latin1_General_CP1_CI_AS, SQLSortOrder=52, IsAutoCreateStatistics, IsAutoUpdateStatistics, IsFullTextEnabled	90

name	fileid	filename	filegroup	size	maxsize	growth	usage
BookStore	1	C:\Program Files\Microsoft SQL Server\MSSQL.1\MSSQL\DATA\BookStore.mdf	PRIMARY	1216 KB	Unlimited	1024 KB	data only
BookStore_log	2	C:\Program Files\Microsoft SQL Server\MSSQL.1\MSSQL\DATA\BookStore_log.LDF	NULL	504 KB	2147483648 KB	10%	log only

How It Works

The system-stored procedure sp_helpdb was used to view the properties of a database. This system-stored procedure takes a single optional parameter, which in this case is the database name:

```
EXEC sp_helpdb 'BookStore'
```

Had the database name been omitted from this stored procedure, information for all the databases on the SQL Server instance would have been returned instead.

This system-stored procedure returns information such as:

- The database name and owner.

- The date that the database was created.

- The various database settings and options, such as its default collation or whether or not it configured to automatically update statistics (database options are described later in the chapter).

- A list of individual files that make up the database, along with their size, file group, and growth options.

The output also includes the database's compatibility level. For example, a SQL Server 2005 database by default will have a compatibility level of "90." SQL Server 2000 compatibility would be a level of "80," SQL Server 7.0 "70," and SQL Server 6.5 "65." Compatibility level allows you to keep databases in SQL Server 2005 that remain compatible with prior versions of SQL Server. This also means that you cannot use Transact-SQL extensions introduced in SQL Server 2005 with a SQL Server 2000-compatible database. You can set this level using the sp_dbcmptlevel system-stored procedure.

Creating a Database Using File Options

Using the default options from the model system database to create a new database is fine if you're simply looking to create a quick-and-dirty test database, but in a production environment you'll usually want to put more thought into the location, size, and growth options of the database data and log files. This recipe will demonstrate the use of specifying explicit file options when creating a new database.

The abridged syntax for CREATE DATABASE, as presented in this recipe, is as follows:

```
CREATE DATABASE database_name
    [ ON
        [ <filespec> [ ,...n ] ] ]
[ [ LOG ON { <filespec> [ ,...n ] } ] ]
```

The arguments of this syntax are briefly described in Table 22-1.

Table 22-1. *CREATE DATABASE File Arguments*

Argument	Description
database_name	The name of the database.
[ON [<filespec> [,...n]]]	Designates one or more explicitly defined data files for the database.
[LOG ON { <filespec> [,...n] }]	Designates one or more explicitly defined transaction log files for the database.

The syntax for the `filespec` argument, used both in creating a data file and a log file, is as follows:

```
[ PRIMARY ]
(
    [ NAME = logical_file_name , ]
    FILENAME = 'os_file_name'
        [ , SIZE = size [ KB | MB | GB | TB ] ]
        [ , MAXSIZE = { max_size [ KB | MB | GB | TB ] | UNLIMITED } ]
        [ , FILEGROWTH = growth_increment [ KB | MB | % ] ]
) [ ,...n ]
```

The `filespec` arguments are described in Table 22-2.

Table 22-2. *Filespec Arguments*

Argument	Description
PRIMARY	This optional keyword designates the data file in the `filespec` as the primary data file (entry point of the database which contains pointers to other files and is typically named with an .mdf file extension). Only one primary file can exist for a database, and if it is not explicitly designated, the first data file listed in `CREATE DATABASE` is used as the primary file.
logical_file_name	The logical name of the database file.
os_file_name	The physical path and file name of the database file.
size [KB	MB	GB	TB]	The initial size of the file, based on the sizing attribute of choice (kilobytes, megabytes, gigabytes, terabytes).
MAXSIZE = { max_size [KB	MB	GB	TB]	UNLIMITED }	The maximum allowable size of the file. If `UNLIMITED` is chosen, the file can grow to the available space of the physical drive.
FILEGROWTH = growth_increment [KB	MB	%]	The amount that the file size increases when space is required. You can either designate the number of kilobytes or megabytes, or the percentage of existing file size to grow. If you select 0, file growth will not occur.
[,...n]	Indicates that you can have one or more files defined (up to 32767 files per database).

In this recipe, I'll create a new database called `BookStoreArchive` using all the aforementioned `CREATE DATABASE` options:

```
USE master
GO
```

```
CREATE DATABASE BookStoreArchive
ON  PRIMARY
(   NAME = 'BookStoreArchive',
    FILENAME = 'F:\MSSQL\DATA\BookStoreArchive.mdf' ,
    SIZE = 2MB ,
    MAXSIZE = UNLIMITED,
    FILEGROWTH = 10MB ),
(   NAME = 'BookStoreArchive2',
    FILENAME = 'G:\MSSQL\DATA\BookStoreArchive2.ndf' ,
    SIZE = 1MB ,
    MAXSIZE = 30,
    FILEGROWTH = 5% )
 LOG ON
(   NAME = 'BookStoreArchive_log',
    FILENAME = 'H:\MSSQL\TLOG\BookStoreArchive_log.LDF' ,
    SIZE = 504KB ,
    MAXSIZE = 100MB ,
    FILEGROWTH = 10%)
GO
```

How It Works

In this recipe, a new database called BookStoreArchive was created. The PRIMARY keyword was used to designate the first file as the primary data file:

```
CREATE DATABASE BookStoreArchive
ON  PRIMARY
```

The first file definition follows in parentheses. The logical file name is called BookStoreArchive:

```
(   NAME = 'BookStoreArchive',
```

The physical filename is designated on the F: drive. In production scenarios, you'll likely be putting your data files on different drive letters (which could support a RAID 5 or RAID 10 array):

```
    FILENAME = 'F:\MSSQL\DATA\BookStoreArchive.mdf' ,
```

Next, the initial data file size is set to two megabytes:

```
    SIZE = 2MB ,
```

The maximum size of the file is set to unlimited, meaning that it can keep growing as long as there is free space on the C: drive:

```
    MAXSIZE = UNLIMITED,
```

The growth increment is set to 10 megabyte chunks. Whenever more space is needed on the file, the file size will expand in 10 megabyte increments:

```
    FILEGROWTH = 10MB ),
```

The previous file definition ended with a comma, followed by a second data file definition:

```
(   NAME = 'BookStoreArchive2',
    FILENAME = 'G:\MSSQL\DATA\BookStoreArchive2.ndf' ,
```

The second data file is given a different logical name and physical filename. The physical filename ends in an .ndf file extension. Although that specific file extension isn't required, it does make it easier to identify the file type if you use .mdf for the primary file, and .ndf for all secondary data files. Adding multiple files that are spread out over different drive letters can, assuming each drive letter is RAID enabled and on a separate channel or controller, allow you to spread out I/O activity and potentially improve performance for larger, high traffic databases.

The size of the second file is set to one megabyte, with a cap on the maximum size of 30 megabytes. File growth was set to increment in 5% chunks, instead of in megabytes as the first data file was defined:

```
SIZE = 1MB ,
MAXSIZE = 30,
FILEGROWTH = 5% )
```

After the two data files were defined, the LOG ON keywords marked the beginning of the transaction log file definition:

```
LOG ON
(   NAME = 'BookStoreArchive_log',
```

The physical file name used an .ldf file extension, which is the standard for transaction log files:

```
FILENAME = 'H:\MSSQL\TLOG\BookStoreArchive_log.LDF' ,
```

The initial size was set to 504 kilobytes with a maximum transaction log size of 100 megabytes, with a 10% file growth rate.

```
SIZE = 504KB ,
MAXSIZE = 100MB ,
FILEGROWTH = 10%)
```

Once the CREATE DATABASE command is executed, the associated files are automatically created on the server, and the database is then available for use.

Later on in the chapter, there will be recipes showing you how to modify existing file properties, as well as how to add new data or transaction files to the database.

Creating a Database with a User-Defined Filegroup

A database must have, at a minimum, one data file and one transaction log file. These files belong to a single database and therefore are not shared with other databases. By default, when a database is created, the data files belong to the primary filegroup. A *filegroup* is a named grouping of files for administrative and placement reasons. The primary filegroup contains the primary data file, as well as other data files that have not been explicitly assigned to a different filegroup. Data files (but *not* transaction log files) belong to filegroups.

In addition to the primary filegroup (which all SQL Server databases have), you can create secondary user-defined filegroups for placing your files. User-defined filegroups are often used in very large databases (VLDB), allowing you to partition the database across several arrays and manage backups at the filegroup level instead of the entire database.

■**Note** You can place tables or indexes on specific filegroups. See Chapter 4 for a review of filegroups and tables, and Chapter 5 for a review of filegroups and indexes.

In this recipe, I demonstrate how to create a database with files on a user-defined filegroup. The syntax for doing so is as follows:

```
CREATE DATABASE database_name
[ ON
        FILEGROUP filegroup_name [ DEFAULT ]
    <filespec> [ ,...n ]
]
```

```
[
    [ LOG ON { <filespec> [ ,...n ] } ] ]
```

The syntax arguments are detailed in Table 22-3.

Table 22-3. *CREATE DATABASE Arguments*

Argument	Description
database_name	The name of the database.
FILEGROUP filegroup_name [DEFAULT]	Designates the logical name of the filegroup. If followed by the DEFAULT keyword, this filegroup will be the default filegroup of the database (meaning all objects will by default be created there).
<filespec> [,...n]	Designates one or more explicitly defined data files for the database.
[LOG ON { <filespec> [,...n] }]	Designates one or more explicitly defined transaction log files for the database.

This recipe creates a new database called BookStoreInternational, which uses two filegroups. One is the required primary filegroup and the other, the new user-defined FG2 filegroup, is created in the CREATE DATABASE command:

```
USE master
GO

CREATE DATABASE BookStoreInternational
ON  PRIMARY
(   NAME = 'BookStoreInternational',
    FILENAME = 'C:\Program Files\Microsoft SQL
➥ Server\MSSQL.1\MSSQL\DATA\BookStoreInternational.mdf' ,
    SIZE = 2MB ,
    MAXSIZE = UNLIMITED,
    FILEGROWTH = 5MB ),
FILEGROUP FG2 DEFAULT
(   NAME = 'BookStoreInternational2',
    FILENAME = 'C:\Program Files\Microsoft SQL
➥ Server\MSSQL.1\MSSQL\DATA\BookStoreInternational2.mdf' ,
    SIZE = 1MB ,
    MAXSIZE = UNLIMITED,
    FILEGROWTH = 1MB )
 LOG ON
(   NAME = 'BookStoreInternational_log',
    FILENAME = 'C:\Program Files\Microsoft SQL
➥ Server\MSSQL.1\MSSQL\DATA\BookStoreInternational_log.LDF' ,
    SIZE = 504KB ,
    MAXSIZE = 100MB ,
    FILEGROWTH = 10%)
GO
```

How It Works

In this recipe, a new database was created with two data files and one transaction log file. The first data file was created on the PRIMARY filegroup:

```
CREATE DATABASE BookStoreInternational
ON  PRIMARY
(   NAME = 'BookStoreInternational',
    FILENAME = 'C:\Program Files\Microsoft SQL
➡ Server\MSSQL.1\MSSQL\DATA\BookStoreInternational.mdf' ,
    SIZE = 2MB ,
    MAXSIZE = UNLIMITED,
    FILEGROWTH = 5MB ),
```

The second database data file was created in a new user-defined filegroup called FG2, using the FILEGROUP keyword. This filegroup was marked as the default filegroup, so that any new database objects created in the database will be created in this filegroup:

```
FILEGROUP FG2 DEFAULT
(   NAME = 'BookStoreInternational2',
    FILENAME = 'C:\Program Files\Microsoft SQL
➡ Server\MSSQL.1\MSSQL\DATA\BookStoreInternational2.mdf' ,
    SIZE = 1MB ,
    MAXSIZE = UNLIMITED,
    FILEGROWTH = 1MB )
```

Since transaction logs are not placed in filegroups, the LOG ON keywords were used with the standard filespec definition:

```
 LOG ON
(   NAME = 'BookStoreInternational_log',
    FILENAME = 'C:\Program Files\Microsoft SQL
➡ Server\MSSQL.1\MSSQL\DATA\BookStoreInternational_log.LDF' ,
    SIZE = 504KB ,
    MAXSIZE = 100MB ,
    FILEGROWTH = 10%)
GO
```

In this recipe, a single file was placed in the FG2 filegroup, though you can put multiple files in a single filegroup. With multiple files in a filegroup, SQL Server will fill each in a proportional manner, instead of filling up a single file before moving on to the next.

Setting Database User Access

SQL Server 2005 provides three database user access modes that affect which users (and how many) can access a database: SINGLE_USER, RESTRICTED_USER, and MULTI_USER. The SINGLE_USER and RESTRICTED_USER options are methods used to "shut the door" on other users performing activities in the database. This is often useful if you need to perform database configuration changes that do not allow other users to be in the database at the same time. These options are also used when you need to undo a data change, or force users out prior to a cutover to a new system or application upgrade. The upcoming table describes each option in more detail.

The syntax for modifying user access is as follows:

```
ALTER DATABASE database_name
SET  { SINGLE_USER | RESTRICTED_USER | MULTI_USER }
[WITH { ROLLBACK AFTER integer [ SECONDS ]
   | ROLLBACK IMMEDIATE
   | NO_WAIT
}]
```

The arguments of this syntax are described in Table 22-4.

Table 22-4. *ALTER DATABASE Arguments*

Argument	Description
database_name	The name of the existing database to modify user access for.
SINGLE_USER | RESTRICTED_USER | MULTI_USER	When SINGLE_USER is selected, only one user is allowed to access the database at a time. When this option is selected, unless the termination options are used (see the next row for a description of termination options), the modification is blocked until all other users disconnect from the database. With RESTRICTED_USER selected, only members of the sysadmin, dbcreator, or db_owner roles can access the database. With MULTI_USER, all users with permissions to the database are allowed access.
ROLLBACK AFTER integer [SECONDS] | ROLLBACK IMMEDIATE | NO_WAIT	These termination options allow you to roll back incomplete transactions for the database during the ALTER DATABASE statement. If you don't use a termination option, your ALTER may have to wait for however long the locking connection needs to complete its task. Termination options can actually be used with any SET clause; however they are most often used when changing a database to SINGLE_USER or RESTRICTED_USER modes. ROLLBACK AFTER integer [SECONDS] specifies that open database transactions be rolled back after a specified number of seconds. ROLLBACK IMMEDIATE rolls back open transactions immediately. NO_WAIT, when specified, causes the statement to fail if it cannot complete immediately (using this option requires that there are no open transactions in the database in order to succeed).

This recipe demonstrates taking the AdventureWorks into a SINGLE_USER mode, rolling back any open transactions, and then putting the database back into MULTI_USER mode:

```
SELECT user_access_desc
FROM sys.databases
WHERE name = 'AdventureWorks'

ALTER DATABASE AdventureWorks
SET  SINGLE_USER
WITH ROLLBACK IMMEDIATE

SELECT user_access_desc
FROM sys.databases
WHERE name = 'AdventureWorks'

ALTER DATABASE AdventureWorks
SET  MULTI_USER

SELECT user_access_desc
FROM sys.databases
WHERE name = 'AdventureWorks'
```

This returns:

```
user_access_desc
-----------------------------------------------------------
MULTI_USER

(1 row(s) affected)

user_access_desc
-----------------------------------------------------------
SINGLE_USER

(1 row(s) affected)

user_access_desc
-----------------------------------------------------------
MULTI_USER

(1 row(s) affected)
```

How It Works

In this recipe, the system catalog view sys.databases was queried to check the current user access mode. The database was then changed to SINGLE_USER mode, and included a termination of all open transactions in other database user sessions:

```
ALTER DATABASE AdventureWorks
SET  SINGLE_USER
WITH ROLLBACK IMMEDIATE
```

The user access mode was then checked again via sys.databases, and the database was changed back to MULTI_USER:

```
ALTER DATABASE AdventureWorks
SET  MULTI_USER
```

After that, the access mode was checked again via sys.databases:

```
SELECT user_access_desc
FROM sys.databases
WHERE name = 'AdventureWorks'
```

It is important to note that canceling open transactions in this manner may cause issues in your application, depending on how your application handles incomplete processes. When possible, try to change user access during periods of inactivity or when no transactions are active. You need to set the database to SINGLE_USER for certain operations, such as for the READ_ONLY and READ_WRITE options. Another reason to close all current user connections may be, for example, to put in an emergency object fix without having to deal with blocking or errors from the calling application.

Renaming a Database

In this recipe, I demonstrate how to change the name of an existing database using ALTER DATABASE.

The syntax is as follows:

```
ALTER DATABASE database_name
MODIFY NAME = new_database_name
```

The two arguments for this command include the original database name and the new database name.

This recipe demonstrates changing the name of the BookWarehouse database to the BookMart database. ALTER DATABASE...SET SINGLE USER is also executed in order to clear out any other con-current connections to the database:

```
USE master
GO

ALTER DATABASE BookWarehouse
SET SINGLE_USER
WITH ROLLBACK IMMEDIATE
GO

ALTER DATABASE  BookWarehouse
MODIFY NAME = BookMart
GO

ALTER DATABASE BookMart
SET MULTI_USER
GO
```

This returns (results may vary depending on activity in the database during the termination of connections):

```
Nonqualified transactions are being rolled back. Estimated rollback completion: 100%.
The database name 'BookMart' has been set.
```

How It Works

In this recipe, a database was renamed from BookWarehouse to BookMart. Before doing so, the query session's context was changed to the master database (because you can't change the name of the database using a connection to the database itself):

```
USE master
GO
```

The database was placed into single user mode and all active transactions against the database were rolled back (except for transactions existing within the current session):

```
ALTER DATABASE BookWarehouse
SET SINGLE_USER
WITH ROLLBACK IMMEDIATE
GO
```

The database name was then changed using ALTER DATABASE and MODIFY NAME:

```
ALTER DATABASE  BookWarehouse
MODIFY NAME = BookMart
GO
```

Even though the database was put in single user mode under its original name, it will remain in single user mode until it is explicitly set back to MULTI_USER access:

```
ALTER DATABASE BookMart
SET MULTI_USER
GO
```

Dropping a Database

You can remove a user database from SQL Server using the DROP DATABASE command. DROP DATABASE removes references to the database from SQL Server system tables. If the underlying files are online, it also removes the physical files from the SQL Server machine.

The syntax is as follows:

```
DROP DATABASE database_name
```

In this recipe, the BookStoreArchive_Ukrainian database is dropped:

```
USE master
GO

ALTER DATABASE BookStoreArchive_Ukrainian
SET SINGLE_USER
WITH ROLLBACK IMMEDIATE
GO

DROP DATABASE BookStoreArchive_Ukrainian
GO
```

How It Works

In this recipe, I started off by switching the current query session to the master database, because you cannot drop a database while you are also connected to it. The recipe also set the database into single user mode and forced any open transactions to be rolled back immediately. Finally, within the same query session, the database was dropped using the DROP DATABASE command.

Detaching a Database

When you drop a database, it is removed from the SQL Server instance along with its physical files. If you wish to remove a database from a SQL Server instance, but still retain the physical files (for archiving or to migrate the database to another SQL Server instance), you can *detach* the database instead. You can also move a database from one SQL Server instance to another, by detaching it from one instance and adding it to the other.

In order to detach a database, you use the system-stored procedure sp_detach_db, which uses the following syntax:

```
sp_detach_db [ @dbname= ] 'dbname'
    [ , [ @skipchecks= ] 'skipchecks' ]
    [ , [ @KeepFulltextIndexFile= ] 'KeepFulltextIndexFile' ]
```

The parameters for the procedure are described in Table 22-5.

Table 22-5. *sp_detach_db Parameters*

Parameter	Description
dbname	The name of the database to detach.
skipchecks	This option allows a true or false value. When this option is true, statistics are not updated prior to detaching the database. By default statistics are updated.
KeepFulltextIndexFile	This option allows a true or false value. When this option is true, full-text index files associated with the detached database are not dropped. If this option is not designated or is false, full-text files associated with the database are dropped.

In this recipe, I will create, and then detach, a database using sp_detach_db:

```
-- Create a default example database to detach
USE master
GO

CREATE DATABASE TestDetach
GO

-- Kick out any users currently in the database

ALTER DATABASE TestDetach
SET SINGLE_USER
WITH ROLLBACK IMMEDIATE

-- Detach the database

EXEC sp_detach_db 'TestDetach',
                'false', -- don't skip checks
                'false' -- drop any full-text indexes
```

This returns:

```
Nonqualified transactions are being rolled back. Estimated rollback completion: 100%.
Updating [sys].[queue_messages_1977058079]
    [queue_clustered_index], update is not necessary...
    [queue_secondary_index], update is not necessary...
    0 index(es)/statistic(s) have been updated, 2 did not require update.

Updating [sys].[queue_messages_2009058193]
    [queue_clustered_index], update is not necessary...
    [queue_secondary_index], update is not necessary...
    0 index(es)/statistic(s) have been updated, 2 did not require update.

Updating [sys].[queue_messages_2041058307]
    [queue_clustered_index], update is not necessary...
    [queue_secondary_index], update is not necessary...
    0 index(es)/statistic(s) have been updated, 2 did not require update.

Statistics for all tables have been updated.
```

How It Works

In this recipe, a new database called TestDetach was created. After that, I used ALTER DATABASE to set the TestDetach database into single user mode, while also kicking out any open database connections using the ROLLBACK IMMEDIATE option.

The system-stored procedure sp_detach_db was then used to detach the database—but not before updating statistics (designating false in the second parameter) and also dropping any full-text index files (designating false in the third parameter). The database has, for all intents and purposes, been dropped. However the data files still exist on the SQL Server instance's server, and can be recreated on the current or other SQL Server instance if you choose to do so.

Attaching a Database

The previous recipe demonstrated how to detach a database. In this next recipe, I'll demonstrate how to attach a database. Using the detach/attach method is a clean way to migrate a database from one SQL Server instance to another, assuming that a copy of the database needn't remain on both SQL Server instances.

■**Caution** Detaching and attaching a database from one server to the other doesn't also move the SQL Server logins associated to users in the database. You must move logins to the new SQL Server instance as a separate operation.

In previous versions of SQL Server, the system-stored procedure sp_attach_db was used to attach a database to a SQL Server instance. Now in SQL Server 2005, the CREATE DATABASE FOR ATTACH command is used instead.

The syntax is as follows:

```
CREATE DATABASE database_name
    ON <filespec> [ ,...n ]
    FOR { ATTACH
        | ATTACH_REBUILD_LOG }
```

The arguments for this command are described in Table 22-6.

Table 22-6. *CREATE DATABASE...FOR ATTACH*

Parameter	Description
database_name	The name of the database to attach.
<filespec> [,...n]	The name of the primary data file and any other database files. If the file locations of the originally detached database match the existing file location, you only need to include the primary data file reference. If file locations have changed, however, you should designate the location of each database file.
ATTACH | ATTACH_REBUILD_LOG	The ATTACH designates that the database is created using all original files that were used in the detached database. When ATTACH_REBUILD_LOG is designated, and if the transaction log file or files are unavailable, SQL Server will rebuild the transaction log file or files.

In this recipe, the TestDetach database detached in the previous recipe will now be reattached to the SQL Server instance using the same files and file paths. The database, however, will be re-attached with a new name of TestAttach:

```
CREATE DATABASE TestAttach
    ON (FILENAME = 'C:\Program Files\Microsoft SQL
➥ Server\MSSQL.1\MSSQL\DATA\TestDetach.mdf')
    FOR ATTACH
```

How It Works

In this recipe, a database was reattached by using CREATE DATABASE FOR ATTACH. The command referenced the primary data file name, which contains references to the location of the other files (in this case, the transaction log file).

If you detach a database, and then relocate the secondary data files and/or transaction log files, you will also need to explicitly reference the new location of each file in the CREATE DATABASE...FOR ATTACH command. The new path of the files is designated in the filespec. If the transaction log or logs had been unavailable, you could have used the ATTACH_REBUILD_LOG instead of ATTACH to rebuild the transaction log file.

Configuring Database Options

This next set of recipes covers how to configure database options which impact the behavior of activities performed within the database. Specifically, I'll be showing you how to:

- View database options currently configured for the database.
- Configure ANSI SQL options.
- Configure automatic options. Automatic database options impact the behavior of the SQL Server database engine, enabling or disabling automatic maintenance or meta-data updates.
- Configure external access options, including DB_CHAINING and TRUSTWORTHY.
- Create or modify a database to use a specific collation.
- Configure cursor options.
- Enable date correlation optimization. In this new SQL Server 2005 functionality, two tables that are related by a datetime foreign key reference can benefit from enabling the DATE_CORRELATION_OPTIMIZATION option.
- Modify database parameterization behavior. Introduced in SQL Server 2005, the PARAMETERIZATION option is used with ALTER DATABASE and controls whether all or some queries against the database are parameterized.
- Enable row versioning. SQL Server 2005 introduces two new database options that allow for statement-level and transaction-level read consistency: ALLOW_SNAPSHOT_ISOLATION and READ_COMMITTED_SNAPSHOT.
- Configure database recovery models. SQL Server 2005 uses three different recovery models that define whether or not transaction log backups can be made, and if so, what database activities will write to the transaction log.
- Configure page verification. SQL Server 2005 has three modes for handling and detecting incomplete I/O transactions caused by disk errors: CHECKSUM, TORN_PAGE_DETECTION, and NONE.

I'll begin by reviewing how to see the current database options for a database using the sys.databases system catalog view.

Viewing Database Options

This recipe demonstrates how to view database options using the sys.databases system catalog view for the AdventureWorks database:

```
SELECT name, is_read_only, is_auto_close_on, is_auto_shrink_on
FROM sys.databases
WHERE name = 'AdventureWorks'
```

This returns:

```
name                 is_read_only is_auto_close_on is_auto_shrink_on
-------------------  ------------ ---------------- -----------------
AdventureWorks       0            0                0

(1 row(s) affected)
```

How It Works

In this recipe, a query was used to view three database options: is_read_only, is_auto_close_on, and is_auto_shrink_on. The sys.databases system catalog view can be used to view many other database options for both user and system databases. Other columns of interest exposed by this view (related to recipes shown in this book) include:

```
collation_name                  compatibility_level             create_date
database_id                     is_ansi_null_default_on         is_ansi_nulls_on
is_ansi_padding_on              is_ansi_warnings_on             is_arithabort_on
is_auto_create_stats_on         is_auto_update_stats_async_on   is_auto_update_stats_on
is_broker_enabled               is_concat_null_yields_null_on
is_cursor_close_on_commit_on
is_date_correlation_on          is_db_chaining_on               is_fulltext_enabled
is_master_key_encrypted_by_server  is_numeric_roundabort_on
is_parameterization_forced
is_quoted_identifier_on         is_read_committed_snapshot_on
is_recursive_triggers_on
is_trustworthy_on               recovery_model_desc             service_broker_guid
snapshot_isolation_state        snapshot_isolation_state_desc   state_desc
user_access_desc
```

Configuring ANSI SQL Options

This recipe demonstrates how to set ANSI (American National Standards Institute) SQL compliance defaults for a database. These settings impact a number of behaviors which are detailed in Table 22-7.

Table 22-7. *ANSI SQL Options*

Option	Description
ANSI_NULL_DEFAULT	When set to ON, columns not explicitly defined with a NULL or NOT NULL in a CREATE or ALTER table statement will default to allow NULL values. The default is OFF, which means a column will be defined as NOT NULL if not explicitly defined.
ANSI_NULLS	When enabled, a comparison to a null value returns UNKNOWN. The default for this setting is OFF, meaning that comparisons to a null value will evaluate to TRUE when both values are NULL.
ANSI_PADDING	This option pads strings to the same length prior to inserting into a varchar or nvarchar data type column. The default setting is OFF, meaning that strings will not be padded.
ANSI_WARNINGS	This setting impacts a few different behaviors. When ON, any null values used in an aggregate function will raise a warning message. Also, divide-by-zero and arithmetic overflow errors will roll back the statement and return an error message. When this setting is OFF (the default), null values in an aggregate function return no warning and divide-by-zero and arithmetic overflow errors will return a NULL value instead of rolling back the statement.

Option	Description
ARITHABORT	When ON, a query with an overflow or division by zero will terminate the query and return an error. If this occurs within a transaction, then that transaction gets rolled back. When this option is OFF (the default), a warning is raised, but the statement continues to process.
CONCAT_NULL_YIELDS_NULL	When set to ON, concatenating a null value with a string produces a NULL value. When OFF (the default), a null value is the equivalent of an empty character string.
NUMERIC_ROUNDABORT	When set to ON, an error is produced when a loss of precision occurs in an expression. When OFF (the default), no error message is raised, but the result is rounded to the precision of the destination column or variable.
QUOTED_IDENTIFIER	When set to ON, identifiers can be delimited by double quotation marks, and literals with single quotation marks. When OFF (the default), only literals can be delimited with single or double quotation marks.
RECURSIVE_TRIGGERS	When this option is ON, triggers can fire recursively (trigger 1 fires trigger 2, which fires trigger 1 again). When OFF (the default), trigger recursion is not allowed.

The syntax for setting these options is as follows:

```
ALTER DATABASE database_name
SET  ANSI_NULL_DEFAULT { ON | OFF }
   | ANSI_NULLS { ON | OFF }
   | ANSI_PADDING { ON | OFF }
   | ANSI_WARNINGS { ON | OFF }
   | ARITHABORT { ON | OFF }
   | CONCAT_NULL_YIELDS_NULL { ON | OFF }
   | NUMERIC_ROUNDABORT { ON | OFF }
   | QUOTED_IDENTIFIER { ON | OFF }
   | RECURSIVE_TRIGGERS { ON | OFF }
```

This statement takes two arguments: the database name you want to modify, and the name of the ANSI SQL setting you wish to enable or disable.

Note The default options for any newly created databases will depend on the values in the model database at the time the new database is created. However out-of-the-box, SQL Server defaults are those that were underlined in the syntax.

In this recipe, ALTER DATABASE is used to set the ANSI_NULLS option to OFF. This means that that comparisons to a null value in a query will evaluate to TRUE when both values are NULL:

```
SELECT is_ansi_nulls_on
FROM sys.databases
WHERE name = 'AdventureWorks'

ALTER DATABASE AdventureWorks
SET  ANSI_NULLS  OFF

SELECT is_ansi_nulls_on
FROM sys.databases
WHERE name = 'AdventureWorks'
```

This returns:

```
is_ansi_nulls_on
----------------
1

(1 row(s) affected)

is_ansi_nulls_on
----------------
0

(1 row(s) affected)
```

How It Works

This recipe demonstrated using ALTER DATABASE to change an ANSI SQL setting. The recipe started by querying the sys.databases system catalog view to see the current setting of the database. After that, the ANSI_NULLS setting was turned off, using ALTER DATABASE and SET ANSI_NULLS OFF, and then the sys.databases system catalog view was queried again to confirm the change.

It is important to note that database ANSI options *can still be overridden* by SET statement connection-level settings. For example, even though the AdventureWorks database has the ANSI_NULLS setting OFF, using SET ANSI_NULLS ON in a query batch will override the database setting behavior for the query session.

Some of the options reviewed here are required to be turned ON before manipulating indexes on computed columns or indexed views. Those options include ARITHABORT, QUOTED_IDENTIFIER, CONCAT_NULL_YIELDS_NULL, ANSI_NULLS, ANSI_WARNINGS, and ANSI_PADDING. The NUMERIC_ROUNDABORT, however, must be OFF.

Configuring Automatic Options

Automatic database options impact the behavior of the SQL Server database engine, enabling or disabling automatic maintenance or metadata updates. Table 22-8 describes each of the automatic options.

Table 22-8. *Automatic Options*

Option	Description
AUTO_CLOSE	When AUTO_CLOSE is enabled, the database is closed and shut down when the last user connection to the database exits and all processes are completed.
AUTO_CREATE_STATISTICS	When enabled, SQL Server automatically generates statistical information regarding the distribution of values in a column. This information assists the query processor with generating an acceptable query execution plan (the internal plan for returning the result set requested by the query).
AUTO_SHRINK	When enabled, SQL Server shrinks data and log files automatically. Shrinking will only occur when more than 25 percent of the file has unused space. The database is then shrunk to either 25 percent free, or the original data or log file size. For example, if you defined your primary data file to be 100MB, a shrink operation would be unable to decrease the file size smaller than 100MB.
AUTO_UPDATE_STATISTICS	When enabled, this option automatically updates statistics already created for your tables.

Option	Description
AUTO_UPDATE_STATISTICS_ASYNC	An option that was introduced in SQL Server 2005. When ON, if a query initiates an automatic update of old statistics, the query will not wait for the statistics to be updated before compiling. When OFF (the default), a query that initiates statistics updates will wait until the update is finished before compiling a query plan.

The syntax for configuring automatic database options is as follows:

```
ALTER DATABASE database_name
SET   AUTO_CLOSE { ON | OFF }
  | AUTO_CREATE_STATISTICS { ON | OFF }
  | AUTO_SHRINK { ON | OFF }
  | AUTO_UPDATE_STATISTICS { ON | OFF }
  | AUTO_UPDATE_STATISTICS_ASYNC { ON | OFF }
```

The first argument is the database name you want to modify. The second argument is the name of the option you wish to either enable (ON) or disable (OFF). This recipe will demonstrate enabling the AUTO_UPDATE_STATISTICS_ASYNC automatic database option for the AdventureWorks database:

```
SELECT is_auto_update_stats_async_on
FROM sys.databases
WHERE name = 'AdventureWorks'

ALTER DATABASE AdventureWorks
SET   AUTO_UPDATE_STATISTICS_ASYNC   ON

SELECT is_auto_update_stats_async_on
FROM sys.databases
WHERE name = 'AdventureWorks'
```

This returns:

```
is_auto_update_stats_async_on
-----------------------------
0

(1 row(s) affected)

is_auto_update_stats_async_on
-----------------------------
1

(1 row(s) affected)
```

How It Works

This recipe demonstrated using ALTER DATABASE to change the AUTO_UPDATE_STATS_ASYNC automatic database setting. The recipe started by querying the sys.databases system catalog view to see the current setting of the database. After that, the AUTO_UPDATE_STATS_ASYNC setting was turned ON using ALTER DATABASE, and then the sys.databases system catalog view was queried again to confirm the change.

Some automatic settings can have a *negative* impact on performance when set to ON—including AUTO_CLOSE and AUTO_SHRINK. For AUTO_CLOSE, the overhead of opening the database after cleanly shutting down can cause performance issues in a high traffic database that has moments where no user is currently logged in (the overhead of starting up and shutting down a database repeatedly). For AUTO_SHRINK, SQL Server may initiate a database shrink operation during an inopportune moment, slowing down query performance of regular end-users. Also, database size may expand and contract repeatedly when this option is on. When it's possible, let the free space in the database remain, so that SQL Server isn't continually expanding and contracting the same files.

Other options should *not* be set OFF without a very good reason, including AUTO_CREATE_STATISTICS and AUTO_UPDATE_STATISTICS. Statistics help SQL Server compile the best query optimization plan, and the overhead of creating and maintaining statistics automatically is usually not significant compared to the benefits they provide to query performance.

Creating or Modifying a Database to Allow External Access

The CREATE DATABASE command provides two external access database options: DB_CHAINING and TRUSTWORTHY. Both of these options are OFF by default. The DB_CHAINING option, when enabled, allows the new database to participate in a cross-database ownership chain. In its simplest form, an ownership chain occurs when one object (such as a view or stored procedure) references another object. If the owner of the schema that contains these objects is the same as the referenced object, permissions on the referenced object are not checked. *Cross-database chaining* means that one object references another object in a different database. Ownership chaining can result in inappropriate or unintended data access—for example if a dbo-owned schema in a view references a different database's dbo-owned data table, security will not be checked if the DB_CHAINING option is enabled.

New in SQL Server 2005, the TRUSTWORTHY option is used to specify whether or not SQL Server will "trust" any modules or assemblies within a given database. When this option is OFF, SQL Server will protect against certain malicious EXTERNAL_ACCESS or UNSAFE activities within that database's assemblies, or from malicious code executed under the context of high-privileged users.

The syntax for creating a database with external access options enabled or disabled is as follows:

```
CREATE DATABASE database_name
   [ ON
     [ <filespec> [ ,...n ] ]
     [ , <filegroup> [ ,...n ] ]
   ]
[ [ LOG ON { <filespec> [ ,...n ] } ] ]
   [ WITH  { DB_CHAINING { ON | OFF }
        |TRUSTWORTHY { ON | OFF }]]
```

Both options appear in the WITH clause following the transaction log LOG ON option. They can be enabled in the same statement, and both are OFF by default.

You can also set these options for an existing database using ALTER DATABASE:

```
ALTER DATABASE database_name
{
SET   DB_CHAINING { ON | OFF }
| TRUSTWORTHY { ON | OFF }
}
```

This recipe demonstrates how to create a database with the database chaining option enabled, and then modify the new database to also allow external database access within database objects:

```
USE master
GO
-- Create a database with the model database defaults
CREATE DATABASE BookData
WITH DB_CHAINING ON
GO
```

```
USE master
GO
-- Now modify the new database to also have the
-- TRUSTWORTHY option ON
ALTER DATABASE BookData
SET TRUSTWORTHY ON
GO
```

How It Works

In this recipe, database ownership chaining was enabled within the CREATE DATABASE statement. The BookData database was created using default options (filename, size, growth) based on the model system database. After that, the WITH clause was used to enable database ownership chaining:

```
WITH DB_CHAINING ON
```

After that, the ALTER DATABASE command was used to enable the TRUSTWORTHY setting. Instead of the WITH keyword, the SET keyword was used, followed by the external access option name and the ON keyword:

```
ALTER DATABASE BookData
SET TRUSTWORTHY ON
GO
```

Creating or Changing a Database to Use a Non-Server Default Collation

In this recipe, I demonstrate how to create or modify a database to use a specific collation. SQL Server collations determine how data is sorted, compared, presented, and stored. The database collation can be different from the server-level collation defined when the SQL Server instance was installed, for those times that that you may wish to store data with a differing code page or sort order from the SQL Server instance default.

The syntax for designating the collation using CREATE DATABASE is as follows:

```
CREATE DATABASE database_name
    [ ON
        [ <filespec> [ ,...n ] ]
        [ , <filegroup> [ ,...n ] ] ]
[ [ LOG ON { <filespec> [ ,...n ] } ] ]
    [ COLLATE collation_name ]]
```

The COLLATE command is used after the transaction log definition to explicitly define the default database collation.

To change the default collation for an existing database, the syntax for ALTER DATABASE is as follows:

```
ALTER DATABASE database_name
{COLLATE collation_name}
```

This recipe demonstrates creating a new database with a default Ukrainian collation, with case and accent insensitivity settings. After creating the database, the database will then be altered to use a case and accent *sensitive* collation instead:

```
CREATE DATABASE BookStoreArchive_Ukrainian
ON   PRIMARY
(   NAME = 'BookStoreArchive_UKR',
    FILENAME = 'C:\Program Files\Microsoft SQL
```

```
➥ Server\MSSQL.1\MSSQL\DATA\BookStoreArchive_UKR.mdf' ,
   SIZE = 2MB ,
   MAXSIZE = UNLIMITED,
   FILEGROWTH = 10MB )
 LOG ON
(   NAME = 'BookStoreArchive_UKR_log',
   FILENAME = 'C:\Program Files\Microsoft SQL
➥ Server\MSSQL.1\MSSQL\DATA\BookStoreArchive_UKR_log.LDF' ,
   SIZE = 504KB ,
   MAXSIZE = 100MB ,
   FILEGROWTH = 10%)
COLLATE Ukrainian_CI_AI
GO

ALTER DATABASE BookStoreArchive_Ukrainian
COLLATE Ukrainian_CS_AS
GO
```

How It Works

Both the `CREATE DATABASE` and `ALTER DATABASE` examples used the `COLLATE` statement, followed by the collation name, to designate the default collation of the database:

```
COLLATE Ukrainian_CI_AI
```

Once the database default collation is set, new tables containing character data type columns (varchar, nvarchar, char, nchar, text, ntext) will use the database default collation as the column collation.

■**Caution** Creating a user-defined database with a default collation different from the SQL Server instance default (system database), can cause collation conflicts (cross-collation data cannot be converted or joined in a query). For example, the tempdb system database uses the same collation as the model database, which may cause temporary table data operations to fail in conjunction with a different collation. Always test cross-collation operations thoroughly.

Configuring Cursor Options

In Chapter 9 I discussed how to create and use Transact-SQL cursors. SQL Server 2005 has two database options that control the behavior of Transact-SQL cursors, as you can see in Table 22-9.

Table 22-9. *Cursor Options*

Option	Description
CURSOR_CLOSE_ON_COMMIT	When enabled, Transact-SQL cursors automatically close once a transaction is committed.
CURSOR_DEFAULT { LOCAL | GLOBAL }	If CURSOR_DEFAULT LOCAL is enabled, cursors created without explicitly setting scope as GLOBAL will default to local access. If CURSOR_DEFAULT GLOBAL is enabled, cursors created without explicitly setting scope as LOCAL will default to GLOBAL access.

The syntax for configuring cursor options is as follows:

```
ALTER DATABASE database_name
SET CURSOR_CLOSE_ON_COMMIT { ON | OFF }
  | CURSOR_DEFAULT { LOCAL | GLOBAL }
```

The statement takes two arguments, the database name you want to modify, and the option that you want to configure on and off.

This recipe will demonstrate enabling the CURSOR_CLOSE_ON_COMMIT for the AdventureWorks database:

```
SELECT is_cursor_close_on_commit_on
FROM sys.databases
WHERE name = 'AdventureWorks'

ALTER DATABASE AdventureWorks
SET  CURSOR_CLOSE_ON_COMMIT   ON

SELECT is_cursor_close_on_commit_on
FROM sys.databases
WHERE name = 'AdventureWorks'
```

This returns:

```
is_cursor_close_on_commit_on
----------------------------
0

(1 row(s) affected)

is_cursor_close_on_commit_on
----------------------------
1

(1 row(s) affected)
```

How It Works

This recipe demonstrated using ALTER DATABASE to change the CURSOR_CLOSE_ON_COMMIT automatic database setting. The recipe started by querying the sys.databases system catalog view to see the current setting of the database. After that, the CURSOR_CLOSE_ON_COMMIT setting was turned ON using ALTER DATABASE, and then the sys.databases system catalog view was queried again to confirm the change.

Enabling Date Correlation Optimization

SQL Server 2005 introduces a new option that allows you to enhance query performance between foreign-key related datetime data type columns. Two tables that are related by a datetime foreign key reference can benefit from enabling the DATE_CORRELATION_OPTIMIZATION option. When enabled, SQL Server 2005 collects additional statistics, which in turn help improve the performance of queries that use a join between the two datetime data type columns (foreign key and primary key pair).

The syntax for enabling this option is as follows:

```
ALTER DATABASE database_name
SET DATE_CORRELATION_OPTIMIZATION { ON | OFF }
```

The command takes two arguments: the database name you want to modify, and whether to set the DATE_CORRELATION_OPTIMIZATION ON or OFF. This option is defaulted to OFF, as having it ON adds extra overhead for those tables that meet the criteria for date correlation optimization.

This option, when ON, can benefit queries that join two table datetime values, which are related by a foreign key reference. SQL Server will then maintain additional correlation statistics, which may allow, depending on your query, SQL Server to generate more efficient, less I/O intensive query plans.

In order to take advantage of this database setting and for the statistics to be created automatically, at least one of the datetime columns (primary key or foreign key) has to be the first key column in a clustered index or the partitioning column in a partitioned table.

Be aware that there is extra overhead in updating the statistics, so you should monitor performance for databases that have heavy updates to the primary-key and foreign-key datetime-related tables, as the benefits of the query optimization may not outweigh the overhead of the statistics updates.

In this recipe, the AdventureWorks will have this option turned ON:

```
SELECT is_date_correlation_on
FROM sys.databases
WHERE name = 'AdventureWorks'

ALTER DATABASE AdventureWorks
SET DATE_CORRELATION_OPTIMIZATION ON

SELECT is_date_correlation_on
FROM sys.databases
WHERE name = 'AdventureWorks'
```

This returns:

```
is_date_correlation_on
----------------------
0

(1 row(s) affected)

is_date_correlation_on
----------------------
1

(1 row(s) affected)
```

How It Works

In this recipe, the sys.databases system catalog view was used to check the state of date correlation of the AdventureWorks database. After that, ALTER DATABASE and SET DATE_CORRELATION_OPTIMIZATION ON was issued. The sys.databases system catalog view was checked again, confirming the new setting.

Modifying Database Parameterization Behavior

Introduced in SQL Server 2005, the PARAMETERIZATION option is used with ALTER DATABASE and controls whether all or just some queries against the database are parameterized.

Parameterization occurs when a query is submitted to SQL Server. SQL Server looks at literal values in a SELECT, INSERT, UPDATE, and DELETE statement and seeks to parameterize them (make a placeholder) so that query execution plans can be reused when similar queries are executed, instead of a new plan being made for each query. Execution plans are created for the parameterized query at the statement level, so that each statement in a batch of statements can be individually parameterized.

The syntax for enabling this option is as follows:

```
ALTER DATABASE database_name
SET PARAMETERIZATION { SIMPLE | FORCED }
```

The command takes two arguments: the database name, and the parameterization option. You have two choices with parameterization, SIMPLE (the default) or FORCED. With SIMPLE parameterization (the default value), SQL statements are parameterized for a smaller population of queries (at SQL Server's discretion). Setting parameterization to FORCED increases the population of queries that become parameterized, which can benefit query performance as more query execution plans are created and potentially reused.

This recipe demonstrates how to enable this option using ALTER DATABASE, check the value in sys.databases, and then show the results of parameterization using the sys.dm_exec_cached_plans system catalog view and the sys.dm_exec_cached_plans dynamic management function. First, the AdventureWorks database is checked to see if the parameterization option is set to forced:

```
SELECT is_parameterization_forced
FROM sys.databases
WHERE name = 'AdventureWorks'
```

The results of this query confirm that this option is *not* enabled:

```
is_parameterization_forced
--------------------------
0
```

Next , the parameterization option is changed to FORCED using ALTER DATABASE:

```
ALTER DATABASE AdventureWorks
SET PARAMETERIZATION FORCED
```

The change is then confirmed by querying sys.databases:

```
SELECT is_parameterization_forced
FROM sys.databases
WHERE name = 'AdventureWorks'
```

This returns:

```
is_parameterization_forced
--------------------------
1
```

Next, the DBCC FREEPROCCACHE command is used to clear out the procedure cache; in order to demonstrate the use of the FORCED option:

```
-- CAUTION!  Don't run this on a production SQL Server instance.
-- This clears out the procedure cache and will cause all
-- new queries to recompile.
DBCC FREEPROCCACHE
```

The following query is then executed:

```
USE AdventureWorks
GO
```

```
SELECT ManagerID
FROM HumanResources.Employee
WHERE EmployeeID BETWEEN 1 AND 2
```

This returns the following results:

```
ManagerID
-----------
16
6
```

Now the sys.dm_exec_cached_plans system catalog view is queried. This view returns information about the query execution plans cached in the SQL Server instance. The view column plan_handle contains an identifier that references the query plan in memory. To view this plan in memory, the query uses the sys.dm_exec_query_plan dynamic management function, which takes the plan_handle as a parameter and returns the execution plan in XML format. This query searches for any reference to EmployeeID from the previous query, for prepared, cached plans:

```
SELECT query_plan
FROM sys.dm_exec_cached_plans p
CROSS APPLY sys.dm_exec_query_plan(p.plan_handle)
WHERE CAST(query_plan as varchar(max))
    LIKE '%EmployeeID%' AND
    objtype = 'Prepared'
```

This returns the following abridged results (I'm showing a small fragment of the XML formatted plan):

```
<StmtSimple StatementText="(@0 int,@1 int)select ManagerID from
HumanResources . Employee where EmployeeID between @0 and @1"
StatementId="1" StatementCompId="1" StatementType="SELECT"
StatementSubTreeCost="0.0032842" StatementEstRows="2"
StatementOptmLevel="TRIVIAL">
```

This example of parameterization could have also occurred in the SIMPLE parameterization setting, only the FORCED setting increases the chances that the parameterization *will* occur.

To set the database option back to SIMPLE, ALTER DATABASE is used again:

```
ALTER DATABASE AdventureWorks
SET PARAMETERIZATION SIMPLE
GO
```

How It Works

This recipe demonstrated how to change a database to use forced parameterization and then back again to simple parameterization. I began the recipe by checking the parameterization state of the AdventureWorks database using the sys.databases system catalog view. After that, ALTER DATABASE and SET PARAMETERIZATION FORCED was used. The sys.databases system catalog view was checked again to confirm that the option was changed.

After that, DBCC FREEPROCCACHE was used to clear out the procedure cache.

■**Caution** Only use DBCC FREEPROCCACHE on a test, non-production SQL instance, as it removes all plans from the procedure cache, which can negatively impact performance.

Next, a query was executed against the HumanResources.Employee table, using a WHERE clause that qualified EmployeeIDs between 1 and 2:

```
SELECT ManagerID
FROM HumanResources.Employee
WHERE EmployeeID BETWEEN 1 AND 2
```

A query was then executed using the sys.dm_exec_cached_plans system catalog view and the sys.dm_exec_query_plan dynamic management function:

```
SELECT query_plan
FROM sys.dm_exec_cached_plans p
CROSS APPLY sys.dm_exec_query_plan(p.plan_handle)
WHERE CAST(query_plan as varchar(max))
   LIKE '%EmployeeID%' AND
   objtype = 'Prepared'
```

The results showed an XML formatted SQL plan (your results may vary) with parameter place holders for use in the WHERE clause:

```
where EmployeeID between @0 and @1"
```

Enabling Read Consistency for a Transaction

SQL Server 2005 introduces two new database options that allow for statement-level and transaction-level read consistency: ALLOW_SNAPSHOT_ISOLATION and READ_COMMITTED_SNAPSHOT (which will be demonstrated after this recipe).

■**Note** Both of the database options are discussed in the same recipe, because they both impact read consistency. They do not, however, need to be used together. They are independent options. Use ALLOW_SNAPSHOT_ISOLA-TION if you want transaction-level read consistency and READ_COMMITTED_SNAPSHOT if you are looking for statement-level read consistency.

The ALLOW_SNAPSHOT_ISOLATION database option enables a snapshot of data at the transaction level. When ALLOW_SNAPSHOT_ISOLATION is enabled, you can use the snapshot transaction isolation level to read a transactional consistent version of the data as it existed *at the beginning* of a transaction. Using this option, data reads don't block data modifications. If data was changed while reading the snapshot data, and an attempt was made within the snapshot transaction to change the data, the change attempt will *not* be allowed and will end with a warning from SQL Server's update conflict detection support. Once this database setting is enabled, snapshot isolation is initiated when SET TRANSACTION ISOLATION LEVEL with SNAPSHOT isolation is specified before the start of the transaction.

■**Note** For an example of ALLOW_SNAPSHOT_ISOLATION in action, see Chapter 3's recipe "Using SET TRANSAC-TION ISOLATION LEVEL."

The READ_COMMITTED_SNAPSHOT setting enables row versioning at the *individual statement level*. Row versioning retains the original copy of a row in tempdb whenever the row is modified, storing the latest version of the row in the current database. For databases with a large amount of transactional activity, you'll want to make sure tempdb has enough space in order to hold row versions. The READ_COMMITTED_SNAPSHOT setting enables row versioning at the individual statement level for the query session. When enabling `READ_COMMITTED_SNAPSHOT`, locks are not held on the data. Row versioning is used to return the statement's data as it existed at the beginning of the statement execution. Data being read during the statement execution still allows updates by others, and unlike snapshot isolation, there is no mandatory update conflict detection to warn you that the data has been modified during the read. Once this database option is enabled, row versioning is then initiated when executing a query in the default read-committed isolation level or when `SET TRANSACTION ISOLATION LEVEL` with `READ COMMITTED` is used before the statement executes.

The main benefit of using these options is the reduction in locks for read operations. If your application requires real-time data values, these two options *are not* the best choice. However if snapshots of data are acceptable to your application, setting these options may be appropriate.

The syntax for enabling these options is as follows:

```
ALTER DATABASE database_name
   SET ALLOW_SNAPSHOT_ISOLATION {ON | OFF }
   | READ_COMMITTED_SNAPSHOT {ON | OFF }
```

The command takes two arguments: the database name, and the snapshot option of enabling or disabling. This recipe will demonstrate enabling both row versioning options for the AdventureWorks database. First, the current database settings are validated by querying `sys.databases`:

```
SELECT snapshot_isolation_state_desc,
     is_read_committed_snapshot_on
FROM sys.databases
WHERE name = 'AdventureWorks'
```

This returns:

snapshot_isolation_state_desc	is_read_committed_snapshot_on
OFF	0

Next, `ALTER DATABASE` is used to enable both options (although both options needn't be chosen, because you can choose to enable one type of read consistency option and not another):

```
ALTER DATABASE AdventureWorks
SET ALLOW_SNAPSHOT_ISOLATION ON

ALTER DATABASE AdventureWorks
SET READ_COMMITTED_SNAPSHOT ON
```

Next, the database settings are validated again, post-change:

```
SELECT snapshot_isolation_state_desc,
     is_read_committed_snapshot_on
FROM sys.databases
WHERE name = 'AdventureWorks'
```

This returns:

snapshot_isolation_state_desc	is_read_committed_snapshot_on
ON	1

How It Works

This recipe started off by checking the current state of row versioning in the AdventureWorks database by querying `sys.databases`. After that, two separate `ALTER DATABASE` commands were executed to enable snapshot isolation and read-committed isolation levels in the database. The system catalog view sys.databases was queried again to confirm the changes. Keep in mind that both options do not need to be enabled—you can pick and choose whether or not you want both statement and transaction-level read consistency, both, or neither.

Configuring Database Recovery Models

A full database backup is a full copy of your database. Transaction log backups, on the other hand, only back up the transaction log from the latest full backup or latest transaction log backup. When the backup completes, SQL Server truncates the inactive portion of the log. Aside from allowing a restore from the point that the transaction log backup completed, transaction log backups also allow point-in-time and transaction mark recovery. Point-in-time recovery allows you to restore the database as of a specific time period, for example, restoring a database prior to a database modification or failure. *Transaction mark recovery* recovers to the first instance of a "marked" transaction and includes the updates made within this transaction.

Note For more information on transaction log backups, see Chapter 29.

SQL Server 2005 uses three different recovery models that define whether or not transaction log backups can be made, and if so, what database activities will write to the transaction log. The three recovery models are FULL, BULK_LOGGED, and SIMPLE:

- When using SIMPLE recovery, the transaction log is automatically truncated after a database backup, removing the ability to perform transaction log backups. In this recovery mode, the risk of data loss is dependent on your full or differential backup schedule—and you will not be able to perform the point-in-time recovery that a transaction log backup offers.

- The BULK_LOGGED recovery model allows you to perform full, differential, and transaction log backups; however there is minimal logging to the transaction log for bulk operations. The benefit of this recovery mode is reduced log space usage during bulk operations, however the trade off is that transaction log backups can only be used to recover from the end of the transaction log backup (no point-in-time recover or marked transactions allowed).

- The FULL recover model fully logs all transaction activity, bulk operations included. In this safest model, all restore options are available, including point-in-time transaction log restores, differential backups, and full database backups.

The syntax for changing the database recovery mode is as follows:

```
ALTER DATABASE database_name
SET RECOVERY { FULL | BULK_LOGGED | SIMPLE }
```

In this recipe, the AdventureWorks database will be set to the FULL recovery model:

```
SELECT recovery_model_desc
FROM sys.databases
WHERE name = 'AdventureWorks'
GO

ALTER DATABASE AdventureWorks
SET RECOVERY FULL
GO
```

```
SELECT recovery_model_desc
FROM sys.databases
WHERE name = 'AdventureWorks'
```

This returns:

```
recovery_model_desc
------------------------------------------------------------
SIMPLE

(1 row(s) affected)

recovery_model_desc
------------------------------------------------------------
FULL

(1 row(s) affected)
```

How It Works

The initial recovery model when a database is created depends on the recovery mode of the model database. After creating a database, you can always modify the recovery model using ALTER DATABASE and SET RECOVERY.

In this recipe, the sys.databases system catalog view was used to check on the recovery model of the AdventureWorks database. Once it was confirmed that it was currently using a SIMPLE model, ALTER DATABASE and SET RECOVERY were used to change the database to FULL mode.

■Tip After changing a database's recovery model, it is a good practice to perform a full backup of your database.

Configuring Page Verification

Disk errors can occur when a data page write to the physical disk is interrupted due to a power failure or other physical issue. SQL Server 2005 has three modes for handling and detecting incomplete I/O transactions caused by disk errors: CHECKSUM, TORN_PAGE_DETECTION, and NONE.

- The CHECKSUM option (the model database default) writes a checksum value to the data page header based on the contents of the entire data page. If a page is corrupted or partially written, SQL Server will detect a difference between the header and the actual page contents.

- The TORN_PAGE_DETECTION option (the main option used in previous versions of SQL Server) detects data page issues by reversing a bit for each 512-byte sector of the data page. When a bit is in the incorrect state when read by SQL Server, a "torn" page is identified.

- When NONE is selected, neither CHECKSUM nor TORN_PAGE_DETECTION handling is used in allocating new data pages nor identified by SQL Server during a read.

Unless you have a good reason for doing so (such as a requirement for unfettered query performance for a benchmark test, for example), keeping the default option of CHECKSUM is a good idea. Although CHECKSUM has more overhead than TORN_PAGE_DETECTION, it is also more comprehensive in its ability to identify data page errors. The syntax for setting the page verification mode is as follows:

```
ALTER DATABASE database_name
SET PAGE_VERIFY { CHECKSUM | TORN_PAGE_DETECTION | NONE }
```

In this recipe, the AdventureWorks database is modified to *not* perform page verification:

```
SELECT page_verify_option_desc
FROM sys.databases
WHERE name = 'AdventureWorks'
GO

ALTER DATABASE AdventureWorks
SET PAGE_VERIFY NONE
GO

SELECT page_verify_option_desc
FROM sys.databases
WHERE name = 'AdventureWorks'
GO
```

This returns:

```
page_verify_option_desc
------------------------------------------------------------
CHECKSUM

(1 row(s) affected)

page_verify_option_desc
------------------------------------------------------------
NONE

(1 row(s) affected)
```

Now it will be added back:

```
ALTER DATABASE AdventureWorks
SET PAGE_VERIFY CHECKSUM
GO

SELECT page_verify_option_desc
FROM sys.databases
WHERE name = 'AdventureWorks'
GO
```

This returns:

```
page_verify_option_desc
------------------------------------------------------------
CHECKSUM
```

How It Works

This recipe started off by validating the current page verification state in the AdventureWorks database by querying the sys.databases system catalog view. After that, ALTER DATABASE and SET PAGE_VERIFY were executed to disable page verification. The sys.databases system catalog view was queried again, validating the change.

Controlling Database Access and Ownership

In these next two recipes, I'll cover how to control the access and ownership of user databases. First off, I'll show you how to change a database's accessibility using three different states: online, offline, or emergency. The next recipe after that demonstrates how to change the owner of the database using the sp_changedbowner system-stored procedure.

Changing a Database State to Online, Offline, or Emergency

A database can be in one of three states: online, offline, or emergency.

The *online state* is the default, meaning that the database is open and available to be used. When in *offline status*, the database is "closed" and cannot be modified or queried by any user. You may wish to take a database offline in situations where you need to move the data files to a new physical location, and then use ALTER DATABASE to modify the metadata for that file's new location (demonstrated later in the chapter). Unlike detaching the database, the database is still kept in the metadata of the SQL Server instance, and can then be taken back online later on.

Lastly, if the database is corrupted, setting a database to an emergency state allows read-only access to the database for sysadmin server role logins, allowing you to query any database objects that are still accessible (depending on the nature of the problem).

The syntax for configuring the database state is as follows:

```
ALTER DATABASE database_name
SET { ONLINE | OFFLINE | EMERGENCY }
```

This recipe demonstrates how to bring the database offline, attempt a read, and then bring it online again. Keep in mind that if active connections are in the AdventureWorks database, your command will have to wait for them to disconnect unless you force them out (using techniques discussed in the previous "Setting Database User Access" recipe):

```
USE master
GO

ALTER DATABASE AdventureWorks
SET OFFLINE
GO

-- Attempt a read against a table
SELECT COUNT(*)
FROM AdventureWorks.HumanResources.Department
GO
```

This returns:

```
Msg 942, Level 14, State 4, Line 3
Database 'AdventureWorks' cannot be opened because it is offline.
```

Now to bring the database back online again:

```
ALTER DATABASE AdventureWorks
SET ONLINE
GO
```

How It Works

In this recipe, the AdventureWorks database was taken offline by using ALTER DATABASE and the SET OFFLINE command. After taking the database offline, a query against a table in the database was attempted, causing an error to be raised. The database was then brought back online using ALTER DATABASE and the SET ONLINE option.

Changing a Database Owner

In this recipe, I demonstrate how to change the owner of an existing database using the sp_changedbowner system-stored procedure.

The syntax for this system-stored procedure is as follows:

```
sp_changedbowner [ @loginame = ] 'login'
          [ , [ @map= ] remap_alias_flag ]
```

The parameters for the procedure are described briefly in Table 22-10.

Table 22-10. *sp_changedbowner Parameters*

Parameter	Description
'login'	The new SQL Server login that will own the database. This login cannot already be mapped to an existing database user (without dropping this user first).
remap_alias_flag	The optional flag references alias functionality which was used in previous versions of SQL Server and allowed you to map users to a database. Alias functionality is going to be removed in a future version of SQL Server, so don't use it.

This recipe creates a new login and then makes the new login the database owner of the Book-Warehouse database:

```
CREATE LOGIN NewBossInTown WITH PASSWORD = 'HereGoesTheNeighborhood10'
GO

USE BookData
GO

EXEC sp_changedbowner 'NewBossInTown'
GO

SELECT p.name
FROM sys.databases d
INNER JOIN sys.server_principals p ON
   d.owner_sid = p.sid
WHERE d.name = 'BookData'
```

This returns:

```
name
----------------------------------------------------------------------
NewBossInTown
```

How It Works

An owner is mapped from an existing SQL Server login to the dbo user in the database. Once this happens, the new owner has permissions to perform all database-specific operations (for example, creating tables, granting object permissions, deleting data, and so on).

In this recipe, a new login was created and the database context was switched to the BookWarehouse database. The sp_changedbowner system-stored procedure was used to set the new login as the owner:

```
EXEC sp_changedbowner 'NewBossInTown'
```

The new owner was then mapped to the dbo database user. Once set, the sys.databases and sys.server_principals system catalog views were queried in order to confirm that the owner was actually changed.

Managing Database Files and Filegroups

This next set of recipes covers how to manage database files and filegroups. Specifically, I'll be showing you how to:

- Add a data or log file to an existing database.
- Remove a data or log file from a database.
- Relocate a data or transaction log file on the operating system.
- Change a file's logical name.
- Increase a database file size and modify growth options.
- Add a filegroup to an existing database.
- Set the default filegroup for a database.
- Remove a filegroup from a database.
- Make a database or filegroup read-only.

This next recipe demonstrates how to use ALTER DATABASE to add a data or log file to an existing database.

Adding a Data File or Log File to an Existing Database

Once a database is created, assuming that you have available disk space, you can add additional data or transaction logs to it as needed. This allows you to expand to new drives if the current physical drive/array is close to filled up, or if you are looking to improve performance by spreading I/O across multiple drives. It usually only makes sense to add additional data and log files to a database if you plan on putting these files on a separate drive/array. Putting multiple files on the same drive/array doesn't improve performance, and may only benefit you if you plan on performing separate file or filegroup backups for a very large database (VLDB).

Adding files doesn't require you to bring the database offline. The syntax for ALTER DATABASE in order to add a data or transaction log file is as follows:

```
ALTER DATABASE database_name
{ADD FILE <filespec> [ ,...n ]
        [ TO FILEGROUP { filegroup_name | DEFAULT } ]
  | ADD LOG FILE <filespec> [ ,...n ] }
```

The syntax arguments are described in Table 22-11.

Table 22-11. *ALTER DATABASE...ADD FILE*

Argument	Description
database_name	The name of the existing database.
<filespec> [,...n]	Designates one or more explicitly defined data files to add to the database.
filegroup_name | DEFAULT	Designates the logical name of the filegroup. If followed by the DEFAULT keyword, this filegroup will be the default filegroup of the database (meaning all objects will by default be created there).
[LOG ON { <filespec> [,...n] }]	Designates one or more explicitly defined transaction log files for the database.

In this recipe, a new data and transaction log file will be added to the BookData database:

```
ALTER DATABASE BookData
ADD FILE
(   NAME = 'BookData2',
    FILENAME = 'C:\Program Files\Microsoft SQL Server\MSSQL.1\MSSQL\DATA\BD2.NDF' ,
    SIZE = 1MB ,
    MAXSIZE = 10MB,
    FILEGROWTH = 1MB )
TO FILEGROUP [PRIMARY]
GO

ALTER DATABASE BookData
ADD LOG FILE
(   NAME = 'BookData2Log',
    FILENAME = 'C:\Program Files\Microsoft SQL Server\MSSQL.1\MSSQL\DATA\BD2.LDF' ,
    SIZE = 1MB ,
    MAXSIZE = 5MB,
    FILEGROWTH = 1MB )
GO
```

How It Works

In this recipe, a new data and transaction log file were added to the BookData database. To add the data file, ALTER DATABASE was used with the ADD FILE command, followed by the file specification:

```
ALTER DATABASE BookData
ADD FILE
...
```

The filegroup where the new file was added was specified using the TO FILEGROUP clause, followed by the filegroup name in brackets:

```
TO FILEGROUP [PRIMARY]
GO
```

In the second query in the recipe, a new transaction log file was added using ALTER DATABASE and the ADD LOG FILE command:

```
ALTER DATABASE BookData
ADD LOG FILE
...
```

Neither file addition required the database to be offline.

Removing a Data or Log File from a Database

This recipe demonstrates how to remove a data or transaction log file from an existing database. You may wish to do this if you need to relocate files from one drive/array to a different drive/array by creating a file on one drive and then dropping the old one.

The syntax for removing a file (data or transaction log) is as follows:

```
ALTER DATABASE database_name
REMOVE FILE logical_file_name
```

The syntax arguments are described in Table 22-12.

Table 22-12. *ALTER DATABASE...REMOVE FILE*

Argument	Description
database_name	The name of the existing database.
logical_file_name	The logical file name of the file to be removed from the database.

This recipe will first check for the logical file names for the BookData database, then empty the contents of the file (which moves the data to the remaining data files), and, finally, will drop the file from the database:

```
USE BookData
GO

SELECT name
FROM sys.database_files

DBCC SHRINKFILE(BookData2, EMPTYFILE)

ALTER DATABASE BookData
REMOVE FILE BookData2
```

This returns:

```
name
----------------------
BookData
BookData2
BookData_log
BookData2Log

(3 row(s) affected)

The file 'BookData2' has been removed.
```

How It Works

The recipe started by switching to the BookData database so that the query against sys.database_files would return all logical file names from the current connection's database.

You can't remove the primary data or primary transaction log file from the database, nor can you remove a file that contains data or active transactions logging within it. DBCC SHRINKFILE was used to remove existing data from the file to be dropped. This was done by using the EMPTYFILE parameter (see later on in the chapter for a review of this command).

After that, `ALTER DATABASE` was used with the `REMOVE FILE` command to remove the file from the database. Removing the file from the database also removes the underlying file from the file system.

Relocating a Data or Transaction Log File

Sometimes you may find it necessary to relocate a database file for an existing database. Your reasons for doing this may vary—you might need to do this because a physical drive is running out of space, or to improve performance (placing files on separate RAID arrays).

This recipe demonstrates how to move a database file's location using the `ALTER DATABASE` command. In SQL Server 2000, you had to detach the database, move the file, and then attach the database again from the new location. Another option was to back up the database and restore it to the new location. In SQL Server 2005, you don't have to detach the database in order to move the file, although you *do* need to take the database offline.

The syntax for changing the file's location is as follows:

```
ALTER DATABASE database_name
MODIFY FILE
{NAME = logical_file_name , FILENAME = 'new_physical_file_name_and_path')
```

The arguments of this syntax described in Table 22-13.

Table 22-13. *ALTER DATABASE...MODIFY FILE*

Argument	Description
database_name	The name of the existing database.
logical_file_name	The logical file name of the physical file to be relocated.
new_physical_file_name_and_path	The new file path and location.

In this recipe, a new database called `BookWarehouse` will be created using the default settings. After that, the database will be taken offline and then copied to the new location on the server. Once moved, the file will be relocated using `ALTER DATABASE`:

```
USE master
GO

-- Create a default database for this example
CREATE DATABASE BookWarehouse
GO

ALTER DATABASE BookWarehouse
SET OFFLINE
GO
```

Now move the file "C:\Program Files\Microsoft SQL Server\MSSQL.1\MSSQL\DATA\Book-Warehouse.mdf" to the C:\MSSQL\Data directory. After that, execute the following:

```
ALTER DATABASE BookWarehouse
MODIFY FILE
(NAME = 'BookWarehouse', FILENAME = 'C:\MSSQL\Data\BookWarehouse.mdf')
GO
```

This returns:

```
The file "BookWarehouse" has been modified in the system catalog. The new path will be
used the next time the database is started.
```

Finally, the database must then be brought back online:

```
ALTER DATABASE BookWarehouse
SET ONLINE
GO
```

How It Works

The recipe started by creating a new database with default options. The database was then taken offline. Once offline, the data file was copied to the new location.

Once the file was moved, SQL Server was informed of the change by using the ALTER DATABASE and the MODIFY FILE statement:

```
ALTER DATABASE BookWarehouse
MODIFY FILE
(NAME = 'BookWarehouse', FILENAME = 'C:\MSSQL\Data\BookWarehouse.mdf')
GO
```

After that, the database was brought back online by using ALTER DATABASE and SET ONLINE.

Changing a File's Logical Name

You can change a database file's logical name without having to bring the database offline. The logical name of a database doesn't affect the functionality of the database itself, allowing you to change the name for consistency and naming convention purposes. For example, if you restore a database from backup using a new database name, you may wish for the logical name to match the new database name.

The syntax for changing a logical file name is as follows:

```
ALTER DATABASE database_name
{NAME = logical_file_name
    [ , NEWNAME = new_logical_name ] }
```

The arguments of this syntax are briefly described in Table 22-14.

Table 22-14. *ALTER DATABASE...NEWNAME*

Argument	Description
database_name	The name of the existing database.
logical_file_name	The logical file name to be renamed.
new_logical_name	The new logical file name.

This recipe changes the logical data file name of the BookWarehouse data file in the BookWarehouse database:

```
ALTER DATABASE BookWarehouse
MODIFY FILE
(NAME = 'BookWarehouse', NEWNAME = 'BookWarehouse_DataFile1')
GO
```

This returns:

```
The file name 'BookWarehouse_DataFile1' has been set.
```

How It Works

This recipe modified the BookWarehouse logical file name to BookWarehouse_DataFile1 by using ALTER DATABASE with the MODIFY FILE command. The command used the original NAME value and the NEWNAME value in order to make the change.

Increasing a Database's File Size and Modifying Its Growth Options

The previous recipe demonstrated how to change the logical filename using ALTER DATABASE and MODIFY FILE. With the MODIFY FILE command you can also change the file sizing settings.

The syntax is as follows:

```
ALTER DATABASE database_name
MODIFY FILE
(
NAME = logical_file_name
[ , SIZE = size [ KB | MB | GB | TB ] ]
[ , MAXSIZE = { max_size [ KB | MB | GB | TB ] |
UNLIMITED } ]
[ , FILEGROWTH = growth_increment [ KB | MB | % ] ]
)
```

The arguments of this syntax are briefly described in Table 22-15.

Table 22-15. *ALTER DATABASE...MODIFY FILE*

Argument	Description
database_name	The name of the existing database.
logical_file_name	The logical file name to change size or growth options for.
size [KB	MB	GB	TB]	The new size (must be larger than the existing size) of the file based on the sizing attribute of choice (kilobytes, megabytes, gigabytes, terabytes).
{ max_size [KB	MB	GB	TB]	UNLIMITED }]	The new maximum allowable size of the file based on the chosen sizing attributes. If UNLIMITED is chosen, the file can grow to the available space of the physical drive.
growth_increment [KB	MB	%]]	The new amount that the file size increases when space is required. You can either designate the number of kilobytes or megabytes, or the percentage of existing file size to grow. If you select 0, file growth will not occur.

In this recipe, a file is increased to 6MB in size and given a maximum allowable size of 10MB:

```
ALTER DATABASE BookWarehouse
MODIFY FILE
(NAME='BookWarehouse_DataFile1', SIZE=6MB, MAXSIZE=10MB)
```

How It Works

This recipe used ALTER DATABASE and MODIFY FILE to change a specific file's existing size as well as its maximum allowable size. The NAME option was referenced to specify which file was to be modified. The other two options, SIZE and MAXSIZE, were used to configure the new file size and maximum file size values.

Adding a Filegroup to an Existing Database

This recipe demonstrates how to add a filegroup to an existing database using ALTER DATABASE. Once the filegroup is created, you can then add a file or files to it.

The syntax is as follows:

```
ALTER DATABASE database_name
ADD FILEGROUP filegroup_name
```

The arguments of this syntax are described in Table 22-16.

Table 22-16. *ALTER DATABASE...ADD FILEGROUP*

Argument	Description
database_name	The name of the existing database.
filegroup_name	The name of the new filegroup.

This recipe adds a new filegroup to the BookWarehouse database:

```
ALTER DATABASE BookWarehouse
ADD FILEGROUP FG2
GO

ALTER DATABASE BookWarehouse
ADD FILE
(   NAME = 'BW2',
    FILENAME = 'C:\Program Files\Microsoft SQL Server\MSSQL.1\MSSQL\DATA\BW2.NDF' ,
    SIZE = 1MB ,
    MAXSIZE = 50MB,
    FILEGROWTH = 5MB )
TO FILEGROUP [FG2]
GO
```

How It Works

This recipe used ALTER DATABASE and ADD FILEGROUP to add a new filegroup called FG2 to an existing database. A new file was then added to the filegroup using ALTER DATABASE, ADD FILE, and the TO FILEGROUP command.

Setting the Default Filegroup

This recipe demonstrates how to change a filegroup into the default filegroup, meaning that the filegroup will contain all newly created database objects by default (unless database objects are explicitly put in a different filegroup during their creation).

The syntax for setting a filegroup to the database default is as follows:

```
ALTER DATABASE database_name
MODIFY FILEGROUP filegroup_name
DEFAULT
```

This recipe sets the FG2 filegroup in the BookWarehouse database to the default filegroup:

```
ALTER DATABASE BookWarehouse
MODIFY FILEGROUP FG2 DEFAULT
```

This returns:

```
The filegroup property 'DEFAULT' has been set.
```

How It Works

This recipe used ALTER DATABASE and MODIFY FILEGROUP to change an existing filegroup to the default filegroup. The DEFAULT keyword was used after the name of the new default filegroup.

Removing a Filegroup

This recipe demonstrates how to remove a user-defined filegroup. You can remove an empty filegroup using the following syntax:

```
ALTER DATABASE database_name
REMOVE FILEGROUP filegroup_name
```

The arguments of this syntax are briefly described in Table 22-17.

Table 22-17. *ALTER DATABASE...REMOVE FILEGROUP*

Argument	Description
database_name	The name of the database to drop the user-defined filegroup from.
filegroup_name	The name of the user-defined filegroup to drop.

In this recipe, I'll add a new filegroup called FG3 to the BookWarehouse database. A new file will then be created within the filegroup. After that, the file will be removed, and then the user-defined filegroup will be removed:

```
ALTER DATABASE BookWarehouse
ADD FILEGROUP FG3
GO

ALTER DATABASE BookWarehouse
ADD FILE
(   NAME = 'BW3',
    FILENAME = 'C:\Program Files\Microsoft SQL Server\MSSQL.1\MSSQL\DATA\BW3.NDF' ,
    SIZE = 1MB ,
    MAXSIZE = 10MB,
    FILEGROWTH = 5MB )
TO FILEGROUP [FG3]
GO

-- Now, the file in the filegroup is removed
ALTER DATABASE BookWarehouse
REMOVE FILE BW3
GO

-- Then the filegroup
ALTER DATABASE BookWarehouse
REMOVE FILEGROUP FG3
GO
```

This returns:

```
The file 'BW3' has been removed.
The filegroup 'FG3' has been removed.
```

How It Works

A user-defined filegroup can be removed once it is empty. In this recipe, ALTER DATABASE and REMOVE FILE were used to first empty the FG3 user-defined filegroup of files. Once empty of files, ALTER DATABASE and REMOVE FILEGROUP were used to remove the filegroup from the database.

Making a Database or Filegroup Read-Only

You can use ALTER DATABASE to set the database or specific user-defined filegroup to read-only access. Making a database or filegroup read-only prevents data modifications from taking place, and is often used for static reporting databases. Using read-only options can improve query performance, because SQL Server no longer needs to lock objects queried within the database due to the fact that data and object modification in the database or user-defined filegroup is *not* allowed (although this isn't a replacement for setting up appropriate security permissions for data and object modifications).

The syntax for changing a database's updateability is as follows:

```
ALTER DATABASE database_name
SET { READ_ONLY | READ_WRITE }
```

The arguments for this statement only require the database name, and the updateability option to be set.

The syntax for changing a filegroup's updateability is as follows:

```
ALTER DATABASE database_name
MODIFY FILEGROUP filegroup_name
{ READ_ONLY | READ_WRITE }
```

All that is needed in this syntax block is the database name, filegroup, and updateability option.

This recipe demonstrates setting the entire BookWarehouse to read-only mode, and then setting it back to read-write mode (where modifications can then be made again). After this, the recipe demonstrates setting the updateability of a specific filegroup:

```
-- Make the database read only
ALTER DATABASE BookWarehouse
SET READ_ONLY
GO

-- Allow updates again
ALTER DATABASE BookWarehouse
SET READ_WRITE
GO

-- Add a new filegroup
ALTER DATABASE BookWarehouse
ADD FILEGROUP FG4
GO

-- Add a file to the filegroup
ALTER DATABASE BookWarehouse
ADD FILE
```

```
(    NAME = 'BW4',
     FILENAME = 'C:\Program Files\Microsoft SQL Server\MSSQL.1\MSSQL\DATA\BW4.NDF' ,
     SIZE = 1MB ,
     MAXSIZE = 50MB,
     FILEGROWTH = 5MB )
TO FILEGROUP [FG4]
GO

-- Make a specific filegroup read-only
ALTER DATABASE BookWarehouse
MODIFY FILEGROUP FG4 READ_ONLY
GO

-- Allow updates again
ALTER DATABASE BookWarehouse
MODIFY FILEGROUP FG4 READ_WRITE
GO
```

How It Works

This recipe demonstrated changing the updateability of both a database and a specific filegroup. To modify the database, ALTER DATABASE and SET READ_ONLY were used. SET READ_WRITE was used to allow updates again. The last two queries in the recipe updated a specific filegroup, using ALTER DATABASE and MODIFY FILEGROUP to change updateability.

Viewing and Managing Database Space Usage

The last set of recipes in this chapter covers how to manage and view database disk storage usage. You'll learn how to shrink an entire database, or just the individual files within, depending on your needs. This next recipe demonstrates how to view space usage with the sp_spaceused system-stored procedure.

Viewing Database Space Usage

This recipe demonstrates how to display database data disk space usage using the sp_spaceused system-stored procedure. To view transaction log usage, I'll also demonstrate the DBCC SQLPERF command.

The syntax for sp_spaceused is as follows:

```
sp_spaceused [[ @objname = ] 'objname' ]
[,[ @updateusage = ] 'updateusage' ]
```

The parameters of this procedure are briefly described in Table 22-18.

Table 22-18. *sp_spaceused Parameters*

Parameter	Description
'objname'	The optional object name (table, for example) to view space usage. If not designated, the entire database's space usage information is returned.
'updateusage'	This parameter is used with a specific object, and accepts either true or false. If true, DBCC UPDATEUSAGE is used to update space usage information in the system tables.

The syntax for DBCC SQLPERF is as follows:

```
DBCC SQLPERF ( LOGSPACE )
[WITH NO_INFOMSGS ]
```

This DBCC command's arguments are briefly described in Table 22-19.

Table 22-19. *DBCC SQLPERF Arguments*

Parameter	Description
LOGSPACE	This is the only documented parameter allowed, and when designated, returns transaction log space information for the entire SQL Server instance.
WITH NO_INFOMSGS	When included in the command, WITH NO_INFOMSGS suppresses informational messages from the DBCC output.

In this recipe, database and transaction log space will be viewed for the AdventureWorks database:

```
USE AdventureWorks
GO

EXEC sp_spaceused
```

This returns:

```
database_name    database_size  unallocated space  reserved    data       index_size  unused
AdventureWorks   192.63 MB      26.09 MB           168480 KB   84416 KB   77584 KB    6480 KB
```

Next, transaction log information is displayed for the entire SQL Server instance:

```
DBCC SQLPERF ( LOGSPACE )
```

This returns:

```
Database Name         Log Size (MB) Log Space Used (%) Status
--------------------- ------------- ------------------ -----------
master                0.4921875     69.02437           0
tempdb                0.4921875     62.50349           0
model                 0.4921875     69.04762           0
msdb                  0.7421875     53.15789           0
AdventureWorksDW      1.992188      20.58824           0
AdventureWorks        1.992188      33.33333           0

(6 row(s) affected)

DBCC execution completed. If DBCC printed error messages, contact your system
administrator.
```

How It Works

In this recipe, space usage for the AdventureWorks database was returned using the system-stored procedure sp_spaceused and the DBCC SQLPERF command.

In the results of sp_spaceused, the database_size column showed the current size of the database (including both the data and log files). The unallocated space column showed unused space in the database and the reserved column the amount of space used by database objects. The data column showed the amount of space used by the object data, and index_size the amount of space used by indexes.

The output of DBCC SQLPERF returned data for all databases on the SQL Server instance, showing the log size in megabytes and the percentage of the log file currently being used with active or inactive log information.

Shrinking the Database or a Database File

In this recipe, I demonstrate how to shrink an entire database using DBCC SHRINKDATABASE or a specific database file using DBCC SHRINKFILE. When following this recipe, keep in mind that shrinking databases and database files is a relatively expensive operation, and should only be performed when necessary.

Database files, when auto-growth is enabled, can expand due to index rebuilds or data modification activity. You may have extra space in the database due to data modifications and index rebuilds. If you don't need to free up the unused space, you should allow the database to keep it reserved. However, if you do need the unused space and want to free it up, use DBCC SHRINKDATABASE or DBCC SHRINKFILE.

The DBCC SHRINKDATABASE command is use to shrink data and log files in a database.

Note This command will shrink individual data files (MDF, NDF) on an individual basis, but will shrink the transaction log file or files (LDF) as if the multiple transaction log files were one continuous file.

The syntax is as follows:

```
DBCC SHRINKDATABASE
( 'database_name' | database_id | 0
    [ ,target_percent ]
    [ , { NOTRUNCATE | TRUNCATEONLY } ]
)
[ WITH NO_INFOMSGS ]
```

The arguments for this command are described in Table 22-20.

Table 22-20. *DBCC SHRINKDATABASE Arguments*

Argument	Description
'database_name' | database_id | 0	You can designate a specific database name to shrink the system database id, or if 0 is specified, the current database your query session is connected to.
target_percent	The target percentage designates the free space remaining in the database file after the shrinking event.
NOTRUNCATE | TRUNCATEONLY	NOTRUNCATE performs the data movements needed to create free space, but retains the freed space in the file without releasing it to the operating system. If NOTRUNCATE is not designated, the free file space is released to the operating system. TRUNCATEONLY frees up space without relocating data within the files. If not designated, data pages are reallocated within the files to free up space, which can lead to extensive I/O.
WITH NO_INFOMSGS	Prevents informational messages from being returned from the DBCC command.

The DBCC SHRINKFILE command is use to shrink a specific database file in a database. The syntax is as follows:

```
DBCC SHRINKFILE
(
    { ' file_name ' | file_id }
    { [ , EMPTYFILE]
    | [ [ , target_size ] [ , { NOTRUNCATE | TRUNCATEONLY } ] ]
    }
)
[ WITH NO_INFOMSGS ]
```

The arguments for this command are described in Table 22-21.

Table 22-21. *DBCC SHRINKFILE Arguments*

Argument	Description
' file_name '	file_id	The specific logical file name or file id to shrink.
EMPTYFILE	Moves all data off the file so that it can be dropped using ALTER DATABASE and REMOVE FILE.
target_size	The free space to be left in the database file (in megabytes). Leaving this blank instructs SQL Server to free up space to the default file size.
NOTRUNCATE	TRUNCATEONLY	NOTRUNCATE relocates allocated pages from within the file to the front of the file, but does not free the space to the operating system. Target size is ignored when used with NOTRUNCATE. TRUNCATEONLY causes unused space in the file to be released to the operating system, but only does so with free space found at the end of the file. No pages are rearranged or relocated. Target size is also ignored with the TRUNCATEONLY option. Use this option if you must free up space on the database file with minimal impact on database performance (rearranging pages on an actively utilized production database can cause performance issues, such as slow query response time).
WITH NO_INFOMSGS	Prevents informational messages from being returned from the DBCC command.

In this recipe, the AdventureWorks will have its files expanded by allocating additional space using ALTER DATABASE...MODIFY FILE, and then shrunk using the two DBCC file and database shrinking commands. In the first example, the AdventureWorks data and transaction log file are both expanded to larger sizes, and then shrunk using a single DBCC operation:

```
ALTER DATABASE AdventureWorks
MODIFY FILE (NAME = AdventureWorks_Data , SIZE= 250MB)
GO

ALTER DATABASE AdventureWorks
MODIFY FILE (NAME = AdventureWorks_Log , SIZE= 500MB)
GO
```

The sp_spaceused system-stored procedure is then used to return the space usage for the AdventureWorks database:

```
USE AdventureWorks
GO

EXEC sp_spaceused
GO
```

This returns:

database_name	database_size	unallocated space
AdventureWorks	750.00 MB	85.45 MB

reserved	data	index_size	unused
168496 KB	83896 KB	78024 KB	6576 KB

Next, the size is reduced using DBCC SHRINKDATABASE:

```
DBCC SHRINKDATABASE ('AdventureWorks', 10)
```

This returns:

DbId	FileId	CurrentSize	MinimumSize	UsedPages	EstimatedPages
6	1	23416	15360	21064	21064
6	2	8224	256	8224	256

In the second example of this recipe, only the transaction log file is expanded, and then shrunk using DBCC SHRINKFILE:

```
ALTER DATABASE AdventureWorks
MODIFY FILE (NAME = AdventureWorks_Log , SIZE= 150MB)
GO
```

The sp_spaceused system-stored procedure is then used to return the space usage for the AdventureWorks database:

```
USE AdventureWorks
GO

EXEC sp_spaceused
GO
```

This returns:

database_name	database_size	unallocated space
AdventureWorks	332.31 MB	17.77 MB

reserved	data	index_size	unused
168496 KB	83896 KB	78024 KB	6576 KB

Next, the size is reduced using DBCC SHRINKDATABASE:

```
DBCC SHRINKFILE ('AdventureWorks_Log', 100)
```

This returns:

DbId	FileId	CurrentSize	MinimumSize	UsedPages	EstimatedPages
6	2	13696	256	13696	256

How It Works

DBCC SHRINKDATABASE shrinks the data and log files in your database. The behavior of this DBCC command is deceptively simple; but there are many details you should be aware of:

- DBCC SHRINKDATABASE shrinks each data file on a per-file basis, but treats the transaction log or logs as a single entity.
- The database can never shrink smaller than the model database.
- You cannot shrink a database past the target percentage specified.
- You cannot shrink a file past the original file creation size, or size used in an ALTER DATABASE statement.

In this recipe, the AdventureWorks data and log files were both increased to a larger size. After that, the DBCC SHRINKDATABASE command was used to reduce it down to a target free space size of 10%:

```
DBCC SHRINKDATABASE ('AdventureWorks', 10)
```

After execution, the command returned a result set showing the current size (in 8KB pages), minimum size (in 8KB pages), currently used 8KB pages, and estimated 8KB pages that SQL Server could shrink the file down to.

DbId	FileId	CurrentSize	MinimumSize	UsedPages	EstimatedPages
6	1	23416	15360	21064	21064
6	2	8224	256	8224	256

In the second part of the recipe, DBCC SHRINKFILE was demonstrated. DBCC SHRINKFILE is very similar to DBCC SHRINKDATABASE, only it allows you to shrink the size of individual data and log files instead of all files in the database. In this recipe, the AdventureWorks transaction log file was expanded, and then shrunk down to a specific size (in megabytes):

```
DBCC SHRINKFILE ('AdventureWorks_Log', 100)
```

This command shrinks the physical file by removing inactive virtual log files. Virtual log files (VLFs), which range in size from a minimum 256 kilobytes and larger, are the unit of truncation for a transaction log and are created as records are written to the transaction log.

Within the transaction log is the "active" logical portion of the log. This is the area of the transaction log containing active transactions. This active portion does not usually match the physical bounds of the file, but will instead "round robin" from VLF to VLF. Once a VLF no longer contains active transactions, it can be truncated through a BACKUP LOG operation or automated system truncation. This truncation doesn't reduce the size of the transaction log file; it only makes the VLFs available for new log records.

DBCC SHRINKFILE or DBCC SHRINKDATABASE will make its best effort to remove inactive VLFs from the end of the physical file. SQL Server will also attempt to add "dummy" rows to push the active logical log towards the beginning of the physical file—so sometimes issuing a BACKUP LOG after the first execution of the DBCC SHRINKFILE command, and then issuing the DBCC SHRINKFILE command again, will allow you to free up the originally requested space.

■ ■ ■

Database Integrity and Optimization

In the previous chapter, I showed you how to create, configure, modify and drop a database. In this chapter I'll show you how to maintain your database using the Transact-SQL language, including ways to use SQL Server 2005's new ALTER INDEX command for rebuilding or defragmenting indexes, and DBCC commands for helping identify database integrity problems.

In previous versions of SQL Server, DBCC commands such as DBCC CHECKDB were resource-intensive, and could adversely affect performance if executed on a busy SQL Server instance. In SQL Server 2005, Microsoft has enhanced several of the DBCC commands to use internal database snapshots of target data instead of using table or database locks. Several of the commands are also more thorough in their checking routines than in previous versions of SQL Server.

■**Caution** Several of the DBCC commands reviewed in this chapter have REPAIR options. With SQL Server 2005, Microsoft now recommends that you solve data integrity issues by restoring the database from the last good backup rather then resorting to a REPAIR option. If restoring from backup is not an option, the REPAIR option should be used only as a last resort. Depending on the REPAIR option selected, data loss can occur, and the problem may still not be resolved.

This chapter contains recipes that you can run periodically to check for database integrity issues. Running periodic checks (daily, weekly, and so on) will allow you to identify internal errors that can occur in various areas of the database.

As data is modified in your databases, the tables and indexes can become fragmented. The more fragmented a clustered or nonclustered index becomes, the more potential pages are required to be returned by the database engine in order to fulfill the same query request. The last two recipes in this chapter will address how to rebuild or defragment these indexes on a periodic basis, using Transact-SQL.

Database Checking

Database integrity errors are rare, but do occur. The next two recipes will review the commands used to validate and check for issues within a database. You'll learn how to check page usage and allocation in the database by using DBCC CHECKALLOC. You'll also learn how to check the integrity of database objects using DBCC CHECKDB.

Before getting into the recipes, however, I think that a quick discussion of disk space allocation structures is in order. When I talk about page allocation and integrity of database objects, it is important to understand what exactly is being verified. At a high level, I'm talking about verification of SQL Server's central unit of storage, the 8KB page. SQL Server reads and writes data at the page level. Pages are stored in blocks called extents, which consist of eight contiguous 8KB pages. Internally, a page includes header information which tracks the free space and usage of that page. There are different page types used to store varying types of data. These page types include data pages (storing data types such as char, int, datetime), index data pages, and large data type data pages (for example varchar(max), xml, varbinary(max)). There are also varying page types used to track system metadata, including information for where pages and extents are allocated, where free space is available, which extents contain table or index data, the extents last modified by bulk operations, and more.

Checking Consistency of the Disk Space Allocation Structures with DBCC CHECKALLOC

DBCC CHECKALLOC checks page usage and allocation in the database, and will report on any errors that are found (this command is automatically included in the execution of DBCC CHECKDB too).

The syntax is as follows:

```
DBCC CHECKALLOC
(
    [ 'database_name' | database_id | 0 ]
        [ , NOINDEX
    |
    { REPAIR_ALLOW_DATA_LOSS
    | REPAIR_FAST
    | REPAIR_REBUILD
    } ]
)
    [ WITH { [ ALL_ERRORMSGS ]
            [ , NO_INFOMSGS ]
            [ , TABLOCK ]
            [ , ESTIMATEONLY ]
        }
    ]
```

The arguments of this command are described in Table 23-1.

Table 23-1. *DBCC CHECKALLOC Arguments*

Argument	Description
'database_name' | database_id | 0	The database name or database ID that you want to check for errors. When 0 is selected, the current database is used.
NOINDEX	When used, nonclustered indexes are not included in the checks.
REPAIR_ALLOW_DATA_LOSS | REPAIR_FAST | REPAIR_REBUILD	See the beginning of the chapter regarding a warning on using repair options. REPAIR_ALLOW_DATA_LOSS attempts a repair of the table or indexed view, with the risk of losing data in the process. REPAIR_FAST and REPAIR_REBUILD are maintained for backward-compatibility only.
ALL_ERRORMSGS	When ALL_ERRORMSGS is chosen, every error found will be displayed. If this option isn't designated, a maximum of 200 error messages can be displayed.
NO_INFOMSGS	NO_INFOMSGS represses all informational messages from the DBCC output.
TABLOCK	When selected, an exclusive table lock is placed on the table instead of using an internal database snapshot, thus potentially decreasing query concurrency in the database.
ESTIMATEONLY	Provides the estimated space needed by the tempdb database to execute the command.

In this brief recipe, data page usage and allocation will be checked for errors in the AdventureWorks database:

```
DBCC CHECKALLOC ('AdventureWorks')
```

This returns the following results (abridged). It includes information about pages used, and extents for each index. The key piece of information is in the final line, where you can see the reporting of the number of allocation errors and consistency errors encountered:

```
DBCC results for 'AdventureWorks'.
...
*****************************************************************
Table Person.Address            Object ID 53575229.
Index ID 1, partition ID 72057594042974208, alloc unit ID 72057594048086016 (type
...
Index ID 4, partition ID 72057594047627264, alloc unit ID 72057594053066752 (type
In-row data). 29 pages used in 4 dedicated extents.
Total number of extents is 76.
*****************************************************************
...
   Object ID 2130106629, index ID 1, partition ID 72057594046840832, alloc unit ID
72057594052214784 (type In-row data), data extents 13, pages 103, mixed extent pages
2.
...
CHECKALLOC found 0 allocation errors and 0 consistency errors in database
'AdventureWorks'.
DBCC execution completed. If DBCC printed error messages, contact your system
administrator.
```

How It Works

In this brief recipe, the DBCC CHECKALLOC command was used to verify the allocation of all database pages and internal structures in the AdventureWorks database. Informational data was returned, including the internal page information, number of extents, and pages. At the end of the command, any allocation or consistency errors were reported (in this case, none were found).

When DBCC CHECKALLOC is executed, an internal database snapshot is created to maintain transactional consistency during the operation. If for some reason a database snapshot can't be created, or if TABLOCK is specified, an exclusive database lock is acquired during the execution of the command (thus potentially hurting database query concurrency). Unless you have a good reason not to, you should allow SQL Server 2005 to issue an internal database snapshot, so that concurrency in your database is not impacted.

Checking Allocation and Structural Integrity of All Database Objects with DBCC CHECKDB

The DBCC CHECKDB command checks the integrity of objects in a database. Running DBCC CHECKDB periodically against your databases is a good maintenance practice. Weekly execution is usually sufficient; however, the optimal frequency all depends on the activity and size of the database in question. If possible, DBCC CHECKDB should be executed during periods of light database activity. Doing it this way will allow DBCC CHECKDB to finish faster, and keep other processes from being slowed down by its overhead.

Like the other commands I've described in this chapter, an internal database snapshot is created to maintain transactional consistency during the operation when this command is executed. If for some reason a database snapshot cannot be created (or the TABLOCK option was specified), shared table locks are held for table checks, and exclusive database locks for the allocation checks.

As part of its execution, DBCC CHECKDB executes other DBCC commands that are discussed elsewhere in this chapter, including DBCC CHECKTABLE, DBCC CHECKALLOC, and DBCC CHECKCATALOG. In addition to this, the integrity of SQL Server 2005 Service Broker data is validated as well.

The syntax for DBCC CHECKDB is as follows:

```
DBCC CHECKDB
(
        'database_name' | database_id | 0
    [ , NOINDEX
    | { REPAIR_ALLOW_DATA_LOSS
    | REPAIR_FAST
    | REPAIR_REBUILD
    } ]
)
    [ WITH        {
            [ ALL_ERRORMSGS ]
            [ , [ NO_INFOMSGS ] ]
            [ , [ TABLOCK ] ]
            [ , [ ESTIMATEONLY ] ]
            [ , [ PHYSICAL_ONLY ] ]
            [ , [ DATA_PURITY ] ]
        }
    ]
```

The arguments of this command, which will look familiar based on previous commands reviewed in this chapter, are described in Table 23-2.

Table 23-2. *DBCC CHECKDB Arguments*

Argument	Description
'database_name' | database_id | 0	The database name or database ID that you want to check for errors. When 0 is selected, the current database is used.
NOINDEX	Nonclustered indexes are not included in the integrity checks when this option is selected.
REPAIR_ALLOW_DATA_LOSS | REPAIR_FAST | REPAIR_REBUILD	See the beginning of the chapter regarding a warning on using repair options. REPAIR_ALLOW_DATA_LOSS attempts a repair of the table or indexed view, with the risk of losing data in the process. REPAIR_FAST is maintained for backward compatibility only and REPAIR_REBUILD performs fixes without risk of data loss.
ALL_ERRORMSGS	When ALL_ERRORMSGS is chosen, every error found will be displayed (instead of just the default 200 error message limit).
NO_INFOMSGS	NO_INFOMSGS represses all informational messages from the DBCC output.
TABLOCK	When selected, an exclusive database lock is used instead of an internal database snapshot. Using this option decreases concurrency with other queries being executed against objects in the database.
ESTIMATEONLY	Provides the estimated space needed by the tempdb database to execute the command.

Argument	Description
PHYSICAL_ONLY	Limits the integrity checks to physical issues only, skipping logical checks.
DATA_PURITY	For use on upgraded databases (from previous versions of SQL Server), this instructs DBCC CHECKDB to detect column values that do not conform to the data type (for example if an integer value has a bigint-sized value stored in it). Once all bad values in the upgraded database are cleaned up, SQL Server 2005 maintains the column-value integrity moving forward.

Despite all of these syntax options, the common form of executing this command is also most likely the simplest. This brief recipe executes DBCC CHECKDB against the AdventureWorks database. For thorough integrity and data checking of your database, the default is often suitable:

```
DBCC CHECKDB('AdventureWorks')
```

This returns the following informational results detailing the database objects evaluated within the database, including the number of rows, pages, and—most importantly at the end—number of allocation or consistency errors found:

```
DBCC results for 'AdventureWorks'.
Service Broker Msg 9675, State 1: Message Types analyzed: 14.
Service Broker Msg 9676, State 1: Service Contracts analyzed: 6.
...
DBCC results for 'sys.sysrowsetcolumns'.
There are 1301 rows in 9 pages for object "sys.sysrowsetcolumns".
DBCC results for 'sys.sysrowsets'.
...
There are 6 rows in 1 pages for object "Person.AddressType".
DBCC results for 'Production.ProductSubcategory'.
There are 37 rows in 1 pages for object "Production.ProductSubcategory".
DBCC results for 'AWBuildVersion'.
There are 1 rows in 1 pages for object "AWBuildVersion".
DBCC results for 'Production.TransactionHistoryArchive'.
There are 89253 rows in 620 pages for object "Production.TransactionHistoryArchive".
...
CHECKDB found 0 allocation errors and 0 consistency errors in database 'AdventureWorks'.
DBCC execution completed. If DBCC printed error messages, contact your system
administrator.
```

How It Works

In this recipe a thorough integrity check was performed against the AdventureWorks database using DBCC CHECKDB, including the name of the database within parentheses:

```
DBCC CHECKDB('AdventureWorks')
```

This command returned several lines of information, including the final information about the number of allocation or consistency errors.

As I warned in the beginning of this chapter, you should be aware that if DBCC encounters errors, Microsoft now recommends that you solve data integrity issues by restoring the database from the last good backup rather then resorting to REPAIR options. If restoring from backup is not an option, the REPAIR options should be used only as a last resort. Depending on the REPAIR options selected, data loss can occur, and the problem may still not be resolved.

Tables and Constraints

The next set of recipes demonstrates DBCC commands used to validate integrity at the constraint and table level. Specifically, I'll be demonstrating how to use:

- DBCC CHECKFILEGROUP, which is very similar to DBCC CHECKDB, but limits integrity and allocation checking to objects within a specified filegroup.

- DBCC CHECKTABLE, which is used to identify any integrity issues for a specific table or indexed view.

- DBCC CHECKCONSTRAINTS, which alerts you to any CHECK or constraint violations found in a specific table or constraint.

Lastly, I'll review how to check for consistency in and between system tables using the DBCC CHECKCATALOG command.

Checking Allocation and Structural Integrity of All Tables in a Filegroup Using DBCC CHECKFILEGROUP

The DBCC CHECKFILEGROUP command is very similar to DBCC CHECKDB, only it limits its integrity and allocation checking to objects within a single filegroup. For very large databases (VLDB) performing a DBCC CHECKDB operation may be time-prohibitive. If you use user defined filegroups in your database, you can use DBCC CHECKFILEGROUP to perform your weekly (or periodic) checks instead—spreading out filegroup checks across different days.

When this command is executed, an internal database snapshot is created to maintain transactional consistency during the operation. If, for some reason, a database snapshot can't be created (or the TABLOCK option was specified), shared table locks are created by the command for table checks, as well as an exclusive database lock for the allocation checks.

Again, if errors are found by DBCC CHECKDB, with SQL Server 2005, Microsoft now recommends that you solve any discovered issues by restoring from the last good database backup. Unlike other DBCC commands in this chapter, DBCC CHECKFILEGROUP doesn't have repair options (although repair options are no longer recommended by Microsoft anyhow).

The syntax is as follows:

```
DBCC CHECKFILEGROUP
(
[ { 'filegroup' | filegroup_id | 0 } ]
[ , NOINDEX ]
)
    [ WITH
        {
            [ ALL_ERRORMSGS | NO_INFOMSGS ]
            [ , [ TABLOCK ] ]
            [ , [ ESTIMATEONLY ] ]
        }
        ]
```

The arguments of this command are described in Table 23-3.

Table 23-3. *DBCC CHECKFILEGROUP Arguments*

Argument	Description
`'filegroup'` | `filegroup_id` | `0`	The filegroup name or filegroup ID that you want to check. If 0 is designated, the primary filegroup is used.
`NOINDEX`	When designated, nonclustered indexes are not included in the integrity checks.
`ALL_ERRORMSGS`	When ALL_ERRORMSGS is chosen, all errors are displayed in the output, instead of the default 200 message limit.
`NO_INFOMSGS`	NO_INFOMSGS represses all informational messages from the DBCC output.
`TABLOCK`	When selected, an exclusive database lock is used instead of using an internal database snapshot (using this option decreases concurrency with other database queries, but speeds up the DBCC command execution).
`ESTIMATEONLY`	Provides the estimated space needed by the tempdb database to execute the command.

In this recipe, the primary filegroup integrity will be checked in the AdventureWorks database:

```
USE AdventureWorks
GO
DBCC CHECKFILEGROUP('PRIMARY')
```

This returns the following abridged results:

```
DBCC results for 'AdventureWorks'.
DBCC results for 'sys.sysrowsetcolumns'.
There are 1301 rows in 9 pages for object "sys.sysrowsetcolumns".
DBCC results for 'sys.sysrowsets'.
There are 248 rows in 2 pages for object "sys.sysrowsets".
DBCC results for 'sysallocunits'.
...
There are 10 rows in 1 pages for object "Sales.SalesReason".
DBCC results for 'Sales.Individual'.
There are 18484 rows in 3082 pages for object "Sales.Individual".
DBCC results for 'Sales.SalesTaxRate'.
...
CHECKFILEGROUP found 0 allocation errors and 0 consistency errors in database
'AdventureWorks'.
DBCC execution completed. If DBCC printed error messages, contact your system
administrator.
```

How It Works

In this recipe, allocation and structural integrity were checked for all objects in the PRIMARY filegroup in the AdventureWorks database. The result output showed row and page counts for filegroup objects and a sum total of the number of allocation and consistency errors found (reported at the end). Like the other DBCC commands, the second to last line is most critical for knowing if there are any issues:

```
CHECKFILEGROUP found 0 allocation errors and 0 consistency errors
in database 'AdventureWorks'.
```

Checking Data Integrity for Tables and Indexed Views Using DBCC CHECKTABLE

Although stability has increased with each version of SQL Server, data integrity issues can still occur. In order to identify issues in a specific table or indexed view, you can use the DBCC CHECKTABLE command. (If you want to run it for all tables and indexed views in the database, use DBCC CHECKDB instead, which performs DBCC CHECKTABLE for each table in your database).

In SQL Server 2005, when DBCC CHECKTABLE is executed, an internal database snapshot is created to maintain transactional consistency during the operation. If for some reason a database snapshot can't be created, a shared table lock is applied to the target table or indexed view instead (thus potentially hurting database query concurrency against the target objects).

The syntax is as follows:

```
DBCC CHECKTABLE
(
        'table_name' | 'view_name'
    [ , NOINDEX
    | index_id
    | { REPAIR_ALLOW_DATA_LOSS
    | REPAIR_FAST
    | REPAIR_REBUILD }
    ]
)
    [ WITH
        { [ ALL_ERRORMSGS | NO_INFOMSGS ]
          [ , [ TABLOCK ] ]
          [ , [ ESTIMATEONLY ] ]
          [ , [ PHYSICAL_ONLY ] ]
        }
    ]
```

The arguments of this command are described in Table 23-4.

Table 23-4. *DBCC CHECKTABLE Arguments*

Argument	Description
'table_name'	'view_name'	The table or indexed view you want to check.
NOINDEX	This keyword instructs the command not to check nonclustered indexes.
index_id	The specific ID of the index to be checked (if you are checking a specific index).
REPAIR_ALLOW_DATA_LOSS | REPAIR_FAST | REPAIR_REBUILD	See the warning on using REPAIR options at the beginning of the chapter. REPAIR_ALLOW_DATA_LOSS attempts a repair of the table or indexed view, with the risk of losing data in the process. REPAIR_FAST is no longer used, and is kept for backward compatibility only. REPAIR_REBUILD does repairs and index rebuilds without any risk of data loss.
ALL_ERRORMSGS	NO_INFOMSGS	When ALL_ERRORMSGS is chosen, every error found during the command execution will be displayed. NO_INFOMSGS represses all informational messages from the DBCC output. If neither option is designated, up to 200 error messages could be displayed.
TABLOCK	When selected, a shared table lock is placed on the table instead of using an internal database snapshot. Using this option decreases concurrency with other database queries accessing the table or indexed view.

Argument	Description
ESTIMATEONLY	Provides the estimated space needed by the tempdb database to execute the command (but doesn't actually execute the integrity checking).
PHYSICAL_ONLY	Limits the integrity checks to physical issues only, skipping logical checks.

This recipe provides a few examples of using the command. In the first example, the integrity of the Production.Product table will be checked in the AdventureWorks database:

```
DBCC CHECKTABLE ('Production.Product')
WITH ALL_ERRORMSGS
```

This returns (results vary based on your environment):

```
DBCC results for 'Production.Product'.
There are 504 rows in 13 pages for object "Production.Product".
DBCC execution completed. If DBCC printed error messages, contact your system
administrator.
```

In the next example in the recipe, we return an estimate of tempdb space required for a check on the Sales.SalesOrderDetail table. This allows you to know ahead of time if a specific CHECKTABLE operation requires more space than you have available:

```
DBCC CHECKTABLE ('Sales.SalesOrderDetail')
WITH ESTIMATEONLY
```

This returns (these results may differ from yours, since they are based in part on your local environment):

```
Estimated TEMPDB space needed for CHECKTABLES (KB)
--------------------------------------------------
1121

(1 row(s) affected)

DBCC execution completed. If DBCC printed error messages, contact your system
administrator.
```

This last example executes DBCC CHECKTABLE for a specific index, checking for physical errors only (no logical). First, however, the index ID needs to be determined:

```
SELECT index_id
FROM    sys.indexes
WHERE   object_id = OBJECT_ID('Sales.SalesOrderDetail')
AND name = 'IX_SalesOrderDetail_ProductID'
```

This returns:

```
index_id
-----------
3
```

Next, the index_id will be used in the command:

```
DBCC CHECKTABLE ('Sales.SalesOrderDetail', 3)
WITH PHYSICAL_ONLY
```

This returns:

```
DBCC execution completed. If DBCC printed error messages, contact your system
administrator.
```

How It Works

In this recipe, the first example demonstrated how to check the integrity of a single table, showing all error messages if they exist (instead of the 200 message maximum default). The name of the table to check was included as the first argument:

```
DBCC CHECKTABLE ('Production.Product')
```

The second argument, ALL_ERRORMSGS, designated that any and all error messages found would be returned:

```
WITH ALL_ERRORMSGSx
```

DBCC CHECKTABLE checks for errors regarding data page linkages, pointers, verification that rows in a partition are actually in the correct partition, and more.

In the second example, a tempdb size requirement estimate was returned for the Sales.SalesOrderDetail table by designating the WITH ESTIMATEONLY argument:

```
DBCC CHECKTABLE ('Sales.SalesOrderDetail')
WITH ESTIMATEONLY
```

In the last example, the index ID of the IX_SalesOrderDetail_ProductID index on the Sales.SalesOrderDetail table was retrieved from the sys.indexes system catalog view. After retrieving the index ID, it was used in the DBCC CHECKTABLE command along with the PHYSICAL_ONLY argument, which was used to skip logical integrity checks against that index.

Checking Table Integrity with DBCC CHECKCONSTRAINTS

DBCC CHECKCONSTRAINTS alerts you to any CHECK or foreign key constraint violations found in a specific table or constraint. This command allows you to return the violating data so that you can correct the constraint violation accordingly (although this command does not catch constraints that have been disabled using NOCHECK).

The syntax is as follows:

```
DBCC CHECKCONSTRAINTS
[( 'table_name' | table_id | 'constraint_name' |
constraint_id )]
[ WITH
{ ALL_CONSTRAINTS | ALL_ERRORMSGS } [ , NO_INFOMSGS ] ] ]
```

The arguments of this command are described in Table 23-5.

Table 23-5. *DBCC CHECKCONSTRAINTS Arguments*

Argument	Description
`'table_name' | table_id | 'constraint_name' | constraint_id`	The table name, table ID, constraint name, or constraint ID that you want to validate. If a specific object isn't designated, all the objects in the database will be evaluated.
`ALL_CONSTRAINTS | ALL_ERRORMSGS`	When `ALL_CONSTRAINTS` is selected, all constraints (enabled or disabled) are checked. When `ALL_ERRORMSGS` is selected, all rows that violate constraints are returned in the result set (instead of the default maximum of 200 rows).
`NO_INFOMSGS`	`NO_INFOMSGS` represses all informational messages from the DBCC output.

In this recipe, I demonstrate how to check the constraints of a table after a CHECK constraint has been violated:

```
ALTER TABLE Production.WorkOrder  NOCHECK CONSTRAINT CK_WorkOrder_EndDate
GO

-- Set an EndDate to earlier than a StartDate
UPDATE Production.WorkOrder
SET EndDate = '1/1/2001'
WHERE WorkOrderID = 1
GO

ALTER TABLE Production.WorkOrder  CHECK CONSTRAINT CK_WorkOrder_EndDate
GO

DBCC CHECKCONSTRAINTS ('Production.WorkOrder')
```

This returns the following results:

```
Table                      Constraint            Where
[Production].[WorkOrder]   [CK_WorkOrder_EndDate]   [StartDate] = '2001-07-04
00:00:00.000' AND [EndDate] = '2001-01-01 00:00:00.000'
```

How It Works

In this recipe, the check constraint called CK_WorkOrder on the Production.WorkOrder table was disabled, using the ALTER TABLE...NOCHECK CONSTRAINT command:

```
ALTER TABLE Production.WorkOrder  NOCHECK CONSTRAINT CK_WorkOrder_EndDate
GO
```

This disabled constraint restricted values in the EndDate column from being less than the date in the StartDate column.

After disabling the constraint, a row was updated to violate this check constraint's rule:

```
UPDATE Production.WorkOrder
SET EndDate = '1/1/2001'
WHERE WorkOrderID = 1
GO
```

The constraint was then re-enabled:

```
ALTER TABLE Production.WorkOrder
CHECK CONSTRAINT CK_WorkOrder_EndDate
GO
```

The DBCC CHECKCONSTRAINTS command was then executed against the table:

```
DBCC CHECKCONSTRAINTS('Production.WorkOrder')
```

The command returned the table name, constraint violated, and the reason why the constraint was violated:

```
Table                        Constraint                  Where
[Production].[WorkOrder]     [CK_WorkOrder_EndDate]      [StartDate] = '2001-07-04
00:00:00.000' AND [EndDate] = '2001-01-01 00:00:00.000'
```

Unlike several other database integrity DBCC commands, DBCC CHECKCONSTRAINTS is *not* run within DBCC CHECKDB, so you must execute it as a stand-alone process if you need to identify data constraint violations in the database.

Checking System Table Consistency with DBCC CHECKCATALOG

DBCC CHECKCATALOG checks for consistency in and between system tables (this is another command that is automatically included in the execution of DBCC CHECKDB).

The syntax is as follows:

```
DBCC CHECKCATALOG
[ ( 'database_name' | database_id | 0)]
    [ WITH NO_INFOMSGS ]
```

The arguments of this command are described in Table 23-6.

Table 23-6. *DBCC CHECKCATALOG Arguments*

Argument	Description
'database_name'	database_id	0	The database name or database ID to be checked for errors. When 0 is selected, the current database is used.
NO_INFOMSGS	NO_INFOMSGS represses all informational messages from the DBCC output.

In this brief recipe, system table consistency checks are performed for the entire AdventureWorks database:

```
DBCC CHECKCATALOG ('AdventureWorks')
```

This returns (assuming no errors found):

```
DBCC execution completed. If DBCC printed error messages, contact your system
administrator.
```

How It Works

In this recipe, the system catalog data was checked in the AdventureWorks database. Had errors been identified, they would have been returned in the command output. If errors are found, DBCC CHECKCATALOG doesn't have repair options, and a restore from the last good database backup may be your only repair option.

Like the other commands I've described in this chapter, when DBCC CHECKCATALOG is executed, an internal database snapshot is created to maintain transactional consistency during the operation. If for some reason a database snapshot cannot be created, an exclusive database lock is acquired during the execution of the command (thus potentially hurting database query concurrency).

Index Maintenance

Fragmentation is the natural byproduct of data modifications to a table. When data is updated in the database, the logical order of indexes (based on the index key) gets out of sync with the actual physical order of the data pages. As data pages become further and further out of order, more I/O operations are required in order to return results requested by a query. Rebuilding or reorganizing an index allows you to defragment the index by synchronizing the logical index order and reordering the physical data pages to match the logical index order. In the next two recipes, I'll demonstrate two methods you can use to defragment your indexes.

■**Tip** See Chapter 28 to learn how to display index fragmentation.

Rebuilding Indexes

If you've used previous versions of SQL Server, you may be searching this chapter for the DBCC DBREINDEX or DBCC INDEXDEFRAG commands, which were used to rebuild indexes and defragment indexes, respectively. DBCC DBREINDEX has been deprecated in place of the ALTER INDEX REBUILD command. DBCC INDEXDEFRAG, used to defragment an index while allowing access to the data, has been deprecated in place of ALTER INDEX REORGANIZE (covered in the next recipe).

Rebuilding an index serves many purposes, the most popular being the removal of fragmentation that occurs as data modifications are made to a table over time. As fragmentation increases, queries can slow. Rebuilding an index removes fragmentation of the index rows and frees up physical disk space.

Large indexes that are quite fragmented can reduce query speed. The frequency of how often you rebuild your indexes depends on your database size, how much data modification occurs, and how much activity occurs against your tables.

The syntax for ALTER INDEX in order to rebuild an index is as follows:

```
ALTER INDEX { index_name | ALL }
    ON <object>
    { REBUILD
    [ [ WITH ( <rebuild_index_option> [ ,...n ] ) ]
    | [ PARTITION = partition_number
[ WITH ( <single_partition_rebuild_index_option>
                        [ ,...n ] )
                ]
            ]
        ]
    }
```

The arguments of this command are described in Table 23-7.

Table 23-7. *ALTER INDEX...REBUILD Arguments*

Argument	Description
index_name | ALL	The name of the index to rebuild. If ALL is chosen, all indexes for the specified table or view will be rebuilt.
<object>	The name of the table or view that the index is built on.
<rebuild_index_option> [,...n]	One or more index options can be applied during a rebuild, including:
	FILLFACTOR = fillfactor: The FILLFACTOR percentage of an index refers to how full the leaf level of the index pages should be when the index is first created.
	PAD_INDEX = { ON | OFF }: When designated, used only in conjunction with FILLFACTOR, specifies a percentage of free space to be left open on the intermediate level pages of an index.
	SORT_IN_TEMPDB = { ON | OFF }: Stores intermediate index results in the tempdb system database.
	IGNORE_DUP_KEY = { ON | OFF }: When enabled, duplicate key values inserted into a unique index raise a warning, and only unique rows are inserted. When OFF, any non-unique value causes the entire transaction to fail.
	STATISTICS_NORECOMPUTE = { ON | OFF }: When enabled, automatic statistics updates no longer occur on the index.
	ONLINE = { ON | OFF }: If enabling this option and using SQL Server 2005 Enterprise Edition, the index will be available for queries and data modification during the rebuild process. When this option is OFF, the data in the index being rebuilt will be unavailable.
	ALLOW_ROW_LOCKS = { ON | OFF }: Specifies if row locks are allowed when using the index.
	ALLOW_PAGE_LOCKS = { ON | OFF }: Specifies if page locks are allowed when using the index.
	MAXDOP = max_degree_of_parallelism: This option overrides the "max degree of parallelism" server option, and is only available in SQL Server 2005 Enterprise Edition. When specifying a "1," processor parallelism won't be used during the index rebuild. If greater than "1" is specified, the number of processors used cannot exceed that number. If "0" is specified, SQL Server can use one or more processors (depending on your hardware).
partition_number	If using a partitioned index, the partition_number designates that only one partition of the index is rebuilt.
<single_partition_rebuild_index_option> [,...n]	If designating a partition rebuild, you are limited to using the following index options in the WITH clause: SORT_IN_TEMPDB and MAXDOP (both described in the rebuild_index_option description.

This recipe demonstrates `ALTER INDEX REBUILD`, which drops and recreates an existing index. It demonstrates a few variations for rebuilding an index in the AdventureWorks database:

```
-- Rebuild a specific index

ALTER INDEX PK_ShipMethod_ShipMethodID
ON Purchasing.ShipMethod  REBUILD

-- Rebuild all indexes on a specific table

ALTER INDEX ALL
ON Purchasing.PurchaseOrderHeader REBUILD

-- Rebuild an index, while keeping it available
-- for queries (requires Enterprise Edition)

ALTER INDEX PK_ProductReview_ProductReviewID
ON Production.ProductReview REBUILD
WITH (ONLINE = ON)

-- Rebuild an index, using a new fill factor and
-- sorting in tempdb

ALTER INDEX PK_TransactionHistory_TransactionID
ON Production.TransactionHistory REBUILD
WITH (FILLFACTOR = 75,
SORT_IN_TEMPDB = ON)
```

How It Works

In this recipe, the first `ALTER INDEX` was used to rebuild the primary key index on the Purchasing.ShipMethod table (rebuilding a clustered index does not cause the rebuild of any nonclustered indexes for the table):

```
ALTER INDEX PK_ShipMethod_ShipMethodID
ON Purchasing.ShipMethod  REBUILD
```

In the second example, the `ALL` keyword was used, which means that any indexes, whether nonclustered or clustered (remember, only one clustered index exists on a table) will be rebuilt:

```
ALTER INDEX ALL
ON Purchasing.PurchaseOrderHeader REBUILD
```

The third example in the recipe rebuilt an index *online*, which means that user queries can continue to access the data of the PK_ProductReview_ProductReviewID index while it's being rebuilt. In SQL Server 2000, the data included in an index being rebuilt using `DBCC DBREINDEX` was *not* available at certain stages due to locking:

```
WITH (ONLINE = ON)
```

The ONLINE option requires SQL Server 2005 Enterprise Edition, and can't be used with XML indexes, disabled indexes, or partitioned indexes. Also, indexes using large object data types or indexes made on temporary tables can't take advantage of this option.

In the last example, two index options were modified for an index—the fill factor and a directive to sort the temporary index results in tempdb:

```
WITH (FILLFACTOR = 75,
SORT_IN_TEMPDB = ON)
```

Defragmenting Indexes

In SQL Server 2005, DBCC INDEXDEFRAG was deprecated in place of the ALTER INDEX REORGANIZE command. ALTER INDEX REORGANIZE reduces fragmentation in the leaf level of an index, causing the physical order of the database pages to match the logical order. During the process, the indexes are also compacted based on the fill factor, resulting in freed space and a smaller index. ALTER TABLE REORGANIZE is automatically an online operation, meaning that you can continue to query the target data during the reorganization process.

The syntax is as follows:

```
ALTER INDEX { index_name | ALL }
    ON <object>
    { REORGANIZE
        [ PARTITION = partition_number ]
        [ WITH ( LOB_COMPACTION = { ON | OFF } ) ]
    }
```

The arguments of this command are described in Table 23-8.

Table 23-8. *ALTER INDEX...REORGANIZE Arguments*

Argument	Description
index_name | ALL	The name of the index that you want to rebuild. If ALL is chosen, all indexes for the table or view will be rebuilt.
<object>	The name of the table or view that you want to build the index on.
partition_number	If using a partitioned index, the partition_number designates that partition to reorganize.
LOB_COMPACTION = { ON | OFF }	When enabled, large object data types (varchar(max), navarchar(max), varbinary(max), xml, text, ntext, and image data) are compacted.

This recipe demonstrates how to defragment a single index, as well as all indexes on a single table:

```
-- Reorganize a specific index
ALTER INDEX PK_TransactionHistory_TransactionID
ON Production.TransactionHistory
REORGANIZE

-- Reorganize all indexes for a table
-- Compact large object data types
ALTER INDEX ALL
ON HumanResources.JobCandidate
REORGANIZE
WITH (LOB_COMPACTION=ON)
```

How It Works

In the first example of this recipe, the primary key index of the Production.TransactionHistory table was reorganized (defragmented). The syntax was very similar to rebuilding an index, only instead of REBUILD, the REORGANIZE keyword was used.

In the second example, all indexes (using the ALL keyword) were defragmented for the HumanResources.Jobcandidate column. Using the WITH clause, large object data type columns were also compacted.

Use ALTER INDEX REORGANIZE if you cannot afford to take the index offline during an index rebuild (and if you cannot use the ONLINE option in ALTER INDEX REBUILD because you aren't running SQL Server 2005 Enterprise Edition). Reorganization is always an online operation, meaning that an ALTER INDEX REORGANIZE operation doesn't block database traffic for significant periods of time, although it may be a slower process than a REBUILD.

CHAPTER 24

■ ■ ■

Maintaining Database Objects and Object Dependencies

This chapter contains a few recipes that you can use to maintain database objects and view object dependencies. You'll see recipes used to:

- Change the name of user-created database objects.
- Change an object's schema.
- Display information about object dependencies.

These recipes got their own chapter because they can be applied to more than one database object type.

Database Object Maintenance

In these next two recipes I'll show you how to change the name of an existing user-created database object using the sp_rename system-stored procedure and how to transfer an existing object from its existing schema to a different schema using ALTER SCHEMA.

Changing the Name of a User-Created Database Object

This recipe demonstrates how to rename objects using the sp_rename system-stored procedure. Using this procedure, you can rename table columns, indexes, tables, constraints, and other database objects.

The syntax for sp_rename is as follows:

```
sp_rename [ @objname = ] 'object_name' , [ @newname = ] 'new_name'
    [ , [ @objtype = ] 'object_type' ]
```

The arguments of this system-stored procedure are described in Table 24-1.

Table 24-1. *sp_rename Parameters*

Argument	Description
object_name	The name of the object to be renamed.
new_name	The new name of the object.
object_type	The type of object to rename: column, database, index, object (for renaming a database, you can also use ALTER DATABASE MODIFY NAME, as detailed in Chapter 22's recipe, "Renaming a Database").

This recipe demonstrates how to rename a table, column, and index:

```
USE AdventureWorks
GO

-- Add example objects

CREATE TABLE HumanResources.InsuranceProvider
(InsuranceProviderID int NOT NULL,
 InsuranceProviderNM varchar(50) NOT NULL
)
GO

CREATE INDEX ni_InsuranceProvider_InsuranceProviderID
ON HumanResources.InsuranceProvider (InsuranceProviderID)

-- Rename the table
EXEC sp_rename 'HumanResources.InsuranceProvider',
          'Provider',
          'Object'

-- Rename a column
EXEC sp_rename 'HumanResources.Provider.InsuranceProviderID',
          'ProviderID',
          'Column'

-- Rename the primary key constraint
EXEC sp_rename 'HumanResources.Provider.ni_InsuranceProvider_InsuranceProviderID',
          'ni_Provider_ProviderID',
          'Index'
```

This returns the following message for each sp_rename execution:

```
Caution: Changing any part of an object name could break scripts and stored procedures.
```

How It Works

This recipe began with you creating a new table called HumanResources.InsuranceProvider with an index on the new table called InsuranceProviderID. After that, the system-stored procedure sp_rename was used to rename the table:

```
EXEC sp_rename 'HumanResources.InsuranceProvider',
          'Provider',
          'Object'
```

Notice that the first parameter uses the fully qualified object name (schema.table_name), whereas the second parameter just uses the new table_name. The third parameter used the object type of "object."

Next, sp_rename was used to change the column name:

```
EXEC sp_rename 'HumanResources.Provider.InsuranceProviderID',
          'ProviderID',
          'Column'
```

The first parameter used the schema.table_name.column_name to be renamed and the second parameter the new name of the column. The third parameter used the object type of "column."

In the last part of the recipe, the index was renamed:

```
EXEC sp_rename 'HumanResources.Provider.ni_InsuranceProvider_InsuranceProviderID',
          'ni_Provider_ProviderID',
          'Index'
```

The first parameter used the schema.table_name.index_name parameter. The second parameter used the name of the new index. The third used the object type of "index."

This recipe returned a warning about "changing any part of an object name could break scripts and stored procedures." In a real life scenario, before you rename an object, you'll also want to ALTER any view, stored procedure, function, or other programmatic object which contains a reference to the original object name. To find out which objects reference an object, see this chapter's recipe, "Displaying Information on Database Object Dependencies."

Changing an Object's Schema

In SQL Server 2000, before the concept of schemas, an object's owner was changed using the sp_changeobjectowner system-stored procedure. Now in SQL Server 2005, users (owners) and schemas are separate, and to change an object's schema you use the ALTER SCHEMA command instead.

The syntax is as follows:

```
ALTER SCHEMA schema_name TRANSFER object_name
```

The command takes two arguments: the first being the schema name you want to transfer the object to, and the second the object name that you want to transfer.

This recipe demonstrates transferring a table from the Sales to the HumanResources schema:

```
Use AdventureWorks
GO

CREATE TABLE Sales.TerminationReason
(TerminationReasonID int NOT NULL PRIMARY KEY,
TerminationReasonDESC varchar(100) NOT NULL)
GO

ALTER SCHEMA HumanResources TRANSFER Sales.TerminationReason
GO
```

How It Works

In this recipe a new table was created in the Sales schema. With SQL Server 2005, an object is no longer *owned* by a specific user, but is instead contained within a schema. After creating the table, it was then transferred to the HumanResources schema using the ALTER SCHEMA TRANSFER command.

> ■**Caution** Permissions granted to the original `schema.object` will be dropped after the transfer (for example `SELECT` permissions for `USER1`). If these permissions need to be maintained in the new schema, be sure to script them out prior to using `ALTER SCHEMA`. See Chapter 18 for instructions on how to see what permissions are currently allocated to a securable.

Object Dependencies

The next two recipes will demonstrate how to display database object dependencies using the `sp_depends` system-stored procedure, and how to view the definition of a module using the `OBJECT_DEFINITION` function.

Displaying Information on Database Object Dependencies

This recipe demonstrates how to view the database object dependencies of a specific database object using the `sp_depends` system-stored procedure. A dependency in this context is a database object that depends upon another database object in order to function properly. Dependencies can be formed when a module (such as views, stored procedures, user-defined functions, or triggers) references another module or table. You'll most likely want to report object dependencies prior to removing a database object or changing its name, so that you can change the referencing objects accordingly.

The syntax for `sp_depends` is as follows:

```
sp_depends [ @objname = ] '<object>'
```

The object parameter designates the object to report dependencies for. If the object is a table, for example, the output of the procedure will show all objects that reference that table (in a view, stored procedure, user-defined function, trigger, etc.). If the object is modular code, such as a user-defined function, for example, the output would show all database objects that are referenced within the Transact-SQL definition of the function.

This first example in the recipe demonstrates using `sp_depends` to view dependencies of a user-defined function in the `AdventureWorks` database:

```
EXEC sp_depends 'dbo.ufnGetContactInformation'
```

This returns:

name	type	updated	selected	column
Sales.StoreContact	user table	no	yes	ContactID
Sales.StoreContact	user table	no	yes	ContactTypeID
Person.Contact	user table	no	yes	ContactID
Person.Contact	user table	no	yes	FirstName
Person.Contact	user table	no	yes	LastName
Purchasing.VendorContact	user table	no	yes	ContactID
Purchasing.VendorContact	user table	no	yes	ContactTypeID
Person.ContactType	user table	no	yes	ContactTypeID
Person.ContactType	user table	no	yes	Name
HumanResources.Employee	user table	no	yes	ContactID
HumanResources.Employee	user table	no	yes	Title
Sales.Individual	user table	no	yes	ContactID

This second example demonstrates viewing all objects that depend on a specific table (the reverse of the previous example):

```
EXEC sp_depends 'Purchasing.VendorContact'
```
This returns:

name	type
dbo.ufnGetContactInformation	table function
Purchasing.uVendorContact	trigger
Purchasing.vVendor	view

How It Works

The sp_depends stored procedure returns two different results sets: a result set of the objects that the procedure argument database object depends on, and a result set of the objects that depend on the procedure argument database object.

The first example in this recipe used the sp_depends system-stored procedure to show all object dependencies for a user-defined function. The result set returned the name and column of each object that the user-defined function was dependent on, as well as the object type. The selected column indicates if the object/column is referenced in a SELECT statement. The updated column in the result set indicates if the object/column is modified.

The second example in this recipe showed all programmatic objects dependent on the Purchasing.VendorContact table, which included a table function, trigger, and view.

Viewing an Object's Definition

Once you've identified an object that is dependent on a module that you need to modify, you can have a look at its definition using the OBJECT_DEFINITION function. This function can be used to return the Transact-SQL definition of user-defined and system-based constraints, defaults, stored procedures, functions, rules, schema-scoped DML and DDL triggers, and views.

The syntax is as follows:

```
OBJECT_DEFINITION ( object_id )
```

The only argument for this command is the object ID, which is the unique object identifier (each object identifier uniquely identifies a database object within a database).

In this example, the Transact-SQL definition is returned for an AdventureWorks database's user-defined function and the OBJECT_ID function is used within the OBJECT_DEFINITION function to get that user-defined function's identifier:

```
USE AdventureWorks
GO

SELECT OBJECT_DEFINITION
(OBJECT_ID('dbo.ufnGetAccountingEndDate'))
GO
```

This returns the Transact-SQL definition:

```
CREATE FUNCTION [dbo].[ufnGetAccountingEndDate]()
RETURNS [datetime]
AS
BEGIN
 RETURN DATEADD(millisecond, -2, CONVERT(datetime, '2004-07-01', 101));
END;
```

If you're curious about how Microsoft programs its own system objects, you can also use OBJECT_DEFINTION to peek at their Transact-SQL. In this example, the system-stored procedure code for the sp_depends stored procedure is revealed:

```
USE AdventureWorks
GO

SELECT OBJECT_DEFINITION(OBJECT_ID('sys.sp_depends'))
GO
```

This returns the following abridged results:

```
create procedure sys.sp_depends
--- 1996/08/09 16:51  @objname nvarchar(776)
...
select @dbname = parsename(@objname,3)

if @dbname is not null and @dbname <> db_name()
begin    raiserror(15250,-1,-1)
return (1)
end
...
```

How It Works

In this recipe I demonstrated using OBJECT_DEFINITION to return the Transact-SQL code for a user-defined function and for a system-stored procedure. In both cases, the OBJECT_ID function was nested within the function in order to pass the object identifier ID as an argument:

```
OBJECT_DEFINITION
(OBJECT_ID('dbo.ufnGetAccountingEndDate'))
```

The object name was fully qualified, using the schema.object_name format.

Both examples returned the Transact-SQL code definition for the database objects. Had those objects been encrypted, you would have gotten a NULL result set instead.

CHAPTER 25

■ ■ ■

Database Mirroring

Introduced in SQL Server 2005, *database mirroring* provides high availability at the user database level. High availability in this case refers to the SQL Server databases being available to end-users to query with little or no unplanned downtime. Database mirroring allows database redundancy, by synchronizing a primary (principal) database on one server with a second copy of a database on a second server. This second copy can be used as a hot standby, allowing for fast failover in the event you need to take your primary copy off-line for any reason. Unlike failover clustering, database mirroring doesn't require expensive hardware such as shared disk arrays or SAN. At a minimum, all you need are two SQL Server 2005 instances on the same network.

Caution Unlike failover clustering, database mirroring operates at the user database level. You cannot mirror system databases (master, msdb, tempdb).

In this chapter, I'll review how to set up, configure, monitor, and remove database mirroring. At the time this chapter was written, Microsoft decided to hold off on full support of database mirroring functionality, and are instead planning to make it fully supportable at a later date. This doesn't, however, keep you from testing it out. To enable your SQL Server instances for use in database mirroring, you must enable trace flag 1400.

To enable this flag so that it is enabled when your SQL Server instances start, follow these steps for each SQL Server instance participating in database mirroring:

1. In the SQL Server Configuration Manager, with SQL Server Services selected in the left pane, go to the right pane, right-click the SQL Server instance you wish to configure, and select Properties.

2. Click the Advanced Tab.

3. Scroll down to the Startup Parameters configuration. Append the following (prefixed by a semicolon) to the end of the Startup Parameters value:

    ;-T1400

4. Restart the SQL Server service in order for the change to take effect. Repeat for each participating SQL Server instance.

Before I get into the specifics of database mirroring in the next section, I'll first talk about database mirroring in the context of other SQL Server high availability options.

Database Mirroring in Context

Although database mirroring was introduced in SQL Server 2005, SQL Server 2000 included other methods for enabling high availability. These 2000 technologies have been carried over into SQL Server 2005 as well, and in most cases, with enhancements. Some of the high availability technologies include:

- *Failover clustering.* Available in previous versions of SQL Server, failover clustering allows you to maintain high-availability at the SQL Server instance level, using two or more nodes that are connected to shared disks. When you install a SQL Server instance on a failover cluster, the user and system database files are installed on the shared disk, and the regular binary install files are written to all nodes (servers) participating in the cluster. One physical node "controls" the SQL Server instance at a time, and if something happens to that node that makes it unavailable, a second node in the cluster can take over the duties of serving that SQL Server instance. Depending on the settings of the SQL Server instance, a failover from one server to another can take just a few seconds.

- *Log shipping.* Also available in previous versions, log shipping is the most similar to database mirroring functionality. Log shipping enables high availability at the database level, and involves keeping a primary online database on one SQL Server instance and a continuously recovering database on a second SQL Server instance. As transaction log backups are performed on the primary database, the transaction log backups are copied to the second SQL Server instance and continuously applied to the database copy. In the event of a failure , either on the primary database or on the server where it resides, the second database copy can be brought online by applying the last of the transferred transaction log backups.

- *Replication.* Also available in previous versions, replication allows you to move data and object definitions (tables, views, and more) to a second database copy on one or more SQL Server instances. Depending on the type of replication you've chosen, you can push data changes on a specific schedule, migrate data as changes are made, or synchronize data changes across multiple data sources. Replication provides high availability in a lesser form, focusing on specific objects and data, but not allowing you to automate the transfer of all database object types. This means that you cannot depend on it to produce an identical copy of your database (something that database mirroring *can* do).

There are several ways in which database mirroring differentiates it from these high availability options:

- Database mirroring doesn't require shared disks or special hardware required by failover clustering. Failover clustering protects the entire SQL Server instance, but database mirroring only allows high availability at the user database scope. System databases cannot be mirrored.

- Unlike log shipping, setup of a database mirror can be performed entirely with Transact-SQL. Log shipping requires manual configurations and is considered to be a warm standby solution. Database mirroring is integrated into the database engine and allows for a hot database standby, allowing failover within seconds.

> ■**Note** A "hot" standby server is one that receives frequent updates from a production server and is immediately available for use in the event of a failure on the production server. A "warm" standby server is one that receives updates, but may require adjustments or a few minutes of transition before taking over in the event of a failure on the production server.

- Replication allows you to push or pull specific database objects, but doesn't allow you to pull all database objects. Database mirroring, however, creates an exact copy of the database.

In the next section I'll discuss the database mirroring architecture.

Database Mirroring Architecture

Database mirroring involves a principal server role, a mirroring server role, and an optional witness server (shown in Figure 25-1). The database on the principal server is actively used, and as transactions are applied to the principal server's database, they are also submitted to the mirror server's database. The mirror server database is left in a recovering state, where it receives changes made on the principal copy, but it cannot be used while the principal mirror database is still available.

Principal Server Role
1. Has the active database
2. Allows user updates and reads
3. Pushes all modifications to mirror copy

Principal Mirror Server
1. Has the recovering copy of the principal database
2. Receives updates as they are made
3. If the principal database becomes unavailable, the mirror database can switch roles and become the principal

Witness Server Role
1. Is required for automatic failover
2. Helps make the decision that the principal database is "unavailable".
3. Doesn't contain a copy of the database.

Figure 25-1. *Database Mirroring Basic Architecture*

If an issue occurs on the principal server database, which then makes it unavailable, the mirror server can take on the role of the primary database. When the other database (the original principal) comes back online, the former primary database takes on the mirrored server database role, receiving transactions from the principal server.

Failover from principal to mirror databases can be initiated manually or automatically, depending on the database mirroring mode (which is described in detail later in this chapter). If automatic failover is required, a third server must join the mirroring session as a witness server. The *witness server* monitors the principal and mirror servers. In a database mirroring session that consists of these three servers (principal, mirror, and witness), two of the three connected servers can make the decision (called a *quorum*) as to whether or not an automatic failover should occur.

Database mirroring sessions can run in a synchronous or asynchronous mode. When in synchronous mode, transactions written to the principal server database must also be written to the mirror server database before any containing transaction can be committed. This option guarantees data redundancy, but has a trade-off of potential performance degradation.

Asynchronous mode allows transactions to commit on the principal database mirroring session before actually writing the transaction to the mirror server database. This option allows for faster transaction completion on the principal database, but also poses the risk of lost transactions if a failure occurs on the principal server before updates can be reflected on the mirror database.

With regards to application and client connectivity to the principal database, SQL Server 2005 maintains metadata that allows .NET application redirection in the event of a failover. Specifically, you can use the SQL Native Client in your .NET code to connect to the mirrored database and the code can be configured such as to be aware of the locations of the mirrored databases. With the SQL Native Client, you can designate both the principal and mirroring SQL Server instances in the connection string, allowing the application connection to be transparently redirected to the newly active principal when the primary database is unavailable.

Setting Up Database Mirroring

In this chapter, I'll demonstrate one scenario across several smaller recipes, much like I did in the Service Broker chapter. In this scenario, I'll be setting up a database mirroring session on the BookStore database. One SQL Server instance will house the principal database, another will house the mirrored database, and another will act as the witness (no database needed).

The following is a general list of steps used to enable database mirroring:

1. *Create endpoints.* You should create mirroring endpoints, which will allow the SQL Server instances (principal, mirror, and witness) to communicate with each other. You have your choice regarding which authentication method is used, and I'll discuss that issue in the upcoming recipe.

2. *Create the database mirror copy.* Before doing this, though, you need to make sure the principal database is in FULL recovery mode, because transaction log backups are applied to the mirror database from the principal database, in order to propagate principal database modifications. To make the mirror database copy, a full database backup is made to the principal database and is then restored to the mirror SQL Server instance WITH NORECOVERY (this option also leaves the database in a state to receive additional transaction log restores). After the full database backup is made on the principal, a transaction log backup must also be made, and then restored on the database mirror copy.

3. *Initialize the database mirroring session.* These last steps involve designating the role of each database using ALTER DATABASE. This command tells SQL Server which SQL Server endpoints connect to the partners and which connect to the witness. *Partner databases* have the principal and/or mirror database, and can also change roles if the principal database becomes unavailable.

The first recipe in this scenario will show you how to create mirroring endpoints that can be used to define which SQL Server instances participate in which actions within the database mirroring session.

Creating Mirroring Endpoints

In order to establish a mirroring session, the participant servers must be able to communicate with one another on their own dedicated TCP port. These endpoint ports will be dedicated to listening for mirroring messages and operations.

In getting ready to set up a new database mirroring session, the mirroring server is the first to have an endpoint created, followed then by the primary server, and then the optional witness server (designated if you wish to have automatic failover). Although no special hardware is needed, SQL Server 2005 must be used for the principal, mirror, and witness SQL Server instances.

The `CREATE ENDPOINT` command is used to create the mirroring endpoints. Recall from the previous chapters in this book that `CREATE ENDPOINT` is also used to create HTTP endpoints and to enable Service Broker cross-server communication. The syntax is as follows:

```
CREATE ENDPOINT endPointName [ AUTHORIZATION login ]
STATE = { STARTED | STOPPED | DISABLED }
AS TCP (LISTENER_PORT = listenerPort )
FOR DATABASE_MIRRORING (
   [ AUTHENTICATION = {
            WINDOWS [ { NTLM | KERBEROS | NEGOTIATE } ]
       | CERTIFICATE certificate_name
   } ]
   [ [ , ] ENCRYPTION = { DISABLED |SUPPORTED | REQUIRED }
       [ ALGORITHM { RC4 | AES | AES RC4 | RC4 AES } ]
]
   [,] ROLE = { WITNESS | PARTNER | ALL }
)
```

The arguments of this command are described in Table 25-1.

Table 25-1. *CREATE ENDPOINT...FOR DATABASE MIRRORING Arguments*

Argument	Description
endPointName	The name of the new server endpoint.
login	The owning SQL Server or Windows login of the endpoint. When not designated, the default owner is the creator of the new endpoint.
STATE = { STARTED | STOPPED | DISABLED }	This argument defines what state the endpoint is created in. STARTED means the endpoint will immediately be active. DISABLED means that the endpoint will not listen or respond to requests. STOPPED means that the endpoint listens to requests, but returns errors back to the caller.
listenerPort	The free TCP port on which the mirroring session will listen for incoming communications.
WINDOWS [{ NTLM | KERBEROS | NEGOTIATE }] | CERTIFICATE certificate_name	This option designates the authentication method of connection to the endpoint, using either NTLM, KERBEROS, or NEGOTIATE (which allows Windows negotiation protocol to choose from NTLM or Kerberos). If not designated, NEGOTIATE is the default authentication option. The CERTIFICATE option allows a certificate to be used for authentication, requiring the calling endpoint.
ENCRYPTION = { DISABLED| SUPPORTED | REQUIRED }	This option applies encryption to a mirroring process. When DISABLED is selected, data sent between mirroring sessions isn't encrypted. When SUPPORTED is selected, if both communicating endpoints support encryption, encryption is used (otherwise it is not). REQUIRED designates that communicating endpoints must support encryption.
ALGORITHM { RC4 | AES | AES RC4 | RC4 AES }	This option designates the encryption algorithm used in encrypted data transmission.
WITNESS | PARTNER | ALL	These options designate the database mirroring server role. When PARTNER is designated, the created endpoint can be used for either primary or mirrored session communications. If WITNESS is selected, the endpoint is used for the witness role in a mirroring session. The ALL session allows the endpoint to be used for the primary, mirroring, and witness mirroring session roles.

Before starting with the recipe, we need to first discuss authentication options that are required in order for the three SQL Server instances to communicate with one another. First of all, as long as each of the SQL Server instances is running under the same domain service account, and if you use the WINDOWS option to create your endpoint, your SQL Server instances will automatically have access to one another for the database mirroring session. If, however, these SQL Server instances are *not* running under the same domain user account, you'll need to create the Windows login of the remote SQL Server instance on each participating SQL Server instance. For example, let's say the SQL Server instance that is housing the principal database has a startup service account [JOEPROD\SQLAdmin]. Assume also that the SQL Server instance that is going to house the mirror database copy uses a startup service account of [JOEPROD\Node2Admin]. In order to allow the mirror SQL Server access to the principal SQL Server, the [JOEPROD\Node2Admin] must be added to the principal database. For example:

```
USE master
GO
CREATE LOGIN [JOEPROD\Node2Admin]
FROM WINDOWS
GO
```

The same thing must be done on the mirror SQL Server instance, in order to allow access to the principal and witness SQL Server instances. If these new accounts are also in the Windows administrator groups on the other SQL Server servers, those logins will automatically have access to connect to the database mirroring endpoint. If they are not members of this group, however, you must also explicitly grant the remote login access to the endpoint. For example:

```
GRANT CONNECT ON ENDPOINT::JOEPROD_Mirror
TO [JOEPROD\Node2Admin]
GO
```

In this chapter's scenario, I'll be using three SQL Server instances that run under the same Windows service account. In the first part of this example, a new endpoint is created on the SQL Server instance that will hold the mirrored copy of the database:

```
-- Create an Endpoint on the Mirror SQL Server Instance

CREATE ENDPOINT JOEPROD_Mirror
    STATE = STARTED
    AS TCP ( LISTENER_PORT = 5022 )
    FOR DATABASE_MIRRORING (
        AUTHENTICATION = WINDOWS NEGOTIATE,
        ENCRYPTION = SUPPORTED,
        ROLE=PARTNER)
GO
```

This next step is to create a new endpoint on the SQL Server instance that will hold the principal database:

```
-- Create an Endpoint on the Primary SQL Server Instance

CREATE ENDPOINT JOEPROD_Mirror
    STATE = STARTED
    AS TCP ( LISTENER_PORT = 5022 )
    FOR DATABASE_MIRRORING (
        AUTHENTICATION = WINDOWS NEGOTIATE,
        ENCRYPTION = SUPPORTED,
        ROLE=PARTNER)
GO
```

In the third step, a new endpoint is created on the SQL Server instance that will act as the witness in the mirrored database session:

```
-- Create an Endpoint on the Witness SQL Server Instance

CREATE ENDPOINT JOEPROD_Witness
    STATE = STARTED
    AS TCP ( LISTENER_PORT = 5022 )
    FOR DATABASE_MIRRORING (
        AUTHENTICATION = WINDOWS NEGOTIATE,
        ENCRYPTION = SUPPORTED,
        ROLE=WITNESS)
GO
```

After creating the endpoints, you can verify the endpoint settings by querying the `sys.database_mirroring_endpoints` system catalog view.

On the SQL Server instance that will eventually house the database mirror copy, the following query confirms the name of the endpoint, the state (meaning, whether it is started), and its mirroring role:

```
SELECT name, state_desc, role_desc
FROM sys.database_mirroring_endpoints
```

This returns:

name	state_desc	role_desc
JOEPROD_Mirror	STARTED	PARTNER

This query is then executed on the SQL Server instance that will house the principal database:

```
SELECT name, state_desc, role_desc
FROM sys.database_mirroring_endpoints
```

This returns:

name	state_desc	role_desc
JOEPROD_Mirror	STARTED	PARTNER

Next, the SQL Server instance that will assume the witness role is queried:

```
SELECT name, state_desc, role_desc
FROM sys.database_mirroring_endpoints
```

This returns:

name	state_desc	role_desc
JOEPROD_Witness	STARTED	WITNESS

How It Works

Before you can set up a database mirroring session, you must add endpoints to the participating SQL Server instances. These endpoints use the TCP/IP protocol to listen in on a designated port.

In this recipe, an endpoint called `JOEPROD_Mirror` was first created on the mirroring SQL Server instance:

```
CREATE ENDPOINT JOEPROD_Mirror
```

The initial state was set to `STARTED`, meaning that the endpoint was created in a state that can be used right away. The listening port was set to 5022:

```
STATE = STARTED
```

The TCP listening port was set to 5022. This is the port that the endpoint will listen on for database mirroring communication:

```
AS TCP ( LISTENER_PORT = 5022 )
```

The port number choice was arbitrary; just make sure the port is available. If your SQL Server instances communicate over a firewall, the designated mirroring ports must be opened for those machines in order to allow communication.

For the authentication, WINDOWS NEGOTIATE was chosen, which means that Windows authentication will be used to communicate between the participating SQL Server instances:

```
FOR DATABASE_MIRRORING (
    AUTHENTICATION = WINDOWS NEGOTIATE,
```

For encryption, SUPPORTED was designated, meaning that if both communicating sessions support encryption, encryption will be used in the data transmission:

```
ENCRYPTION = SUPPORTED,
```

The ROLE for the mirrored server was PARTNER, which means that the endpoint can be used for principal database or the mirror:

```
ROLE=PARTNER)
```

In exactly the same fashion, CREATE ENDPOINT was then executed on the principal SQL Server instance (again, using PARTNER) and then executed on the witness SQL Server instance with a role of WITNESS.

Finally, I queried the system catalog view, sys.database_mirroring_endpoints, which contains information on any database mirroring endpoints that may exist on each SQL Server instance. (In this scenario, there was one endpoint per SQL Server instance.)

Backing Up and Restoring Principal Databases

Once the endpoints are created, the next step in creating a database mirroring session is to create a database backup of the principal database and then restore it to the mirrored SQL Server instance. After restoring a full database backup, a transaction log backup should be made and then applied to the database mirror copy.

■**Note** This chapter demonstrates BACKUP and RECOVERY techniques. These commands are reviewed in more detail in Chapter 29.

Prior to backing up the database, and in order to use database mirroring, the database needs to use the FULL recovery model. In this example, I demonstrate making this change on the principal database SQL Server instance:

```
-- This is executing on the principal database SQL Server instance
USE master
GO

-- Make sure the database is using FULL recovery

ALTER DATABASE BookStore
SET RECOVERY FULL
GO
```

Next, a full database backup is performed:

```
-- Backing up the BookStore DATABASE

BACKUP DATABASE BookStore
TO DISK =
'C:\Apress\Recipes\Mirror\principalbackup_BookStore.bak'
WITH INIT
```

Once the database backup is complete on the primary SQL Server instance, the .bak file is then manually copied to the mirroring SQL Server instance, where it will be restored using NORECOVERY. NORECOVERY mode leaves the database in a state where additional transaction logs can be applied to it:

```
RESTORE DATABASE BookStore
FROM  DISK = 'C:\Apress\Recipes\principalbackup_BookStore.bak'
WITH MOVE 'BookStore' TO 'C:\Apress\Recipes\Mirror\BookStore.mdf',
    MOVE 'BookStore_log' TO 'C:\Apress\Recipes\Mirror\BookStore_log.ldf',
    NORECOVERY
GO
```

Keep in mind that the database that you restore must use the same name as the principal database in order for database mirroring to work.

If any transaction log backups occur *after* you perform a full backup on the principal SQL Server instance and *before* you perform the restore on the mirrored server, you must also apply those transaction log backups (using RESTORE) to the mirrored server database. Before enabling mirroring, you also must perform one more transaction log backup on the principal database and then restore it to the mirrored copy.

This example demonstrates backing up the transaction log of the principal database:

```
BACKUP LOG BookStore
TO DISK =
'C:\Apress\Recipes\Mirror\BookStore_tlog.trn'
WITH INIT
```

Once the transaction log backup is complete on the primary SQL Server instance, the .trn file is then manually copied to the mirroring SQL Server instance, where it is restored using NORECOVERY:

```
RESTORE LOG BookStore
FROM DISK = 'C:\Apress\Recipes\Mirror\BookStore_tlog.trn'
WITH FILE = 1, NORECOVERY
```

Tip Restoring a user database doesn't bring along the necessary SQL or Windows logins to the server containing the mirrored database. Any SQL or Windows logins mapped to database users in the principal database should also be created on the mirrored SQL Server instance. These logins should be ready in the event of a failover, when the mirror database must take over the role as the principal. If the logins are not on the mirror database SQL Server instance, the database users within the mirrored database will be orphaned. See Chapter 17 for more information on logins and database users.

How It Works

In this recipe, the principal database was first modified to a FULL recovery mode so that it could participate in a database mirroring session:

```
ALTER DATABASE BookStore
SET RECOVERY FULL
```

After that, a full database backup was made of the BookStore database. The INIT option was used to entirely overlay the database file with just the most recent full backup (in case an older backup already existed on the specified file):

```
BACKUP DATABASE BookStore
TO DISK =
'C:\Apress\Recipes\Mirror\principalbackup_BookStore.bak'
WITH INIT
```

The backup file was then manually copied to the second SQL Server instance, which would house the mirrored copy of the database. A new database was then restored using the MOVE and NORECOVERY option. You should use the MOVE option when you want to relocate *where* the database files are restored, versus *how* they were stored when the original backup was created:

```
RESTORE DATABASE BookStore
FROM  DISK = 'C:\Apress\Recipes\principalbackup_BookStore.bak'
WITH MOVE 'BookStore' TO 'C:\Apress\Recipes\Mirror\BookStore.mdf',
     MOVE 'BookStore_log' TO 'C:\Apress\Recipes\Mirror\BookStore_log.ldf',
     NORECOVERY
GO
```

After that, back on the principal database server, a transaction log backup is created:

```
BACKUP LOG BookStore
TO DISK =
'C:\Apress\Recipes\Mirror\BookStore_tlog.trn'
WITH INIT
```

The transaction log backup file was then manually copied to the second SQL Server instance prior to restoring it on the mirrored copy of the database (again using the NORECOVERY option):

```
RESTORE LOG BookStore
FROM DISK = 'C:\Apress\Recipes\Mirror\BookStore_tlog.trn'
WITH FILE = 1, NORECOVERY
```

Now you have a second copy of the database in a NORECOVERY state, and you are ready to proceed to the next step in this example scenario, which involves creating the database mirroring session.

Creating a Database Mirroring Session

Once the database is restored and in recovering mode on the mirror server, the mirroring session can then be started using the ALTER DATABASE command. This is achieved in two steps (three, if you are using a witness SQL Server instance, which in this scenario, you are). First, ALTER DATABASE will be executed on the mirror SQL Server instance to set it as a partner with the principal server endpoint. After that, ALTER DATABASE will be executed on the principal SQL Server instance to set the mirroring partner and witness endpoint locations.

The specified syntax for using ALTER DATABASE to enable database mirroring is as follows:

```
ALTER DATABASE database_name
[PARTNER { = 'partner_server'
  | FAILOVER
  | FORCE_SERVICE_ALLOW_DATA_LOSS
  | OFF
  | RESUME
  | SAFETY { FULL | OFF }
  | SUSPEND
  | REDO_QUEUE ( integer { KB | MB | GB } | UNLIMITED )
  | TIMEOUT integer
          } |
```

```
WITNESS { = 'witness_server'
        | OFF
        }]
```

The arguments of this command are described in Table 25-2. Keep in mind that several of these options touch on the functionality demonstrated later on in the chapter:

Table 25-2. *ALTER DATABASE Arguments*

Argument	Description
database_name	The name of the database participating in the mirror session (the name must be the same on both the principal and mirror servers).
partner_server	The name of the partner server, which expects the following format: TCP://fully_qualified_domain_name:port.
FAILOVER	The FAILOVER option manually fails over the principal database to the mirror database. This option requires that the SAFETY option is FULL.
FORCE_SERVICE_ALLOW_DATA_LOSS	FORCE_SERVICE_ALLOW_DATA_LOSS forces the failover to the mirrored database without fully synchronizing the latest transactions (thus potentially losing data). This operation requires that the principal server database is unavailable, the SAFETY option is OFF, and no witness is designated.
OFF	The OFF option stops the database mirroring session.
RESUME	Starts back up a suspended database mirroring session.
SAFETY { FULL | OFF }	The SAFETY setting has two values, FULL or OFF. When FULL, the database mirroring session works in synchronous mode, requiring transactions on the principal database to be written to the mirror database before the transaction is allowed to commit. When SAFETY is OFF, the mirroring session is asynchronous, meaning that transactions at the principal don't wait to be applied at the mirror before committing (which introduces the potential for data loss).
SUSPEND	The SUSPEND mode suspends the database mirroring session.
REDO_QUEUE (integer { KB | MB | GB } | UNLIMITED)	The REDO_QUEUE affects the size of the queue that holds log records that have been committed to disk, but have not yet rolled forward on the mirrored database. The default size is UNLIMITED, however you can adjust the sizes by kilobytes, megabytes, or gigabytes. This option applies to synchronous mode. Reducing the size of this queue helps reduce the amount of time it takes to failover to the mirror, but can also slow down updates on the principal database, as it may need to wait for the mirror server to catch up.
TIMEOUT integer	The TIMEOUT option designates how long a server instance will wait to receive a PING message back (the heartbeat method between the partner servers) from the other partner before deeming that connection to be unavailable (thus causing a failover). The minimum wait time is five seconds, with a default value of ten seconds.
witness_server	This is the name of the witness server, which expects the following format: TCP://fully_qualified_domain_name:port.
OFF	OFF removes the witness from the database mirroring session.

Continuing with the example scenario, on the mirrored SQL Server instance, the following command is executed to begin the mirroring process by referencing the principal SQL Server instance and TCP port number (where the endpoint listens):

```
-- Set on the mirrored SQL Server instance
-- Default SAFETY is FULL - synchronous mode
ALTER DATABASE BookStore
    SET PARTNER = 'TCP://NODE2.JOEPROD.COM:5022'
GO
```

Next, ALTER DATABASE is executed on the principal SQL Server instance, designating the mirror server's name and TCP port number:

```
-- Enable the mirroring session on the principal SQL Server instance
-- Default SAFETY is FULL - synchronous mode
ALTER DATABASE BookStore
    SET PARTNER = 'TCP://NODE1.JOEPROD.COM:5022'
GO
```

After setting up both the mirror and principal, you can then optionally add a witness server, which is configured on the principal SQL Server instance, as this example demonstrates:

```
-- Enable the witness on the principal SQL Server instance
-- Default SAFETY is FULL - synchronous mode
ALTER DATABASE BookStore
    SET WITNESS = 'TCP://NODE3.JOEPROD.COM:5022'
GO
```

Mirroring is now configured in this example with the optional witness server. Any data modifications or schema changes made on the principal database will be logged to the mirror database. The mirror database will *not* be available for activity, unless it becomes the principal database either by an automatic or manual failover (discussed and demonstrated later in the chapter).

How It Works

In this example, the ALTER DATABASE command was used to start a database mirroring session. You started off on the mirrored SQL Server instance. ALTER DATABASE was executed using SET PARTNER:

```
ALTER DATABASE BookStore
    SET PARTNER = 'TCP://NODE2.JOEPROD.COM:5022'
GO
```

The PARTNER of this command pointed to the principal database SQL Server server name, and the listening endpoint port of that SQL Server instance. Recall earlier that the endpoint was configured to listen on port 5022 in a partner (not witness) capacity.

Next, on the principal database SQL Server instance, the ALTER DATABASE command was used to set the database mirroring partner, this time pointing to the mirrored database node and listening to the TCP port:

```
ALTER DATABASE BookStore
    SET PARTNER = 'TCP://NODE1.JOEPROD.COM:5022'
GO
```

The SQL Server instance containing the principal database is also where you need to configure the witness for the database mirroring session. Recall from the earlier recipe that you created a database mirroring endpoint on the witness SQL Server instance. When you use ALTER DATABASE and SET WITNESS, the name of the witness machine and listening TCP port are designated (from the principal database SQL Server instance):

```
ALTER DATABASE BookStore
    SET WITNESS = 'TCP://NODE3.JOEPROD.COM:5022'
GO
```

The database mirroring session has now been configured. Any database objects that have been added or modifications that have been made in the BookStore database will be transferred to the mirror copy. If the principal database becomes unavailable, a failover can occur, changing the mirrored database's role to the principal role. Before you get into these tasks, however, I'll quickly recap what was accomplished in these last few recipes.

Setup Summary

The general steps for setting up database mirroring spanned the last three recipes, so here is a step-by-step review of how it was done:

- First, on the mirror SQL Server instance, an endpoint was created using CREATE ENDPOINT and designating the role of PARTNER, using the TCP port of 5022.

- On the principal SQL Server instance, an endpoint was created using a role of PARTNER and using a listener port of 5022 (because these are separate servers, you can use the same TCP port on each, so long as the port is available for use).

- Next, on the witness SQL Server instance, an endpoint was created with a role of WITNESS, using a listener port of 5022.

- Back on the principal SQL Server instance, the BookStore database (the database to be mirrored) was set to FULL recovery mode using ALTER DATABASE (if it was already using FULL, this step wouldn't have been necessary).

- Still, on the principal SQL Server instance, a full database backup was performed on the BookStore database.

- On the mirror SQL Server instance, the database was then restored using the NORECOVERY option, leaving it in a state to receive transactions from the mirroring process. Had additional transaction log backups been made on the principal database after the last full backup, those transaction log backups would need to be applied to the mirrored, restored copy too.

- On the principal SQL Server instance, a transaction log backup was performed on the BookStore database.

- On the mirror SQL Server instance, the transaction log backup was then restored using the NORECOVERY option, leaving it in a state to receive transactions from the mirroring process.

- Still on the mirror SQL Server instance, the ALTER DATABASE...SET PARTNER command was executed, pointing to the fully qualified *principal* server name and TCP port that the *principal* SQL Server instance endpoint listens on.

- On the principal SQL Server instance, ALTER DATABASE...SET PARTNER was executed pointing to the fully qualified name of the *mirrored* server and TCP port that the *mirror* SQL Server instance endpoint listens on.

- Lastly, still from the principal, ALTER DATABASE...SET WITNESS was executed, pointing to the fully qualified name of the *witness* server and TCP port that the *witness* SQL Server instance endpoint listens on.

After all of this, the database mirror session begins. Modifications to the principal database will be logged to the awaiting mirror database. The witness server will be keeping an eye on the connection between the principal and mirror databases, making sure that if there are any problems, the appropriate actions are taken (such as automatic failovers). Before I discuss failovers, however, in the next section I'll discuss the various operating modes of a mirroring session, and how they can be both modified and controlled.

Operating Database Mirroring

Database mirroring sessions operate in three modes; high availability (used in the previous example), high protection, or high performance.

High availability mode means that transactions committed on the principal database require the availability of both the principal and mirror databases before the transaction can commit. This mode also requires a witness server, which allows automatic failover to occur. The owner of the principal database is determined by a quorum, which is the presence of at least two servers that can communicate with each another. If the witness loses contact with the mirror, but keeps contact with the principal, the principal database will remain in its role. If the witness loses contact with the principal, however, but can still see the mirror, in high availability mode the mirror assumes the role of principal. If the witness becomes unavailable for whatever reason, the principal and mirror form the quorum, and remain in their present roles. In short—it takes two to make a quorum, and a quorum decides which partner controls the principal database.

High protection mode, just like high availability mode, means that transactions committed on the principal database require the availability of both the principal and mirror databases before the transaction can commit. Unlike high availability mode, however, there isn't a witness server in the mix. This means that while a manual failover can occur, an automatic failover can't. High protection mode still forms a quorum (of just the two partner servers) with the mirror database, however if the mirror database becomes unavailable, SQL Server will make the database unavailable (meaning, take it out of service). This is because high protection mode requires the mirror in order to commit transactions.

Both of the aforementioned modes suggest data protection and availability as the primary emphasis. With this functionality, however, comes performance overhead. If your mirrored database has significant update activity, each transaction on the principal database must wait for an acceptance from the mirrored copy before a commit can happen.

Enter high performance mode, which allows asynchronous updates on the principal database (no waiting for the mirror before committing the transaction), and no witness server. This mode emphasizes transaction speed, but not data availability (because of the lack of manual or automatic failover) and minimal data recoverability (asynchronous modifications allow for the potential of lost transactions on the mirror database).

In this next recipe, I'll demonstrate how to use ALTER DATABASE to configure the high availability, high protection, and high performance modes.

Changing Operating Modes

Both high availability and high protection modes use the FULL safety mode (which is the default mode when you start a mirroring session). You can, however, turn this setting off by using ALTER DATABASE...SET SAFETY. This command takes two options: OFF or FULL.

In this first example, the safety of a specific mirrored session is turned OFF for a database (putting it in high performance mode) by executing the command on the principal SQL Server instance:

```
ALTER DATABASE BookStore SET SAFETY OFF
```

This second example demonstrates turning safety back on again, and changing from high performance to high availability mode:

```
ALTER DATABASE BookStore SET SAFETY FULL
```

High protection mode was not demonstrated here, as it also has FULL safety mode enabled, only without the use of a witness in the database mirroring session.

How It Works

In this example, the mirroring session safety was turned off and then on again by referencing the database name, followed by the new safety mode (either OFF or FULL). With the presence of a witness and the safety on FULL, your database mirroring session will operate in high availability mode. If you aren't using a witness, but safety is still FULL, the database mirroring session is operating in high protection mode. With safety OFF, the database is in asynchronous, high performance mode. See Table 25-3 for a summary of these different modes.

Table 25-3. *Database Mirroring Operating Modes*

Mode	Safety Configuration	Witness?
High Availability	FULL	Yes
High Protection	FULL	No
High Performance	OFF	No

■**Tip** As a best practice, use synchronous, high availability mode with mission critical databases. Only use asynchronous, high performance mode for databases where you can easily recover the lost data through other mechanisms or sources. Of the synchronous choices, use a witness server whenever possible (high availability) in order to take advantage of automatic failover.

Performing Failovers

A failover involves switching the roles of the principal and mirror database, with the mirror copy becoming the principal and the principal becoming the mirror. Existing database connections are broken during the failover, and the connecting application must then connect to the new principal database (and with the new 2005 .NET functionality, the connection string can be database-mirror aware).

You can manually set databases participating in a mirroring session to failover in synchronous high performance or high availability modes using the ALTER DATABASE...SET PARTNER FAILOVER command.

In this example, a failover is initiated from the principal server (which becomes the mirror server after the operation):

```
USE master
GO
ALTER DATABASE BookStore SET PARTNER FAILOVER
```

How long the actual failover operation takes depends on the time it takes to roll forward the logged transactions on the mirrored copy.

If the database session is running in asynchronous, high performance mode, you cannot initiate a manual failover. Instead, if the principal becomes unavailable, you can either wait for the database to become available again, or you can force the service on the mirror copy. To force the service, use the ALTER DATABASE...SET PARTNER FORCE_SERVICE_ALLOW_DATA_LOSS command. After forcing the service, the mirrored database will roll forward logged transactions (and in asynchronous mode, the principal could have lost some of the transactions in transit prior to the outage). The mirrored database then takes over as the principal.

■**Caution** Force service on a mirrored database only if absolutely necessary as data can be lost from the unavailable principal database.

In this example, the mirrored database in a database session using asynchronous, high performance mode is forced into service (requires that the actual principal database be unavailable to the mirroring session):

```
ALTER DATABASE ReportCentralDB SET PARTNER FORCE_SERVICE_ALLOW_DATA_LOSS
```

How It Works

These examples demonstrated failover options, which depend on the database mirroring session mode. You may decide to perform a manual failover, for example, in order to perform maintenance activities on the principal database server.

For asynchronous, high performance mode, however, if the principal database becomes unavailable, you'll only want to force service on the mirror session when absolutely necessary, as data can be lost from any unsent transactions on the unavailable principal database.

Pausing or Resuming a Mirroring Session

If your mirrored principal database is undergoing a significant amount of updates, which are then being bottlenecked by the synchronous updates to the mirror, you can temporarily pause the mirroring session using ALTER DATABASE...SET PARTNER SUSPEND. This option keeps the principal database available, and preserves changes in the log, which will then be sent to the mirroring database once it's resumed. The database mirroring session should only be paused for a short period of time, as the transaction log will continue to grow, causing it to fill up if the transaction log file size is fixed or expand until the drive is full (if the transaction log is not fixed).

In this example, the BookStore database mirroring session is paused from the principal server:

```
ALTER DATABASE BookStore SET PARTNER SUSPEND
```

The state is then confirmed by querying the sys.database_mirroring system catalog view on the principal server:

```
SELECT mirroring_state_desc
FROM sys.database_mirroring
WHERE database_id = DB_ID('BookStore')
```

This returns:

```
mirroring_state_desc
SUSPENDED
```

This next example demonstrates resuming the database mirroring session, causing the mirror database to synchronize with the pending log transactions:

```
ALTER DATABASE BookStore SET PARTNER RESUME
```

How It Works

You can pause or resume a database mirroring session without removing it entirely. Use the techniques demonstrated in this recipe to allow the removal of performance bottlenecks that may appear on high activity databases. Be mindful, however, of the transaction log size, and don't keep the mirroring session disabled longer than is strictly necessary.

Stopping Mirroring Sessions and Removing Endpoints

The previous example demonstrated briefly pausing and resuming a mirroring session, however if you wish to remove it altogether, you can use the ALTER DATABASE...SET PARTNER OFF command.

In this example, the BookStore database mirror is stopped and removed (mirroring meta-data is removed):

```
ALTER DATABASE BookStore SET PARTNER OFF
```

You can remove the mirroring endpoints on each SQL Server instance using the DROP ENDPOINT command, for example:

```
-- Executed on the witness server
DROP ENDPOINT JOEPROD_Witness

-- Executed on the mirror server
DROP ENDPOINT JOEPROD_Mirror

-- Executed on the principal server
DROP ENDPOINT JOEPROD_Mirror
```

How It Works

Use ALTER DATABASE...SET PARTNER OFF to stop and remove the database mirroring session. Connections will be broken in the principal database, but are allowed back in again for regular activity after the mirroring session is removed. The mirrored copy is left in a restoring state, where you can either recover or drop it. If you wish to reinstate mirroring, you have to follow the steps of setting up the principal, mirror, and witness from scratch.

If you remove mirroring, it's best to also remove the endpoints using DROP ENDPOINT, so that you don't forget that they are there holding on to the TCP port (which you may decide to use for other things).

Monitoring and Configuring Options

The last batch of recipes in this chapter will show you how to:

- Monitor the status of the database mirror using the sys.database_mirroring system catalog view.

- Reduce the time it takes for a failover to occur using the ALTER DATABASE...PARTNER REDO_QUEUE command.

- Configure the connection timeout period using the ALTER DATABASE...SET PARTNER TIMEOUT command.

You'll begin with learning how to monitor a database mirroring session's current status.

Monitoring Mirror Status

You can confirm the status of your mirroring session by querying the sys.database_mirroring system catalog view.

For example, this view is executed on the principal and shows the state of the mirror, the role of the current database, the safety level (described in the next recipe), and the state of the witness connection to the principal:

```
SELECT mirroring_state_desc, mirroring_role_desc, mirroring_safety_level_desc,
mirroring_witness_state_desc
FROM sys.database_mirroring
WHERE database_id = DB_ID('BookStore')
```

This returns:

mirroring_state_desc	mirroring_role_desc	mirroring_safety level_desc
mirroring_witness_state_desc		
SYNCHRONIZED	PRINCIPAL	FULL CONNECTED

How It Works

The SYNCHRONIZED state, when seen for the default FULL safety mode, means that the principal and mirrored database contain the same data. Other states you can see in this view include:

- SYNCHRONIZING, which means that the principal is sending log records that the mirror is still in the process of applying.

- SUSPENDED, which means that either the mirrored copy of the database is unavailable, errors have occurred, or the database has been manually put in this state. In a SUSPENDED state, the principal database runs without sending log records to the mirror.

- PENDING_FAILOVER, which is seen when a manual failover request has been made, but not yet executed.

- DISCONNECTED, which means that the partner has lost communication with the partner and witness.

Reducing Failover Time

Log transactions during periods of high activity on the principal database are continuously sent to the mirror copy, in spite of how far behind the mirror copy may be in applying the changes. Databases use a *redo queue*, containing the pending changes to roll forward on the mirror copy. By default, the redo queue has unlimited size (limited to the disk space, of course), and the larger the redo queue is, the longer the failover can take. Consequently, a smaller redo queue can reduce the amount of time a failover can take. Although limiting the size of the queue allows the database mirror copy to catch up with changes, it can also slow down updates that occur on the principal database copy, because the principal database cannot push more changes to the queue than its current size allows. So you must balance failover speed to overall update speed on the principal.

For synchronous database mirroring sessions, you can limit the size of the redo queue by using the ALTER DATABASE...PARTNER REDO_QUEUE command.

The syntax is as follows:

```
REDO_QUEUE ( integer { KB | MB | GB } | UNLIMITED)
```

This command uses an integer value, followed by the increment (kilobytes, megabytes, gigabytes, or the default, unlimited). This example sets the redo queue to 50MB in size (executed on the principal server):

```
ALTER DATABASE BookStore SET PARTNER REDO_QUEUE 50MB
```

The sys.database_mirroring system catalog view is then queried to validate the change:

```
SELECT mirroring_redo_queue
FROM sys.database_mirroring
WHERE database_id = DB_ID('BookStore')
```

This returns:

```
mirroring_redo_queue
--------------------
50
```

How It Works

In this recipe, the ALTER DATABASE command was used to set the REDO_QUEUE to 50MB:

```
ALTER DATABASE BookStore SET PARTNER REDO_QUEUE 50MB
```

By limiting the redo queue size, the pending transactions are forced to write to the mirror copy sooner. The actual size depends on the size of your database and the amount of data modification activity. Remember that the tradeoff to a faster failover may also result in slower updates on the principal database. The default behavior is for changes to be sent from the principal to the mirror without restriction, even if the database mirror falls behind in applying the log changes to disk. Restricting the queue size allows the database mirror to "catch up," resulting in a faster failover if the principal database goes down, but may have a negative impact on overall principal database performance.

Configuring the Connection Timeout Period

Database mirroring uses a default connection timeout period of ten seconds. If a connection cannot be made after ten seconds, a failure occurs, and depending on the role of the database (principal, mirror, or witness) or the mirroring session mode (synchronous, asynchronous), a failover or mirroring shut-down can occur.

If your network latency causes premature failures in the database mirroring session, you can configure the connection time-out period using the ALTER DATABASE...SET PARTNER TIMEOUT command. This command configures the timeout period in seconds (with a minimum of five seconds allowed).

In this example, the connection time-out period is increased to 15 seconds on the principal server:

```
ALTER DATABASE BookStore SET PARTNER TIMEOUT 15
```

You can confirm the new setting by querying the sys.database_mirroring system catalog view:

```
SELECT mirroring_connection_timeout
FROM sys.database_mirroring
WHERE database_id = DB_ID('BookStore')
```

This returns:

```
mirroring_connection_timeout
----------------------------
15
```

How It Works

In this recipe, the connection timeout period was modified using the ALTER DATABASE...
SET PARTNER TIMEOUT command:

```
ALTER DATABASE BookStore SET PARTNER TIMEOUT 15
```

When a mirroring session is active, PING communication messages are sent between the participating servers. When a server instance has to wait longer than the configured timeout, a failure occurs. The reaction to the failure depends on the role of the server, how quorum is defined (which two servers still see one another), and the database mirroring mode (high availability, high protection, or high performance).

Database Snapshots

With the release of SQL Server 2005 Enterprise Edition came the ability to create *database snapshots*, which are read-only, static copies of a database, representative of a specific point in time. You can connect to these snapshots just as you would any other database, allowing you to use them for reporting, testing, training or data recovery purposes. Before you conduct large or potentially hazardous database updates, you can use database snapshots as a just-in-case precaution when you may need to undo your work.

In this chapter, I demonstrate how to create, query, and drop database snapshots, as well as how to use database snapshots for data recovery purposes.

Snapshots Basics

Database snapshots can be created from user databases, providing a read-only view of the data, from the specific point in time when the snapshot was generated. Multiple snapshots can be created for a single database, allowing you, for example, to create a snapshot of a database at the end of each day or week, or at month's end.

Database snapshots are also space efficient, because they use *sparse files*. A sparse file is a file that contains no user data when first created. Snapshots reserve a minimum amount of space, in order to maintain the original snapshot's data. When first created, a database snapshot does *not* produce an extra copy of all data in the source database, but as database changes occur over time in the source, a copy of the pre-changed data is placed in the sparse file. The snapshot will then contain the contents of the database as it appeared the moment the snapshot was created.

Queries against the snapshot will return data from either the snapshot, the database, or both. Unchanged source database data will still be retrieved from the source database. But, if the data has been changed on the source database since the snapshot database was created, it will be retrieved from the snapshot.

As the percentage of changed data in the database source approaches 100%, the database snapshot will approach the size of the original database at the time the snapshot was originally created. Keep in mind that if the same data is modified on the source database multiple times, no additional updates are made to the database snapshot. Once a data page is updated on the source, the pre-changed data page is only moved once to the snapshot database.

There are a few limitations to keep in mind when deciding whether to use snapshots. For example, snapshots can't be created for the system databases. And, database snapshots can't be backed up, restored over, attached, or detached like regular databases. Also, snapshots do add performance overhead to the source database. This is because you'll see increased I/O activity for each modification that causes a data page to be moved to the snapshot file. If you have multiple snapshots on the same source database, the I/O activity will increase for each snapshot that requires page updates.

Limitations aside, database snapshots offer an excellent means of preserving point-in-time data, separating out reporting queries from the source database, and allowing quick data recovery. The next set of recipes will demonstrate database snapshots in action.

Creating and Querying Database Snapshots

You create a database snapshot using the CREATE DATABASE command.

The syntax for this command is as follows:

```
CREATE DATABASE database_snapshot_name
    ON
        (
        NAME = logical_file_name,
        FILENAME = 'os_file_name'
        ) [ ,...n ]
    AS SNAPSHOT OF source_database_name
```

The arguments for this command are described in Table 26-1.

Table 26-1. *CREATE DATABASE...AS SNAPSHOT Arguments*

Argument	Description
database_snapshot_name	The name of the database snapshot that you want to create.
(NAME = logical_file_name,FILENAME = 'os_file_name') [,...n]	logical_file_name is the logical filename of the source database data files. os_file_name is the physical filename to be created for the snapshot file. For each source database data file, there must be a snapshot file defined.
source_database_name	The source database that the snapshot is based on.

In this recipe's example, a snapshot is generated for the AdventureWorks database:

```
CREATE DATABASE AdventureWorks_Snapshot_Oct_08_2005
ON
( NAME = AdventureWorks_Data,
  FILENAME =
'C:\Apress\Recipes\AdventureWorks_Snapshot_Oct_08_2005.mdf
')
AS SNAPSHOT OF AdventureWorks

GO
```

Next, an update is made in the source data of the AdventureWorks database, in order to demonstrate the database snapshot's functionality:

```
USE AdventureWorks
GO

INSERT HumanResources.Department
(Name, GroupName)
VALUES ('Accounting Temps', 'AR')
GO
```

A new row was inserted into the source database. The HumanResources.Department table in the AdventureWorks source database and the database snapshot AdventureWorks_Snapshot_Oct_08_2005 are both queried for the newly inserted row:

```
SELECT Name
FROM AdventureWorks.HumanResources.Department
WHERE GroupName = 'AR'
```

This returns:

```
Name
Accounting Temps
```

Now the snapshot is queried:

```
SELECT Name
FROM
AdventureWorks_Snapshot_Oct_08_2005.HumanResources.➥
Department
WHERE GroupName = 'AR'
```

No data is returned from the snapshot, as the snapshot contains data *prior* to the change:

```
Name

(0 row(s) affected)
```

How It Works

In this recipe, a database snapshot was created using the CREATE DATABASE command:

```
CREATE DATABASE AdventureWorks_Snapshot_June_26_2005
```

The ON clause included the logical name of the data file from the AdventureWorks database, followed by the physical path and filename of the new database snapshot data file (since the snapshot is read-only, no transaction log file is needed):

```
ON
(   NAME = AdventureWorks_Data,
    FILENAME = 'C:\Apress\Recipes\AdventureWorks_Snapshot_June_26_2005.mdf')
```

The AS clause designated which database the snapshot would be based on:

```
AS SNAPSHOT OF AdventureWorks
```

Once the snapshot was created, an insert was performed on the AdventureWorks database. Behind the scenes, SQL Server copied the pre-change data pages to the database snapshot file. Queries against the snapshot that require data that has changed in the source database since the snapshot was created will be read from the snapshot database. This copy-on-write functionality allows the size of the snapshot file to remain relatively small, meaning that only the data affected by any changes would need to be stored in the snapshot data file.

Removing a Database Snapshot

To remove a database snapshot, use the DROP DATABASE command.

The syntax is as follows:

```
DROP DATABASE database_snapshot_name
```

This command uses just one argument: the name of the database snapshot.

In this next example, I demonstrate dropping the database snapshot created in the previous recipe:

```
DROP DATABASE AdventureWorks_Snapshot_Oct_08_2005
```

How It Works

The snapshot was removed in this recipe using DROP DATABASE. This removed the snapshot from the SQL Server instance, along with the removal of the underlying physical snapshot file.

Recovering Data with a Database Snapshot

Consider this not so uncommon scenario: you get a call from a database end-user telling you that he has accidentally updated a column's value for all rows in a table. The database he modified is very large, and restoring the data from backup will first require that you retrieve the backup file from tape. Once retrieved, you'll have to restore the database under a separate database name, and then INSERT...SELECT out the missing data into the production database. In addition to the pain of doing all of this, you may also find that you don't have the required disk space to store both the backup file and additional restored copy of the database.

Now imagine that you had created periodic snapshots of your database after significant data update events. Depending on the volatility of the data in your source database, database snapshots may only consume a fraction of the space required for a full database restore. With a snapshot, you can restore/update the data affected by the previous example by updating the source database with data from the snapshot database.

Or, if you can afford to do so, you can overlay the existing source database, recovering data as of the last snapshot using the RESTORE...FROM DATABASE_SNAPSHOT command. Using RESTORE...FROM DATABASE_SNAPSHOT, SQL Server will copy over the existing source database with the database snapshot. The RESTORE...FROM DATABASE_SNAPSHOT command is only used in conjunction with snapshots.

■**Note** For other uses of the RESTORE command, see Chapter 29.

The syntax for reverting from a database snapshot is as follows:

```
RESTORE DATABASE <database_name>
FROM DATABASE_SNAPSHOT = <database_snapshot_name>
```

This command takes two arguments: the name of the source database that you want to restore over, and the name of the database snapshot that you want to revert from.

Using RESTORE...FROM DATABASE_SNAPSHOT, you'll lose any data modifications made to the source database since the last snapshot, only recovering your data as of the point in time when the snapshot was created. But, with only having to update information that was modified since the snapshot was created, RESTORE...FROM DATABASE_SNAPSHOT operations can take significantly less time than regular database restores. You are achieving similar results to those in a regular database restore, in that your database state is reverted to the contents as they were when the snapshot was created.

■**Caution** Only revert to a snapshot if you can afford to lose all the changes you made in the source database since the last snapshot! This method is most useful for "scratch" databases, such as the ones used for training or testing. Also, although database snapshots are a convenient means of recovering data, database snapshots should not be considered a replacement for a good data recovery plan.

If you plan on using database snapshots to recover data in your SQL Server instance, note that other database snapshots (snapshots you are not recovering from) must be deleted prior to the `RESTORE...FROM DATABASE_SNAPSHOT` operation. Otherwise you will receive an error message similar to this:

```
Msg 3137, Level 16, State 4, Line 2
Database cannot be reverted. Either the primary or the snapshot names are improperly
specified, all other snapshots have not been dropped, or there are missing files.
Msg 3013, Level 16, State 1, Line 2
RESTORE DATABASE is terminating abnormally.
```

In addition to database snapshots, any full-text catalogs in the database must be removed prior to a database snapshot `RESTORE...FROM DATABASE_SNAPSHOT` operation, and your source database can't contain read-only or offline filegroups.

■**Note** Since a restore from a snapshot file breaks the transaction log backup sequence (see Chapter 29), it is a good idea to perform a full database backup after performing the `RESTORE` operation.

In this recipe, a new database snapshot is created on the AdventureWorks database:

```
CREATE DATABASE AdventureWorks_Snapshot_Oct_09_2005
ON
(   NAME = AdventureWorks_Data,
    FILENAME = 'C:\Apress\Recipes\AdventureWorks_Snapshot_Oct_09_2005.mdf')
AS SNAPSHOT OF AdventureWorks
GO
```

Next, the CustomerType column of the Sales.Customer table is accidentally updated to be 'S' for all rows (as no WHERE clause was used):

```
UPDATE Sales.Customer
SET CustomerType = 'S'
```

A query is executed to validate what happened in the AdventureWorks database:

```
SELECT CustomerType, COUNT(*) RowCnt
FROM Sales.Customer
GROUP BY CustomerType
```

This returns the following results, confirming that all rows now have a single CustomerType value of 'S':

```
CustomerType RowCnt
------------ -----------
S                  19185
```

Next, the AdventureWorks database is reverted back to the state it was in as of the database snapshot. No sessions can be connected to the source database during the RESTORE, so this example changes the database context to the master database. The AdventureWorks database is offline during the operation:

```
USE master
GO
```

```
RESTORE DATABASE AdventureWorks
FROM DATABASE_SNAPSHOT = 'AdventureWorks_Snapshot_Oct_09_2005'
```

The validation query is executed again to see if the data in the CustomerType column was corrected by the database snapshot revert:

```
USE AdventureWorks
GO

SELECT CustomerType, COUNT(*) RowCnt
FROM Sales.Customer
GROUP BY CustomerType
```

This returns confirmation that the CustomerType values have been recovered:

```
CustomerType RowCnt
------------ -----------
S            701
I            18484
```

How It Works

The RESTORE...FROM DATABASE_SNAPSHOT command allows you to undo any changes you made to the source database after the date and time of the creation of the designated database snapshot. This operation can also take less time to perform than a regular restore operation (for more on this topic, see Chapter 29).

In this recipe, the data in a column was unintentionally updated. A database snapshot was then used to revert to the data as of the point when the database snapshot was created. During the RESTORE...FROM DATABASE_SNAPSHOT operation, the database was offline and unavailable for use. After the operation completed, any changes made to AdventureWorks since the database snapshot were lost.

CHAPTER 27

■ ■ ■

Linked Servers and Distributed Queries

Linked servers provide SQL Server with access to data from remote data sources. Using linked servers, you can issue queries, perform data modifications, and execute remote procedure calls. Remote data sources can be homogeneous (meaning that a source is another SQL Server instance) or heterogeneous (from other relational database products and data sources such as DB2, Access, Oracle, Excel, and text files). A query that joins or retrieves data across multiple platforms is a cross-platform query. Using a cross platform query, you can access legacy database systems without the cost of merging or migrating existing data sources.

The remote data sources are connected to via an OLE DB provider. OLE DB, created by Microsoft, is a set of COM (component object model) interfaces used to provide consistent access to varying data sources. To establish access from a SQL Server 2005 instance to another data source requires that you choose the correct OLE DB provider. How the OLE DB provider was designed determines what kind of distributed query operations can be implemented through a distributed query (whether SELECT, INSERT, UPDATE, or DELETE stored-procedure execution).

So in a nutshell, a linked server is a means of establishing a connection to a remote data source. Depending on the OLE DB driver used to set up the linked server, you can execute distributed queries to retrieve data or perform operations on the remote data source.

Distributed queries can also be run without having to define linked servers, for example by using the Transact-SQL function OPENROWSET. In addition to querying a remote data source without a linked server, OPENROWSET has been enhanced in SQL Server 2005 to allow BULK reads of ASCII, Unicode, and binary files. Using OPENROWSET and BULK, you can read tabular data from a text file, or use it to import an ASCII, Unicode, or binary type file into a single large data type column and single row (such as varchar(max), nvarchar(max), or varbinary(max)).

Also new in SQL Server 2005, Microsoft has introduced the SYNONYM object, which allows you to reference an object that has a long name with a shorter name. This can be useful for long identifiers in general, but particularly for distributed queries that reference a four-part linked server name, using a shorter name for the data source instead.

This chapter contains recipes for creating linked servers, executing distributed queries, reading from a text file using OPENROWSET and BULK, and using the new SYNONYM object.

Linked Server Basics

This next set of recipes will demonstrate how to use linked servers. Specifically, I'll be demonstrating how to

- Create a linked server connection to another SQL Server 2005 instance.
- Configure the properties of a linked server.
- View information about configured linked servers on the SQL Server instance.
- Drop a linked server.

I'll start off by discussing how to use the system stored procedure sp_addlinkedserver to create a new linked server.

Creating a Linked Server to Another SQL Server Instance

Linked servers allow you to query external data sources from within a SQL Server instance. The external data source can either be a different SQL Server instance, or non-SQL Server data source such as Oracle, MS Access, DB2, or MS Excel.

To create the linked server, use the system stored procedure sp_addlinkedserver. The syntax is as follows:

```
sp_addlinkedserver
    [ @server= ] 'server' [ ,
    [ @srvproduct= ] 'product_name' ]
    [ , [ @provider= ] 'provider_name' ]
    [ , [ @datasrc= ] 'data_source' ]
    [ , [ @location= ] 'location' ]
    [ , [ @provstr= ] 'provider_string' ]
    [ , [ @catalog= ] 'catalog' ]
```

The parameters of this system stored procedure are described in Table 27-1.

Table 27-1. *sp_addlinkedserver Arguments*

Argument	Description
Server	Local name used for the linked server. Instance names are also allowed, for example MYSERVER\SQL1.
product_name	Product name of the OLE DB data source. For SQL Server instances, the product_name is 'SQL Server'.
provider_name	This is the unique programmatic identifier for the OLE DB provider. When not specified, the provider name is the SQL Server data source. The explicit provider_name for SQL Server is SQLNCLI (for Microsoft SQL Native Client OLE DB Provider). MSDAORA is used for Oracle, OraOLEDB.Oracle for Oracle versions 8 and higher, Microsoft.Jet.OLEDB.4.0 for MS Access and MS Excel, DB2OLEDB for IBM DB2, and MSDASQL for an ODBC data source.
data_source	This is the data source as interpreted by the specified OLE DB provider. For SQL Server, this is the network name of the SQL Server (servername or servername\instancename). For Oracle, this is the SQL*Net alias. For MS Access and MS Excel, this is the full path and name of the file. For an ODBC data source, this is the system DSN name.
Location	The location as interpreted by the specified OLE DB provider.

Argument	Description
provider_string	The connection string specific to the OLE DB provider. For an ODBC connection, this is the ODBC connection string. For MS Excel, this is Excel 5.0.
Catalog	The catalog definition varies based on the OLE DB provider implementation. For SQL Server, this is the optional database name. For DB2, this catalog is the name of the database.

In a network environment with multiple SQL Server instances, linked servers provide a convenient method for sharing SQL Server data without having to physically push or pull the data and replicate the schema.

■**Tip** In this chapter, I cover examples of communication between SQL Server instances. For heterogeneous data sources such as DB2, Access, and Oracle, parameters will vary substantially. For an extensive table of required sp_addlinkedserver options, see the SQL Server Books Online topic "sp_addlinkedserver (Transact-SQL)."

The configurations used to connect to heterogeneous data sources vary, based on the OLE DB provider. If you're just connecting to a different SQL Server instance, however, Microsoft makes it easy for you. In this recipe, I demonstrate creating a linked server connection to another SQL Server instance:

```
EXEC  sp_addlinkedserver @server=  'JOEPROD',
            @srvproduct=  'SQL Server'
```

You can also create linked servers to connect to SQL Server named instances, for example:

```
EXEC  sp_addlinkedserver @server=  'JOEPROD\NODE2',
            @srvproduct=  'SQL Server'
```

How It Works

Adding a linked server to an external data source allows you to perform distributed queries (distributed queries are reviewed later in this chapter). When adding a SQL Server linked server to a SQL Server instance, whether it's a default or named instance, Microsoft makes it easy for you by requiring just the server and product_name values.

What about the security method for connecting to the SQL Server instance? When creating a new linked server, the current user's login security credentials (SQL or Windows) will be used to connect to the linked server. You can also create explicit remote login mapping for the linked server, which you'll see discussed later on in the chapter.

Configuring Linked Server Properties

There are a number of different settings you can use to configure a linked server after it has been created. These settings are described in Table 27-2.

Table 27-2. *Linked Server Properties*

Setting	Description
collation compatible	Enable this setting if you are certain that the SQL Server instance has the same collation as the remote SQL Server instance. Doing so can improve performance, as SQL Server will no longer have to perform comparisons of character columns between the data sources, as the same collation is assumed.
collation name	If use remote collation is enabled and the linked server is for a non-SQL Server data source, collation name specifies the name of the remote server collation. The collation name must be one supported by SQL Server.
Connect timeout	Designates the number of seconds a connection attempt will be made to the linked server before a timeout occurs. If the value is "0", the sp_configure server value of remote query timeout is used as a default.
data access	If enabled, distributed query access is allowed.
lazy schema validation	If set to true, schema is not checked on remote tables at the beginning of the query. Although this reduces overhead for the remote query, if the schema has changed and you are not schema-checking, the query may raise an error if the referenced objects used by the query no longer correspond with the query command.
query timeout	Determines the number of seconds it takes for a waiting query to time out. If this value is 0, then the sp_configure value configured for the query wait option will be used instead.
rpc	Enables remote procedure calls from the server.
rpc out	Enables remote procedure calls to the server.
use remote collation	Determines if remote server collation is used (true) instead of the local server collation (false).

To change linked server properties, use the sp_serveroption system stored procedure. The syntax is as follows:

```
sp_serveroption [@server =] 'server'
     ,[@optname =] 'option_name'
   ,[@optvalue =] 'option_value'
```

The arguments of this system stored procedure are described in Table 27-3.

Table 27-3. *sp_serveroption Arguments*

Argument	Description
server	The name of the linked server to configure properties for.
option_name	The option to configure.
option_value	The new value of the option.

In this recipe, the query timeout setting for the JOEPROD\NODE2 linked server will be changed to 60 seconds:

```
EXEC sp_serveroption
   @server = 'JOEPROD\NODE2' ,
   @optname = 'query timeout',
   @optvalue = 60
```

How It Works

In this recipe, the linked server JOEPROD\NODE2 was modified to a query timeout limit of 60 seconds. The first parameter, called server, designated the linked server name. The second parameter, option_name, designated the option to configure, and the third parameter, option_value, configured the new value.

Viewing Linked Server Information

You can use the sys.servers system catalog view to view linked servers defined on a SQL Server instance. For example:

```
SELECT name, query_timeout, lazy_schema_validation
FROM sys.servers
WHERE is_linked = 1
```

This returns:

name	query_timeout	lazy_schema_validation
JOEPROD\NODE2	60	0

How It Works

The system catalog view sys.servers can be used to retrieve information about linked servers defined on your SQL Server instance. Other options you can view from sys.servers include: product, provider, data_source, location, provider_string, catalog, is_linked, is_remote_login_enabled, is_rpc_out_enabled, is_data_access_enabled, is_collation_compatible, use_remote_collation, and collation_name. The is_linked column was qualified in the query to return only linked servers (excluding the local SQL Server instance settings).

Dropping a Linked Server

The sp_dropserver system stored procedure is used to drop a linked server. The syntax for sp_dropserver is as follows:

```
sp_dropserver [ @server= ] 'server'
    [ , [ @droplogins= ] { 'droplogins' | NULL} ]
```

The parameters of this system stored procedure are described in Table 27-4.

Table 27-4. *sp_dropserver Arguments*

Argument	Description
server	The name of the linked server to remove from the SQL Server instance.
droplogins	If droplogins is specified, login mappings (described later in this chapter) are removed prior to dropping the linked server.

This recipe demonstrates dropping a linked server:

```
EXEC sp_dropserver
    @server= 'JOEPROD',
@droplogins= 'droplogins'
```

How It Works

This recipe demonstrated removing a linked server from your SQL Server instance using the system stored procedure sp_dropserver. The droplogins option was designated in the second parameter to drop any existing login mappings (I'll review linked server logins in the next block of recipes) prior to removing the linked server. If you try to drop a linked server before removing logins, you'll get the following message:

```
There are still remote logins for the server.
```

Linked Server Logins

In the next three recipes, I'll demonstrate how to work with linked server login mappings. Specifically, I'll cover how to

- Create a linked server login mapping.
- View linked server login mappings configured on the SQL server instance.
- Drop a linked server login mapping.

I'll start off by discussing how to use the system stored procedure sp_addlinkedsrvlogin to create a login mapping.

Adding a Linked Server Login Mapping

When executing a distributed query against a linked server, SQL Server maps your local login and credentials to the linked server. Based on the security on the remote data source, your credentials are either accepted or rejected. When sp_addlinkedserver is executed and a linked server is created, the default behavior is to use your local login credentials (either SQL or Windows) to access data on the linked server. Even if you don't have the proper permissions to connect to a linked server, security on the linked server is not checked until you attempt a distributed query. Since security configurations, logins, and database users vary by SQL Server instance, you may need to set up a different mapping from your local login to a different remote login.

The login mapping information is stored on the SQL Server instance where the linked server is defined. To create a login mapping, you use the sp_addlinkedsrvlogin system stored procedure.

The syntax is as follows:

```
sp_addlinkedsrvlogin [ @rmtsrvname = ] 'rmtsrvname'
    [ , [ @useself = ] 'useself' ]
    [ , [ @locallogin = ] 'locallogin' ]
    [ , [ @rmtuser = ] 'rmtuser' ]
    [ , [ @rmtpassword = ] 'rmtpassword' ]
```

The parameters of this system stored procedure are described in Table 27-5.

Table 27-5. *sp_addlinkedsrvlogin Arguments*

Argument	Description
rmtsrvname	The local linked server that you want to add the login mapping to.
Useself	When the value true is used, the local SQL or Windows login is used to connect to the remote server name. If false, the locallogin, rmtuser, and rmtpassword parameters of the sp_addlinkedsrvlogin stored procedure will apply to the new mapping.

Argument	Description
locallogin	This is the name of the SQL Server login or Windows user to map to a remote login. If this parameter is left NULL, the mapping applies to all local logins on the SQL Server instance.
rmtuser	The name of the user/login used to connect to the linked server.
rmtpassword	The password of the login/user used to connect to the linked server.

In this recipe, a login mapping is created for all local users—mapping to a login named "test" on the JOEPROD\NODE2 linked server:

```
EXEC sp_addlinkedsrvlogin
    @rmtsrvname = 'JOEPROD\NODE2',
    @useself = false ,
    @locallogin = NULL,  -- Applies to all local logins
    @rmtuser = 'test',
    @rmtpassword = 'test1!'
```

How It Works

In this recipe, a login mapping was explicitly created using the sp_addlinkedsrvlogin system stored procedure. The first parameter @rmtsrvname contained the name of the linked server you are connecting to. The second parameter, @useself, was a false value, so that the defined login and password in @rmtuser and @rmtpassword on the remote server will be used. The @locallogin was set to NULL, meaning that the test login will be used to map from any login on the local SQL Server connection. Now when a query is executed against the TESTSRV linked server, those queries will run under the test remote user.

Viewing Linked Logins

To see explicit local login mappings to remote logins, you can query the sys.server_principals, sys.linked_logins, and sys.servers system catalog views, as this query demonstrates:

```
SELECT s.name LinkedServerName, ll.remote_name, p.name LocalLoginName
FROM sys.linked_logins ll
INNER JOIN sys.servers s ON
   s.server_id = ll.server_id
LEFT OUTER JOIN sys.server_principals p ON
   p.principal_id = ll.local_principal_id
WHERE s.is_linked = 1
```

This returns:

LinkedServerName	remote_name	LocalLoginName
JOEPROD\NODE2	test	NULL

How It Works

This recipe retrieved explicit login mappings to remote logins by querying the sys.linked_logins, sys.servers, and sys.server_principals system catalog views. The query returned the name of the linked server, the remote login on the remote data source, and the local login that was mapped to it. In this case, the results returned the remote login name of test and NULL for the local login name (meaning that all local connections will map to the remote test login).

Dropping a Linked Server Login Mapping

Use the sp_droplinkedsrvlogin system stored procedure to drop a linked server login mapping. The syntax for sp_droplinkedsrvlogin is as follows:

```
sp_droplinkedsrvlogin [ @rmtsrvname= ] 'rmtsrvname' ,
    [ @locallogin= ] 'locallogin'
```

The parameters of this system-stored procedure are described in Table 27-6.

Table 27-6. *sp_droplinkedsrvlogin Arguments*

Argument	Description
rmtsrvname	The linked server name of the login mapping.
locallogin	This is the name of the SQL Server login or Windows user mapping to drop from the linked server.

This recipe demonstrates dropping the login mapping created in an earlier recipe:

```
EXEC sp_droplinkedsrvlogin
    @rmtsrvname= 'JOEPROD\NODE2' ,
    @locallogin=  NULL
```

How It Works

In this recipe, the default login mapping for all local users was removed by sending the linked server name in the first parameter, and a NULL value in the second @locallogin parameter.

Executing Distributed Queries

So far in this chapter, I've demonstrated how to create and configure linked servers. In this next set of recipes, you'll learn how to execute distributed queries against the linked server remote data source. You aren't limited to using a linked server to connect to a remote data source, however, and the next few recipes will also demonstrate how to access external data using commands such as OPENQUERY and OPENROWSET. You'll also lean how to create and use an alias to a linked server name.

Executing Distributed Queries Against a Linked Server

Distributed queries are queries that reference one or more linked servers, performing either read or modification operations against remote tables, views, or stored procedures. The types of queries (SELECT, INSERT, UPDATE, DELETE, EXEC) that are supported against linked servers depend on the level of support for transactions present in the OLE DB providers. You can run a distributed query referencing a linked server by using either a four-part name of the remote object in the FROM clause, or using the OPENQUERY Transact-SQL command (OPENQUERY is reviewed later in the chapter).

The basic syntax for referencing a linked server using a four-part name is as follows:

```
linked_server_name.catalog.schema.object_name
```

The parts of the four-part name are described in Table 27-7.

Table 27-7. *Linked Server Four-Part Name*

Part	Description
linked_server_name	The linked server name.
catalog	The catalog (database) name.
schema	The schema container of the data source object.
object_name	The database object (for example the view, table, data source, or stored procedure).

This distributed query selects the performance counter value from the sys.dm_os_performance_counters dynamic management view on the linked server:

```
SELECT object_name, counter_name, instance_name,
cntr_value, cntr_type
FROM JOEPROD.master.sys.dm_os_performance_counters
WHERE counter_name = 'Active Transactions' AND
  instance_name = '_Total'
```

This returns:

object_name	counter_name	instance_name	cntr_value	cntr_type
SQLServer:Databases	Active Transactions	_Total	0	65792

This next query demonstrates executing a system-stored procedure on the linked server (for a SQL Server named instance). The linked server is a named instance, so the full name is put in square brackets:

```
EXEC [JOEPROD\NODE2].master.dbo.sp_monitor
```

This returns various statistics and result sets about the remote SQL Server instance:

last_run	current_run	seconds
2005-09-02 22:47:26.770	2005-10-09 10:52:27.007	3153901

cpu_busy	io_busy	idle
53(53)-0%	22(21)-0%	10433(10192)-0%

packets_received	packets_sent	packet_errors
182(154)	377(349)	0(0)

total_read	total_write	total_errors	connections
693(693)	201(201)	0(0)	8091(8079)

How It Works

As you can see, executing a distributed query simply involves referencing the database object using the four-part name. If you need to reference a linked server that is a SQL Server named instance, use square brackets around the linked server name.

Creating and Using an Alias to Reference Four-Part Linked Server Names

Introduced in SQL Server 2005, you can create an alias for a database object (including stored procedures, functions, tables, and views). This alias can then be referenced in your code, allowing you to shorten a long name, or obscure changes to the underlying object source (switching from a development to production linked server name, for example).

This functionality is performed using CREATE SYNONYM, which uses the following syntax:

```
CREATE SYNONYM [ schema_name. ] synonym_name
FOR < object >
```

The arguments for this command are detailed in Table 27-8.

Table 27-8. *CREATE SYNONYM*

Argument	Description
[schema_name.] synonym_name	The optional schema name and required synonym name.
object	The object that will be aliased. This can be of the format server_name.database_name.schema_name.object_name, database_name.schema_name.object_name, or schema_name.object_name.

Also, to drop a synonym, use the DROP SYNONYM command. The syntax is as follows:

```
DROP SYNONYM [ schema. ] synonym_name
```

The command takes the optional schema of the synonym and the required synonym name. In this recipe, a synonym is created on a linked server:

```
CREATE SYNONYM dbo.PerfInfo
FOR JOEPROD.master.sys.dm_os_performance_counters
```

Next, the linked server synonym is referenced in the FROM clause of the query using the new synonym name:

```
SELECT cntr_value
FROM dbo.PerfInfo
WHERE counter_name = 'Active Transactions' AND
instance_name = '_Total'
```

After that, the synonym is dropped from the database:

```
DROP SYNONYM dbo.PerfInfo
```

Lastly, a new synonym is created with the same name as before, but this time pointing to a different SQL Server instance:

```
CREATE SYNONYM dbo.PerfInfo
FOR [JOEPROD\NODE2].master.sys.dm_os_performance_counters
```

How It Works

In this recipe, a synonym called PerfInfo was created to represent a four-part linked server table name. Synonyms can reduce keystrokes by allowing you to use a shorter name to represent a linked server four-part name. The PerfInfo synonym was then used in the FROM clause in order to query the underlying linked server table. After that, the synonym was dropped (although in real life you would have kept the synonym around for future use). Lastly, a new synonym was created with the previous name, referencing a new data source. This means the original query against dbo.PerfInfo will now access a different SQL Server instance. Synonyms can give you the ability to change underlying data sources without changing the referencing synonym name.

Executing Distributed Queries Using OPENQUERY

SQL Server provides a different method for executing distributed queries other than using the four-part naming method.

OPENQUERY is a function that issues a pass-through query against an existing linked server and is referenced in the FROM clause of a query just like a table. The syntax is as follows:

```
OPENQUERY ( linked_server ,'query' )
```

The parameters for this command are described in Table 27-9.

Table 27-9. *OPENQUERY Arguments*

Argument	Description
linked_server_name	The linked server name that you want to query.
Catalog	The actual query to issue against the linked server connection.

The OPENQUERY command queries a linked server by sending it as a pass-through query instead of referencing the four-part name. A pass-through query executes entirely on the remote server and then returns the results back to the calling query.

Why use one over the other? Some OLE DB providers that you can use to create a linked server may have varying abilities to be referenced using the four-part name in the FROM clause. OPENQUERY is an alternative method for retrieving distributed data, and may work correctly where a four-part name query does not.

This recipe demonstrates querying a linked server with the same query as the previous recipe, only this time the actual query in the second parameter of the OPENQUERY command uses the three-part, not four-part, name in the FROM clause:

```
SELECT cntr_value
FROM OPENQUERY ( [JOEPROD] ,
'SELECT object_name, counter_name, instance_name, cntr_value, cntr_type
FROM JOEPROD.master.sys.dm_os_performance_counters
WHERE counter_name = ''Active Transactions'' AND
instance_name = ''_Total''' )
```

How It Works

In this recipe, the first parameter of the OPENQUERY command was the name of the linked server. The second parameter was the query itself. Notice that the WHERE clause contains double-ticked values, which serve as delimited single ticks.

Executing Ad Hoc Queries Using OPENROWSET

Like OPENQUERY, the OPENROWSET command is referenced in the FROM clause and acts like a table in a SELECT statement. Unlike OPENQUERY however, OPENROWSET creates an ad hoc connection to the data source. It does *not* use an existing linked server connection to query the remote data source. This is a good function to use if you don't wish to retain a linked server for a remote data source on the SQL Server instance.

The syntax for `OPENROWSET` is as follows:

```
OPENROWSET
( { 'provider_name' ,
{ 'datasource' ; 'user_id' ; 'password' | 'provider_string' }
, { [ catalog. ] [ schema. ] object | 'query' }
```

The parameters for this command are described in Table 27-10.

Table 27-10. *OPENROWSET Arguments*

Argument	Description
provider_name	The unique programmatic identifier for the OLE DB provider.
datasource ; user_id ; password | provider_string	This is the connection string expected by the OLE DB provider. Either you designate the datasource, user_id, and password, *or* you can designate the provider string.
catalog.schema.object| query	The object name to return results for or the query to execute.

■**Note** The ability to use OPENROWSET to query remote data sources is off by default in SQL Server 2005. To enable use of OPENROWSET you must enable it using SQL Server 2005 Surface Area Configuration. Under the "Ad Hoc Remote Query" section, check the "Enable OPENROWSET and OPENDATASOURCE support checkbox."

In this recipe, a query is issued against a SQL Server 2005 named instance:

```
SELECT *
FROM OPENROWSET
('SQLNCLI','TESTSRV\NODE2';'test';'test1!',
'SELECT * FROM AdventureWorks.HumanResources.Department
WHERE GroupName = ''Research and Development''')
```

This returns:

DepartmentID	Name	GroupName	ModifiedDate
1	Engineering	Research and Development	1998-06-01 00:00:00.000
2	Tool Design	Research and Development	1998-06-01 00:00:00.000
6	Research and Development	Research and Development	1998-06-01 00:00:00.000
18	Misc	Research and Development	2005-09-20 19:20:25.570

How It Works

In this recipe, I used `OPENROWSET` to query a remote data source without having to define a linked server. The first parameter of the command designated `SQLNCLI`, which is the provider name for the Microsoft SQL Native Client OLE DB Provider. The second parameter included three semicolon delimited values—the SQL Server 2005 instance name, login, and password. The last parameter for the command included a query against the `AdventureWorks` database on the remote SQL Server instance.

OPENROWSET can be used in the FROM clause of a SELECT and can also be used as the target table of an INSERT, UPDATE, or DELETE operation—depending on the update support of the OLE DB Provider.

Reading Data from a File Using OPENROWSET BULK Options

Introduced in SQL Server 2005, you can now query data from an ASCII, Unicode, or binary file using the new BULK options in the OPENROWSET command. With this functionality, you can query a file and also use the result set in a data modification statement—all without having to first physically import the data from the file into a SQL Server table.

The syntax for the BULK options in OPENROWSET is as follows:

```
OPENROWSET
( { BULK 'data_file' ,
      { FORMATFILE = 'format_file_path' [ <bulk_options> ]
      | SINGLE_BLOB | SINGLE_CLOB | SINGLE_NCLOB }
} )
```

The parameters for this command are described in Table 27-11.

Table 27-11. *OPENROWSET...BULK Arguments*

Argument	Description
data_file	The name and path of the file to read.
format_file_path	The name and path of the format file—which lays out the column definitions in the data file. In SQL Server 2005, you have a choice of two format file layouts—XML or non-XML.
bulk_options	These options define how the data is read, as well as which rows are retrieved. See the next table for details.
SINGLE_BLOB | SINGLE_CLOB | SINGLE_NCLOB	When designated, the format file parameter is ignored. Instead, the data file is imported as a single row, single column value. For example if you wish to import a document or image file into a large data type column, you would designate one of these flags. Designate the SINGLE_BLOB object for importing into a varbinary(max) data type, SINGLE_CLOB for ASCII data into a varchar(max) data type, and SINGLE_NCLOB for importing into a nvarchar(max) Unicode data type.

The BULK options syntax is as follows:

```
<bulk_options> ::=
   [ , CODEPAGE = { 'ACP' | 'OEM' | 'RAW' | 'code_page' }]
   [ , ERRORFILE = 'file_name' ]
   [ , FIRSTROW = first_row ]
   [ , LASTROW = last_row ]
   [ , MAXERRORS = maximum_errors ]
   [ , ROWS_PER_BATCH = rows_per_batch ]
```

These options are described in Table 27-12.

Table 27-12. *BULK Options*

Option	Description
`'ACP'` | `'OEM'` | `'RAW'` | `'code_page'`	This defines the chosen source data code page of character data to be converted to the destination SQL Server code page. OEM is the default. ACP is the ISO 1252 code page, RAW implies no conversion, and code_page is a specific encoded code page number.
`file_name`	The error file name used to hold any reject rows from the BULK process.
`first_row`	The first row in the result set to load (default is 1). If the first row includes column names, you can designate a first_row of "2" to skip the first column.
`last_row`	The last row in the result set to load (default is 0, the last row of the result set).
`maximum_errors`	The maximum number of errors in the load process before the load fails (default is 10).
`rows_per_batch`	This value indicates the number of rows to import per batch; however OPENROWSET should always import the data as a single batch. Specifying a number here may help the query processor allocate appropriate resources. However, in most cases this option can be ignored or set to 0.

In this recipe, I'll demonstrate two examples of reading from an external text file.

The first example demonstrates using a SELECT statement to read data from a text file. The text file has the following comma delimited data in a text file called ContactType.txt:

```
21,Sales Phone Rep,2005-06-01 00:00:00
20,Sales Phone Manager,2005-06-01 00:00:00
```

The columns in this file will be defined using a format file called ContactTypeFormat.Fmt which contains the following format file definition (SQL Server 2005 allows both XML formatted and regular text format files):

```
9.0
3
1 SQLCHAR 0 2 "," 1 ContactTypeID ""
2 SQLCHAR 0 20 "," 2 Name SQL_Latin1_General_CP1_CI_AS
3 SQLCHAR 0 19 "\r\n" 3 ModifiedDate ""
```

This query reads from the ContactType.txt file in a SELECT query:

```
SELECT ContactTypeID, Name, ModifiedDate
FROM OPENROWSET( BULK 'C:\Apress\Recipes\ContactType.txt',
          FORMATFILE = 'C:\Apress\Recipes\ContactTypeFormat.Fmt',
          FIRSTROW = 1,
          MAXERRORS = 5,
          ERRORFILE = 'C:\Apress\Recipes\ImportErrors.txt' )
          AS ContactType
```

This returns:

ContactTypeID	Name	ModifiedDate
21	Sales Phone Rep	2005-06-01 00:00:00
20	Sales Phone Manager	2005-06-01 00:00:00

The second example in this recipe will import the ContactType.txt file into a single column and single row (instead of breaking it out into a tabular result set as was done in the previous query). First, a table is created to hold the imported document:

```
-- Create a table to hold import documents
CREATE TABLE dbo.ImportRepository
   (ImportHistoryID int IDENTITY(1,1) NOT NULL PRIMARY KEY,
    ImportFile varchar(max) NOT NULL)
GO
```

Next, the value is imported into a new row using OPENROWSET...BULK:

```
INSERT dbo.ImportRepository
(ImportFile)
SELECT BulkColumn
FROM OPENROWSET( BULK 'C:\Apress\Recipes\ContactType.txt',
           SINGLE_CLOB) as ContactTypeFile
```

Now to confirm the contents:

```
SELECT ImportFile
FROM dbo.ImportRepository
```

This returns:

```
ImportFile
21,Sales Phone Rep,2005-06-01 00:00:00    20,Sales Phone Manager,2005-06-01 00:00:00
```

How It Works

In the first example in this recipe, a data file was queried using the OPENROWSET BULK option. The SELECT clause included the columns from the data file, as defined by the format file:

```
SELECT ContactTypeID, Name, ModifiedDate
```

The OPENROWSET command was then included in the FROM clause. The BULK option was the first parameter in the command, followed by the data and data format file:

```
FROM OPENROWSET( BULK 'C:\Apress\Recipes\ContactType.txt',
FORMATFILE = 'C:\Apress\Recipes\ContactTypeFormat.Fmt',
```

Three options were also included, designating the first row of the data file to be imported:

```
        FIRSTROW = 1,
```

The number of allowable errors for the import before failure was also designated, along with an error file to contain the rejected rows:

```
        MAXERRORS = 5,
        ERRORFILE = 'C:\Apress\Recipes\ImportErrors.txt' )
```

After the closed parenthesis, a table name alias was required in order to be used in the SELECT query:

```
        AS ContactType
```

The second example used OPENROWSET to insert the entire contents of a single file into a single column and single row. After creating a table to store the results, an INSERT SELECT was used:

```
INSERT dbo.ImportRepository
(ImportFile)
```

The SELECT referenced the BulkColumn system column name, which is returned from OPENROWSET when using any of the SINGLE_* options:

```
SELECT BulkColumn
```

The OPENROWSET is held in the FROM clause of the SELECT statement, followed by the name of the file and the SINGLE_CLOB option (which imports the data as ASCII text):

```
FROM OPENROWSET( BULK 'C:\Apress\Recipes\ContactType.txt',
         SINGLE_CLOB) as ContactTypeFile
```

This is a much easier method of importing files (ASCII, Unicode, or Binary) using Transact-SQL than was available in previous versions of SQL Server. A query is executed against the table, and the results of the raw file format are displayed in a single column/row (with delimiting commas intact).

CHAPTER 28

■ ■ ■

Performance Tuning

When you're talking about database queries, performance is a subjective term. While one end-user could be happy with a query that takes ten seconds to execute, another user might not be happy unless all queries run under one second. While performance requirements are certainly diverse, so are the methods used to improve performance. A few key factors that impact SQL Server query performance include:

- *Database design.* Probably one of the most important factors influencing both query performance and data integrity, design decisions impact both read and modification performance. Standard designs include OLTP-normalized databases, which focus on data integrity, removal of redundancy, and the establishment of relationships between multiple entities. This is a design most appropriate for quick transaction processing. You'll usually see more tables in a normalized OLTP design, which means more table joins in your queries. Data warehouse designs, on the other hand, often use a more denormalized Star or Snowflake design. These designs use a central fact table, which is joined to two or more description dimension tables. For Snowflake designs, the dimension tables can also have related tables associated to it. The focus of this design is on query speed and not on fast updates to transactions.

- *Physical hardware.* I once spent a day trying to get a three second query down to one second. No matter which indexes I tried to add, or query modifications I made, I couldn't get its duration lowered. This was because there were simply too many rows required in the result set. The limiting factor was the I/O. A few months later, I migrated the database to the higher-powered production server. Lo and behold, the query executed consistently in less than one second. This underscores the fact that CPU, memory, and RAID subsystems can have a significant impact (both positive and negative) on query performance. As a matter of fact, memory is one of the most critical resources for the SQL Server, allowing it to cache data and execution plans for faster data retrieval and query execution. If you're prioritizing where your server dollars go, don't be stingy with the memory.

- *Network throughput.* The time it takes to obtain query results can be impacted by a slow or unstable network connection. This doesn't mean that you should blame the poor network engineers whenever a query executes slowly—but do keep this potential cause on your list of areas to investigate.

- *Index fragmentation.* As data modifications are made over time, your indexes will become fragmented. As fragmentation increases, data will become spread out over more data pages. The more data pages your query needs to retrieve, the slower the query.

- *Appropriate indexing.* In addition to watching for fragmentation, you need to make sure only useful indexes are kept on your tables. Your table indexes should be based on your high priority or frequently executed queries. If a query is executing thousands of times a day and is completing in two seconds, but could be running in less than one second with the proper index, adding this index could reduce the I/O pressure on your SQL Server instance significantly. You should create indexes as needed, and remove indexes that aren't being used (this chapter shows you how to do this). Each index on your table adds overhead to data modification operations, and can even slow down SELECT queries if SQL Server decides to use the less efficient index. When you're initially designing your database, it is better for you to keep the indexes at a minimum (having at least a clustered index and nonclustered indexes for your foreign keys). Instead, wait to add additional indexes until after you have a better idea about the queries that will be executed against the database.

- *Up-to-date statistics.* As I discussed in Chapter 22, the AUTO_CREATE_STATISTICS database option enables SQL Server to automatically generate statistical information regarding the distribution of values in a column. If you disable this behavior, statistics can get out of date. Since SQL Server depends on statistics to decide how to execute the query, SQL Server may choose a less than optimal plan if it is basing its execution decisions on stale statistics.

In this chapter, I'll demonstrate the commands and techniques you can use to help troubleshoot and evaluate your query performance. You'll also learn how to address fragmented indexes and out-of-date statistics, and evaluate the usage of indexes in the database. I'll introduce you to a few graphical interface tools such as SQL Server Profiler, graphical execution plans, and the Database Engine Tuning Advisor. This chapter will also review a few miscellaneous performance topics, including how to use sp_executesql as an alternative to dynamic SQL, how to apply query hints to a query without changing the query itself, and how to force a query to use a specific query execution plan.

Query Performance Tips

Before I start the discussion of the commands and tools you can use to evaluate query performance, I'd first like to briefly review a few basic query performance tuning guidelines. Query performance is a vast topic, and in many of the chapters I've tried to include small tips along with the various content areas (such as stored procedures, views, and triggers). Since this is a chapter that discusses query performance independently of specific objects, the following list details a few query-performance best practices to be aware of when constructing SQL Server 2005 queries (note that indexing tips are reviewed later in the chapter) :

- In your SELECT query, only return the columns that you need. Don't underestimate the impact of narrow result sets. Fewer columns in your query translate to less I/O and network bandwidth.

- Along with fewer columns, you should also be thinking about fewer rows. Use a WHERE clause to help reduce the rows returned by your query. Don't let the application return twenty thousand rows when you only need to display the first ten.

- Keep the FROM clause under control. Each table you JOIN to in a single query can add additional overhead. I can't give you an exact number to watch out for, as it depends on your database's design, size, and columns used to join a query. However, over the years, I've seen enormous queries that are functionally correct, but take much too long to execute. Although it is convenient to use a single query to perform a complex operation, don't underestimate the power of smaller queries. If I have a very large query in a stored procedure that is taking too long to execute, I'll usually try breaking that query down into smaller intermediate result sets. This usually results in a significantly faster generation of the final desired result set.

- Use ORDER BY only if you need ordered results. Sorting operations of larger result sets can incur additional overhead. If it isn't necessary for your query, remove it.

- Beware of testing in a vacuum. When developing your database on a test SQL Server instance, it is very important that you populate the tables with a representative data set. This means that you should populate the table with the estimated number of rows you would actually see in production, as well as a representative set of values. Don't use dummy data in your development database and then expect the query to execute with similar performance in production. SQL Server performance is highly dependent on indexes and statistics, and SQL Server will make decisions based on the actual values contained within a table. If your test data isn't representative of "real life" data, you'll be in for a surprise when queries in production don't perform as you saw them perform on the test database.

- I pushed this point hard in Chapter 10, and I think it is worth repeating here. Stored procedures can often yield excellent performance gains over regular ad hoc query calls. Stored procedures also promote query execution stability (reusing existing query execution plans). If you have a query that executes with unpredictable durations, consider encapsulating the query in a stored procedure.

When reading about SQL Server performance tuning (like you are now), be careful about the words "never" and "always." Instead, get comfortable with the answer "it depends." When it comes to query-tuning, results may vary. There are certainly many good and bad practices to be aware of, but performance tuning is both art and science. Keep your options open and feel free to experiment (in a test environment, of course). Ask questions and don't accept conventional wisdom at face value.

Capturing and Evaluating Query Performance

In this next set of recipes, I'll demonstrate how to capture and evaluate query performance. This book has focused almost entirely on SQL Server 2005's flavor of Transact-SQL, and hasn't touched on the various graphical interface tools much. I'll be breaking with this tradition in this chapter to briefly show you how to use SQL Profiler to capture query activity. Also, I'll demonstrate how to graphically display the actual or estimated execution plan of a query so that you can understand the decisions that SQL Server is making in order to generate the query result set. I'll also demonstrate several other Transact-SQL commands, which can be used to return detailed information about the query execution plan.

Capturing High Duration Queries Using SQL Server Profiler

There are usually two branches of query performance tuning: proactive and reactive. Proactive query tuning usually occurs during development. You design the database, populate it with data, and then start building queries. You build the queries based on application and end-user requirements. For those queries that don't perform well, you can tune them before deploying out in the stored procedure or to the application developer.

Reactive performance involves capturing poor performance after the code has already been deployed to production. Data changes over time, and so does the effectiveness of indexes and the queries that use them. Queries that once performed well may execute longer than they did originally. You may hear complaints from end-users, or you might actually seek out poorly performing queries yourself.

One of the most valuable graphical interface tools in the SQL Server 2005 toolset is SQL Server Profiler. With SQL Server Profiler, you can monitor query activity as it occurs against your SQL

Server instance. There are many potential uses for this tool, but this recipe specifically demonstrates how to use SQL Server Profiler to capture high duration queries.

In this recipe, SQL Server Profiler is launched and configured to capture high duration queries. Then, a query is executed in SQL Server Management Studio that will be captured in SQL Server Profiler:

1. The recipe begins by going to Start, Programs➤Microsoft SQL Server 2005➤Performance Tools➤SQL Server Profiler.

2. Once in SQL Server Profiler, go to File➤New Trace. This brings up the Connect to Server dialog box (see Figure 28-1). It is here that you select the name of the SQL Server instance to connect to, and the authentication method (either Windows or SQL). When you're finished designating these values, click the Connect button.

Figure 28-1. *The Connect to Server dialog box*

3. This brings up the Trace Properties dialog box (see Figure 28-2). In the Trace name field, type in **Queries with a Duration > 5 seconds**. SQL Server Profiler comes with a set of various trace templates. These templates contain pre-defined event selections, which allow you to get started with monitoring specific types of SQL Server instance activity. In this recipe, the TSQL_Duration template is selected from the Use the template field:

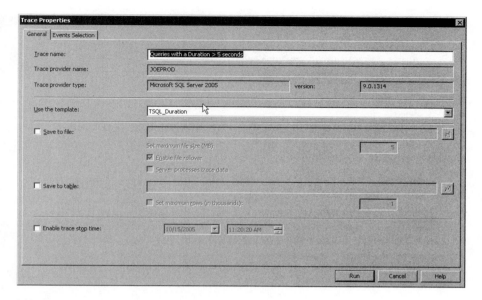

Figure 28-2. *The Trace Properties dialog box*

4. Next, click the Events Selection tab in the Trace Properties dialog box (see Figure 28-3). It is here that the traced events from the pre-canned TSQL_Duration template are loaded. Currently two different events will be monitored, RPC:Completed and SQL:BatchCompleted. This means that SQL Server Profiler will return a row for every remote procedure call or Transact-SQL statement that has completed on the SQL Server instance. This window also shows the columns which will be returned in the trace data, in this case including the Duration (duration of the completed query), TextData (capturing the actual Transact-SQL), SPID (the server process id of the caller), and BinaryData (returns different data depending on the event).

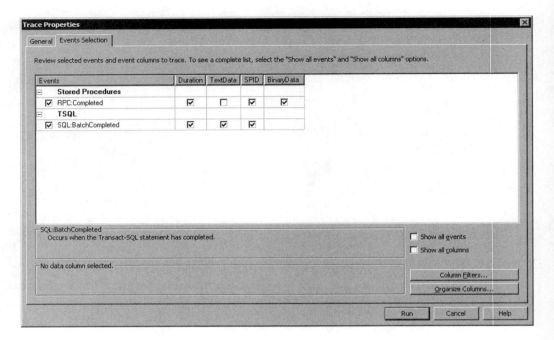

Figure 28-3. *Events Selection*

5. To see some other events and columns that can be added to the trace, click the Show all events and Show all columns checkboxes (see Figure 28-4). This adds several Event categories which can be expanded or contracted to show the events classes within. Available columns that are associated to the individual events can be checked or unchecked accordingly:

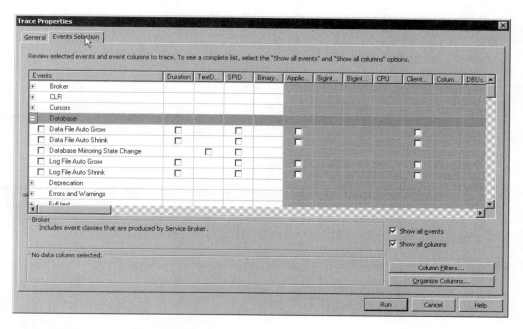

Figure 28-4. *Expanded events and columns*

6. Next, you'll want to configure this trace to only show events where the duration of the query is longer than five seconds. To do this, click the Column Filters button in the Events Selection window. This brings up the Edit Filter dialog box (see Figure 28-5). To filter query duration, click the Duration column in the left list box. In the right list box, expand the Greater than or equal filter and type in **5001** (this is a time measurement in milliseconds). To finish, select OK.

Figure 28-5. *Edit Filter dialog box*

7. To kick off the trace, click Run in the Trace Properties dialog box.

8. In SQL Server Management Studio, within a Query Editor, the following query is executed:

```
SELECT CustomerID, ContactID, Demographics, ModifiedDate
FROM Sales.Individual
```

9. Switching back to the SQL Server Profiler, you can see that the query was indeed captured in the trace (see Figure 28-6). In order to stop the trace, go to the File menu and select Stop Trace. By highlighting the SQL:BatchCompleted row, you can see the full SELECT statement in the lower pane. The duration shows that the query took 7.8 seconds, and originated from server process ID 52.

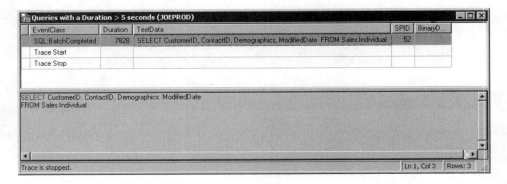

Figure 28-6. *SQL Server Profiler results*

How It Works

In this recipe, I demonstrated using SQL Server Profiler to identify a long running query. I filtered the list based on the query's duration in this example, but you can also add additional filters based on your needs. For example, you can add an additional filter to only include activity for the AdventureWorks database. Or, you could add filters to only include queries that reference a specific database object or column name. Once you've captured the activity you are looking for, you can save the trace output to a file or table. You can also launch the Database Engine Tuning Advisor to evaluate the trace data for potential index improvements. I'll cover the Database Engine Tuning Advisor later on in the chapter.

Capturing Executing Queries Using sys.dm_exec_requests

In addition to capturing queries in SQL Server Profiler, you can also capture the SQL for currently executing queries by querying the sys.dm_exec_requests dynamic management view, as this recipe demonstrates:

```
SELECT r.session_id, r.status, r.start_time, r.command, s.text
FROM sys.dm_exec_requests r
CROSS APPLY sys.dm_exec_sql_text(r.sql_handle) s
WHERE r.status = 'running'
```

This captures any queries that are currently being executed—even the current query used to capture those queries:

session_id	status	start_time	command	text
55	running	2005-10-16 13:53:52.670	SELECT	SELECT r.session_id, r.status, r.start_time, r.command, s.text FROM sys.dm_exec_requests r CROSS APPLY sys.dm_exec_sql_text(r.sql_handle) s WHERE r.status = 'running'

How It Works

The sys.dm_exec_requests dynamic management view returns information about all requests executing on a SQL Server instance.

The first line of the query selects the session ID, status of the query, start time, command type (for example SELECT, INSERT, UPDATE, DELETE), and actual SQL text:

```
SELECT r.session_id, r.status, r.start_time, r.command, s.text
```

In the FROM clause, the sys.dm_exec_requests dynamic management view is cross-applied against the sys.dm_exec_sql_text dynamic management function. This function takes the sql_handle from the sys.dm_exec_requests dynamic management view and returns the associated SQL text:

```
FROM sys.dm_exec_requests r
CROSS APPLY sys.dm_exec_sql_text(r.sql_handle) s
```

The WHERE clause then designates that currently running processes be returned:

```
WHERE r.status = 'running'
```

Viewing a Query's Graphical Execution Plan

Knowing how SQL Server executes a query can help you determine how best to fix a poorly performing query. Common operations that you can identify by viewing a query's execution plan (graphical or command based) include:

- Identifying whether the query is performing scans (looking at all the pages in a heap or index) or seeks (only accessing selected rows).

- Identifying missing statistics or other warnings.

- Performing costly sort or calculation activities.

In this recipe, I'll demonstrate how to view the estimated and actual execution plans for a query. I'll start by using the previous recipe's long duration query in SQL Server Management Studio, using the AdventureWorks database context (see Figure 28-7):

```
SELECT CustomerID, ContactID, Demographics, ModifiedDate
FROM Sales.Individual
```

Figure 28-7. *SQL Server Management Studio*

Next, I'm going to display the *estimated* query execution plan. This returns what operations SQL Server thinks it will perform without actually executing the query. To do this in SQL Server Management Studio, select Query and Display Estimated Execution Plan. This returns the query plan in the lower pane beneath the query (see Figure 28-8). The execution plan is represented by a tree that contains one or more operators.

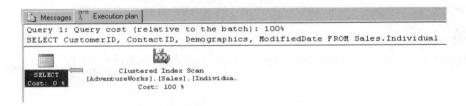

Figure 28-8. *Estimated Execution Plan graphical output*

The icons in Figure 28-8 represent each operator that SQL Server performs in order to produce the result set. An *operator* is an action SQL Server takes to execute a query. There are two types of operators: logical and physical. *Logical operators* describe an operation in conceptual terms, while *physical operators* are used to perform the actual implementation of the logical operator. For example, a logical operator may be INNER JOIN, but the physical method to perform an INNER JOIN is a Hash Match (one of the physical methods for joining two result sets).

■**Note** For a complete list of all available operators and their descriptions, see the SQL Server 2005 Books Online topic "Graphical Execution Plan Icons (SQL Server Management Studio)."

One of the operations returned in this example's execution plan is the Clustered Index Scan. This tells us that the entire clustered index was read in order to return the result set, which makes sense because the query doesn't use a WHERE clause to filter the result set.

The execution plan includes two different Cost % areas. The first Cost % can be found in the header of each query, where you see "Query 1: Query cost (relative to the batch)." This tells you what percentage of the query's duration was due to the specific query in the batch of queries. You'll also see percentage of cost underneath each of the icons in the execution plan results. In this example, the Clustered Index Scan accounted for 100% of the query's cost.

In addition to the estimated plan, you can also display the actual execution plan. This means the query itself is executed, returns results, and returns the execution plan as a separate tab. For example, to do this, select Query and Include Actual Execution Plan.

This time you'll change the query to include a defined range of customers, ordering the results by the ContactID:

```
SELECT CustomerID, ContactID, Demographics, ModifiedDate
FROM Sales.Individual
WHERE CustomerID BETWEEN 11000 AND 11020
ORDER BY ContactID
```

You then execute the query as normal in order to return the results, and the actual execution plan. After executing the query, three tabs are spawned: one for the results, one for any messages, and one containing the execution plan. Click the Execution plan tab to see the results (see Figure 28-9).

Figure 28-9. *Actual execution plan graphical output*

This time you'll see three operations in the execution plan output. With the graphical execution plan output, you read the icons from right-to-left, and top-to-bottom. You'll see that with the addition of the WHERE clause's CustomerID search condition in the query, the data retrieval operation changed from a Clustered Index Scan to a Clustered Index Seek operation. A scan retrieves all rows from a heap or index. A seek operation is more selective, retrieving specific rows from an index. Also, notice that the cost of this operation was 32%. The remaining cost percentage of the query was due to the Sort operator (at 68% cost), which appeared in the execution plan results because of the addition of our query's ORDER BY clause.

If you have multiple queries in a batch, for example when executing a stored procedure, you can use the graphical output to pinpoint which batch of the group has the highest cost %. For example, in this scenario you are going to execute the sp_help stored procedure with the Include Actual Execution Plan still enabled:

```
EXEC sp_help
```

This returns two result sets (abridged):

Name	Owner	Object_type
vAdditionalContactInfo	dbo	view
vEmployee	dbo	view
vEmployeeDepartment	dbo	view
vEmployeeDepartmentHistory	dbo	view
...		

User_type	Storage_type	Length	Prec	Scale	Nullable	Default_name	Rule_name	Collation
AccountNumber	nvarchar	30	15	NULL	yes	none	none	SQL_Latin1 General_CP1 _CI_AS
...								

Because there are two queries, you'll also see two actual execution plans (See Figure 28-10).

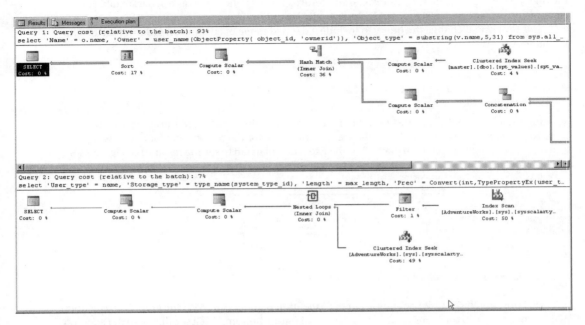

Figure 28-10. *Actual execution plan of sp_help*

The results of this stored procedure show two different execution plan panes within the stored procedure, with each pane showing the various operations used to generate the result sets. You can see in the header of the first query that the query cost is 93% (see Figure 28-11) versus the second query's 7% cost (see Figure 28-12)—as a percentage of the whole stored procedure execution:

```
Query 1: Query cost (relative to the batch): 93%
select 'Name' = o.name, 'Owner' = user_name(ObjectProperty( object_id, 'ownerid')), 'Object_type' = substring(v.name,5,31) from sys.all_
```

Figure 28-11. *Cost relative to Batch Query 1*

```
Query 2: Query cost (relative to the batch): 7%
select 'User_type' = name, 'Storage_type' = type_name(system_type_id), 'Length' = max_length, 'Prec' = Convert(int,TypePropertyEx(user_t_
```

Figure 28-12. *Cost relative to Batch Query 2*

So, if your job was to troubleshoot the performance of a stored procedure, your first step would be to identify the batch in the procedure with the highest cost. After identifying the highest cost batch, you should then focus in on the highest cost operations within that batch. For example, within the sp_help system-stored procedure, Query 1 consumed 93% of the total cost. Looking within Query 1's operators, you can then look for the higher percentage operations. For example in Figure 28-13, you can see that the Hash Match Inner Join operator has a cost of 36%, while the two Clustered Index Scan operations take 16% for one operation and 26% for another.

Figure 28-13. *Cost relative to Batch Query 2*

To get more information about an individual operation, you can hover your mouse pointer over it. This returns a ToolTip window which shows information about the specific operation, including a description of what each operator actually does, the number of rows impacted, and more (see Figure 28-14).

Hash Match

Use each row from the top input to build a hash table, and each row from the bottom input to probe into the hash table, outputting all matching rows.

Physical Operation	Hash Match
Logical Operation	Inner Join
Actual Number of Rows	2383
Estimated I/O Cost	0
Estimated CPU Cost	0.0312801
Estimated Operator Cost	0.0312831 (36%)
Estimated Subtree Cost	0.072014
Estimated Number of Rows	257.082
Estimated Row Size	176 B
Actual Rebinds	0
Actual Rewinds	0
Node ID	2

Output List
Union1048, Union1049, Expr1063
Probe Residual
[Expr1065]=[Expr1064]
Hash Keys Probe
Expr1065

Figure 28-14. *A ToolTip*

Other visual indicators you can look out for include *thick arrows*. Arrows become thicker based on the number of rows being passed from operator to operator. Hovering over the arrow gives you ToolTip information for the number of rows being passed to the next operation. Figure 28-15 shows the ToolTip for a Hash Match operator:

Figure 28-15. *A ToolTip for an arrow*

The color of the operator icon also has meaning. If the operator is red, this indicates a warning of some kind—for example, it could be telling you that the statistics on the table are missing. Yellow icons are used to represent cursor operations. Green icons represent language elements such as IF and WHILE. Blue icons are used for the remainder of the physical and logical operations.

Concluding this recipe, to stop the Query Editor from returning the Actual Execution Plan each time a query is executed, go to the Query menu and deselect Include Actual Execution Plan.

How It Works

In this recipe, I walked through how to view the estimated and actual query execution plans in a graphical format. This is by far the easiest way to visually understand what operations are taking place within your query. If a query is taking too long to execute, you can check the output for the higher cost query batches and within that query batch, the higher cost operators. Once you find a high percentage operator, you can hover your mouse pointer over it to see the ToolTip.

You don't, however, have to use the graphical tools in order to view a query's execution plan. SQL Server 2005 includes Transact-SQL commands which can also provide this information in result set form, as you'll see in the next recipe.

Viewing Estimated Query Execution Plans Using Transact-SQL Commands

In SQL Server 2005, there are three commands that can be used to view detailed information about a query execution plan for a SQL statement or batch: SET SHOWPLAN_ALL, SET SHOWPLAN_TEXT, and SET SHOWPLAN_XML. The output of these commands helps you understand how SQL Server plans to process and execute your query, identifying information such as table join types used and the indexes accessed. For example, using the output from these commands, you can see whether SQL Server is using a specific index in a query, and if so, whether it is retrieving the data using an index seek (nonclustered index is used to retrieve selected rows for the operation) or index scan (all index rows are retrieved for the operation).

When enabled, the SET SHOWPLAN_ALL, SET SHOWPLAN_TEXT, and SET SHOWPLAN_XML commands provide you with the plan information without executing the query, allowing you to adjust the query or indexes on the referenced tables before actually executing it.

Each of these commands returns information in a different way. SET SHOWPLAN_ALL returns the estimated query plan in a tabular format, with multiple columns and rows. The output includes information such as the estimated IO or CPU of each operation, estimated rows involved in the operation, operation cost (relative to itself and variations of the query), and the physical and logical operators used.

■ **Note** Logical operators describe the conceptual operation SQL Server must perform in the query execution. Physical operators are the actual implementation of that logical operation. For example a logical operation in a query, INNER JOIN, could be translated into the physical operation of a Nested Loop in the actual query execution.

The SET SHOWPLAN_TEXT command returns the data in a single column, with multiple rows for each operation.

Introduced in SQL Server 2005, you can also return a query execution plan in XML format using the SET SHOWPLAN_XML command.

The syntax for each of these commands is very similar:

```
SET SHOWPLAN_ALL  { ON | OFF }
SET SHOWPLAN_TEXT { ON | OFF}
SET SHOWPLAN_XML  { ON | OFF }
```

Each command is enabled when set to ON, and disabled when set to OFF.

This recipe's example demonstrates returning the estimated query execution plan of a query in the AdventureWorks database using SET SHOWPLAN_TEXT and then SET SHOWPLAN_XML (SET SHOWPLAN_ALL is not demonstrated in this book because it returns seventeen columns and multiple rows which are not easily presented in print):

```
SET SHOWPLAN_TEXT ON
GO

SELECT p.Name, p.ProductNumber, r.ReviewerName
FROM Production.Product p
INNER JOIN Production.ProductReview r ON
    p.ProductID = r.ProductID
WHERE r.Rating > 2
GO

SET SHOWPLAN_TEXT OFF
GO
```

This returns the following estimated query execution plan output:

```
StmtText
------------------------------------------------------------------

SELECT p.Name, p.ProductNumber, r.ReviewerName
FROM Production.Product p
INNER JOIN Production.ProductReview r ON
    p.ProductID = r.ProductID
WHERE r.Rating > 2

(1 row(s) affected)

StmtText
------------------------------------------------------
  |--Nested Loops(Inner Join, OUTER REFERENCES:([r].[ProductID]))
       |--Clustered Index
Scan(OBJECT:([AdventureWorks].[Production].[ProductReview].[PK_ProductReview_Product
ReviewID] AS [r]), WHERE:([AdventureWorks].[Production].[ProductReview].[Rating] as
[r].[Rating]>(2)))
       |--Clustered Index
Seek(OBJECT:([AdventureWorks].[Production].[Product].[PK_Product_ProductID] AS [p]),
SEEK:([p].[ProductID]=[AdventureWorks].[Production].[ProductReview].[ProductID] as
[r].[ProductID]) ORDERED FORWARD)

(3 row(s) affected)
```

The next example returns estimated query plan results in XML format:

```
SET SHOWPLAN_XML ON
GO

SELECT p.Name, p.ProductNumber, r.ReviewerName
FROM Production.Product p
INNER JOIN Production.ProductReview r ON
    p.ProductID = r.ProductID
WHERE r.Rating > 2
GO
```

```
SET SHOWPLAN_XML OFF
GO
```

This returns the following (this is an abridged snippet, because the actual output is more than a page long):

```
<ShowPlanXML xmlns="http://schemas.microsoft.com/sqlserver/2004/07/showplan"
Version="0.5" Build="9.00.1187.07">
  <BatchSequence>
    <Batch>
      <Statements>
...
 <RelOp NodeId="0" PhysicalOp="Nested Loops" LogicalOp="Inner Join" EstimateRows="3"
EstimateIO="0" EstimateCPU="1.254e-005" AvgRowSize="105"
EstimatedTotalSubtreeCost="0.00996111" Parallel="0" EstimateRebinds="0"
EstimateRewinds="0">
                <OutputList>
                   <ColumnReference Database="[AdventureWorks]" Schema="[Production]"
Table="[Product]" Alias="[p]" Column="Name" />
                   <ColumnReference Database="[AdventureWorks]" Schema="[Production]"
Table="[Product]" Alias="[p]" Column="ProductNumber" />
                   <ColumnReference Database="[AdventureWorks]" Schema="[Production]"
Table="[ProductReview]" Alias="[r]" Column="ReviewerName" />
                </OutputList>
...
```

How It Works

You can use SHOWPLAN_ALL, SHOWPLAN_TEXT, or SHOWPLAN_XML to tune your Transact-SQL queries and batches. These commands show you the estimated execution plan without actually executing the query. You can use the information returned in the command output to take action towards improving the query performance (for example, adding indexes to columns being using in search or join conditions). Looking at the output, you can determine whether SQL Server is using the expected indexes, and if so, whether SQL Server is using an index seek, index scan, or table scan operation.

In this recipe, the SET SHOWPLAN for both TEXT and XML was set to ON, and then followed by GO:

```
SET SHOWPLAN_TEXT ON
GO
```

A query referencing the Production.Product and Production.ProductReview was then evaluated. The two tables were joined using an INNER join on the ProductID column, and only those products with a product rating of 2 or higher would be returned:

```
SELECT p.Name, p.ProductNumber, r.ReviewerName
FROM Production.Product p
INNER JOIN Production.ProductReview r ON
   p.ProductID = r.ProductID
WHERE r.Rating > 2
```

The SHOWPLAN was set OFF at the end of the query, so as not to keep executing SHOWPLAN for subsequent queries for that connection.

Looking at snippets from the output, you can see that a nested loop join (physical operation) was used to perform the INNER JOIN (logical operation):

```
|--Nested Loops(Inner Join, OUTER REFERENCES:([r].[ProductID]))
```

You can also see from this output that a clustered index scan was performed using the PK_ProductReview_ProductReviewID primary key clustered index to retrieve data from the ProductReview table:

```
|--Clustered Index Scan
(OBJECT:([AdventureWorks].[Production].[ProductReview].[PK_ProductReview_ProductReviewID]
AS [r]),
```

A clustered index *seek*, however, was used to retrieve data from the Product table:

```
|--Clustered Index
Seek(OBJECT:([AdventureWorks].[Production].[Product].[PK_Product_ProductID] AS [p]),
```

The SET SHOWPLAN_XML command returned the estimated query plan in an XML document format, displaying similar data as SHOWPLAN_TEXT. The XML data is formatted using attributes and elements.

For example, the attributes of the RelOp element shows a physical operation of Nested Loops and a logical operation of Inner Join—along with other statistics such as estimated rows impacted by the operation:

```
<RelOp NodeId="0" PhysicalOp="Nested Loops" LogicalOp="Inner Join" EstimateRows="3"
EstimateIO="0" EstimateCPU="1.254e-005" AvgRowSize="105"
EstimatedTotalSubtreeCost="0.00996111" Parallel="0" EstimateRebinds="0"
EstimateRewinds="0">
```

The XML document follows a specific schema definition format which defines the returned XML elements, attributes, and data types. This schema can be viewed at the following URL: http://schemas.microsoft.com/sqlserver/2004/07/showplan/showplanxml.xsd.

Forcing SQL Server 2005 to Use a Query Plan

SQL Server 2005 introduces the new USE PLAN command, which allows you to force the query optimizer to use an existing, specific query plan for a SELECT query. You can use this functionality to override SQL Server's choice, in those rare circumstances when SQL Server chooses a less efficient query plan over one that is more efficient. Like plan guides (covered later), this option should only be used by an experienced SQL Server professional, as SQL Server's query optimizer usually makes good decisions when deciding whether or not to reuse or create new query execution plans.

The syntax for USE PLAN is as follows:

```
USE PLAN N'xml_plan'
```

The xml_plan parameter is the XML data type representation of the stored query execution plan. The specific XML query plan can be derived using several methods, including: SET SHOWPLAN_XML, SET STATISTICS XML, the sys.dm_exec_query_plan dynamic management view, and via SQL Server Profiler's Showplan XML events.

In this example, SET STATISTICS XML is used to extract the XML formatted query plan for use in the USE PLAN command:

```
SET STATISTICS XML ON

SELECT TOP 10 Rate
FROM HumanResources.EmployeePayHistory
ORDER BY Rate DESC

SET STATISTICS XML OFF
```

The XMLDocument results returned from SET STATISTICS XML are then copied to the next query. Note that all the single quotes (') in the XML document, have to be escaped with an additional single quote (except for the quotes used for USE PLAN):

```
SELECT TOP 10 Rate
FROM HumanResources.EmployeePayHistory
ORDER BY Rate DESC
OPTION (USE PLAN
'<ShowPlanXML xmlns="http://schemas.microsoft.com/sqlserver/2004/07/showplan"
Version="1.0" Build="9.00.1314.06">
  <BatchSequence>
    <Batch>
      <Statements>
        <StmtSimple StatementText="SELECT TOP 10 Rate&#xD;&#xA;FROM
HumanResources.EmployeePayHistory&#xD;&#xA;ORDER BY Rate DESC&#xD;&#xA;&#xD;"
StatementId="1" StatementCompId="2" StatementType="SELECT"
StatementSubTreeCost="0.019825" StatementEstRows="10" StatementOptmLevel="TRIVIAL">
          <StatementSetOptions QUOTED_IDENTIFIER="false" ARITHABORT="true"
CONCAT_NULL_YIELDS_NULL="false" ANSI_NULLS="false" ANSI_PADDING="false"
ANSI_WARNINGS="false" NUMERIC_ROUNDABORT="false" />
          <QueryPlan DegreeOfParallelism="0" MemoryGrant="64" CachedPlanSize="8">
            <RelOp NodeId="0" PhysicalOp="Sort" LogicalOp="TopN Sort"
EstimateRows="10" EstimateIO="0.0112613" EstimateCPU="0.00419345" AvgRowSize="15"
EstimatedTotalSubtreeCost="0.019825" Parallel="0" EstimateRebinds="0"
EstimateRewinds="0">
              <OutputList>
                <ColumnReference Database="[AdventureWorks]"
Schema="[HumanResources]" Table="[EmployeePayHistory]" Column="Rate" />
              </OutputList>
              <MemoryFractions Input="0" Output="1" />
              <RunTimeInformation>
                <RunTimeCountersPerThread Thread="0" ActualRows="10"
ActualRebinds="1" ActualRewinds="0" ActualEndOfScans="1" ActualExecutions="1" />
              </RunTimeInformation>
              <TopSort Distinct="0" Rows="10">
                <OrderBy>
                  <OrderByColumn Ascending="0">
                    <ColumnReference Database="[AdventureWorks]"
Schema="[HumanResources]" Table="[EmployeePayHistory]" Column="Rate" />
                  </OrderByColumn>
                </OrderBy>
                <RelOp NodeId="1" PhysicalOp="Clustered Index Scan"
LogicalOp="Clustered Index Scan" EstimateRows="316" EstimateIO="0.00386574"
EstimateCPU="0.0005046" AvgRowSize="15" EstimatedTotalSubtreeCost="0.00437034"
Parallel="0" EstimateRebinds="0" EstimateRewinds="0">
                  <OutputList>
                    <ColumnReference Database="[AdventureWorks]"
Schema="[HumanResources]" Table="[EmployeePayHistory]" Column="Rate" />
                  </OutputList>
                  <RunTimeInformation>
                    <RunTimeCountersPerThread Thread="0" ActualRows="316"
ActualEndOfScans="1" ActualExecutions="1" />
                  </RunTimeInformation>
                  <IndexScan Ordered="0" ForcedIndex="0" NoExpandHint="0">
                    <DefinedValues>
                      <DefinedValue>
                        <ColumnReference Database="[AdventureWorks]"
Schema="[HumanResources]" Table="[EmployeePayHistory]" Column="Rate" />
```

```
                     </DefinedValue>
                   </DefinedValues>
                   <Object Database="[AdventureWorks]" Schema="[HumanResources]"
Table="[EmployeePayHistory]"
Index="[PK_EmployeePayHistory_EmployeeID_RateChangeDate]" />
                 </IndexScan>
               </RelOp>
             </TopSort>
           </RelOp>
         </QueryPlan>
       </StmtSimple>
     </Statements>
   </Batch>
 </BatchSequence>
</ShowPlanXML>'
```

How It Works

USE PLAN allows you to capture the XML format of a query's execution plan and then force the query to use it on subsequent executions. In this recipe, I used SET STATISTICS XML ON to capture the query's XML execution plan definition. That definition was then copied into the OPTION clause. The USE PLAN hint requires a Unicode format, so the XML document text was prefixed with an N'.

Both USE PLAN and plan guides should be used only as a *last resort*—after you have thoroughly explored other possibilities such as query design, indexing, database design, index fragmentation, and out-of-date statistics. USE PLAN may have short term effectiveness, but as data changes, so too will the needs of the query execution plan. In the end, the odds are that, over time, SQL Server will be better able to dynamically decide on the correct SQL plan than you. Nevertheless, Microsoft provided this option for those advanced troubleshooting cases when SQL Server doesn't choose a query execution plan that's good enough.

Viewing Execution Runtime Information

SQL Server 2005 provides four commands that are used to return query and batch execution statistics and information: SET STATISTICS IO, SET STATISTICS TIME, SET STATISTICS PROFILE, and SET STATISTICS XML.

Unlike the SHOWPLAN commands, STATISTICS commands return information for queries that have actually executed in SQL Server. The SET STATISTICS IO command is used to return disk activity (hence I/O) generated by the executed statement. The SET STATISTICS TIME command returns the number of milliseconds taken to parse, compile, and execute each statement executed in the batch. SET STATISTICS PROFILE and SET STATISTICS XML are the equivalents of SET SHOWPLAN_ALL and SET SHOWPLAN_XML, only the actual (*not* estimated) execution plan information is returned along with the actual results of the query.

The syntax of each of these commands is similar, with ON enabling the statistics, and OFF disabling them:

```
SET STATISTICS IO { ON | OFF }

SET STATISTICS TIME { ON | OFF }

SET STATISTICS PROFILE { ON | OFF }

SET STATISTICS XML { ON | OFF }
```

In the first example, STATISTICS IO is enabled prior to executing a query that totals the amount due by territory from the Sales.SalesOrderHeader and Sales.SalesTerritory tables:

```
SET STATISTICS IO ON
GO

SELECT  t.name TerritoryNM,
        SUM(TotalDue) TotalDue
FROM Sales.SalesOrderHeader h
INNER JOIN Sales.SalesTerritory t ON
    h.TerritoryID = t.TerritoryID
WHERE OrderDate BETWEEN '1/1/2003' AND '12/31/2003'
GROUP BY t.name
ORDER BY t.name

SET STATISTICS IO OFF
GO
```

This returns the following (abridged) results:

```
TerritoryNM         TotalDue
Australia           4547123.2777
Canada              8186021.9178
...
Southwest           11523237.5187
United Kingdom      4365879.4375
```

```
Table 'Worktable'. Scan count 1, logical reads 39, physical reads 0, read-ahead reads 0,
lob logical reads 0, lob physical reads 0, lob read-ahead reads 0.
Table 'SalesOrderHeader'. Scan count 1, logical reads 703, physical reads 3, read-
ahead reads 699, lob logical reads 0, lob physical reads 0, lob read-ahead reads 0.
Table 'SalesTerritory'. Scan count 1, logical reads 2, physical reads 0, read-ahead
reads 0, lob logical reads 0, lob physical reads 0, lob read-ahead reads 0.
```

Substituting SET STATISTICS TIME with SET STATISTICS IO would have returned the following
(abridged) results for that same query:

```
TerritoryNM         TotalDue
Australia           4547123.2777
...
Southeast           3261402.9982
Southwest           11523237.5187
United Kingdom      4365879.4375
```

```
SQL Server parse and compile time:
   CPU time = 50 ms, elapsed time = 117 ms.

(10 row(s) affected)

SQL Server Execution Times:
   CPU time = 40 ms,   elapsed time = 87 ms.
```

How It Works

The SET STATISTICS commands return information about the actual execution of a query or batch
of queries. In this recipe, SET STATISTICS IO returned information about logical, physical, and large

object read events for tables referenced in the query. For a query that is having performance issues (based on your business requirements and definition of "issues"), you can use SET STATISTICS IO to see where the I/O hot spots are occurring. For example, in this recipe's result set, you can see that the SalesOrderHeader had the highest number of logical reads:

```
...
Table 'SalesOrderHeader'. Scan count 1, logical reads 703, physical reads 3, read-
ahead reads 699, lob logical reads 0, lob physical reads 0, lob read-ahead reads 0.
...
```

Pay attention to high physical (reads from disk) or logical read values (reads from the data cache)—even if physical is zero and logical is a high value. Also look for worktables (which were also seen in this recipe):

```
Table 'Worktable'. Scan count 1, logical reads 39, physical reads 0, read-ahead
reads 0, lob logical reads 0, lob physical reads 0, lob read-ahead reads 0.
```

Worktables are usually seen in conjunction with GROUP BY, ORDER BY, hash joins, and UNION operations in the query. Worktables are created in tempdb for the duration of the query, and are removed automatically when SQL Server has finished the operation.

In the second example in this recipe, SET STATISTICS TIME was used to show the parse and compile time of the query (shown before the actual query results), and then the actual execution time (displayed after the query results):

```
SQL Server parse and compile time:
   CPU time = 50 ms, elapsed time = 117 ms.

(10 row(s) affected)

SQL Server Execution Times:
   CPU time = 40 ms,  elapsed time = 87 ms.
```

This command is useful for measuring the amount of time a query takes to execute from end-to-end, allowing you to see if precompiling is taking longer than you realized, or if the slowdown occurs during the actual query execution.

The two other STATISTICS commands, SET STATISTICS PROFILE and SET STATISTICS XML, return information similar to SET SHOWPLAN_ALL and SET SHOWPLAN_XML, only the results are based on the *actual*, rather than the estimated execution plan.

Viewing Performance Statistics for Cached Query Plans

In this recipe, I demonstrate using SQL Server 2005 dynamic management views and functions to view performance statistics for cached query plans.

In this example, a simple query that returns all rows from the Sales.Individual table is executed against the AdventureWorks database. Prior to executing it, you'll clear the procedure cache so that you can identify the query more easily in this demonstration (remember that you should only clear out the procedure cache on test SQL Server instances):

```
DBCC FREEPROCCACHE
GO

SELECT CustomerID, ContactID, Demographics, ModifiedDate
FROM Sales.Individual
```

Now, I'll query the sys.dm_exec_query_stats dynamic management view, which contains statistical information regarding queries cached on the SQL Server instance. This view contains a sql_handle, which I'll use as an input to the sys.dm_exec_sql_text dynamic management function. This function is used to return the text of a Transact-SQL statement:

```
SELECT   t.text,
      st.total_logical_reads,
      st.total_physical_reads,
      st.total_elapsed_time/1000000 Total_Time_Secs,
      st.total_logical_writes
FROM sys.dm_exec_query_stats st
CROSS APPLY sys.dm_exec_sql_text(st.sql_handle) t
```

This returns:

text	total logical_reads	total_physical_reads	Total_Time_Secs	total_logical_writes
SELECT CustomerID, ContactID, Demographics, ModifiedDate FROM Sales.Individual	3092	3	7	0

How It Works

This recipe demonstrated clearing the procedure cache, then executing a query that took a few seconds to finish executing. After that, the sys.sm_exec_query_stats dynamic management view was queried to return statistics about the cached execution plan.

The SELECT clause retrieved information on the Transact-SQL text of the query, number of logical and physical reads, total time elapsed in seconds, and logical writes (if any):

```
SELECT   t.text,
      st.total_logical_reads,
      st.total_physical_reads,
      st.total_elapsed_time/1000000 Total_Time_Secs,
      st.total_logical_writes
```

The total elapsed time column was in microseconds, so it was divided by 1000000 in order to return the number of full seconds.

In the FROM clause, the sys.dm_exec_query_stats dynamic management view was cross applied against the sys.dm_exec_sql_text dynamic management function in order to retrieve the SQL text of the cached query:

```
FROM sys.dm_exec_query_stats st
CROSS APPLY sys.dm_exec_sql_text(st.sql_handle) t
```

This information is useful for identifying read- and/or write-intensive queries, helping you determine which queries should be optimized. Keep in mind that this recipe's query can only retrieve information on queries still in the cache.

This query returned the totals, but the sys.dm_exec_query_stats also includes columns that track the min, max, and last measurements for reads and writes. Also note that the sys.dm_exec_query_stats has other useful columns that can measure CPU time (total_worker_time, last_worker_time, min_worker_time, and max_worker_time) and .NET CLR object execution time (total_clr_time, last_clr_time, min_clr_time, max_clr_time).

Statistics

As I discussed in Chapter 22, the AUTO_CREATE_STATISTICS database option enables SQL Server to automatically generate statistical information regarding the distribution of values in a column. The AUTO_UPDATE_STATISTICS database option automatically updates existing statistics on your table or indexed view. Unless you have a *very* good reason for doing so, these options should never be disabled in your database, as they are critical for good query performance.

Statistics are critical for efficient query processing and performance, allowing SQL Server to choose the correct physical operations when generating an execution plan. Table and indexed view statistics, which can be created manually or generated automatically by SQL Server, collect information that is used by SQL Server to generate efficient query execution plans.

The next few recipes will demonstrate how to work directly with statistics. When reading these recipes, remember to let SQL Server manage the automatic creation and update of statistics in your databases whenever possible. Save most of these commands for special troubleshooting circumstances or when you've made significant data changes (for example, executing sp_updatestats right after a large data load).

Manually Creating Statistics

SQL Server will usually generate the statistics it needs based on query activity. However, if you still wish to explicitly create statistics on a column or columns, you can use the CREATE STATISTICS command.

The syntax is as follows:

```
CREATE STATISTICS statistics_name
ON { table | view } ( column [ ,...n ] )
    [ WITH
        [ [ FULLSCAN
          | SAMPLE number { PERCENT | ROWS }
          | STATS_STREAM = stats_stream ] [ , ] ]
        [ NORECOMPUTE ]
    ]
```

The arguments of this command are described in Table 28-1.

Table 28-1. *CREATE STATISTICS Arguments*

Argument	Description
statistics_name	The name of the new statistics.
table	view	The table or indexed view which the statistics are based off of.
column [,...n]	One or more columns used for generating statistics.
FULLSCAN| SAMPLE number { PERCENT	ROWS }	FULLSCAN, when specified, reads all rows when generating the statistics. SAMPLE reads either a defined number of rows or a defined percentage of rows.
STATS_STREAM = stats_stream	Reserved for Microsoft's internal use.
NORECOMPUTE	This option designates that once the statistics are created, they should not be updated —even when data changes occur afterwards. This option should rarely, if ever, be used. Fresh statistics allow SQL Server to generate good query plans.

In this example, new statistics are created on the Sales.Customer CustomerType column:

```
CREATE STATISTICS Stats_Customer_CustomerType
ON Sales.Customer (CustomerType)
WITH FULLSCAN
```

How It Works

This recipe demonstrated manually creating statistics on the Sales.Customer table. The first line of code designated the statistics name:

```
CREATE STATISTICS Stats_Customer_CustomerType
```

The second line of code designated the table to create statistics on, followed by the column name used to generate the statistics:

```
ON Sales.Customer (CustomerType)
```

The last line of code designated that all rows in the table would be read in order to generate the statistics:

```
WITH FULLSCAN
```

Updating Statistics

After you create statistics, if you wish to manually update statistics, you can use the UPDATE STATISTICS command.

The syntax is as follows:

```
UPDATE STATISTICS table | view
    [
        {
            { index | statistics_name }
        | ( { index |statistics_name } [ ,...n ] )
            }
    ]
    [    WITH
        [
            [ FULLSCAN ]
            | SAMPLE number { PERCENT | ROWS } ]
            | RESAMPLE
        ]
        [ [ , ] [ ALL | COLUMNS | INDEX ]
        [ [ , ] NORECOMPUTE ]
    ]
```

The arguments of this command are described in Table 28-2.

Table 28-2. *UPDATE STATISTICS Arguments*

Argument	Description
table | view	The table name or indexed view for which to update statistics.
{ index | statistics_name}| ({index| statistics_name} [,...n]) }	The name of the index or named statistics to update.
FULLSCAN| SAMPLE number { PERCENT | ROWS } |RESAMPLE	FULLSCAN, when specified, reads all rows when generating the statistics. SAMPLE reads either a defined number of rows or a percentage. RESAMPLE updates statistics based on the original sampling method.

Argument	Description
[ALL | COLUMNS | INDEX]	When ALL is designated, all existing statistics are updated. When COLUMN is designated, only column statistics are updated. When INDEX is designated, only index statistics are updated.
NORECOMPUTE	This option designates that once the statistics are created, they should not be updated—even when data changes occur. Again, this option should rarely, if ever, be used. Fresh statistics allow SQL Server to generate good query plans.

This example updates the statistics created in the previous recipe, populating statistics based on the latest data:

```
UPDATE STATISTICS Sales.Customer
Stats_Customer_CustomerType
WITH FULLSCAN
```

How It Works

This example updated the statistics created in the previous recipe, refreshing them with the latest data. The first line of code designated the table name containing the statistics to be updated:

```
UPDATE STATISTICS Sales.Customer
```

The second line designated the name of the statistics to be updated:

```
Stats_Customer_CustomerType
```

The last line of code designated that all rows in the table would be read in order to update the statistics:

```
WITH FULLSCAN
```

Generating and Updating Statistics Across All Tables

You can also automatically generate statistics across all tables in a database for those columns that don't already have statistics associated to them, by using the system-stored procedure sp_createstats.

The syntax is as follows:

```
sp_createstats [ [ @indexonly = ] 'indexonly' ]
    [ , [ @fullscan = ] 'fullscan' ]
    [ , [ @norecompute = ] 'norecompute' ]
```

The arguments of this command are described in Table 28-3.

Table 28-3. *sp_createstats Arguments*

Argument	Description
indexonly	When indexonly is designated, only columns used in indexes will be considered for statistics creation.
fullscan	When fullscan is designated, all rows will be evaluated for the generated statistics. If not designated, the default behavior is to extract statistics via sampling.
norecompute	The norecompute option designates that once the statistics are created, they should not be updated—even when data changes occur. Like with CREATE STATISTICS and UPDATE STATISTICS, this option should rarely, if ever, be used. Fresh statistics allow SQL Server to generate good query plans.

If you wish to update all statistics in the current database, you can use the system-stored procedure `sp_updatestats`. Improved in SQL Server 2005, this stored procedure only updates statistics when necessary (when data changes have occurred). Statistics on unchanged data will not be updated.

This example demonstrates creating new statistics on columns in the database that don't already have statistics created for them:

```
EXEC sp_createstats
GO
```

This returns the following (abridged) result set:

```
Table 'AdventureWorks.Production.ProductProductPhoto': Creating statistics for the
following columns:
    Primary
    ModifiedDate
Table 'AdventureWorks.Sales.StoreContact': Creating statistics for the following columns:
    ModifiedDate
Table 'AdventureWorks.Person.Address': Creating statistics for the following columns:
    AddressLine2
    City
    PostalCode
    ModifiedDate
...
```

This next example automatically updates all statistics in the current database:

```
EXEC sp_updatestats
GO
```

This returns the following (abridged) results. Notice the informational message of `'update is not necessary'`. The results you see may differ based on the state of your table statistics:

```
Updating [Production].[ProductProductPhoto]
    [PK_ProductProductPhoto_ProductID_ProductPhotoID], update is not necessary...
    [AK_ProductProductPhoto_ProductID_ProductPhotoID], update is not necessary...
    [_WA_Sys_00000002_01142BA1], update is not necessary...
    [Primary], update is not necessary...
    [ModifiedDate], update is not necessary...
    0 index(es)/statistic(s) have been updated, 5 did not require update.
...
```

Viewing Statistics Information

If you suspect that the statistics on a specific table are *not* being updated appropriately, or contain out-of-date information, you can use the DBCC SHOW STATISTICS command to view detailed statistics information in order to verify.

The syntax is as follows:

```
DBCC SHOW_STATISTICS ( 'table_name' | 'view_name' , target )
[ WITH [ NO_INFOMSGS ]
< STAT_HEADER | DENSITY_VECTOR | HISTOGRAM > [ , n ] ]
```

The arguments of this command are described in Table 28-4.

Table 28-4. *DBCC SHOW_STATISTICS Arguments*

Argument	Description
'table_name' | 'view_name'	The table or indexed view to evaluate.
target	The name of the index or named statistics to evaluate.
NO_INFOMSGS	When designated, NO_INFOMSGS suppresses informational messages.
STAT_HEADER |DENSITY_VECTOR | HISTOGRAM [, n]	Specifying STAT_HEADER, DENSITY_VECTOR, or HISTOGRAM designates which result sets will be returned by the command (you can display one or more). Not designating any of these means that all three result sets will be returned.

This example demonstrates how to view the statistics information on the Sales.Customer Stats_Customer_CustomerType statistics:

```
DBCC SHOW_STATISTICS ( 'Sales.Customer' , Stats_Customer_CustomerType)
```

This returns the following result sets:

Name	Updated	Rows	Rows Sampled	Steps	Density	Average key length	String Index
Stats_Customer_ CustomerType	Oct 15 2005 2:32PM	19185	19185	2	0	2	YES

All density	Average Length	Columns
0.5	2	CustomerType

RANGE_HI_KEY	RANGE_ROWS	EQ_ROWS	DISTINCT_RANGE_ROWS	AVG_RANGE_ROWS
I	0	18484	0	1
S	0	701	0	1

How It Works

In the results of this recipe's example, the All density column indicates the *selectivity* of a column:

All density	Average Length	Columns
0.5	2	CustomerType

Selectivity refers to the percentage of rows that will be returned given a specific column's value. A low All density value implies a high selectivity. Columns with high selectivity often make for useful indexes (useful to the query optimization process).

In the third result set returned by SHOW_STATISTICS, CustomerType had only two values, I and S (which you can see in the RANGE_HI_KEY in the third result set):

RANGE_HI_KEY	RANGE_ROWS	EQ_ROWS	DISTINCT_RANGE_ROWS	AVG_RANGE_ROWS
I	0	18484	0	1
S	0	701	0	1

With such a high density of similar values, and low selectivity (one value is likely to return many rows), you can make an educated assumption that an index on this particular column is unlikely to be very useful to SQL Server in generating a query execution plan.

Removing Statistics

To remove statistics, use the DROP STATISTICS command.

The syntax is as follows:

```
DROP STATISTICS table.statistics_name | view.statistics_name [ ,...n ]
```

This command allows you to drop one or more statistics, prefixed with the table or indexed view name.

In this example, the Sales.Customer Stats_Customer_CustomerType statistics are dropped from the database:

```
DROP STATISTICS Sales.Customer.Stats_Customer_CustomerType
```

How It Works

This recipe dropped user-created statistics using DROP STATISTICS. The statistics were dropped using the three part name of schema.table.statistics_name.

Index Tuning

This next batch of recipes demonstrates techniques for managing indexes. Specifically, I'll be covering how to:

- Identify index fragmentation, so you can figure out which indexes should be rebuilt or reorganized.

- Display index usage, so you can determine which indexes *aren't* being used by SQL Server.

- Use the Database Tuning Advisor tool to analyze a workload file containing a query and make index suggestions.

Before getting into the recipes, I'd like to take a moment to discuss some general indexing best practices. When considering these best practices, always remember that like query tuning, there are few hard and fast "always" or "never" rules. Index usage by SQL Server depends on a number of factors, including, but not limited to, the query construction, referenced tables in the query, referenced columns, number of rows in the table, and uniqueness of the index column(s) data. Some basic guidelines to keep in mind when building your index strategy:

- Add indexes based on your high priority and high frequency queries. Determine ahead of time what acceptable query execution durations might be, based on your business requirements.

- Don't add multiple indexes at the same time. Instead, add an index and test the query to see that the new index is used. If it is not used, remove it. If it is used, test to make sure there are no negative side effects to other queries. Remember that each additional index adds extra overhead to data modifications to the base table.

- Unless you have a very good reason *not* to do so, always add a clustered index to each table. A table without a clustered index is a heap, meaning that the data is stored in no particular order. Clustered indexes are ordered according to the clustered key and its data pages re-ordered during an index rebuild or reorganization. Heaps, however, are not rebuilt during an index rebuild or reorganization process, and therefore can grow out of control, taking up many more data pages than necessary.

- Monitor query performance over time. As your data changes, so too will the performance and effectiveness of your indexes.

- Fragmented indexes can slow down query performance since more I/O operations are required in order to return results for a query. Keep index fragmentation to a minimum by rebuilding and/or reorganizing your indexes on a scheduled or as-needed basis.

- Select clustered index keys that are rarely modified, highly unique, and narrow in data type width. Width is particularly important because each nonclustered index also contains within it the clustered index key. Clustered indexes are useful when applied to columns used in range queries. This includes queries that use the operators BETWEEN, >, >=, <, and <=. Clustered index keys also help reduce execution time for queries that return large result sets or depend heavily on ORDER BY and GROUP BY clauses. With all these factors in mind, remember that you can only have a single clustered index for your table, so choose carefully.

- Nonclustered indexes are ideal for small or one-row result sets. Again, columns should be chosen based on their use in a query, specifically in the JOIN or WHERE clause. Nonclustered indexes should be made on columns containing highly unique data. As discussed in Chapter 5, don't forget to consider using covering queries and the new SQL Server 2005 INCLUDE functionality for non-key columns.

- Use a 100% fill factor for those indexes that are located within read-only filegroups or databases. This reduces I/O and can improve query performance because less data pages are required to fulfill a query's result set.

- Try to anticipate which indexes will be needed based on the queries you perform—but also don't be afraid to make frequent use of the Database Engine Tuning Advisor tool. Using the Database Engine Tuning Advisor, SQL Server can evaluate your query or batch of queries and determine what indexes could be added (or removed) in order to help the query run faster. I'll demonstrate this later on.

The next recipe will now demonstrate how to display index fragmentation.

Displaying Index Fragmentation

In SQL Server 2000, the DBCC SHOWCONTIG command was used to display index fragmentation. Fragmentation is the natural byproduct of data modifications to a table. When data is updated in the database, the logical order of indexes (based on the index key) gets out of sync with the actual physical order of the data pages. As data pages become further and further out of order, more I/O operations are required in order to return results requested by a query. Rebuilding or reorganizing an index allows you to defragment the index by synchronizing the logical index order, re-ordering the physical data pages to match the logical index order.

■**Note** See Chapter 5 for a review of index management and Chapter 23 for a review of index defragmentation and reorganization.

Now in SQL Server 2005, DBCC SHOWCONTIG has been deprecated in place of the new dynamic management function, sys.dm_db_index_physical_stats. The sys.dm_db_index_physical_stats dynamic management function returns information that allows you to determine an index's level of fragmentation.

The syntax for sys.dm_db_index_physical_stats is as follows:

```
sys.dm_db_index_physical_stats (
    { database_id | NULL }
    , { object_id | NULL }
    , { index_id | NULL | 0 }
    , { partition_number | NULL }
```

```
    , { mode | NULL | DEFAULT }
)
```

The arguments of this command are described in Table 28-5.

Table 28-5. *sys.dm_db_index_physical_stats Arguments*

Argument	Description
database_id | NULL	The database ID of the indexes to evaluate. If NULL, all databases for the SQL Server instance are returned.
object_id | NULL	The object ID of the table and views (*indexed* views) to evaluate. If NULL, all tables are returned.
index_id | NULL | 0	The specific index ID of the index to evaluate. If NULL, all indexes are returned for the table(s).
partition_number | NULL	The specific partition number of the partition to evaluate. If NULL, all partitions are returned based on the defined database/table/indexes selected.
LIMITED | SAMPLED | DETAILED | NULL | DEFAULT	These modes impact how the fragmentation data is collected. The LIMITED mode scans all pages for a heap and the pages above the leaf-level. SAMPLED collects data based on a 1% sampling of pages in the heap or index. The DETAILED mode scans all pages (heap or index). DETAILED is the slowest, but most accurate option. Designating NULL or DEFAULT is the equivalent of the LIMITED mode.

In this example, the sys.dm_db_index_physical_stats dynamic management view is queried for all objects in the AdventureWorks database with an average fragmentation percent greater than 30:

```
USE AdventureWorks
GO

SELECT OBJECT_NAME(object_id) ObjectName,
       index_id,
       index_type_desc,
       avg_fragmentation_in_percent
FROM sys.dm_db_index_physical_stats
(DB_ID('AdventureWorks'),NULL, NULL, NULL, 'LIMITED')
WHERE avg_fragmentation_in_percent > 30
ORDER BY OBJECT_NAME(object_id)
```

This returns the following (abridged) results:

```
ObjectName       index_id   index_type_desc        avg_fragmentation_in_percent
BillOfMaterials  2          NONCLUSTERED INDEX     33.3333333333333
CountryRegion    1          CLUSTERED INDEX        50
DatabaseLog      0          HEAP                   54.1666666666667
Employee         1          CLUSTERED INDEX        57.1428571428571
Employee         2          NONCLUSTERED INDEX     66.6666666666667
...
```

This second example returns fragmentation for a specific database, table, and index:

```
SELECT OBJECT_NAME(f.object_id) ObjectName,
       i.name IndexName,
       f.index_type_desc,
       f.avg_fragmentation_in_percent
FROM sys.dm_db_index_physical_stats
```

```
        (DB_ID('AdventureWorks'),
         OBJECT_ID('Production.ProductDescription'),
         2,
         NULL,
         'LIMITED')  f
INNER JOIN sys.indexes i ON
    i.object_id = f.object_id AND
    i.index_id = f.index_id
```

This returns:

ObjectName	IndexName	index_type_desc	avg_fragmentation in_percent
ProductDescription	AK_ProductDescription_rowguid	NONCLUSTERED INDEX	66.6666666666667

How It Works

The first example started off by changing the database context to the AdventureWorks database:

```
USE AdventureWorks
GO
```

Since the OBJECT_NAME function is database-context sensitive, changing the database context ensures that you are viewing the proper object name.

Next, the SELECT clause displays the object name, index ID, description, and average fragmentation percent:

```
SELECT OBJECT_NAME(object_id) ObjectName,
       index_id, index_type_desc,
       avg_fragmentation_in_percent
```

The index_type_desc column tells you if the index is a heap, clustered index, nonclustered index, primary XML index, or secondary XML index.

Next, the FROM clause referenced the sys.dm_db_index_physical_stats catalog function. The parameters were put in parentheses, and include the database name and NULL for all other parameters except the scan mode:

```
FROM sys.dm_db_index_physical_stats
(DB_ID('AdventureWorks'),NULL, NULL, NULL, 'LIMITED')
```

Since sys.dm_db_index_physical_stats is referenced like a table (unlike 2000's DBCC SHOWCONTIG), the WHERE clause is used to qualify that only rows with a fragmentation percentage of 31% or greater be returned in the results:

```
WHERE avg_fragmentation_in_percent > 30
```

The query returned several rows for objects in the AdventureWorks database with a fragmentation greater than 30%. The avg_fragmentation_in_percent column shows logical fragmentation of nonclustered or clustered indexes, returning the percentage of disordered pages at the leaf level of the index. For heaps, avg_fragmentation_in_percent shows extent level fragmentation. Regarding extents, recall that SQL Server reads and writes data at the page level. Pages are stored in blocks called *extents*, which consist of eight contiguous 8KB pages. Using the avg_fragmentation_in_percent, you can determine if the specific indexes need to be rebuilt or reorganized using ALTER INDEX.

In the second example, fragmentation was displayed for a specific database, table, and index. The SELECT clause included a reference to the index name (instead of index number):

```
SELECT OBJECT_NAME(f.object_id) ObjectName,
       i.name IndexName,
```

```
    f.index_type_desc,
    f.avg_fragmentation_in_percent
```

The FROM clause included the specific table name, which was converted to an ID using the OBJECT_ID function. The third parameter included the index number of the index to be evaluated for fragmentation:

```
FROM sys.dm_db_index_physical_stats
(DB_ID('AdventureWorks'),
OBJECT_ID('Production.ProductDescription'),
2,
NULL,
'LIMITED')  f
```

The sys.indexes system catalog view was joined to the sys.dm_db_index_physical_stats function based on the object_id and index_id.

```
INNER JOIN sys.indexes i ON
    i.object_id = f.object_id AND
    i.index_id = f.index_id
```

The query returned the fragmentation results just for that specific index.

Displaying Index Usage

Similar to query performance tuning, creating useful indexes in your database is often part art and part science. Indexes can slow down data modifications while at the same time speeding up SELECT queries. You must balance the cost/benefit of index overhead with read activity versus data modification activity. Every additional index added to a table may improve query performance at the expense of data modification speed. On top of this, index effectiveness changes as the data changes, so an index that was useful a few weeks ago may no longer be useful today. One great difficulty in SQL Server 2000 was figuring out which indexes were *not* being used—either never or rarely used at all. This is important because adding indexes slows down updates. If you're going to have indexes on a table, they should be put to good use on high priority queries. If an index is unused by SQL Server, it's just dead weight.

Now in SQL Server 2005, you can see whether or not an index is being used by querying the sys.dm_db_index_usage_stats dynamic management view. This view returns statistics on the number of index seeks, scans, updates, or lookups since the SQL Server instance was last restarted. It also returns the last dates the index was referenced.

In this example, the sys.dm_db_index_usage_stats dynamic management view is queried to see if the indexes on the Sales.Customer table are being used. Prior to referencing sys.dm_db_index_usage_stats, two queries will be executed against the Sales.Customer table, one returning all rows and columns and the second returning the AccountNumber column for a specific TerritoryID:

```
SELECT *
FROM Sales.Customer

SELECT AccountNumber
FROM Sales.Customer
WHERE TerritoryID = 4
```

After executing the queries, the sys.dm_db_index_usage_stats dynamic management view is queried:

```
SELECT i.name IndexName, user_seeks, user_scans,
last_user_seek, last_user_scan
FROM sys.dm_db_index_usage_stats s
INNER JOIN sys.indexes i ON
    s.object_id = i.object_id AND
    s.index_id = i.index_id
WHERE database_id = DB_ID('AdventureWorks') AND
      s.object_id = OBJECT_ID('Sales.Customer')
```

This returns:

IndexName	user_seeks	user_scans	last_user_seek	last_user_scan
IX_Customer_TerritoryID	1	0	2005-10-15 17:13:35.487	NULL
PK_Customer_CustomerID	0	1	NULL	2005-10-15 17:13:34.237

How It Works

The sys.dm_db_index_usage_stats dynamic management view allows you to see what indexes are being used in your SQL Server instance. The statistics are valid since the last SQL Server restart.

In this recipe, two queries were executed against the Sales.Customer table. After executing the queries, the sys.dm_db_index_usage_stats dynamic management view was queried.

The SELECT clause displayed the name of the index, the number of user seeks and user scans, and the dates of the last user seeks and user scans:

```
SELECT i.name IndexName, user_seeks, user_scans,
last_user_seek, last_user_scan
```

The FROM clause joined the sys.dm_db_index_usage_stats dynamic management view to the sys.indexes system catalog view (so the index name could be displayed in the results) on the object_id and index_id:

```
FROM sys.dm_db_index_usage_stats s
INNER JOIN sys.indexes i ON
    s.object_id = i.object_id AND
    s.index_id = i.index_id
```

The WHERE clause qualified that only indexes for the AdventureWorks database be displayed, and of those indexes, only those for the Sales.Customer table. The DB_ID function was used to get the database system ID, and the OBJECT_ID function was used to get the table's object ID:

```
WHERE database_id = DB_ID('AdventureWorks') AND
      s.object_id = OBJECT_ID('Sales.Customer')
```

The query returned two rows, showing that the PK_Customer_CustomerID clustered index of the Sales.Customer table had indeed been scanned recently (most likely by the first SELECT * query) and the IX_Customer_TerritoryID nonclustered index had been used in the second query (which qualified TerritoryID = 4).

Indexes assist with query performance, but also add disk space and data modification overhead. Using the sys.dm_db_index_usage_stats dynamic management view, you can monitor if indexes are actually being used, and if not, replace them with more effective indexes.

Using the Database Engine Tuning Advisor

If a performance issue is stumping you, or you'd like to check your current indexing strategy for possible improvements, use the Database Engine Tuning Advisor tool.

This recipe will demonstrate how to use the Database Engine Tuning Advisor to create recommendations for a specific query used in the AdventureWorks database:

```
SELECT  Production.Product.Name,
        Production.Product.ProductNumber,
        Production.ProductModel.Name AS ModelName,
        Production.ProductInventory.LocationID,
        Production.ProductInventory.Shelf,
        Production.ProductInventory.Bin,
        Production.ProductCostHistory.StartDate,
        Production.ProductCostHistory.EndDate,
        Production.ProductCostHistory.StandardCost
FROM    Production.Product
INNER JOIN   Production.ProductCostHistory ON
    Production.Product.ProductID = Production.ProductCostHistory.ProductID
INNER JOIN   Production.ProductInventory ON
    Production.Product.ProductID = Production.ProductInventory.ProductID
INNER JOIN   Production.ProductModel ON
    Production.Product.ProductModelID = Production.ProductModel.ProductModelID
WHERE Production.ProductInventory.LocationID IN (60)
ORDER BY Production.Product.Name
```

For this recipe, the query is saved as a file to C:\Apress\ProductsByLocation.sql where it will be evaluated later on.

First, however, Figure 28-16 shows the graphical execution plan of this query. For larger result sets, one common goal for index tuning is to reduce the number of scans in favor of seeks. As you can see from this query's execution plan, some tables use index scan operations while only one table (the ProductCostHistory table) uses an index seek.

Figure 28-16. *Execution plan for the Products by Location query*

You'll use the Database Engine Tuning Advisor to evaluate the query and make recommendations to improve its performance. The Database Engine Tuning Advisor is launched by going to Start➤Programs➤Microsoft SQL Server 2005➤Performance Tools➤ Database Engine Tuning Advisor.

You'll be prompted for the Server name and authentication method in the Connect to Server dialog box (see Figure 28-17). After selecting these options, click the Connect button.

Figure 28-17. *Connect to Server dialog box*

The main screen now appears, showing the connected SQL Server instance in the left Session Monitor window, and the General configuration tab in the right window (see Figure 28-18). In the General tab, you can select the file containing the SQL you wish to tune by selecting the File option under the Workload section, in this case C:\Apress\ProductsByLocation.sql. You also select the database where the tuning recommendations should be focused by selecting the checkbox next to the AdventureWorks database.

Figure 28-18. *General options for the Database Engine Tuning Advisor*

Clicking the Tuning Options tab shows more options used to evaluate the workload (see Figure 28-19). Using options on this screen, you can set the maximum amount of time the tool can take to evaluate a workload. You can also specify which physical design structures can be recommended (in this example, you'll be keeping the default of indexes), whether or not partitioning strategy recommendations are given, and whether or not all existing objects (indexes, indexed views) should be kept in the database.

Figure 28-19. *Tuning Options tab*

To begin analysis, go to the Actions menu and select Start Analysis. This opens up a new Progress screen (see Figure 28-20).

Figure 28-20. *Progress tab*

Once finished, two more tabs appear: the Recommendations tab and the Reports tab. The Recommendations tab contains a list of recommendations generated to improve the performance of the query. Notice at the top of the screen in Figure 28-21 that the estimated improvement of the query is 22%. The Database Engine Tuning Advisor has recommended the creation of three new indexes which are listed in the Index Recommendations section. It is here that you can see which tables the indexes are to be added to, which columns will be indexed, and the index size in KB.

Figure 28-21. *Recommendations tab*

The Reports tab (see Figure 28-22) displays a summary of the tuning statistics in the upper window, and in the lower screen, the ability to view other tuning reports (Figure 28-22 shows results of the index usage report, for example).

Figure 28-22. *Report tab*

Back on the Recommendations tab, you have the choice to either disregard the recommendations, apply the recommendations immediately, or save them off to a .sql file. In this recipe, you'll apply the recommendations immediately by going to the Actions menu and selecting Apply Recommendations.

This brings up the Apply Recommendations dialog box (see Figure 28-23). It is here that you can apply the index changes right away, or schedule them for a later time. Select Apply now and click the **OK** button.

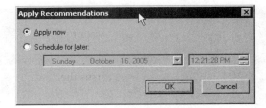

Figure 28-23. *Apply Recommendations dialog box*

This launches the Applying Recommendations status dialog (see Figure 28-24). When the process is finished, click the Close button.

Figure 28-24. *Applying Recommendations status dialog box*

At this point, you can re-test the original recipe query and view any impact on the execution plan. In this case, as you can see in Figure 28-25, two tables (instead of just the original one) are now using Index Seek operations.

Index Seek
[AdventureWorks].[Production].[Prod..
Cost: 26 %

Index Seek
[AdventureWorks].[Production].[Prod..
Cost: 20 %

Figure 28-25. *Post Recommendation execution plan*

Testing the query duration, you can decide if the time saved by creating the index is worth the additional disk and database modification overhead of keeping the newly recommended indexes.

How It Works

This recipe gave a brief introduction on how to use the Database Engine Tuning Advisor to make index recommendations based on a Transact-SQL query. You can use this tool to evaluate and make recommendations based on a query workload.

As a best practice, always be sure to evaluate the benefit of faster query time versus the disk space and data modification overhead. You should also check the impact of any new indexes on the duration of existing queries.

Also, be sure to tune your database only during slow periods on your SQL Server instance. This is because the Database Engine Tuning Advisor can consume significant CPU and memory resources while analyzing a workload. To reduce unnecessary overhead of the tool, be sure to remove objects types that you don't want recommendation on from the Tuning Options tab.

Miscellaneous Techniques

The next two recipes detail a few techniques which don't cleanly fall under any of the previous sections in this chapter. These recipes will demonstrate how to use an alternative to dynamic SQL and stored procedures using the sp_executesql system-stored procedure. The last recipe in the chapter will show you how to apply query hints to an existing query without having to actually modify the application's SQL code using plan guides.

Using an Alternative to Dynamic SQL

Using the EXECUTE command, you can execute the contents of a character string within a batch, procedure, or function. You can also abbreviate EXECUTE to EXEC.

For example, the following statement performs a SELECT from the Sales.Currency table:

```
EXEC ('SELECT CurrencyCode FROM Sales.Currency')
```

Although this technique allows you to dynamically formulate strings which can then be executed, this technique comes with some major hazards.

The first and most important hazard is the risk of SQL injection. SQL injection occurs when harmful code is inserted into an existing SQL string prior to being executed on the SQL Server instance. Allowing user input into variables that are concatenated to a SQL string and then executed can cause all sorts of damage to your database (not to mention the potential privacy issues). The malicious code if executed under a context with sufficient permissions can drop tables, read sensitive data, or even shut down the SQL Server process.

The second issue with character string execution techniques is in their performance. Although performance of dynamically generated SQL may sometimes be fast, the query performance can also be unreliable. Unlike stored procedures, dynamically generated and regular ad hoc SQL batches and statements will cause SQL Server to generate a new execution plan each time they are run.

If stored procedures are not an option for your application, an alternative, the sp_executesql system-stored procedure, addresses the dynamic SQL performance issue by allowing you to create and use a reusable query execution plan where the only items that change are the query parameters. Parameters are also type-safe, meaning that you cannot use them to hold unintended data types. This is a worthy solution, when given a choice between ad hoc statements and stored procedures.

■**Caution** sp_executesql addresses some performance issues, but does not entirely address the SQL injection issue. Beware of allowing user-passed parameters that are concatenated into a SQL string! Stick with the parameter functionality described next.

The syntax for sp_executesql is as follows:

```
sp_executesql [ @stmt = ] stmt
[
{, [@params=] N'@parameter_name data_type [ [ OUTPUT ][,...n]' }
{, [ @param1 = ] 'value1' [ ,...n ] }
]
```

The arguments of this command are described in Table 28-6.

Table 28-6. *sp_executesql Arguments*

Argument	Description
stmt	The string to be executed.
@parameter_name data_type [[OUTPUT][,...n]	One or more parameters that are embedded in the string statement. OUTPUT is used similarly to a stored procedure OUTPUT parameter.
'value1' [,...n]	The actual values passed to the parameters.

In this example, the Production.TransactionHistoryArchive table is queried based on a specific ProductID, TransactionType, and minimum Quantity values:

```
EXECUTE sp_executesql
N'SELECT TransactionID, ProductID,
        TransactionType, Quantity
FROM    Production.TransactionHistoryArchive
WHERE   ProductID = @ProductID AND
        TransactionType = @TransactionType AND
        Quantity > @Quantity',
        N'@ProductID int,
          @TransactionType char(1),
          @Quantity int',
              @ProductID =813,
              @TransactionType = 'S',
              @Quantity = 5
```

This returns the following results:

```
TransactionID    ProductID    TransactionType    Quantity
28345            813          S                  7
31177            813          S                  9
35796            813          S                  6
36112            813          S                  7
40765            813          S                  6
47843            813          S                  7
69114            813          S                  6
73432            813          S                  6
```

How It Works

The sp_executesql allows you to execute a dynamically generated Unicode string. This system procedure allows parameters, which in turn allow SQL Server to re-use the query execution plan generated by its execution.

Notice in the recipe that the first parameter was preceded with the N' Unicode prefix, as
sp_executesql requires a Unicode statement string. The first parameter also included the SELECT
query itself, including the parameters embedded in the WHERE clause:

```
EXECUTE sp_executesql
N'SELECT TransactionID, ProductID,
TransactionType, Quantity
FROM Production.TransactionHistoryArchive
WHERE ProductID = @ProductID AND
            TransactionType = @TransactionType AND
            Quantity > @Quantity',
```

The second parameter further defined the data types of each parameter that was embedded in
the first parameter's SQL statement. Each parameter is separated by a comma:

```
N'@ProductID int,
@TransactionType char(1),
@Quantity int',
```

The last parameter assigned each embedded parameter a value, which was put into the query
dynamically during execution.

```
@ProductID =813,
@TransactionType = 'S',
@Quantity = 5
```

The query returned eight rows based on the three parameters provided. If the query is executed
again, only with different parameter values, it is likely that the original query execution plan will be
used by SQL Server (instead of creating a new execution plan).

Applying Hints Without Modifying Application SQL

As was discussed at the beginning of the chapter, troubleshooting poor query performance involves
reviewing many areas such as database design, indexing, and query construction. You can make
modifications to your code, but what if the problem is with code that you *cannot* change? If you are
encountering issues with a database and/or queries that are not your own to change (in shrink-
wrapped software, for example)—then your options become more limited. Usually in the case of
third party software, you are restricted to adding new indexes or archiving off data from large tables.
Making changes to the vendor's actual database objects or queries is usually off limits.

SQL Server 2005 provides a new solution to this common issue using *plan guides*. Plan guides
allow you to apply hints to a query without having to change the actual query text sent from the
application. Plan guides can be applied to specific queries embedded within database objects
(stored procedures, functions, triggers) or specific, stand-alone SQL statements.

A plan guide is created using the sp_create_plan_guide system-stored procedure:

```
sp_create_plan_guide [ @name = ] N'plan_guide_name'
 , [ @stmt = ] N'statement_text'
 , [ @type = ] N' { OBJECT | SQL | TEMPLATE }'
 , [ @module_or_batch = ]
    {
      N'[ schema_name.]object_name'
      | N'batch_text'
      | NULL
    }
 , [ @params = ] { N'@parameter_name data_type [,...n ]' | NULL }
 , [ @hints = ] { N'OPTION ( query_hint [,...n ] )' | NULL }
```

The arguments of this command are described in Table 28-7.

Table 28-7. *sp_create_plan_guide Arguments*

Argument	Description
plan_guide_name	The name of the new plan guide.
statement_text TEMPLATE	The SQL text identified for optimization. OBJECT | SQL | When OBJECT is selected, the plan guide will apply to the statement text found within a specific stored procedure, function, or DML trigger. When SQL is selected, the plan guide will apply to statement text found in a stand-alone statement or batch. The TEMPLATE option is used to either enable or disable parameterization for a SQL statement. Recall from Chapter 22, in the topic "Modify Database Parameterization Behavior" that the PARAMETERIZATION option, when set to FORCED, increases the chance that a query will become parameterized, allowing it to form a reusable query execution plan. SIMPLE parameterization, however, affects a smaller amount of queries (at SQL Server's discretion). The TEMPLATE option is used to override either a database's SIMPLE or FORCED parameterization option. If a database is using SIMPLE parameterization, you can force a specific query statement to be parameterized. If a database is using FORCED parameterization, you can force a specific query statement to *not* be parameterized.
N'[schema_name.]object_name' | N'batch_text' | NULL	Specifies either the name of the object the SQL text will be in, the batch text, or NULL, when TEMPLATE is selected.
N'@parameter_name data_type [,...n]' | NULL	The name of the parameters to be used for either SQL or TEMPLATE type plan guides.
N'OPTION (query_hint [,...n])' | NULL	The query hint or hints to be applied to the statement.

To remove or disable a plan guide, use the sp_control_plan_guide system-stored procedure:

```
sp_control_plan_guide
[ @operation = ]
N'[    DROP
  | DROP ALL
  | DISABLE
  | DISABLE ALL
  | ENABLE
  | ENABLE ALL ]',
[ @name = ] N'plan_guide_name' ]
```

The arguments of this command are described in Table 28-8.

Table 28-8. *sp_control_plan_guide Arguments*

Argument	Description
DROP	The DROP operation removes the plan guide from the database.
DROP ALL	DROP ALL drops all plan guides from the database.
DISABLE	DISABLE disables the plan guide, but doesn't remove it from the database.
DISABLE ALL	DISABLE ALL disables all plan guides in the database.
ENABLE | ENABLE ALL	ENABLE enables a disabled plan guide, and ENABLE ALL does so for all disabled plan guides in the database.
plan_guide_name	The name of the plan guide to perform the operation on.

In this recipe's example, a plan guide is used to change the table join type method for a stand-alone query. In this scenario, your third-party software package is sending a query which is causing a LOOP join. In this scenario, you want the query to use a MERGE join instead.

■**Caution** SQL Server should usually be left to make its own decisions regarding how a query is processed. Only under special circumstances, and administered by an experienced SQL Server professional, should plan guides be created in your SQL Server environment.

In this example, the following query is executed using sp_executesql:

```
EXEC sp_executeSQL N'SELECT v.AccountNumber, p.PostalCode
FROM Purchasing.Vendor v INNER JOIN Purchasing.VendorAddress a
ON v.VendorID = a.VendorID
INNER JOIN Person.Address p ON a.AddressID = p.AddressID'
```

Looking at this query's execution plan in Figure 28-26 shows that the Vendor and VendorAddress table are joined together using a Nested Loop operator.

Figure 28-26. *Query execution plan prior to applying a Plan Guide*

If, for example, you wanted SQL Server to use a different join method, but without having to change the actual query sent by the application, you can apply this change by creating a plan guide.

The following plan guide is created to apply a join hint onto the query being sent from the application:

```
EXEC sp_create_plan_guide
   @name = N'Vendor_Query_Loop_to_Merge',
   @stmt = N'SELECT v.AccountNumber, p.PostalCode FROM Purchasing.Vendor v INNER
JOIN Purchasing.VendorAddress a ON v.VendorID = a.VendorID INNER JOIN Person.Address
p ON a.AddressID = p.AddressID',
@type = N'SQL',
@module_or_batch = NULL,
@params = NULL,
@hints = N'OPTION (MERGE JOIN)'
```

After creating the plan guide, the query is executed using sp_executesql:

```
EXEC sp_executeSQL N'SELECT v.AccountNumber, p.PostalCode
FROM Purchasing.Vendor v INNER JOIN Purchasing.VendorAddress a
```

```
ON v.VendorID = a.VendorID
INNER JOIN Person.Address p ON a.AddressID = p.AddressID'
```

Looking at the graphical execution plan in Figure 28-27, you'll now see that the Nested Loop joins have changed into Merge join operators instead—all without changing the actual query being sent from the application to SQL Server.

Figure 28-27. *Query execution plan after applying a Plan Guide*

If it is decided that this Merge join is no longer more effective than a Nested loop join, you can drop the plan guide using the sp_control_plan_guide system-stored procedure:

```
EXEC sp_control_plan_guide N'DROP', N'Vendor_Query_Loop_to_Merge'
```

How It Works

Plan guides allow you to add query hints to a query being sent from an application without having to change the application itself. In this example, a particular SQL Statement was performing Nested Loop joins. Without changing the actual query itself, SQL Server "sees" the plan guide and matches the incoming query to the query in the plan guide. When matched, the hints in the plan guide are applied to the incoming query.

The sp_create_plan_guide allows you to create plans for stand-alone SQL statements, SQL statements within objects (procedures, functions, DML triggers), and for SQL statements that are either being parameterized or not, due to the database's PARAMETERIZATION setting.

In this recipe, the first parameter sent to sp_create_plan_guide was the name of the new plan guide:

```
EXEC sp_create_plan_guide
    @name = N'Vendor_Query_Loop_to_Merge',
```

The second parameter was the SQL statement to apply the plan guide to (white space characters, comments, and semicolons will be ignored):

```
@stmt = N'SELECT v.AccountNumber, p.PostalCode FROM Purchasing.Vendor v INNER JOIN
Purchasing.VendorAddress a ON v.VendorID = a.VendorID INNER JOIN Person.Address p ON
a.AddressID = p.AddressID',
```

The third parameter was the type of plan guide, which in this case was stand-alone SQL:

```
@type = N'SQL',
```

For the fourth parameter, since it was not for a stored procedure, function, or trigger, the `@module_or_batch` parameter was `NULL`:

```
@module_or_batch = NULL,
```

The `@params` parameter was also sent `NULL` since this was not a `TEMPLATE` plan guide:

```
@params = NULL,
```

The last parameter contained the actual hint to apply to the incoming query—in this case forcing all joins in the query to use a `MERGE` operation:

```
@hints = N'OPTION (MERGE JOIN)'
```

Finally, the `sp_control_plan_guide` system-stored procedure was used to drop the plan guide from the database, designating the operation of `DROP` in the first parameter, and the plan guide name in the second parameter.

■■■

Backup and Recovery

One of the most critical responsibilities of a SQL Server professional is to protect data. Like many features in SQL Server 2005, you can perform database backups and restores without using any Transact-SQL code at all (with SQL Server Management Studio). However, during an emergency, you cannot always count on graphical user interfaces to help you restore data.

This chapter contains various recipes for backing up your database, be it a full, file, filegroup, transaction log, or differential backup (all of these backups will be described in more detail). You'll also learn methods for using these backup types to recover (restore) your database.

■Note There are BACKUP and RESTORE features in SQL Server 2000 that have been deprecated in SQL Server 2005. These include BACKUP LOG WITH NO_LOG, BACKUP LOG WITH TRUNCATE_ONLY, BACKUP / RESTORE WITH MEDIAPASSWORD, and BACKUP / RESTORE WITH PASSWORD.

Creating a Backup and Recovery Plan

Before getting too far into the details of *how* to perform backups and restores for your SQL Server databases, I'd first like to discuss how to generate a database recovery plan. In general, you should think about answering the following questions:

- Which of your databases are important? If a database is important, and is not used just for throwaway work, it should be backed up.

- How much data can you lose? Can you lose a day's worth of data? An hour's worth? A minute's? The less data you can afford to lose, the more often you should be backing up your databases.

- Do you have an off-site storage facility? Disasters happen. Equipment gets wet or catches on fire. If the data is important to you, you need to be moving it to a separate, offsite location via tape or over the network.

- How much downtime can your business handle? How much time would it currently take you to get everything up and running after a loss of all your databases? If your databases are large, and your downtime allowance very small, you may need to consider duplication of your existing databases (database mirroring, log shipping, replication).

Recovery plans are based on the value your company places on the SQL Server instance and its databases. The business value placed on an individual instance can range from "crash-and-burn" to mission critical, or "can't lose a single bit of data." It almost goes without saying that business-critical databases must be backed up. If you cannot afford to lose or reproduce the data within a database, you should be backing it up. This chapter will review how to use Transact-SQL to perform backups, and will discuss the various types of backups that can be performed.

Another consideration with backups is the backup frequency. How much data can you afford to lose? Can you lose a day's worth of work? A few minutes? None? If you can afford to lose 24 hours-worth of data, then, depending on the database size, a full database backup scheduled to run once a day may be acceptable. If you cannot lose more than 30 minutes worth of modifications, you should consider executing transaction log backups every 30 minutes as well. If you cannot afford to lose any data at all, then you should investigate such solutions as log shipping, database mirroring, RAID mirroring, or vendor solutions offered with storage area networks (SAN) and split-mirror software. The implication being, of course, that the closer you want to get to a guarantee for no data loss, the more money you must potentially spend.

Along with backups, you should also be thinking about archiving the files generated from the backup to another server on the network or to tape. If your SQL Server instance machine is destroyed, you definitely need backups from an off-server and offsite source.

The last major point to consider is the maximum allowable downtime for the SQL Server instance and databases. Aside from the data that is lost, how much time can you afford to spend before everything is up and running again? How much money does your business lose for each hour of database downtime? If the number is high, you need to invest in redundancy to offset this outage. If a database restore operation for a single database takes eight hours, you may need to reevaluate whether restoring from backup is appropriate or cost-effective. In this situation, you may choose to use replication, log shipping, database mirroring, or other third-party solutions that involve making copies of the data available across two or more SQL Server instances. Failover clustering can also help you with your SQL Server instance's availability by eliminating several single points of failure (except for shared disks). If your hardware goes bad, do you have replacement parts on site? Or, do you need to run to the nearest store to buy them? For high-availability requirements, you need to think about any single points of failure, and address them with redundant parts and processes.

As a DBA, you should consider and act upon all the questions raised in this section in order to create a SQL Server backup and recovery plan. At a lower level, you should also know the details of who to contact in the event of a disaster. The following is a list of items that you should document along with your backup and recovery strategy:

- You will need to know the primary contact or contacts for each application connecting to a database. Who handles the communication with end users? If a database is corrupted, who makes the decision to restore from a backup (and potentially lose some recent data updates) rather than work with Microsoft to potentially save the corrupted data?

- If you have a standby server, who on your IT staff needs to be involved to get the standby server up and running? Who installs the OS, moves files, swaps DSN names, and so on? Do you have a list of these people and their pager/email/contact info?

- Do you have a support plan with your hardware and software vendors? Do you have a central document listing license keys, service codes, and phone numbers?

- Do you have spare parts or an available spare part server?

- If your entire site is down, do you have an alternative site? Do you have a documented process for moving to this alternate site?

If you lose an entire server, and must rebuild it from scratch, you should have even more information available to you. Your company should have the following information documented (and available for reference):

- Who on your team needs to be involved in a server rebuild? Can they be available at two in the morning? Will they be available when you need them?

- Where do you keep your SQL Server backup files? What types of backups were you performing and how often were they run?

- Were there any other applications installed or configured on the SQL Server server? (Remember, aside from performance improvements, making your SQL Server machine a dedicated server reduces the complexity of reinstalling third-party or home-grown applications.)

- What operating system version were you running on? Do you have the CDs needed to reinstall the OS? Reinstall SQL Server? Do you have all necessary license keys?

- Did you document the steps used to install SQL Server 2005? What collation did you choose? Did you install all available components (Integration Services, Analysis Services, for example) or just the database engine?

The more databases and applications you have running on the SQL Server instance, the more documentation you'll need to keep, in order to be prepared for the worst. The important thing is to prioritize accordingly, first forming plans for your organization's most critical databases and then enlisting the help of business partners to help keep your backup and recovery plan both updated and useful.

Backups

In this next set of recipes, I'll show you different methods for backing up SQL Server 2005 databases. Specifically, I'll be showing you how to perform full, transaction log, and differential backups.

A *full backup* makes a full copy of your database. While the database backup is executed, the database remains available for database activity (since this is an online activity). Of all the database backup options, full database backups are the most time-consuming. The full backup includes all changes and log file entries as of the point in time when the backup operation completes. Once created, a full database backup allows you to restore your entire database. A full backup is the core of your data recovery plan, and it's a prerequisite for taking advantage of transaction log or differential backups (as you'll see later). When creating a backup, you have the option of creating a file on a disk drive or writing directly to tape. In general, SQL Server backups execute and complete more quickly when written directly to disk. Once the backup has been created, you can then copy it to tape.

A SQL Server 2005 database requires a transaction log file. A transaction log tracks transactions that have committed, or those that are still open and not yet committed. This file contains a record of ongoing transactions and modifications in the database. *Transaction log backups* back up the transaction log's activity that has occurred since the last full or transaction log backup. When the backup completes, SQL Server truncates the inactive portion of the log (the part not containing open transaction activity). Transaction log backups have low resource overhead and can be run frequently (every 15 minutes, for example).

Transaction log backups can only be performed on databases using a FULL or BULK_LOGGED recovery model. Recall from Chapter 22 that the three database recovery models are FULL, BULK_LOGGED, and SIMPLE:

- When using SIMPLE recovery, the transaction log is automatically truncated by SQL Server, removing the ability to perform transaction log backups. In this recovery mode, the risk of data loss is dependent on your full or differential backup schedule, and you will not be able to perform point-in-time recovery that a transaction log backup offers.

- The BULK_LOGGED recovery model allows you to perform full, differential, and transaction log backups—however, there is minimal logging to the transaction log for bulk operations. The benefit of this recovery mode is reduced log space usage during bulk operations, however the trade-off is that transaction log backups can only be used to recover to the time the last transaction log backup was completed (no point-in-time recover or marked transactions allowed).

- The FULL recovery model fully logs all transaction activity, bulk operations included. In this safest model, all restore options are available, including point-in-time transaction log restores, differential backups, and full database backups.

Aside from allowing a restore from the point that the transaction log backup completed, transaction log backups also allow for point-in-time and transaction mark recovery. Point-in-time recovery is useful for restoring a database prior to a database modification or failure. Transaction marking allows you to recover to the first instance of a marked transaction (using BEGIN TRAN...WITH MARK) and includes the updates made within this transaction.

The size of the transaction log backup file depends on the level of database activity and whether or not you are using a FULL or BULK_LOGGED recovery model. Again, the SIMPLE recovery model does not allow transaction log backups.

■**Caution** Although RESTORE is covered in a later recipe in this chapter, it is important to first understand how the sequence and frequency of transaction log backups impacts your database recoverability plan.

To recover from transaction logs backups, you must first restore from the full backup, and then apply the transaction log backups. Transaction logs are cumulative, meaning each backup is part of a sequential line of transaction log backups, and must be restored sequentially in the same order. You cannot, for example, restore a full database backup and then restore the third transaction log backup, skipping the first two transaction log backups.

A database also should not be recovered (meaning, brought online and made available for use), until you are finished applying all the transaction logs that you wish to apply in order chronologically by backup date and time. Recovery is handled by the RECOVERY and NORECOVERY clauses of the RESTORE command, reviewed later in the chapter.

You must understand the backups that have been made, what is contained in them, and when they were performed before you can restore them. Later on in the chapter I'll demonstrate the various commands that you can use to view this information. The following list details a typical backup sequence:

```
Time     Backup Type
8AM      Full database backup
10AM     Transaction log backup
1PM      Transaction log backup
```

If you wanted to recover the database as of 1pm, you would need to restore the 8am full backup first, the 10AM transaction log backup next, and finally the 1pm transaction log backup. If using differential backups, you must restore the full backup first, the differential backup next, and then transaction log backups created after the differential backup.

Differential backups copy all the data and log pages that have changed since the last full backup. Since the database is online when it's being backed up, the differential backup includes changes and log file entries from the point the backup began to when the backup completes. The files generated by differential backups are usually smaller than full database backups, and are created more quickly too.

Differential backups, unlike transaction log backups, are self-contained and only require the latest full backup from which to restore. Transaction log backups, however, are sequential files that don't include data from previous transaction log backups. For example, if you run a full backup at 8am, a differential backup at 10am, and an additional differential backup at 1pm, the 1pm differential backup will still include all changes since the 8am full backup:

```
Time      Backup Type
8AM       Full database backup
10AM      Differential backup (captures changes from 8am - 10am)
1PM       Differential backup (captures changes from 8am - 1pm)
```

Differential backups can still work side-by-side with transaction log backups, although transaction log backups can't be restored until any full and differential backups have been restored first.

The first recipe in this set of backup recipes will demonstrate how to perform a full backup in its simplest form.

Performing a Basic Full Backup

To perform a full backup, you use the BACKUP DATABASE command. The simplified syntax for performing a full backup to disk is as follows:

```
BACKUP DATABASE { database_name | @database_name_var }
TO DISK  = { 'physical_backup_device_name' | @physical_backup_device_name_var }
[ ,...n ]
```

The arguments of this command are described in Table 29-1.

Table 29-1. *BACKUP DATABASE Arguments*

Argument	Description
database_name | @database_name_var	The database name to be backed up (either designated as a string or local variable).
'physical_backup_device_name' | @physical_backup_device_name_var	The physical path and filename, or a local variable containing the physical path and filename.
[,...n]	You can designate up to 64 backup device names for a single BACKUP DATABASE command.

The BACKUP command also includes several options, many of which are demonstrated in this chapter (this syntax block omits command arguments that are deprecated in SQL Server 2005):

```
[ WITH
    [ BLOCKSIZE = { blocksize | @blocksize_variable } ]
    [ [ , ] { CHECKSUM | NO_CHECKSUM } ]
    [ [ , ] { STOP_ON_ERROR | CONTINUE_AFTER_ERROR } ]
    [ [ , ] DESCRIPTION = { 'text' | @text_variable } ]
    [ [ , ] EXPIREDATE = { date | @date_var }
    | RETAINDAYS = { days | @days_var } ]
    [ [ , ] { FORMAT | NOFORMAT } ]
    [ [ , ] { INIT | NOINIT } ]
    [ [ , ] { NOSKIP | SKIP } ]
    [ [ , ] MEDIADESCRIPTION = { 'text' | @text_variable } ]
    [ [ , ] MEDIANAME = { media_name | @media_name_variable } ]
```

```
    [ [ , ] NAME = { backup_set_name | @backup_set_name_var } ]
    [ [ , ] { NOREWIND | REWIND } ]
    [ [ , ] { NOUNLOAD | UNLOAD } ]
    [ [ , ] STATS [ = percentage ] ]
    [ [ , ] COPY_ONLY ]
]
```

These options are described in Table 29-2.

Table 29-2. *Backup Options*

Argument	Description
BLOCKSIZE	Sets the block size in bytes (it is almost never necessary to configure this option).
CHECKSUM | NO_CHECKSUM	Using CHECKSUM adds page-write backup file validity-checking. NO_CHECKSUM skips this validation (which is the default behavior).
STOP_ON_ERROR | CONTINUE_AFTER_ERROR	STOP_ON_ERROR stops the backup if a CHECKSUM error is found. CONTINUE_AFTER_ERROR keeps backing up even after a validation error.
DESCRIPTION	Free-form text describing the backup set, helping identify the contents of the backup device.
EXPIREDATE |RETAINDAYS	EXPIREDATE indicates the date that the backup set expires and can be overwritten. RETAINDAYS specifies the days before the backup media set can be overwritten.
FORMAT | NOFORMAT	FORMAT generates a media header for all volumes used for the backup. Existing headers are overwritten. This renders a backup set unusable if a stripe (stripes will be demonstrated later) exists on the device. NOFORMAT indicates that a media header should not be written on all volumes.
INIT | NOINIT	INIT overwrites existing backup sets, but preserves the media header. Backup sets are not overwritten if they have not expired yet, or the name set in the BACKUP statement doesn't match the name on the backup media. NOINIT appends the backup set to the disk or tape device. NOINIT is the default option.
NOSKIP | SKIP	NOSKIP checks the date and name, and is an extra safeguard to ensure the backup is not overwritten improperly. SKIP does not check expiration and name verification.
MEDIADESCRIPTION	Free-form text description of media set, helping identify the contents of the media.
MEDIANAME	Name of entire backup media set, limited to 128 characters.
NAME	Name of backup set.
NOREWIND | REWIND	NOREWIND prevents applications from using the tape until SQL Server issues a BACKUP or RESTORE command. Sometimes not supported by the tape device. REWIND makes SQL Server rewind the tape and release control.
NOUNLOAD | UNLOAD	UNLOAD specifies that the tape is automatically rewound and unloaded after the backup. NOUNLOAD means that the tape is not unloaded from the tape drive after backup, and can be used by other backup operations.
STATS	Returns feedback to the client on the backup progress. Default is 10 percent update increments.
COPY_ONLY	A new option in SQL Server 2005, allowing you to create a database backup without breaking a backup sequence (chain of full database backup and transaction log backups, for example).

In this recipe, I'll perform a simple, full database backup of the TestDB database to a disk device (file). Used for demonstrating BACKUP DATABASE, I'll first create a new scratch database which is also populated with a few objects from the AdventureWorks database:

```
USE master
GO

CREATE DATABASE TestDB
GO

USE TestDB
GO

SELECT *
INTO dbo.SalesOrderDetail
FROM AdventureWorks.Sales.SalesOrderDetail
GO

SELECT *
INTO dbo.SalesOrderHeader
FROM AdventureWorks.Sales.SalesOrderHeader
GO
```

Now, the new database will be backed up:

```
BACKUP DATABASE TestDB
TO DISK = 'C:\Apress\Recipes\TestDB_Oct_14_2005_1617.BAK'
```

This returns:

```
Processed 2456 pages for database 'TestDB', file 'TestDB' on file 1.
Processed 5 pages for database 'TestDB', file 'TestDB_log' on file 1.
BACKUP DATABASE successfully processed 2461 pages in 4.210 seconds (4.788 MB/sec).
```

How It Works

In this simple recipe, a full database backup was created for the TestDB database. The first line of code designated the name of the database to be backed up:

```
BACKUP DATABASE TestDB
```

The second line of code designated the file to backup the database to:

```
TO DISK = 'C:\Apress\Recipes\TestDB_Oct_14_2005_1617.BAK'
```

A backup file was created with a *.bak file extension. The name of the backup showed the date and military time. Although including a timestamp in the filename helps you identify the time the backup was created, it isn't a requirement. After executing, information was returned regarding the number of data pages processed, and the amount of time the backup process took.

Naming and Describing Your Backups and Media

In the age of government regulation of information and retention laws, your company policies may require that you keep database backups for longer periods of time. With longer retention periods, backup set metadata becomes more important. Naming your database backup file with the database name and time stamp is usually sufficient, however SQL Server includes other options you can take advantage of as well for describing and naming your backups. These options include:

```
[ WITH
    [ [ , ] DESCRIPTION = { 'text' | @text_variable } ]
    [ [ , ] MEDIADESCRIPTION = { 'text' | @text_variable } ]
    [ [ , ] MEDIANAME = { media_name | @media_name_variable } ]
    [ [ , ] NAME = { backup_set_name | @backup_set_name_var } ]
]
```

These options are described in Table 29-3.

Table 29-3. *Backup Media Options*

Argument	Description
DESCRIPTION	Free-form text describing the backup set, helping identify the contents of the backup device.
MEDIADESCRIPTION	Free-form text description of media set, helping identify the contents of the media.
MEDIANAME	Name of entire backup media set, limit to 128 characters.
NAME	Name of backup set.

Two terms related to SQL Server backups are used in the previous table: backup set and media set. A *backup set* is simply the result of a database backup operation. The backup set can span one or more backup devices (disk or tape). The *media set* is the collection of one or more backup devices that the backup set is written to.

This example demonstrates designating a description and name for both the backup and media sets:

```
BACKUP DATABASE TestDB
TO DISK  = 'C:\Apress\Recipes\TestDB.bak'
WITH  DESCRIPTION = 'My second recipe backup, TestDB',
    NAME = 'TestDB Backup October 14th',
    MEDIADESCRIPTION = 'Backups for October 2005, Week 2',
    MEDIANAME = 'TestDB_October_2005_Week2'
```

This returns:

```
Processed 144 pages for database 'TestDB', file 'TestDB' on file 1.
Processed 1 pages for database 'TestDB', file 'TestDB_log' on file 1.
BACKUP DATABASE successfully processed 145 pages in 0.461 seconds (2.576 MB/sec).
```

How It Works

This recipe has demonstrated how to add more descriptive information with your database backup. The additional options were added to the BACKUP DATABASE command using the WITH clause. The DESCRIPTION described the backup set:

```
WITH DESCRIPTION = 'My second recipe backup, TestDB',
```

The NAME identified the backup set name:

```
NAME = 'TestDB Backup June 4th',
```

The MEDIADESCRIPTION designated the description of the media set:

```
MEDIADESCRIPTION = 'Backups for June 2005, Week 1',
```

MEDIANAME designated the name of the entire backup media set:

```
MEDIANAME = 'TestDB_June_2005_Week1'
```

This information can be retrieved using RESTORE commands (such as RESTORE HEADERONLY), which will be covered later on in the chapter.

Configuring Backup Retention

In the first recipe of this chapter, if the backup file (device) hadn't already existed before the backup, it would be created during execution of the BACKUP command. If the file *did* already exist, the default behavior of the backup process would be to append the backup to the existing backup file (retaining any other backups on the file).

There are several BACKUP options that impact the backup set retention:

```
[ WITH
    [ [ , ] EXPIREDATE = { date | @date_var }
    | RETAINDAYS = { days | @days_var } ]
    [ [ , ] { FORMAT | NOFORMAT } ]
    [ [ , ] { INIT | NOINIT } ]
    [ [ , ] { NOSKIP | SKIP } ]
]
```

These options are described in Table 29-4.

Table 29-4. *Backup Retention Options*

Argument	Description
EXPIREDATE | RETAINDAYS	EXPIREDATE indicates when the date the backup set expires and can be overwritten. RETAINDAYS specifies the days before the backup media set can be overwritten.
FORMAT | NOFORMAT	FORMAT generates a media header to all volumes used for the backup. Existing headers are overwritten. This renders a backup set unusable if a stripe (stripes are demonstrated later) exists on the device. NOFORMAT indicates that a media header should not be written on all volumes.
INIT | NOINIT	INIT overwrites existing backup sets, but preserves the media header. Backup sets are not overwritten if they have not expired yet, or the name set in the BACKUP statement doesn't match the name on the backup media. NOINIT appends the backup set to the disk or tape device. NOINIT is the default option.
NOSKIP | SKIP	SKIP does not check expiration and name verification. NOSKIP checks the date and name, and is an extra safeguard to ensure the backup is not overwritten improperly.

This recipe demonstrates performing a full database backup while setting a backup set retention period of 30 days, after which it can be overwritten:

```
BACKUP DATABASE TestDB
TO DISK  = 'C:\Apress\Recipes\TestDB_Oct.bak'
WITH RETAINDAYS = 30
```

Now an attempt will be made to overwrite existing backups on the TestDB_June.bak file:

```
BACKUP DATABASE TestDB
TO DISK  = 'C:\Apress\Recipes\TestDB_Oct.bak'
WITH INIT
```

This returns:

```
Msg 4030, Level 16, State 1, Line 1
The medium on device 'C:\Apress\Recipes\TestDB_June.bak' expires on Nov 13 2005 ➡
  5:34:05:000PM and cannot be overwritten.
Msg 3013, Level 16, State 1, Line 1
BACKUP DATABASE is terminating abnormally.
```

How It Works

In this recipe, a new database backup was created with a backup set retention of 30 days. After the backup was created, another backup was executed, this time using the INIT switch (which overwrites existing backup sets). This attempt failed with an error warning that the backup set hasn't expired yet, and therefore cannot be overwritten.

Striping Backup Sets

Striping backups involves using more than one device (disk or tape) for a single backup set operation. In fact, when performing a database backup, you can use up to 64 devices (disk or backup) in your backup operation. This is particularly useful for very large databases, because you can enhance backup performance by striping the backup files across separate drives/arrays. Striping the backup files means each file is written to proportionately, and simultaneously. Striped backups use parallel write operations, and can significantly speed up backup operations.

This recipe demonstrates striping a backup across three disk devices:

```
BACKUP DATABASE TestDB
TO DISK  = 'C:\Apress\Recipes\TestDB_Stripe1.bak',
   DISK  = 'D:\Apress\Recipes\TestDB_Stripe2.bak',
   DISK  = 'E:\Apress\Recipes\TestDB_Stripe3.bak'
```

This backup creates three files which are each used to store one third of the backup information needed to restore the database.

If you try to use any one of the devices independently for a backup, you'll get an error message, as this next example demonstrates:

```
BACKUP DATABASE TestDB
TO DISK  = 'C:\Apress\Recipes\TestDB_Stripe1.bak'
```

This returns:

```
Msg 3132, Level 16, State 1, Line 1
The media set has 3 media families but only 1 are provided. All members must be provided.
Msg 3013, Level 16, State 1, Line 1
BACKUP DATABASE is terminating abnormally.
```

How It Works

In this recipe, a backup was created using three devices, which are also called *media families*. The three media families are used as a single *media set*, which can contain one or more *backup sets*. After creating the media set made up of three media families, the second part of the recipe attempted a backup using one of the existing media families. An error occurred because until that file or files(s) are formatted (using WITH FORMAT), they must be used together and not separately in a backup operation.

Using a Named Backup Device

You can define a logical name for a tape or disk device that can be used in your BACKUP or RESTORE command. Defining a device adds it to the sys.backup_devices catalog view and saves you from having to type in a disk's path and file or tape name.

To add a new backup device definition, use the sp_addumpdevice system-stored procedure:

```
sp_addumpdevice [ @devtype = ] 'device_type'
        , [ @logicalname = ] 'logical_name'
        , [ @physicalname = ] 'physical_name'
    [ , { [ @cntrltype = ] controller_type |
          [ @devstatus = ] 'device_status' }
    ]
```

The arguments of this command are described in Table 29-5.

Table 29-5. *sp_addumpdevice Arguments*

Argument	Description
device_type	Used to specify the device type: disk or tape.
logical_name	Name of the backup device that will be used in the BACKUP and RESTORE syntax.
physical_name	Operating system file name, universal naming convention name (UNC), or tape path.
controller_type	Not a required field: used to designate 2 for disk, 5 for tape.
device_status	This option determines whether ANSI tape labels are read (noskip), or ignored (skip), prior to usage. noskip is the default for type tape. Either this option or controller_type can be specified, but not both.

To view the definition of a backup device, use the sp_helpdevice system-stored procedure, which only takes the logical_name as a parameter:

```
sp_helpdevice [ [ @devname = ] 'name' ]
```

To delete a backup device, use sp_dropdevice:

```
sp_dropdevice [ @logicalname = ] 'device'
    [ , [ @delfile = ] 'delfile' ]
```

The first parameter is the name of the backup device, and when DELFILE is designated in the second parameter, the actual backup device file is deleted.

In the first part of the example, a backup device is created called TestDBBackup, which is mapped to the C:\Apress\Recipes\TestDB_Device.bak file:

```
USE master
EXEC sp_addumpdevice 'disk', 'TestDBBackup', 'C:\Apress\Recipes\TestDB_Device.bak'
```

This returns:

```
Command(s) completed successfully.
```

Next, information regarding the device is queried using sp_helpdevice:

```
EXEC sp_helpdevice 'TestDBBackup'
```

This returns:

device_name	physical_name	description	status	cntrltype	size
TestDBBackup	C:\Apress\Recipes\TestDB_Device.bak	disk, backup device	16,	2,	0

Next, a backup is performed against the device:

```
BACKUP DATABASE TestDB
TO TestDBBackup
```

This returns:

```
Processed 160 pages for database 'TestDB', file 'TestDB' on file 1.
Processed 8 pages for database 'TestDB', file 'TestDB2' on file 1.
Processed 8 pages for database 'TestDB', file 'TestDB3' on file 1.
Processed 8 pages for database 'TestDB', file 'TestDB4' on file 1.
Processed 1 pages for database 'TestDB', file 'TestDB_log' on file 1.
BACKUP DATABASE successfully processed 185 pages in 0.602 seconds (2.517 MB/sec).
```

Lastly, the device is dropped using sp_dropdevice (since the second DELFILE option is not designated, the physical backup file will remain on the operating system):

```
EXEC sp_dropdevice 'TestDBBackup'
```

This returns:

```
Device dropped.
```

How It Works

In this recipe, I demonstrated how to create a named backup device, allowing you to skip the keystrokes you would need to designate a full disk or tape name in your BACKUP or RESTORE commands.

The first example in the recipe created a device using sp_addumpdevice. The first parameter of the stored procedure took the device type disk. The second parameter was the logical name of the device, and the third parameter was the actual physical file path and name. The second query in the recipe demonstrated returning information about the device using sp_helpdevice. The status field relates to the description of the device, and the cntrltype column designates the device type (2 for disk device, 5 for tape). The third query in the recipe demonstrated using the device in a backup, which involved simply designating the device name instead of using the DISK or TAPE options: In the last query of the recipe, the device was dropped using sp_dropdevice.

Mirroring Backup Sets

Introduced in SQL Server 2005, you can now mirror a database, log, file, or filegroup backup. Mirroring creates backup redundancy by creating two, three, or four copies of a media set. This redundancy can come in handy if one of the media sets is corrupted or invalid, because you can use any of the other valid mirrored media sets instead.

The syntax is as follows:

```
BACKUP DATABASE { database_name | @database_name_var }
TO < backup_device > [ ,...n ]
[ [ MIRROR TO < backup_device > [ ,...n ] ] [ ...next-mirror ] ]
```

The MIRROR TO command is used in conjunction with a list of one or more backup devices, and up to three mirrors. In this example, a backup is mirrored to three different copies. Unlike the previous striping example, only one of these generated backup files will actually be needed for a database restore operation. Although, if one of the files is invalid, there are three other copies to attempt a restore from instead:

```
BACKUP DATABASE TestDB
TO DISK = 'C:\Apress\Recipes\TestDB_Original.bak'
MIRROR TO DISK = 'D:\Apress\Recipes\TestDB_Mirror_1.bak'
MIRROR TO DISK = 'E:\Apress\Recipes\TestDB_Mirror_2.bak'
MIRROR TO DISK = 'F:\Apress\Recipes\TestDB_Mirror_3.bak'
WITH FORMAT
```

This returns:

```
Processed 2456 pages for database 'TestDB', file 'TestDB' on file 1.
Processed 1 pages for database 'TestDB', file 'TestDB_log' on file 1.
BACKUP DATABASE successfully processed 2457 pages in 11.460 seconds (1.756 MB/sec).
```

This second example demonstrates mirroring a striped backup:

```
BACKUP DATABASE TestDB
TO DISK = 'C:\Apress\Recipes\TestDB_Stripe_1_Original.bak',
DISK = 'D:\Apress\Recipes\TestDB_Stripe_2_Original.bak'
MIRROR TO DISK = 'E:\Apress\Recipes\TestDB_Stripe_1_Mirror_1.bak',
DISK = 'F:\Apress\Recipes\TestDB_Stripe_2_Mirror_1.bak'
WITH FORMAT
```

This returns:

```
Processed 2456 pages for database 'TestDB', file 'TestDB' on file 1.
Processed 1 pages for database 'TestDB', file 'TestDB_log' on file 1.
BACKUP DATABASE successfully processed 2457 pages in 7.883 seconds (2.553 MB/sec).
```

How It Works

In the first example of this recipe, a backup was executed with three mirrors, which resulted in four backup files for the TestDB database. The first line of code designated the database to back up:

```
BACKUP DATABASE TestDB
```

The second line designated the location of the main (non-mirrored) backup file:

```
TO DISK = 'C:\Apress\Recipes\TestDB_Original.bak'
```

The next three lines designated the three mirrored copies of the backup:

```
MIRROR TO DISK = 'D:\Apress\Recipes\TestDB_Mirror_1.bak'
MIRROR TO DISK = 'E:\Apress\Recipes\TestDB_Mirror_2.bak'
MIRROR TO DISK = 'F:\Apress\Recipes\TestDB_Mirror_3.bak'
WITH FORMAT
```

Note that WITH FORMAT is required the first time a mirrored backup set is created. The original backup was placed on the C drive, and then each mirrored copy placed on its own drive (D, E, F). Any one .bak file in this example can then be used to restore the TestDB database, thus providing redundancy in the event of a backup file corruption.

The second example in the recipe demonstrated mirroring a striped backup (two media families in a media set). This time TO DISK included the two files used to stripe the original backup:

```
BACKUP DATABASE TestDB
TO DISK = 'C:\Apress\Recipes\TestDB_Stripe_1_Original.bak',
DISK = 'D:\Apress\Recipes\TestDB_Stripe_2_Original.bak'
```

The MIRROR TO DISK also designates two files that will be the mirror copy of the original striped backup:

```
MIRROR TO DISK = 'E:\Apress\Recipes\TestDB_Stripe_1_Mirror_1.bak',
DISK = 'F:\Apress\Recipes\TestDB_Stripe_2_Mirror_1.bak'
WITH FORMAT
```

Notice that MIRROR TO DISK was only designated once, followed by the two devices to mirror to.

Performing a Transaction Log Backup

The BACKUP LOG command is used to perform a transaction log backup. The following is the basic syntax for performing a transaction log backup:

```
BACKUP LOG { database_name | @database_name_var }
{
    TO <backup_device> [ ,...n ]
[ [ MIRROR TO <backup_device> [ ,...n ] ] [ ...next-mirror ] ]
    [ WITH
    [ BLOCKSIZE = { blocksize | @blocksize_variable } ]
    [ [ , ] { CHECKSUM | NO_CHECKSUM } ]
    [ [ , ] { STOP_ON_ERROR | CONTINUE_AFTER_ERROR } ]
    [ [ , ] DESCRIPTION = { 'text' | @text_variable } ]
    [ [ ,] EXPIREDATE = { date | @date_var }
    | RETAINDAYS = { days | @days_var } ]
    [ [ , ] { FORMAT | NOFORMAT } ]
    [ [ , ] { INIT | NOINIT } ]
    [ [ , ] { NOSKIP | SKIP } ]
    [ [ , ] MEDIADESCRIPTION = { 'text' | @text_variable } ]
    [ [ , ] MEDIANAME = { media_name | @media_name_variable } ]
    [ [ , ] NAME = { backup_set_name | @backup_set_name_var } ]
    [ [ , ] NO_TRUNCATE ]
    [ [ , ] { NORECOVERY | STANDBY = undo_file_name } ]
    [ [ , ] { NOREWIND | REWIND } ]
    [ [ , ] { NOUNLOAD | UNLOAD } ]
    [ [ , ] RESTART ]
    [ [ , ] STATS [ = percentage ] ]
    [ [ , ] COPY_ONLY ]
    ]
}
```

As you can see from the syntax, BACKUP LOG shares many of the same options and functionality as the BACKUP DATABASE command. Options not yet covered in this chapter or specific only to transaction log backups are described in Table 29-6.

Table 29-6. *BACKUP LOG Options*

Argument	Description
NO_TRUNCATE	If the database is damaged, NO_TRUNCATE allows you to back up the transaction log without truncating the inactive portion (the inactive portion contains committed transaction entries). This is often used for emergency transaction log backups, capturing activity prior to a RESTORE operation. Don't run this on a long-term basis, because your log file size will keep expanding.
NORECOVERY | STANDBY = undo_file_name	NORECOVERY backs up the tail of the transaction log and then leaves the database in a RESTORING state (which is a state from which additional RESTORE commands can be issued). STANDBY also backs up the tail of the transaction log but instead of leaving it in a RESTORING state, puts it into a read-only STANDBY state instead (used for log shipping). This option requires a file to be designated to hold changes that will be rolled back if log restores are applied.

In the first query of this recipe, a transaction log backup will be executed on the TestDB database:

```
BACKUP LOG TestDB
TO DISK = 'C:\Apress\Recipes\TestDB_Oct_14_2005_1819.trn'
```

This returns:

```
Processed 13 pages for database 'TestDB', file 'TestDB_log' on file 1.
BACKUP LOG successfully processed 13 pages in 0.448 seconds (0.230 MB/sec).
```

The second example in this recipe demonstrates making a transaction log backup on the tail of the transaction log. This assumes that there has been a database corruption issue—taking a backup of the "tail" means that you are backing up the latest transactions in the database without truncating the inactive portion of the transaction log:

```
BACKUP LOG TestDB
TO DISK = 'C:\Apress\Recipes\TestDB_Oct_14_2005_1820_Emergency.trn'
WITH NO_TRUNCATE
```

How It Works

In this recipe, I demonstrated two examples of transaction log backups Note that BACKUP LOG can't be performed unless the database has had a full database backup in the past. Also, in both examples, the database had to be using either a FULL or BULK_LOGGED recovery model.

The first example was a standard transaction log backup to disk. The first line of code designated the name of the database to backup:

```
BACKUP LOG TestDB
```

The second line of code designated the device to back up to:

```
TO DISK = 'C:\Apress\Recipes\TestDB_Oct_14_2005_1819.trn'
```

After the backup was completed, a file is generated and the inactive portion of the transaction log is truncated automatically. In the second query, the WITH NO_TRUNCATE option was designated, allowing you to back up the active portion of the transaction log without truncating the inactive portion of the transaction log.

Later on in the chapter, you'll learn how to restore data from a transaction log file, including how to use point-in-time recovery.

Using COPY ONLY Backup Sets

Introduced in SQL Server 2005, database and transaction log backups can now use the COPY_ONLY option to create backups that don't impact the backup sequence. As you'll see in future recipes in this chapter, both differential and transaction log backups depend on a full backup being performed first. Whenever other full database backups are created, the sequence restarts again. This means that previous differential or log backups cannot use the later generated full database backups. Only those differential or transaction log backups that are created after the full database backup can be used.

When you use the COPY_ONLY option, however, a full backup does not disrupt the sequence of backups. This is useful for creating ad hoc backups prior to major database changes, where you don't want to disrupt the standard backup schedule, but might like to have a "just-in-case" full backup available to RESTORE from. This example demonstrates how to use COPY_ONLY with a full database backup:

```
BACKUP DATABASE TestDB
TO DISK = 'C:\Apress\Recipes\TestDB_Copy.bak'
WITH COPY_ONLY
```

When you're using COPY_ONLY with transaction log backups, the transaction log is not truncated after the backup is created (leaving an unbroken chain of transaction log backups). This example demonstrates how to use COPY_ONLY with a transaction log backup:

```
BACKUP LOG TestDB
TO DISK = 'C:\Apress\Recipes\TestDB_Copy.trn'
WITH COPY_ONLY
```

How It Works

This recipe demonstrated using COPY_ONLY to create both full and transaction log backups. The syntax was similar to previous recipes, with the difference being that COPY_ONLY was included in the WITH clause. Full database backups using this option will not break the sequence of restores required for previous transaction log or differential backups. Transaction log backups using the COPY_ONLY option will also not break the chronological order of the other transaction log backups.

Performing a Differential Backup

In this next recipe, I demonstrate how to create a differential backup. Recall from earlier in the chapter that differential backups are used to back up all data and log pages that have changed since the last full backup. This differs from transaction log backups which only capture changes made since the last transaction log and/or full database backup.

Differential backups are performed using BACKUP DATABASE and use the same syntax and functionality as regular full database backups—only the DIFFERENTIAL keyword is included. This recipe demonstrates creating a differential backup on the TestDB database:

```
BACKUP DATABASE TestDB
TO DISK = N'C:\apress\Recipes\TestDB.diff'
WITH DIFFERENTIAL, NOINIT, STATS = 25
```

This returns:

```
58 percent processed.
78 percent processed.
Processed 40 pages for database 'TestDB', file 'TestDB' on file 1.
100 percent processed.
Processed 1 pages for database 'TestDB', file 'TestDB_log' on file 1.
BACKUP DATABASE WITH DIFFERENTIAL successfully processed 41 pages in 0.339 seconds (0.989 MB/sec).
```

How It Works

In this recipe, a differential backup was created on the TestDB database. The command usage was similar to previous recipes, only this time the DIFFERENTIAL keyword was included in the WITH clause. Two other options (both available when using different backup types) were used: NOINIT, which appends the backup set to an existing disk or tape device, and STATS, which returns feedback to the client on backup progress.

Differential backups can only be executed after a full database backup, so for a new database, a differential backup can't be the initial backup method.

Backing Up Individual Files or Filegroups

For very large databases, if the time required for a full backup exceeds your backup time window, another option is to back up specific filegroups or files at varying schedules. This option allows recovery in the event of lost files or filegroups. In order to perform file or filegroup backups for read-write enabled databases, the database must be using either the full or bulk-logged recovery models, as transaction log backups must be applied after restoring a file or filegroup backup.

Backing up a file or filegroup uses virtually the same syntax as a full database backup, except you use the FILEGROUP or FILE keywords and you can specify more than one filegroup or file by separating each by a comma.

To demonstrate backing up a filegroup, you'll create a new database that uses a secondary filegroup called FG2:

```
CREATE DATABASE VLTestDB
ON  PRIMARY
( NAME = N'VLTestDB',
FILENAME =
N'C:\Program Files\Microsoft SQL Server\MSSQL.1\MSSQL\DATA\VLTestDB.mdf' ,
SIZE = 2048KB ,
FILEGROWTH = 1024KB ),
 FILEGROUP FG2
( NAME = N'VLTestDB2',
FILENAME =
N'C:\Program Files\Microsoft SQL Server\MSSQL.1\MSSQL\DATA\VLTestDB2.ndf' ,
SIZE = 2048KB ,
FILEGROWTH = 1024KB ),
( NAME = N'VLTestDB3',
FILENAME =
N'C:\Program Files\Microsoft SQL Server\MSSQL.1\MSSQL\DATA\VLTestDB3.ndf' ,
SIZE = 2048KB ,
```

```
FILEGROWTH = 1024KB )
 LOG ON
( NAME = N'VLTestDB_log',
FILENAME =
N'C:\Program Files\Microsoft SQL Server\MSSQL.1\MSSQL\DATA\VLTestDB_log.ldf' ,
SIZE = 1024KB ,
FILEGROWTH = 10%)
GO
```

This first example creates a single filegroup backup:

```
BACKUP DATABASE VLTestDB
FILEGROUP = 'FG2'
TO DISK = 'C:\apress\Recipes\VLTestDB_FG2.bak'
```

This returns the following results:

```
Processed 8 pages for database 'VLTestDB', file 'VLTestDB2' on file 1.
Processed 8 pages for database 'VLTestDB', file 'VLTestDB3' on file 1.
Processed 2 pages for database 'VLTestDB', file 'VLTestDB_log' on file 1.
BACKUP DATABASE...FILE=<name> successfully processed 18 pages in 0.296 seconds
(0.482 MB/sec).
```

This second example demonstrates backing up two specific files for this database. To get a list of file names first, execute sp_helpfile:

```
USE VLTestDB
GO

EXEC sp_helpfile
```

This returns the following (abridged) results:

```
name            fileid    filename
VLTestDB        1         C:\Program Files\Microsoft SQL Server\MSSQL.1\MSSQL\DATA\VLTestDB.mdf
VLTestDB_log    2         C:\Program Files\Microsoft SQL Server\MSSQL.1\MSSQL\DATA\VLTestDB_log.ldf
VLTestDB2       3         C:\Program Files\Microsoft SQL Server\MSSQL.1\MSSQL\DATA\VLTestDB2.ndf
VLTestDB3       4         C:\Program Files\Microsoft SQL Server\MSSQL.1\MSSQL\DATA\VLTestDB3.ndf
```

Using the logical file name from the sp_helpfile results, this example demonstrates backing up the TestDB3 file in the TestDB database:

```
BACKUP DATABASE VLTestDB
FILE = 'VLTestDB2',
FILE = 'VLTestDB3'
TO DISK = 'C:\apress\Recipes\VLTestDB_DB2_DB3.bak'
```

This returns:

```
Processed 8 pages for database 'VLTestDB', file 'VLTestDB2' on file 1.
Processed 8 pages for database 'VLTestDB', file 'VLTestDB3' on file 1.
Processed 1 pages for database 'VLTestDB', file 'VLTestDB_log' on file 1.
BACKUP DATABASE...FILE=<name> successfully processed
17 pages in 0.278 seconds (0.499 MB/sec).
```

How It Works

This recipe started out by demonstrating backing up a specific filegroup. The syntax is almost identical to a regular full database backup, only the FILEGROUP is specified:

```
...
FILEGROUP = 'FG2'
...
```

The second example demonstrated backing up two specific files using the FILE option, in this case backing up two database files:

```
...
FILE = 'VLTestDB2',
FILE = 'VLTestDB3'
...
```

Restoring from a filegroup or file backup will be demonstrated later in the chapter.

Performing a Partial Backup

Also new in SQL Server 2005, a *partial backup* automatically creates a backup of the primary filegroup and any read-write filegroups in the database. If you back up a database with a read-only filegroup, the partial backup will only back up the primary filegroup. This option is ideal for those very large databases with read-only filegroups that needn't be backed up as frequently as the writable filegroups.

The syntax for performing a partial backup is almost the same as a full backup, except that with a partial you need to designate the READ_WRITE_FILEGROUPS option. If there are read-only files or filegroups you also want to back up, you can explicitly designate them too.

In this first example, only the READ_WRITE_FILEGROUPS option is used (in this example, the filegroup FG3 is read-only):

```
BACKUP DATABASE TestDB
READ_WRITE_FILEGROUPS
TO DISK = 'C:\apress\Recipes\TestDB_Partial.bak'
```

This returns:

```
Processed 160 pages for database 'TestDB', file 'TestDB' on file 1.
Processed 8 pages for database 'TestDB', file 'TestDB2' on file 1.
Processed 8 pages for database 'TestDB', file 'TestDB3' on file 1.
Processed 1 pages for database 'TestDB', file 'TestDB_log' on file 1.
BACKUP DATABASE...FILE=<name> successfully processed 177 pages in 0.638 seconds (2.272 MB/sec).
```

In the second example, a read-only filegroup is explicitly included in the partial database backup. To prep for this example, the VLTestDB's FG2 filegroup will be set to READONLY:

```
USE master
GO
ALTER DATABASE VLTestDB
MODIFY FILEGROUP FG2 READONLY
GO
```

This returns:

```
The filegroup property 'READONLY' has been set.
```

Now, the read-only filegroup is explicitly included in the partial database backup:

```
BACKUP DATABASE VLTestDB
FILEGROUP = 'FG2',
READ_WRITE_FILEGROUPS
TO DISK = 'C:\apress\Recipes\TestDB_Partial_include_FG3.bak'
```

This returns:

```
Processed 160 pages for database 'VLTestDB', file 'VLTestDB' on file 1.
Processed 8 pages for database 'VLTestDB', file 'VLTestDB2' on file 1.
Processed 8 pages for database 'VLTestDB', file 'VLTestDB3' on file 1.
Processed 2 pages for database 'VLTestDB', file 'VLTestDB_log' on file 1.
BACKUP DATABASE...FILE=<name> successfully processed 178 pages in
0.550 seconds (2.638 MB/sec).
```

How It Works

A read-only filegroup contains files that cannot be written to. Since read-only data doesn't change, it only needs to be backed up periodically (as in when it's changed to read-write for updates). For very large databases, unnecessary backups of read-only filegroups can eat up time and disk space. The new partial database backup option allows you to back up just the primary filegroup and any writable filegroups and files, without having to explicitly list each filegroup. If you wish to include a read-only filegroup in the backup, you can still do so.

In the first example of this recipe, the READ_WRITE_FILEGROUPS option was used without designating any files. The primary data file and writable files were all backed up, leaving out the read-only TestDB4 file from the FG3 filegroup. In the second example for this recipe, the filegroup was included in the backup by designating the FILEGROUP option.

In both cases a database restore from a partial backup also assumes that you have a filegroup/file backup for the skipped over files. A restore from a partial backup is demonstrated later on in this chapter.

Viewing Backup Metadata

Once a backup is created, you can view the contents of the media set by using various RESTORE functions, including RESTORE FILELISTONLY, RESTORE HEADERONLY, RESTORE VERIFYONLY, and RESTORE LABELONLY:

- RESTORE LABELONLY is used to return information about backup media on a specific backup device.

- RESTORE HEADERONLY returns a row for each backup set created on a specific device.

- RESTORE FILELISTONLY goes a level deeper by showing the database file names (logical, physical) and other information of the backed up database.

- RESTORE VERIFYONLY pre-validates the backup device to report if a RESTORE operation would succeed without errors.

The syntax is very similar across all four commands. I've combined the four commands into a single syntax block, but note that not all arguments apply to all commands (for example the MOVE argument is used only in RESTORE VERIFYONLY):

```
RESTORE { HEADERONLY | FILELISTONLY | LABELONLY | VERIFYONLY }
FROM <backup_device>
```

```
[ WITH
    [ { CHECKSUM | NO_CHECKSUM } ]
    [ [ , ] { CONTINUE_AFTER_ERROR | STOP_ON_ERROR } ]
    [ [ , ] FILE = file_number ]
    [ [ , ] LOADHISTORY ]
    [ [ , ] MEDIANAME = { media_name | @media_name_variable } ]
  [ [ , ] MOVE 'logical_file_name' TO 'operating_system_file_name' ] [ ,...n ]
    [ [ , ] REWIND | NOREWIND]
 [ [ , ] STATS [ = percentage ] ]
    [ [ , ] { UNLOAD | NOUNLOAD } ]
]
```

The arguments of this command are described in Table 29-7.

Table 29-7. *RESTORE Arguments for Backup Metadata*

Argument	Description
backup_device	The backup device (disk or tape) you want to examine.
CHECKSUM | NO_CHECKSUM	Using CHECKSUM adds page-write backup file validity-checking. NO_CHECKSUM skips this validation (and is the default behavior).
CONTINUE_AFTER_ERROR | STOP_ON_ERROR	CONTINUE_AFTER_ERROR continues the operation even after encountering a validation error. STOP_ON_ERROR stops the operation if a CHECKSUM error is found.
file_number	Used for FILELISTONLY, VERIFYONLY, and HEADERONLY (not LABELONLY); this number specifies the backup set to view, with "1" being the first backup set written to the media, "2" the second, and so forth.
LOADHISTORY	Used in the VERIFYONLY command, when designated, information regarding the backup set and restore operation is saved to the msdb system database history tables.
media_name | @media_name_variable	The name of the media set to validate.
MOVE 'logical_file_name' TO 'operating_system_file_name'	Applies to VERIFYONLY. MOVE allows you to verify that a restore of the database to a different filename and/or path from where it was originally backed up on will succeed.
REWIND	REWIND makes SQL Server rewind the tape and release control.
STATS	Applies to VERIFYONLY. Returns feedback to the client on the command execution progress. Default is 10% update increments.
UNLOAD | NOUNLOAD	UNLOAD specifies that the tape is automatically rewound and unloaded after the validation. NOUNLOAD means that the tape is not unloaded from the tape drive after validation, and can be used by other backup operations.

In most cases, you'll use these RESTORE commands to identify the contents of the device prior to writing your actual RESTORE DATABASE operation.

In this first example in the recipe, the media set information is returned for the TestDB.bak device:

```
RESTORE LABELONLY
FROM DISK = 'C:\apress\Recipes\TestDB.bak'
```

This returns the following (abridged) results:

MediaName	MediaDate
TestDB_October_2005_Week2	2005-10-14 16:23:30.000

In this second query, the same device is evaluated to see what backup sets exist on it:

```
RESTORE HEADERONLY
FROM DISK = 'C:\apress\Recipes\TestDB.bak'
```

This returns the following (abridged) results:

Position	DatabaseName	DatabaseCreation	DateBackupTypeDescription
1	TestDB	2005-2005-10-14 16:15:03.000	Database

In the third example of this recipe, the individual files backed up in the backup sets of a device are validated:

```
RESTORE FILELISTONLY
FROM DISK = 'C:\apress\Recipes\TestDB.bak'
```

This returns the following (abridged) results:

LogicalName	PhysicalName	Type
TestDB	C:\Program Files\Microsoft SQL Server\MSSQL.1\MSSQL\DATA\TestDB.mdf	D
TestDB_log	C:\Program Files\Microsoft SQL Server\MSSQL.1\MSSQL\DATA\TestDB_log.LDF	L

In the last example of this recipe, the backup device's RESTORE validity is checked:

```
RESTORE VERIFYONLY
FROM DISK = 'C:\Apress\Recipes\TestDB.bak'
WITH FILE = 1,
LOADHISTORY
```

This returns:

```
The backup set on file 1 is valid.
```

How It Works

The four commands, RESTORE FILELISTONLY, RESTORE HEADERONLY, RESTORE VERIFYONLY, and RESTORE LABELONLY, are each useful for gathering the information that you'll need prior to performing a RESTORE operation.

In the first example in this recipe, RESTORE LABELONLY was used to return information on the media set of a specific backup device.

The second example used RESTORE HEADERONLY to see what backup sets actually existed on the device, so that when you restore you can specify the backup set file number to restore from (also making sure you are restoring from the correct date and backup type).

The third example in the recipe used RESTORE FILELISTONLY to return the actual database files that were backed up in the device's backup sets. This is particularly useful information if you want to restore a database to a different server, because the drive and folder structures could be different on the new server versus the old. In later recipes in this chapter, you'll learn how to move the location of database files during a restore.

The last example checked the backup device to make sure it was valid for the RESTORE DATABASE operation. The backup set was designated using FILE = 1. Also, history regarding the backup set was saved to the msdb system database using the LOADHISTORY option.

Restoring a Database

The first part of this chapter was dedicated to reviewing how to back up a database, including how to perform a full, transaction log, differential, file, and filegroup backup. The second half of this chapter will discuss how to restore a database from a backup file. A restore operation copies all data, log, and index pages from the backup media set to the destination database. The destination database can be an existing database (which will be overlaid) or a new database (where new files will be created based on the backup). After the restore operation, a "redo" phase ensues, rolling forward committed transactions that were happening at the end of the database backup. After that, the "undo" phase rolls back uncommitted transactions (in SQL Server 2005, the database becomes available to users once the "undo" phase begins).

This next set of recipes will demonstrate database restores in action.

Restoring a Database from a Full Backup

In this recipe, I demonstrate how to use the RESTORE command to restore a database from a full database backup. Unlike a BACKUP operation, a RESTORE is not always an online operation—for a full database restore, user connections must be disconnected from the database prior to restoring over the database. Other restore types (such as filegroup, file, or the new "page" option) can allow online activity in the database in other areas aside, from the elements being restored. For example, if filegroup "FG2" is getting restored, "FG3" can still be accessed during the operation.

■**Note** Online restores are a SQL Server 2005 Enterprise Edition feature.

In general, you may need to restore a database after data loss due to user error, file corruption, needing a second copy of a database, or if you are moving a database to a new SQL Server instance.

The following is syntax for the RESTORE command:

```
RESTORE DATABASE { database_name | @database_name_var }
[ FROM <backup_device> [ ,...n ] ]
[ WITH
    [ { CHECKSUM | NO_CHECKSUM } ]
    [ [ , ] { CONTINUE_AFTER_ERROR | STOP_ON_ERROR } ]
    [ [ , ] FILE = { file_number | @file_number } ]
    [ [ , ] KEEP_REPLICATION ]
    [ [ , ] MEDIANAME = { media_name | @media_name_variable } ]
    [ [ , ] MOVE 'logical_file_name' TO 'operating_system_file_name' ] [ ,...n ]
    [ [ , ] { RECOVERY | NORECOVERY | STANDBY =
          {standby_file_name | @standby_file_name_var }
    } ]
    [ [ , ] REPLACE ]
    [ [ , ] RESTART ]
    [ [ , ] RESTRICTED_USER ]
    [ [ , ] { REWIND | NOREWIND } ]
    [ [ , ] STATS [ = percentage ] ]
```

```
      [ [ , ] { STOPAT = { date_time | @date_time_var }
        |   STOPATMARK = { 'mark_name' | 'lsn:lsn_number' }
                  [ AFTER datetime ]
        |   STOPBEFOREMARK = { 'mark_name' | 'lsn:lsn_number' }
                  [ AFTER datetime ]
      } ]
      [ [ , ] { UNLOAD | NOUNLOAD } ]
]
```

The arguments of this command are described in Table 29-8.

Table 29-8. *RESTORE Arguments*

Argument	Description
database_name | @database_name_var	Database name or character variable that you want to restore the database as (can be a new database name or overlay of an existing database).
backup_device	Name of backup device (named backup device, tape, or disk).
CHECKSUM | NO_CHECKSUM	Using CHECKSUM adds page write backup file validity checking. NO_CHECKSUM skips this validation (and is the default behavior).
CONTINUE_AFTER_ERROR | STOP_ON_ERROR	CONTINUE_AFTER_ERROR keeps restoring even after a validation error. STOP_ON_ERROR stops the restore if a CHECKSUM error is found.
file_number | @file_number	File number from the backup set that you want to restore from.
KEEP_REPLICATION	Prevents replication settings from being removed on restore (used in conjunction with log shipping).
media_name | @media_name_variable	If given, must match media name on backup volume. Otherwise the check is not performed.
MOVE 'logical_file_name' TO ' operating_system_file_name'	MOVE allows you to restore the database to a different filename and/or path.
{ RECOVERY | NORECOVERY | STANDBY = {standby_file_name | @standby_file_name_var }	NORECOVERY keeps the database in a restored state that allows more differential or transaction log backups to be applied. RECOVERY designates that no further differential or transaction logs need to be applied. The default option is RECOVERY, which begins both the redo and undo phases. The STANDBY state is used in conjunction with log shipping, designating a database as the warm standby for a primary server. The database will receive and apply transaction logs—until the time that the database must be brought online due to a failure at the primary database.
REPLACE	Overlays an existing database with the name designated in RESTORE DATABASE database_name.
RESTART	If a RESTORE stops prematurely, RESTART allows you to continue with the operation. Recommended for long RESTORE operations (for example, a several-hour operation).
RESTRICTED_USER	Only db_owner, dbcreator, and sysadmin may have access to the newly restored database.
REWIND | NOREWIND	NOREWIND indicates that after the restore, the tape is not rewound. REWIND rewinds the tape at the end of the restore.
STATS [= percentage]	Returns progress percentage of RESTORE operation.

Argument	Description
STOPAT = { date_time | @date_time_var }	STOPAT Allows you to recover to a specific point in time from the transaction log backup.
STOPATMARK = { 'mark_name' | 'lsn:lsn_number' }[AFTER datetime]	STOPATMARK recovers to the first instance of a marked transaction and *includes* the updates made within this transaction. Designating STOPATMARK = 'mark_name' AFTER datetime recovers to the first instance of the marked transaction on or after the specified datetime.
STOPBEFOREMARK = { 'mark_name' | 'lsn:lsn_number' }[AFTER datetime]	STOPBEFOREMARK restores the database up to the first instance of the marked transaction, excluding any activity within this transaction. STOPBEFOREMARK AFTER datetime will restore the database up to the first instance of the marked transaction, on or after the specified datetime, excluding this transaction.
UNLOAD | NOUNLOAD	NOUNLOAD does not eject the tape after the restore. UNLOAD ejects the tape at the end of the restore.

The first example in this recipe is a simple RESTORE from the latest backup set on the device (in this example, two backup sets exist on the device for the TestDB database, and you want the second one). For the demonstration, I'll start by creating two full backups on a single device:

```
BACKUP DATABASE TestDB
TO DISK  = 'C:\Apress\Recipes\TestDB_Oct_15_2005.BAK'
GO

-- Time passes, we make another backup to the same device

BACKUP DATABASE TestDB
TO DISK  = 'C:\Apress\Recipes\TestDB_Oct_15_2005.BAK'
GO
```

Now the database is restored using the second backup from the device (notice that the REPLACE argument is used to tell SQL Server to overlay the existing TestDB database):

```
USE master
GO

RESTORE DATABASE TestDB
FROM  DISK = 'C:\Apress\Recipes\TestDB_Oct_15_2005.bak'
WITH  FILE = 2, REPLACE
```

This returns the following output:

```
Processed 2456 pages for database 'TestDB', file 'TestDB' on file 2.
Processed 1 pages for database 'TestDB', file 'TestDB_log' on file 2.
RESTORE DATABASE successfully processed 2457 pages in 5.578 seconds (3.607 MB/sec).
```

In this second example, a *new* database is created by restoring from the TestDB backup, creating a new database called TrainingDB1. Notice that the MOVE argument is used to designate the location of the new database files:

```
RESTORE DATABASE TrainingDB1
FROM  DISK = 'C:\Apress\Recipes\TestDB_Oct_15_2005.BAK'
WITH  FILE = 2,
MOVE 'TestDB' TO 'C:\apress\Recipes\TrainingDB1.mdf',
MOVE 'TestDB_log' TO 'C:\apress\Recipes\TrainingDB1_log.LDF'
```

This returns:

```
Processed 2456 pages for database 'TrainingDB1', file 'TestDB' on file 2.
Processed 1 pages for database 'TrainingDB1', file 'TestDB_log' on file 2.
RESTORE DATABASE successfully processed 2457 pages in 4.799 seconds (4.193 MB/sec).
```

In the last example for this recipe, the TestDB database is restored from a striped backup set (based on the striped set created earlier in the chapter):

```
USE master
GO

RESTORE DATABASE TestDB
FROM DISK = 'C:\apress\Recipes\TestDB_Stripe1.bak',
DISK = 'C:\apress\Recipes\TestDB_Stripe2.bak',
DISK = 'C:\apress\Recipes\TestDB_Stripe3.bak'
WITH FILE = 1, REPLACE
```

This returns:

```
Processed 152 pages for database 'TestDB', file 'TestDB' on file 1.
Processed 1 pages for database 'TestDB', file 'TestDB_log' on file 1.
RESTORE DATABASE successfully processed 153 pages in 0.657 seconds (1.907 MB/sec).
```

How It Works

In the first example, the query began by setting the database to the master database. This is because a full RESTORE is not an online operation, and requires that there be no active connections to the database that is being restored in order to run.

The RESTORE is for the TestDB database and overlays the current database with the data as it existed at the end of the second backup set on the TestDB_Oct_15_2005.bak backup device. The first line of the command details the database to RESTORE over:

```
RESTORE DATABASE TestDB
```

The second line of this example designates the location of the backup device:

```
FROM  DISK = 'C:\Apress\Recipes\TestDB_Oct_15_2005.bak'
```

The last line of this example designates which backup set from the backup device should be used to RESTORE from (recall from earlier in this chapter that you can use RESTORE HEADERONLY to see what backup sets exist on a backup device):

```
WITH  FILE = 2, REPLACE
```

Any data that was updated since the last backup will be lost, so it is assumed in this example that data loss is acceptable, and that data as of the last backup is desired.

In the second example, a new database was created based on a RESTORE from another database. The example is similar to the previous query, only this time the MOVE command is used to designate where the new database files should be located (and the new database name is used as well):

```
MOVE 'TestDB' TO 'C:\apress\Recipes\TrainingDB1.mdf',
MOVE 'TestDB_log' TO 'C:\apress\Recipes\TrainingDB1_log.LDF'
```

RESTORE FILELISTONLY (demonstrated earlier) can be used to retrieve the logical name and physical path of the backed up database.

Tip Using the RESTORE...MOVE command is often used in conjunction with database migrations to different SQL Server instances that use different drive letters and directories.

In the last example of the recipe, the TestDB was restored from a striped backup set. FROM DISK was repeated for each disk device in the set:

```
RESTORE DATABASE TestDB
FROM DISK = 'C:\apress\Recipes\TestDB_Stripe1.bak',
DISK = 'C:\apress\Recipes\TestDB_Stripe2.bak',
DISK = 'C:\apress\Recipes\TestDB_Stripe3.bak'
WITH FILE = 1, REPLACE
```

In each of these examples, the database was restored to a recovered state, meaning that it was online and available for users to query after the redo phase (and during/after the undo phase). In the next few recipes, you'll see that the database is often *not* recovered until a differential or transaction log backup can be restored.

Restoring a Database from a Transaction Log Backup

Transaction log restores require an initial full database restore, and if you're applying multiple transaction logs, they must be applied in chronological order (based on when the transaction log backups were generated). Applying transaction logs out of order, or with gaps between backups, isn't allowed. The syntax for restoring transaction logs is RESTORE LOG instead of RESTORE DATABASE, however the syntax and options are the same.

To set up this demonstration, a new database is created called TrainingDB:

```
USE master
GO

CREATE DATABASE TrainingDB
GO

-- Add a table and some data to it
USE TrainingDB
GO

SELECT *
INTO dbo.SalesOrderDetail
FROM AdventureWorks.Sales.SalesOrderDetail
GO
```

This database will be given a full backup and two consecutive transaction log backups:

```
BACKUP DATABASE TrainingDB
TO DISK = 'C:\Apress\Recipes\TrainingDB.bak'
GO

BACKUP LOG TrainingDB
TO DISK = 'C:\Apress\Recipes\TrainingDB_Oct_14_2005_8AM.trn'
GO

-- Two hours pass, another transaction log backup is made
```

```
BACKUP LOG TrainingDB
TO DISK = 'C:\Apress\Recipes\TrainingDB_Oct_14_2005_10AM.trn'
GO
```

The previous RESTORE examples have assumed that there were no existing connections in the database to be restored over. However, in this example I demonstrate how to kick out any connections to the database prior to performing the RESTORE:

```
USE master
GO

-- Kicking out all other connections
ALTER DATABASE TrainingDB
SET SINGLE_USER
WITH ROLLBACK IMMEDIATE
```

Next, a database backup and two transaction log backups are restored from backup:

```
RESTORE DATABASE TrainingDB
FROM DISK = 'C:\Apress\Recipes\TrainingDB.bak'
WITH NORECOVERY, REPLACE

RESTORE LOG TrainingDB
FROM DISK = 'C:\Apress\Recipes\TrainingDB_Oct_14_2005_8AM.trn'
WITH NORECOVERY, REPLACE

RESTORE LOG TrainingDB
FROM DISK = 'C:\Apress\Recipes\TrainingDB_Oct_14_2005_10AM.trn'
WITH RECOVERY, REPLACE
```

This returns:

```
Processed 1656 pages for database 'TrainingDB', file 'TrainingDB' on file 1.
Processed 2 pages for database 'TrainingDB', file 'TrainingDB_log' on file 1.
RESTORE DATABASE successfully processed 1658 pages in 4.164 seconds (3.260 MB/sec).
Processed 0 pages for database 'TrainingDB', file 'TrainingDB' on file 1.
Processed 2 pages for database 'TrainingDB', file 'TrainingDB_log' on file 1.
RESTORE LOG successfully processed 2 pages in 0.066 seconds (0.186 MB/sec).
RESTORE LOG successfully processed 0 pages in 0.072 seconds (0.000 MB/sec).
```

In this second example, I'll use STOPAT to restore the database and transaction log as of a specific point in time. To demonstrate, first a full backup will be taken of the TrainingDB database:

```
BACKUP DATABASE TrainingDB
TO DISK = 'C:\Apress\Recipes\TrainingDB_Oct_14_2005.bak'
```

Next, rows will be deleted out of the table, and the current time after the change will be queried:

```
USE TrainingDB
GO

DELETE dbo.SalesOrderDetail
WHERE ProductID = 776
GO

SELECT GETDATE()
GO
```

This returns:

```
(228 row(s) affected)
```

```
(1 row(s) affected)
2005-10-14 20:18:57.583
```

Next, a transaction log backup is performed:

```
BACKUP LOG TrainingDB
TO DISK = 'C:\Apress\Recipes\TrainingDB_Oct_14_2005_2022.trn'
```

This returns:

```
Processed 18 pages for database 'TrainingDB', file 'TrainingDB_log' on file 1.
BACKUP LOG successfully processed 18 pages in 0.163 seconds (0.876 MB/sec).
```

Next, the database is restored from backup, leaving it in NORECOVERY so that the transaction log backup can also be restored:

```
USE master
GO

RESTORE DATABASE TrainingDB
FROM  DISK = 'C:\Apress\Recipes\TrainingDB_Oct_14_2005.bak'
WITH  FILE = 1,  NORECOVERY,
STOPAT = '2005-10-14 20:18:56.583'
GO
```

Next, the transaction log is restored, also designating the time of one second prior to the data deletion (which was made at 2005-10-14 20:18:57.583):

```
RESTORE LOG TrainingDB
FROM  DISK = 'C:\Apress\Recipes\TrainingDB_Oct_14_2005_2022.trn'
WITH  RECOVERY,
STOPAT = '2005-10-14 20:18:56.583'
GO
```

Next, the following query confirms that you have restored just prior to the data deletion that occurred at 2005-10-14 20:18:57.583:

```
USE TrainingDB
GO

SELECT COUNT(*)
FROM dbo.SalesOrderDetail
WHERE ProductID = 776
GO
```

This returns:

```
228
```

How It Works

In the first example for this recipe, the TrainingDB database was restored from a full database backup and left in NORECOVERY mode. Being in NORECOVERY mode allows other transaction log or differential backups to be applied. In this example, two transaction log backups are applied in chronological order, with the second using the RECOVERY option to bring the database online.

The second example in the recipe demonstrated restoring a database as of a specific point in time. Point-in-time recovery is useful for restoring a database prior to a database modification or failure. The syntax was similar to the first example, only the STOPAT was used for both the RESTORE DATABASE and RESTORE LOG. Including the STOPAT for each RESTORE statement makes sure that the restore doesn't recover past the designated date.

Restoring a Database from a Differential Backup

The syntax for differential database restores is identical to full database restores, only full database restores must be performed *prior* to applying differential backups. When restoring the full database backup, the database must be left in NORECOVERY mode. Also, any transaction logs you wish to restore must be done *after* the differential backup is applied, as this example demonstrates.

First however, I'll set up the example by performing a full, differential, and transaction log backup on the TrainingDB database:

```
USE master
GO

BACKUP DATABASE TrainingDB
TO DISK = 'C:\Apress\Recipes\TrainingDB_DiffExample.bak'

-- Time passes

BACKUP DATABASE TrainingDB
TO DISK = 'C:\Apress\Recipes\TrainingDB_DiffExample.diff'
WITH DIFFERENTIAL

-- More time passes

BACKUP LOG TrainingDB
TO DISK = 'C:\Apress\Recipes\TrainingDB_DiffExample_tlog.trn'
```

Now, I'll demonstrate performing a RESTORE, bringing the database back to the completion of the last transaction log backup:

```
USE master
GO

-- Full database restore
RESTORE DATABASE TrainingDB
FROM DISK = 'C:\Apress\Recipes\TrainingDB_DiffExample.bak'
WITH NORECOVERY, REPLACE

-- Differential
RESTORE DATABASE TrainingDB
FROM DISK = 'C:\Apress\Recipes\TrainingDB_DiffExample.diff'
WITH NORECOVERY

-- Transaction log
RESTORE LOG TrainingDB
FROM DISK = 'C:\Apress\Recipes\TrainingDB_DiffExample_tlog.trn'
WITH RECOVERY
```

This returns:

```
Processed 152 pages for database 'TrainingDB', file 'TrainingDB' on file 1.
Processed 2 pages for database 'TrainingDB', file 'TrainingDB_log' on file 1.
RESTORE DATABASE successfully processed 154 pages in 0.443 seconds (2.831 MB/sec).
Processed 40 pages for database 'TrainingDB', file 'TrainingDB' on file 1.
Processed 1 pages for database 'TrainingDB', file 'TrainingDB_log' on file 1.
RESTORE DATABASE successfully processed 41 pages in 0.069 seconds (4.860 MB/sec).
RESTORE LOG successfully processed 0 pages in 0.070 seconds (0.000 MB/sec).
```

How It Works

Differential backups capture database changes that have occurred since the last full database backup. Differential restores use the same syntax as full database restores, only they must always follow a full database restore (with NORECOVERY) first. In this recipe, the database was initially restored from a full database backup, then followed by a restore from a differential backup, and then lastly a restore from a transaction log backup. The differential RESTORE command was formed similarly to previous RESTORE examples, only it referenced the differential backup file. On the last restore, the RECOVERY option was designated to make the database available for use.

Restoring a File or Filegroup

Restoring a file or filegroup uses virtually the same syntax as a full database restore, except you also use the FILEGROUP or FILE keywords. To perform a restore of a specific read-write file or file-group, your database must use either a full or bulk-logged recovery model. This is required because transaction log backups must be applied after restoring a file or filegroup backup. In SQL Server 2005, if your database is using a simple recovery model, only read-only files or read-only filegroups can have file/filegroup backups and restores.

To set up this recipe's example, a filegroup backup is taken for the VLTestDB database:

```
USE master
GO

BACKUP DATABASE VLTestDB
FILEGROUP = 'FG2'
TO  DISK = 'C:\Apress\Recipes\VLTestDB_FG2.bak'
WITH NAME = N'VLTestDB-Full Filegroup Backup',
SKIP, STATS = 20
GO
```

Time passes, and then a transaction log backup is taken for the database:

```
BACKUP LOG VLTestDB
TO DISK = 'C:\Apress\Recipes\VLTestDB_FG_Example.trn'
```

Next, the database filegroup FG2 is restored from backup, followed by the restore of a transaction log backup:

```
USE master
GO

RESTORE DATABASE VLTestDB
FILEGROUP = 'FG2'
FROM  DISK = 'C:\Apress\Recipes\VLTestDB_FG2.bak'
WITH  FILE = 1, NORECOVERY, REPLACE
```

```
RESTORE LOG VLTestDB
FROM DISK  = 'C:\Apress\Recipes\VLTestDB_FG_Example.trn'
WITH  FILE = 1, RECOVERY
```

This returns:

```
Processed 8 pages for database 'VLTestDB', file 'VLTestDB2' on file 1.
Processed 8 pages for database 'VLTestDB', file 'VLTestDB3' on file 1.
RESTORE DATABASE ... FILE=<name> successfully processed 16 pages in 0.119 seconds (1.101 MB/sec).
Processed 0 pages for database 'VLTestDB', file 'VLTestDB2' on file 1.
Processed 0 pages for database 'VLTestDB', file 'VLTestDB3' on file 1.
RESTORE LOG successfully processed 0 pages in 0.062 seconds (0.000 MB/sec).
```

How It Works

Filegroup or file backups are most often used in very large databases, where full database backups may take too long to execute. With filegroup or file backups comes greater administrative complexity, because you'll have to potentially recover from disaster using multiple backup sets (one per filegroup, for example).

In this recipe, the VLTestDB database filegroup named FG2 was restored from a backup device and left in NORECOVERY mode so that a transaction log restore could be applied. The RECOVERY keyword was used in the transaction log restore operation in order to bring the filegroup back online. In SQL Server 2005 Enterprise Edition, filegroups other than the primary filegroup can be taken off-line for restores while leaving the other active filegroups available for use (this is called an ONLINE restore).

Performing a Piecemeal (PARTIAL) Restore

The PARTIAL command can be used with the RESTORE DATABASE command to restore secondary filegroups in a piecemeal fashion. This variation of RESTORE brings the primary filegroup online, letting you then restore other filegroups as needed later on. If you're using a database with a full or bulk-logged recovery model, you can use this command with read-write filegroups. If the database is using a simple recovery model, you can only use PARTIAL in conjunction with read-only secondary filegroups.

In this example, the VLTestDB is restored from a full database backup using the PARTIAL keyword, and designating that only the PRIMARY filegroup be brought online (and with filegroups FG2 and FG3 staying offline and unrestored).

First, to set up this example the primary and FG2 filegroups in the VLTestDB are backed up:

```
USE master
GO

BACKUP DATABASE VLTestDB
FILEGROUP = 'PRIMARY'
TO  DISK = 'C:\Apress\Recipes\VLTestDB_Primary_PieceExmp.bak'
GO

BACKUP DATABASE VLTestDB
FILEGROUP = 'FG2'
TO  DISK = 'C:\Apress\Recipes\VLTestDB_FG2_PieceExmp.bak'
GO
```

After that, a transaction log backup is performed:

```
BACKUP LOG VLTestDB
TO DISK = 'C:\Apress\Recipes\VLTestDB_PieceExmp.trn'
GO
```

Next, a piecemeal RESTORE is performed, recovering just the PRIMARY filegroup:

```
RESTORE DATABASE VLTestDB
FILEGROUP = 'PRIMARY'
FROM DISK = 'C:\Apress\Recipes\VLTestDB_Primary_PieceExmp.bak'
WITH PARTIAL, NORECOVERY, REPLACE

RESTORE LOG VLTestDB
FROM DISK = 'C:\Apress\Recipes\VLTestDB_PieceExmp.trn'
WITH RECOVERY
```

The other filegroup, FG2, now contains unavailable files. You can view the file status by querying sys.database_files from the VLTestDB database:

```
USE VLTestDB
GO

SELECT name,
    state_desc
FROM sys.database_files
```

This returns:

name	state_desc
VLTestDB	ONLINE
VLTestDB_log	ONLINE
VLTestDB2	RECOVERY_PENDING
VLTestDB3	RECOVERY_PENDING

How It Works

In this recipe, the VLTestDB was restored from a full backup, restoring just the PRIMARY filegroup. The WITH clause included the PARTIAL keyword and NORECOVERY, so that transaction log backups can be restored. After the transaction log restore, any objects in the PRIMARY filegroup will be available and objects in the secondary filegroups are unavailable until you restore them at a later time.

For very large databases, using the PARTIAL keyword during a RESTORE operation allows you to prioritize and load filegroups that have a higher priority, making them available sooner.

Restoring a Page

SQL Server 2005 has introduced the ability to restore specific data pages in a FULL or BULK_LOGGED recovery model database. In the rare event that a small number of data pages become corrupted in a database, it may be more efficient to restore individual data pages than the entire file, filegroup, or database.

The syntax for restoring specific pages is similar to restoring a filegroup or database, only you use the PAGE keyword coupled with the page ID. Bad pages can be identified in the msdb.dbo.suspect_pages system table, in the SQL error log, or returned in the output of a DBCC command.

To set up this example, a full database backup is created for the TestDB database:

```
BACKUP DATABASE TestDB
TO DISK = 'C:\Apress\Recipes\TestDB_PageExample.bak'
GO
```

Next, a restore is performed using the PAGE argument:

```
RESTORE DATABASE TestDB
PAGE='1:8'
FROM DISK = 'C:\Apress\Recipes\TestDB_PageExample.bak'
WITH NORECOVERY, REPLACE
GO
```

This returns:

```
Processed 1 pages for database 'TestDB', file 'TestDB' on file 1.
RESTORE DATABASE ... FILE=<name> successfully processed 1 pages
in 1.107 seconds (0.007 MB/sec).
```

At this point, any differential or transaction log backups taken after the last full backup should also be restored. Since there were none in this example, no further backups are restored. Next, and this is something that departs from previous examples, a new transaction log backup must be created that captures the restored page:

```
BACKUP LOG TestDB
TO DISK  = 'C:\Apress\Recipes\TestDB_PageExample_tlog.trn'
GO
```

This returns:

```
Processed 2 pages for database 'TestDB', file 'TestDB_log' on file 1.
BACKUP LOG successfully processed 2 pages in 0.840 seconds (0.014 MB/sec).
```

To finish the page restore process, the latest transaction log taken after the RESTORE...PAGE must be executed with RECOVERY:

```
RESTORE LOG TestDB
FROM DISK = 'C:\Apress\Recipes\TestDB_PageExample_tlog.trn'
WITH RECOVERY
```

How It Works

In this recipe, a single data page was restored from a full database backup using the PAGE option in the RESTORE DATABASE command. Like restoring from a FILE or FILEGROUP, the first RESTORE leaves the database in a NORECOVERY state, allowing additional transaction log backups to be applied prior to recovery. You can restore up to 1000 individual pages using this technique.

Index